Deaton Dary Cartwright James Fallow

Griffin Smith L william c. martin John van ...

... Lyons TR Fehrenbach Shelby Hearon

Brazier Paul Burka Gregory Curtis John Deaton

... Cockburn Bill Martin field Al Reinert Griff

... Mackintosh ... Lucy L. King Gene

... Graves Billy Lee Brammer Richard West William

... Dary Cartwright James Fallows A.C. Greene

Griffin Smith L william c. martin John Davidson Stephen

... Lyons TR Fehrenbach Shelby Hearon

Brazier Paul Burka Gregory Curtis John Deaton

... Cockburn Bill Martin field Al Reinert Griff

... Mackintosh ... Lucy L. King Gene

... Graves Billy Lee Brammer Richard West William

... Dary Cartwright James Fallows A.C. Greene

Griffin Smith L william c. martin John Davidson Stephen

... Lyons TR Fehrenbach Shelby Hearon

Brazier Paul Burka Gregory Curtis John Deaton

# THE FIRST FIVE YEARS
# The Best of Texas Monthly
## 1973–1978

**Texas Monthly Press**

Austin, Texas

*The covers of* Texas Monthly,
*from February 1973 to January 1978.*

© 1978 by TEXAS MONTHLY PRESS
P. O. Box 1569, Austin, Texas 78767
All Rights Reserved
ISBN 0-932012-02-7
First Printing

Designed by Sybil Newman Broyles
Project coordinated by Judy Benson and Betty Moore

Type set by G&S Typesetters, Inc.
Printed by Best Printing Company, Inc.
Bound by Universal Bookbindery

# CONTENTS

This volume contains only a sampling of what I consider to have been some of the best journalism published anywhere between February 1973 and January 1978, the first five years of *Texas Monthly*. Those of us involved in the selection process each had his own idea of what was the best of our publishing efforts for this period. While the choice was difficult, I believe the articles selected are fine representatives not only of our commitment to excellence in reporting and writing but also of the excitement, innovation, and integrity of our magazine, which quickly captured our readers' trust and loyalty and made *Texas Monthly* the most influential publication in the state.

Unfortunately, readers of this collection cannot begin to appreciate the incredibly hard work on the part of our editorial and business staff and our contributors, all of whom have helped to give *Texas Monthly* its success. To them this collection is dedicated.

Michael R. Levy
*Publisher*

At five years old a magazine, like a child, should probably be seen and not heard. But these days, five years is practically middle-aged for a magazine, what with more than 300 new ones started last year alone. Among this flood *Texas Monthly* is special, mainly because Texas is special. The 46 articles in this collection amply illustrate just how remarkable our state is. Texas itself, raw and cosmopolitan, raucous and sophisticated, intolerable and absolutely indispensable, dominates these pages. This book is a monument more to a state than a magazine, because the state made the magazine possible and sustains it still. But since *Texas Monthly* first provided a home for these stories, as its editor I would like to describe how *Texas Monthly* came to be.

On a beautiful spring day in 1972 a man named Mike Levy burst into my office in the Houston Public Schools building. In one hand he carried a large suitcase. "I've just got fifteen minutes!" he said, without introduction. "I've got to see eight more people before I drive back to Austin!" He yanked open the suitcase, which turned out to be full of magazines, and spread them on my desk. "You see these magazines? We can do better than that! Texas is better than that! Texas needs a great magazine! We can do it! Are you interested?" I said, "Wha . . . wha . . . what?" Then he was gone. Later that evening, making his way from his last interview in a blinding rainstorm, Levy stepped—suitcase in hand—into a swimming pool.

There were other false steps along the way, and more than once Levy was told he was all wet, that he didn't have enough money, that he didn't know what he was doing. But Levy was convinced a magazine of quality would work in Texas, so he persisted. At 25, after graduating from the University of Texas law school, he took some savings given him by his father and set about to bring his idea to life. On the surface, the skeptics were right: his idea had all the attraction of becoming a stockbroker in 1929. *Life*, *Look*, the *Saturday Evening Post* were dead or dying. The magazines like the one Levy had in mind served single cities, not a state that was virtually a nation.

It was Levy, however, who was right. In spite of the conventional wisdom that the Panhandle had nothing in common with East Texas, East Texas with the Valley, the Valley with the Trans-Pecos, Texans were in fact united by something indefinable yet powerful: being Texan. On its native born being Texan was an indelible birthmark. For its millions of immigrants it was an adopted creed in a way that being Ohioan or being New Jerseyan simply couldn't be. Even as the legendary Texans—cowboys, wildcatters, and wheeler-dealers—disappeared into the reality of an increasingly urban Texas, so being

*Michael Levy,* Publisher *(left)*
*and William Broyles,* Editor    *Bill Brammer*    *Paul Burka*    *Gary Cartwright*    *Alexander Cockburn*    **9**

Texan became more and more a state of mind. In an America homogenized by mass media and a restless, mobile society, Texas stood for something separate and permanent: while Texans might live in Houston or Dallas or Amarillo, they were still *Texans*, and Levy was convinced Texans would buy a magazine that explored Texas honestly, not as it wanted to be but in the full splendor of what it was, warts and all. Levy felt Texas was both ready to be taken seriously and confident enough to laugh at itself. The audience for his magazine would be there because Texas was there.

"Can you make sense of it?" Levy asked me. He proposed that he would be publisher and I editor. He would keep the magazine afloat; I would fill its pages. What Texan could turn down such a challenge? I was so infected by Levy's enthusiasm that I didn't reflect until too late that my experience in journalism consisted of three months as a summer intern on the *Houston Post* and of writing some columns for the Oxford University magazine. My year with the Marines in Viet Nam would be about as helpful. I didn't know any established journalists and we couldn't afford to hire them anyway. Most of the first staff had no more experience than I did. We paid ourselves subsistence salaries, although we did only charge a nickel for the office coffee.

Griffin Smith, jr., who had been editor of the *Rice Thresher* when I was in college, was too good a writer ever to be content practicing law; he agreed to start part-time in January 1973, while remaining active with the State Legislature. I called my old college roommate, Gregory Curtis, who was running a printing press in San Francisco. "Say," I said, "do you know anybody out there who'd like to work for a magazine that may never get out an issue? I'll pay $500 a month as long as it lasts." "You've got your man," Curtis said. The late Bill Brammer, author of *The Gay Place*, the novel about Texas politics that had first made me take the state seriously, was earning a living chopping cedar while on an extended temporary sabbatical from writing. I told him about the magazine and offered him a job while he was rubbing flea powder on his black poodle. "Why not?" he said. Bill Berry, an art professor at the University of Texas, agreed to do the original design, and Richard West, who seemed to know everyone in Texas from his tour as Lieutenant Governor Ben Barnes' press secretary, became our first ad salesman. West was a strange sort of salesman, riding the roads in his VW bus, reading magazines as he drove. As it turned out, West would have had trouble selling matches to an arsonist, but he loved the nooks and crannies of Texas and he could write; soon he switched to the editorial staff. With production supervisor Sandra Beddow, and Anne Barnstone, who joined the magazine as editorial secretary and soon became managing editor, this first group was the core of the magazine.

Levy and I found offices in a small, dank building near the state Capitol. We filled a U-Haul with secondhand furniture, and Curtis, Levy, and I carried everything up the steep stairs. The copying machine was in Levy's office. The only way to the art room was through my office. The low ceilings leaked, the carpet was old and moldy, and the heater seeped gas. We coexisted with mice, ants, and cockroaches, and on more than one occasion we had to call animal rescue to rid us of bats. We added typewriters one by one; if writers wanted to type amid the chaos, they had to bring their own. My wall soon sported large blotches of blood where a contributor had repeatedly slammed his fist in frustration with my editing (editors have that effect on writers sometimes). Our lights burned far into the night while next door a nocturnal dental technician pounded out false teeth, adding an Edgar Allan Poe touch to our deadlines. The offices were cramped, miserable, and completely unworkable. They were, however, the appropriate backdrop for the hundreds of phone calls that went "Hello, I'm working for *Texas Monthly* . . . No, it's a magazine . . . Well, actually we haven't published an issue yet . . . I know, but could he talk for just a minute . . . Hello? Hello?"

We were all justifiably proud of our first issue, but it proved to us that good magazines are made, not

*Gregory Curtis*

*John Davidson*

*John Deaton*

*James Fallows*

*T. R. Fehrenbach*

born. For some reason I had believed that simply putting the name "Texas" on a magazine, like on an ashtray or a sweatshirt, would sell it, that Texas chauvinists would overlook any deficiencies in quality. Of course, I was wrong, as the thousands of copies of the first issue that went unsold amply attest. It was clear that we would have to become—and quick—as good as the best magazines on the newsstands. To reach that level we sought out established Texas writers who knew Texas far better than we did. Gary Cartwright anchored our first issue and has appeared in twenty more since then; Larry L. King, the poet laureate of redneck, also came on early. T. R. Fehrenbach, John Graves, A. C. Greene, and Bill Porterfield, each successful in his own right, lent their names and talents to a new magazine and helped us put down our roots. I'm sure each of them had his reasons for helping out, but I liked King's best. "Damnation, Broyles! If you'd had your little pissant magazine when I was a kid I wouldn't have had to have moved up with all these Yankees just to scratch out a living!"

But no matter how much the proven Texas writers helped us, we knew that the magazine would ultimately be defined by the writers it discovered and developed, the ones we could provide a home for here. We found writers wherever they happened to be and encouraged, browbeat, cajoled, and intimidated them to grow, just as we were trying to learn and grow as fledgling editors. Al Reinert, who in our first year tracked down astronauts, private eyes, hit men, gamblers, and girls at the Chicken Ranch, was an ex-Aggie and ex-*Houston Chronicle* reporter; Stephen Harrigan, a poet who was working as a yardman, lent his gentle irony to a long string of articles on ordinary people. In the early sixties I spent an evening helping a friend put out the sports page of UT's *Daily Texan*. In six-point type I noticed the name of the winner of the women's shuffleboard intramurals—Prudence Mehaffey. The next day I was joking with my friend about the preposterousness of such a name when a girl standing nearby turned around and said: "I'm Prudence Mehaffey, and who are you?" In January 1974, Prudence Mehaffey Mackintosh, then a Dallas housewife, published the first of the nineteen stories she has written for us on child rearing and contemporary life. My friend from the *Daily Texan*, Paul Burka—lawyer, political pro, sports fan, and nationally ranked bridge player—joined the magazine in 1974.

Over the past five years these writers and our other contributors have explored Texas thoroughly. They have spied on trysts behind a bedroom wall with a private detective, ridden a kayak alone through an ocean storm, lived with a welfare family, met a hit man in a lonely motel room, visited massage parlors, strip joints, and the Petroleum Club, forded the Rio Grande with two wetbacks, and, greatest challenge of all, covered the Texas Legislature. They have profiled cowboys, wildcatters wheeler-dealers, sorority sisters, and football players, not to mention big-time attorneys, ministers, politicians, and housewives. They have befriended pit bulldogs, dolphins, and sharks and stared, perhaps too many times, into the baleful gaze of a steer. Since Texans take both their politics and their food seriously, our writers have rated not only the best and worst state legislators and congressmen, but also barbecue and Mexican food, and for their labors have received the supreme compliment of having one state representative tear a copy of the magazine to shreds and stomp it into the august floor of the House chambers.

If any one quality unites these farflung efforts, it is a boundless curiosity. Most of our stories began with one of us saying "I wonder . . ." I wonder why some women are rebelling against feminism, why hippies are dressing like rednecks, why fathers want to be present in the delivery room; I wonder what Barbara Jordan, the Marlboro Man, or Jay J. Armes is really like; I wonder what it's like to be an illegal alien, to live in Highland Park, to be a stripper, to have cancer; I wonder what goes on in those big law firms, during sorority rush, or at the Super Bowl, the Miss Texas pageant, or the county coroner's; I

*John Graves*          *A. C. Greene*          *Stephen Harrigan*          *Shelby Hearon*          *Harry Hurt, III*

wonder how it feels to work a ranch, to canoe the canyons of the Rio Grande, to be hooked on drugs. The only way to satisfy our curiosity is to send a writer to find out, and give to him enough time and room to report what he sees. Since we are a monthly magazine, we can't cover the news as a newspaper does. But we can parallel the news, poke around in it, and try to figure out what it means.

In many ways a magazine is like a hotel. Some writers only stay overnight on their way to or from other destinations; other writers like the place and more or less settle in. But the permanent residents are the magazine's staff, from secretaries to editors, ad salesmen to circulation data processors, who labor in frantic obscurity to maintain its standards, give it continuity, and keep it financially healthy. When the writer returns with his story, the editorial staff works with him, often through several drafts, to help his story become even better than the author thought it could be. Copy editors Suzanne Winckler and Chester Rosson are artists at this process, while David Moorman, our researcher, tracks down the facts of a story quite literally to the ends of the earth. *Texas Monthly* has both a visual and a verbal dimension. The visual dimension—the graphics that are its "look"—catches the reader's eye first and sets the tone for the stories he reads later. Using Texas illustrators and photographers, the art staff has stamped a relaxed, open, and brassy Texas brand on the magazine's graphics. This task is as challenging as bringing in a difficult story. Art directors Sybil Newman Broyles and Jim Darilek have, among other things, coaxed a herd of cattle to stand for a camera, posed Richard West as a flasher on Main Street in Houston, and assembled a motorcycle gang. As does the rest of the editorial and production staff, they labor long hours under mounting pressure every month, scrapping covers at the last minute, haunting the bus station for the arrival of that final photograph, filling unexpected holes, and generally giving a planned, finished look to what is really an exercise in improvisation.

As our sixth year began *Texas Monthly* was in the midst of considerable change. Change is nothing particularly new; a magazine that doesn't change doesn't grow. We have had, for example, three art directors and five managing editors (the latest is Nancy Smith), not to mention countless changings of the guard in other areas. Our listings of entertainment and capsule restaurant reviews, consistently the most popular section of the magazine, have been successively edited by Gregory Curtis, Griffin Smith, jr., and Anne Barnstone. Since 1975 they have been under the wing of Patricia Sharpe, who can tell homemade cheesecake from the Sara Lee variety at twenty paces. Our cultural criticism has been edited by Anne Barnstone and Gregory Curtis and is now supervised by Alice Gordon. In January 1978, Curtis, author of 48 articles, became executive editor. Writers Griffin Smith, jr., and James Fallows left the magazine in 1977 to compose speeches for President Jimmy Carter. Larry L. King has been engrossed in shepherding his first play on to Broadway, and Al Reinert is cloistered with his first novel. At the same time young writers like John Bloom, John Davidson, Harry Hurt III, and Dick Reavis are coming into their own. Richard West, after three years as the *Texas Monthly* Reporter, has taken on one of the magazine's more ambitious assignments, chronicling daily life in each of the major geographical regions of Texas, beginning with West Texas and the Big Bend. In addition to all these people changes, we have also, mercifully, changed our offices.

Looking back through the issues of the first five years and trying to pick the best stories among the 778 we published is like choosing one's favorite children. Many of my own personal favorites simply could not fit in this volume. And, although they all could not be mentioned by name, the two hundred or so people who have worked for us and the four hundred or so who have contributed articles or graphics are neither forgotten nor unappreciated. In 1973 we could comfortably convene the magazine's staff and contributors in one office; today we would need an auditorium. It would not have taken much more than an auditorium to contain those discerning readers who bought our first issue; today no structure in the

*Larry L. King*

*Beverly Lowry*

*Gene Lyons*

*Prudence Mackintosh*

*William Martin*

state would hold the 230,000 people who buy each issue of *Texas Monthly*.

A successful magazine is a dialogue between its contributors and its readers; each learns from the other, no matter how large the magazine or how numerous its audience. We have been well taught by our readers during the past five years, and a sampling of what we have learned appears on the pages of this book. An editor, however, can only discourse so much on his magazine, on what he has in mind for it, what its goals are, what its stories mean. But *Texas Monthly* really belongs to the people who read it. What the editor thinks he is doing with it is of mild interest, but to the true owners of a magazine, the proof is in the pudding.

One Friday every month all the stories and photographs and illustrations—whether exactly as we want them to be or not—are jammed into a packing crate and driven to catch—just—the 6:55 p.m. plane from Austin to the printer in Dallas. That departure is always cause for celebration, but there's also something about it that leaves us all a little sad. Every issue is, in a way, a failure. No matter how good it seems, we know each issue is never as good as it could have been *if we'd just had another week*. But now that these stories from so many such issues have been given permanence by this book, they seem exactly as they should be. Together they testify to how much the people who write, edit, and publish this magazine love Texas.

Loving Texas is not a simple affair. Oklahomans like to tell the story of how pioneers moving west would come across a sign that said "Texas begins here." Those who could read, so the story goes, turned back. Texans—even though now we can read—are used to being laughed at. With the possible exception of New Yorkers, no other Americans are more ridiculed or less loved. And just as New York stands for the melting pot in American history, so Texas symbolizes the frontier. For most Americans, the frontier has been something to put behind them, a passage on the way to paradise in California. To a sophisticated slice of America, the typical Texan is like an ill-mannered, unwelcome ancestor who still has the rough edges our country once had. The problem with this image, of course, is that the typical Texan is no more. Fifty years ago, about the time most of the state's leaders were born, eighty per cent of Texans lived in rural areas; today, eighty per cent live in cities. This change is more than statistical. It goes to the heart of how we live and who we are. Texas is an urban state now, the third most populous in the nation, with three of America's ten largest cities. The frontier that gave us the typical Texan is long since tamed. What New York and other cities of the East did for the children of European immigrants, the cities of Texas are doing for the children of cowboys, wildcatters, and wheeler-dealers: smoothing out the rough edges, civilizing, giving a common language and a common experience, churning out modern Americans. But something uniquely Texan survives: not far from where the moon landing was directed at NASA, for example, cattle are still rounded up on horseback. To be Texan is to embrace such contradictions. But, ultimately, defining Texan is like defining jazz. As Louis Armstrong once said, "If you don't know what it is, then I can't tell you." I can, however, recommend this book as the best place to start finding out.

William Broyles
*Editor*

*Bill Porterfield*

*Al Reinert*

*Jan Reid*

*Griffin Smith, jr.*

*Richard West*

# IT WOULDN'T BE HOME WITHOUT 'EM

**B**eing Texan is not just living in a state, it's sharing a state of mind. With all due respect to Oregonians, New Jerseyites, Arkansans, Michiganders, and all other undifferentiated Americans, being Texan just seems to mean a little more. This section examines some of the traditions which make us special.

For one thing, being a Texan has to do with how we grew up. For many Texas women, their rites of passage begin with summer camps, continue through a sorority, and culminate in living the "good life" in a posh suburb. What gives this segment of Texas femininity its special polish are all the rituals that produce the Kiowas, Tonkawas, and Ideal Girls at summer camp, that teach sorority girls the crucial difference between flowers and pots, and that on an unspoken level define the daily routines of the society woman. Prudence Mackintosh returned to the camps and sororities of her youth to write "The Greatest Experience of Your Life," and "Sisterhood Is Powerful," while Dallas' gentle curmudgeon A. C. Greene reconstructed the special world of "The Highland Park Woman."

Other Texas women travel different roads, but with no less style. In "The Sweet Smile of Success," Shelby Hearon spent a couple of tension-filled weeks with a Miss Texas contestant, from the preparations of the contest gown to the last walk down the runway. Al Reinert's "Closing Down La Grange" gives a fitting tribute to the inhabitants of the famed house of ill repute known as the Chicken Ranch, which Reinert had visited years before as part of the ritual of becoming a Texas Aggie, an equally hallowed institution.

The late Bill Brammer re-created the irresistible effect of those zany border radio stations on the sexual and religious insecurities of Texans in "Salvation Worries? Prostate Trouble?" Until World War II, most Texans lived lives of lonely isolation; since then almost 80 per cent of us have moved to cities, where our loneliness is not so isolated. But we still can't get the country off our minds, as William Martin amply documents in "Growing Old at Willie Nelson's Picnic." Before we romanticize that country past as a time of happy musicians and long-neck beer, we might as well read "Redneck!", Larry L. King's last word on the darker side of our heritage. Our traditions may not all be pretty, but they're all ours.

# REDNECK!

## by Larry L. King

---

*The Redneck is being made into a pop figure, romanticized and defanged. That may be just a tad premature.*

---

The maddest I remember being at my late wife (a Yankee lady, of Greek extraction and mercurial moods) was when she shouted, during a quarrel the origins of which are long lost, that I was "a dumb redneck." My heart dangerously palpitated, my eyes bugged, I ran in tight circles and howled inarticulate general profanities until, yes . . . my neck turned red. Literally. I felt the betraying hot flush as real as a cornfield tan. My wife collapsed in a mirthful heap, little knowing how truly close I felt to righteous killing.

Being called "dumb" wasn't what had excited me. No, for I judged myself ignorant only to the extent that mankind is and knew I was no special klutz. But being called a "redneck," now, especially when you know in your genes and in the dirty back roads of your mind that you *are* one—despite having spent years trying not to be—well, that just don't constitute fair fighting. I do not cherish Rednecks, which means I dislike certain persistent old parts of myself.

Of late the Redneck has been wildly romanticized; somehow he threatens to become a cultural hero. Perhaps this is because heroes are in short supply in these Watergate years, or maybe it's a manifestation of our urge to return to simpler times: to be free of computers, pollution, the urban tangle, morally bankrupt politicians, shortages of energy or materials or elbow room, and other modernist curses threatening to make our lives increasingly grim. Even George Wallace is "respectable" now, the news media boys tell us and tell us, having been semi-martyred by gunfire. Since 'Necks have long been identified with overt racism, we may be embracing them because we tired, in the Sixties, of bad niggers who spooked and threatened us and of laws busing our white children to slum schools; perhaps the revival is a backlash against hippies, peaceniks, weirdos of all stripes. Or the new worship of Redneckism may be no more than the clever manipulations of music and movie czars, ever on the lookout for profitable new crazes. Anyway, a lot of foolish-

*Larry L. King, a contributing editor of* Texas Monthly, *has authored several books and innumerable articles. He lives and writes in New York City.*

ness disguised as noble folklore is going down as the 'Neck is praised in song and story.

There are "good" people, yes, who might properly answer to the appellation "redneck": people who operate Mom-and-Pop stores or their lathes, dutifully pay their taxes, lend a helping hand to neighbors, love their country and their God and their dogs. But even among a high percentage of these salts-of-the-earth lives a terrible reluctance toward even modest passes at social justice, a suspicious regard of the mind as an instrument of worth, a view of the world extending little further than the ends of their noses, and only a vague notion that they are small quills writing a large history. They are often friendly in their associations and may sincerely believe themselves to accept "ever feller for what he is"; generally, however, they own more prejudices than a U-Haul could carry.

Not that these are always mindless. No, some value "common sense" or "horse sense" and in the basics may be less foolish than certain sophisticates or academicians. Some few may read Plato or Camus or otherwise astonish: it does not necessarily follow that he who is poor knows nothing or cares little. By the same token, you can make a lot of money and still be a Redneck in your bones, values, and attitudes. But largely, I think—even at the risk of being accused of elitism or class prejudice—the worse components of 'Neckery are found among the unlettered poor.

Attempts to deify the Redneck, to represent his life style as close to that of the noble savage are, at best, unreal and naive. For all their native wit—and sometimes they have keen senses of the absurd as applied to their daily lives—Rednecks generally are a sorry sad lot. They flounder in perilous financial waters and are mired in the socio-political shallows. Their lives are hard: long on work and short on money; full of vile bossmen, hounding creditors, quarrels, disappointments, confrontations, ignorance, a treadmill hopelessness. It may sound good on a country-western record when Tom T. Hall and Waylon Jennings lift their voices, baby, but it neither sounds nor feels good when life is real and the alarm clock's jarring jangle soon must be fol-

*Illustrated by Ron Scott and Sybil Newman Broyles*

lowed by the timeclock's tuneless bells. No, we need not perpetuate the Redneck myth. Indeed, our mudball ideally might show a net gain if it were possible not to perpetuate Rednecks themselves.

Now, the Rednecks I'm talking about are not those counterfeit numbers who hang around Austin digging the Cosmic Cowboy scene, sucking up to Jerry Jeff Walker and Willie Nelson, wearing bleached color-patched overalls and rolling their own dope, saying how they hanker to go live off the land and then stay six weeks in a Taos commune before flying back on daddy's credit card. Fie and a pox on such damn fakers; may such toy Rednecks choke on their own romantic pretensions.

No, and I'm not talking about Good Ole Boys. Do not, please, confuse the two; so many have. A Good Ole Boy is a Redneck who has acquired a smidgen or much more of polish; I could call him a "former Redneck" except that there ain't no such. One born a 'Neck of the true plastic-Jesus and pink-rubber-haircurlers-in-the-supermarket variety can no more shuck his key condition than may the Baptist who, once saved, becomes doctrinairely incapable of talking his way into Hell.

And here a warning against ersatz Good Ole Boys, too: those who find it advantageous to employ exaggerated country drawls, cracker-barrel observations, and instant histories of their raggedy-ass downtrodden childhoods. On investigation, however, these prove to have been no worse than the proletariat elite; probably they lived in a big white house on the hill with daddies who owned the region's biggest farm or the town gas works; their mommies belonged to bridge clubs or Book-of-the-Month or better. Lyndon B. Johnson was a fake Good Ole Boy; sometimes, when he's drunk, so is Norman Mailer. And Willie Morris misses it by no more than a freckle and a hair. Such people are trying to rise below their raising, to attain a common touch not necessarily natural to their roots. Don't ask me why: I got the other problem.

The *bona fide* Good Ole Boy may or may not have been to college. But bet your ass he's a climber, an achiever, a con man looking for the edge. He'll lay a lot of semi-smarmy charm on you, and middling-to-high-grade bullshit. He acts dumber than he is when he knows something, and smarter than he is when he doesn't. Such parts of his Redneck heritage as may be judged eccentric or humorous enough to be useful will be retained in his mildly self-deprecating stories, and may come in handy while he's working up to relieving you of your billfold or your panties. On the other hand, such Redneck parts as no longer serve him, he attempts to bury in the mute and dead past. And he becomes terribly manic when, say, a domestic quarrel causes him to blow his cool enough that those old red bones briefly rise from their interment so that others may glimpse them.

A Good Ole Boy turns his radio down at red lights so other drivers won't observe him enjoying Kitty Wells singing through her nose. He carefully says "Negro," though it slips to "Nigra" with a shade much Scotch, or even—under stress, or for purposes of humor among close associates—slides all the way down to "Nigger." He does not dip snuff or chaw tobacco, preferring cigarettes or cigars or perhaps an occasional hip toke of pot. He has semi-forgotten the daily fear of being truly dirt-poor—and, perhaps, how to ride a horse, or the cruel tug of the cotton

sack, or the strength of the laborer's sun. He may belong to a civic club, play golf, travel, own his own shop or run somebody else's. For a long time he's been running uphill; sometimes he doesn't know when he's reached level ground and so keeps on struggling.

Who may I furnish as examples? Ah, yes. It may not be perfect, but maybe it'll help you with the shadings: take two old Dallas Cowboys, sports fans, who began in redneck precincts at an approximate parallel. Where Don Meredith may be the quintessential Good Ole Boy, Walt Garrison is mighty like a Redneck. Meredith more than holds his own in chatting with senators, authors, mystics, and drag queens on late-night talk shows; Garrison actually dips the snuff he touts on TV commercials played mainly in Rock Hill, South Carolina. Dandy Don lives in a big house on twenty-odd landscaped acres in rich Bucks County, Pennsylvania; Wild Walt is often found ropin' and brandin' in the dustier sections of Oklahoma. Meredith bawls country-western songs with a wink in his voice; Garrison might not hear the wink. I can't tell it no better than that. It has a little to do with relative smarts and luck and blood attitudes and maybe potty training. Whatever.

While all true, bona fide Good Ole Boys have been at least fringe Rednecks, not all Rednecks rise to be Good Ole Boys. No. Their gizzards don't harbor enough of something—ambition, good fortune, con, education, opportunity, flint, self-propellants, saddle burrs, chickenshit, whatever—and so they continue to breed and largely perpetuate themselves in place, defanged Snopeses never to attain, accumulate, bite the propertied gentry, or smite their tormentors. These are no radicals; they can't find the handle on it and don't have time to think it through. Though generalities are dangerous, one risks the judgment that always they shall vote to the last in number for the George Wallaces or Lester Maddoxes of their time; will fear God at least in the abstract and Authority and Change even more; will become shadetree mechanics, factory robots, salesmen of small parts, peacetime soldiers or sailors; random serfs. (Yes, good neighbors, do you know what it is to envy the man who no longer carries the dinner bucket, and hope that someday you'll reach his plateau: maybe sell for Allstate?) The women of such men are beauticians and waitresses and laundry workers and pregnant. Their children may be hauled in pickup trucks or old Fords dangling baby booties, furry dice, plastic saints. Or be plastered with bumper stickers: *Honk If You Love Jesus*, maybe, or *Goat Ropers Need Love Too*.

We are talking, my friends, about America's white niggers: the left behind, the luckless, and the doomed. It is these we explore: my clay, native roots, mutha culture. . . .

I didn't know I was a Redneck as a kid. The Housenrights were Rednecks, I knew—even though I didn't know the term; couldn't have defined it—and so were the Spagles and certain branches of the Halls, the Peoples, the Conines. These were the raggedest of the ragged; there was a hopelessness about them, a wildness possible only in the surrendered, a community sense that their daddies didn't try as hard as some or, simply, had been born to such ill luck, silly judgments, whiskey thirsts, or general rowdiness as to preclude twitches of upward mobility. Such families were less likely than others to seek church; their breadwinners idled more; their children came barefoot to school even in winter. They were more likely to produce domestic violence, blood feuds, boys who fought their teachers. They no longer cared and, not caring, might cheerfully flatten or stab you in a playground fight or at one of the Saturday night country dances held in rude plank homes along the creek banks. Shiftless badasses. Poor white tacky Rednecks who did us the favor of providing somebody to look down on. For this service we children of the "better" homes rewarded them with rock fights or other torments: *Dessie Hall, Dessie Hall/Haw Haw Haw/Your Daddy Never Bathes/But He's Cleaner Than Your Maw.*

Ours was a reluctant civilization. Eastland County, Texas, in 1920—less than a decade before my birth—had 58,500 people; by the U.S. Census count that year, more than 46,000 of these had attained the age of ten or above without having learned to read or write in any language. Yes, you read the figures right. I recall old nesters who "made their marks" should documents require their signatures. A neighboring farmer in middle-age boasted that his sons had taught him simple long-division; on Saturdays he sat on the wooden veranda of Morgan Brothers General Store in Scranton, demonstrating on a brown paper sack exactly how many times 13 went into 39, while whiskered old farmers gathered for their small commerce looked on as intently as if he might be revealing the internal rules of Heaven.

We lived in one of the more remote nooks of Eastland County, in cotton and goober and scrub oak country. There were no paved roads and precious few tractors among that settlement of marginal farms populated by snuff-dippers, their sunbonneted women, and broods of jittery shy kids who might regard unexpected visitors from concealment. We were broken-plow farmers, holding it all together with baling wire, habit, curses, and prayers. Most families were on FDR's "relief agency" rolls; county agriculture agents taught our parents to card their cotton by hand so they might stuff home-made mattresses. They had less success in teaching crop rotation, farmers feeling that the plot where Daddy and Grandaddy had grown cotton remained a logical place for cotton still. There were many who literally believed in a flat earth and the haunting presence of ghosts; if the county contained any individual who failed to believe that eternal damnation was a fair reward for the sinner, he never came forward to declare it.

Churches grew in wild profusion. Proud backwoodsmen, their best doctrines disputed by fellow parishioners, were quick to establish their rival rump churches under brush arbors or tabernacles or in plank cracker-boxes. One need have no formal training to preach: The Call was enough, a personal conviction that God had beckoned one from a hot cornfield to spread the Word. Converts were baptized in muddy creeks or stock tanks, some flocks—in the words of the late Uncle Earl Long of Louisiana—"chunking snakes and catching fevers."

It was not uncommon for righteous vigilantes to pay nocturnal calls on erring wife-beaters or general ne'er-do-wells, flogging them with whips and prayers while demanding their immediate improvement. Such Godly posses did not seek to punish those who lived outside the law, however, should commerce be involved: times were hard, and so were the people. Bootleggers flourished in those woods, and even cattle thieves were ignored so long as they traveled safe dis-

tances to improve their small herds.

My father's house was poor but proud: law-abiding, church-ridden, hard-working, pin-neat; innocent, it seems in retrospect, of conscious evil, and innocent, even, of the modern world. Certainly we had good opinions of ourselves and a worthy community standing. And yet even in that "good" family of workworn self-starting country aristocrats there were tragedies and explosions as raw as the land we inhabited: my paternal grandfather was shot to death by a neighbor; an uncle went to the pen for carnal knowledge of an under-aged girl; my father's fists variously laid out a farmer who had the temerity to cut in front of his wagon in the cotton gin line, a ranch hand who'd reneged on a promise to pay out of his next wages for having his horse shod, a kinsman who threatened to embarrass the clan by running unsuccessfully for county commissioner a ninth straight time. My father was the family enforcer, handing out summary judgments and corporal punishments to any in the bloodline whose follies he judged trashy or a source of community scorn or ridicule. It was most tribal: Walking Bear has disgraced the Sioux; very well, off with Walking Bear's head.

So while we may have had no more money than others, no more of education or raw opportunity, I came to believe that the Kings were somehow special. A certain deference was paid my parents in their rural domain: they gave advice, helped shape community affairs, were arbiters and unofficial judges. I became a leader at the country school and in Bethel Methodist Church, where we took pride in worships free of snake-handling or foot-washings—although it was proper to occasionally talk in tongues or grovel at the Mourner's Bench.

I strutted when my older brother, Weldon, returned in his second hand Model-A Ford to visit from Midland. I imagined him a leading citizen there; he had found success as manager of the lunch counter and fountain at Piggly Wiggly's and announced cowpoke melodies part-time over the facilities of Radio Station KCRS. More, he was an outfielder with the semi-professional Midland Cowboys baseball team.

Weldon epitomized sophistication in my young mind: he wore smart two-toned shoes with air holes allowing his feet to breathe, oceans of Red Rose hair oil, and a thin go-to-hell mustache. In the jargon of the time and place he was "a jellybean." Where rustics rolled their own from nickel bags of Duke's Mixture or Country Gentleman, my brother puffed luxurious "ready rolls." When he walked among local stay-at-homes on his rare visits, he turned the heads of milkmaids and drew the dark envied stares of male contemporaries who labored on their fathers' farms or, if especially enterprising, had found jobs at the broom factory in Cisco. He was walking proof of the family's industry and ambition, and he reinforced my own dreams of escape to bigger things.

Imagine my shocked surprise, then, when—in my early teens—I accompanied my family in its move to Midland city, there to discover that *I* was the Redneck: the bumpkin, the new boy with feedlot dung on his shoes and the funny homemade haircuts. Nobody in Midland had heard of the Kings; nor did anyone rush to embrace them. Where in the rural consolidated school I had boasted a grade average in the high 90s, in Midland the mysteries of algebra, geometry, and biology kept me clinging by my nails to scholastic survival. Where I had captained teams, I now stood uninvited on the fringes of playground games. My clothes, as good as most and better than some in Eastland County, now betrayed me as a poor clod.

I withdrew to the company of other misfits who lived in clapboard shacks or tents on the jerrybuilt South Side, wore time-faded jeans and stained teeth, cursed, fought, drank beer, and skipped school to hang around South Main Street poolhalls or domino parlors. These were East Texans, Okies, and Arkies whose parents—like mine—had starved off their native acres and had followed the war boom west. Our drawls and twangs and marginal grammar had more of the dirt farmer or drifting fruit-picker in them than of the cattleman or small merchant; our homes utilized large lard buckets as stools or chairs and such paltry art as adorned them likely showed Jesus on the cross suffering pain and a Woolworth's framing job; at least one member of almost every family boasted its musician: guitar or banjo or mandolin pickers who cried the old songs while their instruments whined or wailed of griefs and losses in places dimly remembered.

We hated the Townies who cat-called us as Shitkickers . . . Plowboys . . . Luke Plukes. We were a sneering lot, victims of culture shock, defensive and dangerous as only the cornered can be. If you were a Townie you very much wished not to encounter us unless you had the strength of numbers: we would whip your ass and take your money, pledging worse punishments should the authorities be notified. We hated niggers and meskins almost as much as we hated the white Townies, though it would be years before I knew how desperately we hated ourselves.

In time, deposits of ambition, snobbery, and pride caused me to work very hard at rising above common Redneckery. Not being able to beat the Townies, I opted to join them through pathways opened by athletics, debating, drama productions. It was simply better to be In than Out, even if one must desert his own kind. I had discovered, simply, that nothing much on the bottom was worth having.

I began avoiding my Redneck companions at school and dodging their invitations to hillbilly jam sessions, pool hall recreations, forays into the scabbier honky-tonks. The truth is, the Rednecks had come to depress me. Knowing they were losers they acted as such. No matter their tough exteriors when tormenting Townies, they privately whined and sniveled and raged. The deeper their alienations, the smaller they seemed to become physically: excepting an occasional natural jug-butted old boy, Rednecks appeared somehow to be stringier, knottier, more shriveled than others. They hacked the coughs of old men and moved about in old men's motions somehow furtive and fugitive. I did not want to be like them.

Nor did I want to imitate their older brothers or fathers, with whom I worked in the oil fields during summers and on weekends. They lived nomadic lives, following booms and rumors and their restless unguided hearts. It puzzled me that they failed to seek better and more far-flung adventures, break with the old ways and start anew: I was very young then and understood less than all the realities. Their abodes were tin-topped old hotels in McCamey, gasping-hot tents perched on the desert floor near Crane, a crummy tourist court outside Sundown, any number of peeled fading houses decorating Wink, Odessa, Monahans. Such places smelled of sweat, fried foods, dirty socks, the bottoms of the barrel, too much history.

By day we dug sump pits, pissanted heavy lengths of pipe, mixed cement and pushed it in iron wheelbarrows (''wheelbars''), blistered our skins while hot-doping new pipeline, swabbed oil storage tanks, grubbed mesquites and other desert growths to make way for new pump stations. We worked ten hours; the pay ranged from 70 to 94 cents for each of them and we strangely disbelieved in labor unions.

There was a certain camaraderie, yes, a brotherhood of the lower rungs; kidding could be rough, raw, personal. Often, however, the day's sun combined with the evening's beer or liquor to produce a special craziness. Then fights erupted, on the job or in beer joints or among roommates in their quarters. Few rules burdened such fights and the gentle or unwary could suffer real damage. Such people frightened me. They frighten me now, when I encounter them on visits to West Texas beer joints or lollying about a truckstop cafe. If you permit them to know it, however, your life will become a special long-running hell: *Grady, let's me and you whup that booger's ass for him again.* Often, in the oil patch, I acted much tougher than the stuff I knew to be in my bones. It helped to pick a fight occasionally and to put the boots to your adversary once you got him down. Fear and rage being first cousins, you could do it if you had to.

But I can't tell you what it's really like, day to day, being a Redneck: not in the cool language of one whom time has refurbished a bit, nor by use of whatever sensibilities may have been superimposed on me through the years. That approach can hint at it in a gentlemanly way, knock the rough edges off. But it isn't raw enough to put you down in the pit where only the fittest survive: let you smell the blood, know the bone dread, the debts, the pointless migrations, and purposeless days. So I must speak to you from an earlier time, bring it up from the gut, use the language, warts and all— the way it was spoken and the way it was perceived.

You may consider this next section, then, a fictional interlude . . . voices from the past . . . essence of Redneck. Whatever. Anyway, it is something of what life was like for many West Texas people in the late 1940s or early 1950s; I suspect that even today it remains relatively true there and in other sparse grazing places of America's unhorsed riders: those who fight our dirtier wars, make us rich by the schlock and drek they buy and the usurious interest rates they pay, suffer invisible rule and stew in their own poor juices. It is, at once, a story that didn't really happen and one that has happened over and over and over. I am trying to impart, dear reader, something of the constant confrontations, challenges, and survival techniques of white niggers who live on the fringes out near the very edge.

**M**e and Bobby Jack and Red Turpin was feeling real good that afternoon. We'd told this old fat fart bossing the gang to shove his pipeline up his ass sideways and then we'd hitched a ride to Odessa and drawed our time. He was a sorry old bastard, that gang boss. He'd been laying around in such shade as he could find hollaring at us for about six weeks because we didn't pissant pipe fast enough to suit him.

This happened in the morning, just before we would of broke for dinner. Red Turpin was down in the dumps because the finance company had found him and drove his old Chevvy away. We tried to tell him not to sweat it, that it wasn't worth near what he owed on it, but that never wiped out the fact that he was left afoot.

The gang boss had been groaning and moaning more than usual that day. All at once Red spun around to him and said, "I'm ona git a piece of yore ass, Mister Poot, if you don't git offa mine." Well, the gang boss waved his arms and hollared that ole Red was sacked and Red said, "F--- you, Mister Poot. I was a-huntin' a job when I found this 'un."

Me and Bobby Jack was standing there with our mouths dropped open when the gang boss started yelling at us to git back to work, to show him nothing but assholes and elbows. He was jumping around all red in the face, acting like a stroke was on him. Bobby Jack said, "Shit on such as this. Lincoln's done freed the slaves," and about that time he dropped his end of that length of pipe and told the gang boss to shove it. "Sideways, Mister Poot," I hollared. And then I dropped *my* end in the dirt.

Mister Poot squealed like a girl rabbit and grabbed a monkey wrench off the crew truck and warned us not to come no closer. Which would of been hard to do, fast as he was backing up. So we cussed him for seventeen kinds of a fool and peed on the pipe we'd dropped and then left, feeling free as blowing wind.

Out on the Crane Highway we laughed and hooted about calling that old gang boss "Mister Poot," which is what we'd been calling him behind his back on account of he just laid around in the shade by the water cans and farted all day. But finally, after four or five cars and several oil trucks passed us up, we kinda sagged. You could see down that flat old highway for about three days and all there was was hot empty. Red got down-in-the-mouth about his old lady raising hell soon as she learned he'd cussed his way off the job. Bobby Jack said hell, just tell 'er he'd got laid off. "Shit," Red said. "She don't care if it's fared or laid off or carried off on a silk piller. All she knows is, it ain't no paycheck next week."

By the time we'd signed papers and drawed our time at the Morrison Brothers Construction Company there in Odessa, and got a few cool 'uns down in a East Eighth Street beer joint, we was back on top. We played the juke box—Hank Williams, he'd just come out with a new 'un and there was plenty of Tubbs and Tillman and Frizzell—and shot a few games of shuffle board at two-bits a go. It was more fun than a regular day off because we was supposed to be working.

Bobby Jack danced twice with a heavy-set woman in red slacks from Conroe, who'd come to Odessa on the Greyhound to find her twin sister that had been run off from by a driller. But all she'd found was a mad landlord that said the woman's sister had skipped out on a week's rent and had stole two venetian blinds besides. "I called that landlord a damn liar," the Conroe woman said. "My twin sister don't steal. We come from good stock and got a uncle that's been a deputy sheriff in Bossier City, Louisiana, for nearly twenty years."

Bobby Jack had enough nookie in mind to buy her four or five beers, but all she done was flash a little brassiere and give him two different names and tell him about being a fan-dancer at the Texas Centennial in 19-and-36. She babbled on about what all she'd been—a blues singer, a automobile dealer's wife, a registered nurse; everything but a lion tamer it seemed like—until Bobby Jack said, "Lissen, Hon, I don't care what all you been. All I care about is what

you are and what *I* am. And I'm horny as a range bull with equipment hard as Christmas candy. How 'bout you?" She got in a mother huff and claimed it was the worst she'd ever been insulted. When Bobby Jack taken back the last beer he'd bought her, she moved over to a table by herself.

A fleshy ole boy wearing a Mead's Fine Bread uniform straddled a stool by us and said, "Man, I taken a leak that was better'n love. I still say if they'd *give* the beer away and charge a dollar to piss they'd make more money." We talked about how once you'd went to take a beer piss you had to go ever five minutes, where you could hold a gallon up until you'd went the first time.

Red Turpin got real quiet like he does when he's bothered. I whispered to Bobby Jack to keep an eye on the sumbitch because when Red quits being quiet he usually gets real loud and rambunctious in a hurry. Along between sundown and dark, Bobby Jack got real blue. He went to mumbling about owing on his new bedroom set and how much money his wife spent on home permanents and cussing the government for various things. Bobby Jack hated Harry Truman for some reason, and blamed him ever time a barmaid drawed a hot beer or he dropped a dime in a crack. Now it seemed like he was working up to blaming Truman for losing him his job. I didn't much care about Truman either way, but I'd liked President Roosevelt for ending hard times even though ole Eleanor traipsed all over the world and run with too many niggers. My daddy's people come from Georgia before they settled over around Clarksville and hadn't none of us ever been able to stomach niggers.

Bobby Jack kept getting downer and downer. Finally a flyboy from the Midland Air Base tapped his shoulder and asked if he had a match. "Sure, airplane jockey," Bobby Jack said. "My ass and your face." The flyboy grinned sickly. Before he could back off, Bobby Jack asked what he thought of Harry Truman. The flyboy mumbled about not being able to talk about his Commander-in-Chief. "I got your Commander-in-Chief swangin'," Bobby Jack said, cupping his privates in one hand. "Come 'ere and salute 'em." That flyboy set his beer down and took off like a nigger aviator, lurching this way and that.

Bobby Jack felt better for a bit; I even got him and Red Turpin to grinning a little by imitating Mister Poot when we'd cussed him. But it's hard to keep married men perked up very long. I married a girl in beautician's college in Abilene in '46, but we didn't live together but five months. She was a hardshell Baptist and talked to God while she ironed and pestered me to get a job in a office and finish high school at night. Her mother believed that when people died they come back as grubworms.

Red Turpin went to the pay phone back by the men's pisser to tell his wife to borrow her daddy's pickup and come git him. He had to wait a long spell for her to come to the neighbor's phone, and I could tell right off she wasn't doing much rejoicing.

"Goddammit, Emma," Red said. "We'll thresh all that out later. Come git me and eat my ass out in person. It's cheaper than doing it long-distance." Red and Emma lived over in Midland behind the Culligan Bottled Water place. "Lissen," Red said, "*I* sure never stole my own kid's trike today, and I don't know who did. I'll whup his ass when I can find him, but all I'm trying to do right now is git a ride home. What? Well, alright, dammit, *I* don't like hearing the little fartknocker cry neither. Promise 'im we'll buy 'im another 'un.'' He listened for a minute, got real red, and yelled: "Lissen, Emma, *just f--- you*! How many meals you missed since we married?'' From the way he banged the phone down I couldn't tell for sure which one of 'em had hung up first.

Two old cowboys come in about then, the pot-bellied one right tipsy. He was hollaring "*Ah Ha, Santa Flush*!'' and singing of how he was a plumb fool about Ida Red. He slammed me on the back and said, "Howdy, stud! Gettin' any strange?'' He laughed when I said, "It's all strange to me,'' and went on in the pisser real happy. When Red followed the old cowhand in, I just naturally figured he'd went to take a leak.

I moseyed back to the bar. In a little bit Red Turpin slid back on his stool and started drinking Pearl again, big as you please. About a half a beer later the second cowboy went to the pisser and come out like a cannon had shot him, yelling for a doctor and the po-leece. "They done killed ole Dinger,'' he hollared. "I seen that big 'un go in right behind him. They's enough blood in there to float a log.''

Four or five people run back toward the pisser; a general commotion started and I said real quick, "Come on. Let's shuck outta here.'' But Bobby Jack was hopping around cussing Red Turpin, asking what the hell he'd did. Red had a peculiar glaze in his eye; he just kept growling and slapping out at Bobby Jack like a bear swatting with his paw. The barkeep run up and said, "You boys hold what you got.'' He taken a sawed-off shotgun from under the bar and throwed down on us. "Call the po-leece, Skeeter,'' he yelled. "And don't you damn Bohunks move a hair.'' I wouldn't a-moved for big money.

The old cowboy had been helped out of the pisser and was sitting all addled at a back table, getting the blood wiped off his face. He groaned too loud to be good dead and kept asking, "What happened?'' which is what everbody was asking him. The barkeep relaxed his shotgun a smidgen, but when I offered him twelve dollar to let us go on our way, he just shook his head.

Two city cops come in, one fatter than the other; hog fat and jowly. They jangled with cuffs, sappers, and all kinds of hardwear: them sumbitches got more gear than Sears and Roebuck. The biggest cop huffed and puffed like he'd run a hill and said, "What kinda new shit we got stirred up, Frankie?''

The barkeep poked a thumb in our direction and said, "That big ole red-haired booger yonder beat up a Scharbauer Ranch cowboy.''

"What about it, Big 'Un?'' the big cop asked.

"I never hit *him*,'' Red said.

"Oh, I see,'' the big cop said. "That fellow just musta had bad luck and slipped and fell in somebody else's blood.'' I could tell he was enjoying hisself, that he would of po-leeced for free.

"I never hit *him*,'' Red said again. He commenced to cry, which I found disgusting.

"Yeah he did,'' the barkeep said. "Near as I unnerstan it, the boomer hit the cowboy without a word passin'. Far as the cowboy knows, he mighta been hit by a runaway dump truck.''

"On your feet.'' The big cop jerked Red off of the bar stool. He tightened his grip and lowered his voice and said, "You twitch just one of them fat ole shitty muscles, Big

'Un, and I'll sap you a new hat size. And if 'at ain't enough, my partner'll shoot you where you real tender.'' Red kept on blubbering while the short cop fumbled the cuffs on him; me and Bobby Jack looked away and was careful not to say nothing. One time up in Snyder, I ask this constable what a buddy's fine would be when he was being hauled off for common public drunk, and the sumbitch taken me in, too. Next morning in court I found out the fine for common public drunk: $22 and costs.

The big cop went back and talked to the hurt cowboy awhile and wrote down in a notebook; now that his health was better, the hurt cowboy ask for another beer. The cop come walking back to us: "You peckerwoods holding cards in this game?'' We naw-sirred him. The barkeep nodded. The big cop looked us over: "Where you boys work at?'' We told him Morrison Brothers Construction. "Him, too?'' He nodded toward Red. "Well,'' I said, "I heard he quit lately.'' The cop grunted and tapped Bobby Jack on the ass with his billy club and said, "Keep it down to a dull roar, Hoss. I'm tard, and done had six Maggie-and-Jiggs calls. Old ladies throwin' knives and pots at their husbands, or their husbands kickin' the crap out of 'em. I don't wanta come back in this sumbitch 'til my shift's over and I'm scenting beer.''

They taken the old cowboy to the county hospital for stitches. When he passed by, being about half helt-up, I seen his face had been laid open like a busted watermelon. I guess maybe Red's ring that he got in a meskin gyp-joint in that spick town acrost from Del Rio done it. Just seeing it made my belly swim and pitch. One time at Jal, New Mexico, I seen a driller gouge out a roughneck's eye with a corkscrew when they fell out over wages, and I got the same feeling then only more so.

The Conroe woman in red slacks was sashaying around telling everybody with a set of ears how we'd broke a record insulting her just before Red beat up the old cowboy. They all kept looking at us. After we'd drank another beer to show they wasn't spooking us, and dropped a quarter in the juke box like nothing had happened, we eased on out the door.

I wanted to hit Danceland on East Second because a lot of loose hair pie hung out there. Or the Ace of Clubs where they had a French Quarter stripper who could twirl her titty-tassels two different directions at once. But Bobby Jack said naw, hell, he reckoned he'd go on home. I walked with him up to where he turned down the alley running between the Phillips 66 Station and Furr's Cafeteria. "Well,'' Bobby Jack said, "at least ole Emma won't have to sickle over here to give Red a ride to Midland. He's got him a free bed in the crossbar hotel.'' We talked a little about checking on how much Red's bail had been set at, but didn't much come of it. To tell the truth what he had did didn't make much sense and ruined the best part of the night. Without saying so, we kinda agreed he'd brought it on hisself.

I went on over to the Club Cafe and ate me a chicken-fried steak with a bowl of chili-beans on the side and listened to some ole humpbacked waitresses talk about their ailments and how much trouble their kids was. Next day I caught on with a drilling crew up in Gaines County and it wasn't but about six weeks more than I joined the Army just in time to see sunny Korea, so I never did learn what all Red got charged with or how he come out.

*—August 1974*

# SALVATION WORRIES? PROSTATE TROUBLE?

## by Bill Brammer

*"A raffish assortment offering everything from baby chicks to techniques of seduction to stock in gold mines."*

Once upon a time in the real American West, which might have been anyplace people were uprooted, undefined or emotionally underfed, there was seldom heard a word of any kind.

Even now, survivors dwell on that experience best remembered for its intolerable loneliness and the absence of all but the most basic human inputs. Young men would stand at their gateposts all day long for just a glimpse of settlers' wagons heading west. People tended simply to hunker up in a warm place and hope for something to happen: a Bible reading, a laconic exchange, a fragment of correspondence or printed journalism. It could not be long endured, of course, and yet it was—right up until free enterprise, culture, and technology combined to effect a rescue of sorts for all those devastated folks out there on the wretched edge of Western Civilization.

And what was the first message likely to have leaked through by the miracle of radio transmission? Incline your ears to wisdom and rejuvenation:

"Fred's shaking is so much better, friends . . . That old prostate really hurts when it is cold up there in North Dakota."

Who was it? *What* was it? That mesmeric, almost Oracular voice trembling with urgency and unction:

"Folks . . . Friends . . . And all who are weary and oppressed. This is Dr. J. R. Brinkley speaking to you from my home in Del Rio, Texas, with a message for all humanity . . ."

The message, more often than not, dwelt on "the derelictions of this robber gland, the male prostate . . . 90 per cent of all males suffer from the enlarged gland which, if cancerous, eats out the bone marrow and leads to an agonizing end."

Brinkley had hospitals in Del Rio and, later on, San Juan,

*Bill Brammer won the Houghton Mifflin Literary Fellowship Award for his novel,* The Gay Place. *Brammer, one of* Texas Monthly's *first writers, died in February 1978.*

Texas: "San Juan for your rectal problems! Del Rio for the prostate!" He also provided a straight-from-the-hip pocket accounting of available services: a Business Man's Treatment, the Average Man's Treatment, and (as a "humanitarian gesture") the Poor Folks' Treatment. The deal offered businessmen was pegged at $1,000 and was a combination of medical and surgical procedures for relieving "loss of pep and coated tongue." Patients were guaranteed a free urinalysis every six months for the remainder of their lives.

The Doctor's credentials were not impressive by contemporary standards. Gerald Carson, one of his biographers, pointed out that a mail order diploma mill—the "Eclectic Medical University of Kansas City, Mo."—had certified Brinkley in Kansas, and from that point he operated on reciprocal certification in all of eight states. His principal mode of accreditation came through publicity from something they called "goat gland transplantation," which was precisely what it implied.

"So far as I know," he had said, "I was the first man that ever did this operation of taking the goat testicle and putting it in the man's testicle. The glands of a three-weeks-old male goat are laid upon the non-functioning glands of a man. These goat glands do actually feed, grow into and become absorbed by the human glands, and the man is renewed in his physical and mental vigor."

He was cautious enough to disclaim any notion that his operation was in any sense a cure-all, but it was indicated for a remarkably wide range of problems: impotency, insanity, arterio-sclerosis, prostate, high blood pressure, skin diseases, prolonging life and rebuilding the body. His patients were even more impressed, citing success in treating conditions such as "sexual apparatus . . . eyesight . . . influenza, youthful indiscretions, melancholia, hernia, dizzy spells" and such esoteric complaints as "husband acted queerly," or "seemed to be floating through space."

The ether over most of North America was very shortly turbulent with the babble and burble and atmospheric hiss of much of the Republic's long suppressed derangements: mental, emotional, musical, or mercantile. There were hustlers and carny pitchmen, hillbillies and nostrum promoters, minstrels and mind-readers and displaced vaudevilleans and lunatic whoopers from the First Testament. There were tips on horses, astrological revelations, stock market scams, occult intuitions, even a down-home strategist on the hatching of baby chicks.

But always, inescapably, there was Brinkley. He had in fact been broadcasting four times a day since 1923, four years before the creation of the Federal Radio Commission, the first broadcast regulatory agency. He had always owned his own stations, the first of them in Milford, Kansas, a tiny village which nonetheless boasted one of the most powerful signals in North America.

Brinkley had been there from the beginning—loud, clear, cantankerous, and ultimately outrageously rich from his hospital in Milford and a radio prescription dodge which exploited studio-to-patient consultations. He prescribed his own patent elixirs "from any druggist selling my remedies." His earnings on prescriptions alone averaged $14,000 weekly or $728,000 a year—and he managed to keep the whole improbable hustle going for 13 years!

The right to operate a radio station was easily secured in those days of freewheeling enterprisers, and Brinkley's original vision seemed modest enough, giving little hint of the grandiose reality that would soon materialize. He had already made a name for himself at a time when "rejuvenation fever" swept the country. More than 700 surgeons, charlatans, mentalists, necromancers and religious healers were hustling gland therapies of one sort or another to trembling, underpowered aging Americans. Brinkley had also made $12 million on transplants. Among the early Brinkley clients was Harry Chandler, owner of *The Los Angeles Times*. Early in 1922, Brinkley was on the West Coast renovating the libidos of Chandler and his circle of friends. The visit coincided with construction of the Chandler-backed KHJ, first radio station in Los Angeles. Brinkley was intrigued, and said so:

"I thought it would be a nice thing to entertain my patients (back in Milford) by having a radio station close to the hospital where they could lay in bed and listen on their earphones, and so I bought the station and gave lectures over it . . ." Construction was underway by the summer of 1923; a broadcasting license came through in September, and within a few days Brinkley's messages to humanity could be plainly heard in the middle of the Atlantic Ocean:

"A man is as old as his glands. All energy is sex energy! Of all afflictions that men are heir to, impotency is the worst. Who wants to be made young again?"

And so on, through the nights, through the years, ambushing the lonely, unfulfilled, vaguely paranoid and always unsuspecting wooly-hatted frontier Americans. Persons deprived of all sensory input will presently begin to hallucinate. Catch them at that low ebb, exposed and vulnerable, and no information seems too outrageous or fanciful.

Yet, for a time it appeared even Brinkley might have gone too far. In 1930 he lost both his radio and medical licenses—the lure and the cure—but it was soon apparent he had merely been pressed into vastly more ambitious media thrills. He had already made an accommodation with the Mexican government for creation of a 75,000 watt sta-

tion at Villa Acuna, Coahuila, across the International Bridge from Del Rio. Brinkley's Kansas operation had been sustained by a mere 1,000 watts of power. His new acquisition, XER, was suddenly pumped into operation as the second most powerful station in the world. Within two years and a quantum leap to a half-million watts of power, XER ruled them all with enough juice to blot out any U.S. or Canadian station operating on channels within 50 kilocycles of its wavelength. The mighty voice of XER—"Mexico's radio outlaw . . . bootlegger of the air"—washed far and wide over the Western Hemisphere.

Thus was spawned the phenomenon of border radio, and Brinkley very nearly on his own had created the mode and the manner, the shape and substance and money-grubbing dynamic that has scarcely altered in 40 years.

Brinkley himself built two more stations: XEPN in Piedras Negras and XEAW in Reynosa. He also set the pattern closely followed by later entrepreneurs. There was Norman Baker, who promoted his cancer cure over XENT across from Laredo before he was convicted of using the mails to defraud. Brinkley sold his Reynosa station to Carr P. Collins who made a fortune pushing Crazy Water Crystals, an elixir which claimed relief for many complaints but especially constipation.

These stations sold commercial time to a raffish assortment of patent medicine men, evangelists, hate-mongers, mystics, diploma mills, handwriting analysts, personality therapists and merchandisers offering everything from baby chicks to techniques of seduction to stock in gold mines. The real gold mine, of course, was right down there among the sweltering palms of Tex-Mex country. If Wayne Rainey could strike it rich selling over seven million "talking harmonicas," one could only imagine what profit could be made by stations selling nothing more substantial than broadcast time.

William Burns, now operating the International Advertising Agency in San Antonio but once a sales representative for the Brinkley station in the late Thirties, explains part of the edge: "We were selling air time in exchange for good U.S. dollars—while our overhead was in pesos. Operational costs were negligible."

Burns also recalls Del Rio at a time when the environment was quite literally electric. "With half a million watts coming out of those transmitters, the whole place seemed energized. You could touch a wire fence and pick up a mild shock. Try to use a telephone and you were likely to hear old Brinkley's voice leaking out of the earpiece. The air was just charged with the stuff."

And Larry King comes up with this reminiscence from his hard-scuffling Horatio days in West Texas:

"One time in 1951 I was doing local news and spinning country records for Station KCRS in Midland, all for the grand sum of $70 a week, when this thin fella with a prominent adam's apple and sporty two-tone shoes walked in and introduced himself. Looked something like a 1930's road drummer come on good times: big sparkly rings and gaudy string tie and big car and hard essence of ambition. Said he had heard me on his car radio, just passing through, and I had the kind of palaver and down-home delivery that would make me a fortune if I would let it—and him—just do it. I said for money I would just about do anything, and he explained how he was connected with that Del Rio/Villa Acuna station. Described himself as an independent time contractor, which meant he bought up time in blocks of 60 minutes from the station and used it as he wished. He then subcontracted to guys like me who could impersonate some evangelist, say, preach a little, sing a little, then give a spiel for etchings of the Last Supper or prayer cloths to be placed anywhere you happen to hurt. He said they even once tried selling bottled Holy Water from the Rio Grande.

"Or I might come on as Uncle Buddy or Cowboy Jim or whatever, so long as people liked me enough to buy tonics or hymnals or unsexed baby chicks or genuine simulated diamond rings. Yes, the deal was he would pay me $125 weekly to start, and more if I was good at it, plus a percentage of whatever came in from the good folks out there in Radio Land. If I liked it, and proved to have the talent he thought he saw in me, then he would sell me some of his own time and I could invent my own programs and characters and keep all I made—and conceivably become a big-time independent contractor like himself."

King remembers it as "about the best offer I ever had, and I damn near took it." Then he adds: "After a week, maybe, of searching what little soul I had, I decided that life called me surely to more noble roles, so I declined . . ."

Brinkley and his imitators along the border were never diverted by such irrelevant concerns. Not that there weren't casualties now and again along the way. There was Norman Baker, the cancer quack who served time for mail fraud. Up until the early Sixties there was the Rev. Charles Jessup who nightly appealed for assistance in his own personal care and feeding: "Keep this little ole boy from the clay hills of Alabama on the air. I'm your brother, and I'm doin' the best I can. Won't you, dear friends, send me your offering today?"

In 1964 Jessup was arrested and charged with mail fraud, specifically for the use of donations to buy property, big cars, boats, seaplanes, and dabble in illegal cock fighting. The indictment claimed Jessup represented himself as "a holy and devout man whose whole life was devoted to God's work, a man who had talked with God." He had also talked with lady friends, the indictment charging him with concealing the fact he had been married four times, obtaining two divorces by false statements and courting and marrying a 15-year-old while still married to his third wife. His Fellowship Revival Association, the indictment claimed, was used to solicit donations, evade taxes, maintain reduced mailing privileges, and otherwise enrich himself personally.

Jessup was subsequently fined a few thousand dollars, and sentenced to a year in prison plus five years probation during which he would be forbidden to engage in any self-promotion ventures.

Bringing down the Brinkley empire was considerably more complicated. It was not until 1941 that pressure from the U.S. finally provoked the Mexican government to deny XERA its wave-length assignment and send in the Mexican Army to tear down the station and its towers. And before Brinkley could be brought to trial for mail fraud in 1942, he was dead of larger-than-life natural causes: heart blockage, kidney ailments, incomplete healing of an amputated leg. Within a few years, Brinkley's former associates were back in business and carrying on the glorious tradition—XERF was established as a successor to XERA, and the U.S. continued to be jolted nightly by the big voice from little Del

Rio advertising pyorrhea cures, penny-a-day burial insurance, engraved tombstones.

The formula has seldom been tampered with to this day. The format of Station XEG in Monterrey is practically identical to XERF, and XELO in Juarez tailored much of its broadcast time to similar programming until a recent change of ownership signaled a perceptible shift to soul-station trappings. Other faces in the cloud are PJB, powered by half a million watts from the Netherlands Antilles, beaming a signal north *and* south, and XETRA in Rosarita Beach, Mexico, covering Tijuana, San Diego, all of Southern California and just about anyplace else an effective signal strength of a quarter-million watts might reach.

The superpowered border radio has been more or less condoned by Mexican authorities from the outset, presumably because the U.S. and Canadian governments had arrogantly divided between themselves the entire long-wave broadcast band, leaving neither Cuba nor Mexico any clear channels at all. The border stations, traditionally owned by American investors, have always cut into wave lengths used by U.S. and Canadian stations which are forbidden by law from stoking up their own transmission facilities. With the border stations' more powerful means of transmission, American advertisers were able to exploit their products throughout most of the U.S.

The hellfire and lamentation manner might have caused more sophisticated listeners to view the programs with contempt, but the economic rationale was incontestably sound.

The boondock listening audience was enormous, intensely loyal and infinitely patient—always desperate to invest a few more hard-earned dollars in suitably-packaged propositions guaranteeing anything from guitar lessons ("Don't you-all know guitar players make lots of money?") to relief from hemorrhoidal pain to mere eternal nirvana in the heavenly kingdom. Even conventional broadcasters began marketing products chiefly popular with country people: Black Draught, Wine of Cardui, Garrett Snuff, Nehi and Royal Crown, Redman Chewing Tobacco and Light Crust Flour.

In *The Story of Country Music*, the border stations were credited with the principal role in the dissemination of country music throughout the U.S. "If one could endure the seemingly never ending advertising," the book notes, "he could occasionally hear a hillbilly song of the best quality." XERA, for example, carried the Carter Family in the last three years of their professional recording career (1938 to 1941), and other stations carried such strong traditionalist groups as Mainer's Mountaineers, the Callahan Brothers, the Delmore Brothers, the Pickard Family and Cowboy Slim Rinehart. It was generally assumed that New York and New England were the only areas where such programming did not claim wide appeal.

Nor do operational problems differ markedly from the time 40 years ago when Brinkley was obliged to prettify his own house with at least the appearance of nominal Mexican ownership. The stock ownership of the Villa Acuna Broadcasting Company was shifted, by bearer certificates, to Brinkley friends on the Mexico side of the river who just as obligingly handed the stock back to Brinkley. Whereupon the Mexican Department of Communications concluded that XER belonged to a group composed entirely of Mexican nationals, that the station was run legally and in accordance

25

with all regulations, that it did not interfere with U.S. stations, and that any person could use it for "business, scientific, cultural or literary broadcasting."

A contemporary broadcaster is compelled to play similar games. Border stations are ostensibly owned by Mexican nationals with exclusive sales rights leased to U.S. corporations which handle actual station operations. In practice, all shares of stock are signed over (as "bearer certificates") at the time of issuance and are held in American banks. The procedure is standard for American companies doing business in revolutionary Mexico—and a matter of well-rehearsed negotiable routine for Mexico City law firms.

A broadcaster with a good many years of experience along both sides of the border states flatly: "There is no problem in successfully operating a Mexican radio station in the United States. If the Federal Communications Commission was as easy to get along with as the Mexican government, there would be few problems in operating any stations today!" He admits that there are, of course, "basic techniques" of ownership of Mexican stations which must be followed, but these present no problem with proper legal guidance.

Then, too, and surely not the least among the plus factors of such operations, there is the delightful fact that Mexican stations are licensed for 30 years rather than the three years common in the United States.

Just how staggeringly lucrative a border station beamed toward Yankee buying power can be is suggested by the example of XELO in Juarez, recently purchased for close to a million dollars by a group of El Paso businessmen-investors. The seller was one Jack McVeigh, also from El Paso, whose father-in-law had personally built the station before the war. When prospective buyers began appraising current profits and future possibilities, it was noted straightaway that the broadcast concession was good until 1989 and that there was virtually no upward limitation on its broadcast frequency. Current gross revenues were $300,000 yearly, which, with low operating costs typical of border facilities, produced a cash flow of $130,000 a year. This was the kind of money still circulating even *after* the McVeigh family had paid themselves approximately $70,000 in salaries as employees of both the station and their own advertising sales agency.

None of which, however, should suggest the McVeigh ownership was realizing XELO's full potential. Consultants were quick to point out that refinements in equipment and in programming would produce dramatic results—juicing up effective signal strength from 50 to 100 per cent and attracting a vastly larger listenership on both sides of the river. One critic noted the station was about where it was in 1944: "It simply does not program in a modern manner and thus fails to attract the Mexican audience in El Paso to the degree it logically should."

And another observer commented: "With a station of this power, the number of formats in which success is possible is limited only by the imagination and promotional ability of the operator . . . It is likely that a new owner might consider retention of an improved format of Spanish programming until sunset when the skywave effect makes the station really begin to reach out . . . Additional opportunities arise in an expansion of the religious category in the evening hours and a strong format after the religious block. The greatest opportunity exists for the station as an absolute

maximum power operation, one which could become a legend in broadcasting within a short time. That the present owner is short-sighted in this regard is shown clearly by the fact that he chooses to sign off the finest night signal in North America at 12 midnight."

Short-sighted, just conceivably, but one wonders how listeners might ever feel short-rationed or vaguely deprived by premature signoffs of contemporary border programming. Take a quick, dial-spinning tour almost any evening and then reflect upon the losses.

There is Reverend Ike, the free-wheeling black evangelist out of Boston who is almost continuously on tour (taped rebroadcasts heard on XERF) and makes no apologies for his preoccupations: "The lack of money is the root of all evil!" He goes on to celebrate the coin of the realm and anybody's steady accumulation thereof:

"I don't care what you say, money is wonderful stuff . . . Don't care how much holy ghost or holy goose you got, you need money! When people are broke and down and out, that's sickness and I'm against sickness . . . You don't think money is dirty or evil do you? Everybody give money a great big hand and say MONEY! That's right. Everybody needs money, and even I need money. It takes millions of dollars to keep this ministry going. Now I didn't say thousands, I said millions! One issue of our magazine we send out, which tells you how to use your mind power to get what you want, to attain financial success, one issue costs $350,000 for printing alone."

And Brother Carroll in Dallas plugs appearances on his Southern tour and on his "great crusade in Toronto, ministering under the big tent," before asking to support his worthy cause: "We're helping orphans and widows and the needy everywhere. Sit down right now and make out a check. You'll be prospered by it. You'll be blessed four fold. Look for the signs! Renewed strength and health, and a healing will come to your body, giving you an abundance of power . . . God bless you and keep you over Christmas."

It is almost a relief to come upon Don and Earl, who have been picking and singing gospel music on XEG for 20 years and have nothing to sell except a few more songs—101 songs, to be exact: "Now we gonna sang you 'nother song in jus' a minnit. We been on the radio twenny years and here's the biggest offer ever—we'll send you six different gospel record albums, featuring 101 songs by Don and Earl, for only $5, and we pay the postage!"

The Rev. George Cooper of San Antonio supports his programs with a grab-bag of items: calendars, ballpoint pens, 13 multicolored Bible pictures, a biography of his life "from start to finish," an automatic needle-threader, and "a large-print red-letter Bible approximately one-inch thick."

Is there no relief from the seemingly rigid format, scarcely modified in 40 years? Well, change is not likely so long as those cards, letters and dollar bills keep coming. Yearly billings for English-language religious programs on XELO, for example, totaled more than $170,000 in 1971. There is the shift to after-midnight soul station formats, sponsored by the likes of "Hollywood Discount Records" and perhaps some merchandisers for Bikini underwear.

There's also Brother Human, barely hanging in there for 15 minutes a week (Fridays, 11:30 p.m., Station XEG), paid for and performed by a group of Austin provocateurs masquerading as the Church of the Coincidental Metaphor. Even Brother Human needs help to carry on his guerrilla raids against the old hucksters:

"Humble natives! I come here tonight as a messenger of your great white friend Brother Human, who has commissioned me to indoctrinate you, here in this last stronghold of ignorance, in the principles of humility and servitude which enable great men such as himself to lead you in prayerful obedience . . .

"And what a trip I been on! Permit me to enlighten you as to what is real and what ain't real . . . Every aspect of your life must be examined—what you eat, what you drive, what you sit on, who you walk on, what you live in, what you sleep in, who you give money to . . . . I know there are lots of artificial things that Satan tempts you to buy . . . Says, that shiny, gas-eatin' car is better than the plain economy model, says frozen foods are better than fresh food, says two more inches of shag carpet can cushion you from the reality of everyday evil . . . Says pave those forests and level those trees . . . Says give that money to a flashy, pile-drivin', triple-clutchin', nonstop religion that only seeks to bankroll a few high-rollin' reverends.

"But stop right there, hallelujah brothers, for I'm bringing you the message that will unseat Satan! Brother Human and all of us here at the Church of the Coincidental Metaphor are askin' you for money. But in return we're givin' you that good-mileage economy religion, that natural divinity untainted by preservatives of man-made hype, that solid wood floor on which to build a real faith! Friends, our religion is no limousine; we got no continental kits; we're not white-walled evangelists with padded dashes. We're straight stick, standard shift, four-door everyday evangelists bringing you the non-polluted word. But even our little car burns gas, brothers, and we got no divine credit card. So help us out and send those dollars to Brother Human!"

Move over Marjoe, you ain't heard nuthin'!

*—March 1973*

*Photography by Constance Ashley*

# SISTERHOOD IS POWERFUL

## by Prudence Mackintosh

*One of the most important decisions in a girl's life may be made in her first week of college—at sorority rush.*

Of all the trappings of my four years at the University of Texas, only one followed me to Dallas and appears destined to be with me the rest of my life: my sorority. Maligned and revered, the butt of jokes and jibes and the goal of countless anxious mothers for their daughters, sororities have kept their place in the rites of passage of a whole segment of Texas society that moves from summer camp to sorority to Junior League, with the same basic rituals serving at each level to strengthen the bond of women together. When I returned to Austin last fall to witness sorority rush, I had expected that the intervening years of the late sixties and the seventies would have changed things utterly. Instead, I found my memories going back to my own rush.

It was the fall of 1962, and I had just hobbled in ill-fitting stiletto-heeled shoes from the Chi Omega house on Wichita to the Tri Delt house on 27th Street in Austin. Word had not reached Texarkana that during rush week, regardless of the University policy which forbade freshmen to have cars, it was unseemly to walk from sorority house to sorority house. Socially astute and ambitious mothers from Houston and Dallas had willingly stranded themselves at the Villa Capri motel near campus, so that their daughters could drive the family car and arrive poised and oblivious to the beastly Austin September sun in their de rigueur dark cottons.

My dark cottons were severely circled under the armpits and the humidity made me regret the tight permanent wave that my mother had felt was necessary to keep my already naturally curly hair out of my eyes. The lengthy walk had made me late, and I half hoped that I could sit this one out. But before I could blot the sweat from my upper lip, a vivacious girl costumed like Judy Garland's dog Toto pinned a huge nametag on me and led me down a cardboard yellow

*Prudence Mackintosh is a contributing editor of* Texas Monthly *and winner of a 1976 Penney-Missouri Award.*

brick road into the cool interior of her sorority house.

Like young Jay Gatsby, I had seldom been in such beautiful houses before. Although F. Scott Fitzgerald never mentioned Daisy's sorority affiliation, these houses—particularly the Tri Delt and Pi Phi houses—could have been hers. Like Gatsby, I suspected that these houses held "ripe mystery . . . a hint of bedrooms upstairs more beautiful and cool than other bedrooms, of gay and radiant activities taking place through its corridors." I was much too naive to recognize voices "full of money," but I did marvel at the inexhaustible charm of these breathless beauties. I wrote to my parents after that first day of parties with Pi Phis, Tri Delts, Zetas, Chi Omegas, Kappas, and Thetas that I had never seen such a gathering of beautiful girls in my life. "High in a white palace, the king's daughters, the golden girls"—in Pappagallo shoes.

Sororities at the University of Texas in 1962 were large by national standards. If all pledges remained active, a UT sorority could usually boast close to 150 active members. Even if only half of them were really beauties, the effect was overwhelming when you saw them—exquisitely groomed—in one large room.

After what seemed interminable non-conversation and punch which never really quenched one's thirst, the lights dimmed at the Tri Delt house, and Toto gave me a quick squeeze, "You just sit right here on the front row. I'll be back when the skit is over." My naiveté once again kept me from being impressed by this privileged front-row position. Being squired around by a costumed sorority personality, I would later learn, also might indicate favoritism. The skits blur a little in my mind, but they were nothing less than major musical productions, often with professional lighting and costumes. We were the tail end of a generation raised on Broadway musicals and consequently were prime suckers for lyrics lifted from *Carousel*, *Showboat*, or *South*

*Pacific* and altered for sorority purposes. I distinctly remember a green-eyed Tri Delt named Kay dressed as the carnival barker from *Carousel* sending shivers down my spine with "When you walk through a storm, hold your head up high . . ." It was that unflinching eye contact that got me every time, and by the end of the week, if you were a desirable rushee, someone might be squeezing your elbow by the time Kay's voice reached the final "You'll never walk aaalone." Although the songs varied, that was the pitch at most of the houses. The girls locked arms around the room and swayed gently as they sang, all to remind you that it was a big University and that joining these self-confident beauties meant not having to face it alone.

As I watched these sorority girls flash their perfect teeth and sing and dance, I surmised that they possessed secrets that they might share if I managed to get out of the foyer and into those upstairs rooms. They not only knew their way to class on the 150 acres that then composed the University, but they also knew appropriate retorts when drunk Kappa Sigs pulled their skirts up at parties and howled, "Look at the wheels on this woman!" I knew they could hold their beer and their cool when someone "dropped trou" or toga at a Fiji Island party. I was sure that they did not worry—as I did—about where one slept when one accepted an OU-Texas date to Dallas or when one made the bacchanalian pilgrimage to Laredo for George Washington's Birthday.

**B**ut the week was not all costumed escorts, squeezes, and front-row seats. Sometimes the carefully concealed rushing machinery broke down and the party lost its air of graciousness. A survivor recalls that in the grand finale of the *Carousel* skit, performers tossed bags of popcorn to prize rushees on the front row. One player overshot the front row, but remedied her error by wrenching the popcorn bag from the second-row innocent's hand and restoring it to its intended mark. More often the embarrassing moments were brought on by a provincial rushee. It's probably apocryphal, but the story floated around for years that, on being passed a silver tray of cigarettes, a rushee at the Zeta house looked puzzled for a moment, then reached furtively into her purse, emptied her cigarette pack on the tray, and quickly passed it on.

At the Pi Phi house I once held four "floaters" (sorority members who moved in and out of many circles at each party to get an overall picture of the rushees) captive with a fifteen-minute maudlin tale about the day my dog died when I was eleven. They feigned intense interest, their eyes brimming at appropriate times, but doubtless they collapsed in spasms of laughter and goose calls when I made my exit. The next day, to my horror, I was repeatedly introduced at the Pi Phi house with, "This is Prudence. Get her to tell you that neat story about her dog."

But despite our faux pas, my roommates and I had an easy time of it. We were under no parental pressure to pledge at all. Totally ignorant of the machinations of rush, we innocently perceived the whole rush week scene as one exhausting and bewildering but happy experience in which we were to decide whom we liked best. We had only the vaguest notions about sorority rankings on campus. Although there were twenty sororities on the UT campus in 1962, for many girls, accepting a bid from other than the "big six" was apparently unthinkable. We were aware of tears down the hall as first- and second-period "cuts" were

made by the sororities, but we could not appreciate the pain of the "legacy" (the daughter of a sorority alum) whose mother responded to her daughter's rejection with, "Pack your bags, honey, SMU has deferred rush." Or the one who declared, "See, I told you you should have gone to Tech first"—where it was easier to make it into an elite sorority and then transfer to UT.

The third period of rush week consisted of two Saturday evening parties. It was tense, and girls on both sides were exhausted. Members had culled their rushee lists to approximately 100. Too many rushees at a final period party could scare top rushees away. ("There were ten Houston girls at that party; they won't take us all.") In 1962 rushees were required to wear "after-five" dresses to these parties. Members usually dressed in white or, in the case of the Kappas, in sepulchral black. Sidewalks were lined with hurricane lamps and the houses were candlelit. This was the party for sentimental tearjerkers. The Thetas were renowned for leaving no dry eyes. The Tri Delts put a string of pearls around your neck and instructed you to toss a wishing pearl in a shell fountain while an alumna with a haunting voice sang mysteriously from an upstairs window. The Kappas still croon in four-part harmony.

*And when we tell you*
*How wonderful you are,*
*You'll never believe it.*
*You'll never believe it.*
*That girls so fine could ever be united in fraternity*
*And they all wear the little golden key.*
[descant: *ah-ah-ah-ah*]
*And when you wear one,*
*And you're certainly going to wear one.*
[This is when the not so subtle elbow squeeze came.]
*The proudest girl in this wide world you'll be*
*You'll never believe it.*
*You'll never believe it.*
*That from this great wide world*
*We've chosen YOU.*
[Really look 'em in the eye.]

After two such parties (a first and second preference), the rushees departed for Hogg Auditorium to sign preference cards, which would be sorted by computer. Needless to say, no one folded, spindled, or mutilated her card. Sorority members would be up in all-night final hash sessions to determine their top 50 choices. On Sunday afternoon, the computer would print out the results. Panhellenic representatives sat with boxes of alphabetized envelopes. For appearances' sake, there was an envelope for every girl who had attended a final party, but some contained cards with the message, "You have received no sorority bid at this time. Please feel free to come by the Panhellenic office to register for open rush." Amid the squealing and squeezing that went on as envelopes were ripped open, perhaps it was possible to run unnoticed from the room with such an envelope and back to a lonely dorm room for a bitter cry. We were among the shriekers and squeezers and we did not notice. My three roommates and I had received bids to the same sorority, and our course was set.

**A**lthough we were to become somewhat aberrant sorority members, we had unwittingly chosen our bridesmaids, the godmothers for our future children, and access to certain social circles.

Others in our pledge class already had this social entree by virtue of their birth; numerous legacies recall hearing Kappa songs as lullabies. I remember being fascinated by a framed family tree that hung in the study hall of the Kappa house. The genealogy was illustrated by linking Kappa keys (the sorority symbol) indicating that all of the women in this family had been Kappas for four generations. I distinctly remember feeling sorry for these girls whose choices were made inevitable by long family tradition. Still others had simply been born in the right neighborhoods and had distinguished themselves in the privileged big-city high schools—which then were Lamar (Houston), Alamo Heights (San Antonio), Highland Park (Dallas), and Arlington Heights (Fort Worth). Small-town sorority members might have already joined these elite circles at expensive summer camps. Only one of my new Kappa roommates had done any of these things. She was a product of Camp Mystic, had attended a boarding school, recognized prestige clothing labels, and generally knew her way around the social scene into which the other three of us had stumbled. She was appalled at our ignorance. We had blindly selected our sorority because we liked each other and because we agreed that the Kappas' whole rush setup was pleasantly amateurish and not at all intimidating. Quite frankly, we felt like we might be able to help them out. In a small-town high school, where rivalry was not particularly fierce, one tended to get an inflated idea of one's abilities and talents. In a competitive big-city high school, one might be a cheerleader or serve on the student council, but in a smaller pond like ours, it was entirely possible to be cheerleader, star in the senior play, editor of the school paper, and a member, and probably an officer, in every school organization and still do well scholastically.

When we expressed these reasons for pledging later in a rush evaluation questionnaire, our active "sisters," knowing that our egos could obviously take it, were quick to inform us that our pledge class had been a tremendous disappointment.

There were other illusions destroyed that freshman year. Girls who had chastely sung of truth, beauty, and honor during rush and had even lectured our pledge class on ladylike behavior befitting a sorority member would be seen holding forth with sloshing beer cup atop the toilet seat in the powder room during a Sigma Chi match party, "Furthermore, remember, you *can* drink like a lady."

But the scales would not really drop from our eyes until rush the following year. We had spent many summer hours rewriting and casting skits and painting new scenery, and though exhausted we looked forward to rush with the enthusiasm that only one who has not already endured it can possess. The business of UT rush was mind boggling. Every member was required to attend unless she was out of the country. On arrival in Austin the week before rush week, members were handed a schedule of workshop activities and a list of at least 300 names containing pertinent information about each rushee. Hours and hours were spent in the basement with a slide projector flashing pictures of rushees on a screen while we shouted names, hometowns, and other key information. I was totally unprepared for the power blocs from the big cities. Houston might send twenty highly recommended girls through our rush, but the actives from Houston already knew which ones were to be eliminated before the end of the week. Gradually, as the pictures be-

came more familiar on the screen during workshop, someone would shout out in the darkened room, "Gotta get that girl!" or "Key to Houston—get her, we get 'em all" or "Theta legacy-Theta pledge, forget her." As the sessions got longer, girls became giddy and pictures of less than beautiful girls would be greeted with uncharitable mooing. I learned to become exceedingly wary of those air-brushed Gittings portraits of girls in their Hockaday graduation gowns.

Besides giving us some sight recognition of the rushees, I think "the flicks," as we called the grueling picture sessions in the basement, served another purpose. When combined with song memorizing, skit practices, loss of sleep, and evangelical exhortations to "fire up!" they produced a certain singlemindedness that would enable almost-grown women to revert to what in retrospect seems incredibly childish behavior. Happenings in the outside world had no bearing on our lives that week. What really mattered was stealing Houston's adorable Jo Frances Tyng away from the Pi Phis. By the end of rush week, when all but the die-hards had conceded loss, we dubbed her "Ring-ching-Tyng" (as in "Ring-Ching Pi Beta Phi," a song sung to the jingle of gold charm bracelets at the Pi Phi house).

"Silence rules" prescribed by Panhellenic to prevent undue pressure on any rushee only contributed to the unreality of the whole experience. From the time they arrived in Austin until the end of rush week, rushees could associate only with the other rushees. They could not have dates or talk to their parents. Sorority members were isolated in their respective houses with all telephones disconnected except one. Such isolation on both sides set the scene for considerable emotional buildup, hence the tears by third-period party, which were variously interpreted as "she loves us—we've got her" or "she loves us, but her mother was a Zeta and called her, crying." In retrospect, I think all the tears were small nervous breakdowns."

When rush week began that year, we poured through the front door clapping and yelling, "I'm a Kappa Gamma, awful glad I amma, a rootin-tootin' K-K-G." I remember being slightly embarrassed by the peculiar stares we received from nonparticipants passing by, but nevertheless I sought out my assigned rushee and did my best to "give her a good rush" (introduce her to as many people as I could). By the third party of the day, our mouths were so dry that we sometimes had trouble getting our lips down over our teeth when the perpetual rush smile was no longer required. I was chastised more than once by a rush captain who saw me monopolize a rushee by having some "meaningful conversation" with her away from the babbling crowds, thus spoiling her chances for maximum recognition in the cut sessions that night.

The language of rush week almost requires a special lexicon. After the first round of parties, I was bewildered by the basement voting sessions. The rush captain had to keep things moving and be sure that sufficient people were dropped from our list each night to keep subsequent parties from being overcrowded. Certain signals developed for expedience. Members in agreement with a favorable comment being made on a rushee would begin to snap their fingers. Widespread finger snapping meant the rushee had sufficient support and that discussion could be curtailed. I also encountered that wonderful euphemism, "the courtesy cut."

The rush captain carefully explained that we owed it to legacies to cut them after first-period parties if we did not intend to pledge them. ''That way they can go another direction,'' she reasoned with us. We never allowed ourselves to consider that other houses were cutting the girl that night because she was *our* legacy—leaving her *no* ''direction'' to go. To avoid gossipy invasions of a rushee's past indiscretions, any doubts about a girl's reputation were phrased, ''I don't believe she is Kappa material.'' From a reasonably credible source, this phrase could utterly destroy the rushee's chance—no further discussion needed. Another shorthand signal that either cut a rushee from the list or initiated a lengthy debate was, ''Y'all, I just think she'd be happier elsewhere.'' I remember one particularly stormy evening when this phrase was used on an active member's sister.

It took me until the second year of rush to perceive the battle lines that inevitably were drawn within chapters during rush. We dubbed it ''the flowers versus the flower pots.'' One ludicrous evening the debate in the basement had gone hot and heavy over a girl who had outstanding recommendations, scholastic average, activity record, and family background. She simply wasn't ''beautiful, adorable, or precious.'' Just as the fingers began to snap favorably, a member whom I recall as being particularly nonproductive except during rush, gained the floor and whined, as only Texas girls can, ''But yew-all, would you ask your boyfriend to get her a date?'' The strongest proponent of the girl rose to her feet and shouted, ''We've got enough flowers in this chapter! What we need are some pots to put them in.'' My sentiments were usually with the pots, the solid citizens who kept the chapter machinery rolling by doing the undesirable jobs, kept the grade-point average high, and generally provided the diversity and good humor that flowers who rose at 5:30 a.m. to begin teasing and spraying their hair so often lacked. Flowers, of course, performed the essential function of keeping the sorority's reputation with fraternities high enough to insure a steady stream of eligible males in and out the front door.

Although alumnae money and time kept the sorority houses well furnished, alumnae pressure varied from house to house. During rush week only one alum adviser was allowed at voting sessions, but alumnae could attend the parties. Aside from the pressure they exerted in the cities as to who received recommendations, alums had little influence in our rush. This was not the case at other houses. Friends from other sororities say that they were constantly plagued with alumnae who could not resist offering unauthorized ''oral bids'' at their parties. The Thetas, in those days, were traditionally beset by alumnae, not only from Austin but also from Houston and Dallas. Making an impression on Mrs. Alum at a party might be just as important as being labeled ''precious'' by the entire Houston active contingent. One former rush captain recalled a very persistent alum who as a last resort threatened to keep all the active members from her hometown out of the Junior League if they didn't see to it that a certain legacy was pledged. The girl was pledged, but regrettably her pledge pin was jerked before the year was out for swimming nude with a dozen boys at their fraternity house after curfew.

At the end of the week the final vote was taken. The final usually included about three-fourths flowers and one-fourth

pots, with legacies who had survived the courtesy cut securely listed at the top. Other names could be shifted around in the last-minute voting session held after the tearful final preference party. This was the party where oral bids, strictly prohibited by Panhellenic, slipped out. Rushees hoping for some assurance or just overcome by emotion would weep and hug their active friends at the end of the party and say, ''Oh, I just wish I could stay here forever.'' Statements like these would cause an uproar in the downstairs sessions. A cynic would rise and say, ''Yeah, she said the same thing to the Pi Phis an hour ago.'' But a believer would respond, ''Y'all, I know she has a Pi Phi mother and two active sisters, but she wants us . . . I know she does. We've got to move her up the list.''

The computer had its final say, and by Sunday afternoon, since several sororities were fiercely competing for the same 50 girls, everyone's list had been altered somewhat. New pledges were greeted once again with hugging and squealing and after a quick supper were lined up like so many prize cattle in an auction to be inspected by the ultimate judges—the fraternity men. One of my favorite flowerpots recalled it this way. ''If you were a beauty, you were immediately asked for a date and taken out of the gruesome inspection line. Because we were arranged alphabetically, I got to stand next to someone named Tancy, five-feet-two, curvy, giggly . . . well, precious. Ten minutes after we lined up, she was surrounded with guys elbowing and shoving to get closer. I was ignored unless someone needed to know Tancy's name. I vividly remember standing there, awkward and skinny, alternately wishing painful and exotic diseases on Tancy and at the same time cursing my parents for spending all that money on my 'intellectual development' instead of taking me to a good plastic surgeon in Dallas. I felt a little guilty when cute little Tancy was pregnant by December and had to depledge.''

Pledges were guaranteed a date every night during University registration week, thanks to the efforts of fraternity and sorority social chairmen who laboriously matched girl pledge class with boy pledge class and posted the lists at the respective houses. At least two of my ''match'' dates took one look at my name and were suddenly called away to their grandmothers' funerals. It was just as well; I could never drink enough beer to get into the swing of fraternity parties anyway. Even after I became an active member, no one ever shared the secrets of the cool retort, and sure enough tears came to my eyes when a drunk Kappa Sig pulled my dress up in the middle of the dance floor. I often wonder if some of my contemporaries who married their fraternity boyfriends, and have since divorced, perhaps mistook three years of standing arm-in-arm with sloshing beer cups in front of blaring bands as real intimacy. Could it be that when the keg stopped flowing and the music quit playing, they found they hardly knew each other?

Within the sorority system, however, good friendships did develop. Perhaps we would have experienced the same bonding in a dorm or co-op; however, I doubt that I would have known 150 women on the University campus as well as I did these without such a formal structure.

My sorority sisters and I did serve at each other's weddings, and my children *do* have a Kappa godmother. We still exchange the Christmas cards with the long notes attached. Although we were frequently stereotyped as "look-alike-think-alikes" by our critics, within a group of 150 girls there was inevitable diversity. These were the days when the Bored Martyrs (a notorious women's drinking society) were witty girls who truly could have been Mortar Boards (an honor society) if they hadn't become cynical so young. We also had our share of philosophy majors, musicians, artists whose rooms were boycotted by the maids and labeled fire hazards by the fire marshal, campus politicians, professional bridge players, and party girls who frequently majored in elementary education or jumped from college to college fleeing scholastic probation. Most were, of course, from wealthy families, and for me, who had attended a high school where only 15 per cent went to college, it was an education in how the other half lived. I'll never forget my father's first visit to the Kappa house. He stood in the foyer gazing at the lovely furnishings and curved stairway. "Honey," he said, "why do you bother to come home?" The sorority parking lot was filled with the latest model automobiles; one sister drove a classy vintage Mercedes. When a fire damaged the Dallas Neiman-Marcus one fall, there was genuine distress over whether Christmas would come that year. Being a part of the Greek community in the early sixties was a way of feeling rooted in a big University and eventually rooted in the state. These were privileged little girls, and their daddies and some of their mothers were powerful people—University regents, renowned doctors, influential lawyers, judges, king makers, or politicians themselves. The young fraternity men we dated became lawyers, doctors, bankers, went into "investments" or joined their fathers' successful businesses. In the course of an afternoon spent doing volunteer work in Parkland Hospital's emergency room recently, I heard the names of three blind dates from my freshman year being paged as resident doctors. Texas Law Review banquets and Bar conventions are like homecomings where the men still greet the women with the standard fraternity embrace. Even after fourteen years, the wives, especially the Houston flowers, are still quite glamorous. Flowerpots are more scattered as they frequently pursued careers that took them out of the South. One writes from New York as an assistant editor of a magazine, "Remember, I may have been a late bloomer—but I bloomed!" Others have become artists, lawyers, biologists, or academicians at universities where sororities are once again on the upswing. "I was invited with five other faculty members to a sorority house recently for what I think we called apple-polishing night," writes one who is now an English professor. "After dinner the girls sang to us. The four male profs looked delighted, but I couldn't resist searching the crowd to discern the pots from the flowers."

With such continuity of friendship, social education, and broad acquaintance across the state, I can hardly dismiss my sorority experience. However, by the time we reached our junior year in college, many of us had begun to sense that something was amiss. There were strong conflicts between belonging to a sorority and trying to pursue an education. Why did we volunteer our time to help the Phi Delts gather wood for the Aggie bonfire when I could have been with my English class buddies hearing Tom Wolfe and Truman Capote? I missed Igor Stravinsky's visit to campus because I was the song leader at chapter dinner. In retrospect, the conflict was most apparent when the sorority pretended to

serve academic purposes. The poet John Crowe Ransom joined us for dinner one evening, and the only sustained conversation we could handle was "How are your grandchildren?" Even worse was the night William Sloane Coffin, the activist chaplain from Yale, came for dinner. If I led the chapter in singing "Kayappa, Kayappa, Kayappa, Gayamma, I am so hayuppy tha-ut I yamma . . ." that night I have thankfully blocked it from my memory. Coffin, of course, was already condemning the escalating war in Viet Nam and generally taking a few cracks at lifestyles like ours. We, who had spent the previous weekend parading around in initiation sheets and performing the solemn Victorian rituals required to initiate our pledges, were ill-equipped to defend ourselves. The chaplain so easily trapped us that we could hardly say no when he challenged us to follow him to the SDS (Students for a Democratic Society) meeting he was scheduled to address when he left our house. Slipping our pearl-encrusted Kappa keys into our pockets, we followed him with great trepidation down the alley to the University Christian Church where the meeting was to be held. We had seen these humorless campus radicals on the Union steps. Some of us had given token support to slightly suspect University "Y" activities; others had at least signed the petition to integrate Roy's Lounge on the Drag, but we had never sat in the midst of such a group, and we shivered that our opinion on the Gulf of Tonkin might be sought. Fortunately the SDS was much too taken with Coffin even to notice us, much less explore our ignorance.

Besides the educational conflicts, the sorority could also be indicted for providing a womblike environment in which one could avoid practically all contact with the unfamiliar or unknown. Many of my sorority sisters now freely admit that they never even knew how to get to the Main Library, nor did they ever darken the door of the Chuck Wagon in the Student Union where my roommates and I frequently drank dishwater-colored iced tea with foreign students or "rat-running" psychology lab instructors. This same narrow environment also kept the haves from developing much sensitivity for the have-nots. Sorority alumnae groups are generous philanthropists, but in college our philanthropy was usually limited to a Christmas party for blind children or an Easter egg hunt for the retarded. The only have-nots sorority girls encountered on a regular basis were the servants in the house. I often wondered how the cook felt when the KAs rode up on horseback and sent a small black boy to the door with "Old South Ball" invitations on a silver tray.

Perhaps the worst indictment of the sorority system, however, is the damage done to the self-esteem of many girls either by the selection process or the values that may predominate after pledging. The same friend who recalled the gruesome pledge line insists that flowerpots dwindled after my class graduated and the standards of beauty, money, and cheerleader rah-rah became entrenched. "It was an unhappy time for me," she writes. "I wasn't like the rest and yet I didn't know what else to be. Half the time I hated myself for not being able to fill the sorority mold I had been raised to believe was what a girl should be; half the time I hated myself for even considering becoming like them. Ultimately I led a double life, holding minor service offices and doing those daring 'radical' things, like introducing motions to allow Jewish girls to go through our rush. Graduate school was my lifesaver. My experience there was so good that it tends to block out the mindlessness, the social superiority, and the hypocrisy of those undergraduate days. Looking back, I see my two years in the house as most men regard their Army duty—only mine was service to my family and their values instead of my country. It was such a waste of potential and time. My life goes so fast now, when I compare it with those hours spent on phone duty as a pledge at the sorority house.''

Shortly after our graduation in 1966, a very different generation appeared, provoking many changes at the University—the Drag vendors, the use of drugs, massive demonstrations against the war, the no-bra look, the pass-fail grading system, bicycles as an acceptable mode of transportation, beer in the Student Union, the lifting of curfews in women's housing, and courses called ''Women's Studies.'' The whole Greek system suddenly was viewed as an anachronism surely doomed to extinction. Indeed, the Panhellenic Council removed itself in 1967 as a recognized campus organization, hence no longer subject to University regulation or eligible to use University facilities. Some say this became necessary when the University discontinued supervision of student housing except that which it actually owned and operated. Sorority alums were not yet ready to abandon curfews and needed an independent body to govern such regulations. Others insist that sororities with racial and religious discriminatory clauses in their bylaws felt threatened. In truth most sororities had purged their charters of such clauses long before civil rights unrest became a reality on campus. Numbers going through rush dropped drastically then; several fraternities and sororities folded, and living space in sorority houses went begging as girls moved to apartments.

The hypocrisy of the ''standards committee,'' which served as a self-policing morals squad within most sororities, finally crumbled in many houses. In our day, the standards committee had served without much question. Headed by the sorority vice president and assisted by an alum adviser, the committee was usually composed of girls of good character who ideally were imbued with discretion and compassion for the weaker sisters in their midst. They were charged with preserving the sorority's reputation, which occasionally involved admonishing, disciplining, or expelling those who strayed. One contemporary of mine recalled that ''nymphomania'' was the big scare word in standards committee. ''Pledge an ugly girl, but for God's sake, don't let a nymphomaniac slip through!'' The fact was most standards committee members were intimidated by candidly rebellious behavior, and those girls who openly marched to a different moral drummer often escaped unpunished. It was the poor timid soul who, after two cups of spiked punch, vomited in the stall next to the alum chaperone at the spring formal that got called on the carpet. Apparently when birth control pills and drugs became readily available in the late sixties, it became difficult in many houses to assemble enough straight arrows to form such a committee. Rebellion widened the gulf that already existed between sorority members and what they regarded as ''interfering'' alumnae. University curfews were lifted, but sorority girls were still required to be in their houses at 11:30 on weeknights. Repeated violations of the curfew threatened to expel even the officers in some of the sororities. Pappagallo shoes were being exchanged for bare feet

and Army fatigues. Housemothers resigned, and alumnae wrung their hands.

So I went back to rush week in 1975. I had heard that the number of girls going through rush was rising again, but I was skeptical. I still expected to see a tired old dinosaur ready for the last rites—or a vastly revolutionized sorority system. I found neither. There I was again in the Tri Delts' front yard wiping the sweat off my upper lip. Well, a few things had changed. Panhellenic no longer lobbies for dark cottons. Dallas and Houston rushees were classy in their cool summer dresses worn fashionably three inches below the knee with rope wedges and bangle bracelets. My counterparts—girls from Edinburg and Fort Stockton—were most often represented by polyester church dresses worn three inches above the knee with pumps. Nervous conversation was unchanged. ''Sounds like a mob scene in there. I'm not sure I wanta go in . . .'' ''I didn't even know she was an A Chi O, y'all, I hope I don't get in trouble.'' In the minutes before the doors burst open, there was much flopping of long hair behind ears and finally, nail biting. The yellow brick road was gone, but the gushing enthusiasm was unchanged. The rush captain, or maybe she was the president, looked like Margaux Hemingway. In fourteen years, the beauty standards had been upgraded. I wasn't permitted inside the houses—not even my own sorority house (alum pressure is out)—but from the curb I spotted the same machinery still in motion. I overheard a frantic active begging another, ''Please take my second girl; I've just got to give Sally a good rush.'' I watched as they unselfconsciously clapped, squealed, or ran out for a second goodbye hug even though a Panhellenic representative had signaled the end of the party.

In talking with active members later, I was amazed to learn how little rush really had changed. The songs, the finger snapping, and even the language were essentially the same. ''She's the key to Houston'' had become ''She's the ticket,'' just as a much admired fraternity man had gone from ''stud'' to ''stallion.'' Fatigue and giddiness still prevailed in the late-night voting sessions with a few cynical seniors sometimes tossing panties in the air and yelling, ''We really rushed her pants off!'' Skits are no longer the major productions they once were, but the silence rules, the maudlin sentimentality, and the weeping are still an integral part of the rush week scene. I asked about the tears. ''Aren't girls just too sophisticated now for that sort of gimmickry?''

''Well,'' the innocents replied, ''they really are a lot smarter these days and they know if you're not really sincere. But that last night, well, you just look around the room and know how glad you are to be a Kappa—well, it's just like the last night at camp, you just can't keep from crying.''

''But what about the changes?'' I asked. I was relieved to learn that girls receiving no bids are now called by a Panhellenic representative to spare them the public humiliation of the old no-bid envelope. I was not surprised to learn that sorority pins are never worn on campus, since they were beginning to fade from the scene even while I was in school. ''Dressing'' to go on campus has returned. I doubt seriously if the gold earrings were ever abandoned even when revolutionary garb was in fashion. Jewish girls are no longer restricted to Jewish sororities, but I saw no Spanish surnames other than Valley aristocracy. Black sororities still exist and since 1967 have participated in Panhellenic activities with the white sororities.

But I also wanted to know whether the outside world had forced many changes on the sororities. "What impact has the women's movement had on sororities?" I asked.

"Not much," they shrugged. "Oh, almost everybody majors in business or communications or elementary education, but it's not because they really want careers. They just know that they've got to get a job when they graduate." I suppose I should have anticipated this response. The women's liberation movement had begun with an intellectual appeal, but most Texas women have been brought up to trust their charm more than their intellect.

"What about marriage? Do you still pass the lighted candle at chapter meetings while singing,

*I found my ma-an.*
*He's my Kappa ma-an.*
*He's my sweetheart for evermore.*
*I'll leave him never,*
*I'll follow wherever he goes.*

"We still pass the candle, but it hardly ever gets blown out. Not many of us are getting married after graduation, but it's not because we wouldn't like to," they giggled.

"What about no curfew?" I asked, recalling how many of my sisters had sustained injuries while sneaking out of the house. One of my contemporaries had actually broken a foot in a fall from the fire escape and had to be hauled back up through a window. She awakened the housemother with a lame story about falling down the carpeted stairway.

"Well, everybody is usually in by two a.m. and usually earlier on the week-nights," they assured me. Their parents, I learned, pay an extra $50 per semester for a security guard to let the girls in and out at night.

There was so much more that I wanted to know, but they were eager to hear about my bygone era. "Oooooh, you were here when they had Ten Most Beautiful and Bluebonnet Belles and Round Up Revue." I could tell from their curiosity that they felt cheated.

Because I sensed that I had been talking to the straight-arrow public relations team of the sorority, I deliberately sought out one of the two acknowledged scholars within their membership, a law-school-bound Plan II student. Plan II (a liberal arts honors program), the college of humanities, and the college of natural sciences were poorly represented in the sorority houses I investigated. This young lady was indeed very bright, and I pressed her to justify her Greek affiliation.

"Plan II is really a tough academic program," she said, "and I study so hard during the week that if someone didn't plan some mindless social activity for me on the weekend, I'd probably crack. My friends who came here from the same private high school and didn't pledge are beginning to drop out. They just can't face four years of college without ever going to a big party."

I had called her away from an SAE street dance. She freely admitted that none of her dates on the weekend were intellectual types. "I talk about Kant and Hegel all week. I don't want any more on Saturday." She doesn't live in the house because she needs the silence of her own apartment to carry such an academic load. "I sometimes wish I'd pledged a fraternity," she grinned, "They have such a good time, dropping by their fraternity houses to shoot a game of pool, play cards, or just shoot the breeze. We only go to our

sorority houses for some organized meeting—never just for the fun of it."

The Greek system died out on many campuses across the country during the late sixties. The president of UT's Interfraternity Council, noting that pledge classes and houses are full again, says, "The Greek system is definitely thriving." Of course the 5000 people who participated in rush last year are still quite a minority on a campus of more than 40,000, even more of a minority than in the sixties when the 5000 Greeks made up about a fifth of the campus population of 27,000. However, after several years during which rush was totally ignored by the *Daily Texan*, the irate September letters have begun to crop up again in the "Firing Line" letters column: "Only a moron would pay someone to impose rules upon them of the 'don't speak to boys during rush week' variety." "Big sisters and study buddies, indeed!" "They remind me of swine at auction." "The Greek system is composed of people with Pat Boone/Ann Landers mentality who insist on segregating themselves socially, sexually, and racially." "I often wanted to become friends with one of those beautiful chicks with the long, flowing hair, but most of them are such conceited social climbers that I just stay away from them."

Sorority members continue to dominate certain campus activities, such as Student Union committees, simply because they are joiners and organizers by nature. The University Sweetheart is invariably a sorority girl principally because no one else is interested and because the Greeks have the organizational power to get out the vote.

Certainly, the intimidating size of the University of Texas student body and physical plant had something to do with the returning strength of the Greek system. As one Highland Park mother put it, "When these affluent high school kids around here visit the University, they visit the sorority and fraternity people. That *is* the University to them. Not to pledge is to step into an unfathomable void." Another mother admitted that her daughter was not a particularly independent spirit. "If she's going to be a follower, we'd just as soon she be in a group where she'll at least keep up her appearance."

The nostalgia craze is certainly another factor in sorority revival in the seventies. When I visited the campus briefly in the spring of 1976, I saw freshmen spending hours stuffing crepe paper in chicken-wire floats for the Round Up parade, a spectacular phenomenon discontinued during the sixties at UT. Sigma Chi Derby Day, with its sorority relays and "tug o'war" over mudpits, has reappeared, and Greek-sponsored dance marathons for charity have been held in Gregory Gym. Indeed the current self-described absurdist student body president and vice president, Jay Adkins and Skip Slyfield, make the absurdities of Greek life seem quite in tune with the times.

And perhaps it's more than just nostalgia. Some have suggested that it's a longing for tradition. You're supposed to feel something for your alma mater, aren't you? At the University of Texas, if you don't "feel it" for the Longhorns and Darrell's winning tradition, the Orange Tower, and the "Eyes," you have little else to come back for. UT has no ivied halls or picturesque chapels and few legendary professors. Most students graduate by mail rather than attend the massive impersonal graduation ceremonies. There are no formal homecomings or reunions unless you "belonged" to something while you were there—the Texas Cowboys, the Friars, the Longhorn Band, or even a sorority or fraternity, each with its own rituals and traditions.

I suppose the wisest answer to the survival question came from another sorority sister of mine. "Well, why do girls still make their debut in Dallas?" she asked. "Because people long for exclusivity, because their parents want them to, because they are only nineteen years old and are not asking the same questions that we ask at thirty-two."

I think she's right. I was recently perusing a copy of the *Kappa Key*, my sorority's national magazine that finds me no matter where I hide. An interview with a bright-eyed blonde coed caught my eye. She had been Miss Everything on her campus, and, when questioned about the value of being cheerleader, homecoming queen, and sorority president, she replied, "I don't think it's always nice to question the relevance of things that are fun."

You can always wait to do that when you're thirty-two.

*—September 1976*

# GROWING OLD AT WILLIE NELSON'S PICNIC

## by William Martin

---

### *The last, positively the last, word on rock festivals.*

---

Idon't much like heat or dirt or loud noise or even being outdoors for long stretches at a time, but I do like picnics and special events and crowds and country music and Willie Nelson. So when Willie first announced he was organizing a three-day Fourth of July Picnic featuring 36 hours of traditional and progressive country music, and expected 50,000 people to be there, I made up my mind to go, and I went. I thought you might like to hear about it.

The picnic was held in the 160-acre infield of the Texas World Speedway south of College Station, an inhospitable site attractive to promoters because it is highly resistant to gate-crashers but as barren of trees or other shade as it has been of auto races. Yet as I joined the crowd walking through two long tunnels to the infield, I sensed that we had come because we knew the stark landscape and three days of searing heat would inflict great suffering, and since our lives are so easy and our chances to test ourselves against the elements so few, we grimly determined to pursue a happiness of discomfort on this our nation's birthday.

At the top of the grade coming out of the tunnels, where we had felt the last coolness of the day, members of the volunteer medical staff handed out free salt tablets with the promise they would help us last two extra hours if we drank a lot of liquids. Most of the people walking in with me looked prepared to heed the advice on liquids, having estimated their needs at approximately one case of beer per person. I was impressed. Even at the American Legion picnics I went to when I was a boy, nobody would come close to drinking that much beer except oilfield workers and Catholics.

The crowd was not quite what I had expected. It was probably no larger than half the hoped-for 50,000, but what surprised me more was its composition. I had expected thousands of cosmic cowboys and assorted freaks, but I had

*William Martin is associate professor of sociology at Rice University and author of several books and magazine articles. He is a contributing editor of* Texas Monthly.

also expected fairly large numbers of authentic rednecks, and I knew if I got uncomfortable with the freaks I could go sit with the kickers. I am not trying to pretend I grew up a redneck, because I didn't. We were town people. My daddy ran the feed store and was president of the school board, my mama was big in the PTA, and I knew when I was five years old that I was going to college. But I also knew a lot of rednecks and, if it came right down to it, I figured I might feel more at home with them than with long-haired hippie weirdos eating toadstools and smoking LSD.

There were some kickers there, all right. About six. The other 25,000 were freaks or freak-ish, all under 25. I began to realize that I stood out, because I was wearing an honest-to-goodness western shirt with pearl grippers and, at age 36, I was a Senior Citizen. Clearly, I was a stranger in a strange land. Since the closest I had ever been to an event like this was watching the first half of the Woodstock movie, I found a spot to set my cooler down and spent most of the Fourth just paying attention.

For those interested in fashion, it can be reported that the Gatsby look has not taken over everywhere. It's probably just as well, since white is not practical without a certain commitment to cleanliness. Still, observable regularities of dress indicated the young folk had indeed thought about what they were going to wear. The standard uniform for "dudes"—a useful designation for someone no longer a boy but not quite a man—consisted of jeans and sleeveless shirts. With rare exceptions, "chicks" wore shorts and halters. A lot of the dudes walked around with jockey shorts sticking out of the waist of their Levis. I used to have nightmares about showing up in public places in my underwear, but it didn't seem to bother them. Sometimes they had holes in their pants and you could tell they didn't even have on any underwear or, if they did, that it was all worn out and torn. What if they were in an accident? The police would take one look at their underwear and send them to the charity hospital.

If there was sameness in Levis and shorts and sleeveless shirts and halters, there was marvelous variety in cap and hat. There were derbies and dapper Panamas, porkpies and pith helmets, hard hats and Hombergs, mountaineer hats and Mexican sombreros, Navaho hats and Scottish tams, Budweiser hats and Lone Star visors, golf hats and tennis hats and fishing hats, fatigue caps and baseball caps and railroad caps, Dodge Truck and Yamaha Motorcycle and York Air Conditioning caps, International Harvester caps and Caterpillar caps just like the man wore in the cafe in *Easy Rider*, lumberyard caps and polka-dot paint caps, and caps advertising Lone Star Feed and Fertilizer, Equidyne Horse Pellets, and the Athens Livestock Commission. Those who had neglected to bring hats fashioned substitutes from T-shirts and jockey shorts, or by jamming a six-pack carton on their heads, or by combining a Budvisor with a Holiday Inn towel to create the look of an ersatz A-rab from the burning sands of Cairo, Illinois. Most common, of course, were beat-up western hats, with the brims flattened out or bent down in front to look mean. At kicker dance halls, skilled laborers try to look like ranchhands. Here, unemployed students were trying to look like rustlers. I understand the desire to dress up, but if I were picking a costume, I would choose a black and silver outfit and pretend I was a town tamer. My name would be Johnny Laredo.

After I got my bearings I began to pay closer attention to the music. I had been a bit apprehensive about how I would respond to three days of what has come to be called "progressive country" or, more recently, "redneck rock." I like country music because the tunes are easy to remember and I can understand the words. I don't like most rock music because it is too loud and straining for the words seldom proves worth the effort. I just didn't see how country music was going to gain much from crossbreeding. I do like some rock, of course. I've got two Carole King albums and a Neil Diamond tape and I really enjoy the Living Strings version of "Hey Jude" and "Let It Be" on KYND ("All Music, All the Time"). I had liked a good bit of what I had heard of progressive country, especially Jerry Jeff Walker and Michael Murphey and the Nitty Gritty Dirt Band, and I had been told I would like Greezy Wheels and Freda and the Firedogs and several others, but I had never gone to hear them in person because they usually appear in places where people stand up and walk around and make a lot of noise. So, really, I was open, and I'm glad I was. I picked up some new enthusiasms.

One of the groups I enjoyed most was Jimmy Buffett and his Coral Reefer Band. Buffett started out with a song about wishing he had "a pencil-thin moustache, a two-toned Ricky Ricardo jacket, and an autographed picture of Andy Devine." It made me think about the time I got Lash LaRue's autograph—for all you older people who have wondered whatever happened to Lash, he did a night-club act in Juarez for awhile and is now a street preacher in Florida, bullwhipping for the Master. Buffett claimed the fellow who wrote "Pencil-thin Moustache" is named Marvin Gardens; I imagine he lives in a yellow house near the water works and pays $24 rent. When Jimmy rendered a lament for the fact that "They don't dance like Carmen Miranda anymore," I was about to decide I could come to like his work. Then he sang a number called "Why Don't We All Get Drunk and Screw?" which I found not only a sharp break with nostalgic themes, but a rather more direct

sentiment than I like in my love songs. I really prefer something a bit more sensitive and delicate, like Snooky Lanson and Dorothy Collins singing "Lavender Blue—Dilly Dilly."

The sound system was excellent, performers were reasonably good about sticking to half-hour sets, and in the relatively short exchange time between groups we got to hear Kris Kristofferson records, which was fine with me since I think Kristofferson is the greatest living American next to Carl Yastrzemski. At the beginning of an act, or at any point when enthusiasm seemed to be waning, most of the performers could be counted on to say something like "Hot Damn! Aren't we having a good time at the Willie Nelson Picnic?" or "Who in the entire globe of the planet earth could ever put something on like this but Willie Nelson?" which inevitably drew automatic shouts and applause of the sort right-wing politicians trigger by calls for law and order or tent preachers get when they ask their flocks to say Amen if they love Jesus. Despite these periodic outbursts, however, the crowd paid no more than half-hearted attention during most of the acts. They knew the music was playing and moved their feet or hands or something, but treated it rather as if it were background music, except that it was hard to determine what it was background *to*. They really did very little except drink and smoke and stare.

There were exceptions, of course. When Augie Meyers and his Western Headband played, a dude with a benign but decidedly crazy look danced around off the beat, blowing a harmonica and kicking dirt on the folk around him. Even though he had lost a lot of his fine motor control and could never have handled the Samba, especially on the trickier steps like the Copa Cabana, he did have spirit, a quality that marked him from his peers. Directly in front of me three of the most taciturn young men I have seen in some time, including one who was a dead ringer for my Cousin Bolo (that's not his real name, of course; his real name is Little Walter), sat for ten hours passing beer and dope but no more than 50 words. Once, the one in the middle leaned over and threw up between his feet. A girl stepped over and rubbed his back with his wadded-up shirt and in a few minutes he straightened up and resumed his torporous attitude. As far as I could tell, his friends did not notice. Behind me, four boys about the age of my sons—thirteen and fourteen— managed to sustain a state of unbroken somnambulance by alternating between beer and marijuana. A couple of times, the youngest, who might have been no more than twelve, offered me a joint, for which I thanked him but no-thanked him. I'm pretty sure there is a law against taking dope from a twelve-year-old.

Picking one's way through a crowd of 25,000 people, sitting or lying next to one another like stricken pilgrims at the Ganges, is a delicate maneuver at best. For those whose sense of height and depth had been altered by marijuana, it became an assignment of mammoth proportion. I watched one boy make three unsuccessful attempts to lift his foot high enough to get over the edge of an army blanket lying flat on the ground. He finally gave up and took another route. But perhaps what was lost in precision of movement was regained in a greater capacity for informal adaptive measures. A chick clad in shorts and two bandanas tied loosely above her breasts, managed the task more effectively by offering people a hit off her Schlitz in return for safe passage. She will be a good wife for some nice young man. She's frugal, friendly, resourceful, and makes her own clothes.

On another occasion, a dude with a pleasant grassy look stumbled into the neighborhood and announced he felt a certain sexual tension, or words to that effect: "Anybody wants me, come on. I don't mean to be nasty, but come on. Right here." In a similar spirit of forthrightness, a wild-looking youth lurched into the vicinity and began to ask loudly, "Would anybody mind if I take a piss right here? Be honest." I admired his direct approach; I recognize that urination is just another bodily function and nothing to be ashamed of, and because I was a member of a minority group, I was somewhat reluctant to insist that his needs violated my sense of territoriality. Still, I was as relieved as he was not, when my younger neighbors suggested he move on. No more than twenty feet behind us, however, he found an accommodating group willing to step aside for him, and he took his ease for all to see. As a reciprocal gesture—and we know that reciprocity is essential to community—he offered us a good price on that which had so relaxed his inhibitions: "Anybody want any Quaaludes? Anybody want any reds?" His sense of enterprise encouraged me about his generation. As my father used to point out, being able to sell is the best job security a man can have. It's as good as a teaching certificate for a woman.

By late afternoon, the combination of sun, alcohol, and drugs had taken a terrible toll. The heat, though relieved slightly by a brief shower, was simply awful. I was uncomfortable, but managed to avoid collapse by continual intake of liquid. I don't know what the record is but I was quite surprised to learn that it is possible to eliminate through the pores of one's skin the liquid from twelve cans of assorted beverages and a 70-cent sack of ice. No lie. Members of the medical staff circulated through the crowd, pushing salt pills and spraying Solarcaine on the lobstered backs of people who had gone to sleep or passed out. The medical center itself resembled a ward for the insane as kids jammed in for treatment. Many were badly burned and crying, others were upset and uncomfortable from the unhappy effects of mixing Quaaludes or other downers with alcohol, a few who had taken LSD worked with modeling clay and colored pens, and half a dozen kids had to be sent on to the hospital after what a sadist had sold them as THC or given them as salt tablets turned out to be either rat poison or strychnine. A staff member who worked in the medical center all weekend said later, "It was really very sad. So many were having such a horrible time. They were hot and dirty and really, really sick, and wishing so much they had not come."

Of those who never made it to the medical center, hundreds slumped around in a red-eyed stupor, as if the life had gone out of them. They may have been watching *Fantasia* in a theater-of-the-mind that was twenty degrees cooler inside; on the outside, they looked hot, tired, and miserable. But they had told their friends they were coming and they would want to tell them they had had a good time, so it was necessary for them to stick it out.

Even after blessed night finally came and the temperature dropped into the bearable range, it was hard to strike and hold a truly festive mood. A little after ten p.m., Jerry Jeff Walker began a highly promising set, but was interrupted repeatedly by unscheduled fireworks and emergency medical announcements. Most of the fireworks were roman candles and cluster rockets, but a few less socially conscious persons threw large firecrackers into clumps of people and one of the rockets zipped into the crowd and burned a spectator rather badly. The management declared there would be no more music until the fireworks stopped and the pyromaniacs eased off momentarily, but when the music started up again, so did the fireworks. Unnerving as they were, they added a nice touch when Jerry Jeff sang "Up Against the Wall, Redneck Mother." At precisely the moment that 25,000 peopled yelled "REDNECK!" the biggest and most spectacular rocket of the night burst into a sparkling cluster high over the stage. It was the sort of thing that happens in movies.

What followed was the sort of thing that happens in bad dreams. The medical staff had gotten a report that a woman somewhere in the crowd was in a coma from insulin shock and needed immediate attention if she were not to die. Trouble was, they didn't know just exactly where she was, so would we check out the unconscious chicks around us and see if any of them appeared to be in insulin shock and if we found one, would we please yell out while everybody else got quiet? Most of the crowd got quiet but a good many yelled out from different parts of the audience—for a joke, probably, but given the number of unconscious people strewn about, perhaps not—and one guy got a good laugh when he called out, "Anybody got any downers?" I wondered how many of those who laughed were diabetics, and I wondered at the capacity of my fellows to laugh when one of their number might be dying. But, as someone called out, we had come to hear music, not to look for sick chicks, and after a bit the show resumed. As it turned out, the delay and search had been unnecessary. The diabetic in question was not a girl but a boy named Val, and he had already been treated before the announcement was made, but the irritation of the crowd at having their concert interrupted by what appeared to be a hoax did not augur well for the survival chances of other medical emergencies.

In fact, the medical people did report some difficulty with the crowd, especially on the first two days. Rory Harper, one of the supervisors of the medical staff, said, "Occasionally, people even pushed the stretcher crews back and wouldn't let them through. Or we would be trying to treat someone who had passed out and somebody would yell, 'Give her a couple of Quaaludes and she'll be all right.' They were either stoned or just didn't give a damn."

To climax the confusion, operations manager Tim O'Conner took the microphone to announce that a peculiar Texas law governing mass gatherings required that the show end promptly at eleven o'clock. Not only would the last four scheduled acts be cancelled, but Jerry Jeff would not be allowed to come back for an encore. As the young folk began yelling about rip-offs and suggesting that the law and its agents occupy themselves in acts of sexual self-gratification, I feared there might be some unpleasantness. But this was not a violent crowd and the height of the objection came when a young man stood on a beer chest and screamed frustratedly at O'Conner: "You're a fart!" It is possible to be irritated with a person so designated but one does not lynch him. Defeated, perhaps at some level relieved to have the ordeal ended without having to admit they were ready to quit, the crowd filed out peaceably.

It may be that anything worth doing is worth doing to excess, but as I eased my ravaged body into the soft bucket seats of my little red station wagon, I reckoned that the folks who schedule three-hour concerts in air-conditioned auditoriums have a basically sound idea. And as I drove past the tired, dirty kids bedding down in the Willie Nelson Approved Campsites next to the Speedway, I was pleased that because I have this good job teaching school and writing stories, I could afford to stay at the Ramada Inn. I caught the last part of *No Time for Sergeants* on the motel TV. I could have seen all of *China Gate* if I had wanted to.

On Friday, July 5th, I awoke at noon and enjoyed a delightful breakfast of pizza and iced tea, which I preferred to the Alice B. Toklas brownies and Kool-Aid I imagined the kids were eating out at the Speedway. I didn't go back to the picnic until about four o'clock, but that was early enough. I still managed to get in a full day's entertainment.

Despite what was probably greater heat—reports of 103 may have been exaggerated but indicated what folk thought of the weather—most people seemed to be suffering less than on the Fourth. Hundreds of umbrellas and makeshift sunshelters had been erected, creating the appearance of vacationers who had headed for the beach but missed. Apparently because most people took salt tablets and upped their liquid intake, the medical staff had far fewer cases of heat prostration. But in its place, they treated thousands of cuts that resulted when the threshing action of a grounds-cleaning machine left millions of small chunks and shards of glass lying in wait for romantically bare feet.

I roamed a good bit on the Fifth and found the much smaller crowd friendly and relaxed, even though the young folk kept confirming my sense of strangerhood by asking, "Are you having a good time, Sir?" and "What's happening, Daddy?" I wanted to point out to them that most of the performers they liked best were a lot closer to my age than theirs, and that my having never heard of the Lost Gonzo Band or the Neon Angels did not mean I had ridden into town on a head of cabbage. I wanted to tell them about the time I had breakfast at Cisco's Bakery in Austin with Willie Nelson and Tom T. Hall and Coach Darrell Royal, or about hearing Bill Monroe when Lester Flatt and Earl Scruggs were part of his Blue Grass Boys. I even considered telling them about the time I heard Gene Krupa and Charlie Parker on the same night, but I didn't want to have to explain who they were. Mostly, I just smiled and said, "Fine." But when the third person of the day asked me if I was a sheriff, I asked him whatever had made him think I might be. He said, "Well, it's your shirt." I asked him what was wrong with my shirt. It's a good shirt. My wife gave it to me for Christmas. "That's just it," he said. "It's too good. You need an old shirt." I don't go along with that. It seems to me that pretending I am poor isn't taking poverty seriously. Besides, I don't have any old shirts. I give them to the Goodwill and take it off my income tax.

While wandering around, I ran into several fine folk of maturity comparable to my own, but none delighted me more than Mr. and Mrs. Weldon Wilson from Wharton. Mr. Wilson, who had on grey trousers and a peach-colored shirt with the short sleeves rolled up a couple of turns and who wears his thin grey hair in a close trim, fixes TVs for Sears over at Bay City. He and Mrs. Wilson, who wore a navy blue shorts outfit with white socks and sneakers and had a chain fastened to her grey half-rim glasses so she wouldn't have to put them down when she took them off, were enjoying themselves. "The main reason I am here," he said, "is because I like country music. And I haven't seen any of the kids that I don't like. They are going to be running this world in the future and from what I have seen here, I think I'll enjoy living with them. I really do. A little girl asked me while ago why I was here. I asked her why she asked me that question and she said, 'Well, usually only kids come to these things. Do you enjoy it?' I said, 'Definitely!' She said, 'You don't think we're wrong?' I said, 'Definitely not! When I was your age I did things the older people thought I was wrong in doing.' And, you know, she just loved my neck. Anyone that would say that all these kids are out here for is to get doped up, there's something wrong with them. There might be some of it I don't agree with, but they've got their own lives to live and they are going to live them, one way or another. They'll have to pay for their mistakes, the same as you and I did, but I haven't seen them doing that much wrong yet."

Mrs. Wilson said, "Neither one of us has ever smoked marijuana or taken dope and we probably never will, but there is something that is funny to me. Out of all them I know that are smoking it, there is not but one I know that wasn't a cigarette smoker first. So smoking can lead to marijuana just like marijuana can lead to heroin. And, you know, if this had been the thing to have done when I was this age, I don't know that I wouldn't have tried it." Mr. Wilson wasn't sure about that. "I've got enough adrenalin in my body that I don't need anything to slow it down or speed it up. Anything they can use their smoking or their dope to do, I can do the same things naturally. Say, would you like a beer? We've got Coors."

Late Friday afternoon, the Nitty Gritty Dirt Band galvanized the audience into the form it would hold until well after midnight as hundreds, maybe thousands, of young people wedged themselves into a sweating, writhing, ecstatic mass of back-to-front bodies that stretched outward from the wide stage in a 50-yard-wide semicircle. As the Dirt Band raised the speed and volume of its excellent music, the crowd raised the intensity of its response. Five attractive chicks persuaded their dudes to lift them onto their shoulders that they might better see and perchance be seen. I thought about how much it would make my neck hurt to have a girl sit up on my shoulders like that and how I would resent not being able to put my hands in my pockets because I would have to hold her by the thighs to keep her from falling off, but the dudes seemed to bear up under their burdens rather well.

Eventually, inevitably, one of the girls untied her halter and threw it onto the stage. Within seconds, three of the remaining four had done likewise, to the delight of the gathered multitude. As they jiggled and swayed barebreasted through several long numbers, the plight of the fifth girl became apparent and poignant. Less abundantly blessed than her sisters, she had not foreseen, as I am relatively certain they had, that matters might come to this. As the others grew more wanton by the bar, she tightened her lips and stiffened noticeably. She could not climb down without losing face; she could not disrobe without revealing less than she cared to. I remembered young teenaged boys, friends of mine mostly, who dreaded gym classes because of the showers that followed, and I hoped she would think of a graceful exit. She did not: but as she suffered, others prospered. A striking blonde girl, whom I suspect I would recognize if I were to see her at any point during the next twenty years, slowly but surely stole the show from the others. When Willie Nelson came out to finish up with the Dirt Band, he tossed her a fine straw hat which she set at what had to be the most provocative angle possible—people who wear clothes well have a knack for that sort of thing—then threw back her head, shouted, "I love it!" and went into a magnificent shiver of the sort one seldom experiences alone. Her actions seemed to set up needs in others for similar release of tension. Several girls stripped buck-naked and tried to climb onto the stage. Most were beaten back by heartless security guards but one streaked briefly to the rear of the platform. God knows what happened to her back there with all those musicians.

As I watched this scene which did not remind me much of the dances at the Faculty Club, I thought of a sober colleague who recently confided that his secret fantasy was to be a rock star and to enjoy the adulation of hundreds of nubile young women. I remember what Mark Twain had said about naked people having little influence in society. And I wondered what the odds were, given the fact that man has been on the earth for thousands, perhaps millions of years, that one would miss the sexual revolution by less than ten. I'm sure Weldon Wilson is right. They'll have to pay for their mistakes the same as he and I did. But I don't think he and I were ever offered such an impressive line of credit.

Actually, I face my missing the sexual revolution without much difficulty. I acknowledge there is a certain attractiveness to a firm, smooth, tan, lissome young body with well-fitted parts, but I have come to appreciate, perhaps even prefer, the sensual beauty of women in their mid- to late thirties, women whose eyes and smiles reflect experience not just with sex but with love, and whose softer bosoms and the gentle ring of stretch-marked waists that will not quite be contained inside their swimsuits or jeans give tangible evidence of time shared by man and child. I pondered the casualness of sexual display and of sex itself in this age group and thought that, for all its momentary allure, sex not undergirded by love, sex between people who seek their own pleasure rather than a true experience of mutuality, sex with a person one may hardly know, however attractive that person may be physically, could never be as meaningful and fulfilling as sex with a person to whom one has made a lifetime commitment and with whom one has shared the bad times as well as the good. Probably.

And I thought that if I had a hat like Willie Nelson's I would have put a tether on it before tossing it out to that blonde girl.

All the naked bodies and reveling and such during the peak of the Nitty Gritty set had led me to believe that we might, following parallels in nature, expect things to tail off for a spell, that folk would find seats and smile about what a nice time they were having, and respond a bit more passively to the efforts of the next group or two. Probably because I failed to take into account that most of them don't have jobs that demand much physical or mental effort—peeling avocados in health-food restaurants, sitting on the sidewalk selling jewelry, things like that—I had seriously underestimated the amount of reserve energy these young folk still possessed after two days of grooving in the sun. Here I was, trapped and unable to move, slumping under the years of gravity's relentless pull, feet aching despite special arch supports and Comfisoles, and realizing that they intended to stay there right up to the end, which obviously was not coming soon. A friendly, smiling dumpy-pretty sort of girl explained it was precisely this kind of experience that had attracted many to the picnic. "It's a stimulus, just like the dope and the music. It keeps you going. It's a weird high."

As I gathered such bits of intelligence, I recorded them for later retrieval by speaking into a small microphone tucked deep within my fist to shut out the noise of the speakers. The microphone was attached by a cord to a superb little tape recorder fastened to my belt and covered with a black leather case. When a gat-toothed young man inquired as to what I was doing when I put my mouth up to my obviously-wired fist, I told him it was electric dope, expecting no more than a smile or agreeable chuckle. Instead, his face exploded in delight and he asked if he could try it. I handed him the microphone, he took a couple of hits, shouted "Far f . . . . . g out!" (an expression more freighted with enthusiasm than substantive content), declared to his friends that it was first-rate stuff, and demanded to know where he could get some for himself.

The Friday evening program was marred somewhat by the fact that it was being filmed by the Midnight Special television show. As members of the film crew walked in and out among performers and as the cameras swept around without concern for the fact that soft human bodies were in the vicinity, one got the impression the crowd was being regarded less as primary consumer than as studio audience. Even more offensive was the presence and behavior of Leon Russell, who would serve as Wolfman Jack's co-host for the Special when it aired in early August. Russell is a darling of the progressive country set, for reasons I cannot fathom. For three days he wandered around in what appeared to be a chemical daze, his pasty white pot-belly poking through an unbuttoned shirt and his wasted face peering out from under a straw hat perched on top of the grey hair that flowed down the sides of his face for at least two feet. Because he had obviously ordained himself to be the Big Star of the picnic, Leon felt free to walk onstage whenever an act was reaching its peak and share in the applause, just as if he had earned it. On one of his early appearances, he sprinkled beer on the crowd with his fingertips, in the manner of a Great High Priest. On another, when a groupie-aspirant handed him a box of strawberries, he took small bites from each and threw them into the crowd, to be shared in sacramental fashion. Most of the time, though, he just stood and gazed through eyes that betrayed a mind suffering from severe brown-out.

But not even Russell could ruin the evening. The Main Coonass, Doug Kershaw, gave a typically superlative performance. With his rubber face changing in an instant from Bayou Prince to Lunatic Frog, and his body contorting like a package of pipe cleaners on an acid trip, he bounded all over the stage, playing his gaudy fiddle at maniacal speed and working himself, his band, and the audience into a frenzied lather. Michael Murphey, splendid in his white cosmic cowboy suit, did a fine job with some exceptional songs and

Waylon Jennings got a good reception with his hard-driving music about men that represent poor marital risks. I think things closed down about one a.m. but I don't honestly know, because I finished before they did. As I was walking out, I heard Leon Russell take credit for getting the mass-gathering law suspended and then declare that ''I never expected the Good Lord to bless me so much by having so many beautiful faces look at me at one time on the Fourth of July.'' It was actually the sixth of July, but I doubt Russell knew it. In any case, his pronouncement strained my doctrine of special providence considerably, and I wished I knew where to find the young man who had hollered at Tim O'Conner late the night before. I think he might have had an appropriate word for Leon.

More from a sense of duty than desire, I went back again on Saturday. The main attraction of the afternoon was a middle-aged man who both looked and claimed to be a deputy sheriff, but who walked around giving freaks the soul-brother handshake and spending what time he could bridg-ing the generation gap with a topless chick of generous endowment. Among the invited performers, Greezy Wheels, Doug Sahm, Spanky and Our Gang, and some others did a nice job, but Rick Nelson and David Carradine helped convince the faithful it was time to go home.

I suspect most of the people who stayed all three days managed to have a good time and would probably show up if Willie announced a similar event for next week. And I'm glad I went. I enjoyed myself, as well as a lot of other people, and I came to like redneck rock better than before. But late Saturday night, as I sat all showered and shampooed in my cool two-story house with the lawn and the shrubs and the birdfeeder and the basketball goal and the hopscotch grid, drinking iced tea and talking to my friends, admiring my teenaged boys and eight-year-old daughter, and thinking about my prize wife whose eyes and smile reflect experience not just with love but with sex, I decided this year's picnic would probably last me a good long while.

*—October 1974*

# THE HIGHLAND PARK WOMAN

by A. C. Greene

*Some are born into the club, others never quite make it.*

The Highland Park woman is thirty-two or thirty-three. She says she honestly forgets sometimes. She's not particularly afraid to tell her age (she's not *that* old) but she seldom does. It's not really necessary: a ten-year-old son in St. Mark's and a seven-year-old daughter in Lamplighter, three bedrooms and three baths on one end of Beverly Drive, her station wagon, his 98. Although she isn't *young* young anymore. Last summer, in Acapulco with the Frasers, she gave up her bikini. And came back and enrolled in Louise Williams' exercise class. She likes ballet better but thinks it doesn't keep the tummy quite as flat.

Early thirties, but downright good-looking, seated in Houlihan's and having a Bloody Mary—one Bloody Mary—with Judy and Anne. She easily passes for late twenties, although the men who eye her probably don't demand that kind of youthfulness and girlish charm. She's the woman they have in mind when they get back to Detroit and Denver and tell their associates about those wonderful Dallas women.

Her hair is, or was, blonde, but that was a good many streakings and tintings and tippings ago. Pulled back, short, cool. Her eyes are blue or hazel according to whether or not she has on her tinted contacts. Or prescription sunglasses. Big, oval or round. She never leaves home, summer or winter, without her glasses, of course, so unless you know her *very* well you don't know what color her eyes really are. Probably not even John, her husband, remembers. Her figure is much more important, and it's still competitive. Although the Highland Park woman hates to compete, if you want to call it that. There's something so lower middle class about competition. Dallas is full of young stewardess types. It would be foolish and wasteful at her age to compete with them. And she certainly does not consider wait-

*A. C. Greene, a contributing editor of* Texas Monthly, *is the author of books and articles. He created his Highland Park woman with inspiration from Charles Willeford.*

resses and bar girls to be competition at *any* age. God forbid.

The Highland Park woman is on a permanent diet, of course, and the only reason she doesn't go to Louise Williams' as often as she's paid for is that she can't always get one of the other girls to go with her. The Highland Park woman rarely does anything alone. She would never, for instance, go to a movie alone, even Cinema I or II. Neither would she drive all the way out to the Dallas Museum of Fine Arts unless she was meeting someone there for soup-and-sandwich. One of her friends, Laura, drives alone to Fort Worth from time to time to see an exhibit at the Kimbell or the Amon Carter, but the Highland Park woman would never do that. She can't remember, since she was a little girl chasing butterflies, when she didn't like doing things in groups. Oh, there were one or two special close friends when she was in Hockaday, but they were in Cotillion and Junior Assembly like everyone else. Even in college—at The University—her sorority was mainly girls from Highland Park she'd known all her life.

"Maybe it's some kind of social phobia we have," she says of this insistence on doing things together. By herds, her friend Dick says. Dick says things like that and she's never sure how he means it. She's not sure he does either. Dick doesn't work in an office and he didn't grow up in Highland Park. Or Dallas. But she likes him despite the cynical way he has of teasing and referring to her social instincts. But alone too much, she becomes uneasy. It's not the fear you read about in newspapers of muggers and rapists. It's a funny little constant fear of being caught out in the open without an umbrella when it rains. A fear that one of those women who wears rollers to grocery shop will suddenly push in line. Will invade, Dick says. Oh well, she supposes it comes from her mother's narrow social views. The Highland Park woman vows secretly and sometimes sincerely she will not rear her daughter the way she was reared. She stops just short of vowing she will not rear her

*Photography by Constance Ashley*

daughter to be a Highland Park woman.

The Highland Park woman is married, like most of her friends, to her first husband. If she divorces John, if she's widowed too young, or if he deserts her—thinking the unthinkable—she can rarely get another one in Highland Park. She must be willing to leave for a happier hunting ground. That is, if she convinces some married girl friend she is safe to have around at Cozumel or La Jolla. Eligible males between the ages of 35 and 55 are few to nonexistent in Highland Park. Or gay. And the men control the money. Knowing this, even if she has a bad marriage a Highland Park woman will put up with the husband she has much longer than will, say, her Houston counterpart.

Her younger sister, who is 28, is in what the Highland Park woman calls "a fix." She is currently unattached, unhappy, and sleeping around. Although to hear her tell it, it's simply divine. She has made all the mistakes younger sisters usually make, but in spades. She had an abortion in high school—wouldn't go to Hockaday because there were no boys—then dropped out of The University to get married (slightly pregnant, of course) and never got her degree. Instead she got Bennie. Then Bennie, Jr. Then Earl. And for a while thought there'd be another name to inscribe in the family Bible. But the Highland Park woman told her, "Get rid of it." And she did. "Just don't think about what it was. Or whose it was, if there's any doubt." Well, there was some doubt, perhaps, because Bennie moved out on her. Although now he's always trying to patch things up "for the good of the kids." The Highland Park woman doesn't like to think about her younger sister or her two darling boys or her abortions or Bennie or whomever she's sleeping with currently. Which is generally an airline pilot or somebody from television.

But why does John act as if there's something decadent and rare about her younger sister? Look at *his* sister. Older sister, too. Third husband meekly sending her $2500 a month and her supporting a lover somewhere in France who is old enough to be her father and who is Jewish. Or, as if John hadn't ever indulged. As if *they* hadn't. Well, even her own mother pretended there was something evil about being attracted to men. Thank God, she'll never be that way with *her* daughter. She doesn't think it necessary to go back and recall certain times and certain boys but she's too straightforward to make believe they never occurred. Well, at least, both her children were planned. And when she watches her younger sister, alternately in love and in depression, having a quiet marriage doesn't seem all that dull.

The Highland Park woman's husband earns $40,000 a year, which is nearly three times as much as he earned when he went into business with his father and his brother. His family isn't one of the old, *old* Highland Park families—neither is hers—so they'll never be really rich. But they'll have enough to live a certain way. And herd or not, she likes it. Better than the alternatives she grew up with. John isn't a lush, like her father was, and even though she's never able to buy all she wants at Marie Leavell's, not to mention Neiman-Marcus, life could be worse. But it's almost impossible to save, really save, anything. If she didn't have her trust fund, small though it is, well, they might be peering over the edge the way some couples their age were. Thank God for that quarterly check. And thank God for Daddy, even if he was a

lush and spent more nights in bed with prostitutes than with mother. According to mother. It gives them a slight edge and keeps her from having to take a genteel part-time job. And keeps John III (whom they already call Trey) in St. Mark's and Missy in Lamplighter. The house will be theirs in twenty more years and fortunately they inherited a Dallas Country Club membership—through John's parents—and don't need a swimming pool.

Domestic relations? Okay, there's John's mother and her mother. That's quite enough. Sometimes she just wants to point to them and say, "Take your pick." Her mother lives in a condominium off Reverchon Park, and John's mother, God knows how, stays at the Gold Crest. Or rather, flits down on her leathery bat wings two or three times a week to tell her how to run her home, run her children, run John, and run herself. Of her own mother she sighs and keeps quiet. A face lift and silicone injections. At her age. The silicone injections, that is. The face lift isn't so bad, the Highland Park woman says. In fact, the day may come— may—when she'll want a couple of tucks here and here, too. But silicone injections, at 56? "You just don't know men. They don't change that much when they get old," her mother told her. "I'm still a relatively young woman, dear. Your father never knew it, of course. But there are those who do." It disturbs her, the Highland Park woman says. Her mother and her younger sister might as well be in a race. What might she think if she knew some of the things her own mother did?

Domestic relations. Ha. There is, or was, the matter of John and Miss or Mrs. Nameless. The little bitch. But it is over now, the Highland Park woman says, and forgiven if not totally forgiven. Nobody ever mentions names or anything else. Except, oh, about once a year. And John, damn him, asks for it when she does. "All right . . . all right. Take off," she says she told him, "take right off. But don't take anything with you. Not one damn thing." Or words to that effect. But she didn't. She was scared and sick and frightened—lonely, depthless fright—and went from mirror to mirror asking herself questions, wondering what had happened. And John acting guilty, mean, harsh. The Highland Park woman cut him off at the source when she found out. Click, like that. Except, she discovered herself wanting her husband worse than ever. Maybe to prove to him she was as sexy as Miss or Mrs. Nameless. Maybe to prove it to herself. But she didn't solve it. The "other woman" solved it. She married an oilman from West Texas. Money enough to do things for her and with her John couldn't have done. He says that ended it, but sometimes the Highland Park woman wonders if it might not happen again. Sometimes she can't believe it won't. When he acts discontented and blames things on his career and talks about getting older without having done any of the things he wants to do. The Highland Park woman wonders.

She's never been involved herself, not really. The crowd they run with, their Highland Park herd, gives lots of parties. Flirts a lot and touches. Kitchen kisses and hugging in the hallway after enough scotches and sodas. Some are worse than others. The women, too. Martha, who is so calm and sweet and Eastern finishing school. Give her a few drinks, which she won't turn down if there are enough men around. And Shuggie. Shuggie's the only grown woman she knows of who smokes pot. The Highland Park woman wonders about Martha and John sometimes. Martha's much nearer the kind of woman John thinks he likes than she is, his own wife. Oh, John denies it if she makes some veiled reference to him and Martha in fun. But it's a matter of style. Martha's his style. Shuggie might be even more his style, but the Highland Park woman suspects Shuggie has wider worlds to conquer than John. Shuggie is so chic, so sleek and superior. Thank God, John isn't really up to something like Shuggie—whom she really likes, the Highland Park woman says.

Personally, she's on the pill—has been since college—and there are no problems. But the problem with no problems is the simple fact that there is no problem. She thinks she and John make love twice a month or so. If she kept track of it. Sometimes it may be longer. He works hard and thinks about his work and sits up late and gets up early and plays hard—golf and tennis—and stays on the job, really stays on the job, plenty of evenings. And with all that they just don't make love very much. But no one she knows, except her younger sister, does.

And there is Dick. If Dick were a little younger—he's 44—a little more, should she say, aggressive? Anyhow, if Dick were a little more . . . , well, something. There have been lots of kisses and hand-holding and dates for lunch and desires freely expressed. By Dick. But not involved. Would she get involved? Well, she isn't the type who plans that sort of thing. The answer would have to come simultaneously with the opportunity, and the opportunity has not come. Yes, she might even become his mistress, although she hates that word. But Dick is as caught in it all as she is. Everyone they both know they see constantly. Dallas is small enough: Highland Park is like living in a retirement home when it comes to knowing what everyone is doing. Let Dick take her to Kuby's or Arthur's for lunch and their whole circle would know it by nightfall. Going to bed with him might turn out to be the same thing. If Dick took her to bed. She wonders about Dick, if he's as passionate for her as he says he is. But he's sweet and very clever. And not many men pay the personal attention to her he does. Not even John.

Several hours of every day are spent in the car, driving carpool with her daughter every third week, taking John's shirts to the laundry he likes, picking up the maid at the bus stop three times a week, shopping, shopping and going, going. She's not fond of it, she says, and, the Highland Park woman confesses, she's not a superb driver. But she can still talk a policeman out of a traffic ticket. Especially one of the Highland Park police. Not that she gets *that* many tickets.

She finds plenty to occupy her time, regardless of what Women's Lib says. Volunteering at the museum or Old City Park. Going to ballet and exercise class. Taking Trey to his soccer games. From time to time she enrolls in some continuing education class at SMU. Languages or art. Right now she's taking backgammon lessons at DCC as a sort of lark Dick suggested. Nobody in her crowd plays bridge anymore.

Two days a week she shops. With someone. Sometimes Anne, sometimes Martha. Shuggie's taste is too rich for her, but it's fun going shopping with Shuggie. Fun to watch the saleswomen at Marie Leavell's and Lou Lattimore fall

all over her when she walks in. They will have lunch at the Chimney or the Upper Crust at Olla Podrida, or if it's one of the girls' birthday they'll take her to the Zodiac Room at Neiman-Marcus. They never talk about men. Well, only their husbands and how hard they work. Nobody ever says she's unhappy. Just frustrated. They talk about their children most of all, and about new things they've bought, or some change at home they're planning to make. If they gossip it will be sympathetic and not caustic.

What else?

Well, she belongs to a book review club, one her mother helped start, that meets once a month in some Highland Park home. If it's a particularly interesting home she'll go. She seldom goes to the DCC. She doesn't play golf. Not that age yet, she told Rachel, who's 40 and plays twice a week. And didn't like her remark. The Highland Park woman tried to play several years ago when John wanted her to learn, but that little piece of newly married togetherness dissolved with her first pregnancy.

She makes the mothers meeting at Lamplighter and St. Mark's but never says anything. The super-rich gals run that show and the best she can hope for is to be asked to join a committee with one of them. She wanted to go to the SMU Film Festival last spring but she had an appointment with her hairdresser the morning they showed the Warren Beatty picture, and she had to take Missy to the dentist another afternoon. And she couldn't get anyone to go with her, regardless.

She reads a lot, but it's not very deep. They've been members of Book-of-the-Month Club for years and she automatically reads what they send unless it's too thick. John reads about one book a year, if it's about business or money. He says the *Wall Street Journal* tells him all he needs to know about books. She has an account at Preston Books and the Bookseller at Willow Creek and sometimes she will come away with $20 or $30 worth, and John will say, "When in God's name do you plan to read all that?" John watches more television than she does, although he claims he doesn't have time. She likes an old movie late at night—the only time she can watch TV in peace—and she tried to follow *Upstairs, Downstairs* but gave up because of the kids. A number of magazines come to the house, but the only ones she reads much are *The New Yorker*, *Vogue*, *Time*, *Texas Monthly*, and *D*. Sometimes she finds something in *Harper's* or *Atlantic* someone's said she should read, and she looks at the pictures in *House Beautiful* and *House and Garden* every month. She wishes she had read more of the classics in college; learned to read modern poetry and drama. But she didn't.

All right, so she passed over The Time. He was a lawyer but she met him in a night French class at SMU and he said he was giving up the law and was going to get his PhD in American literature at Harvard. He was divorced. His wife had been from a famous Houston family and was so dumb, he said, he had to remind her every month when it was time for her period. The Highland Park woman went to his apartment at 3525 after their third class and he had champagne in the refrigerator. It hadn't been like a college affair. It was more deliberate on her part. A man can't take off panty hose. He was passionate but no better in bed than John when John is interested. And the whole time she kept thinking she needed to go to the bathroom. After that he begged and begged her to sleep with him again and when he left Dallas to go to Boston he begged her to leave John and marry him. He seemed to have a lot of money and drove one of those little Mercedes 450s that cost so much. But she couldn't picture herself married to him. Not really. He'd never had children and acted as if she could simply take her children along, the way people take poodles with them to Aspen and Santa Fe. For a while he called her once a week, then every month or so. But that was four years ago, and there'd been no more phone calls since, oh, year before last. Except, the Highland Park woman says, thinking about him now makes him seem terribly exciting. If she lets herself she even wonders how long it might have lasted.

What about the future?

"I don't know exactly," she says. "I want a better life for my children, of course. I love my children and I think I'm a good mother. I don't spoil them." Would she like for her children to do more or less the same things she's done? Live the same life? "Well, I expect them to live a certain kind of way—a certain lifestyle, if that doesn't sound too hackneyed."

What about herself?

"I'm happy," the Highland Park woman says. "One thing sure. I'm not ending up like my mother getting silicone injections at 56. Or like John's mother completely wrapped up in her children. I'm going to be a person."

Last week the Highland Park woman and her husband and their children flew down to South Padre for a short vacation. They had a nice room with an ocean view and there were supervised play areas for the children and she and John had, for the first time in years, a few days completely to themselves. They had dinner in the dining room the first evening and sent the kids to a nature show, then returned to their room and had drinks. Later, John sat at the window with a scotch and soda and said, "I ought to call the office, I guess," and shook his head a few times and turned to her and said, very seriously, "Shit." She sat in bed with the sheet up around her, feeling deliciously nude, and smoked a cigarette while he stared out to sea.

The sunset faded in a positively gorgeous pile of pink and gold clouds and the sea birds swirled and darted across the view. The sound of the surf came through the wide window and John finished his drink, dropped his cigarette butt in the glass, and said to her, "We've had dinner, we made love, we had a drink. What do we do now?"

The Highland Park woman, who only smokes with her husband, lit another cigarette and thought about it.

*—April 1976*

Camp Waldemar girls. *Photography by Linda Kerr*

# THE GREATEST EXPERIENCE OF YOUR LIFE

by Prudence Mackintosh

## Fame? Riches? Sex? Nope. Camp.

"I knew I couldn't be a Pi Phi. I went to the wrong camp," the sophisticated Houston coed explained as we walked out of the Junior Ball Room of the University of Texas Student Union with respectable sorority bids in hand. The 1962 rush week "pig squealing" was over. For me, a small-town girl, it had been a week of unconscious blunders, naive assumptions, unwarranted overconfidence, and too much punch. I was forewarned that I would need a jingly (preferably gold) charm bracelet to wear to the Pi Beta Phi rush parties in order to participate in the sisterly singing of "Ring Ching, Pi Beta Phi." The bracelet's symbols of high school accomplishments momentarily buoyed flagging small talk throughout the week; but there were status symbols that had not made their way to my rural province of East Texas. I had never been particularly concerned with Sakowitz and Neiman-Marcus labels or Villager oxford cloth blouses. Pappagallo dress shoes held no majority in my closet. How was I to know about camp?

Certainly no one had asked me about the two weeks I had spent at Girl Scout Camp High Point in Mena, Arkansas, a healthy preadolescent experience that bore no resemblance to the camp stories I would hear about during my four years at The University of Texas. I gradually became aware that the camp one went to made a remarkable difference in all sorts of social endeavors, both in college and in the years that followed it.

My first visit to the Texas Hill Country around Kerrville convinced me that it is a camper's paradise. The cool, clear waters of the Guadalupe River are irresistible, and I waded in before reaching the first camp on my tour. The hills themselves are part of camp life, since they provide a natural setting for secret "tribal" meetings. After you've heard the echoes bounce off Joy Bluff at Camp Stewart, you don't

wonder that a Great Spirit could light the bonfire. With my feet in the Guadalupe, I lost a good bit of my skepticism about Hill Country camps. As one former camper put it, "All I know is, I thought about things on the banks of the Guadalupe that just wouldn't have occurred to me if I'd stayed in Dallas."

In a week I visited seven camps in the Kerrville-Hunt vicinity before going on to Inks Lake to see camps Longhorn and Champion. I wanted to explore the mystique of the legendary girls' camps like Waldemar and Mystic. What was it about them that inspired such loyalty? Why would a college coed wear her diamond camp ring well into her junior year? Was it true that debutante bows were a part of the calisthenic program at Waldemar? Why did wives at lawyers' conventions or medical meetings greet each other with "Kiowa?" "No, Tonkawa"? Or why would a 40-year-old woman squint through binoculars across the Cotton Bowl and nudge her husband, "See that blonde five rows up in the first deck? She was in War Canoe with me at Waldemar." What did these camps offer that would make a Texas daddy who had invested more than $12,000 in 25 cumulative years of summer camp for three daughters say, "It's a bargain."

At fees of $465 to $650 per session (usually four to five weeks), all the private girls' camps along the Guadalupe offer a standard curriculum—swimming, canoeing, archery, riflery, horseback riding, tennis, crafts, tumbling, and dance. Some offer a great deal more. I couldn't help wondering if cheerleading appears as a regular activity in camps in Wisconsin or upstate New York as it does in Texas.

Girls' camps are emotional places. Take little girls away from boys for four weeks and they fall in love with each other. They adore secret clubs and tribes, where they hug and cry a lot and sing tearful, terrible corruptions of 1930s love songs or Broadway musicals. It's a confusing blend of

*Prudence Mackintosh is a contributing editor of* Texas Monthly *and winner of a 1976 Penney-Missouri Award.*

Protestant Christianity and pantheism, with the word "love" used so liberally that a nine-year-old couldn't be sure whether she was crying because she loved Jesus, the Kickapoos, the tribal True Blue, or her counselor.

During my camp sojourn, I kept experiencing *deja vu*. I knew it couldn't be my old Girl Scout days, but it wasn't until I overheard a counselor say, "We've got to get them to crying tonight, so they'll sign up for next year," that I knew. It wasn't camp; it was the sorority house during rush week, with the songs calculated to bring tears, the embraces, the rituals, and the ubiquitous Rodgers and Hammerstein scores.

One of my contemporaries, a Rice graduate, has always been puzzled and slightly amused by a University of Texas phenomenon. "Texas graduates," he says, "do not view their four years in Austin as a terminal experience." He theorizes that it is only a small part of a much larger picture, a place where paths begin to cross from all over the state in ways that will somehow affect the rest of their lives. I could hardly wait to tell him that though the bonding process is galvanized at UT, it does not always begin there. The words of the Houston coed came back, "I went to the wrong camp." I had unwittingly stumbled on one of the earlier threads in the continuum of Texas society.

A remarkably beautiful and healthy fifteen-year-old girl stands on the banks of the Guadalupe to give her inspirational vespers talk. She begins profoundly, "Two roads diverged in a yellow wood." Poor Frost. Would he enjoy the irony of his "The Road Not Taken" read on this hallowed camp ground? Camp, after all, is a decidedly decisionless place to be. As one ingenuous child said, "It's so easy to be good at camp." The other irony, of course, is that for most of these girls the road is already chosen. It goes from Hill Country camp to private school, or at least to an affluent suburban high school, to what Texans regard as Eastern girls' schools: Mary Baldwin, Sweet Briar, Mount Vernon, Hollins, Randolph Macon, or any of those institutions which offer the "Texas Plan." This plan allows girls to have one or perhaps two years out of state before returning to THE University where they can live at Miss Hardin's (Hardin House it's called now), acquire the necessary sorority credentials, marry lawyers, doctors, or inherited wealth, have two to four lovely, wholesome children, run carpools, dance a few years in the Junior League follies or work in the Thrift Shop, and "knowing how road leads on to road," put their children on the appropriate waiting lists.

Counterparts of these Hill Country camps are dying out in the East. Spiraling expense, complaints from kids that camp is boring, and competition from shorter term, specialized camps have taken their toll. Wilderness camps are so popular now that they can often charge more and offer less.

But the Hill Country camps don't seem to be suffering. To be sure, they have problems. Texas camps are currently fighting federal safety regulations, even though the ones I visited could probably pass the most stringent of safety inspections. I suspect the directors' real fear is that any federal interference will not only increase paper work, and hence costs, but also might threaten their prerogative to decide who attends.

Kids themselves have changed in recent years and pose some challenges. Janis Joplin probably never envisioned, "Oh, Lord, Won't You Buy Me a Mercedes Benz" as a song at Camp Kickapoo in Kerrville. Baseball teams at Camp Stewart have names like the Margaritas and the Harvey Wallbangers. Most directors admitted that their campers are more worldly wise and better trained athletically than in years past, but certainly no more mature. Nurses said they were stocking as much Maalox as Mercurochrome since many kids arrive with potential ulcers. They also said that more children are on prescribed medication than ever before.

No director would admit that drugs had ever been a problem at his camp, but all were extremely vigilant. A child at Heart o' the Hills was seen hiding a bag of white powder under her pillow, which a counselor quickly took to the director. Analysis at the Kerr County sheriff's office revealed that the bag contained ascorbic acid, a bittersweet candy substance. Si Ragsdale says that some of his campers wrote home with fictitious claims that they had discovered cannabis growing on Stewart's property and implied that Mr. Ragsdale was raising a bumper crop. Kids are more likely to challenge authority these days. "Why should I have to ride horses? I hate horses."

Some camps are obviously bending with the times. Rio Vista for boys, established in 1921, seems to pay lip service to its Indian tribe traditions while actually becoming more and more a specialty sports camp. Its eight magnificent laykold tennis courts reveal the principal interest of Jack McBride, Rio Vista's director and stockholder, who sees the possibilities of another Lakeway-type resort in the Hill Country. Increasing budgets and a dearth of "good help" are inescapable problems. The cost of sending a child to Mystic increased from $575 last summer to $635 this year. Cafeteria food service has replaced family-style meals in all the camps except Waldemar, Kickapoo, Mystic, and Stewart.

In spite of problems and costs, these camps still have waiting lists. Most of the directors are talented salesmen, and their programs still please Texans. And camp has always been a safe place to park the kids while Mom and Dad were in Europe. But most of the parents I talked with suggested that they weren't so eager to get rid of the kids as they were to go to camp with them. A former Waldemar Ideal Girl whose daughter will soon be a camper recalled how safe and secure she felt at Waldemar. "I'll never forget the time some boys on motorcycles roared into our camp. I was near the kitchen and saw the cook run out brandishing his butcher knife after the hoodlums. I remember thinking, 'Gosh, they really *must* love us.'" These parents have terrific nostalgia for a place that is seemingly unchanged, for a time in their lives when life was uncomplicated by adult responsibility.

Then there are the social implications. These camps are the closest to boarding schools most Texans will ever get, and they perform the similar function of introducing affluent children to one another. "Get to know the boys in your cabin, Son," one Camp Stewart father admonished. "Lamar Hunt was in my cabin and I didn't give a damn. Now I just wish he knew my name."

Heart o' the Hills, its roots in Texas legend, has fewer social pretensions than most of the other camps I visited. Built as a lodge by Dr. E. J. Stewart, who was then the owner of camps

Stewart for boys and Mystic for girls, Heart o' the Hills was intended to house the parents who came to Hunt for camp ceremonies. Arriving in the area without a hotel reservation, Dallas millionaire Colonel D. H. "Dry Hole" Byrd reportedly demanded a room at Heart o' the Hills. The clerk assured him that no rooms were available, so, in fine Texas fashion, Byrd turned to his companion Kenneth Jones, a maintenance man from Camp Mystic, and said, "Kenneth, if I bought this place, would you run it for me? I need a place to stay." Jones agreed, and Byrd told the clerk, "We'll take it."

Jones and his wife turned the lodge into a camp in 1953. Its acreage is decidedly limited as Hill Country camps go, but the beautiful Guadalupe waterfront is accessible by tunnel under the highway, and steep hills rise behind the original lodge to provide the secret tribal grounds for the Heart tribes—Pawnee and Shawnee. Although it has long since been under different ownership, the camp's highest achievement award is still called Jo Jones Girl, a memorial to Jones' daughter who was killed in a car accident.

Heart o' the Hills, now owned by Carl and Diane Hawkins, is the smallest camp I visited. It accepts 125 girls, aged six through sixteen. The Hawkins see the small size as a distinct advantage since it offers each camper a better chance to excel, as well as an opportunity to ride horses every day. Larger camps offer horseback riding only on alternate days.

The Hawkins are hard-working people with extensive professional experience. Hawkins loves what he does and has a genuine concern and sympathetic ear for every girl in the camp. The program is full, but relaxed, with particular emphasis on the kids having a good time and making friends, rather than perfecting the final show for parents. The finale was in fact terrible—the craft display had the usual monstrosities: painted rocks, lap boards, and decoupaged plaques—but the little girls enjoyed it. Tribal competition is fierce between the Pawnees and the Shawnees throughout the session, but is lessened somewhat by the joining of the tribes to form one Heart Tribe at the closing.

Additional hands to do the heavy or tedious camp work are scarce, expensive, and frequently unreliable, so there are few jobs that Carl and Diane Hawkins cannot handle, be it mowing grass, slinging hash in the cafeteria-style dining room, or counting up camp store deposits. Knowing who's who in Texas is simply not a part of the Hawkins' experience, although their camp obviously draws from affluent families around the state and from northern Mexico. I returned from a neighboring camp one afternoon and mentioned to Hawkins that I'd seen one of Ross Perot's children. "Is that someone I should know?" Hawkins asked. Impossible? Not when you understand the news vacuum that exists in Hunt. Television and radio reception are so poor and the *Kerrville Mountain Sun* so completely local in coverage that it took me three days to learn that Fred Carrasco was dead in Huntsville. But it isn't just the inaccessibility of news that insulates you in Hunt. Camp is a cosmos unto itself. Nixon made his resignation speech on the closing day of one of the camp sessions. I was so involved in camp life by that time that I experienced some irritation that parents would delay the Memorial Vespers by refusing to leave their portable radios. Who cared about the American presidency; I wanted to know who had won the Jo Jones award.

"I learned a code at Waldemar that's almost a burden at times," the young woman told me. "Eight years at Waldemar taught me never to settle for anything less than the best in everything—pure quality—no veneer. I learned to do things thoroughly and to expect the same from others." She had been a camper at Waldemar sixteen years ago and, like an amazing number of women I talked with in Dallas, she felt Waldemar was one of the great moral influences in her life.

For sheer natural beauty, Waldemar's 1200 acres along the North Fork of the Guadalupe in Hunt are unparalleled in the Hill Country. Architect Harvey P. Smith, who also restored the Spanish Governor's Palace and several missions in San Antonio, insisted that no trees be cut, and designed native stone structures that seem to grow out of the hillside. Massive trees grow right through the roofs of several cabins. The masonry executed by German immigrant craftsman Ferdinand Rehberger in 1931 is matchless. The perfectly tended plantings suggest that the grounds keepers bear the burden of the Waldemar code, too. The Kampongs (cabins) are not carpeted or air-conditioned as detractors had tried to tell me, but they have a certain Spartan beauty: bunks are dark-stained oak, floors are red Mexican tile, and several cabins have fireplaces. The walls bear no names, carved initials, or tribal slogans. Since Kampongs are inspected twice a day, bedsheets had "hospital corners" and trunks were immaculate. The bathrooms, cleaned by maids, were sparkling.

August 1974 was not a good time to judge camp food. Rampant inflation could not have been foreseen when budgets were drawn up in the spring, but Waldemar was typically unperturbed by it all. None of the mysterious pizza, tamale, noodle, and Frito concoctions I had seen in other camps ever appeared in the polished dining room, where white-coated black waiters attended the tables. The food is legendary: "I ate my first soufflé at Waldemar," a friend recalled. There are few packaged mixes, and the aesthetic manner in which the food is served is deemed as important as nutrition.

But it is not only the setting and the food that place Waldemar apart from other Texas camps. Some say it's the Waldemar spirit, the immutable traditions, the social clout, and the intense loyalty it breeds; others believe it just may be Doris Johnson herself, owner and director of Waldemar and niece of its founder, Miss Ora Johnson. One friend admitted that as a nine-year-old, she had believed that perhaps Miss Ora's ghost floated around the camp site at night.

"Waldemar is the only experience from my own childhood that I can offer unchanged to my daughter," one mother explained, as I needled her about having enrolled her newborn daughter for Waldemar in 1983. Tradition is a big drawing card for any Texas institution, and Texas traditions require only 30 or 40 years to develop. The Hill Country camps, especially Waldemar, have made the most of it. The tribal rituals, the War Canoe picnic, and even a special Victorian vocabulary remain the same at Waldemar. Snack time is called "Nourishment," and who could forget Miss Roe, former calisthenics teacher, calling, "Boozerings up, whosits in, squeeze those legs together." Waldemar standards are traditionally rigid. Right and wrong are so clearly defined at camp that seemingly slight infractions may require a full confession before the entire tribe.

Waldemar offers the standard camp athletic activities, but with strong emphasis on perfecting form. Those who have attended camp long enough to participate in War Canoe, an exhausting activity requiring strength and impressive precision, can undoubtedly identify with the girl who said, "Every year after I got home from camp, I would turn my bare back to the mirror, lift my arms to a ballroom dancing position and watch with tears in my eyes as the muscles rippled across my back like Charles Atlas'."

Even my most cynical friends became a little misty-eyed about Waldemar's tradition of traditions, the Ideal Girl Ceremony. The most loyal return year after year, well past their college days, to participate. The Ideal Girl is elected by the entire camp and staff at the end of a session, and her virtues are extolled in a candlelight ceremony that has not changed since the camp began. Once she is named, she is taken down the Guadalupe in a white canoe paddled only by former Ideal Girls while the entire camp sings, in choked voices, to "the spirit of Camp Waldemar."

Waldemar accepts girls aged nine to sixteen and has a capacity of 306. Present preenrollment applications will fill the camp through 1983. Grandmothers have been known to secretly enroll granddaughters whose mothers were still rebelling against their own upbringing. "Sally will thank me when little Sarah is nine years old." Although there is really no debutante bow practice at Waldemar, the social implications of going there are undeniable. Even the least enthusiastic campers admitted, "I wouldn't have thought of going through rush at Texas without my Waldemar ring." One ex-camper was amazed to hear a friend who had attended another camp admit that she had participated in skits satirizing Waldemar. "I was a little sad to think that they were so aware of us," the Waldemar graduate said. "We never even thought about them."

Indeed, Waldemar has experienced no competition from other camps along the Guadalupe, although "Nakanawa, in Tennessee, once took a lot of our Dallas girls," Doris Johnson conceded. Doris—she is known by her first name to all Waldemar campers—is the embodiment of the Waldemar spirit, high standards, and organization. Always clad in white, this slightly imperial doyenne of the Hill Country camps lives year-round in Rippling Waters, her home on the Waldemar grounds. She has been associated with the camp since 1928.

Doris maintained a certain aloofness throughout our conversation; however, as we strolled the grounds, it was apparent that she never forgets the name or face of any camper. When I mentioned my own contemporaries who had gone to Waldemar, she recalled not only their married names, but also the names of their children. As I sat in her office looking at the massive wooden card catalog that records the pertinent information on every past camper, I couldn't help wondering how many of them regarded Waldemar as the last bastion of civilization. Perusing a Record Card, I noted that table manners are graded on a scale of 1 to 10. "Don't sixteen-year-old girls find this a little silly?" I naively asked. "It's more important than ever now; families eat on TV trays," Doris replied with ill-concealed disgust. I knew that Waldemar attracted girls from New Orleans and Little Rock particularly during the second session, but I saw no evidence of the Mexican aristocracy from Monterrey, Piedras Negras, or Mexico City that I had frequently

encountered in the other Hill Country camps. "We tried that once," Doris explained, "but we saw no need to continue. Their English was poor and, since most of them are raised by servants, they have terrible manners and are much too spoiled for camp life."

"What about notable or famous women who have attended Waldemar?" I asked. An icy hesitation suggested that I had trespassed. She replied with inoffensive though patronizing protectiveness, "No, I can't think of anyone who's made a name for herself."

What will become of Waldemar when Doris is gone? She is seventyish, and there is no clear line of succession. Wealthy parents and former campers, her loyal subjects, stand nervously in the wings awaiting her instruction.

If I asked a Mystic camper about the traditions she learned at camp, she would tell me about the tribes Kiowa and Tonkawa and the training rules—unchanged since 1928—that prohibit bare feet, Coca-Cola, candy, and talking at rest hour. She would tell about living in cabins called Chatter Box or Angels' Attic or Hangover where her mother's name might be found carved in the rafters, or about tribal serenades, or winning Best Posture.

"The Spirit of Camp Mystic is love," says Inez Harrison, the camp's director. "And that spirit pervades our whole camp. Mystic girls learn to love God first, others second, and themselves last." Before the day was over, however, I would know that Inez Harrison is no naive grandmother and that beneath the almost cloying sweetness there is a strong intelligent organizer with a sound visceral sense of what these little girls need and what their parents expect.

Mystic has long been a favorite of the Texas political aristocracy. Texas Governors Dan Moody, Price Daniel, and John Connally have all sent daughters there. Lyndon Johnson's daughters were also Mystic campers. Luci unexpectedly took refuge here after the 1960 Democratic convention. Even now, Luci acknowledges Inez and Frank Harrison as her much beloved summertime parents.

Inez sees Mystic as a retreat. "The world demands too much sophistication of these little girls," she says. Outside that gate these same fourteen-year-olds might talk knowledgeably of birth control or the merits of *The Last Picture Show*, but once inside, they are little girls screaming their hearts out for the Tonkawas. When they return to the real world, they might be a little embarrassed at this display of emotion, but for five weeks they can live without affectation.

Campers come from all over the state. Mystic also welcomes the children of Mexico's affluent families, but Inez admits that language and cultural barriers are not always so smoothly crossed. Imagine the trauma of a little Mexican girl being introduced for the first time to that relic of American pre-Freudian toilet training, the "Health and Happiness Chart," on which each child records her tooth brushing and daily bowel movements. One Mexican camper went for days without brushing her hair. The counselor hated to reprimand her, but by week's end, after swimming and riding horses, the child's hair was hopelessly matted. An older cousin was summoned to ask why she hadn't brushed her hair. "I don't know how," the eight-year-old replied in Spanish. "My ladies have always done it."

Escorted by two counselors, I toured the camp grounds.

Mystic's 650 acres on the South Fork of the Guadalupe are remarkably beautiful, but unmistakably camp. The cabins, although perched aesthetically on a hillside, are still no-nonsense frame or Central Texas stone with concrete floors. Indoor plumbing was added in 1939. A brief trail ride within the camp acreage took me through a clear creek and up to Natural Fountains, a curious basin-shaped stalagmite formation under a cliff, with natural springs bubbling up in it.

While observing the Mystic water-front activities, I was startled to see a white Cadillac driven by what I took to be somebody's grandmother come barreling down to the water's edge. "Oh, that's just Ag," the counselors assured me. Agnes Stacey, an owner of Mystic and a camp personality since 1937, climbed out of her car and headed for the water. After a disciplined number of laps to and from the raft in the middle of the river, she climbed out, blue-rinsed hairdo intact. The counselors introduced me, and Ag said, "You know I used to swim every day to the dam and back, but now they won't let me go alone, and these counselors can't keep up with me. You be at my house in about fifteen minutes. It doesn't take me as long to get into my girdle as you might think."

Born in Dallas in 1887 on a farm where the Cotton Bowl now stands, Agnes Stacey (then Doran) turned down a Dallas debut to attend The University of Texas, against her father's wishes. There she appeared on *Cactus* beauty pages, pledged Kappa Kappa Gamma, received a T Association letter in swimming, maintained a creditable academic record, and met Bill Stacey, a UT tennis champion. Her postgraduate days included graduate work at Wellesley, teaching school in France, and Junior League work in Austin. She and Bill took over Camp Mystic in 1937, possibly the worst time in American history to sell people on the importance of a private camp for girls.

It became apparent during my brief stay that Ag Stacey's stamina and her link with the Texas aristocracy are still a part of Mystic's continuing success story. The actual directing of the camp has been delegated to Inez and Frank Harrison, but this doughty octogenarian has not completely retired. She is still likely to appear in unexpected places doing unexpected things. Campers requesting a song from Ag after dinner may be awed to see her climb up on the piano and belt out, "Oh My Man, I Love Him So."

The camp calendar of activities is largely unchanged since Ag organized it years ago. Mystic offers twenty activities, of which campers select eight. The tribal competition in tennis, swimming, canoeing, and baseball produces amazing athletic prowess among the girls, but their energy is also channeled with equal zeal into cheerleading and twirling activities.

No one leaves Mystic without some sense of personal accomplishment. Even the klutziest kid can stand up straight for a week in order to win Best Posture or get fork to mouth efficiently enough to be named Best Manners. At Final Campfire, no less than 30 awards are bestowed, but there is no Miss Mystic. The honor that most little girls seem to seek is to return as a counselor. Former campers have told me that they were always aware of their counselor's sorority and that considerable preliminary rushing took place at camp. On learning my affiliation, Ag almost upset the mashed potatoes to slip me the Kappa grip across the lunch table.

Most of these private camps have recruiting parties at country clubs in the major cities. I attended a Coke party for Camp Arrowhead in February and couldn't help noting the disparity between the movies of sunny Arrowhead flickering on the screen before the well-groomed audience of mothers and daughters and the camp I had seen on a rainy day the previous summer.

Arrowhead is noticeably more rustic than Waldemar or Mystic and even a little bleak on a rainy day, with muddy paths linking cabins that appear unimproved since the Thirties. The heart of the camp is on very flat terrain with only the clear Guadalupe and its cypress trees beautifying the site. When I saw separate bathhouses between cabins, I thought to myself, "Now this is camp. These little girls don't mind roughing it." The cafeteria-style dining hall, called the Filling Station, suggested that eating was purely for nourishment. "Good manners are encouraged," one mother told me, "but Arrowhead doesn't try to be a finishing school. It's just a place to have fun." The only hint of social pretension I saw at Arrowhead was the naming of the age divisions: Debs, Junior Debs, and Sub-Debs.

Arrowhead is by no means, however, an ugly stepsister of the other Hill Country camps. It offers similar, well-taught activities, equally adequate sports facilities, and it inspires great loyalty among wealthy alumnae across the state. Mothers who had gone to Arrowhead could hardly wait to start packing their daughters' trunks. "It hasn't changed a bit since I was there," one mother said. I could feel mothers around me thrill to Garner Bartell, camp director and owner, saying, "We're just as square as we've always been." Mrs. Bartell's family has been associated with the camp since its founding in 1934.

Arrowhead's tribes, the Kickapoos and the Pawnees, promote teamwork, leadership, and competition. A second-generation camper may choose to be in her mother's tribe, while others are assigned arbitrarily. Other than a few individual certificates and ribbons earned by campers, no awards are given at the Final Campfire. Mrs. Bartell feels that too many awards detract from the lifelong rewards of good camping experiences.

There are private boys' camps in the Hill Country, too. Stewart is widely acknowledged to be the male counterpart of Waldemar and Mystic. Silas B. Ragsdale, Jr., exchanged his coat and tie for shorts and tee shirt when he left the Denton Chamber of Commerce in 1967 to become the owner and director of the socially prestigious camp, but he brought his super-salesmanship abilities with him. Touring Stewart's 500 acres with Si in the camp's orange and white Ford Bronco, I learned a good bit about boys, Stewart's traditions, its problems, and its successes.

As we rode along, I could see that Stewart's site doesn't require much selling. The Guadalupe branches and bends to form four separate water areas—Blue Hole for fishermen; Bathtub, an area of shallow white-water rapids for non-swimmers; a Junior Pool with a Tarzan rope for average swimmers; and a Senior Pool for water skiing and canoeing. Joy Bluff rises above the Senior Pool and provides spooky echoes for nighttime bonfires. Younger campers' stone and frame cabins line the road that follows the athletic playing fields. Older campers stay across the river in Senior Camp.

Si's commentary made me well aware of the special problems that plague a boys' camp. He readily admitted that little boys are destructive, careless, and, most of the time, dirty. They will go to great lengths to avoid taking a shower and can mysteriously break four screens in their cabin during rest hour. "Now, that's what I'm talking about," he said, pointing to the broken window in the back of the camp station wagon. "That got busted during the dance with Waldemar, and no one is even sure how it happened."

Boys do not seem to form the emotional attachment to camp that little girls do, but that doesn't mean that camps like Stewart are devoid of tradition. Si stopped the Bronco long enough for me to meet "Mr. Lip," Stewart's favorite personality and link with the past. For 35 summers, Travis Lipscomb has served the camp in some capacity. Now, as head counselor, he remembers the good old days when "Uncle Bill" James directed Stewart. The place was much smaller then, and campers much less sophisticated. "With Uncle Bill, the boys just did a lot of hiking and sleeping out," he recalls, "but now they require every day to be filled with planned activity."

Our next stop was the dining hall. Like Waldemar, Stewart's bread is homemade and its cooks are a disappearing breed who use no packaged shortcuts. A little camper catching a small catfish in Blue Hole can usually persuade someone in the kitchen to fry it for him any time of the day. I saw the dining hall in action later that evening, a very different story from the kitchen. The noise even while the boys had their mouths full was earsplitting, and I saw one child stuff two pieces of bread into his mouth before attempting to chew. Si apologized for the atrocious manners, "We make some attempts, but it's even hard to find counselors who know how to eat in public anymore." Ben Barnes once won the Double Doily Award for having both elbows on the table while visiting his son Greg at mealtime.

Campers who attend Stewart for five years may get a second chance to polish their manners. Fred Pool, a former executive with the East Texas Chamber of Commerce and Si Ragsdale's long-time friend, takes a group of older Stewart boys for a week in Monterrey and Saltillo every summer during the camp session. Mr. Pool, who speaks fluent Spanish, introduces the boys to the cultural and culinary pleasures of Mexico, considered an essential part of a Texas gentleman's education.

The camp motto hangs on a wall in the dining hall. "Don't Wait Till You Are a Man to be Great—Be a Great Boy." This is implemented with "Thoughts for the Day" and "Pow Wows," brief meetings when distinguished visitors, counselors, or campers share their experiences. Stewart also offers its members a chance to perfect their interests by bringing in specialists like "Rooster" Andrews to teach a football kicking clinic, Rex Cobble for a calf-roping exhibition, or Steve Farish, professor of music at North Texas State University, for vocal instruction. The athletic clinics keep Stewart competitive with the sports specialty camps that have sprung up in recent years. But Stewart is interested in more than building athletes. As Si said, "Parents who send their boys to Stewart don't want their boys to be coaches, so we try to hire college students with professional ambitions, doctors or lawyers, to be in-cabin counselors."

Stewart accepts boys aged six through sixteen. The night I spent there, after a stunt performance before a huge

bonfire, my maternal instincts got the best of me. The youngest campers with meringue crusted in their hair from a pie-eating contest looked too young to be away from their mothers for four or five weeks. Kathy Ragsdale, the camp's business manager, handles homesick boys with aplomb. Giving an extra warm hug to a little camper eyeing the Ragsdale telephone, Kathy, with her Sulfur Springs drawl, quietly comforted, "Sweetheart, we'll call your mama tomorrah, you just go on to sleep tonaht."

Tex and Pat Robertson, the executive directors of Camp Longhorn, are acknowledged by other directors to be Mr. and Mrs. Camp in Texas. Their operation in Burnet on Inks Lake offers three 24-day sessions a summer. Five hundred campers aged eight to sixteen fill each term. Everyone knows someone who's been to Longhorn, and that may in part account for its popularity.

In the truest sense of the word, Longhorn doesn't really qualify as a camp. As one young Stewart camper said, "My friends who go to Longhorn don't do very much that they couldn't do here in Dallas." Longhorn campers don't go on overnights, seldom hike or even ride. (Longhorn has only 38 horses.) Nature study is limited to a small petting zoo in the middle of the complex. Furthermore, it's hot in Burnet, with only an occasional scrub oak for shade. And yet, 1500 kids can hardly wait to go back each summer. Tex says, "Longhorn is so many things—it's health, happiness, love of God and country, manners, friendship, and training in activity skills. It's also a place where young people can be counselors."

I talked with Tex briefly in his office before touring Longhorn. It had been a hard summer for him. Federal hearings in Washington on youth camp safety had been scheduled at a time when directors could least afford to leave their camps to testify. A contemporary of Gerald Ford's at the University of Michigan, Tex is suntanned, silver-haired, and physically fit.

Tex had so much to tell me about the evils of federal control that I hardly had time to get the basics on the camp. Longhorn for Boys and Longhorn for Girls are separate camps; however, Chow Hall is a common dining room, and occasional activities are coeducational. Former campers have assured me that they were very much aware of the opposite sex while at Longhorn.

Quite frankly I have never seen so much teenage pulchritude under one roof as I did at Chow Hall. Features were regular, teeth straight, bodies perfectly proportioned. The most beautiful were the counselors, who were fairly easy to spot since most wore sorority or fraternity tee shirts. Indeed Longhorn seemed to be the most obvious prelude to UT greek life that I had seen all summer; 64 of the 113 college-age counselors were from the University. Orange and white colors everything from camp vehicles to sports equipment.

Longhorn is principally known for its water sports. Tex is a former Olympic swimmer, so it's not surprising that a timed mile swim is one of the major competitive events. Offerings include water skiing, water polo, diving, scuba diving, and "blobbing," a Longhorn original. Created by boys' camp director Bill Johnson, the "blob" is a huge orange and white, whalelike inflated plastic float. It is much like a trampoline, though much harder to stay on.

Another popular activity at Longhorn seems to be collecting Merits, small plastic tokens earned by good behavior that are negotiable only at the camp store. The store is a child's fantasy world of sporting equipment—not just baseballs and Ping-Pong paddles, but ten-speed bicycles, water skis, and expensive tennis racquets. A kid seldom stops to realize that merits sufficient to purchase a bicycle would probably require attending camp at least eight years, which would cost his parents approximately $4000. Merits are also sent to Longhorn campers on their birthdays. Around Christmastime, a staff member delivers the *Longhorn Yearbook*, a thick orange and white volume containing pictures of the campers and counselors and candid shots of the past summer. During this visit, the staff member inspects the camper's room; for every memento of Longhorn found there, another Merit is awarded. Recruiting carnivals at country clubs in major cities allow prospective campers to win Merits playing games. This merit system is apparently so successful in keeping misbehavior down and camp attendance up that it has been adopted by neighboring camps like Champion, a newer camp which boasts Darrell Royal as a stockholder.

Longhorn's site is almost as crowded with buildings as the University of Texas campus. Enough cabins to house 500 somehow diminish the feeling of wide open spaces normally associated with camp. Longhorn's only claim to real rusticity is that cabins lack electricity and running water. (But bathhouses with both are less than ten yards away.) Well-tended carpet grass makes shoes superfluous.

Aside from the chance it offers to glimpse the opposite sex, the dining hall is a purely functional cafeteria. Campers eat on metal army-type trays, which they must wash after each meal. A Waldemar camper who later served as a counselor at Longhorn said, "My father almost didn't let me stay after he saw the food. I couldn't write him that part of my duties as counselor included clipping the hedge."

Counselors told me that they felt a strong obligation to keep the kids happy and entertained. Longhorn is not big on tearful sentiment and its closing ceremonies are quick and painless.

*—May 1975*

Shirley Cothran (center). *Photography by Gary Bishop*

# THE SWEET SMILE OF SUCCESS

## by Shelby Hearon

*What does it take to transform pleasant young women
into beauty queens?*

The annual Miss Texas Scholarship Pageant was held in Fort Worth the second week in June, to select a winner to compete in the 46th Miss America Pageant in Atlantic City the week after Labor Day. This year's 57 contestants were college students between eighteen and twenty-three years old, each of whom had won a local pageant bearing the name of that town or area, and each of whom had polished a talent act to present for this next-to-last competition.

Through the Miss Texas Pageant, I accompanied Miss Austin, Diane (Dina) Elise Elsik, a nineteen-year-old with golden skin, good cheekbones, and nice manners. Although she had been eligible to enter the Austin pageant because of her enrollment at The University of Texas, her family lived in Seguin, where I visited with them the day before we left for Fort Worth.

Dina's warm, outgoing mother, the former Isabel Martinez of San Antonio, reminded me at once of Ethel Merman as Rose in *Gypsy*. Like her, she admitted to being a "stage-struck mother." She was proud to show me around their large ranch-style home, and to catch me up on Dina's past. Inside the front door, much like a shrine, was a life-size oil painting of Dina as the Duchess of the DeMolays, in a pure white dress, holding an armful of red roses. In front of her image was a vase of red velvet roses flanked on either side by red candles. We looked at the framed photographs of her as Albert Pike Priory Queen, second runner-up in the Miss South Texas Pageant, and Miss Guadalupe County. After eight years in a Catholic school where Dina wore a uniform and all the boys and girls were "like brothers and sisters," she entered the public school system, where, as pictures in her high school annual showed, she blossomed more each year: cheerleader, Sophomore Class Favorite, Junior Class Favorite, and, in her senior year, Miss Seguin

*Shelby Hearon's most recent novel is* A Prince of a Fellow. *She is a contributing editor of* Texas Monthly.

High School.

Isabel explained that she had started both her daughters early on dance lessons, both ballet and tap; that for the past twelve years she had put on the annual March of Dimes shows and that Dina had danced in every one; that four years ago Dina had auditioned for Toots Johnson, "who was in movies and on Broadway." She had instructed her younger daughter, Ava, to understudy Dina's week at the pageant. "What a waste, I told her, if she wouldn't learn anything from this opportunity." Of this younger daughter, who was much in evidence, her long hair flying, Isabel said, "She wants to be like her sister, but better, go farther. She really has the competitive instinct."

Also around for most of the day was Dina's boyfriend Doak. Dina was very proud of him and his blond good looks and introduced him to me, "He is Mr. All Jock." He told me that he had been named for Doak Walker, that he had a younger brother named for Kyle Rote, that he played football and baseball for Texas Lutheran College. As he stood with his arm around Dina, he provided her with living proof that one could live up to one's parents' hopes.

Dina's father, Leroy Elsik, and her younger brother, Dutch, were away on a fishing trip for the week to Indianola. Although Leroy had relayed the message that "You can leave my part of the limelight out," he had told Dina, "I may not be there but I'm behind you all the way."

Isabel spoke of Leroy—chiropractor, rancher, and real estate developer—as if he were all that a man should be. "He's as blond as I am dark, and muscular. He's better looking now at 46 than he was when we got married." She bragged that Dina had inherited his good Czech bones. Of his close relationship with his son she related that "I had two girls and he really wanted a boy. Dutch came on New Year's Eve and all day my husband went around saying, 'I got my boy.'" We admired the large oil portraits that showed him in his white coat in his office, and on horseback at the ranch with his son, the two of them painted to look alike.

Most of Dina's day was spent getting together the bare minimum of clothing needed for the coming week of rehearsals and competitions: seven long dresses, eight street dresses, two one-piece bathing suits, twelve pairs of shoes, pants outfits, plus "all the accessories and jewelry you have to have." The contestants' handbook detailed the clothes required for each event: there would be at least four costume changes a day for all 57 entrants.

Isabel showed me the seven long gowns that Dina would take; all except one—a gift from a bridal shop—had been used in other presentations. Each gown wrapped in its plastic bag had a history to go with it: the princess-line white dress which Dina would use for her gown competition was an exact copy of a Thirties dress and was designed and beaded by her mother; the bright orange chiffon was designed for her by a talented boy "who went to fashion design school in Atlanta and is going to make it big in New York."

As part of advancing to the state contest, Dina had changed her talent act from a semi-classical ballet to a jazz number done to Barbra Streisand's recording of "Don't Rain on My Parade." For this Isabel had fashioned a scanty hot-pink suit, based on a leotard, with a pouf of scarves on the hips to wiggle as Dina danced: "This hot pink is really going to catch the judges' eyes."

There were other last minute changes, mostly influenced by word-of-mouth information from the other South Texas contestants, and second-hand stories about what Judy Mallett, the reigning Miss Texas and the carrier of the official gospel, had suggested. One recommendation was the purchase of a fall, bought with the money Dina had earned teaching dancing lessons, to put on top of her own wealth of dark hair; another was adopting the common practice of using padding in her white bathing suit, but this seemed, in Seguin, too deliberate a step to take.

Isabel talked readily about herself. Last year she had taken a course in writing for mass media, which she hoped would be a start in the field of public relations. "For self-improvement if nothing else, and for all the organizations I belong to." But that came second. "I'm Dina's mother and now Ava's mother and even Dutch's mother. You lose your identity." She gestured to her dramatic black-and-white pant suit. "I tell her not to let herself go like I have. [If] you don't watch yourself nobody else will."

She showed me a picture of herself at Dina's age: a slender girl in Portuguese folk costume, ruffled blouse, tiny laced bodice, heart-shaped locket. "[I've] danced since I was young." Danced for her father's band, did old-timey folk dances with her grandfather, then moved on to perform for the San Antonio recreation department, as well as for the air bases, and once, as in that snapshot, at the sunken gardens in Brackenridge Park. "If you have girls," she said, "there's nothing better than dance for grace and charm." We studied the girl whose face looked out at us across the years with startling beauty and unlimited promise.

The morning we left, Dina, Isabel, and I had breakfast at four in the morning at the home of Juanita Taylor, the franchise owner for both the Miss South Texas and Miss San Antonio Pageants. In the past months, Mrs. Taylor had opened her home on Lake McQueeney often to the winners of those two contests, who joined us for breakfast and would ride with us to Ft. Worth.

A former executive with Mutual of Omaha, with no children of her own, Mrs. Taylor was glad to give her time and energy to helping "her girls," since she believed strongly that the Miss America Pageant—as opposed to "the legions of other pageants that get press coverage"—had outstanding talent, was the world's largest scholarship program for women, and, most importantly, was run by people like herself "whose main interest is the girls involved."

Her husband, the owner-publisher of the *Seguin Gazette*, repeated her sentiments, and added that the only real problem was getting the right kind of girl to enter their pageants. He said they did the best they could, checking into a girl's family background and morals, making sure the sponsoring group ("usually a Rotary or Chamber") knew what caliber of girl they were seeking.

Each used the present Miss Texas as a good example. "Judy is a Christian but she's not a fanatic," she said. He agreed. "She made a little prayer last year at the end of each presentation. That's the kind of girl the Miss America Pageant gets."

They felt that the wide community support in Seguin for Dina was because she was the right sort of girl. This support had been evident to us the afternoon before when Isabel and I ran errands and were met everywhere with good wishes: the owner of the music store donated a tape for Dina to use for rehearsal, the assistant deejay who cut the tape reminded us that she had been a high school classmate of Dina's, and the man in the dime store where we got toothpaste said he was rooting for her and welcomed me to town with a postcard showing that Seguin was the Home of the World's Largest Pecan.

The Taylors showed me a copy of the contract that the sponsoring group signed. Each contestant must be of good moral character and shall not have been convicted of any crime and shall possess talent, poise, personality, intelligence, charm, and beauty of face and figure. No contestant will be eligible if she has endorsed or contracted to endorse any product competitive to products sold by the national sponsors of the Miss America Pageant Scholarship program or if she has participated during the franchise year in any other national or international competition of a similar nature which is televised nationally.

After we ate, we loaded more than a dozen suitcases and garment bags into Dina's station wagon and my sedan and took off in the dawn. As Miss San Antonio rode with me to Waco where we all stopped for coffee and Miss South Texas rode with me into Fort Worth, there was a chance to get acquainted with these contestants.

I was interested in what they hoped to do with their lives after the pageant. Earlier Dina had said that she had considered majoring in PE, because she was big for sports, and then drama, because she had always acted in plays at school, but that a high school counselor had told her about the school of communications at The University of Texas and she had "loved it right away, especially TV." Now a junior in summer school, she hoped to get an internship in television production in the fall.

Miss San Antonio, currently a weather-girl on a Spanish-speaking station, had been for four years the solo dancer at Fiesta Nocha del Rio in San Antonio. With the poise of a professional performer she assessed her future: in a few years she would be too old to dance; she hoped the pageant would open up other possibilities. On the contestant fact sheet she had listed her future ambition as becoming a doctor.

Miss South Texas, a charmer who had taken time to attach ''spiders'' (false eyelashes) before our early breakfast, had been in drill teams in high school and college. Unless she broke into show business through the pageant, she planned to get a PE degree and lead a junior college drill team.

None of the three girls, all first-time entrants, expected to win the title of Miss Texas, but each hoped very much to place in the top ten. At the least they could count on television exposure during the finale Saturday night.

Each was certain that, as in the past, the winner would be one of the nine or ten girls who were returning to the pageant for the second or third time. As each contestant is allowed to enter the Miss Texas Pageant up to three times, but can not succeed herself in the same local pageant, this means she has to enter a different one each year by changing her residence to that of her parents or to a school she is currently attending.

**"L**et's all smile; it's pageant time.''
On Monday morning a porcine official paraded the contestants alphabetically by title around the fanshaped swimming pool of the Ramada Inn. The girls had been instructed to remove their beach covers, and were in the outfit prescribed in the contestant handbook for this event: swimsuit, heels, and banner. This was billed as the Press Party and was a chance for photographers to get a few shots for their hometown dailies and weeklies.

It was vital to the backers of the Miss Texas Pageant that publicity about each day's events be favorable and flowing, and that the press feel that information was readily available. Reporters received a fact sheet giving the height, weight, and measurements of all the girls, as well as a schedule telling what each night's events were and where each evening's preliminary swimsuit and talent winners would be available for photos and interviews. Reporters were assured that there would be time to photograph the winner and runners-up on Saturday night, and that all information would be provided well in advance of deadlines.

''This way, darlin','' an official urged, ''get in line.''
Photographers assembled groups of girls from their part of the state and posed them: leaning coyly forward with hands placed on bent knees to reveal cleavage, or tossing beach balls overhead in the wading pool for action shots. Someone in the back hollered: Get out of the way of my Hasselblad! To each other, *sotto* and not so *sotto voce*, they made comparisons between this scene and Fort Worth's annual Fat-Stock Show, an image which was reinforced when an official checked his watch and called out, ''It's ten o'clock and time to start walking them around.''

For this event, as well as the week's other contacts with the media, the pageant had hired the public relations firm that also handled Cycle-Rama, the World's Largest Motorcycle Show, and Ringling Brothers, Barnum & Bailey Circus, the Greatest Show on Earth. While the girls were posing poolside, the PR men dispensed soft drinks and coffee and kept a watchful eye on the tensions between press and pageant officials.

The high priests of the Miss Texas Scholarship Pageant Corporation, the staff and the board of directors, were out in full force. They ranged in size from large to stout and portly, and in image from car salesman to carnival barker. Most wore loud plaid, checked, or paisley knit sports jackets that appeared custom tailored, and most had beepers at their waists like doctors. All wore medallions bearing the pageant's gold seal suspended from a row of gold bars that looked like awards given for perfect church attendance.

The head of the group, the chairman of the board, was B. Don Magness, called by everyone B. Don, a named spelled in diamonds on his tie-clasp. When he is not chairing the pageant or acting as manager for the present Miss Texas, he handles special events at the Will Rogers Convention Center for the City of Fort Worth.

Beginning with that first meeting at poolside, the press tried for an exposé of the officials by slanting all interviews to reveal what had never been concealed: that most of the finalists would have been in the contest before; that B. Don and his wife, a stunning professional model, helped with the hair, clothes, makeup, and talent of any of the contestants who requested it or who appeared to have potential; that the purpose of the pageant was not to discover an unknown girl fresh from her hometown but to produce a winner who would stand a chance at Atlantic City.

The first stories harped on how the preliminary winners almost without exception had been entrants in this pageant before. There were headlines like: *Former Runners-up Show Pageant Experience Counts*.

When Terry Meeuwsen, a former Miss Wisconsin and Miss America (1973) who emceed the 1974 pageant, was asked her views on premarital sex and answered, ''I think that's none of your business,'' her frankness did not make news. But the interview was concluded when reporters got her to say that, well, yes, returning to competitions more than once could make a girl plastic, depending on where her head's at.

A photographer with the local paper summed up the prevailing attitude when he asked me, ''Why don't you write how the press works its butt off to cover all this. There's three of us assigned to it who all hate it.''

**M**eanwhile, it was on with the show: three full nights of well-attended preliminary contests followed by the sold-out grand finale.
The daddy of the reigning Miss Texas (Judy Mallett) opened the first night with an invocation thanking God ''for the greatest chance to be a real American woman that the mind of man has ever devised.''

Seated next to me was a friendly fellow named The Reverend Mr. Billy Cox, who whispered that he hoped someday to be asked to pray at the Miss America Pageant. He revealed also that he was the number-one fan of Miss Toledo Bend, Donna Amos, and that he was here this week to represent the *East Texas Light*: ''Covering Shelby County Like The Pine Straw Covers The Ground.'' When we discovered that our two girls shared the same hostess and that ''we'' were both in Group A, we became friends enough for me to inquire if he had found his Scotch-Taped camera at a pawn shop. At this he vowed to come with a roll of film the following night, and, to show his good intentions, he shared with me his way of rating the girls, beginning at the bottom with ''She barks and chases cars,'' through ''I knew her in high school,'' up to ''I could take her home to mother,'' and the ultimate, ''She teaches Sunday School.''

For the first time that week we heard Judy fiddle her ''Orange Blossom Special'' and Terry sing, with New York polish, ''Bye, Bye Blackbird.'' All the girls were in their long dresses for the opening production number, doing a simple bit of sleight of hand to ''Magic to Do.'' Dina wore her bright green gift from the bridal shop and stood smiling on the front row.

For the competitions the girls had been divided into three groups of nineteen, with the strong talent scattered through the three groups in order to make each evening's performance worth the money for the crowd. Miss Austin and Miss Toledo Bend, in Group A, had gown competition on Wednesday, swimsuit on Thursday, and talent on Friday.

In gown competition each girl had twenty seconds before the microphone to impress both the judges and the audience with her poise and her personality. Each, in a formal evening dress, gave her name, school, ambition, and a smidge of personal philosophy: ''As a Dear Friend said to me, 'Not my will but Thine be done.' '' ''If life hands you a lemon, squeeze it and then set up a lemonade stand.'' ''Live as if we would live a hundred years, pray as if we would die tomorrow.'' ''My object in life is to unite my avocation and my vocation.'' Miss Austin, in the white copy of the Thirties gown, told us in her even voice that she wanted to keep up with the world so ''the world doesn't pass me by.''

No one on the stage was lovelier, or more composed, than Dina in her slim-waisted homemade dress, but in Fort Worth on Wednesday it was already clear that a DeMolay Duchess from Seguin, Texas, could not make it on beauty and naturalness alone against girls who had spent a year or more being groomed and gowned by professionals.

The most well-known designers were a team from El Paso called Guyrex, who last year had created gowns for five girls in the top ten. Richard Guy explained that their secret was in the skirt (''anybody can do a bodice''), that their skirts were very full but were cut on the bias to make a girl look slim on the stage. This illusion ran from $400, he said, for ''your average competition dress,'' to about $800 for a ''top, top.''

Becky Bloomer, the first night's talent winner and the girl considered the favorite to win the Miss Texas title, had been dressed by Guyrex last year. This year, as part of her overall effort to take the crown, an effort which included weightlifting and sessions at a health spa to help in swimsuit competition, she had switched to designer Les Wilk.

She was entered this year as Miss White Settlement, a suburb of Fort Worth, since she was a student at Tarrant County Junior College; last year she had come as Miss Dallas, where her parents reside, and the year before that she was Miss Denton while she attended North Texas State University. Last year, as first runnerup in the Miss Texas Pageant, she qualified automatically for the National Sweetheart Pageant, conducted in conjunction with the Sweet Corn Festival in Hoopeston, Illinois, where she was chosen National Sweetheart. When I asked her if she planned to go back to crown the new Queen of Sweet Corn she answered, ''Not if I'm on my way to Atlantic City.''

There is no preliminary award for gown, as these points are tallied in with the judges' interview, but had there been, Billy and I would have guessed the judges' choice to be Shirley Cothran, this year's Miss Haltom-Richland Area,

who, from her first step on the stage, looked like all the Miss Americas we could remember.

I was interested in how the judges arrived at their final choices as I remembered my single experience as a judge in a Labor Day beauty contest at Austin's Zilker Park. Not only did we tend to select larger finalists with bigger features the farther we sat from the stage, but when we got through, the winner seemed to be everyone's fourth choice.

The judge I interviewed was the district marketing manager for Southeastern Bell Telephone in northern Mississippi, and had judged in Fort Worth before. He repeated what the handbook said: that talent counted 50 points and both swimsuit and the combined gown and judges' interview 25 points each. He said that although each night's preliminary winners competed only within their group, in theory the ten finalists could all come from one group. He said the top ten were selected from the points given during the three days of contests and therefore they were known to the judges at the end of the competition Friday night. The ranking of the top five, also selected from this balloting, was made after the top ten repeated their gown, talent, and swimsuit on Saturday night.

The judge, who was dressed in a black and red paisley tuxedo jacket with bright red shirt and tie, explained that he was giving this week of his vacation to the contest because ''I believe in the Miss America system and what it can do for a lady. I believe in it because of the development of the individual contestant. It takes young ladies who are introverted and shy. It's like a Dale Carnegie course. It gives them self-confidence and self-discipline and exposure to the public. Plus the scholarship they get to pursue the interest of their choice whether it be merchandising or art or whatever. It's something college can't give.''

I asked him about the judges' interviews, which are said to be all-important in screening the candidate, as the South Texas girls had been worried about this on our drive to Fort Worth.

The judge explained that interviews (street dress, heels, rosettes, DO NOT wear hats or gloves) in which the girls are scrutinized three at a time for a total of nine minutes, gave judges a chance to look over a girl's complexion, her features, how she conducts herself. ''For example,'' he said, ''a lady doesn't come into a room and sit down and cross her legs.'' It gave them a chance to spot a noticeable scar or one eye that was larger than the other; ''Sometimes we're amazed at how a girl we've interviewed up close looks on the stage with all her makeup on.''

Dina, on our drive up, had reassured the others that there was no need to read up on the news because the judges wouldn't ask things like what was Kissinger doing in Israel, that they would ask you personal questions about your family and what you liked to do, things like what was your major in school. She had spoken with the assurance of one whose private life had straight-forward answers; appropriately, she had planned to wear a deep red copy of a Victorian dress, complete with cameo at the throat.

One official, who had once been a judge himself, confirmed Dina's belief that the questions themselves did not matter. ''Here's where they cut girls out, weed them out—you can't keep 57 of anything in your head at once—then, if they've got talent you can put them back. You make up a list of questions that they can make an intelligent answer to, like what is the state flower, or what is the state bird. Or you ask them, 'How long you been taking dance lessons?'; then when you see her talent later you think: fourteen years and that's all she can do?'' He supplied the real answer to what judges look for: ''Our contestants are a real contrast to those in Miss USA even though they are really knockout looking, but if you told one of them to go empty the ashtray they would say 'huh?' and dump over a potted plant. We're not like that. We're the image the little girl wants to grow up to be.''

The second night of contests, when our little girls were in the swimsuit competition, Billy, the preacher-photographer from East Texas, had put film in his camera and had adjusted his patches of Scotch Tape for a better look at Miss Toledo Bend.

In the stiff and obviously padded one-piece suits, the contestants walked out one at a time to the mike and then to the edge of the stage. As they showed their poise, Terry Meeuwsen told the audience the name of their sponsor and parents, their height and weight, their majors and interests. A few small concessions had been made to women's lib: gone were the list of their measurements, the quarter-turns that used to show off the body profile, and no longer might the girls lick their lips when their backs were to the audience to make a moist smile.

Dina was slender and self-possessed in a white halterneck suit. Her white V-neck which had been acceptable for the poolside was not proper here: it had fringe on the hips. Miss Toledo Bend looked like a cheerleader at the beach and Billy whispered loudly that everything she had was hers.

The audience was too full of parents and surrogate-parents—hostesses, sponsors, managers, chaperones—for them to see the girls as other than *their* contestants. It was not a sex show: it was like the weekly posture contest at Camp Mystic. The same number of pretty faces and nearly pretty ones, the same good and bad skin, good and bad carriage, awkward and practiced movements. The real drawback was that we on the front row had a view we did not want: bruised thighs, callused heels, streaked leg makeup, as well as all too apparent glimpses of a protruding rubber falsie, or the obvious outline of a mini-sanitary pad. Embarrassed, Billy and I reminisced about other times when you paid to see bodies on display: we talked of pasties and clockwise tassels, and of the Champagne Lady of Bourbon Street who was of course a family friend of his.

This was the competition which brought the sharpest criticism from the press and the most defensive reaction from the pageant people, who felt compelled to repeat that it showed how a girl could hold up under stress.

Those who had the most trouble with swimsuit were the female reporters who were the same age and background as the contestants. For some of them it was an opportunity to work through their own feelings about being, or refusing to be, a sex object; for others it was a lesson in allowing each woman the use of her own body.

One reporter—who had been ambivalent about the pageant as she considered the girls were being exploited although she herself was using them to get a front page story with byline every day—had the difficult job of interviewing the preliminary swimsuit winner, who also had been a very good friend of hers in high school. There was between this intern reporter and Amy Griggs, who was this year's Miss Hurst-Euless-Bedford and a top contender for the title, an

awkwardness, a distance as if each felt the need to justify to the other the different path she had taken. After the interview the reporter confessed her second thoughts, ''At first I wanted to knock it all. At first I thought the girls were doing their whole sex a disservice. It's so absurd; it's not what America is really all about. Now, well, I'd hate to see any of these girls hurt. . . .''

The last night of preliminaries Billy and I watched our girls compete in talent. As we had seen on previous nights, what the judges wanted in a winner was a girl who could create an affinity between performer and audience. They wanted an act which could be repeated on TV talk shows and at other pageants, an act which would play in Atlantic City, an act that would bring the audience to spontaneous clapping and cheering like Terry Meeuwsen belting, in Liza Minelli style, ''You gotta ring them bells.''

Thus the outstanding voice at the pageant did not make the top five, although when Miss Waco came up to the mike and vowed to ''make Rivers Hatchett a name to remember in opera,'' there was not a doubter in the house. The nonfinalist talent award went to Miss Pasadena, Peggy Ruth Oliver, who gave an electrifying performance, in warrior costume with sword upraised, of the war variation from Pandora's Box ballet. It was like seeing Joan of Arc on a Broadway stage. But she was a sleeper: none of the pageant people had caught her act at her local pageant and she had been placed near the end of the program. As Terry explained it to me, as Miss Pasadena had not been noticed in swimsuit or gown earlier, it was too late by the last night for her to be a finalist. (The preliminary winner from her group was an audience-pleasing piano player who did a medley of Floyd Cramer tunes.)

Most of the talent numbers of the non-finalists were either a sensuous jazz dance done in eye-catching red or hot pink, like Dina's, or a night club song, like Miss Toledo Bend's, with the contestant holding the mike in her left hand, her right hand stretched to the sky, in imitation of big-name stars.

The finalists' performances were not different in kind from the efforts of our girls, but their acts were as polished as those on the best TV variety show.

The supporting cast behind the ten finalists, whose names were determined by the end of Friday night's show, was made up of mothers, hostesses, and franchise holders who had worked behind the scenes all week, almost around the clock.

There was little sleep for anyone. My own day began at 6:30 in the morning with the selection of the day's outfit from my wardrobe of four T-shirts and three pairs of slacks, and ended around two in the morning in a hot tub, listening either to the sounds of the truckers' favorite country deejay or to family problems through the paper-thin hotel walls.

The girls came back from the nightly competitions to a midnight spread of hamburgers, homemade cake, and ice cream; then the hostesses helped them with their nerves, hair, and rumors until two or three o'clock. All were up again for a six a.m. breakfast of fruit and pastries served dormitory style in the motel.

While the girls were being put to bed, their friends and family were invited to what was called the Franchise Holders Party (Admission by Badge Only). These gatherings were a chance for B. Don and the other directors to press the flesh and call by name the owners of the 57 local pageants. To keep relations smooth, an open bar and a band that played loud oldies held forth until three in the morning.

Here I visited again with Isabel and the Taylors from Seguin. They crowded around a table in the dark, packed room to discuss their girls' chances and to cling to the hope that at least one of the three would reach the top ten. Isabel wanted to hear that Dina had looked perfect in her white gown, that she had shown herself off as well as anyone in her bathing suit, that she had danced like Cyd Charisse, that the judges had noticed her.

The pageant officials do all they can to keep the local owners content, since they have a strong interest in retaining the location of the Miss Texas franchise in Fort Worth, where it has been for the past twelve years. Under her contract, Miss Texas must go to TCU to receive her scholarship, and, once selected, automatically moves her residence to Fort Worth. In the event she goes on to become Miss America, she still resides in Fort Worth and her time and a percentage of her earnings belong to the pageant.

During her reign, Miss Texas is managed by B. Don, who keeps her working. As one official put it, if she doesn't block out time for her old daddy's birthday, B. Don will fill that day, too. What advertisers can use Miss Texas? The same official said, "All they have to do is contact the manager; she'll do anything for money." Then he amended this quickly, "Not beer, not liquor. We never advertise it; we just drink it. But the girls never see it. And they can't touch it." He explained the girls' abstinence: "It's the Miss America dream. It's what it's all about."

Largely responsible for guarding this dream at the pageant were the hostesses whose job it was not only to keep the girls from drinking, but also from seeing or hearing anything offensive. At all times they were to keep their charges behaving like ladies. Not only were contestants not permitted at any time "to enter a cocktail lounge, private club, night club, bar, inn, tavern or any place where liquor is being served," but they were instructed that a contestant "WILL NOT smoke in public", and "Contestants ARE NOT PERMITTED TO SPEAK TO ANY MAN unless in the company of their hostess." The contestant's own family was not excepted. In addition, the hostesses had instructions to terminate any photographic session or interview which was "improper, indecent, embarrassing, or in poor taste." To help with this they had the resources of a policewoman on duty 24 hours a day to protect against intruders. To prevent obscene phone calls, the girls were not allowed to receive incoming calls.

The hostesses (or "hosteii" as they referred to themselves), were all active in the Fort Worth community as volunteers, and each was fiercely partisan to "her" girl. There was an air about them of sorority sisters at a convention, with much hugging and squealing lines like, "Morning, love. I forgot what I'm supposed to do about whatever we're supposed to do." Many of them stayed all week, some of them came in shifts; all of them took their jobs as chaperones literally and seriously.

From my own experience this protectiveness became tedious. One morning at rehearsal Judy needed a ride back to the motel from the convention center and, after she had asked around twice, I offered to give her one. My offer led to a conference of hostesses, as she still had one more day to reign as Miss Texas. At length, they decided that B. Don would not approve, leaving me feeling somewhat as if I had offered to hijack the President to Cuba. On another occasion, when the subject of suntans versus tan-from-a-tube and sunlamps was being discussed, I decided to ask the pro, Miss White Settlement, how she got her deep and even glow. This required, although we were sitting one row apart, getting permission from a hostess who accompanied us to the stairs where she sat between us while I asked Becky, "Do you use a sun-lamp?" "No, I use the sun."

While the hostesses took over the functions of guard, valet, and mother, the actual mothers were left to hover in the hallways or wait in the registration room which served as a reception room. They waited for hair curlers to be taken down upstairs, or for naps to be over, hoping for a chance to pass (in the presence of a hostess, of course) necessities to their daughters: Tampax, shoeshop glue for a broken heel, a basket of fruit from the hometown Jaycees.

One corner of the registration room was used by hairdressers to coif and comb contestant's hair, a process which left a film of hair spray over the donuts and coffee. From outside in the hall came the effusive voices of visiting Misses from other states, old winners from this pageant, and, always putting out cornpone jocularity for her fans, the ever-present Judy: "I've got me a new dressy-poo, and it really is purty."

While the mothers waited they talked about their glimpses of the inside: "She and her roommate both got constipated, it's just nerves, they sent out for a laxative and now they've got the opposite problem"; "There were three other dresses like the one she wore in the opening number"; "Last night's swimsuit winner is really flat as a pancake, I saw her myself this morning"; "You're not allowed to shed any article of clothing in the talent contest; it might give the impression of stripping."

The mothers' optimism during the course of the week ran at roughly the level of the current day's crop of flowers (dozens and dozens of Tyler roses), telegrams, letters, and gifts waiting for each girl by her name on the counter. By Saturday morning, before the list of the finalists leaked, the room looked like rush week at a big university, and the mothers appeared in their best bonded pant suits, their hair fresh from the beauty shop.

Then a rash of hurt feelings broke out among the girls as the news of the finalists, already released to the press, reached them. There was one finalist who was suspected of having been on a date; there was the feeling that all of the four girls who had not won preliminary contests did not dance as well nor were as pretty as the ones passed over; there was much talk of politics and favoritism as four of the ten were from the Fort Worth area.

This, plus the lack of sleep all week, broke everyone's reserve at the last rehearsal and there was a good measure of spoofing here and there. The men putting on the show relaxed: one of them said he could direct almost anything, that he had directed traffic and he'd directed "a few cows in my time—at the rodeo, of course." One told a very confident contestant, "We've got to stop meeting like this; you're running out of pageants." And to a black girl about to miss her bus someone called out, "You just think this is an equal opportunities pageant."

The hostesses, who had kept up a running commentary about the contestants during rehearsals—"She's had her teeth capped since last year''; ''This is the best Miss Prairie View we've had''; ''She's going to wet on herself she's so nervous''; ''I'm going to kill her and tell the Lord she died''—had an opportunity to do their own musical version of the show.

In a noontime follies that one of the hostesses called ''a chance to have a fling of our own,'' they produced a takeoff on the pageant, complete with song and dance production numbers they had written themselves (for one they sent off for T-shirts that said: You've Come A Long Way Baby), and the presentation of past Misses with names like Miss Take and Miss Guided. There were a number of apt touches: Miss Judged was introduced as a contestant ''who had been an acrobatic dancer but she changed her ambition to brain surgery'' to win the title. Another Miss from the Twenties came out in bathing suit stuffed with two large balloons, one of which was punctured as she made her quarter-turns for the ''judges.''

Even Judy must have been able to see freedom at the end of the rainbow. On the stage, going over a solo number with the tape recording which was used for background music, she said, ''I can't hear that dumb tape. If that happens tonight I'll just stick my tongue out at them and say: nyaahhh, that's the last time I'll have to play this for *you.*''

The pageant officials had all but the two most serious problems under control, and those were at least tamped down for the last night. Already surmounted during the week were such troubles as the judges not being able to get into their hotel suite with the bar the first night, and having the Winnebago which was to convey them to the contest fail to appear; and a water main that broke in the street outside the convention center forcing that day's talent to practice its routines on a concrete floor while two feet of water was pumped out from behind the orchestra pit.

One real problem which would have to wait until next year was the fact that the TV show was going down the tube, meaning that the pageant again had no national sponsor now that neither Toni nor the Miss America parent pageant picked up the tab. The 90 minutes had been sold to local advertisers and was going to lose money, but, as the executive director put it, this was part of the pageant corporation's headache financially and not something to trouble the girls with; all they needed to know was that they would be on TV and they would be seen back home.

The other major problem remained: the press. Saturday morning at rehearsal B. Don flopped down in the seat beside me to give his version. He had been more than affable all week. Smiley the photographer had a blown-up glossy of B. Don's rear end bending over, which they had had Judy sign and had presented to him. Now his face sagged. Convinced the press was out to get him, he had squeezed out the time for a two-hour interview with the local paper and had set up a press conference for UPI, who failed to show. He sweated to remember a similar press attack a few years back when some franchise holders were threatening to defect.

But on the surface everything was prepared for the finale. As the crowd arrived in formal attire, the press ticket table began to crack down on what they called ''the pageant freaks'' who had been milling around all week. The first to go were the trouble-makers. As one PR man said, ''You invent a little local paper and buy a roll of film and we'll let

you watch the early shows and freeload a drink at intermission. There's no need to be obnoxious.'' One of the ones who had appeared all week, purportedly representing a large paper, with a dubious queen in tiara and ballgown on his arm, was bounced for the last night. So was another who pleaded, ''I can't be from the *Dallas Morning News*? Would you believe the *Times Herald*?'' Billy's credentials were called into question, but by Saturday he had learned to charge his camera's batteries, knew everyone from the parking lot attendant to the ticket taker, was also representing another county newspaper, *The Champion*, and, besides, he was in a tuxedo. A little pressure and charm was applied, and Billy was allowed to remain, front and center.

The final curtain up at last, Judy told the audience that this had been the most beautiful year of her life, that without the sacrifice of God's son Jesus, this year would not have been possible. For the next-to-the-last-time as Miss Texas (there was one show at 8:30, a final one televised at 10) she brought out the fiddle and played us the ''Orange Blossom Special.'' As the visiting Misses from other states each got a final turn at the mike (their part was not repeated on TV), Billy reported that Miss Alaska, who had spent all week giving chats in the lobby with her ventriloquist's dummy Stanley, planned to come to East Texas Baptist College next year, and, wonder of wonders, that she taught Sunday School. Miss Florida floated on, reminded us all that she was only seventeen. Then Miss Wyoming, a tall, gorgeous black with a modified afro, gave the show-stopper. After casing her audience for four nights, she leaned into the mike and delivered her lines: ''Someone said I ought to stay out of the sun, that I might get too dark. That's nonsense; everyone knows that the blacker the cherry the sweeter the juice.''

Then, after the top ten (Billy complained that two of them ''barked and chased cars'') had gone through their swimsuit, talent, and gown all over again, first for the judges, and then again on live TV, there was the familiar drum-roll and we had presented to us the top five. And there, after years of work, waited the favorites: Miss Hurst-Euless-Bedford, Amy; Miss White Settlement, Becky; and Miss Haltom-Richland Area, Shirley. Each a finalist before, each waiting for one more chance at the crown.

They were not in this for their picture in the paper and certainly not for the $2500 scholarship to TCU, since each had surely spent well over that to get to that stage on Saturday night. The stakes they played for were much higher, beginning with the $1000 for going to Atlantic City: they were playing for what Judy had—$20,000 in the bank, a $50,000 baby food contract waiting, the chance for contracts up to $250,000, plus exposure before millions of TV viewers on the Jimmy Dean show, the Johnny Carson show, and at Super Bowl VIII.

It was a lot for a college student to win; even more to lose. All of them were already aiming high: Amy had a 4.0 average; Shirley had her master's degree; Becky had had overtures from the Christy Minstrels.

Pageant officials carried in sprays of roses. B. Don brought the red velvet train trimmed in ermine. The envelopes were opened and the names were read. When Amy was announced as second runner-up she turned her face away from the crowd, received her consolation yellow roses through tears; when Becky's name was read as first runner-up the whole auditorium could see her turn ashen as the knife went through her sweet-corn throat. Then it was, of course, Shirley who got the red roses, and the crown, and the future. Shirley who had, from the first night, looked like all the Miss Americas there ever were.

Billy passed judgement: "I could take her home to mother." Then, to give her her full due he added, "But I'm not sure I could trust my daddy."

Shirley's mother, a plain white-haired woman, had told me earlier in the week about the first dress that her daughter had worn in her very first pageant, that she and a neighbor had sewed on it for two weeks, sewed on all those rhinestones at the wrist and neck. "All that work and it was a dress you couldn't wear any place else." Of this daughter she had said, "She and her sister are exactly the opposite of each other." The other daughter loves horses, has a baby, has settled down.

Backstage, Becky and Amy sobbed openly into the arms of parents and friends. The intern reporter turned away from her distressed high-school friend Amy; a photographer debated, then rejected, grabbing a shot of the tearstained Becky. After all, none of them had intended it to mean so much, to matter so badly.

The party afterward was like a dead dance in a high school gym. The red punch was tepid, the food scarce, and most of the girls began to talk slowly of "wait till next year." Miss South Texas planned to transfer to Southwest Texas State University and run from that pageant; Miss Big Thicket's mother told me that her girl was going to come back next year as Miss Austin since she was now at the University of Texas; Miss Toledo Bend, who, Billy told me, was informed that she was number eleven, now planned to go to school in Dallas and study voice next year and return from one of the metroplex pageants.

Isabel, introduced as a former star of stage and screen, grinned and obliged with a little soft shoe. She told us that next year Dina ought to wear a bright orange swim suit to catch the judges' eyes. She described her idea for a new competition gown, a copy of a Guyrex.

But with Doak's arm around her and the thought of a TV internship before her, Dina hesitated. It would be fun to go back to Seguin and walk down the street and have everyone say, "I saw you on TV." But would she try again? "Maybe, if somebody really wanted me to."

But even as tears had been dried and the top five had posed, all smiling, for the photographers, retaliation brewed from the disappointed. In the following weeks the schism among the believers was made public. In the same edition of the Fort Worth *Star-Telegram* that carried an editorial welcoming Shirley, whose crown "looked like it belonged

there," was a front page story claiming that the pageant was "controlled." There were threats to "get" B. Don; franchise holders told anyone who would write it down that it had all been fixed from the start. Two disappointed groups approached a Dallas attorney to start an investigation they hoped could lead to a lawsuit; there were rumors of a Friday night caucus of the judges, of a leak from Shirley's roommate, of a veiled hint from a former Miss Texas. Lubbock's pageant owner sent to all owners an eight-page, single-spaced letter, going over it all, including why his contestant changed her dance at the last minute, and saying what was wrong with the whole pageant was that it did not have Miss Lubbock in the top ten this year.

But even in his anger what he wanted, what they all wanted, was not excommunication from the fold but control of it. In his suggested improvements he still held to the prevailing mystique: "Personally, I would like to see swimsuit competition eliminated from competition in this pageant . . . If they want a leg or bust review, they can watch Miss World, Miss U.S.A., or Miss Universe. . . . Also, there are many very talented young ladies who would never enter because of religious or moral convictions. I don't think swimsuit competition is relevant when we are looking for wholesome, all-American girls with talent."

Richard Guy, of Guyrex, was rumored to want to move the state pageant to El Paso where he had the franchise. In his letter to owners he opted for a three-person jury of owners to be present at all times during the judging, including "during all of the entertainment functions which have been planned for the judges' panel during their entire stay."

The majority of owners did not go along with his protests. By telephone from Seguin, Mrs. Taylor, the franchise holder of Miss South Texas (who was Miss Congeniality) and Miss San Antonio (who was a finalist), declared that in her opinion all the flap was "flat sour grapes," that the other owners were "flat very, very poor losers."

But even as the heathens raged, the pageant machinery continued smoothly—only a scant six weeks remained to get Shirley ready for Atlantic City; and scarcely a year for the losers to get ready for the Miss Texas Pageant, 1975.

---

*Shelby Hearon "called it" when she wrote that Shirley Cothran, first Miss Haltom-Richland Area, then Miss Texas, "looked like all the Miss Americas we could remember." Miss Cothran went on to Atlantic City to be crowned Miss America as we went to press in early September. She is the second Miss America from Texas in four years.*

*—October 1974*

# CLOSING DOWN LA GRANGE

## by Al Reinert

---

*In which the Long Lens of the Law uncovers Sin and Corruption in Babylon-on-the-Brazos, and the Electric Bounty Hunter confronts the Nightmare Sheriff and the Banshee Madam to unearth a Bizarre Tale.*

---

On Wednesday, August 1, 1973, the La Grange Chicken Ranch, the Oldest Continually Operating Non-Floating Whorehouse in the United States, was closed down. The Texas Chamber of Commerce elected to ignore the passage of an establishment possibly older than all its members; and the State Historical Society, equally misfeasant, overlooked the shuttering of the house that slept more politicians than the Driskill Hotel and the Governor's Mansion combined.

You all know about the Chicken Ranch of course. It was just about the first tourist attraction I heard about when I came to Texas. But, then, I came to Texas to be an Aggie, so that explains that. Later on I even learned that there was a town called La Grange nestled somewhere on the outskirts of the whorehouse of the same name.

Hell, I even went to La Grange once. The whorehouse, I mean. Not, mind you, because I had any truly unquenchable perversions that required a trip to La Grange to unleash, but, rather, because I figured that if one was going to be an Aggie, well then, Be An Aggie. The pilgrimage to La Grange sits close to the heart of The Aggie Myth, as central to the catechism as standing at football games and building the Bonfire for the Texas game.

We went on Thursday night when they had the $8 Aggie Special, trekking down in an old Pontiac full of fraudulently-purchased Lone Star and a thousand obscene variants of some drastically original horny Aggie fantasy.

We circled around town for a while, body temperature rising in inverse proportion to the declining stash of Lone Star and the increasing depravity of the fantasy, a deep, twisted well of prurient anxiety gradually filling to the point where no adolescent squeamishness could possibly abort an explosive gusher of Sinful Lust.

How's that for metaphor? eh? Us Aggies get a three-

*Al Reinert is a contributing editor of* Texas Monthly *and has written for several other magazines. He is completing a book for Harcourt Brace Jovanovich.*

syllable handicap in this magazine-writin'. In any case, the air went out of the fantasy as soon as we pulled into the Chicken Ranch parking lot and the first person we spotted was a deputy sheriff. He was just there to help park cars, though, so we proceeded on up to the door where Lilly, the black maid—the only black as a matter of strict fact (historical accuracy being an important part of articles like this) who ever passed the doors of the Chicken Ranch—checked our phony I.D.'s to make sure we were 21 and let us in.

We sauntered into the parlor where we drunkenly introduced ourselves to a half-dozen local farmers, a couple of cross-country truck drivers, and a fellow pilgrim who'd journeyed all the way down from Nebraska—and met three young ladies who either worked there or were truck drivers, too, we weren't sure which.

One of the young ladies offered to sell us a Coke for 50 cents, which we declined, and then one of her friends asked us for a quarter to play the jukebox, which we cheerfully provided. My friend Richard, who was still trying to decide if they worked there or were just visiting truck drivers, thought he'd break the ice a little by asking one of them if she wanted to dance, which she didn't.

"What's with this dancin' stuff, honey?" is what she said. "Ya wanna do some business here or not?" That's when we decided she must be one of the U.T. coeds we'd heard about.

Pretty soon after that I picked one of the ladies (or she picked me, quite possibly, my recollection being sort of hazy) and we wandered off down the hall to one of the bedrooms. The walls of the room possessed an angularity that bespoke distracted carpentry, all of them covered with irregular splotches of pastel paint, and the furnishings consisted of a bed, a dresser and a sink, all rather commonplace in appearance and not at all meeting my expectations.

The top dresser drawer had been left open to reveal an intriguing assortment of oils, photographs, and leather goods, but I held firm for the Aggie Special which didn't include any of its contents. Ruthie, who was the lady I'd picked (or who'd picked me), just rolled her eyes and made a face when I told her I only had the eight dollars anyway. She told me to "Git yer clothes off, honey," and left to go deposit my money someplace.

I thought for a bit about how this wasn't the way we'd planned it on the way down and was consequently a little slow getting undressed, being still garbed in my pants when Ruthie got back. "What's this?" she asked me. "We ain't got all night ya know." I apologized for being so slow and took my pants off.

She then started poking and tugging at me, "checking fer diseases," she said, a bit of foreplay that possessed all the sensuality of my Army physical. Ruthie next threw me down on the bed, took off her own clothes and lay down beside me, and told me that for just eight dollars I didn't get to kiss her.

Pleased that I hadn't brought any more money, we just started pawing and pulling at each other and, next thing I knew, she was on top of me and asking if I was "finished already, honey?" "Well, uuuh . . ." I said. Then she pulled me up off the bed, washed us both off, and told me "ta git yer clothes back on, honey." It had been what's known in the trade as a "Four-get": Get up, Get on, Get off, and Get out.

I met the rest of my cohorts outside, all except for Richard for whom we had to wait another hour and a half. He'd been so abashed at being turned down for his dance that he'd gone and splurged $40 on a lavish degeneracy of sufficient novelty that its graphic description entertained us all the way back to College Station.

When old Frank Lotto published the first *History of Fayette County* back in 1902, he wrote, with what must have been a sly snicker to himself, that "The City of La Grange has made a reputation for sociability over the whole state."

It was nicely located for friendly ambience, being sprawled around high limestone bluffs on a parabolic stretch of the Colorado River in that part of Central Texas where the coastal plains begin gently ballooning into a sinuous undulation that goes westering off to the Hill Country. Dense battalions of age-disfigured live oaks, camouflaged in clouds of hanging moss and sentried by towering cedars, occupy the creek and river bottoms while post oak columns skirt the soft green edges of Bermuda Grass hillsides and cypress files demarcate the boundaries of old Spanish land grants. The Second Congress of the Republic of Texas, enticed by vistas "that but few countryes on Earth can compare with," overwhelmingly voted to establish their permanent capital at La Grange, and only President Sam Houston's self-serving veto kept it in the still-unbuilt jerkwater burg named for himself.

If the easy-rolling richness of Fayette County posed no strong attraction for General Sam, it proved a powerful lure across the world in Central Europe. Beginning in the 1830's it became the terminus for South Germans and Bohemians in flight from famine and persecution. They brought with them an industrious capacity for small farming, which still endures, and an independence of mind bordering on the perverse, which also still endures. Ever since 1860, when they voted not to secede with the rest of the state, Fayette County has maintained a strong tradition of political aberrance.

The immigrants also imported a zesty beer-hall enthusiasm for rowdy pleasures. Indeed, nothing in the county's history has proven so consistently unpopular as Temperance, which went down to its first massive electoral defeat in 1877. It was the kind of indulgent tolerance that could sanction the longest-running brothel ever to open its doors and beds in America.

Just when exactly those doors and beds did open is a point of some contention. Dates offered range all the way from 1844, based largely on myth, to 1915, when the house was installed in its present location on the outskirts of town. The most likely occasion for its founding is somewhere in between, with several La Grange oldtimers remembering its definite existence prior to the turn of the century. Ernest Emmerich, who was town marshal in neighboring Round Top back around the First World War, remembers then-County Sheriff August Loessin telling him it was there when August took office in 1894.

The debate, in any case, is spuriously academic. Just as a history of North America, despite its prior existence, doesn't really commence until Columbus, so the True Story of the Chicken Ranch doesn't begin until the arrival, in about 1905, of Ms. Faye Stewart, alias Jessie Williams, and known to friends, employees, numerous intimate acquaintances and elusive Posterity as Miss Jessie.

Originally from Hubbard, up near Waco, Miss Jessie was a whorehouse madam on an epic scale, prostitution's answer to Casey Stengel or Vince Lombardi, author and actor in one of the great chapters in the journal of her profession. A woman of undeniable personal resonance, with rough-hewn country charm and shrewd backwoods tenacity, she is still discussed with soft-eyed affection and reverential tones by those who knew her.

Buddy Zapalac, the editor of *The La Grange Journal*, says, "She just had ta be one a the most amazin' women who ever lived. She was strong! But she was generous, too. And whoooh, Boy! but she was a smart one."

It was Miss Jessie who somehow brought discipline and profit to the house while making peace with the surrounding community at large and its power center in particular; she also negotiated the tacit treaties that enabled her house to survive in the face of contradiction and indignation, a diplomatic performance rivaling those of Henry Kissinger.

Among the first allies she acquired were the Loessin brothers, August and Will, the former being County Sheriff and the latter, younger, being at once the City Marshal in La Grange and his brother's chief deputy (and later his successor as Sheriff). Widely venerated as peace officers, the brothers Loessin seem genuinely to have been well-respected and able peace-keepers, August being the only Central Texas Sheriff to crush the Ku Klux Klan during its bloody pre-War resurgence and Will earning a statewide reputation for ingenious detective work.

The early basis for their pact with Miss Jessie seems to have been a kind of mutual coexistence. She foreswore many of those sidelines that would seem natural in a country cathouse, liquor most notably, and operated it as peaceably and businesslike as the Post Office. The two sheriffs, for their part, just ignored it.

It was a beneficial relationship. Miss Jessie prospered

and, in 1915, she abandoned the battered downtown hotel they then occupied, and moved her business to the southeastern outskirts of town. She brought in a few new girls as well, including two sisters who learned their craft in the break-hell East Texas oil boom and were to serve as middle-management. The house was by now rooting itself into the communal fabric of La Grange and its resident employees, encouraged by Miss Jessie to stay on a permanent basis, had fashioned a broad array of links with the townsfolk; when the boys from La Grange went overseas to Save Democracy in The Great War, the girls from the Ranch sent them cookies.

Soon after the end of the War, Will Loessin was elected to succeed his brother. At some nebulous, earlier point he had made a discovery that struck a glorious chord in his detective heart, one that would repercuss down through all the following years of Fayette County law enforcement. This was, in essence, that men, significantly including local lawbreakers, are (1) habitually prone to bursts of braggadocio, often self-incriminating and helpfully revealing, when they are in bed with women, and (2) these same men were regularly inclined to go to bed with women out at Miss Jessie's. Wonder of Wonders! Will Loessin, in one of the grandest strokes in the annals of detectivery, had buried deep in the twisted solar plexus of the criminal element an incredibly Organic Wiretap.

And Miss Jessie, not disinterested in further cementing her alliance with the forces of justice, was graciously amenable to stepped-up cooperation. From thence forward, continuing on through all of his 26 years as County Sheriff, Will Loessin would journey nightly out to the edge of town to visit with Miss Jessie and learn what intelligence may have been ferreted out by this subtle pack of eavesdroppers.

The Ranch itself was undergoing a little facelift about this time. Not only had Miss Jessie added on a couple of rooms to accommodate her burgeoning flock, but the Gilded Age of post-war ebullience was sending liberating vibrations even unto the outskirts of La Grange. The girls acquired shiny new cars and flapperish regalia, the rooms received new paint and overstuffed furniture, frenetic snatches of jazz were caught drifting through the woods, and Miss Jessie's unpretentious country whorehouse almost became a bawdy citified "sporting house" as it passed through the gaudiest phase of its lifetime.

The emancipation of the Ranch, though, did not include any creatively expanded repertoire of available pleasures. Waco-bred Miss Jessie had always looked with fundamental distaste on all possible erotic combinations that went beyond the dully conventional missionary position, and the continentally-whetted appetites of war-returned farmboys made her furious.

One La Grange oldtimer, a thrice-weekly regular back in those days, remembers trying to explain to a girl named "Deaf" Eddie how to navigate one pleasantly intricate movement: "See, we called 'er Deaf Eddie cause she really was harda hearin', so I was havin' ta talk purty loud. Well, whut hoppened is thet Miss Jessie heard me an come acrashin' inta there hittin' me with a big iron rod and hollerin' 'bout turnin' her girls inta French whores. She throwed me out an' wouldna let me back fer a month."

Prices at Miss Jessie's then were on an easily computed sliding scale based solely on the time consumed, climbing from $3 up to about a $40 maximum, and not until years later did other variables serve to complicate the equation. The only disruption of these simple accounting procedures came with the Great Depression, when rural economies collapsed into a chaos of barter and salvage.

Miss Jessie, whose Depression-sparked social consciousness would make her one of the fiercest New Dealers in the county, promptly adjusted to the new market by accepting payment in farm produce at the straightforward rate of one chicken, one screw. The backyard was quickly over-run with scratching and fluttering Dominickers and Rhode Island Reds, and the heretofore anonymous whorehouse became the Chicken Ranch.

Thus christened, the Ranch passed quietly through the rest of the decade, the only disruptions caused by a rare and foolish Republican who had the temerity to challenge Miss Jessie's estimation of Franklin Roosevelt.

The Ranch was by then thoroughly imbedded in the webwork of life in Fayette County. Miss Jessie contributed money to local civic clubs and church bazaars, establishing the policy of municipal philanthropy that in later years would see the Ranch become the largest sponsor of the Little League. And, while stopping short of joining the Jaycees, Miss Jessie manipulated capital expenditures in a way that best suited everyone, not excluding herself. Deliveries from groceries, hardware stores, dairies, five and dimes, all were rotated on a weekly basis so that each would receive their share of the Ranch's business.

Early in his tenure, Will Loessin had begun the tradition, which continued on up to this year, of reporting on conditions at the Ranch to the twice-annual Fayette County Grand Jury. Estimates of revenue, reports on fights or arrests or information learned were all provided, and an occasionally rambunctious Grand Jury would troop on out to see for themselves, Miss Jessie pleasantly showing them around. In later years, girls going to work at the Ranch would stop first at the sheriff's office to be mugged and fingerprinted, so that checks could be run to see if they'd ever done something illegal somewhere.

One of those early Grand Juries began the practice of requiring weekly medical exams for the girls at Miss Jessie's, and the office of County Medical Examiner was created solely for that purpose. In more modern times, after the office was abolished, the girls would appear every Thursday at the La Grange Health Clinic to have their non-contaminatory status officially certified.

When America found itself in another war in 1941 and a second generation of Fayette County farmboys left to participate, the girls at Miss Jessie's again sent cookies and wrapped bandages for the Red Cross. The Army moved in a training center at nearby Bastrop and, apparently concerned that indiscriminate whoring might short-circuit the American soldier's innate killer instincts, launched a wide-ranging campaign against prostitution. Life at the Ranch temporarily became a little more circumspect, but the officially subversive operations went unimpaired for the duration.

The end of the War brought, amidst other happenings, the retirement of Will Loessin; his replacement, ascending almost mechanically into the vacancy, was T. J. "Jim" Flournoy, who had been Will's chief deputy for a dozen years before putting in a stint as a Texas Ranger. In the same inevitable manner that a national administration will assume the accumulated allies and obligations of all its predecessors, Jim Flournoy inherited all those instinctive understandings and tacit pacts that Miss Jessie had forged 40 years earlier with the Loessin brothers; the momentum of the Ranch swept past another milepost without a missed step or side glance.

Some of that feisty energy that had driven her thus far had begun to subside, though, and, while post-war prosperity was acknowledged in the form of a couple more tacked-on bedrooms, the attendant post-war exuberance inspired no response at the Ranch. They just settled a few years earlier into that semi-moribund inertia that captured the country through most of the fifties.

Miss Jessie, wheelchair-bound in her last years, watched the decade turn from the front porch of the Chicken Ranch, still firmly in command and admitting respect for no one since Franklin Roosevelt. She died, Faye Stewart died, in 1961, mourned by many who were too embarrassed to demonstrate it and missed by four generations of men whose passage from innocence she had administered.

She had, moreover, wrought permanent change in the world she occupied: her Ranch, at some ephemeral point in its passage through the years, had transcended its role as merely a whorehouse to become an Institution, as important a work in the Gallery of Texana as Spindletop or San Jacinto. The Whorehouse at La Grange had passed mouth-to-ear through the locker-room memories of four generations of Texas men, and its widespread acceptance was tacit acknowledgement of its new status.

The Texas Legislature made reference to it in light-hearted floor debate as early as the forties, and Miss Jessie returned the compliment by amending her cash-only policy to include the acceptance of state payroll checks. Books, magazines, and newspapers all wrote sympathetically of its existence and, as the sixties appeared, adventuresome students would make it a topic for term papers and masters' theses.

Indeed, if the Chicken Ranch is viewed strictly as an illegal brothel, then the largest part of the State of Texas was for 20 years involved in a cover-up of unmatched proportions. More likely, the Ranch had passed beyond reach of The Law into another, more sentimental, dimension where The Law serves no purpose.

Miss Jessie was to be succeeded by a woman as thoroughly schooled for her role as Jim Flournoy had been for his. Edna Milton had come to work at the Ranch in 1952, and by the time Miss Jessie died was chief lieutenant in the management of the house. Red-haired and tough-skinned, with clear-green Laser-piercing eyes, Edna evokes an authoritative confidence that could as easily run a Teamsters local as a whorehouse.

She arranged to purchase the Ranch from Faye Stewart's estate and installed herself as madam, moving into the master bedroom that still contained Miss Jessie's massive four-poster walnut bed. To all appearances the house absorbed the shift in management as effortlessly as it had the paper alteration of ownership, the only real changes being the installation of air-conditioning and the offering of a limited variety of "exotic extras."

Edna, even before Miss Jessie died, had been in charge when the Ranch weathered its greatest crisis: Texas Attorney General Will Wilson, who wanted to be a U.S. Senator,

had sounded the call for a great moral crusade aimed vaguely at making the state safe for the easily outraged, who presumably form an impressive bloc of voters.

State law enforcement officials were dashing hungrily around on the hot trail of sin, very nearly arresting the entire island of Galveston, and it seemed likely that the Chicken Ranch, as the state's most notoriously renowned whorehouse, would be a sure target.

Edna's response was to go underground, making the pretense of shutting down while admitting regular customers through the back door. It was good enough. Like all crusades, Wilson's choked on the heat of its own righteousness and he soon went away. The Ranch slipped back into a normal high gear and went humming along into its future, sweetly indifferent to muffled indignation or pious politicians, prepared to cope when necessary with the inevitable next crusade.

The next crusader, though, would come armed with cameras.

Marvin Zindler was a public curiosity even before he became a nightly refutation of McLuhan's thesis that television is the province of the cool. Marvin is most assuredly not cool, and never has been.

Back when he was heading the Consumer Protection Division of the Harris County Sheriff's Department, he would inveigh against truthless advertisers or fast-dealing car salesmen with all the indignant wrath of a Calvinist preacher accosted in the pulpit by some hot-eyed, leering flasher. And always with an audience. Marvin Zindler was to huckstering what Jehovah's God was to sin, with the exception that Marvin always had cameras there to record the pointing of his vengeful finger.

He had a fair penchant for attracting attention. Stories used to float around the city rooms of Houston newspapers about how Marvin would wait two and three days before serving a warrant until a TV crew was available to immortalize his crimebusting; about how Marvin would deluge courthouse reporters with Agatha Christie-style press releases extolling his exploits; about the time *The Houston Post*, on Marvin's "hot inside tip," bannered the four-inch headline HARRELSON IN MEXICO at the same moment the accused murderer was being arrested in Atlanta.

Back when he was the police reporter for a Houston radio station, Zindler would appear just before his on-air signal to relate action-packed on-the-scene accounts that he'd just read from the morning papers. Other reporters used to substitute dated papers and he'd dash in to announce, over the air, "This is Marvin Zindler, On The Scene . . ." and launch into a breathless blow-by-blow of last month's liquor store holdups.

Zindler even looks the part, which is to say artificial. His nose and chin were metamorphosed long ago to meet superstar specifications, and his head is permanently hidden by a handsome Cary Grant toupee. And his clothes, equally handsome, are custom-tailored to conceal the pads he wears on his shoulders and buttocks to fill out his figure to superstar proportions.

It's always been easy, of course, to make fun of Marvin Zindler, as do most of his colleagues in journalism. But, strangely enough, it just won't wash. For one thing, he's so absurdly up-front about those wigs and pads and nose-jobs of his, and he confesses instantly, cheerfully, to a raging egomania. It's hard to laugh at somebody's closet skeletons when they rattle them at you.

And then there're his eyes, as warmly blue and gentle (and genuine) as any superstar could hope to possess, the only external hint that within that ludicrously handmade body of his there's a soft nub of sincerity and compassion.

Danny, who's sort of a hustler, remembers being arrested by Marvin way back when he was just another deputy in the Warrants Division: "Most of the crooks I know have a lotta respect for Zindler. He was a straight-up cop. After he'd busted ya, he'd stick around till ya were mugged an' printed an' in the tank, an' he'd make sure ya had cigarettes before he'd leave."

He still shows that same concern in his role as Channel 13's consumer affairs reporter, staying long after work to answer a blizzard of phone calls from 12-year-olds with lost bicycles and dowdy matrons who don't like the gas company. He rationalizes his media-mongering by saying "Most corporations involved in, say, false advertising will just laugh at a $50 fine, but if you show up with a TV camera and give 'em bad publicity then they'll shape up."

There's a hard truth there. If Marvin's style, a zany blend of P. T. Barnum and Dudley Do-Right, has made him notorious, it's also made him effective; instead of being just another petty public ombudsman, he's become a kind of Electric Bounty Hunter, striking Media-Terror into the fast-talking hearts of consumer bilkers.

That's why it all seemed a little strange when Marvin set out after the Chicken Ranch: while there may well be lots of people who don't like the place, irate consumers aren't among them. But Marvin says his crusade against the Ranch wasn't based on any righteous shock at all the whoring going down out there. "I'm no moralist," he'll tell you. Marvin's targets were bigger than just sin: political corruption and Organized Crime.

Marvin's story is that he got his hands on a Department of Public Safety (DPS) intelligence report that had been made last year. This report, according to Marvin, says that the Chicken Ranch—together with another, less renowned, little whorehouse in Sealy—grosses "a conservative minimum" of $3 million a year, and that most of this money was going into numbered bank accounts in Mexico by way of lavish payoffs to all manner of corrupt state and local officials. It's these officials, the story goes, who really own the Chicken Ranch and whose power in Austin allows it to stay open.

Then there's the black specter of Organized Crime, whose ruthless involvement Marvin keeps invoking. Marvin's definition of Organized Crime, though, is not exactly what you'd first think. It has nothing to do with the Mafia. Or the Syndicate. Or Chicago or New York or even Houston. It maybe has something to do with a "circuit" of other country whorehouses through which girls are rotated, but it's hard to say. Marvin's definition of Organized Crime is pretty vague.

Nonetheless, Marvin bought this DPS report at face value, lock-stock-and-brothel. He has great faith in the Texas Rangers.

When he first saw the report last January, he says, he was asked by the Rangers not to do anything until they'd had the

chance to "move in." Marvin agreed. Then, along about May, Marvin got word that the DPS-Ranger investigation had been canceled. "That's when I really got mad," remembers Marvin, "cause it proved to me that somebody from higher up was interfering with the enforcing of the law."

That's when Marvin went to work. He recruited as his collaborator Larry Conners, a young TV newsman who is a first-rate investigative reporter and the most hard-ass interviewer this side of Mike Wallace. The Zindler and Conners team went underground to begin their investigation.

They sat in the woods outside the Ranch counting and photographing the patrons. Conners, together with a cameraman (but, sadly, no TV camera) handled the "inside work," discovering first-hand that there really was prostitution going on in there.

After three months of this sort of thing they were able to prove that, sure enough, there's a whorehouse in La Grange. That's when they broke the story and ran up against, or into, County Sheriff T. J. "Jim" Flournoy.

Old Jim Flournoy looks like he leapt full-bodied from one of Bobby Seale's nightmare visions of a county sheriff, a pot-bellied, gun-totin', hulking incarnation of Frontier Justice. Slow-talking, in keeping with his thought patterns, Big Jim's style of dealing with the world is based largely on Threat, and is generally successful. His brother Mike, who is the sheriff over in Wharton County, has a reputation for carrying out *his* threats, but big Jim's never gone overboard with that sort of thing.

Like his predecessors, Big Jim was easily accommodated to the existence of the Chicken Ranch. Back in 1958 he'd even had a Hot Line installed to connect the Ranch and the Sheriff's Office, and he's one of the biggest defenders of its operations. "It's nevrah caused no trouble round here," he says, "no fights or dope or nothin. I ain't nevrah got no complaints."

It's been a positive boon to law enforcement, if you listen to the sheriff. Because of the Ranch, "Thar's nevrah been no rapes while I been Shurff," he relates. "O course thet don't count no nigger rapes," he adds, which is probably fair enough since blacks weren't admitted to the Ranch anyway.

He goes on to tell you about the $10,000 that Edna contributed to the Hospital Building Fund, her other munificences, the economic benefits to the community, the low rate of venereal disease afforded by having county-inspected hookers on hand. As Larry Conners puts it, "He makes that whorehouse sound like a damn non-profit county recreational facility."

Most of Big Jim's arguments are pretty specious as well. His figures on rapes, VD, pregnancies and dope (all of which he says there are none of, excepting for niggers) are all bogus, and the $10,000 bequest about equals the annual take on the jukebox. As for the local impact, one local shopkeeper easily dismissed that: "They only got a payroll of a dozen out thar. Now how much money you figure a dozen whores're gonna spend in this town?"

All sad but true. For all Big Jim's efforts at rationalizing, the Ranch's longevity was built on sentiment rather than cash, and sentiment is a poor defense against either the law or a zealous camera. Once Channel 13 weighed in against the "bawdy houses," as they called them, there was no contest.

That doesn't mean, however, that Zindler ever proved his vague assertions about "corruption and Organized Crime." He never even proved his contention that the two whorehouses grossed over $3 million a year; most local Ranchwatchers think that ludicrously high and the most commonly accepted figure was about $300,000. The IRS, who never failed to collect the government's portion, never questioned Edna's returns.

All that Marvin had to do, really, was haul his cameras out to La Grange and put on the tube what every local farmboy for a hundred miles already knew.

Big Jim, who'd probably never before seen the business end of a TV camera, was mercilessly pinned in one of those Conners interviews. He erupted against those goddam DPS fellers who'd been pokin around last fall, and allowed as how he'd called DPS Chief Col. Wilson Speir to get them off his back. The Colonel, said Big Jim, told him to close down the Ranch until the elections were over with, so Big Jim obliged. It was the kind of interview that could make you wonder whose side he was really on.

After a week of nightly exposes, during which the Ranch kept whoring along with all flags flying, Marvin went up to Austin to interview the Governor, the Attorney General, and Col. Speir. Confronted simultaneously with *prima facie* sin and TV cameras, they all professed outrage that this could be going on and promised to get to the bottom of things.

On Wednesday, the day before he was to go to Austin to answer a summons from the Governor, Big Jim capitulated. He just called Edna and told her to shut it down. Marvin promptly left for Jamaica on vacation.

Within a week of its shuttering, the Ranch is deserted, with only Lilly still hanging around to shoo off curious interlopers. Edna is hiding out with her old man in East Texas, and the girls are in Dallas, Houston, Austin, streetwalking. Big Jim is being especially suspicious of strangers, hinting bluntly to the writer from *Playboy* that he's seen about all the snoopy journalists he cares to.

At Berkelbach's Cafe in Round Top, the hangers-on discuss what to do with Marvin Zindler should he ever chance to pass through town. A petition circulates in La Grange to save the ranch, and bumperstickers make their appearance, proclaiming the same thing. Local opinion, as figured by the owner of the local radio station, breaks about even. A few local tycoons begin making plans to buy the Ranch and turn it into a restaurant, with private dining rooms in each of the bedrooms.

There is, indeed, little evidence of any sort that the ranch had ended its days. It had always existed, really, as a pleasant irrelevance, kind of a collective daydream by a rural people that believed in dreams remnant from a simpler era that had a tolerant niche for such things, along with eccentric uncles and town drunks. Like all the excess baggage from that era, realized day dreams have been burrowed under by the plow of progress. X-rated movies and celluloid sex are alright in the modern age—as is everything that is malleable into legalisms and electricity—but that additional dimension of humanity that the ranch possessed is not obscene, not immoral, just obsolete.

*—October 1973*

# IT TAKES ALL KINDS

At last count there were 12,244,678 Texans, and, as they would have said in *Naked City*, each one is a story. This section contains the stories of Texans both famous and not so famous. Bill Porterfield's "Farewell to LBJ: A Hill Country Valediction" explores our President and the land that nourished him and, in the end, claimed him for its own. Texans are also notorious for being rich eccentrics, and no Texan was richer or more eccentric than H. L. Hunt, as Porterfield shows in "H. L. Hunt's Long Goodbye." Bigun Bradley was also well known, but not as himself. Bradley was a real working cowboy who posed for the Marlboro Man advertisements; Gary Cartwright's chronicle of his famous life and lonely death unites the public and private sides of the Texas cowboy myth.

For all their innate interest, the lives of famous Texans don't always tell us how we live. Gary Cartwright spent two months with a Texas family on welfare, and his story, "The Endless Odyssey of Patrick Henry Polk," is a testimony to the desperation and determination of ordinary people. In "The Long Road North," John Davidson followed two Mexicans from deep in Mexico, across the Rio Grande, through the wastes of South Texas, to the hardships of becoming our newest Texans.

In his first magazine article in America, the Irish journalist Alexander Cockburn introduced us to a Texan in a class by herself, Marguerite Oswald, Lee Harvey Oswald's mother, who ten years after the assassination of John Kennedy was still obsessed, like all of us, with the mystery of her son and what he did that terrible day. They are Texans all, a variety that shows some of the variety of our state.

*Photography by Marlon Taylor*

# THE LONG ROAD NORTH

## by John Davidson

*Hunger, thirst, exhaustion, and snakebite plague the journey of the wetback, but there's only one danger that counts.*

When I asked Javier what it was like to be a wetback, he smiled at the implausibility of summing up five years of experience, and then he looked thoughtfully at his hands. We had just met and were sitting on a shady curb next to a hamburger stand in West San Antonio; it was one of those first hot weeks toward the end of May when you know it won't be cool again till fall. Javier's hands, I noticed, looked too old for his 24 years. The fingers were squeezed out of shape from heavy labor and the skin so thick it was like permanent work gloves. He absently rubbed a scar on the back of his left hand as if it might come off and said:

"Two years I worked on a roofing crew. I worked hard and the boss treated me like I was part of the family. His brother was my supervisor and we became compadres. I went to live in his house and shared a room with his son. His wife cooked and took care of my clothes like she did for all the rest. Every Saturday—we worked six days a week except when it rained—we got paid, and every Saturday the boss said he was holding my Saturday wages to save for me. After almost two years of work, I spilled hot tar on my hand. I went to the boss and said I need to go to a doctor, but he told me to just put dirt on the burn. I went to the doctor anyway and missed a day of work. Not too long after that, I got a cold. It was a bad cold, and I had to stay in bed for a week. When I went back to work, my boss was angry. He told me, 'Javier, you're no good and you're lazy. Get out of here! Go back to Mexico where you belong!' None of what he said was true and it made me mad. I told him I was leaving but I wanted my Saturday wages. That's when he said, 'What wages?' He robbed me of almost two thousand dollars and there was nothing I could do. If I had complained too much, he would have turned me in to the Border Patrol."

I commiserated with Javier and said that if I could spend some time with him in San Antonio, follow him around to see how he lived, I might be able to write his story. Javier shook his head and said he was getting ready to leave for

John Davidson, a freelance writer, is working on a book for Doubleday based on his experiences with Javier.

Jalisco; he had just received word from his family that he was needed at home. Perhaps when he got back.

"How will you come back?" I asked.

"Swim the river and walk."

"Then why don't I go with you," I suggested.

"Do you mean in a car?" Javier asked.

"No, swim and walk." I explained that I didn't want to alter the trip, but would just follow along and do whatever he normally did. "I'll be your shadow," I proposed.

Javier looked at me doubtfully. "It's the wrong time of year. The grass is too high; too many snakes."

"It would make a good story," I countered.

Javier looked away, squinting as if to imagine the trip and then began to smile. "If you made the trip," he nodded his head in approval, "then you would know what it's like to be a wetback. Así podrías sacar el chiste: *that way you could get the joke.*"

And so two hours later we left for Mexico. Nonstop—except for sleeping on bus station floors—we traveled eight hundred miles to Jalisco, spent forty-five minutes with Javier's family, picked up his younger brother, and started back to Texas. Both in Mexico and after we crossed the river and started walking toward San Antonio, I was struck by Javier and his brother's attitude toward time and space. It is based on the active knowledge that distance—fifty to a hundred and fifty miles—breaks down into footsteps, which in time accumulate and overcome terrain. It is reinforced by a dependence on walking as a major means of transportation. Keeping up with them was one of the most strenuous things I've ever attempted.

While in Mexico, I achieved a surprising anonymity in the company of Javier. Unlike other trips I had made, no one treated me like a tourist or showed the least curiosity that I spoke Spanish. In Jalisco, none of Javier's family asked who I was or why I was with him, nor did his brother during the entire trip. It was as if traveling with Javier, speaking nothing but Spanish, I had submerged my identity. By the time we were headed north, I began to feel that I was indeed Javier's shadow.

73

When Javier woke, the bus was splashing slowly through water. It cut a wake that lapped at the houses along the street, and stranded cars rocked gently as the bus proceeded into deeper water. "*Está hundido Nuevo Laredo*," a voice in the dark softly exclaimed the obvious. Looking at the flooded streets, Javier thought of the river. If it was flooding, they couldn't swim. A smuggler would have to take them across. Too tired to worry, Javier leaned his head against the window and closed his eyes.

The bus pulled into the Nuevo Laredo terminal at 3 a.m. Javier shook his brother Juan to wake him, and they gathered their belongings to get off. Downtown, the water had run off into the river, and the streets were deserted. Momentarily lost, the two brothers stood in the milky neon glow in front of the Estrella Blanca bus station until Javier went inside to ask about a cheap hotel. He waited meekly at the counter for the clerk to notice him and finally reached out and touched his sleeve.

In Nuevo Laredo Javier and Juan were as easily identifiable as businessmen on a flight to New York City. Their congenital humility and fundamental silence mark them as campesinos. As does their appearance—strong white teeth from a childhood without Cokes and candy, and whites of the eyes slightly discolored from a lifelong deficiency of vitamins and minerals. An informed observer could accurately speculate that the two brothers were coming from an economically depressed agricultural area, probably from the Central Plateau north of Mexico City, and that they were going to cross the Rio Grande illegally. There would be no other reason for two campesinos to come to the border.

Directed toward a cheap hotel the clerk described as "*baratito*," they started down the empty street, Juan carrying a small cardboard box tied with a string and Javier an orange canvas flight bag with black straps. From Javier's clothes—brown-and-white-plaid double-knit trousers, a dark brown shirt, dark green velvet jacket trimmed with silver braid, and a black baseball cap—it is clear that he's been to Texas before. On a white patch on the front of the cap, a red stitched caption demands, "What's your handle?" and an imperative red thumb indicates an appropriate blank, which Javier left nameless.

At 24, Javier is tall and rangy. Five eleven, he is easily the tallest in his family. He estimates he has between eight and eleven brothers and sisters, but he's uncertain how many have died and been born in the five years since he first left Mexico. As to his exceptional height, Javier alternately attributes it to childhood "exercise"—his father took him out of school after the second grade to work in the fields—and to "medicine"—a car ran over him when he was four and he received considerable doctoring. Sparse black bristles on his face intend a moustache and goatee and recall Oriental villains. High sharp cheekbones, a long, slightly flattened nose, and acne scars contribute to the villainous impression, but it is quickly dispelled when he smiles. Juan, younger and smaller than Javier, wears sky-blue pants, a paler blue shirt, and has heavy black hair, fine features, and a resolutely impenetrable nature.

At the hotel, they got a small windowless room with a double bed for two dollars. Without bothering to remove his clothes or black boots, Juan pulled the green bedspread back and lay down on the spotted gray sheets. Javier took off his shirt and then his cowboy boots, which, to discourage age scorpions, he propped upside down in the corner before switching off the bare bulb in the ceiling and lying down next to Juan.

Tired after the fifteen-hour bus ride from Jalisco they fell asleep and didn't wake until late the next morning. Outside, when they left the hotel, it was already hot, and the humidity rose off the damp ground and pavement. Javier and Juan walked directly to the bridge and followed a chain-link fence west along the riverbank. Garbage thrown from nearby houses was scattered along the trail, and a sweet smell of putrefaction filled the air. At the river's edge, they could see the results of the storm—dense brown water pocked by whirling eddies, and farther out, rafts of river trash and the stately progression of floating tree trunks that marked the current's velocity.

"Can you swim?" Javier asked his younger brother.

"Some," Juan answered.

"But not in this," Javier said, and smiled. "You would get caught in the trash or a log would hit you. Then you would drown." He squatted on his heels to watch the river. "I wonder how many have drowned here?"

Juan looked at him.

"No one knows what happens to the ones trying to cross. In the river, we're neither here nor there, so no one counts."

Juan shrugged indifferently and settled on his heels to watch the river. They turned in unison as a man came around a bend in the trail. His pants legs were rolled above the knee and his bare feet were stuck in an old pair of unlaced shoes. He was carrying his shirt. "Lots of water," Javier greeted him.

"Enough," the man agreed.

"How long will the river be up?"

"Who knows," the man answered as he passed. "A week. Maybe more."

They watched the man till he disappeared around the next bend, then turned back to the river. "What do you think?" Javier asked. "Will we make it or not?"

"*Pues, sí*," Juan shrugged, unconcerned.

"We'll see," Javier said and stood up.

Climbing out of the river bottom, Javier indicated what appeared to be an impenetrable thicket of mesquite. Grass rose a foot and a half to an intricate crisscross of mesquite limbs that formed a green wall. "The first fifty miles," he said, "it's like this. Only worse." He turned and climbed the bank to the railroad tracks.

In town, they waded through the jam of American tourists and Mexican vendors on the narrow sidewalks. Away from the bridge and past the market and curio shops, they found an inexpensive restaurant where each ordered carne guisada, tortillas, frijoles, and Pepsi Cola. They ate slowly, using pieces of tortilla to delicately tear the stewed meat into shreds, which they rolled with beans and *salsa* into small tacos. When he finished, Javier cleaned his teeth with a napkin and got out his cigarettes.

From the restaurant, they walked to a small corner grocery store. Javier selected two plastic net shopping bags: one blue-and-green plaid and the other orange and yellow. He asked the woman behind the counter for six cans of refried beans, six cans of large sardines, a small bottle of *salsa picante*, two loaves of Bimbo white bread, five packages of crackers, four packs of Parade cigarettes, several boxes of matches, and a bottle of rubbing alcohol.

Javier distributed the purchases between the two plastic bags, tied the strap of his canvas bag to the plastic handles of one shopping bag, and draped them both over his right shoulder like saddlebags. Juan transferred the shirt and pair of pants from the cardboard box into his own shopping bag.

At a hardware store, Javier bought a compass for himself and a white straw hat for Juan, which, on closer inspection, turned out to be plastic. So equipped, they retraced their steps down Avenida Guerrero toward the bridge, turned west, and in the early afternoon sun, walked out past the railroad station and the cemetery into the slums of Nuevo Laredo.

On the low side of the streets, the soggy contents of houses were draped on fences and shrubs or piled on any dry surface to catch the sun. Block after block, the houses became poorer until the town finally petered out with one last corner grocery. Squatting in the shade against the wall, a man watched them approach. "Hey, where you going?" he called when they got closer.

"*Más allá*," Javier evaded. Farther on.

"Toward Carrizo?" The man stood to face them. Beneath his straw hat, he had yellow eyes and a three-day growth of beard. "A truck is coming that will take you."

"We'll see," Javier answered and they walked into the store. Inside, he asked the *señora* for a half-gallon plastic milk bottle and then bought himself and Juan a Pepsi. When they walked back out, a man was sitting in an old red pickup parked in the shade of the building next to the man with yellow eyes. The driver looked at Javier and Juan with their boots, hats, and plastic net shopping bags. "I imagine you want to cross the river," he said.

"It is a possibility," Javier admitted.

"I can take you both toward Carrizo where a man has a boat. Twenty dollars."

"Ten each?" Javier asked.

"That's right. Ten each."

Javier gave him a ten and put his bags in the back of the truck. "What about your friend?" the man asked.

Javier looked at Juan and shrugged. "He doesn't have any money."

"You could loan it to him," the man suggested.

"Not when I have barely enough to cross the river," Javier answered and started climbing in.

"Fifteen for both," the man offered.

"Leave him here," Javier said coldly, and sat down in the back of the truck to indicate he was ready to leave. The driver shrugged and started the engine. As the truck drove away from the store, Juan and Javier looked at each other but made no sign. As the truck pulled onto the road, the driver glanced into the mirror and saw Juan standing forlornly with his shopping bag. He stepped on the clutch and brake, leaned out the window, and shouted angrily, "All right. Get in!"

The truck ran west along the gravel road a mile south of and parallel to the river. Where the land was low and flat, standing water came up to the truck's axle and the flooded mesquite flats looked like swamps shimmering with heat, reflecting the blue sky with its stray white clouds. Speaking above the sound of crunching gravel and the partially submerged muffler, Javier touched Juan's arm and said, "We may have to walk all of tonight in water."

Impassive, Juan blinked once like a shiny black crow inwardly focused on not falling off its wire. "We cross today?"

"At sunset. If we can get away from the river at night, the little airplane won't see us."

"Little airplane?"

"From *emigración*. They patrol with the airplane and in jeeps and trucks." Then, pointing at the submerged pasture, "Do you think you can sleep in water?"

"I'd rather walk in it."

"Walk enough, and you can sleep anywhere," Javier assured him.

The truck faltered twice before reaching dry land and going on toward Carrizo. After fifty minutes of driving they came to a large white warehouse closed and overgrown with weeds and sunflowers. On the far side of the building, the driver stopped the truck in front of a solitary shack. "For ten dollars," he complained when he got out of the truck, "this is as far as I can take you."

As Juan and Javier climbed down with their belongings, an undernourished adolescent in a large cowboy hat and black jeans tucked into cowboy boots loped out from the shack and stopped before them. "You want to cross the river," he said, his pale eyes tracking independent of each other. Not knowing which eye focused and which stared into space, Javier hesitated and the driver said, "Hector, where's Rodrigo?"

"He's coming now. Any minute," the boy promised. He was so thin—a backbone inside a ragged white T-shirt—it appeared unlikely that he could propel the cowboy boots. "Three others are already waiting. We'll take them all today."

"Then I'll leave these two with you," the driver said, and got back in his truck. As he drove away, Juan and Javier followed Hector to the shack, which was circumscribed by a ring of trash as far as the arm could throw. Away from the road, the tin shack, its roof weighted down with worn-out tires, had been expanded by a makeshift awning covered with huisache branches and a lean-to kitchen. An old Formica-and-chrome kitchen table and chairs sat in the shade of the awning.

"Perhaps you have a cigarette you can give me?" Hector asked. Javier took out his pack, gave Hector and Juan each a cigarette, and took one himself. He started to sit down at the table beneath the awning after they had lighted the cigarettes. "Not here," Hector stopped him. "Sometimes the *federales* come; you had better hide in the bushes." He led them beyond the circle of trash and into the mesquite, where three men sat at the edge of a clearing around a washed-out campfire. Two of the men had paper bags at their sides and the third a black plastic shaving kit. "They're going too," Hector said by way of introduction, and the three men nodded. Javier and Juan dropped their bags in the ring of ashes and sat down on the ground in the long shadows of the mesquite trees. "Very soon and Rodrigo will be here," Hector assured them one last time before going back to the shack.

They watched Hector leave and then Javier asked the men where they came from. "*Veracruz—donde no vale la vida*," the round-faced man sitting in the middle answered for the three. "And you?"

"Jalisco," Javier echoed. "Where life has no value." Javier stretched out on the ground, put his canvas bag beneath his head, and pulled a weed to chew on. "How long have you been waiting here?"

"Since midday," the same man answered. "What time is it now?"

Javier looked at his wristwatch. "Four o'clock." To the west he could see cumulus clouds building as if for the sunset.

"Rodrigo is probably getting drunk somewhere," the man speculated. "The skinny one with the eyes said they took nine this morning."

"Nine," Javier repeated. "That's a good business."

"Yes, but it's not a regular harvest."

"It never is," Javier agreed. "You've been before?"

"Yes, but not the others," the man answered.

"Then you're the one that knows the way?"

"I can look at the sky and tell which way is north."

"That's good," Javier said and pulled the long stem of the weed through his teeth to shred it. "The first time I went, one of us had a compass. We walked for three days and came to a big river. At last we thought we were getting out of the brush. We were so happy. We spent most of a morning looking for a place to cross before we realized it was the Rio Grande."

"You walked in a circle," the man said.

"That's right," Javier smiled. "The one with the compass didn't know how to read it. Like idiots, we almost crossed back into Mexico."

"But you made it."

"Barely," Javier sat up, stretched, and then propped up on one elbow. "Just barely."

"How many days did it take?"

"Eleven to San Antonio. We almost starved in the brush before we got to Carrizo and had to stop at a ranch and work for food. They gave us each two dollars for three days of cutting mesquite posts and said if we didn't leave they would call *la emigración*."

"Be glad they didn't need more posts. You would have worked more days for the same amount of money."

"True," Javier said and sat up farther. Gazing toward the man, he had noticed that beneath the cuffs of his green polyester trousers hung a set of plaid double-knit cuffs. The two other men also had double sets of cuffs hanging above their boots. "You're wearing two pair of pants," Javier observed.

The three men looked down at their cuffs and then up.

"For the snakes," the man in the middle explained.

"They must be bad now."

"Perhaps the rain makes them crawl up in the trees to stay dry."

Javier studied the mesquite around them for signs of snakes and concluded, "That way they would strike us in the face or on the arms, rather than on our boots." Juan shifted uneasily, attracting Javier's attention. "Are you frightened?" Javier asked.

"Psssh," Juan exhaled genuine disgust and turned away.

"The last time," the man in the middle went on, "we found a corpse. Snakebit, we decided."

"Many say they've seen bodies. Thank god, I never have."

Hector reappeared to say that Rodrigo would be there any minute. Impatient, the man in the middle got up and said they would walk further up the river to see if anyone else had a boat. "Rodrigo comes and you're not here," Hector warned, "he won't wait for you. He'll be angry that you left." The man shrugged; the three of them picked up their belongings and started for the road.

Javier watched them go, then lay back down, resting his head on the canvas bag. "If we cross by sunset," he said, "that's soon enough." He pulled the brim of his baseball cap over his eyes and drifted off to sleep.

It was dusk when they heard the pickup. There was honking, then shouting and drunken laughter. Confident it wasn't *federales*, Javier and Juan picked up their bags and walked out toward the road. In the half-light, they could see a blur of activity between the shack and an old truck. Hector, when he saw them, brought Rodrigo out to talk. Powerfully built, dressed completely in black, Rodrigo acted as surly as he looked. "You want to cross," he said, and hitched his pants higher. When he opened his mouth, splayed, tusklike teeth spouted from his upper gum.

Yes, they wanted to cross, Javier answered politely.

"You can pay?" he looked them over as if it might be by the pound.

Yes, Javier answered, they could pay.

"Tomorrow morning when it gets light, I'll take you across. You can sleep tonight behind the warehouse."

Javier and Juan sat on the warehouse loading dock and ate a can of refried beans. Above them they could hear bats swoop, and before them the tops of six-foot-tall sunflowers swayed at the edge of the dock. Juan reached for the empty milk container and started to get up. "Where are you going?" Javier asked.

"To ask for water."

"Don't ask them for anything. If they don't rob us, we'll be lucky. Let them forget we're here."

At the edge of sleep, Javier heard someone on the steps to the dock. Hector came toward them carrying a large bundle. "You want these?" he said and dropped a couple of blankets. They spread one blanket beneath them and pulled the other over. "Tonight," Javier said happily as dirt sprinkled onto them from the blanket, "we sleep like the president."

Javier woke with the first gray light. He sat on the dock and watched the shack. A rooster crowed, but the shack remained silent. The sun rose and Javier lay back down to wait. When he woke again, Rodrigo was climbing the steps to the dock. He squatted down in a friendly way at the end of their blankets. "How much money do you have?" he asked.

"Twenty."

"Each?" he said and sucked his upper lip down over his teeth.

"Together," Javier answered.

As if annoyed, Rodrigo ran a hand through his wavy hair. On his forearm, a lopsided "lov you" was scratched with blue ink. "You think I can take you for that?"

"It's all we have," Javier replied.

"You'll have to give me more—a wristwatch or something of value," Rodrigo said and left the dock without waiting for a response.

Thirty minutes later, Hector appeared to say they should follow him. Carrying their plastic shopping bags, they trotted behind him across the road and through a cornfield toward the river. Overhead, the sun had broken through the morning haze. The damp ground was steaming. They came out of the field onto a road that turned toward the river. From behind, they heard horses and saw Rodrigo approaching in a wagon, which contained a boat. Hitched to two red nags, the wooden relic, adapted with tires, was too large for the horses, but bolting, eyes rolling, they caught up with Javier and Juan and forced them off the road.

Hector led the two brothers down a path into a ravine where they could see Rodrigo waiting on a small knoll next to the now-empty wagon. The boat—which was actually two automobile hoods welded together—floated below in the water. As if barring the way, Rodrigo stood to face them. "How much can you pay me?" he started over.

"Twenty dollars," Javier repeated.

"That's not enough," Rodrigo said angrily. "I take *la raza* across; I help *la raza*. It's a good thing I do, but I must be paid. If caught, I go to prison and my family starves."

"It's all I have."

"What about your wristwatch? What kind is it?"

Javier looked at the dial. "Timex. It's old but I need it. I can't give it to you."

Rodrigo scowled at Juan. "What about you?"

"*Nada*," Juan said and showed empty hands.

Rodrigo turned his back on them. Hector and the two men looked from Javier to Rodrigo and back to see who would give. The tension mounted until Javier repeated, "I promise, it's all I have."

"Then give me the money," Rodrigo relented.

They slid slowly down the bank on their heels to the boat, which had three crossboards for seats. Rodrigo stationed the two brothers and their belongings at either end and climbed into the middle seat. Before telling Hector to push them out, he studied the dense trees and brush on the opposite bank for movement. The mile of river they could see from bend to bend was clear, and the silence revealed no warning hum of Border Patrol surveillance plane or patrol boat. Hector shoved the boat into the swirling brown water, and Rodrigo dug in with oars made of plywood squares nailed to long sticks. With each heavy stroke, the two ends of the boat twisted at the welded seam, but by keeping within shelter of the bank, Rodrigo managed to row against the current without the two hoods splitting apart. The boat moved laboriously upstream until Rodrigo lifted the left oar and dug hard with the right to swing the boat into the current, and then dug with both oars to propel them across the forty yards of river before it could sweep them too far downstream. Javier started to speak, but Rodrigo hushed him—a voice carries too far on water—and there was only the steady thunk of the oars in the notches cut into the side of the boat.

The prow of the boat hit bank at the edge of a canebrake and the two brothers scrambled out into ankle-deep mud. Rodrigo handed up their bags and Juan shoved the boat back into the current. Staggering from the weight of the mud on their boots, they crashed through the cane to dry ground and pushed their way up an overgrown ravine to a dry bank, where Javier sat down to slice thick wedges of mud off the bottom of his boots with a stick. He handed the stick to Juan and, breathing hard, whispered, "We have to get away from the river fast. No more noise." He stood, swung the plastic shopping bag counterbalanced by the weight of the canvas bag over his shoulder, and started north.

The heat of the river bottom was oppressive. The trees and brush gave off more humidity than shade, and the lack of breeze was claustrophobic. Following behind, Juan noticed Javier's dark brown shirt beginning to soak black and the empty water container bouncing loose in the plastic shopping bag. From the top of a steep dirt bluff, beyond a barbed-wire fence and dirt road that ran along the rim, they could see flat pastureland, and below, a curving sweep of river and the lower Mexican bank. Javier stepped on a fence wire and jumped over. Juan followed and they sprinted across the road and through the open part of the pasture to the cover of a clump of mesquite trees. The ground was clear and they wove quickly through the mesquite until they came to another fence that separated the pasture from a field of corn. Again they jumped the fence and ran crouching between two rows of corn to the next fence. The midday sun was fierce in the open field and they were both covered with sweat and panting for breath. The next pasture, where they spooked a small herd of cows, brought them uncomfortably near a farmhouse. They circled away through the mesquite, crossed another fence, and kept going until they heard the clear whine of pickup tires on hot asphalt.

Breathing hard, Javier came to a halt beneath a large mesquite tree where he dropped his bags and sprawled on the ground. "*Carretera*," he rasped, and nodded toward the highway when Juan dropped beside him; he was so dry, the cotton was edging out in gray flecks at the corner of his mouth. Juan sat fanning himself with his white hat and staring as Javier rummaged in his canvas bag and took out the compass to check directions. Sure they were going north, Javier climbed the mesquite as high as its limbs would take him and looked out toward the road. A car whined past and when it disappeared, he dropped back to the ground. "We have to cross a bridge," he said, and swung his bags over his shoulder.

Through the tops of the mesquite they could see a taller line of cottonwood and sycamore indicating a creek. Thick brush protected their approach to the bridge and from its base they saw the water still running muddy from the storm. Javier dropped his bags at the foot of a concrete rampart. "Stay here," he whispered when Juan started to follow him down to the creek. Juan sat down and watched Javier crouch beyond a clump of willow to fill the water container. From above, he could see a large black water moccasin uncoil in the willow and slide into the water.

"Did you see the snake?" Juan asked when Javier handed up the jug.

"I wish it were the last!" he answered. His baseball cap was tilted back, his face was wet, and drops of water hung in the sparse hairs of his moustache and goatee. He watched Juan drink the brown water from the jug. When Juan finished, Javier refilled the jug and put it in his shopping bag. "One at a time, we cross the bridge," he instructed. "Wait till I'm across and hidden, then you come. Listen for cars." On all fours he crawled up the rampart to the bridge. As he was about to haul himself over the concrete railing, they heard a diesel semitrailer. He squatted down and waited for the truck to swoop thunderously past and drone into the distance. Grinning at Juan, he pulled his ball cap snug, climbed over the railing, and ran crouching across the bridge. In turn, Juan did the same.

On the far side of the bridge, Javier was waiting out of sight at the bottom of the road's embankment. Juan waded down through knee-deep grass, they crossed the fence, and started through another pasture. The grass gave way to a hard sandy crust shaded by mesquite trees where they picked up the parallel tracks of a road. Javier looked back and stopped when he noticed Juan walking in one of the sandy tracks. "Step on the grass," he said. "You won't leave footprints." He turned and walked on.

The terrain began to change to hard rocky ground cut with shallow gullies and covered with low-lying scrub brush. Without the cover of mesquite trees, they were exposed to the hot sky. Looking for relief, Javier cut away from the road through the thickest stand of brush until he came to an eroded ditch. At a clump of scrub oak that spanned the ditch the two men dropped in, crawled into the shade, and got out the water jug. By now it was midafternoon.

"What do you think?" he asked his younger brother.

"It's not so bad," Juan answered.

"We haven't begun."

Javier took a can of sardines out of the net shopping bag and cut it open with a pocketknife. He put a piece of white bred on his palm, laid a large Mexican sardine on the bread, poured a little tomato sauce from the can, and rolled it up like a tortilla.

After they finished the sardines and half the loaf of bread, they drank more water and smoked a cigarette. Javier took the dark green velvet jacket out of his canvas bag and draped it over his head and ball cap to keep off the black flies, then leaned back against the ditch wall. "Rest!" he said from behind the dark veil and snuggled his body against the ground.

Juan tilted his white hat over his eyes and crossed his arms, but a rock beneath his shoulder, then the flies, and finally Javier's heavy breathing distracted him. He crawled up on the edge of the ditch to stretch out flat, found that more comfortable, and dozed off. He woke to the sound of a four-wheel-drive vehicle winding through the brush. Not thinking they could have been seen in the brush, but remembering his footsteps in the road, he cautiously slipped back into the ditch where Javier slept soundly. A pickup door slammed, a dog barked, and he heard a man's voice. In the ensuing silence, Juan sat in the ditch and stared down at the ground before him. Next to a dry leaf on the sand, movement focused his eyes on a scorpion scuttling his way. Meditatively, listening to the silence, Juan picked up a twig and stuck the end of it in the scorpion's path. Violently, the scorpion swung the stinger at the end of its long tail over its back at the twig, turned and crabbed in the opposite direction. Again Juan blocked it with the twig, and again the scorpion swung its stinger and turned. Each time intercepted, the scorpion ran back and forth in the silence, back and forth as the truck started and wound away into the brush, back and forth across the sand until Juan crushed it with the twig.

Javier breathed more deeply beneath his dark veil until abruptly, he pulled away his jacket and blinked.

"I dreamed I was snoring and the dream woke me up."

"It was no dream," Juan said.

Javier shook his head with sleepy amusement and then noticed his wristwatch. "Four o'clock! Two hours I slept!"

"You're sleeping a lot," Juan commented.

"I wonder why," Javier said as he sat up. And then with irony, "I guess because it's my vacation."

Javier checked the compass, and they drank more water before crawling out of the ditch. Beyond the fence, the land turned stony and the low rolling hills were covered with an unbroken thicket of brush. Parting the way with a cedar stick he had picked up at the fence, Javier waded in, Juan following. Thorns snagged each step, and stones, unseen beneath the foliage, staggered them. The brush rolled from from swell to swell; the dark green troughs of blackbrush and ironwood were dappled with ashen ceniza and reefs of pale prickly pear, and the crests were light green with fern-like guajillo. Above, white blocks of cumulus marched east toward the Gulf and a late afternoon breeze rippled the surface of green.

Within the brush, the ground held the afternoon heat. Javier's shirt soaked black with perspiration; their accumulated scratches stung with sweat. They held the shopping bags before them like shields, but the constant nag of thorns was inescapable. The first variation in the landscape, a short caliche ledge, forced them down into a trough of huisache. In the pallid light below the brushes they saw a skeletal lattice of pale branches and a long ditch of stagnant water. The ground was sodden caliche, and white clay clung to their boots miring each step. Slipping and staggering, goaded by moist suffocation, they forced their way through the thicket until the ditch dried and they were able to climb the opposite bank.

Climbing out, Juan stumbled and grabbed a branch of blackbrush, driving three of the long straight thorns into his palm. He gave the branch a careful yank to pluck out the spines and then watched as three drops of dark blood formed at the punctures.

Thirsty, tired, red in the face, they pushed through the brush. At the top of a swell, they saw a small cloud of dust moving along the ground from east to west and, as it came closer, heard the crunch of tires on gravel.

The ground had been cleared for fifty feet on either side of a dirt road, increasing the danger of exposure. At the edge, they listened for traffic before dashing across the open space, crossing the fence, the road, another fence, and back into the brush. They kept going through the thinner secondary growth until Javier dropped his bags in a clearing on a slight rise and sat down in the evening shadow of a mesquite tree. Juan sank to the ground, Javier took out the jug, and they both drank. Due east on the horizon, near the road, they could see a windmill. Javier unbuttoned his soaked shirt and flapped the breeze to dry it. "This is going to smell," he grimaced. And then noticing that Juan was relatively dry, "Why don't you sweat?"

"Too thirsty," he answered.

Javier handed him the jug and watched him tilt it for another swallow. A layer of silt approached the neck of the jug as Juan drank. Javier asked him, "Now, what do you think? Think we'll make it?"

Juan handed him the jug and shrugged.

"At any rate, we've had luck," Javier said. "The little airplane hasn't seen us." He took another swallow of the water and then handed it to Juan. When Juan finished, the jug was essentially empty.

"Where do we get more water?" Juan asked.

"Windmills," Javier answered.

"That one?" Juan pointed to the one in view.

"It's too far out of the way. We'll come to others."

"Yes?"

"There are thirteen before Carrizo. With luck, we will sleep next to one tonight." Javier took the compass out of his bag and checked directions. A light evening breeze had begun to blow and the sun's rays were beginning to lose their intensity. "Let's walk," Javier said, and got to his feet. "These are the good hours."

And on they went, one step after another, Javier always in front carrying a cedar stick he'd picked up, Juan just behind wearing his white plastic hat. They never complained and rarely remarked the armadillos and rabbits that crossed their path.

Two more roads and they came to a windmill. They opened the tap beneath the storage tank, let the water run clear, and Javier leaned down to drink. Juan drank as much of the salty water as he could and they took turns holding their heads beneath the stream and running the cool water over their hands and arms. Javier took off his soaked brown shirt, rinsed it, and stored it in the net shopping bag. He put on a dark green shirt he'd been carrying in his canvas bag, they filled the jug with water, and as there was another hour of light, checked the compass and moved on.

The sun neared the dark horizon, its long rays refracting pink on remnants of cloud: the sky turned an intense and late blue. In the last light, they crossed another dirt road. In the secondary growth of mesquite beyond it, Javier picked out a cleared spot that looked relatively snake-free. The sun touched the edge of the horizon and abruptly, as at sea, was gone.

The two brothers sat on the ground beneath the lilac sky eating refried beans spread thick on pieces of white bread. Juan had discovered that either the jug of water had leaked or Javier's wet shirt had soaked the bread, but after considering spreading the slices out to dry overnight with the shirt, they went ahead and ate the bread wet. With their boots they stamped out places on the ground to sleep. Javier put on his velvet jacket and they both lay down on the ground, their heads resting on their bags. In the dark, his back to Javier, Juan asked, "The life in San Antonio: is it a good life?"

Javier thought a moment before answering, "It's work."

"But it's better than Mexico."

"Harder than Mexico. More work. That's all it is—work."

"But you have a car."

"To go to work." Javier raised himself on one elbow to speak more clearly, "Everyone who goes thinks he'll make lots of money; that he'll have a chance. But you never have a chance."

"Then why are you going?"

"Who knows," Javier said. "For the chance."

Javier lay back and didn't speak again. After a moment, his body jerked once and Juan could sense his falling asleep. In the night air, after the day's heat, it was suddenly cool, and Juan pushed his back to Javier's for warmth. The last thing he heard before dropping off was a high-pitched chorus of coyotes singing in the brush.

A quarter moon rose at eleven. At twelve, they started walking again. The dark shiny leaves of the blackbrush and ironwood reflected the pale light, and the ceniza stood spectral. From the contour of the brush and the feel of the cedar stick, Javier was able to guide them through. When the ground was rough, he warned Juan. When the brush was eye-level thorny, he held it back with the stick. They watched the sky to set their course and stopped often to light matches and look at the compass. What relief there was

from the heat was negated by the insecurity of each step.

At a thicket of prickly pear, they veered to the east to try to outflank it, but, after pushing through dense brush, were stopped by an arm of the thicket. They backtracked and forced their way to the west, but again found themselves outflanked. The prickly pear appeared to encircle them, as if like fish they had swum into a trap. Within the thicket, the brush and the dark prevented their seeing where they had entered, and they were unable to gauge the depth of the prickly pear they would have to penetrate. Slightly disoriented, Javier checked the compass and then sighted a narrow indentation to the north. He placed the end of his cedar stick against a branch of the obtruding cactus and pushed until it broke with a vegetable crunch and fell out of the way. With the end of the cedar stick, he slowly and patiently punched a narrow hole through a four-foot-high wall of prickly pear and on they went.

Coyotes sang in the night, the sky turned gray, they lay down to sleep again. By eight o'clock the next morning it was hot in the brush and again they were walking. By noon, they had all but depleted the salty water just to keep their mouths wet. Their faces were a perpetual shade of red beneath their hats; their clothing soaked with sweat; their eyes stinging with perspiration. They stopped to rest beneath a mesquite, and, too hot and too dry to want them, ate beans spread on soda crackers, which, since they had no saliva, stuck to their teeth and gums.

They rested till two before starting again. The brush quivered with heat under the afternoon sun, and the sky was devoid of clouds. Though they had crossed two dirt roads, they hadn't come to any more windmills and began to think they'd passed them in the night. From the sun and sweat, Javier's left eye started to itch and turn red. Occasionally, when they stopped to wet their mouths—an act that only defined the thirst—Javier would look up at the blank sky and shake his head. *"No quiere nublarse."* It doesn't want to cloud up, he would say, and smile sadly as if it were a small favor that he was being senselessly denied.

One sip after another of the water which, at the end, was merely provocation, and finally the jug was empty. Their lips burned from the sun and they became acutely aware of their thirst. Tongue, palate, lining of the mouth: it felt as if they would slowly swell and stick together. What wasn't the heat, a branch in the face, or the next footstep was beyond their attention. Twice they saw rattlesnakes—one coiled and one moving through the grass—and twice ignored them.

At five they came to a windmill. The water was salty, but they no longer cared. It freed their mouths and they took off their shirts to soak with water and sponge themselves. After they had slaked their thirst, they sat beneath the water tank to rest. "How far?" Juan asked.

Javier thought of how long they had walked before saying, "Tomorrow we come to a highway not far from Carrizo, from there, it's ninety miles to San Antonio."

"Ninety miles," Juan repeated.

"But who knows," Javier consoled him. "Perhaps someone will give us a ride."

They walked till sundown, ate, and slept. When the moon rose, they walked. At dawn, they found a windmill where they rested until the morning heat drove them on. Again the sky was cloudless; the heat, visible, audible. The brush trembled with the transmission of the sun's rays passing through, rebounding up from the ground, and shimmering humidly above; the heat's reverberation climbed slowly, reaching higher and higher cycles, hitting no limit.

During the night, Javier's eye had continued to itch, and with the renewed heat and sweat and rubbing, started to swell closed. By midmorning, his eyelids had swollen into a puffed slit through which Juan could see bloodshot veins radiating out from the black iris. When they stopped at noon, the eye was sealed shut, they were low on water, and they discovered a new torment. Black lusterless flies, small and flat, clung to their pants legs and rode along peacefully until they came to a halt. Then, in a swarm, they attacked hands, faces, and necks, sending the two brothers into a slapping frenzy. Spurred by the flies, they moved on through the heat of the day.

After more than an hour without water, Javier and Juan saw a windmill on the horizon. Their relief, however, slowly turned to despair when, goal in view, they saw how tedious their progress was. With the afternoon heat growing to a crescendo, in their thirst and exhaustion, the windmill appeared to advance before them on the horizon.

The windmill, they found, was surrounded by a deer-proof fence; large mesquite trees drooped around a dark pond of motionless water. The gate to the enclosure was padlocked, and within was a silent and ungrazed sanctuary of green. Javier climbed the gate, then Juan, and they jumped into the lush grass. Like shadows, black peccaries moved away from the far side of the pond. Midway to the windmill, knee-deep in grass, a deliberate and unequivocal rattle struck them like a current of electricity. Rooted to the ground, statues in the glade, they listened to the warning fill the enclosure. Pulse hammering, breath shallow and constricted, neither could see the snake or locate the sound. When it stopped, the silence was absolute and alarming.

They stood paralyzed for a moment, then Javier lifted his cedar stick and tapped the ground before him. When there was no response, he continued to try the grass until sure there was no immediate danger of being struck. They moved forward two steps, prodded the grass, and continued the procedure until they reached the windmill. Still shaking, they washed their hands and faces, ran water over their heads, filled the jug, and left the enclosure.

Hastened by the thought of the road, goaded by their nearness to complete exhaustion, they plodded on. The heat broke at five and there was a light breeze, but by then each step forward was punishment, and Javier's eye was red and swollen. At the top of every crest, they thought they would see the highway. Each time they saw more brush.

The sun set and they stopped. Javier opened a can of sardines, which they ate with the last of the crackers, and sipping the water like expensive whiskey, they sat in the dusk and smoked a cigarette. Juan stood up to kick out a spot to sleep and looked north. "*¿Qué es eso?*" he asked, and pointed toward a red blinking light.

"What?" Javier asked with vague interest.

"There's a light."

Javier raised himself to his knees and sighted north through his good eye. "Carrizo! It must be the radio antenna at Carrizo. Come on," he said, getting to his feet, "we're almost there."

The red light winked at them as they walked, telling them how far they had to go and how slowly they had traveled. At the top of a hill they could see a set of white headlights

flash intermittently through the brush as a vehicle moved east to west. The next time they saw headlights they could hear the faint, mournful whine of a truck approaching and then receding in the night. The two brothers came to a pasture where the underbrush had been cleared and they walked quickly toward the road. At a fence, outside the possible sweep of headlights, they sat down on the ground to watch the pavement. "What do you think?" Javier asked. "If we ask for a ride, we might be in San Antonio tonight." He savored the idea. "Or *la emigración* might catch us."

"And if we don't ask for a ride?" Juan asked.

"Then we walk another seven days. More if we have to work for food."

Juan looked straight ahead at the road and didn't answer.

"There are always risks," Javier decided and started for the fence.

The first car caught them in its headlights—Javier with his swollen eye, and black baseball cap; Juan with his white hat—and speeded up. A pickup passed and then a large Oldsmobile sedan hit its brakes as soon as they appeared in the light. They picked up their bags and ran toward the red taillights. A man on the passenger side leaned out and shouted in a friendly voice, "*Vámanos a San Antonio.*"

Javier and Juan stopped running.

"*¿A dónde van?*" the man called, "*¿Quieren un ride?*" Where you going? Want a ride?

Silence.

"*¿Van a San Antonio?*" he asked again.

Silence.

And then, "*¿Son de México?*" Are you from Mexico?

"*Sí,*" Javier answered, knowing that it was too late. "*Somos de México.*"

"*Bueno, vámanos a México,*" the man said and got out. "*Somos de la emigración.*"

Within two hours, the car erased what it had taken Javier and Juan three days and nights to do and they were back at the border. The next morning they were processed, and in the afternoon they were put on a bus with other illegal aliens and driven across the bridge to be let out in Nuevo Laredo. Between the two of them, they had five dollars that Javier had held back for an emergency and a couple of cans of food. They stood for a minute watching the people stream back and forth across the bridge, and then Javier turned and started west, retracing their steps to the railroad trestle, over the embankment and through the brush, until he came to a stop beneath a large oak next to the river. "Here we rest," he said, and set his bags down.

"Then what?" Juan asked.

"Start again."

For once not impassive, Juan allowed a flicker of surprise to cross his face. "How?" he asked.

"That we'll think about while we rest," Javier said, and squatted down to watch the river. "But we'll make it." He looked up at Juan. "Do you know why?"

Juan shook his head.

"*La necesidad nos obliga,*" Javier said.

Necessity obliges.

*Javier and Juan arrived in San Antonio thirteen days later on Sunday morning; on Monday Javier went back to his roofing job, and Juan began as a carpenter's helper on Wednesday.*

—*October 1977*

# MOTHER OF
# THE DECADE

## by Alexander Cockburn

*Lee Harvey Oswald's mother clings to her conviction that her son
has been wrongly made history's villain.*

Even over 3000 miles of transatlantic cable a BBC
voice is a BBC voice: calm, assured. "You see
we're doing this anniversary thing on the Assassination. We want you to interview Jackie Onassis,
Nellie Connally, Lady Bird Johnson, Marina Oswald, Mrs.
Tippett, Judge Sarah Hughes, and oh, yes, Lee Harvey Oswald's mother." A job is only a job. *This* would be a
career! I became excited. "You mean you want me to fly
to the Greek islands and . . ." "No. Catch her in Central
Park if you can. We've got our trace service in New York
locating the others."

The weeks passed. Jackie Onassis did not seem to be in
Central Park. The trace service could locate no one. Not
even Nellie Connally, even though *McCalls* had just done a
big story on her. The voice from the BBC was turning
testy. "No one? Listen. You've got to find *four women*.
We're planning this big feature. *The Widows of Dealey
Plaza*. Go to Dallas. See what you come up with, and watch
the expenses. We're flying this photographer out from London to meet you there." "You're flying a photographer out
from *London*, and you ask *me* to watch the expense? There
are photographers in Texas, you know." The voice from
BBC didn't believe it.

The photographer came down from New York with me in
the end. He was plump and like most pro photographers he
liked to talk about sex. We rose above LaGuardia in the wet
dawn. The photographer announced he wanted to lay the air
hostess. And that girl three rows back. And that other one.
We flew over Memphis. Nice girls in Memphis, said the
photographer. We landed in Dallas. We checked into the
Holiday Inn on Elm St. It was 10:30 a.m. The photographer beckoned to the bell boy. "Where can we get laid in
this town?" It looked like a long week.

It got longer. Kenneth Porter, Marina Oswald's second

*Alexander Cockburn is an Irish journalist living in New
York City. He writes regular columns about the press and
the economy for the* Village Voice.

and present husband said No. Then he said it again. No.
Finally he seemed to be saying that an interview with photographers would cost $3000. The voice from the BBC indi-
cated surprise and shock. "*Three thousand dollars*. That's
*more* than a thousand pounds." "I know." "So what
you're saying is, no Marina Oswald. Nellie Connally is in
San Diego. Lady Bird won't see you. And Mrs. Tippett,
now Mrs. Thomas, won't return your calls." "I am saying
that." "So at a cost of about $5000 in expenses and air
fares you have interviewed Judge Sara Hughes." "Yes."

It seemed time to play my one card. "I've got Mrs. Marguerite Oswald. I'm seeing her tomorrow. It's costing $400,
but she'll be sensational. I'll do a little round-up on the
others, some atmospherics on Dealey Plaza, and you can
center it round her." There was a long ruminative silence
between room 1827, the Holiday Inn, Dallas and extension
2563, Broadcasting House, London. Finally the great British solution to all tricky problems: "Do the best you can."
The voice added that the pictures better be good. They were
going to put Marguerite on the cover. If the pictures were
good.

I didn't tell the voice that Marguerite had specified One
Pose, Three Pictures. Anyone who has horsed around
watching magazines waste money will know that no picture
editor worth his light box is satisfied with less than ten
poses and a hundred photographs.

We drove nervously to Fort Worth. Even on the phone
Mrs. Marguerite Oswald's commanding personality had
been evident. "You're being paid to do the story. Your
outfit will make money. What about me? I have no money,
but I hold the cards. I am the mother of Lee Harvey Oswald.
I've waited ten long years for this. I always said it would
break in ten years. My son is supposed to have been the
assassin. Yet he was never tried. He died legally innocent.
Unless they prove to me that he killed President Kennedy,
this is my opinion. All I want is the truth."

By and large Marguerite Oswald has not done well out of

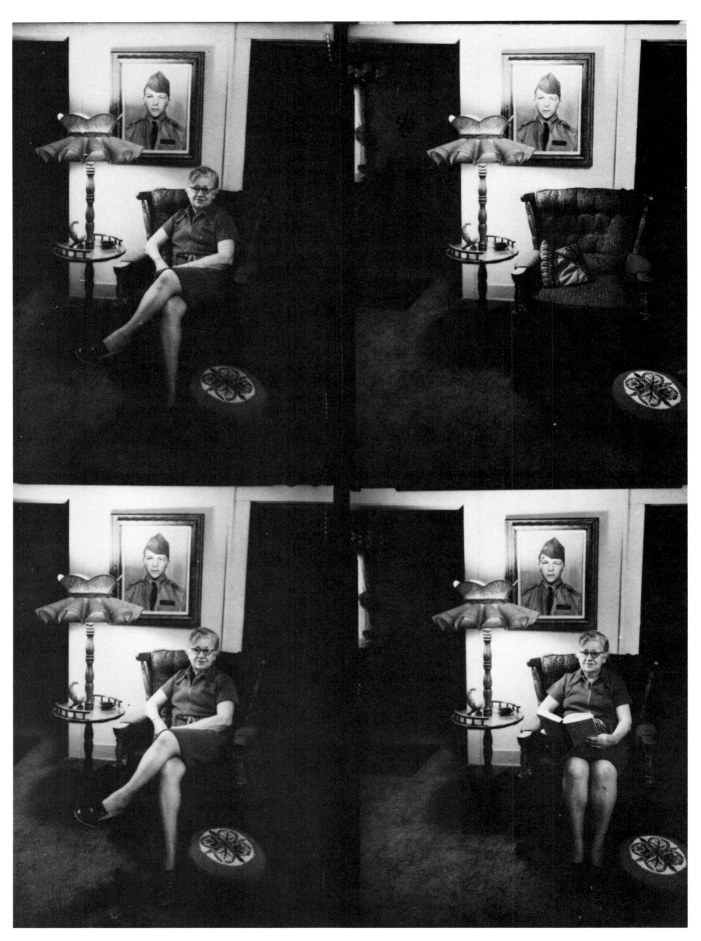

Mrs. Oswald. *Photography by Geoff Winningham (not the photographer mentioned in the story)*

publicity. Writers have described her as a ghoul. She has said she would like to sell Lee's gravestone. She is as briskly businesslike about her son's belongings as a medieval monk selling pieces of the True Cross. She has been married three times. Her second husband divorced her, saying she had knocked him about. Her third husband, Lee's father, died in 1964. William Manchester, no friend of the simple fact, described "her heavy jaw, knotted neck muscles, and face the colour of burnished pewter."

The homely countenance that peered through the door seemed flesh-colored to me. Her eyes do pop a little. Her neck seemed normal. Her house is modest, but pleasant. A little study is crowded with Oswald relics and the bulk of the 350 or so books written on the assassination. Also photos of Lee, and of Marina. A blackboard has chalked on it with deliberate, camera-catching provocation, "They are all making the same mistake." She lives alone, with two large dogs.

The photographer rose to the occasion. Separated momentarily from access to potential lays he threw himself into his role: the distinguished artist asking "as a *privilege*" for a few portraits. He sounded like a bishop saying his prayers. He said, truthfully, that he had photographed the Pope. He let her peer through the camera. He erected umbrellas, strobe lights. He clicked and clicked. Sweat poured off him, as Marguerite graciously inclined this way and that. She changed dresses. Still he clicked. I rejoiced. Even the BBC would be satisfied.

Marguerite Oswald speaks with the passion and truculence of a woman with very little money and only one asset. She is the mother of the man many people think shot the President.

"I am the strongest person in this tragedy, because I have lost everything. But Marguerite Oswald fights the powers. She's the one who speaks out. She believes there has been injustice. This woman [she tapped herself repeatedly] was left with no one and no money. Yet she took the bull by the horns and found a way to survive and support herself. Her attitude is correct, and she will rob Peter to pay Paul occasionally. And Marguerite Oswald *has* survived."

From an even tone her voice rose sharply. "I'm going to fix Mrs. Kennedy and the rest of them. The Kennedy family has known the truth, and they let this family suffer. I would like in this interview to say something controversial about the Kennedys. Mrs. Kennedy bothered me. She was . . . in front of me . . . no, that's not descriptive enough . . . it was as though she was there in person."

"Like a *ghost*? Or was this a dream?"

"No, I never dream. She was always on my mind, even though I had lots of work to do. When she remarried she disappeared entirely."

We moved from the study to the sitting room, where Mrs. Oswald has hung a reproduction of "Whistler's Mother." I asked her if she was persecuted. "I must be careful. They want me to say I'm persecuted so that they can say I'm a psycho, and that I only *think* I'm persecuted. This is what they do to me. The neighbors don't invite me in for coffee, even though I've had them in my house. But I've waited. I've waited ten long years and it's ready to break now. All I'm waiting for is the chance, the offer, to do my book.

"It's all in my book. Ten years everyone said Lee was a Communist, a defector. That's all changed now. If it had been a church man, or a politician of well known integrity would you have jumped to the conclusion that you had the right man. No, no, I said. It was only because he allegedly defected that they said he was the assassin. It took three years for the picture to change, for the critics to get into the Volumes."

The "Volumes" are the Warren Commission findings, which Mrs. Oswald has ever ready to hand. "Imagine *paying* for this trash." She seized a volume and started reading contradictory statements out of it. Her voice grew harsh and very loud.

"They're all scum. I know what they have, and if I know all this I *know* I can survive. They framed him so good, but I'll fix them in my book. That sustains me. I cry a lot. I can hardly pick up the 26 volumes without crying."

She read some more and as she read, tears trickled down from under her spectacles. Then she said in a rasping cry, "If I know all this I can survive. I never see my grandchildren. I want to go away . . . to write my book . . . I want to be free . . . I'm alive, I'd like to get out. I'm stuck here with no money and no friends. My life's not over. I'd like to disappear. Ten years has gone out of my life. I need to be taken out to dinner and dance. I'm not dead yet. I'm only 66. But I need the capital, and *I hold the cards*. Maybe a European publisher would like my book, so I could get away and be free."

For a moment, in the little house on the edge of Fort Worth, it seemed that we were interviewing Emma Bovary, the passion so strong: so bitter the tears. The photographer sweated thoughtfully in a corner, and then to lighten the fraught atmosphere we suggested some exterior pictures. Mrs. Oswald brightened. "The neighbors won't like it. But what the hell. I like you boys. I'll put on my disguise, like when I go out researching. My Jackie Kennedy disguise, with the headscarf."

She posed. He clicked. Then we made our goodbyes. "You see, I am the strongest," she said as we left. "I have nothing and I survive. Be sure and tell publishers I have the book. And I *know*. Because I am the mother of the man they say shot the President."

"She was terrific," I shouted down the line to the voice. "Worth a whole feature. Put her on the cover. Call it 'Mother of the Decade.'" The BBC voice brooded for a moment. Then it brightened. "Well, you've done your best, haven't you?"

*—November 1973*

*Photography by Harry Boyd*

# THE ENDLESS ODYSSEY OF PATRICK HENRY POLK

by Gary Cartwright

*The wanderings of a Texas family on the road to nowhere.*

Patrick Henry Polk III and his brood had been waiting six weeks for their welfare check. It was the worst winter anyone could remember. Henry Polk was 49, destitute, and disabled by a bad heart. He was a rock mason and cedar chopper by trade, though Henry acknowledged that he hadn't "hit a lick at a snake" in months. Piece by piece, he had sold his chain saw, then his tools, and finally his furniture to feed his wife and seven children. They had stuck him in a hospital in Stephenville and scared the fool out of him with that talk about putting a plastic valve on his heart. And that's when Henry Polk did the only thing he could think to do: he put his wife Cynthia and the seven children, ages 4 to 15, in their '67 Chrysler station wagon and he *hooked 'em*. For most of September and October, they lived in their station wagon, cooking and camping on creek banks, accepting handouts from churches and charitable agencies, sometimes stopping to visit relatives as they zigzagged through the cedar brakes of Chalk Mountain, Sipe Springs, Glen Rose, Valley Mills, Cranfills Gap, Lampasas, Marble Falls, and Liberty Hill, moving mostly south toward Austin, where Polk was born and lived most of his life.

By late October Henry was too sick to go on, and so was the baby, Kathy, who had a congenital heart condition. The transmission had fallen out of the station wagon, and they had traded it for a '67 Buick. By Thanksgiving Polk was in Brackenridge Hospital in Austin and Mrs. Polk had applied for welfare. Polk left the hospital a few days later, complaining that they wouldn't let him smoke. By now there was nothing to sell, so Polk and two relatives went down to Onion Creek to look for some fern that they could decorate with holly and sell for Christmas wreaths. Sliding down the creek bank, he felt the familiar flash of pain in his chest and stomach. "The Claw," he called it: just like that wrestler

*Gary Cartwright, author of books and numerous articles, recently won the Texas Institute of Letters award for journalism. He is a contributing editor of* Texas Monthly.

on TV. A week before Christmas Polk was back in the hospital and they were talking again about surgery. By now the family had received $336 in emergency food stamps, and social workers had helped them locate a four-bedroom house in South Austin that would be covered by a federal housing program. But the welfare check for $225 still hadn't arrived.

Damned if Henry Polk was going to spend another Christmas in a hospital. He didn't trust hospitals, or doctors, or the city of Austin for that matter. "You know that song, 'My Kinda Woman'?" he said. "Well, that's Austin to me. I know ever' pig trail in it. You take a woman and seven kids and turn 'em loose in this town with no protection, you just as well tell 'em to go jump off a cliff. I told the doctor that, but he never savvied what I was saying. He just wasn't wearing the right pair of shoes. Long as I can move my hands and feet, there ain't no way I'm gonna let 'em cut me open.

Over his doctor's objections, Polk checked himself out of Brackenridge and went home for Christmas. It was a good Christmas. A Baptist church furnished dinner for the Polks, and a Catholic church brought toys, clothing, and certificates for some groceries and a tank of gasoline. One of Henry Polk's older sisters, who lived a few blocks away, and some other cousins, nephews, nieces, and in-laws found enough used furniture to make the house livable, and Henry borrowed a hammer, saw, and nails from a neighbor and built a kitchen table from an old door and scrap lumber.

"We was all together, that was the thing," said Cynthia Polk. "It was like a miracle." At 32, having given birth to eight children and buried one, having survived two major operations of her own and enough trauma to fill a Russian novel, Cynthia Polk found miracles in the commonplace. She was a woman of faith, moxie, and country wit. When the kids bellyached about something they didn't have, the price of a movie for instance, she would turn it on them and say, "Gimme a dime's worth of dollars and you can keep the change.'' She was physically enormous—after the birth of her six-year-old, Jimmy Joe, or J.J. as he was called, her weight had soared and remained over 225 pounds—but she was amazingly pliable, good-humored, and in a rough way, pretty. Cynthia had married Henry Polk nineteen years ago, when she was thirteen.

On Christmas, as any other day, the Polks clustered together like immigrants in steerage. When they ate, they ate together at the large homemade table. When daddy and mama sat in the living room, the kids congregated there. When the older kids played outside, they checked in every few minutes, reporting on the whereabouts of each member of the family. Four-year-old Kathy, who had epilepsy as well as a heart condition, was seldom out of her mother's sight: the family rule was that she would never be left alone, not for a minute. ''If something was to happen to this baby,'' Cynthia said, ''they'd have to put me in the grave with her.''

Almost everyone in the family had medical problems. Lanette, the beautiful five-year-old with the blond ponytail and imp's grin, had a blood disease one doctor had diagnosed as leukemia. Henry Polk's mother spent $39 on a long-distance telephone call to Oral Roberts, and within a week, through the miracle of faith in Jesus and AT&T, she was pronounced cured. ''The doctor couldn't believe it,'' Cynthia said. ''He accused me of switching babies on him. No doctor cured that baby. It was the Lord.'' Colann, the thirteen-year-old, suffered from occasional convulsions; Cynthia Polk called it a form of epilepsy, though this had never been confirmed. Colann also had a hearing problem. Debby Sue, the brash, chubby eleven-year-old, needed glasses. Lanette needed dental work: her small teeth were already turning black. Billie Jean, the firstborn who would soon be sixteen, had diabetes, as did her mother and grandmother. Billie Jean had also inherited her mother's addiction for sweets and propensity for gaining large amounts of weight.

The two boys, Patrick Henry, Jr. (Buddy Boy), nine, and J. J., six, had inherited their father's ruddy, flinty Anglo features and reddish-blond hair. If you had to guess their genealogy, you would guess Welsh. You could almost see the two boys following their old man down into the coal mines somewhere in South Wales, their fair skin already permanently stained. Though their true origins were long misplaced, Henry Polk and his fourteen brothers and sisters grew up in south-central Texas, mainly in the Clarksville section of West Austin, a community of shacks, neighborhood stores, and churches founded more than a hundred years ago by newly freed slaves. His father was also named Patrick Henry Polk: the old man liked the name so much he named *two* of his sons Patrick Henry—II and III. Cynthia Polk, whose maiden name was Bates, grew up near Gatesville, the oldest girl in a family of eleven.

''We lived in a tent way back in the cedar brakes,'' she would tell her children, who never seemed to tire of the stories their parents told, of hardships endured, of values learned and embraced, of other Christmas days sown along incomprehensible distances and yet ripening before their eyes; there was no tone of embarrassment, no sense of shame or regret or doubt that the ways of their people had happy endings. ''Daddy would always run off, and pretty soon we'd be out of food. We'd look for armadillos or birds or wild onions, anything to eat. Mama was already sick

with cancer and the sugar diabetes, and granny was too old to be much help.''

''Hey, mama,'' Debby Sue would interrupt. ''Tell us again about the man in the truck that broke down and your granny smelling bacon.''

''Your granny always carried a broom,'' Colann prompted.

''Who's telling this story?'' Cynthia Polk barked at her daughters. The other children laughed. They loved their mother's bark, which was considerably worse than her bite. ''Oh, anyhow, we was out in the woods when all of a sudden granny throwed down that old broomstick she always carried and yelled out, 'I smell bacon!' We walked down to the road, and sure 'nuff there was this feller with a pickup load of groceries broke down. Hundred pound sacks of flour, sugar, beans, potatoes, bacon, everything you could think of. Mama said, 'Mister, if you'd like it, I'd be happy to fry you some of that bacon.' I guess he seen all us hungry kids, 'cause he said okay. So mama built a campfire and started fixing the bacon while us kids sneaked back and took some of the provisions from the truck and hid 'em in the woods. He knowed we'd done it right off, and mama said, 'Mister, I ain't gonna lie to you. My kids took them provisions 'cause they was hungry.' He let us keep what we already took, and the next day he come back with more groceries and mattresses and blankets and stuff we didn't even need.''

Cynthia would remember the first time she ever saw Henry Polk, her future husband. Henry had been married and divorced twice by then—he has five grown children and numerous grandchildren from his earlier marriages. Henry had drifted up around Valley Mills where Cynthia Bates was living and it was love at first sight. ''I was outdoors cutting wood,'' she recalled, ''and I looked over and seen him lift this car motor up all by hisself. He was built like a bull back then, back before he took sick. I told my mama, who was sitting on the porch shelling peas, 'I'm gonna marry that man there.' And sure 'nuff I did.''

When Cynthia told her daddy she wanted to marry Henry Polk, he volunteered to drive them to the courthouse. ''He said that would just be one less mouth to feed,'' Cynthia continued, not concealing her rancor. ''After we was married, Henry tried to help out mama and the kids. The last bottle of medicine my mama ever had, Henry bought it with his last ten dollars. When mama finally died, all eat up with cancer and the sugar diabetes, daddy took the nine kids who was still living at home and dropped 'em on the courthouse steps like you would a sack of puppies. We didn't know 'bout what he'd done for a few days. My Uncle Joe got there in time to 'dopt six of 'em. The other three we never saw again.''

''Back then people wasn't so bad off as they are now,'' Henry Polk cut in, stubbing the butt of his Camel on the bare wood floor of the living room. There were not yet any ashtrays and hardly any dishes in the house in South Austin, though ashtrays were not a habit Henry cultivated. ''Back then, we'd find us an abandoned filling station or somewhere and move in. I'd take that double-bit ax and cut me some cedar or post oak and sell 'em fifteen, twenty cents apiece. I was strong as a bull. I could cut wood all day long. When the weather was good, it weren't nothing to make twenty dollars a day.''

Christmas passed, and so did New Year, and as the Legislature convened to consider the problems of the state the Polks still had not received their first welfare check. They didn't know it, but the check was lost in the computer somewhere deep in the heart of the Department of Public Welfare (DPW) bureaucracy. This was partly the Polks' fault. From the time they first applied for welfare back in Stephenville, the family had left such a tangled trail that the DPW computer couldn't cope with their case.

# THE DOLE

Patrick Henry Polk and his brood are not the typical Texas welfare family, but they are a fairly typical poor family. Only a small percentage of the poor in Texas actually receive welfare. There are approximately 500,000 poor families in the state—that's *families*, not people—and only about 18 per cent of them will get any government aid this year. Contrary to prevailing myths, most poor Texans are not black or Chicano: the largest group—almost half—are like the Polks: Anglo-Saxon Protestant, nearly illiterate, and totally puzzled by the complexities of life in the 1970s. Polk is not their real name. I changed names and a few other details because that was the only way the family would agree to a series of interviews that would cover two months. But the Polks are not a composite: details of their case, their medical and social histories, their habits and lifestyle are as accurate as I could report them.

*Welfare* is one of those five-alarm words, like communist or rattlesnake, and is customarily followed by descriptive nouns such as chiseler and bum. You have no doubt heard that welfare recipients drive Cadillacs. The hard fact is, most welfare recipients are barely surviving. Members of an Austin women's club were asked recently to guess how much cash a mother and one child would receive from welfare each month. Guesses ranged from $200 to $500. The actual figure is $86—$24 for the child and $62 for the "caretaker." Only 325,000 Texans, 75 per cent of them children, receive cash payments, or the *dole* as it is sometimes cynically described. That's less than 3 per cent of the state's population. The program that administers the dole is called Aid to Families with Dependent Children (AFDC). The key word here is *children*, though this seems to confuse a lot of us taxpayers. Under the rigid standards set by the Texas Legislature, the only persons who receive welfare are children (and one caretaker) who have lost one or both parents, or (as in the Polks' case) are deprived of basic necessities because the father is disabled. What makes the Polks so rare among welfare recipients is that both parents are living at home. The size of their family and the total amount of cash assistance ($225 a month) place the Polks in the upper 1 per cent of the AFDC rolls.

The "average" AFDC family consists of a mother and two to three children. Daddy is either dead, deserted, or disabled. These children and their caretakers receive on average $32.06 a month (the national average is $72.35). That amounts to about $1 a day for shelter, clothing, laundry, utilities, and other necessities. Twenty to 30 per cent of that $1 goes for the purchase of food stamps, which are not accepted for household items such as soap, detergents, and toilet paper—not to mention cigarettes, beer, or wine. Very few AFDC recipients live in public housing. All AFDC recipients automatically qualify for free medical care

under Medicaid, which in terms of simple survival is far more important than actual cash. If the youngest child is older than five years, the mother is automatically enrolled in a work-training program and in most cases quickly returned to the labor force. The caretaker mother is allowed to deduct job-related expenses from her salary (usually about 30 per cent), but if her bottom line exceeds $86 a month, the mother and child are dropped from AFDC and, after a grace period of ninety days, from Medicaid. The myth of the dole as a permanent gravy train finally collapses when you realize that the average income of a Texas family receiving both AFDC and food stamps is barely half the official poverty level of $5500 for a nonfarm family of four. Hardly your Cadillac crowd. Old Buicks and Oldsmobiles are more like it.

The actual payment to a specific family is calculated by an AFDC caseworker using a sliding scale based on 1969 cost-of-living figures. Because of inflation, the cost of living has increased 56 per cent since 1969, but in the case of AFDC the Legislature has found it politically expedient to ignore this. *Except* for AFDC none of the other 28 programs administered by DPW has gone a single year without a cost-of-living increase. Once the caseworker has calculated the "needs" of the family, the next step is to cut that figure by 25 per cent. The philosophy here is that if the state pays a family less than it "needs" somebody in the family will have to go to work. Even though 75 per cent of the AFDC recipients are *children*, the incentive theory is championed by demagogues and embraced by lawmakers as an excuse to maintain AFDC payments below subsistence levels. "Incentive," says Bill Clayton, Speaker of the Texas House of Representatives, "is the only way we have to break the poverty cycle. Anytime you get support payments to a high level, you discourage incentive." The major flaw in this theory is that by no stretch of the imagination can $1 a day be considered *high level*. More than half the adults living in poverty in Texas are already working full time: they just don't earn enough (the Texas minimum wage is $1.40) to make ends meet. In fact, the incentive is to *stay* on the dole, if for no other reason than to qualify for Medicaid.

There is a technical but highly revealing factor in the Legislature's gut reaction to the Department of Public Welfare. It's not welfare that inspires the sanctimonious preachings in the state house, it's the dole. Welfare in fact embraces dozens of local, state, and federal programs that touch the daily lives of two million Texans (one in six) and cost $2 billion a year—but only $125 million ($92 million of it paid by the federal government) is mailed out each year to AFDC families. When you consider who controls all that money, and where it goes, the incentive theory takes on a new light.

Roughly one-fourth of that $2 billion passes through the cash registers of the grocery stores, then filters down to distributors, processors, teamsters, farmers, and ranchers. "The food stamp program," says a DPW executive, "is heavily supported by the food industry. In fact, it's an industry *subsidy* program." Doctors, pharmacists, hospitals, and nursing homes pocket an enormous share of welfare money. "The strongest lobby in Texas, except maybe the highway lobby, is the nursing home lobby," an executive at DPW claims. "The last Legislature actually gave us *more* than we requested for nursing homes. The figure goes up every year—it'll reach about $436 million by 1978. This doesn't mean the patients are getting more benefits; it simply means the nursing homes are getting more money.'' Welfare in fact is a gigantic public industry controlled largely by special-interest groups.

"The reason AFDC is so unpopular," the DPW executive continued, "is that there isn't any interest group that can control it. It's cash, and it goes directly to the client. It's the only program where the client makes the decision what to do with it."

"I think one reason our welfare rolls are declining is it's easier to get a job in Texas than in most other states," says John Frannea, chief of management assistance at the Department of Public Welfare. "They don't pay very much, but you can get them. It's not the purpose of DPW to compete with the job market—nobody wants that—but we're not even close." Frannea points out that 80 per cent of those being added to welfare rolls are coming on for the first time. On average, a welfare family drops from the rolls after eleven months. "There are few recidivists," Frannea adds. "What this means is that once you've had the experience [of welfare], you don't want it again. There's not much to come back to." Dr. Victor Bach, an expert on urban studies at UT-Austin's LBJ School of Public Affairs, is even more blunt: "The reason there is a low welfare fraud rate in Texas is because it doesn't pay even if you get away with it."

In light of the 56 per cent inflation since 1969, the DPW recommended that the current Legislature increase daily payments from $1 to $1.23—or about $7 a month for each member of the family. The Legislative Budget Board, composed of the Speaker of the House, the Lieutenant Governor, and eight ranking members of the Legislature, rejected the request. With Dolph Briscoe also four-square against it, there seems little chance the increase will be approved.

# THE LONG WAIT

It was the middle of January, and the Polks still hadn't received their welfare check. Henry was getting cabin fever. There was nothing to do with his hands and no way to explain, much less stop, the grinding of time. He had become a statistic. While the kids watched the fuzzy old black-and-white TV set rented from the Seven-Eleven, and mama worked the sewing machine altering hand-me-down jeans and shirts, Henry cut little windows in a piece of cardboard and rolled it into a tube. "What's that, daddy?" Debby Sue asked. "Nothing," he said forlornly, tossing it aside.

"The worst thing I ever did was sell that chain saw," he said.

"Now daddy, don't talk like that," Cynthia said. "We needed the money. 'Sides, that kinda work would kill you now."

"When you get sick," he said, "that's the end of the hump."

Henry remembered that his daddy used to make chairs of green willow and lariats of binder's twine. Henry was thinking of getting himself some binder's twine. Maybe he'd look around for some green willow, though he hadn't seen much willow since they cut the MoPac Expressway through Clarksville. Most of the cedar was gone, too. His daddy had a stationary buzz saw, powered by running a belt around the rear wheel of a '33 Ford, and Henry remembered how they used to pile overlapping layers of cedar posts in a mound, cover the mound with sod and cook it slowly until they had charcoal. They would use the sawdust for fertilizer, and the kids would sell the charcoal from door to door. They hunted coons and rabbits in what would later be called Tarrytown, now a quiet neighborhood of large homes and walled estates. There was always something to do, something to hope for. There were stories of Comanche gold hidden in the caves along the Colorado River, and Henry's daddy claimed there were nine jackloads of Mexican silver buried near the Old Confederates Home, which stood on the southern edge of Clarksville.

Although Clarksville had started as a settlement for newly freed slaves, many poor white families had come later, and by the time Henry and his brothers, sisters, and cousins were growing up, the community was comfortably integrated, making it unique in Austin and probably anywhere else in Texas. "We played and fought with the niggers just like they was our own," Henry said. "There was two old ex-slave ladies, Aunt Eady and Aunt Jenny Moe, lived just down the street from our place. My daddy used to make us call all old folks uncle or aunt no matter what color they was. He said it didn't sound right to call 'em mister or missus. It was unrespectful." In the evenings they used to sit under the large live oak in front of Aunt Eady's frame shanty, which was about the same size and construction as their own place down the block. Aunt Eady would tell about the time of slavery, and about her white folks' pet parrot that would rat on her when she would sneak food from the kitchen or neglect her chores.

"When her white people would leave the house they'd let this parrot out of his cage so he could foller Aunt Eady around and tell on her, then when they come home they'd whup her. But one time they forgot. They left the ol' parrot caged up where the nigger could reach him. 'Nigger gonna get rid of ol' polly parrot,' Aunt Eady said, and the parrot started crying, 'Oh, please, nigger, don't!' But Aunt Eady taken the parrot and socked him in a pot of boiling water, then put him back in the cage like nothing happened, and she never got no more whuppings."

Obie Polk, Henry's older brother, would sometimes drop by the house in South Austin; and—when he wasn't working—so would their cousin, Jake Polk. While Cynthia and the two oldest girls cooked, the men would sit around the kitchen table playing forty-two and talking and drinking strong black coffee. As a young man, Henry had done his share of hooting and drinking—the self-administered tattoo of a spraddle-legged naked woman on his left biceps was a living souvenir of one AWOL bender thirty years ago—but now he was pretty much limited to coffee and cigarettes. He wouldn't want this to get back to his old lady, Henry said in a low voice across the table, but having intercourse, or even urinating, "hurts like somebody cut you between the legs with a hot knife." Doctors at Audie Murphy Veterans Hospital in San Antonio had removed a malignancy from his left testicle two years ago. "They said they cut out the cancer," Henry said, "but I think they just spread it around." Cynthia knew about the claw, of course, but the hot knife in his scrotum was a secret Henry intended to keep among the men. The men nodded. They understood these things. It was like when Cynthia's younger sister's husband put a shotgun in his mouth and pulled the trigger: the men swore it was an accident, even though everyone knew he was dying from cancer.

Jake Polk, who was in his late fifties, earned his living digging, hauling, and laying rocks. He was a rock mason, as opposed to a rock cobbler. "The difference is, a rock mason has to know what he's doing," Jake explained. Henry also took pride in the fact he was a rock mason and regretted that he hadn't gone on to be a brick mason. For reasons that were not clear, Henry never mastered brick masonry. "But there's none better at rocks," he said. "All I gotta do is hang a string from each corner and get after it." Obie Polk, who was two years older than Henry, had never mastered rock or even learned to figure square feet and was something of an outcast. Obie suffered from emphysema and chronic bronchitis and hadn't worked since he loaded watermelons in Weatherford last summer. Obie was a tall, very skinny scarecrow of a man who would have been in a veteran's hospital except for the misfortune of having deserted the Army in 1945. Since Obie had no children to qualify for welfare, he ate and slept wherever he could.

Of the three men at the kitchen table, only Jake Polk was physically able to hold a steady job and now that it was the dead of winter even Jake was idle. So they spent the long afternoons around Henry's kitchen table, talking about rock, about where to buy a rebuilt carburetor, about what they hated most in the Army was saluting, and about mistakes in judgment that might explain their dilemma. Jake remembered the old black man who used to sit on the steps of the Sweet Home Baptist Church and ramble for hours about how someday there would be an expressway right through Clarksville. It would be years before they got around to building MoPac, but the old black man was right about it coming. In time the city would appraise the land in MoPac's projected path at $2000 a lot, peanuts compared to its potential worth. Maybe if Henry's daddy had sold out in time. But he didn't. "The city come and took our homestead for $640 back taxes," Henry said. "Somebody got rich, but it sure wasn't us."

I had been around the Polks for more than a week now, and the hardluck stories had become routine. It wasn't just Henry and his brood: there were brothers, sisters, cousins, in-laws so numerous I couldn't count much less record them, and almost every one of them was a medical and social disaster. When they weren't talking about money they didn't have or hospitals that wouldn't have them, they talked about cancer and bleeding sores and broken hearts and faulty transmissions and relief checks that were nonexistent. When I first knew him, Henry Polk couldn't bring himself to say the word welfare—he called the DPW "those people down there"—but by now the family accepted my presence and even seemed to share a measure of relief that someone from the outside was there to listen. I gradually came to see them as a tribe, a clan of people who had never joined the mainstream culture or had the least desire to. They were almost all cedar choppers and/or rock masons. They worked for cash or sometimes for the cedar itself, which they would sell after clearing land for some developer. They had never belonged to a union or paid Social Security or graduated from a school or had a title. They had never voted, and some of them had never thought of filing an income tax return.

Many of them were unemployed, but only a few qualified for unemployment since they had never worked for anyone except themselves. The ones who were old and disabled like

Troy Tucker and his wife Sara lived on food stamps and Supplemental Security Income (SSI), a federal program for the needy who couldn't qualify for Social Security or state welfare. As in the case of unemployment insurance, only people who have paid into the program are eligible for Social Security. A few of them, such as Cynthia's sister (whose husband died from the shotgun blast), drew AFDC. Almost all of them were eligible for food stamps, but some hadn't got around to applying and others simply refused. Jake Polk never said it out loud, but you could tell that he'd rather die than accept welfare. At one time in his life, Henry Polk must have shared that aversion. Even now, when he heard someone bellyaching, Henry would say: "If you look around, you'll always see somebody worse off than you. God didn't make everybody to be rich. It would be a dull world if everybody was the same."

The house in South Austin, once so government-issue sterile, was gradually taking on personality. Cynthia found some patches of cloth and sewed curtains. One of those velvet bullfighter paintings that you see in Mexican border towns appeared on the wall in the living room. Henry constructed a coffee table from some pieces of plate glass found in the city dump. They got an old king-size mattress and box springs from Goodwill. The two little girls, Kathy and Lanette, shared a cot at the foot of their parents' bed, the three older girls shared a second bedroom, and the two boys slept in the dining room (although the house was supposed to have four bedrooms, the two rooms at the back weren't heated). Apparently the Polks weren't familiar with thermostats, or maybe they were cold-natured—whatever the case, the house was always uncomfortably hot and smelled of used lard and burned sugar. Spectacular amounts of trash accumulated. Billie Jean and Colann swept the kitchen and living room two and sometimes three times a day, and still the floor was littered with crushed candy canes, spilled milk, partly eaten sandwiches, chicken bones, and cigarette butts.

Cynthia Polk had measured out the food stamps carefully, loading up initially on staples like sugar, flour, potatoes, and lard, then falling back on a lifetime habit of planning and shopping one day at a time. While the food stamps lasted, there was always meat or chicken, always fried. Every meal included potatoes, beans, and cake. (Henry's favorite meal was red beans and chocolate cake, mixed together.) Nobody in the family liked tomatoes or lettuce, and they weren't big on fruit either. In the afternoons when the kids came home from school, Cynthia would drive them to the bakery outlet and treat them to day-old fried pies, purchased ten for 99 cents. There was one particular supermarket that the Polks visited daily, the chain that sponsored the TV sweepstakes show called *Let's Go to the Races*. Cynthia would select four or five items, then they would each head to a different checkout line, thereby multiplying their allotment of sweepstakes cards. On Friday nights, Cynthia and the kids would gather in front of the TV and cheer home their horses.

Henry thought this was foolish. Henry's motto was to "believe half of what you see and none of what you hear." It was like the stories about the Mexican silver and Comanche gold. He'd never seen any of it. He had crawled inside every cave along the west bank of the Colorado River and he had never seen any gold. He remembered one cave in particular. It was located straight across the river from the old Deep Eddy grocery store near Clarksville. Henry, Obie, and Troy Tucker discovered it one day as they were hauling rocks across on a rubber raft. In his memory the cave was large as a house, and right in the center, partially covering a seemingly bottomless well lined with cedar posts, was an enormous boulder. The ceiling of the cave was black, suggesting ancient tribal fires. He thought about this cave. He thought about it a lot.

"One of these days," he told his two boys, "we'll go look for it."

# IN THE TRENCHES

**M**arie McAdoo was one of twenty-one AFDC caseworkers assigned to the DPW's Austin office. Each caseworker was responsible for 95 cases. Though she thought of herself as a social worker, her official title was Welfare Service Technician II, the bureaucratic way of saying that her monthly salary was fixed at $820. In a few months she was scheduled for promotion to Public Welfare Worker I, and though her duties would remain the same, her salary would increase to $876. That's tops for a full-time caseworker in this state. Considering their qualifications and work load, DPW's social and clerical workers are among the lowest paid state employees. Many of them are teachers who couldn't find a teaching job. Few started out to be social workers. They majored in math, English, history, economics, in the subjects and skills that the market has little use for. The workers who deal in the food stamps and AFDC programs are the most overworked and the most criticized. "Nobody in those two programs has a good job," says a DPW executive. "Their work load is staggering. They come in daily contact with people who have very serious problems. Quality control is always looking over their shoulder, just like a factory. It's not surprising that they don't last too long." Marie was an exception. She had been with DPW for more than three years and she liked her job. Before joining DPW Marie taught grade school and worked with retarded teenagers. She's 48, a grandmother, and a compulsive problem solver. Her husband makes a good income as manager of an insurance company, but Marie works because she enjoys it.

When Marie first learned of the Polks in early December, the family was camped on Slaughter Creek. She contacted them by telephoning one of Polk's sisters, and an interview was arranged. "The immediate problem was to get them food," she recalled later. "They were down to one can of lard." Normally, emergency food stamps can be obtained in two or three days, but there was a technical problem. Rules set down by the federal Department of Agriculture, which funds the food stamp program (DPW only administers it), require that a family have cooking facilities, and a campfire along Slaughter Creek didn't qualify. Marie requisitioned groceries from the Travis County Department of Human Services, from a church, and from the goodwill of another social worker who was quitting and requested that her fellow workers donate food instead of throwing a going-away party.

Then she contacted David Keene, administrator of the HUD-funded Austin Housing Authority—known in the industry as Section 8. Section 8 is a federal program designed as an alternative to the dreary public housing projects that were in vogue during the Great Society of Lyndon Johnson.

Poor people who qualify are allowed to find low-cost rent property in whatever section of town suits their needs. If the house satisfies government standards, payments are made directly to the landlord. The program is confidential. Since even a next-door neighbor would have no way of knowing that rent was subsidized by Section 8, there is no stigma. It is a very simple, direct program that helps both landlords and poor people and involves a minimum of red tape. The catch is there are never enough suitable houses to go around. In the case of the Polk family, a four- or five-bedroom house was required. But David Keene's office only had allocations for 31 four-bedroom homes. Maybe it *was* a miracle, as Mrs. Polk insisted: at any rate, the Polks located the frame house a few blocks from Polk's sister, and on December 13, after the landlord made some minor repairs, the family moved in.

Now that they had a roof over their heads and cooking facilities, the Polks immediately became eligible for emergency food stamps. Since their application for AFDC had yet to be approved, the food stamps they received were classified as Non-Public Assistance (NPA), which is not to be confused with Public Assistance (PA) food stamps, which go automatically to AFDC recipients. What it meant was that Mrs. Polk paid only $36 for $336 worth of stamps. Later, when their first AFDC check arrived, they would pay $108 for the same amount of stamps. If the Polks came across any additional income, they would pay more.

Meanwhile, Marie McAdoo was pursuing the Polks' case through reams of paperwork. Before their odyssey, the Polks had applied for welfare in Stephenville. For their new application to be accepted, the old one had to be denied in order to "clean the computer." The Stephenville office of DPW had forwarded the Polks' records, but the file was stacked up somewhere in the Christmas mail rush. Marie had verified from her interview that the Polks needed immediate help, but first she had to get Henry Polk's medical records from Brackenridge Hospital. That required a written release. On December 18, she carried a release form to the hospital, but Polk's doctor was out Christmas shopping. She telephoned again two days later, and nobody at the hospital could find the release form. She took a second release form to Brackenridge. She called again on December 23. She was told that the release had been signed, but they couldn't find it. "I told them this was an emergency, so they looked again." Late that afternoon they finally located the form—it had been sent by mistake to the children's section. By the time she got her hands on the release form all state offices had shut down until December 28. It was January 6 before all the records arrived.

By then, Marie had enrolled Colann, Debby Sue, Buddy Boy, and J. J. in school. Billie Jean, who was almost sixteen and had never lived in one place long enough to get past the ninth grade, couldn't be registered until March. Billie Jean wasn't really interested in going back to school. Marie suggested several alternate programs through which Billie Jean could learn a trade. Billie Jean had bad memories of her last encounter with education. When they were living in Lipan, a small community north of Stephenville, she enrolled in a vocational agriculture course and they wanted her to castrate a calf. If that was education, they could have it. Henry and Cynthia Polk didn't encourage Billie Jean. The parents shared an inborn distrust of education, maybe because they feared it would break up their tight family structure. To them children were assets, not too unlike horses and cows. This wasn't cynical or cruel, merely practical: when their own time came years ago both Henry and Cynthia supported their dying parents; now the cycle was being repeated and it would be their children's turn. There were also moral implications. It was Henry's experience that "all schools are good for is sex and dope," and that wasn't what they wanted for their children. Although Billie Jean was already three years older than her mother had been when she married Henry, the girl had never been allowed to date or attend socials.

On January 6, Marie McAdoo filled out DPW Form 1-A, which in most cases goes straight to the computer keypunch operator. But in cases of "medical incapacity" the form must first be approved by the state office. Henry's medical report confirmed his chest pains as angina and myocardial infarction, and indicated it might be necessary to implant a valve to control the flow of blood through the heart. A week after Marie McAdoo completed DPW Form 1-A, the application was approved and sent to the computer where, for reasons no human could explain, it "bounced."

In mid-January, Marie McAdoo had been transferred from "financial needs" to "social services." "I guess you could say that what I'm doing now is dealing with physical instead of financial needs," she explained one afternoon when I dropped by the welfare office in South Austin. "Things like housing, health service—a lot of it is advice and counseling. A *lot* of it is just listening. The people I deal with have such tremendous problems they just need to talk to someone." There were two phones in Marie's tiny office, both ringing at once. Welfare workers joke that the only time the telephones are silent is when *As the World Turns* is on TV. There is a chaotic undercurrent in their work, a rumble like you feel in your legs when a subway train is approaching, an apprehension that an orderly world is only an illusion that protects our sanity. There is always a big rush on welfare after a holiday. One Social Security worker explained: "That's when old-timers sit around the stove and talk about their Social Security checks." It's the same when the weather is bad and arthritis acts up, or when there is an unexpected freeze and thousands of migrant citrus pickers are suddenly out of work. I noticed a mysterious sack of canned goods on the floor by Marie McAdoo's desk, but she didn't volunteer to explain it and I didn't ask.

Jean Bundrant, another social worker who had dropped by Marie's office to deposit two cans of turnip greens in the sack, told me: "Basically, people on welfare do not handle routine things the way you and I do. They don't think in terms of records or forms or programs. It doesn't occur to them to telephone and say they are moving. Right now I'm waiting to interview a mildly retarded woman with two kids. This is the seventh appointment I've set up for her and she's missed them all. Usually, after three times, the application is automatically denied."

"They need an advocate, someone to hear their problems and help solve them," Marie said. "If they can't find their way to Section 8, you take them. If they have problems with the landlord, you try to work it out for them. There are some doctors and pharmacists who won't accept Medicaid because of the red tape, so you help them find a doctor or pharmacist who will."

Sometimes the good intentions backfire. Welfare is so complex and so overweighted with conflicting rules and regulations that only a fool or a politican would pretend to understand it. Businessmen employ platoons of attorneys and accountants to deal with government red tape. Welfare recipients must face it essentially alone.

Jean Bundrant said that what really bothered her was people talking about welfare chiselers and Cadillacs and scrubby hippies on food stamps. Veda Douglas, a Medicaid worker who had come in to drop two cans of vegetable soup in the sack, offered a real case: "The husband had a job paying $600 a month. His wife had to go to a nursing home, which cost $650 a month. Welfare couldn't pay for the nursing home because the income limit in this case is $557.80. This means any kind of income—salary, retirement, Social Security, VA, trust funds."

"It gets very frustrating," Veda Douglas continued. "Every day we see people who need help and can't get it. If we're in the business of helping, we ought to help."

When I couldn't stand it any longer, I asked about the sack of canned goods. Marie McAdoo handed me a clipping from a local newspaper. It told the saga of Slim and Pearl, an elderly couple existing on $38 a month from veteran's disability. Slim should have been eligible for Social Security, except his birth certificate was destroyed in a Colorado courthouse fire. Slim had mailed off $18 trying to get a duplicate, but for some reason it hadn't arrived. The shack where they lived had just been condemned. They were hungry. "If I just had four dollars," Slim said, "I could get me a fishing license and catch some fish." The sack of goods was for Slim and Pearl. Marie McAdoo intended to pay for the fishing license herself. In the two months that I spent hanging around welfare, this went on all the time. People so sensitive somehow coped with human misery in a system so insensitive. And yet almost every social worker I spoke with defended DPW as doing the best it could with what it had. I wondered many times what would happen if you brought the governor and every member of the Legislature down here to the trenches. But that would never happen: political slogans can't deal with specifics.

# MANIFEST DESTINY

It's hard to choose an exact date when Henry Polk became a social problem, but Henry would pick sometime about 1968, when he found the Lucifer bracelet. They were living out on Bluff Springs Road south of Austin, and things looked pretty good. They had collected two goats, three meat hogs, and 175 chickens, and there was plenty of work in the Hill Country cutting cedar or laying rocks. Cynthia, who was pregnant with Buddy Boy, still had an attractive figure. Life had hope and harmony.

Henry found the Lucifer bracelet while digging for worms in the backyard. As he recalls, the bracelet was a devil's head of pure silver with black ruby eyes. A small wooden cross was bound by twine across the devil's face. "I didn't know it at the time, but the Spanish lady next door had tooken it away from her boy and buried it. She had bounded up the devil with that cross. Anyhow, the bracelet was pretty, so I took to wearing it." Looking back on it now, Henry could see that God was punishing him for his backsliding ways. In those days, Jesus frequently spoke to Henry Polk. A few days earlier Henry had been "called" to preach in the Pentecostal church. When it came time to preach his first sermon, God told Henry to wing it. God's exact message, as Henry recalled, was "open your mouth and I will put in the words." As Henry approached the altar there was a great gust of wind from the north and the Bible pages blew open to Matthew 21:31. In a strange voice Henry read: "Jesus saith unto them, Verily I say unto you, That the publicans and the harlots go into the kingdom of God before you." What did that mean? Henry told his flock: "Harlots means whore, and publicans . . . that's like 'Publicans and Democrats. Like senators and governors and hypocrites."

Later, Henry learned to speak in tongues. He took credit for a few modest miracles. The redemption of his nephew, for one. The boy was a disbeliever, so Henry asked the Lord to "not hurt him but scare him a little." That night as the nephew was sleeping on a mattress on the floor "a great ball of fire come rolling through the window" and there appeared Lucifer himself, fire in his eyes and carrying a pitchfork. The next day the boy joined the church. Not long after that, another nephew got in a bit of trouble—police arrested him for robbing a grocery store and shooting the owner. "They was asking the death penalty," Cynthia Polk recalled, "but Henry and his sister got down on their knees and the Lord spared him." His nephew is now doing five–to–ninety-nine.

Anyway, at the time of the Lucifer bracelet, Henry hadn't exactly turned his back on the Lord, but he was standing sideways. Then bad things started happening. His dog jumped through a plate glass window. The son of the Spanish lady next door ran away, then her house burned down. There were weevils in the cornmeal. Henry got another cross and buried the bracelet where he found it, but the bad luck didn't stop. Henry wrecked his car and almost killed himself. One night the Polks came home and found seventeen chickens dead. "We thought the dogs done it," Cynthia said. "We put the dogs in a sack and took 'em out to the country and dumped 'em, and when we come back more chickens was kilt. We discovered it was a polecat done it. We shoulda knowed by the way the chickens was scalped."

Buddy Boy was born healthy, but in 1970 Cynthia gave birth to another boy who was named Oral Roberts Polk. The baby had a bad color and his head seemed too small for his body. He had trouble breathing. Cynthia recalled, "Henry told me right from the start, 'Don't get attached to that 'un, 'cause God never meant him to be raised.' I couldn't believe God just let me borrow him. But one morning when he was a few months old I woke up, saw blood coming from the baby's nose. When I felt him, he was cold as a bucket of ice. We was living then with Henry's cousin Jake and his wife Dora and I screamed, but it weren't no use. I knowed there was a Jonah where we was, and there wasn't nothing nobody could do."

Shortly after they buried the baby, the Polks got together with two of Henry's cousins and their families and reached a decision to move to California. Jake Polk, who was ten years older than Henry, had heard there were millions of acres of wood to be cut in the Sierra Madres west of Bakersfield. Jake and Dora Polk had saved a little money. Their kids were all grown and Jake had bought an Army surplus truck large enough to carry their belongings. Henry bought a 1955 green-and-white Olds from a used car lot on East Second. Cousin Woodrow Polk, along with his wife Betty Frank and their four kids, had an old Ford Ranch

Wagon that the men put in shape. Everything they couldn't carry they sold.

In the spring of 1970, while the bodies of Vietnamese civilians were floating down the Mekong and Richard Nixon was pushing for the confirmation of G. Harrold Carswell to the Supreme Court, the Polk clan set out on a migration that could have happened during the Great Depression. U.S. troops would invade Cambodia and four students would be shot to death at Kent State, but the Polks didn't know it. H. Ross Perot, who had accumulated a fortune of $1.5 billion selling computer time, had chartered a 707 which would fly halfway around the world without reaching its destination in Hanoi, and Woodrow Polk, who had won a Purple Heart in Korea, would sell his broken-down Ford wagon for $50 in Cordes, Arizona. Henry Polk's Olds used half a tank of gas getting up one side of Salt River Canyon, and on the down side the brakes failed. Henry saved the family by bumping against the rear of Jake's truck until they could grind down the canyon to safety. Dandelion soup and organic brown rice were big among movie stars and wealthy faddists in Southern California, and that wasn't too different from what the Polks ate.

Like thousands of migrants before them, the Polks soon experienced the nightmare of California. "You couldn't buy a job," Henry Polk recalled. "The unions had everything locked up." A procurer who worked for a collective of growers still holding out against César Chávez' United Farm Workers union found the Polks destitute in Delano and gave them enough money to reach the fields. For the next three months the Polks picked tomatoes, strawberries, grapefruit, grapes, peaches. "It was like a concentration camp, only it wasn't," Henry recalled. "But you had to do what they said. We lived in little cabins right by the orchards. They'd shake us out at 3:30 in the morning so we could get in eight hours before noon when it got too hot to work." They were paid 22 cents a box for strawberries and 30 cents a box for peaches. The Polks had no way of knowing that César Chávez had just negotiated a contract that would pay farm workers $1.80 an hour, plus 20 cents a box, plus medical benefits. "We'd take the kids out to the orchards with us," Cynthia recalled. "They'd play under the trees while we picked fruit. When it was dinner time we'd build a fire and cook what we had. The grape people was the best. They give us all the free grapes we wanted," Henry said. "We had a hell of a time just keeping from starving that summer. Don't let nobody tell you that money grows on trees in California."

In the late fall of 1970, cold and broke and dispirited, the Polks headed home to Texas. Henry's Olds broke down and had to be abandoned near White Mountain, New Mexico. For the remainder of the trip all fourteen members of the Polk clan rode in Jake's truck. Colann and Debby Sue got whooping cough. When their food supply was down to a few overripe grapes and a little oatmeal, they sold their fishing poles and mattresses. "I happened to tell this woman in New Mexico about the baby dying and she give us a tank of gas and $135 in groceries," Cynthia remembered. "Otherwise, I don't know how we woulda made it home."

Over the next several years the Polks spent a good deal of time moving, looking for wood to cut or rocks to lay. J. J. was born, then Lanette, then Kathy. Lanette got lead poisoning from eating paint. Kathy was born with a heart murmur caused by a defective valve. Fluid had to be pumped from her chest every six months. Jesus still talked to Henry from time to time. "Sometimes He just told me to hook 'em," Henry said. It was Jesus who finally pointed the way to welfare.

Periodic entries in the Polks' thick dossier at the Department of Public Welfare describe what happened after that:

GRANBURY, May 1972—This was the Polks' first encounter with welfare. A DPW caseworker wrote: "Mrs. Polk says that she has been separated four months from her husband Henry. States she doesn't know where he lives. He comes around about once a month to see the seven children and leave $10." Mrs. Polk's application for AFDC in the amount of $146 is approved. She is also granted "commodities." Food stamps weren't available in Texas until the fall of 1973. When her case was next reexamined, additional AFDC payments were denied. The record does not reflect the reason for the denial.

GRANBURY, September 1973—Henry has obviously returned to the fold because this time he is the one who has applied for AFDC, claiming disability because of a bad knee resulting from his car wreck in 1968. The doctor who examined Henry wrote: "This patient's environmental background is poor and he has adapted inadequately to society and is very poorly motivated to improve." The doctor recommended x-rays to the right knee. The heart is listed as "normal." On September 9, the caseworker reported that "this applicant is healthy. He does not appear to meet the agency definition of AFDC incapacity." Application denied.

ROCKWALL, December 1973—Cynthia Polk has applied for welfare. Henry is hospitalized in Dallas with bleeding hemorrhoids. The hemorrhoid operation proves satisfactory, but doctors then discover "a mass in the left testicle." It is diagnosed as "a benign retention cyst." Polk also complains of chest pains. The report states that in the last five months Polk has earned only $278, and that his medical bills are enormous. (The law allows payment of medical bills back to ninety days from the date of the application.) AFDC payments of $245 and food stamps are approved, subject to reexamination on March 1. In another month the federal government will take over all cash-assistance programs except AFDC: the baby, Kathy, who is permanently disabled because of her heart condition, will be eligible for Supplementary Security Income (SSI) checks of $167.80 per month. The Polks don't yet know this, but little Kathy's SSI checks will keep the family going for the next three years.

GRANBURY, May 1974—Polk still complains of chest pains. An appointment is made with a Granbury doctor who will do "an EKG, chest x-ray, and upper G.I." The record shows that Polk never showed up for the appointment.

GRANBURY, July 1974—Cynthia Polk reports that her husband is working again and requests that they be dropped from AFDC rolls. Request approved.

SAN ANTONIO, May 1975—Polk is receiving outpatient care at the Audie Murphy Veterans Hospital. Cancer cells have been found in his testicles.

STEPHENVILLE, August 1976—Mrs. Polk has again applied for AFDC and food stamps. She complains that her husband has "heart trouble" and is hospitalized. The actual medical report is sketchy. A doctor wrote: "Patient complains that he needs to go home to take care of his daughter, Kathy. He seems more concerned with his daughter than his own condition." The doctor suggests heart surgery may be required.

AUSTIN, December 1976—A medical report states: "Chest pains are not brought on by anything particular but exertion definite problem." The diagnosis is "Angina and recent inferior M.I." Application approved.

# GREAT EXPECTATIONS

As January slogged on and the welfare check still hadn't arrived, Henry had a bad case of the *ol' hook 'em blues*. In his depression, he had almost forgotten the claw. This was worse, much worse. The cash from Kathy's December SSI check had completely run out. So had the food stamps. "I can just feel it running all the way through me," he said. "I'm gonna have to make a move. I'm gonna have to do something." Cynthia was unequivocally in favor of hooking 'em back to Lipan, money or not. Kathy's condition appeared to be deteriorating: all day Kathy would sleep in her mother's lap, and all night she would cry. Cynthia had it in her mind that the girl would do better in the country. Cynthia purely hated Austin by now. "The only people I know here are Henry's relatives," she complained. "And the prices here—they'd stop anything. Eggs, ninety cents a dozen. Back home in Lipan you can go to Chicken City and buy a dozen cracked eggs for forty cents. You can get bacon on sale, fifteen pounds for $11.50." Cynthia had a hankering to see her sister, who was consoling the grief of her husband's death by dating a nineteen-year-old neighbor. She even missed her old daddy, who by now had married her mother's sister's oldest daughter.

There were several problems with hooking 'em, aside from the fact they didn't have enough gas to get to Lipan. They worried they might never receive their welfare check if they moved again. But the main consideration was little Kathy. "If that's what's best for the baby," Henry swore, "that's what I'll do. They can keep their checks. They can keep their house. They can sue us. I never asked nobody when and where to go, and I'm not gonna start now." To keep up their spirits—particularly Henry's—the nine Polks would lie for hours jammed together on the king-size bed, trading ideas about what might be done with the welfare money. Cynthia wanted a washing machine. The kids wanted a drive-in movie and a bucket of Kentucky Fried Chicken. Billie Jean wanted something special, but she wouldn't say what. Henry mentioned buying an old pickup truck to haul rocks, or maybe a chain saw, but you knew his heart wasn't in it. On second thought, Henry might buy an old school bus. "I'll fix her up and make us a home," he said. "We're gonna travel. If they got no rock to lay one place, we'll go where they is. If there's no wood to cut, we'll go find some. We'll see how it goes. Nobody's gonna live forever."

There was one day of total panic when Kathy's phenobarbital and Dilantin ran out. Without the medicine she would lapse into a coma. A refill cost $27, and they didn't have anywhere near that amount. Besides, the prescription was written on a drugstore in Lipan. Late that afternoon, when the little girl could no longer keep her eyes open, they rushed her to Brackenridge emergency room where a social worker reminded them that Kathy already *had* a Medicaid card—it comes automatically with SSI, or "Sissy" as they say in the business. A doctor checked Kathy—she had "acute coryza," also known as a common cold—then he wrote a new prescription for her medicine, which Kathy's Medicaid card would pay for. "I had it right there in my purse and didn't know it was any good," Cynthia laughed as she carried her baby back to the car. She kissed Henry on the cheek and laughed again. "I told you it was still good only you wouldn't listen to me." Henry smiled, tugging on the beak of his grimy, "Bowes Seal Fast" mechanic's cap.

On January 20, the day Jimmy Carter was inaugurated, Henry was in the front yard attempting to fix a broken water pump on his '67 Buick. His wife and all seven kids bustled around him, climbing on fenders to watch him work, asking endless questions about when they could go to the drive-in movie and have some fried chicken. Henry's only tools were a borrowed wrench and a piece of scrap metal that he used as a screwdriver, but the work itself was obviously a therapy and Henry seemed as calm and patient as a hound dog with ten pounds of kittens crawling over his back. In the living room a silent television screen showed Jimmy Carter walking up Pennsylvania Avenue, waving, and promising, "No new dream . . . but rather . . . a fresh faith in the old dream." Suddenly, Debby Sue screamed: "It's the mailman, it's the mailman!" Henry kept on working and Cynthia placed his cup of fresh coffee on the fender, pushed through the yammering children, and threatened to "slap that silly off y'all's face if you don't behave." The letter looked official, though it didn't look like the welfare checks they had received in the past. It wasn't. It was a letter from the Texas Rehabilitation Commission (TRC), informing Henry that an appointment had been set for him at the regional headquarters the following Monday. The letter said something about "evaluation, counseling and guidance, training, job training . . . " "What does it mean daddy?" Debby Sue asked. Henry just looked puzzled.

I timed it so that I would arrive at the Polks' home about an hour before Henry's Monday appointment with the TRC. The front door was open. The thermostat was turned to 90° and it was hot enough to bake biscuits in the living room. Henry was lying on the couch with his head in his wife's lap. All the children were sitting around looking at him. "The claw," he told me. "Tell him the truth," Cynthia said. "Over the weekend he climbed up to fix the carport roof and like a fool he jumped off and that's when it got him." After awhile Henry said he was feeling better. Billie Jean brought us two cups of strong black coffee and Henry sat up adjusting his cap. I noticed that the dogs were gone; Henry said he had taken them to the country and dumped them because his sister told him dogs weren't allowed in welfare houses. It turned out the sister was wrong: all he needed was a letter of permission from the landlord, which the landlord was willing to supply. Later that afternoon, when it was too late for the appointment, we all drove out to look for the dogs, but there was no trace of them.

That night I brought over some meat that was wasting in my own refrigerator and we watched the second episode of *Roots*. Cynthia said: "It makes you want to get mad at the white people." Henry retold the story of the old slave lady and the parrot, only this time there were tears in his eyes. I could tell something else was bothering him, and while Cynthia was putting the little girls to bed, Henry offered me some Bull Durham and said: "I'll tell you the truth about that appointment. I was just plain scared." Scared of what?

"Superstition," he said. "I ain't even told my old lady this, but Sunday when we was out driving I saw a roadrunner. Ain't that foolish?" I told Henry I'd heard about black cats, but roadrunners being bad luck was news to me. "That's what I'm talking about. I was a fool. Roadrunners is bad luck for *some*. I got to remembering later, after it was too late to keep that appointment, that the last time I seen one I got a check for $1100 in back payments on Kathy's SSI. Don't that beat all?" I agreed that it did. "But I'll do it yet," he promised. "I'll have my old lady make me a new appointment. I don't know from A to B what they're talking about, but if they'll help me get some tools . . . or a job I can cope with . . . they can keep their damn check."

But Henry Polk wasn't about to report to the TRC. When a man is hanging by his fingernails, it takes a mighty promise for him to lift a hand.

# THE CIRCLE IS UNBROKEN

This may be difficult to believe, but Department of Public Welfare Commissioner Raymond Vowell's habitual tie clasp is a silver and turquoise *roadrunner*. Vowell is a sturdy, balding man with quick-study eyes and the practiced poise of a man accustomed to making large decisions. He might be a retired Air Force colonel, or the president of a small college, which he did once aspire to be. In fact, Vowell is a professional administrator, the presiding officer of a public-owned industry that employs 14,000 people and operates with a biennial budget of $2.3 billion. If you thought of DPW's budget as "industrial sales" it would rank among the nation's 100 largest industrial corporations; it would also rank among the top 300 in employees. Of all the state agencies, his is the least popular and the first to feel the heat when something goes wrong. It's also the first to duck when it is politically expedient.

"The Commissioner," as he is always called around DPW, is admired among rank-and-file welfare workers, particularly those who worked for DPW before his appointment in 1971. They feel that he has streamlined procedures, improved welfare's public image, and reordered priorities where they rightly belong—in favor of the welfare recipient, or "client" as they say. "You feel that he really cares about the clients," says a social worker. The commissioner's passion for bettering the lot of his fellow man does not automatically extend to his own employees. "The commissioner will bust his ass for recipient benefits, but not for his own staff," says a DPW executive.

While administering DPW is the chief purpose of Vowell's $42,000-a-year job, an equally important function is selling his department's biennial budget to the Legislature. Vowell enjoys pointing out that this year the department actually turned back to the state a $40.5 million *surplus* in its food stamp and AFDC programs. The reasons for the surplus were higher employment and a decline in AFDC families. Figures like this make good reading back in the legislators' home districts, but in fact this is an example of the way the lawmakers arbitrarily tangle the department in red tape. By budgeting each DPW program separately (which pleases the various lobbies), the Legislature also makes it unlawful for the DPW to transfer state funds where they are needed. Health service premiums paid to Blue Cross, for example, were projected and budgeted at $159.7

million, but the actual cost was $177.9 million. The department couldn't use the food stamp surplus to make up the difference but had to find surplus federal funds. Since individual members of the Legislature possess an abysmal understanding of the welfare system, Vowell must know at all times who to see and what to say.

Vowell's most popular decision was the creation in 1974 of the department's investigation division which claims to "uncover a half-million dollars a month" in welfare fraud. That is uncover, not *recover*. Last year $871,000 was recovered, or about $72,600 a month. The cost of recovering this money is $1.7 million a year, almost double the reward, but of course there is a principle involved. Not all the criticism Vowell hears in his daily routine concerns welfare chiselers. At almost every subcommittee meeting some black legislator is certain to ask Vowell how many blacks DPW employs at the executive level. "None," Vowell says. Then he smiles and adds, "With the salaries we pay and the services we provide, qualified blacks won't take the job."

Pointing proudly to his charts and graphs, Vowell offers evidence that the state's welfare rolls are steadily declining: when Vowell became commissioner in July 1971, there were 384,682 persons on the Texas AFDC rolls. After peaking at 449,000 in the fall of 1972 (during the national recession), the rolls have dropped to under 325,000. This doesn't mean, though, that there are fewer impoverished Texans; strict enforcement of eligibility standards is cited as the main reason for this decline. Only 2.4 per cent of the Texans on welfare shouldn't be there: no other state has such coldly impressive statistics. The national average is 7.5 per cent. Increases in the state's per capita income levels mean that federal matching funds are decreasing proportionately. Seven years ago, for example, the federal share of medical assistance programs was almost 80 per cent. That figure has dropped to 63.5 per cent, and beginning next fiscal year it will drop again to 60.6. And yet, for all the billions spent, man-hours utilized, charts and graphs and reports, Texas still has the highest number of illiterates and the highest number of poor people in the country. There is absolutely no evidence that the state's stop-gap approach to welfare is doing anything to solve the real problem: what welfare experts call the poverty cycle.

"Before clients come into our system," Vowell told me, "something [bad] has already happened to them. In most cases you can track it back to the time they dropped out of school. If we would go back to the roots of the problem and start doctoring it there, we could break or at least reduce the poverty cycle." Vowell cited a recent study that claimed that of the students who entered the first grade last year in Texas, 40 per cent will never receive high school diplomas. Vowell suggested that I go the the DPW library and read the report of "The White House Conference on Child Health and Protection," convened by President Herbert Hoover in 1930. "I think you'll see that we're dealing with the same problems today as we were then," the commissioner said. "The truth is, we haven't come very far."

The DPW librarian seemed surprised when I asked to see the 1930 White House report, which is about the size of a junior high school history book. "The commissioner is the only one who ever asks for that one," she said. The bulk of the report consists of flowery speeches and high-principled declarations from Hoover and lesser lights. The report

claims that of 45 million children, ten million were "other than normal" because they were improperly nourished. One million suffered from defective speech, and another one million had weak or damaged hearts. Lesser numbers had behavior problems, were mentally retarded, tubercular, deaf, crippled, blind, or delinquent. Hoover begins his speech extolling the virtues of motherhood (the Great Engineer added that he wasn't so sure about fatherhood), then there was a sentence underlined in red pencil, possibly by Commissioner Vowell himself:

*"If we could have but one generation of properly born, trained, educated, and healthy children, a thousand other problems of government would vanish."*

And finally this warning, also underlined in red.

*". . . if we do not perform our duty to the children, we leave them dependent, or we provide . . . the major recruiting ground for the army of ne'er-do-wells and criminals."*

Ray Lyman Wilbur, Hoover's Secretary of Interior and chairman of the conference, tacked on a final philosophical note, claiming that education, health, and welfare were jobs for "the local unit" of government. "We want a minimum of national legislation in this field," he said. "No one should get the idea that Uncle Sam is going to rock the baby to sleep."

You probably remember what happened next: The Great Depression. Then the New Deal. The New Frontier. The Great Society. Always, welfare was supposed to be a leg up. It never worked, possibly because politicians could never agree on whose leg needed the helping hand. Farmers, miners, small businessmen, even Lockheed got a nice share, but many of the states, Texas in particular, never got around to doing much about the crippled, the blind, the deaf, the disabled, the young, the old, or the plain old down-and-outer. There was hardly a trace of uniformity among the states, which of course precipitated migration, putting unbearable burdens on high-welfare states such as New York and California, and at the same time did little to alleviate poverty in tightfisted states like Texas. Uncle Sam's first all-out attempt at what welfare people call "whole income subsidy" was the food stamp program which became mandatory for every state in 1973. On January 1, 1974, the federal government took over all cash-assistance programs except AFDC, which remained the province of each state. In other words, while the federal government set amounts for *adult* welfare, it remained for each state to determine cash payments for dependent children.

Like the commissioner says, we haven't come very far.

"The most difficult problem that we face is the attitude of the people," says Ed Horne, an attorney in charge of one of the DPW's regional Child Support Collection Units. "We have one of the most efficient welfare departments anywhere, but when people read wild stories about welfare fraud in New York they automatically assume that goes for Texas, too. We need to advertise, like the telephone company or Mobil. We're not going to change a lifetime of thinking overnight, but if people could at least understand welfare, society might be able to prevent the cycle sometime in the future."

"The average legislator knows little or nothing about the welfare system," says Representative Mickey Leland of Houston, the only black on the powerful Legislative Budget Board (LBB) which routinely trims the DPW budget and

95

sends it out to be rubber-stamped. "Fraud is used as an excuse to cut back or vote against welfare programs. The LBB doesn't have the resources to investigate the complexity of welfare, and what's more they don't want to investigate." I asked Leland how long it took the LBB to hear testimony and consider the DPW's 2000-page budget proposal. "There wasn't any testimony," he said. "I'd guess we spent about an hour on the total budget, maybe ten minutes of that hour discussing the constitutional limitations of AFDC." After sixty minutes of deliberation, the LBB voted to whack $231 million from the DPW request.

Representative Sarah Weddington of Austin told me, "When you reach the bottom line, welfare comes into collision with other programs—highways, prison systems, new parks. If you ask us to vote a $5 increase to an AFDC recipient or $5 for a new park, we'll vote for the park. It's something lasting. The letters we receive say *don't raise taxes*, not *don't raise welfare*, but there is no effective lobby for poor people. The teachers are organized, the highway lobby is very organized, but when the poor try to organize they usually end up hurting their own cause. The poor are not people that a legislator feels comfortable with, nor are they influential in terms of votes." A member of the state Senate, who asked to remain anonymous, told me: "It's not that members of the Legislature are all that insensitive, it's just that it's politically expedient to vote against welfare. Poor people don't vote."

The mood of the current Legislature is to raise penalties for welfare fraud. Senator Bill Meier of Euless introduced legislation to make welfare fraud of more than $200 a felony (it is now a misdemeanor) punishable by up to ten years in prison. Meier's proposal originated at DPW, which claims that the bill is not designed to slap welfare mothers in jail but to prosecute major offenders, such as the Houston nursing home that collected $120,000 from phony billings, or the DPW worker in Dallas who made off with $14,000 in food stamps. Senator Carlos Truan of Corpus Christi views the bill as a method for legislators to score political points by punishing the poor. Says Truan, "This is a class of people that doesn't have an understanding of the law and its consequences. These are the most illiterate, most ill-educated, most ill-prepared people in our society. I'm sure that it is politically expedient to vote for this bill. Members of the Legislature are fearful that the folks back home wouldn't understand a vote against it. There is no concern for the effects of this legislation. The only concern is to demagogue."

Another "reform" bill that demagogues can write home about is a piece of legislation that would prevent elderly persons from *giving away* property in order to get into a nursing home. An individual who owns at least $1500 in assets is not eligible for nursing home assistance. The maximum for a couple is $2250. Social workers cite numerous cases in which elderly couples have been forced to divorce in order for one of them to qualify for nursing home assistance.

# BURIED TREASURE

**H**enry Polk and his brood were watching *As the World Turns* when the mailman finally arrived. They had returned the night before from a quick trip to Lipan with an old treadle sewing machine and a dog in the trunk of the Buick. Henry had insisted on doing the driving, and now the claw had him again. His spirits were at rock bottom. "I'm just a backsliding Christian, banged up, beat up, wore out," he moaned to the children, who had stayed home from school out of sympathy for his condition. "Just a ol' holer roller. In my soul I don't believe I'm gonna prosper til I get down to the very bottom where I started."

But on January 26, the welfare checks arrived, two at once. The computer finally spit out both December and January. Combined with Kathy's $167 SSI check, the Polks suddenly found $617 in their pockets, though they had already spent $50 of it on the trip to Lipan.

Thirty minutes after the checks arrived the entire family was at Pay-Less Shoes, purchasing tiny cowboy boots ($12 a pair) for the little girls, Kathy and Lanette. It had been almost two weeks since they had eaten meat, so the next stop was the supermarket where they got five dollars' worth of round steak, some cigarettes and candy, and a stack of *Let's Go to the Races* cards. Debbie Sue was still bellowing for some Kentucky Fried Chicken, so that was their next stop. Billie Jean now admitted a hankering for some peach-scented stationery at the drugstore. Henry gave her a dollar, then peeled off a dollar for each one of the kids. While Cynthia was purchasing some thread, Henry and I admired what had to be the world's largest American flag across the street in front of the American Dream Mobile Home Center.

The following day the Polks bought a used washing machine ($35), a new water pump for the Buick ($27), and paid $92.82 to the gas company and $65.80 for water and electricity. They ordered a telephone, which cost $45 for deposit and installation, plus an extra $5 for the privilege of having their number unlisted. They spent $108 for a new supply of food stamps. Cable TV installation cost $4.95. They selected a used 25-inch color TV in a dark oak Mediterranean-style cabinet, paying $55 down and signing a lease-purchase agreement to pay $59 a month for 18 months (or a total of $1117). Then they bought another bucket of chicken, filled the Buick with gasoline, and went to see *The Town That Dreaded Sundown* at the drive-in. Two days after the arrival of the welfare checks, the $617 had been reduced to $60. It would be even tighter in future months when the combined AFDC and SSI checks would amount to only $392. Meeting payments on the car, TV, and utilities would eat up $300. There was definitely going to be a problem figuring out how to find $108 for the purchase of food stamps. When Cynthia mentioned this, Obie Polk, Henry's older brother, said: "Do what ol' Granny Tate used to do. She always carried a six-foot coil of barbwire in her apron. She be out gatherin' wild onions or poke salad, she'd come across a holler log and figure there's gotta be a rabbit in there. She'd just throw that barbwire in the holler and twist that little dickens out and have him for supper."

"Yeah," Henry said glumly. "Only I 'member one time it wasn't no rabbit, it was a ol' rooter polecat. She musta used a gallon of tomato juice and cedar oil getting that stink off her and the dogs."

"Some days it don't hardly pay to try," Obie admitted. Obie had more or less moved in with his brother's family. It had occurred to Cynthia that her brother-in-law's residency might qualify them for extra food stamps, but it had also occurred to her that an extra boarder might disqualify the family for the Section 8 rent program; she decided to let it go. It was never clear where Obie got his money, but he always had a few bucks in the pockets of the green twills that he always wore. One day in early February, Obie came home with something he called a "dowsing instrument." He had paid $25 for it. It looked like a cheap, finger-size piece of hollow aluminum dangling from a cheap chain, but Obie believed it could be used to detect the presence of water, oil, and precious metals. He opened a badly soiled copy of a magazine called *Treasure Hunting Unlimited* and pointed to a diagram for aligning dowsing instruments with the shadows and the rays of the sun. "Exactly halfway between the marks is where the treasure is buried," Obie read.

"What treasure?" Henry asked.

"Them nine jackloads of Meskin silver buried by the Old Confederates Home," Obie told him. All the kids started yammering at once, but Henry told them to shut up. "Obie," he said, "You're touched is what you are." Obie looked hurt. He took his dowsing instrument to his cot in the dining room and stashed it under a pillow. "Don't pay no 'tention to Obie," Henry told me. "He's a little touched is all." Henry took his Bible from the top of the new color TV and walked to the bedroom.

One warm day in late February, Henry loaded his two boys in the Buick and we started out to visit his old friend, Troy Tucker. Troy, who is 72 and nearly blind, lives with his wife Sara in a picture-perfect one-bedroom fieldstone house they built themselves. The house sits on a ridge of cedars and boulders, hidden from the neighboring $100,000 homes and the highway that connects Westlake Hills with South Austin. Three dogs and about two dozen brightly plumed red-and-black chickens scrabble about the carcass of an ancient Dodge truck on blocks. Next to the house is the Tucker family cemetery, where four generations of Troy's people are buried. Years ago Grandma Tucker, who was born just below the ridge on Barton Creek, owned more than 1000 acres around here, but the family had sold it off a little at a time to stay alive and now all that remains is the cemetery and the three acres where Troy and Sara live. The most Grandma Tucker ever got for her land was $20 an acre; now it sells for up to $12,000 an acre. Troy had been one of the best rock masons around until failing eyesight and various other infirmities forced his retirement. "My wind's gone," he told Henry, who out of respect for the old man insisted on hunkering on the floor by Troy's rocking chair. "When your wind's gone, that's it." Troy had worked hard

all his life. He remembered working a full year cutting wood along the Blanco River, and when the boss had subtracted his food and shelter only $394 remained. "That was for a full year's work, mind you," Sara said. Troy had never paid any Social Security. He had no savings, no retirement. He and Sara lived on two $125.90 SSI checks a month, plus $92 worth of food stamps which cost them $62.

They talked about welfare, and about how bad it was to lose your health, and about the rock they had worked, then Henry got around to what was really on his mind. He asked Troy: "You 'member that big ol' cave we found that time when we was building that well-house across the river from Deep Eddy? *Big* sucker . . . with that big boulder in the middle of it mostly covering up that ol' Indian well?"

Troy said that he remembered it.

"You'd drop a rock down that well, you couldn't even hear it hit bottom it was so deep," Henry went on. "It was lined with cedar posts, like maybe it had been a ladder at one time?"

Troy said that was as he recalled.

"Well, me and the boys gonna go look for it," Henry said. "I been telling this man here about it, by golly I'm gonna find it for him."

"It's still there," Troy said. "I don't 'spect anybody come and moved it."

It was almost dark when we stopped searching for the cave. For the better part of three hours we had climbed steep bluffs and bellied along the edges of sheer limestone cliffs with nothing but air at our backs, through cactus and dense underbrush, climbing and dropping back and climbing again until we had covered every inch of the cliff as carefully as a hungry man might eat an ear of corn. We located several smaller caves with blackened ceilings and strange isinglass formations, and we happened across some rich man's trolley tracks used no doubt to transport family and guests from the hilltop mansion to the lake below, but we didn't find anything like the cave that Henry Polk had described. "Let's go back and look again," Buddy Boy suggested as we rested and picked stickers from our hands near the wellhouse that Henry and Troy Tucker had built years ago. Henry's face was beet red and he was blowing hard. As a matter of fact, so was I. He swallowed some nitroglycerin tablets.

"It's gotta be there," he kept repeating. "They couldn't just come and move it. I know it's there. We'll come back some other day. We'll find her yet."

*—May 1977*

LBJ's ranch house. *Photography by Richard Pipes*

# FAREWELL TO LBJ: A HILL COUNTRY VALEDICTION

by Bill Porterfield

*The land that made him takes him back,*
*and many of the goodbyes aren't said at the funeral.*

Never in memory had the hill winter been so hard and insistent and the sun so shy. Men talked of it on the town squares as they backed up to stoves and toasted their behinds. It wasn't idle talk of weather, but the real thing, as if some elemental malevolence was in the air. Twice an icy sheet had covered the whole of Texas, and out here in these runty ruins of some ancient, geologic upheaval, young and old counted a dreary run of coughs and colds and liniment-filled nights.

He, of course, had not died of pneumonia, being too robust for that. Like strong men do, he had been up one day, planting trees, and was gone the next. A turbulence inside himself that had nothing to do with the weather.

That day of his burial we all looked to the sky, and the sun tried to show itself, kept poking here and there through the pall over the Twin Sister Mountains, giving rise to all kinds of false hopes and comment in the people about.

The matriarch of the Johnson clan was Aunt Jessie Hermine Johnson Hatcher, at 88 the ninth and last surviving child of Grandfather Sam Ealy Johnson, Sr. Now there was never any question about Aunt Jessie's attendance at the graveside services. The doughty old girl would be there to see her Lyndon off. The prayer was that she would not catch her death of cold.

•

The petition on Red Casparis' chapped lips was that he could wet a few whistles before George Byars' proclamation went into effect. George, being the mayor of Johnson City, had deemed it proper that business establishments close for the funeral, so Red got up early that dark Thursday to try to sneak a little daylight by the rooster that would crow on curfew.

It isn't that Red is a crassly commercial man; he couldn't be and keep the kind of saloon he does on the square behind

*Bill Porterfield is a contributing editor of* Texas Monthly. *A freelance writer, Porterfield has worked in television and as a newspaper reporter.*

the courthouse. All he sells is beer. It is about as private a club as goat ropers can have. And innocent, I thought. You never see any women in there and the male mainstays seem to be Red and Ted and Austin, Casparises all, Pancho Althaus, the barber, and Lyndon Johnson's common cousin, James Ealy. Ted is Red's cousin and Austin is Red's daddy. Austin is 94. Austin and his late wife, Fannie, used to serve Lyndon chili a lot when they had a cafe and he was a kid, so I asked Red if the old man would make it to the cemetery. He smiled and said he doubted it.

"Like to," he allowed in his gravelly whisper, "Sure Daddy'd like to, but he's a little under the weather, too much to drink last night. Yessir, he put one on."

As I left, Red had lit the stove and was, with a feather duster in hand and an appreciative smile on his round, rich face, carefully examining and dusting what he called his Texas primitives—a rusty assortment of odds and ends he had found in the ruins of barns and artfully arranged about the walls of his joint.

It was hard to imagine the authorities closing him down from time to time for fights and trouble there. Hell, who would be fighting? Not Red and surely not Ted. Behind the Falstaff fog or whatever brand of balm he used, Ted Casparis was a man of mind who hid behind his war wounds. The barber was a good humored man, well known and respected. Old Austin was out of the question and as for James Ealy, well, heck, he wasn't that ambitious. Had to be out of town tush hogs. Damn shame what a little boom like the Presidency will do to the old hometown.

The air was a damp fist in the face as I walked out Red's door and stumbled over a dog that had taken shelter there. The mutt whined and shivered, its thin legs veined as thermometers. Rain. It had begun again, the kind of drizzle that gives gravediggers a bailing-out fit. Down the street the mercury on Pancho's barber pole was just a little above freezing.

Sure, I thought, he had his fat-butted cronies in boots,

greed and gabardine, but he also had Roosevelt and Rayburn.

•

By noon, everything in Johnson City was shut down, even the cafes out on the highway, and by one o'clock a steady stream of cars began heading out Highway 290 toward Stonewall and the LBJ Ranch, where, in the old family cemetery beside the Pedernales, he would be placed beside his mother and daddy. The ceremony was not to start until four o'clock, when Lyndon's body would be flown in from the state funeral at the cathedral in Washington. But the impulse, in spite of the cold, was to hurry to the cemetery and get a good spot before the crush came. What you did if you were an ordinary citizen was park your car in the LBJ State Park on Ranch Road 1 south of the Johnson place, and catch one of the army shuttle buses that took you across the river and into the trees that hung like mourners over the huddle of tombstones. Thousands did this, or walked the winding road to the graveyard where they stood in puddles for hours awaiting his last trip home. What you did if you were the press was sign in at the park office and get a badge which gave you precedence over the run-of-the-mill mourner for a bus and a front row position. Still the press bitched, because the dignitaries were given reserved seats on exclusive buses, because there were only nine phones for calling out, because it was wet and cold and difficult to set men and machinery into motion.

•

Sam Wood, the veteran Austin editor, was in a better humor than most. He sat in one of the shuttle buses beside his reporter, Nat Henderson, his head down in a deep study. Directly he looked up and out at the clouds. "Say," he said to Henderson, "I'll bet you $10 it stops raining and the sun comes out."

"Why?"

"Because," Wood chuckled, "St. Peter doesn't know what he's up against."

Lyndon would have loved that.

The little rotund Lutheran pastor, Wunibald Schneider, was of the same mind, only in his German way much more earnest about the theological import of rain or shine. He stepped out of his church across the river from the cemetery and looked up for a sign, for some show of a benign and benevolent benediction on what was about to transpire.

I doubt Lyndon would have liked that. If the sun had come out it probably would have scared hell out of him.

•

Between 9th and 12th I think, somewhere in there between Grover Cleveland, James K. Polk and Dwight Eisenhower. That's what I would tell Saul when we got back to Austin and the Villa Capri. It would enrage him I knew. I hadn't seen Friedman in years, but he'd never liked LBJ. But I'd hold to it, warts and the war and all.

•

Word came that the body would not arrive by plane at the airstrip on the ranch, but was being brought by hearse from Austin, down 290 through Oak Hill and Dripping Springs and Henly, Johnson City and Hye. I looked at Bo Byers' watch: 3:15. Wally Pryor said the entourage was now passing through Oak Hill, less than an hour away. Was it sudden sentiment to have him brought by car along that road he had known so well? Whatever, I approved, and thought of the places along the way, the people I knew who might watch the procession pass. Dick Polk, the calf-roping, guitar-picking, gas-jockeying postmaster and feedman at Oak Hill. At Henly if they knew maybe the twin sisters who had married brothers would be out on their porches. That would be Ella Mae and Hazel Herbest, who had got the Smitherman boys. Hondo Crouch wouldn't be at Hye but at Luckenbach.

•

Wayne Jackson and I were crunched up against the low stone wall that rectangled the cemetery, but we made room for Ronnie Dugger. The rest of the reporters were exchanging stories but Ronnie remained quiet. I wondered what sense he would make of it. For years, he had been coming to grips with Lyndon Johnson, mostly in *The Texas Observer*. Now he was writing a book about Johnson, had been for some time. Dugger is a discerning man, mentally quick on his feet but deliberate and philosophical in print, and since the fifties he had quarreled with most that Johnson had stood for. Saul came up, and we asked Ronnie to join us later at the Villa Capri. It really wasn't hard to understand the Texas liberals' long war with Lyndon. On the Potomac he may have made like FDR with his programs for the poor, but down here on the Pedernales he ran with men who put more money in a fat steer than they would in a house full of starving Mexicans.

•

I looked at the hole they would lower him into and wondered if he had ever heard of the Smithermans. I doubted it, though he must have passed their place hundreds of times over the past 55 years. Of course they knew him, as obscure and modest neighbors know a great and public figure, but they also knew him better than that implies. Part of it, I figured, had to do with the Presidency itself. For the Smithermans and for most Americans, I felt, there was still a magic in that office. Yes, because of its incredible and growing power, but also because it was, in Clinton Rossiter's words, "a breeding ground of indestructible myth." As soon as a man stepped into that office he became a flesh and blood democratic distillation of us all. If we loved and hated him, it was because we loved and hated ourselves. And there was no question about it. Lyndon Johnson had engendered those extremes. Why, I asked myself, when I thought of LBJ did I always think of old D and Jody and Jesse?

They had moved into Blanco County back in the summer of '27, just a few months after Lyndon had left for college. He had gone off to San Marcos with $75 borrowed money, a hell of a lot less than D and Jody and Jesse had brought with them. Why, they had something like 2000 head of cattle, which they pastured on a 1280-acre lease along Flat Creek.

Funny how things turn out.

For the next 36 years—the time it took Lyndon to rise to the Presidency—D and Jody and Jesse wore themselves to a frazzle trying to make a living out there on what has to be the sorriest land since Terlingua. While Lyndon had gone from student to teacher to congressional secretary to bureaucrat to Congressman, Senator, Vice President and President, the Smithermans had gone from 2000 cows to less than 50, from 1000 acres to 300. Why, they'd even gone to sheep and goats, which made them beyond redemption as far as cowmen were concerned. About the only thing sassy they managed to bring off was marrying sisters, Jody and Jesse that is. D never married. Jody finally removed himself from the partnership and he and Hazel moved into Henly. Out on the ranch fat D spent most of his time trying to coax fig trees out of the caliche and limestone, and out in the barn frail Jesse was always raising a racket inventing contraptions like self-feeders and hayloft lifts which never got off the place. And all the time Lyndon Johnson making millions and moving in high cotton. Did they give him hell like J. Evetts Haley? Were they bitter? When he passed on the road in his Lincoln did they cuss? Why hell no, D told me one day as he fried a sausage patty to a black crisp, it was nice to see somebody get ahead. And when he became president, it kind of perked them up.

Ella Mae, Jesse's wife, started melting down beer bottles which she made into LBJ ashtrays to sell to tourists.

Jesse commenced to talk seriously about putting in a barbecue stand on 290. Why, it was bound to be a money maker. It looked like Lyndon was going to be president for nine years, and if he wasn't the best advertisement for barbecue and beer Jesse didn't know one. Might even put in a motel. Ella Mae could sell her ceramics and D could do the cooking. Jesse got so excited he poked a finger into D's chest. "I'll tell you somethin' else," he declared. "We ought to think about gettin' some Holstein cows, some milkers." He knew damn good and well people were going to keep on drinking milk. By God, the country was beginning to look up with Lyndon in there.

Well, none of it came to pass.

Not the Great Society.

Not the nine years.

Oh, Ella Mae sold a few ashtrays, but not from any Smitherman Bros. Barbecue Stand.

Jesse got sick and died and that was that.

D, in his seventies, had no heart for it or for the milkers.

And when Ella Mae got glaucoma and had to have two eye operations, she stopped melting down beer bottles.

I spent a few hours with them, the widow and the bachelor, one day back in January of 1969, shortly after Lyndon Johnson had called it quits to retire to the ranch. Ella Mae hadn't missed her ceramics. "It's a small thing to have to give up after losing a husband," she said. "Just look what Lyndon's given up."

And we did look, for there on the television screen was Richard M. Nixon, taking the oath as 37th president.

The inauguration saddened them, not because they had anything against Nixon, but because they felt so sorry for Lyndon Johnson.

"I know that seems a silly thing to say," Ella Mae said, "especially when you consider how far he has gone in the world, and from such a little place like Johnson City! But I feel for him and I can't help it. The country turned crazy on him, and he had to step down to save it. People don't seem to appreciate that."

•

D Smitherman died in April of '72. I knew that as I stood next to the cemetery wall. But I did not know that at that moment Jody Smitherman lay in a San Antonio hospital trying to make it back from a heart attack. As Hazel was to put it, "They helicoptered him there just ahead of Lyndon."

•

Now, just behind Lyndon, after the hearse that bore his body, came the family in limousines, and after the family came friends and business associates in limousines, and after them came buses, many buses, unloading important people, many of whom we recognized—Hubert Humphrey, Ed Muskie—but mostly they were VIP's of the Texas Establishment who had not made it to Washington for the more formal services. Anyone who was anybody or who wanted to be was there. One fair young man caught my eye in the forest of great coats. Although he stood taller than the men around him he was somehow subdued and lacking in stature. Perhaps it was what I knew of Ben Barnes that gave him this rather contradictory diminution.

The man whose body the military pallbearers were carrying now to the grave had singled out this young man as his political son, had coached and counseled and favored him to the point that everyone said it was a matter of time before Barnes would be governor and maybe president. It was said that the mantle of greatness had been laid upon him. But just as the young man made his first big move he stumbled, badly, and the people turned from him. I looked at him now and wondered if the men who used to buoy him up had also left him like a leper. I had never thought much of him myself, but now he fascinated me. He was becoming either a very wise man or a very bitter one, depending upon his inner character, and the latter, of course, had never come to light in the days of his public apprenticeship.

•

Before that particular young man had been favored by the departed, another had been his favorite from the time they had been novices in the pursuit of power. Now he came, tall and handsome in his maturity, to eulogize the dead man. And surely the common thought—it caught your breath—was that here, embodied in both, might well be the once and future kings.

•

At one point in his eulogy, John Connally quoted Lyndon Johnson as having said, "I guess I've come a long way for a boy from Johnson City, Texas." Certainly Connally had come a long way himself, but I couldn't help but think, as we watched him read over his friend, that the truly stunning turn in his life was not the years between the Floresville farm and the governor's mansion, but rather those of late.

Who would have thought, say in 1960, when John Kennedy and Lyndon Johnson sent Richard Nixon and Henry Cabot Lodge to the sidelines and beckoned Mr. Connally to Washington as their Secretary of the Navy, that it would be President Nixon, not President Kennedy or President Johnson, who would set John Connally up for a run at the White House? Not even our knowledge then that Connally was a counterfeit Democrat would have prepared us for such a turn of events.

•

Maybe that was premature, putting Connally in the White House when we still had a Texas President to put in the ground. Well what of him, this Lyndon Johnson who yet made such sounds in the earth? The Graham cracker generalities that the Rev. Billy Graham was serving up over his grave did not hit home. What occurred to me then (and I hold to it now) is that not since Andrew Jackson had a President contained such an abundance of both virtue and flaw. In his character and manner and sympathies, Lyndon Johnson was in that great rough-hewn line of succession that began with Old Hickory and found such full expression in our towering genius, Abraham Lincoln. It was passed down, in part, to Theodore Roosevelt and then to Truman, this rude kind of humanity, but of all of them, LBJ was the closest to Jackson.

It doesn't surprise me that Jackson's great friend and spiritual brother was Sam Houston. If Houston was a colossus in buckskin, LBJ was the colossus in khaki. It is uncanny how alike they were. Houston was in Texas because of President Jackson's bidding, and their intent was empire. Sam Houston came to Texas on borrowed money and made a pot while becoming President of the Republic. His sins were human ones. Lyndon Johnson went to Washington on borrowed money and made a pot while becoming President of the United States. His sins were human ones.

They wanted everything, and they went out and got it: power, money, land, a place in history among the titans. Everything but love in their own time and on their own terms.

Both Houston and Johnson were larger than life incarnations of Western Man. They believed, by God and by their own prowess and passions, that everything was possible in this world. Chaotic men of massive contradictions, they ruled with rage as well as reason, and left in their wake both good fortune and calamity.

Both fell from power because the people turned against them, Houston for trying to prevent a war, Johnson for pursuing one. Both retired from the public arena with heavy hearts and died, if not in disrepute, then in disregard.

•

The way we stood in concentric circles about the casket reminded me of the circles of life in a fallen oak, with the dead man our common core. The simile even carried over into how we were arranged about the grave. The first influences on Lyndon Johnson had been those of his hill country boyhood, but as he grew they receded from his center toward the bark of his background, to make room for each succeeding stage of his life. And indeed the ''plain people'' as John Connally called them, were at our backs, making a great outward circle of several thousand persons. In front of them, in a smaller circumference, were the politicians he had known in his middle stage, and in front of them were those who had served him in the White House. And at the heart of the goodbyes, of course, were the old friends and business associates, and the kin.

A fifth circle was wedged in as close to the family as the stone wall and the secret service would allow: the press, rapacious and rude in its appetite for one final insight and intimacy into the man and what he had meant.

•

History redeemed Houston.

•

We tended to think of him as a consummate politician, but I wonder. Of course he was with the boys in the backrooms of Congress. He came to rule the Senate as no man in our history. If it hadn't been for Senator Johnson and his majority whip and carrot, Eisenhower would have been left out on the fairway.

But God was he a bore on the podium, speechmaking! Somebody's middleclass Masonic Uncle, beaming a benign conservatism through his bifocals, when you knew damn well he had just broken somebody's back for crossing him. Up close, pressing your flesh and looking you in the eye, or at his leisure with a Pearl beer in one hand (Jesse was right) and a barbecued rib in the other, he was as winning as John

Wayne.

The cinematic Wayne.

Not the new nominating one. He's as dull on the podium as Johnson was.

•

As Billy Graham.

•

Lady Bird and her girls bore up beautifully, Lynda in her proud, Protestant singing along with Anita Bryant (who was magnificent), Lucy in her Catholic quiet.

But the old aunts, Aunt Jessie Hatcher in particular, you could tell they were chilled to the bone.

•

He was a genius in the Senate, gloried in it. The Presidency was something else. I don't think he ever felt quite at home there, never really hit his stride. Like Andrew Johnson after Lincoln and Chester A. Arthur after James Garfield, he came to it sadly with a nation in tears. Jack Kennedy had been so beautifully young and vibrant.

But after a time, he made it his, came into his own enough to pass the most comprehensive and far-reaching civil rights legislation of any President. In this he was a second Lincoln. He put into law what Lincoln had dreamed of and what Kennedy had schemed of. What he did for the minorities was the high mark of his five years in the White House.

But it was not legislation calculated to make him a popular President. In this he led the people and the Congress instead of following. Our inclination as a people was toward racial injustice, and had Lyndon Johnson been a weaker man, it would have been easier to ignore the militants and go along with the country's prevailing opinion. But he saw the light, and the right, though it was against our grain. The irony, and it was a bitter pill for Johnson to swallow, was that not even the black people loved him for it.

Our mood, as a people, was contentious, as it was in Jackson's time, Lincoln's time, and we barked and bit at him, and at one another, like dogs.

It was not consensus, but contention; and he was miserable and must have commiserated with the ghosts of past Presidents. Now he knew why Washington had left the Presidency sore in heart and mind, eager for the seclusion of Mt. Vernon. Jefferson had called the Presidency the road to splendid misery and Jackson had sworn it more curse than honor.

That was what Viet Nam was for Lyndon Johnson. More curse than honor was his Waterloo, and it doesn't take history's long view to see how tragically absurd his position was. Here, on the one hand, he was pouring manpower and billions of dollars into the making of our own Great Society, while, on the other, waging one of the longest and costliest wars in our history, not against a major power, but on a tiny country in support of a corrupt regime.

It is true he inherited the commitment from Kennedy and the policy of containment from Truman, but he let both get away from him. He paid for it, and we are still paying for it.

•

The 21-cannon salute fell short by two. A howitzer misfired twice.

•

It hurt me to think back over his last lameduck days in the White House. No President since James Polk had worked harder and enjoyed it less. He had wanted to take the country by the tail, but gargantuan that he was, he reached for more than he could handle.

But great men always do. Because, I guess, they are metaphors for the best and worst in all of us.

•

Red sold four beers all that morning.

Dugger never did make it to the Capri, and Saul and I talked of Nixon.

Neither did Jody make it out of the hospital. Hazel said he died two weeks later.

So did Aunt Jessie Hatcher, two weeks to the day. She caught a cold and it went into pneumonia. They buried her in the same cemetery.

*—May 1973*

# THE DEATH OF THE MARLBORO MAN

## by Gary Cartwright

---

*He was a real cowboy who worked every day of his life
and was a lot bigger than even Marlboro made him out to be.*

---

*A world big enough to hold a rattlesnake and a purty woman is big enough for all kinds of people*—oldtime cowboy saying.

I never realized that the Marlboro cowboy was real until I read last May that he had drowned on a bucking bronco. *Drowned* . . . incredible . . . drowned on a nervous young colt in a newly-dug stock tank on the Bill Flowers Ranch near Old Glory, in the starkly beautiful Marlboro country north of Sweetwater. No one knows exactly how it happened; as usual, Carl (Bigun) Bradley was alone at the time.

Bigun and his daddy, Carl (Banty) Bradley, had just sold the colt to Bill Flowers, but Flowers' foreman couldn't handle him. Bigun saddled the horse late that afternoon, cinching the flank rope tight as he could so the horse would feel pain every time he bucked, then he rode off toward what they call Cemetery Pasture.

Bigun was 36 and for as long as anyone could remember his workday started before sunup and ended after sundown, never varying except for the two days he took off to get married, and the few times he was off in South Dakota doing a Marlboro commercial; it was seven days a week, week after week, it was the repetition as well as the work that kept him at it. But this particular day, for no particular reason, Glenda Bradley was worried. She telephoned Susann Flowers at ranch headquarters just after dark.

"You know how cowboys are," Susann Flowers told Glenda. "You gotta hit them in the head to get them off their horse. He'll be in in a while." Nevertheless, Bill Flowers and his foreman would take a pickup out to Cemetery Pasture and see about Bigun. "I'll call you back," Susann told Glenda.

The Flowers were not only Bigun's employers, they were

*Gary Cartwright, contributing editor of* Texas Monthly, *is the author of two books, a screenplay, and many articles.*

his friends, and Glenda's too, a couple about their own age. Bill Flowers was a famous rodeo roper and heir to old Pee Wee Flower's four-ranch spread of 80,000 acres. Bill was a real cowboy, too, but not in the way Bigun was—Bigun was a working cowboy, the son of a working cowboy, the grandson of a working cowboy, all of them born and raised on the same tenant ranch outside of Knox City, simple men working for wages and living their unrelenting existence in a world that could go mad without them knowing or even caring. Bill Flowers and Bigun Bradley had ridden together when Bigun was wagon boss of the Four Sixes (6666) Ranch near Guthrie—"neighboring" they called it, helping out when there is branding or gathering to be done—there was one stretch, Bill recalled, when they were out 41 days, miles from the nearest asphalt or bathtub or woman or child or roof or television set. But there was always this difference—Bill Flowers was rich, he could quit anytime and go back to running his own ranch and rodeoing. Bigun Bradley never had time for the rodeo. And he didn't live long enough to own his own spread.

Bill Flowers and his foreman found nothing in Cemetery Pasture, but returning to the ranch house late that night they saw something in the headlights that sent cold chills up their boots—a horse's leg and part of a saddle blanket protruding from the muddy water near the edge of the new stock tank.

"Get the rope," Bill yelled, jumping from the pickup before it had even stopped rolling. But they had made a mistake that Bigun Bradley would never make: they had forgotten their rope.

About midnight, Bill and Susann Flowers drove over to Glenda's house and told her they had found the horse. There was no trace of Bigun, except his lip ice, gloves and a package of Kools. Sheriff Marvin Crawford and other volunteers had come over from Aspermont, and the dragging operation had begun. The Flowers drove Glenda and her 18-month-old son, Carl Kent Bradley, back to the ranch house where they would wait out the night.

"It was the longest night ever," Susann Flowers would say later. "We kept hoping that maybe he had been bucked and was unconscious somewhere out there. Almost the same thing had happened to my daddy's foreman in Pecos —they found his body in the Pecos River. We never knew what happened."

Working in the lights of a circle of pickup trucks and a fire truck beacon, the cowboys told stories and speculated. There were three possibilities: Bigun could have been bucked off; the horse could have spooked and charged into the water, taking Bigun with him; or Bigun could have deliberately rode the bronco into the tank. "Some people think every horse will swim, but every horse won't swim," Sheriff Crawford said. "I've rode horses up to drink tubs . . . you get a bronco around water, the cinches tight up, they're liable as not to turn and pitch. You get a horse in water, most of them will swim right across, but they's a few'll just turn on their sides and go straight to the bottom."

"Bigun has been known to ride 'em into water," another cowboy recollected. "I seen him one time after a big rain take his chestnut right into the Little Wichita, trying to get the cattle to follow him."

Back at the ranch house, George Humphrey, an oldtime cowboy who managed the Four Sixes for 40 years (Bigun left the 6's when George retired four years ago), told stories to the gathering of women and children. How in the old days when cattle were cheap the best way to subdue an old mossy horn was to shoot it through the thick part of the horns, aiming for dead center so that the pain would calm the steer and make it manageable. "What if you misshot?" Glenda Bradley asked, laughing the nervous schoolgirl laugh that was maintaining her. "You'd kill the animal," George Humphrey said. "Cattle was cheap and it was an advantage to get rid of these outlaws at any price. They spoiled the other cattle. They had to be either shot or driven off."

They dragged Bigun Bradley's body from the tank around 2 a.m. There were signs of a blow over one eye and behind his ear. "Either one was hard enough to kill him," Sheriff Crawford told Glenda Bradley.

Glenda went outside and cried, then she came back and helped fix breakfast.

**H**e preferred to work alone," Glenda Bradley is telling me. Her voice has started to quiver, and she clasps her hands tightly in her lap. "That's very dangerous, but he was so good . . . I think anyone will tell you this . . . he *was* good with horses. He just wasn't afraid. He didn't think anything could happen."

We are sitting in the kitchen of her parents' home in Westbrook, a tiny farming town near Colorado City. This is where Glenda grew up, and this is where she returned after Bigun's death. It has been two months since the funeral: only yesterday Glenda finally forced herself back to Old Glory, and having made the trip she feels better. Old friends and memories are too dear to ignore.

"I interviewed for a job teaching homemaking at Jayton High School—that's east of Knox City. When we were first married and Bigun was wagon boss of the Four Sixes, I taught homemaking in Guthrie. It's a comfort to at least know what I'm going to do. People in that part of the country, especially around Guthrie, they're not very progressive. They want things the way they were in the old times and do a pretty good job keeping it that way. Oh, they use pickups and butane branding irons, but that's about it. At first I thought I could never go back, but . . . "

Carl Kent Bradley, called Kent, now 20 months old, rides a stick horse around the table where we talk.

"I guess he'll be a cowboy, too," Glenda says. "I hate for him to do it, but that's what Bigun would want, and I know Banty (Bigun's daddy) is going to have it that way. Bigun was never allowed to be a little boy. Banty had him out breaking horses when he was old enough to ride. I mean breaking *horses* . . . *colts.* . . . not riding old nags." Glenda says this without rancor. She is more composed now, and there is that nervous, laughing edge to her voice. "Bigun and Banty and all their people, cowboying is all they've ever known or wanted. To be on a horse chasing a cow was what Bigun enjoyed. Kent has already turned that way. Unless I ever remarry and my husband is so different . . . but I don't think I'd like any other life except cowboying."

Glenda Bradley is pretty, the way a high school majorette is pretty, a way that is difficult to describe. She is what you would call "a sweet girl," but tough and proud. As she talks about her five-and-one-half-year marriage to Bigun Bradley, she admits that she never knew him very well. No one did. "The truth is," she says, "we never had much time together, and when we did he didn't say much. He'd leave the house at three or four in the morning and come home after dark. He'd eat and go to bed. Every day, no days off. About the only socializing we did, every July Fourth the cowboys would take off and go to the Stamford Cowboy Reunion Rodeo."

Bigun was a 30-year-old bachelor when Glenda met him at a rodeo dance. She was 22 and had just graduated from Texas Tech. He was the Marlboro man and wagon boss of the 6666. She had never met Bigun Bradley, but she knew him, knew him in a way that always embarrassed Bigun when she told the story.

"Bigun would kill me for telling you, but . . . well, it was a big joke at school [Texas Tech] that I liked *cowboys*. A friend of mine cut out Bigun's picture from a Marlboro ad in *Life* magazine . . . here's your cowboy, Sis, she said. . . . I said, Fine, I'll just *marry* him, and put the picture on my dorm wall . . . you know, a silly girl thing. That summer another friend sent an article out of *Western Horseman* that gave his name—Carl B. Bradley, Jr. He got the name Bigun from his Uncle Guy who use to call him Bigun and his little brother (Doug Bradley) Littleun. Actually, Bigun wasn't all that tall, only about five-eleven, but very strong. Anyway, on July Fourth that summer I went to the Stamford Cowboy Reunion Rodeo Dance with a girl friend and there he was. He took my girl friend home that night. Two nights later, I went back to the dance and he pretty well ignored me, but he did ask me for a date."

Six months later, after a courtship that consisted of going to an occasional cowboy movie in Bigun's pickup, they were married. As wagon boss at the Four Sixes, Bigun was making $310-a-month, but Glenda started teaching and there was extra money from the Marlboro commercials, not all that much, but enough to get by. The Marlboro people had "discovered" Bigun Bradley while shooting some background film at the Four Sixes. He was one of several real cowboys who posed for commercials.

"One of the first things he told me," Glenda says, "is about the Marlboro deal—he'd been offered a fulltime contract that included a part in a movie. He'd turned it down, but now, with us getting married, he didn't know if he'd done the right thing. But he decided he wouldn't be happy not cowboying . . . and he wouldn't, 'cause he was good and he liked it."

Bigun did not speak of the future, but it was his dream to someday own a small ranch. They put a little money in the bank . . . . $120 every time Marlboro used him on TV, $1,500 for a few cover ads in *Life* or *Look* . . . and Bigun bought a few horses and cattle and went in partnership with Banty, who was now leasing the land where they had always worked for wages. Then the government banned cigarette commercials on TV. Glenda had to quit her job when Kent was born, and the savings account quickly evaporated. Bigun hadn't posed for a commercial in the two years befor his death. "We were barely getting by," Glenda says. "And I mean barely."

It cost money to cowboy. Four hundred dollars for a saddle . . . $40 for a pair of chaps . . . $100 for shopmade boots. Except on the rare occasion when he accompanied Glenda to the First Methodist Church ("He never felt comfortable in a crowd"), Bigun wore Levis, white shirt, boots, hat and, in the winter, a neck scarf. He never walked outside without his hat and boots.

"He was always giving things away," Glenda recalls. "Bridles . . . spurs . . . if he thought someone wanted his boots he'd sit down and take them off right there. That's just how he was. He was the most patient, most courteous man I ever knew. Even after we were married and had the baby, he would still open doors for me . . . yes ma'am and no ma'am . . . he wouldn't even take a serving of food off the table until I'd served myself first. That's the way May (Bigun's mother) raised her two boys. Even after we were married, whatever Mama and Daddy said do, he'd do, regardless of my opinion."

J. Frank Dobie once described the cowboy as "a proud rider, skilled, observant, alert, resourceful, unyielding, daring, punctilious in a code peculiar to his occupation, and faithful to his trust."

That's a pretty good description of Bigun Bradley.

Joe Thigpen, the young county attorney of Stonewall County, tosses a pack of Kools on his desk and tilts his straw hat on the back of his head. In his wilder days, before he finished law school, Thigpen worked for Bigun Bradley at the Four Sixes.

"I knew about the Marlboro cowboy—everybody around here did," he tells me. "It was a thrill meeting him." The first thing Bigun Bradley did was send Joe home for his saddle and bedroll; it hadn't occurred to Joe that he would need a bedroll. This was in 1968, the Four Sixes still had a chuck wagon drawn by four mules, a kind of traveling headquarters; they slept under the stars, bathing maybe twice a month. The wagon was already out when Joe Thigpen hired on, and they stayed out another two-and-a-half months.

Joe Thigpen tells me: "I never met a man as patient and completely dedicated as Bigun. I never knew a man who worked harder. I don't think he ever asked for a day off.

He'd wake me up every morning and tell what we had to do that day. Then we'd do it.

"Now I'm not saying he couldn't be tough on you. There was one day we were flanking cattle and I was always in the wrong place, spooking the yearlings. Bigun roped this calf . . . must of weighed 450 pounds . . . and said, 'you been messing up all day so you just flank (ie: throw) this one by yourself.' Now there's no way one man can throw a 450-pound yearling. The calf stepped on my toes and like to of broke them . . . I was sweating and puffing, all the way given out . . . never did get that yearling down. Another fellow finally had to help me. But Bigun wasn't doing it for meanness—he was teaching me a lesson."

I asked Joe Thigpen what it is that makes a man cowboy. He thought for a while, then said, "I can't tell you exactly, but I loved it better than anything I've ever done. You're outdoors, doing what you like to do. I probably never would of gone back to school, except Bigun told me that's what I ought to do. It was the best advice I ever got—a cowboy can't afford a family."

Thigpen took a check stub from his wallet and showed me his final month's pay at the 6's—$162.50. Then he offered me a Kool and told me a story: "We had about 125 horses in the remuda, we were moving them one day . . . I guess we must of rode 22 miles . . . me being the low man on the totem pole, I had to ride drag . . . you know, back at the end, hollering and yelling and pushing horses. It was just dusty as the dickens. I was trying to smoke those Marlboros . . . I thought that's what I oughta smoke . . . but they were burning me up . . . I'd take one puff and throw it way. That's when Bigun came riding back. He didn't say a word. He just took a pack of Kools out and offered me one."

Joe Thigpen takes another cigarette and shakes his head. Hard to believe. Hard to believe that a man who knew so much about horses could be killed by one. "It's something I'll never be able to get out of my mind," he says.

It doesn't take long to tour the Old Glory community, but the tour is fascinating. Seated in a flat, green valley of windmills and skeleton mesquites that have been poisoned because they take too much water from the land, Old Glory is an abandoned cotton gin, a general store and post office, and a scattering of quaint old homes. One of the homes is the old Raynor Court House which sits now like a feudal castle on a high mound. It looks like the house in the movie *Giant* I think as I drift below on the farm road from Aspermont, and it turns out they modeled the movie set after the Raynor Court House. An old couple whose name I didn't catch live there now. No one ever goes up there, they told me at the general store.

The Germans who settled here called the spot New Brandenburg until World War I when, in a fit of patriotism, they decided the name sounded too un-American and asked the oldest woman in town, Mrs. Weinke, what they should do about it. She told them to change it to Old Glory, and that's what it's been ever since.

I'm in the passenger side of a station wagon with Susann Flowers and her two young boys. Bill Flowers has been off since before daylight, buying cattle in a market that is on the verge of Nixonian panic, and Susann is showing me the ranch. We drive through Cemetery Pasture, where the old German cemetery is preserved by a fence—judging from the grave stones, an unusual number of children died here in the late 1800's, a time of epidemic, perhaps—and now we slow down near the stock tank where Bigun Bradley died.

"You know what I always think when I drive by here?" Susann Flowers says. "I think about Bigun's hat. We never found it. It's down there somewhere.

"Bigun couldn't swim, you know. Neither can Bill. It scares the hell out of me to see them swimming their horses, but they do it all the time. There's no reason for it, it's just something they do. We're not supposed to question what happens on this earth, but I can't help wonder what happened that night. He could have been bucked, or the horse could have gone into the tank, but I can't help feel that Bigun rode in on purpose."

We stop in a warm summer rain while Susann fills the tank of her station wagon from a gasoline drum near the foreman's house. In an adjoining pasture there is a modern house trailer where old Pee Wee Flowers still comes occasionally to play dominoes with the hands. Susann wants to change the name of the Bill Flowers Ranch to 'something Spanish," but Bill and Pee Wee won't hear of it. Susann Flowers doesn't want her two children to cowboy, but that's what they will do—cowboy like their daddy, not like Bigun Bradley. Meanwhile, Susann is organizing a college scholarship fund for little Carl Kent Bradley.

"Bigun wasn't afraid of anything," she says as we drive back to the ranch headquarters. "I heard him say one time . . . he was talking about this cowboy we all knew . . . Bigun said: 'Charley's afraid of dying.' It was something Bigun couldn't understand. He was tough as hell—that's what he was. Yet he was the most considerate, most dependable man I ever knew. I'd known him for years before he stopped calling me Mrs. Flowers—and I was younger than he was."

Jeff Flowers, age 5, tells me what he remembers about Bigun— Jeff remembers Bigun brought him a tiny rabbit they caught in post hole. Jeff wears spurs on his little boots and has two horses. They're not very good horses, he tells me.

In a driving rainstorm, I turn toward Knox City, thinking about women and glasses of beer.

I stop to consult my crude map. The rain has stopped and the sun is slipping behind Buzzard Peak when I find the muddy, rutty, unmarked road which leads to the tenant house where Bigun and all his people grew up—the ranch that Banty Bradley now leases. A sign at the main-gate cattleguard identifies this as the "General American Oil Co.," and it is still another ten miles to the house, which sits on a crest overlooking miles of green hills and naked brown peaks. Fat quail and jack rabbits big as dwarf deer bounce in front of my car, and horses and cattle look me over without judging my intentions.

Banty and May Bradley are out by the stable, hoeing weeds. There are miles of weeds, weeds far as you can see, but the apron of ground around the stable is clean as a dinner plate. They hoe patiently, like people listening to the radio, like they don't care if there is an end to their struggle.

Banty is a short, husky, red-faced cowboy with wide spaces between his teeth to spit tobacco through. They say Bigun was a younger exact replica of his daddy. May, though, is pure Texas mule-iron, a lean, severe, outspoken woman who hasn't smiled since Christmas. There is no tele-

phone here; I couldn't call in advance, and now they decline to be interviewed. I stand by my open car door, asking questions, while they go on hoeing, then I get an idea. I tell them that I saw "Sis" (Glenda's nickname) yesterday, she says hidy and she's feeling much better. She's got a new teaching job at Jayton. Banty and May brighten as I play them a part of the tape I did with Glenda.

"Did you see Bigun's boy?" Banty asks, eagerly breaking the silence.

I describe meeting Carl Kent Bradley.

"That baby of Carl B.'s is a natural-born cowboy," May says. May is the only person I met who doesn't call her son Bigun. She calls him Carl B. "Look at him ride his rocky horse . . . natural saddle gait."

"It's getting harder," May says, "harder to go on. There is very little neighboring anymore. It's every man for himself. You used to be able to tell a cowman by his boots," she tells me. "If he was worth a speck, he had $100 shop-made boots. Now days, you tell a cowboy by his woreout brogans. Real cowboys can't hardly afford boots. One thing about Carl B., he couldn't care less about money. There was a pattern in his life. Things came his way. He didn't ever ask for things, we taught him that, but things came his way. He didn't ask for all that publicity. He got plenty of it, but he wasn't a *seeker*."

May does most of the talking, deferring occasionally to Banty, reminding him of a particular story. They tell me about Banty buying Bigun's first saddle when Bigun was three. May talks about their other son, Doug, how Doug never wanted to be a cowboy. Doug drives a bulldozer. Doug was always building things, while Bigun played cowboy. Blocks and stickhorses. "Bigun wore out many a stick horse before he could ride," May says. "He'd play cowboy and Doug was always his calf. Doug had all the hide wore off his neck by the rope."

At May's urging, Banty tells me about Bigun snitching the latch pin off the barn door, and how Bigun was afraid of the dark but Banty made him go back alone in the dark and replace the latch pin. Bigun never again messed with the barn latch. They tell me about the agonizing weeks it took before Bigun would mount his first wild bronco. And how, once he had done it, he never stopped. Why does a man cowboy? I ask. Banty grins and points to his head, as though to say that's where his heart is. If Bigun was as good as they say, and I believe he was, why didn't he join the rodeo circuit? "Too many people," Banty grins.

Later, May takes me up to the house and shows me her clippings, the clippings describing the deeds of the Marlboro cowboy. Best all-around boy at Knox City High, senior class favorite, FFA president, co-captain of his football team, honorable mention all-district. Carl B. (Bigun) Bradley, Jr.'s plain moon face, his eyes tinted Paul Newman blue, barely seen in the shadow of his hat, smoking what is alleged to be a Marlboro cigarette. Why? Why would Marlboro pick Bigun Bradley? I guess because they saw he was a real cowboy.

There is a Marlboro sunset as I slide back along the mud road and turn toward Guthrie. Two horses in the road ahead turn flank and trot off into the brush. There is a silence that lasts forever—if there were such a word, *forever*. A windmill is silhouetted against the dark fire of the horizon, and I can't help thinking it's a long way home.

—*September 1973*

H. L. Hunt. *Photography by UPI*

# H. L. HUNT'S LONG GOODBYE

## by Bill Porterfield

*Like they said, you can't take it with you.*

That last weekend in November was almost too much, even for astrologers and students of the absurd. It began predictably enough—former President Nixon was too ill to testify at the Watergate cover-up trial, doctors had decided—but then strange headlines began to hop out. Popular Princess Elizabeth Bagaya, the foreign minister of Uganda, was dismissed by President Idi Amin after he charged that she had made love to a European in the restroom of the Orly Airport in Paris. In Philadelphia, family pressure and the delicate political position of Vice-President designate Nelson Rockefeller forced Happy Rockefeller's 77-year-old millionaire aunt, Rachel Fitler, to call off her engagement to Michael Wilson, her 29-year-old chauffer. In our other staid, conservative, old-line town, Harvard students were giving standing ovations to none other than Fanne Fox, the Tidal Basin Bombshell who had stripped Congressman Wilbur Mills of his doughty dignity and made of him a dirty old man.

It was a seductive, if lurid, time to be alive, and every health faddist knew that H. L. Hunt was trying. At 85 he was munching dates and doing the full lotus and aiming at a century and more. But then secretly, before only family and friends, he began to fail. And on that last Friday in November, he died in Dallas' Baylor University Medical Center, of pneumonia and complications from cancer. The weekend was yet full of surpises. The Bears of Baylor University, some fellow Baptists, were outscoring the Rice University football team to cap off their first conference championship in 50 years. It would have been a fitting final balm for the world's richest Baptist and football fan.

But perhaps it is just as well Hunt was not aware of the events that transpired on the last day of his life. For transcending everything was the news—in a surprise an-

*Bill Porterfield is a contributing editor of* Texas Monthly. *A freelance writer, Porterfield has worked in television and as a newspaper reporter.*

nouncement from Secretary of State Henry Kissinger—that President Ford would visit Peking in 1975. What an irony to go down to! Haroldson Lafayette Hunt, Jr., had been notoriously stingy with his money, except in one endeavor. Like a Daddy Warbucks, he had waged a long and expensive crusade against communism and what he considered its influence here. Joe McCarthy and Douglas MacArthur had been his idols, Nixon a dupe for allowing Kissinger to subvert us into a rapprochement with China and Soviet Russia. Hunt's last hope lay in Gerald Ford, whom he had recommended to Nixon as a vice-president back before 1960. Yes, it was just as well.

If the highest estimates of H. L. Hunt's wealth are true, he was not only four times as rich as all the Rockefellers, he was nine times richer than all the accumulated wealth of all the presidents of the United States—all 38 of them from George Washington to Gerald Ford. Some sheiks of Araby may scoff at that two or five billion now—whatever it is—but if they hadn't taken the Libyan fields from him two years ago, he'd still be the richest man in the world. I'm not hung up on his money, though. What I liked about old H. L. was the originality and richness of his character.

The big rich are not always fascinating, but Hunt was. Take *Fortune* Magazine's head count on the new centimillionaires in America. The Yellow Pages make better reading. Once it was at least vulgar to have suddenly made a fortune. Now it's just dull. Can you imagine squeezing oranges for a living? That's what Anthony Rossi does down in Florida, and in the last six years it has made him $70 million. He's one of 39 men in the country *Fortune* says has made at least $50 million since 1968. The list doesn't include people who have inherited that much or who made it before 1968, so it's an interesting insight into our newest crop of Croesuses. What emerges is not a saga of flamboyant wheeling and dealing, but rather a parade of pedestrian types who have cornered the market on faucets and tire treads, of people who purvey pet foods and discount clothing. I didn't see a sugar daddy among them. If they throw their money away, it is not to blondes but to Baptist churches and Bible colleges.

But H. L., now, he was many men in one, multitudinous and contradictory. Good and bad, but on a larger scale, right out of Ayn Rand. In an age of midgets and conformists, he was a rogue who broke rules and cut a large swath and then, at last, lay down with a smile and allowed the ubiquitous and unctuous preachers to make of him a monument to nobility. He knew they would because he knew human nature. The will, after all, was still to be read. If ever a dead man looked satisfied with himself, at peace and in repose and yet somehow expectant, it was Mr. Hunt.

He lay in an open casket at First Baptist, the world's largest and richest Baptist church. The church, a mighty fortress covering several downtown blocks in Dallas, is noted as a rock against theological and social heresy. Only recently has the congregation, which numbers 20,000, been moved to accept a Negro member. Hunt was not necessarily the most famous First Baptist; Billy Graham is also a member, though he was not at the funeral. The presiding preacher was the pastor, Dr. W. A. Criswell, a compelling and charismatic fundamentalist who helped convert Hunt after his second marriage seventeen years ago. That was a conversion to match Saul's when he became Paul. Perhaps a more profane comparison would be the transfiguration of that old rip-roaring, foul-mouthed drunk, Sam Houston. It was a woman that helped old Sam see the light: his second wife, the resourceful and enduring Margaret Lea. Legend has it that H. L. was equally rollicking, and history knows that Ruth Ray Wright brought him to heel in a chorus of hallelujahs.

Ruth was a Hunt Oil secretary H. L. married in 1957, two years after the death of his first wife, Lyda Bunker. This marriage, when Hunt was 68, confronted the six children of his first bed—Lamar, Nelson Bunker, W. Herbert, H. L. III, Margaret, and Caroline—with a stepmother 30 years younger than their father. They also faced four sibling rivals in the children of Ruth: Ray Lee, June, Helen, and Swanee, the issue of "a former marriage." After Hunt formally adopted them, Ruth revealed that Hunt was, indeed, their true father. Ruth, a pretty blonde with Southern belle manners, seemed just the right tonic for the old rascal. It wasn't long before she and the preacher put the Lord on H. L., turned him away from gambling and cigars, and led him up the aisle to salvation. Dr. Criswell baptized Hunt and his new family—and from then on they were all devout in the faith.

In his last years Hunt was a doting family man, a moulty old lion in winter. He loved to lie up there in his out-sized replica of Mount Vernon and sing hymns with Ruth and the youngest girls. As he began to fail, there was one song he could not bear to hear: "Swing Low, Sweet Chariot," where it keeps repeating, "comin' for to carry me home. . . ."

It was my first time to hear Brother Criswell preach, and I waited expectantly as the pews filled. People quietly streamed in, filling up the benches except for a few in the balcony. It was more like a theater than a church. There were even little traffic signs and admonitions. I dutifully took note that "In Case of Emergency," I was to "Please Use Exit 2." Another said "Please Be Reverent." Tommy Brinkley, the organist, began to play. First, "The Solid Rock," and then, "This is My Country." Every now and then, a knot of mourners would get up from their seats and go gaze at the body. Mr. Hunt was laid out in a dark, pinstriped suit. He was a beautiful man, his pink and fine, bold head more delicately carved than pictures had portrayed. He was thinner than I had thought, his nose as aristocratic as his Huguenot forbearers. Others had compared him in the flesh to Herbert Hoover, but I saw in him a Leopold Stokowski. He was a genius in a way, an entrepreneur, an impresario, a maestro of money. Most of us pass through town unnoticed. He made ripples, made men note his passing. He had made his mark, like the conquistador of old who, traveling in the wilderness of New Mexico, had inscribed upon the rock, "Pasó por Aquí."

The day before the funeral I had walked to the Kentucky Fried Chicken stand and had ordered a box of No. B, regular, and an iced Coke. They were selling copies of Colonel Harland Sanders' autobiography, so I bought one. My mind was on Hunt and his death, and it struck me, in an amused way, that he and the old bird-cook shared some similarities. The Colonel called his book *Life As I Have Known It Has Been FINGER LICKIN' GOOD*, and inside the jacket was a rundown of the Colonel's checkered career. Sixth grade dropout, farmhand at age twelve, army muletender, locomotive fireman, railroad section hand, aspiring lawyer, insurance salesman, ferryboat entrepreneur, chamber of commerce secretary, tire salesman, amateur obstetrician, unsuccessful political candidate, gas station dealer, motel operator, restaurateur . . . until finally, at the age of 65, a new interstate highway snatched the traffic away from his corner, leaving the Colonel with nothing but a Social Security check and a secret recipe for fried chicken. Dad-gummit! The Colonel was 74 before someone paid him $2 million for his fried chicken franchise. He went on to get religion and sue the people who bought him out something like 22 times, for various and sticky reasons.

Sitting there licking my fingers, I decided to outline Hunt's career the way the Colonel had his. This is what I came up with, and it probably isn't complete: never went to school, farmhand till fifteen, freight train and flophouse hobo, dishwasher, cowboy, lumberjack, laborer, sheepherder, carpenter, mule-team driver, card shark gambler, cotton planter, oil lease hound, oil operator, big-time gambler, farmer, rancher, real estate man, food processor, manufacturer, author, philosopher, political propagandist, unsuccessful advisor to four presidents, and, of course, at one time or another the world's richest man. Compared to Hunt, the Colonel was chicken feed.

Hunt's life was highly American—as bodacious and ungoverned as the age that made him. He was born and raised on a 500-acre farm near Ramsey, Illinois, the youngest of eight children in a well-to-do family. The early years of his youth were among the most prosperous in American history, as the great captains of industry followed the pioneers' movement to the west. There was the Panic of 1893, when Hunt was four and Grover Cleveland was president, and it grew into our first serious depression, but that soon was dispelled by a resurgence of production and patriotism—the latter culminating in Teddy Roosevelt's charge up San Juan

Hill. The rough rider was Hunt's hero; when Roosevelt tried to make a comeback in 1912 as the "old Bull Moose," Hunt, then 23 and running a cotton plantation down in Mississippi, rode all the way back to Illinois to vote for Roosevelt for president. Hunt himself seemed to imitate, throughout his long life, the vim and vigor of the president.

The Land Panic of 1921 destroyed his cotton venture, and Hunt moved on to El Dorado, Arkansas. Oil had been found and the town was booming. Oldtimers claim H. L. came to town as a gambler, and won his first oil well in a game of five-card stud. Hunt admitted he was something of a hustler, but he insisted that he had gotten his stake by shrewdly trading leases. From El Dorado he moved to Smackover in Arkansas, Urania in Louisiana, and out to West Texas—anywhere there was the smell of oil and a sucker at a card table.

As his luck held, Hunt began to form a political philosophy to match his new fortune. Where once he had admired a strong man in the White House, such as Teddy Roosevelt, now he came to value weak men at the helm of government. Young Hunt was not alone. The 1920s was an era of giants in every endeavor except the presidency. There were great heroes in sports—men such as Dempsey and Cobb and Ruth, Thorpe and Red Grange—and as president, a congenital weakling, a bag of wind named Warren G. Harding. There was Man of War on the race track, Lucky Lindy in the sky, George Gershwin on radio, Mary Pickford on the silver screen, and in the White House that old corpse, Calvin Coolidge. And H. L. Hunt loved him. By the end of the decade, when the country was going from riches to rags, Herbert Hoover was in the White House, a rags to riches man. It was all caterwampus. But not for Hunt, because out in the dogwood and deep red clay of East Texas there was a fortune to be made.

H. L. Hunt was already a millionaire, when, at the height of the panic in 1930, he bought out Dad Joiner's strike in East Texas. Joiner had drilled with money raised among the poor farmers of the area, but by the time he had brought the first few wells in, he found that the Depression had created an oil glut, and he couldn't sell his leases to the majors because of some clouded titles. But Hunt didn't lie back. For $50,000 in cash, $45,000 in notes, and a guarantee of $1.3 million from future production, he took over a field that turned out to tap a lake of oil 43 miles long and up to nine miles wide. Hunt's share of the profits came to $100 million, at least. By 1940, H. L. was a billionaire and expanding into the Middle East. During World War II, he produced more oil, here and abroad, than did Germany, Italy, and Japan. By 1960, he was the world's richest man. By this time, his old partner in East Texas, Columbus Marvin (Dad) Joiner, had been broken and buried thirteen years.

A murmur arose from the congregation. A small black man, who seemed to materialize from nowhere, stood before the coffin and drew a sword. He waved it before the dead man, sheathed it, and exited by a side door. It seemed an act of defiance, and I—and I'm sure others—thought, my God, is he some revolutionary, some Symbionese Liberationist come to defame the dead capitalist's memory? Later the mysterious man identified himself as Louis Lyons, a 44-year-old ex-convict Hunt had befriended. He had come to salute the old Caesar, not to damn him.

The family had not yet entered the sanctuary, but at our backs we were startled to see an unmistakable likeness of the dead man standing in the doorway. It could have been Hunt himself, 30 years younger. "Hassie!" someone whispered. And indeed it was. Haroldson Lafayette Hunt III, the old man's eldest son, the gentle one who was said to live in a world all his own. Some great tragedy had befallen him, and he had lived close to the side of his father. Once, it was said, he had shown the same managerial genius as the father, only to retreat from the world of men and affairs. Some said Hassie's tragedy was his experience in the Second World War. Others said he had never gone to war, that he had changed because he could not stand up to the pressure of being a great man's son. Is it indelicate and inaccurate of me to slip here into hearsay? What the mourners said that day, and what the press and other people wrote and said, were the stuff of the Hunt legend. For a man so prominent yet so private, this legend is what lives on, just as it bathes the children in the same light. In a moment Brother Criswell himself would be myth-making, and I would listen to that. Right now I watched Hassie Hunt. He walked down the aisle, looked at his dead father, and wept. Then he returned to his post behind us, near the door. There was in him a sad dignity.

The organist launched into "God Bless America," the cue for Brother Criswell, followed by the family, to enter the stage. The casket was closed. The family sat to the left down front, and Brother Criswell stood at the pulpit above the casket. He is in his 60s, a silver-haired, handsome man with a large head and lantern jaw. Many of his parishioners drive great distances—past closer Baptist churches—to hear him preach. His Wednesday night prayer meetings had to be moved from a hall seating 700 into the main auditorium to handle the crowd. On Sundays the crush is like a small Cotton Bowl. Worshippers often have to stand. Parking lot attendants with walkie-talkies are all about the grounds. Criswell has written at least a dozen books, the most recent entitled *Why I Believe In The Literal Word of The Bible*. The literal fact of First Baptist is extraordinary, approaching legend. Housed in a complex which includes an eleven-story office building, First Baptist Church is a publishing house; a television and recording studio which broadcasts Sunday services; a credit union; a country club and health spa which includes gymnasiums, bowling lanes, skating rink, and snack bars; as well as, of course, the church school and the church itself. First Baptist has 22 choirs, one of which travels throughout the world. The pastor's wife plays saxophone in the church's swing band, and H. L. Hunt's third daughter, June, used to sing solo in one of the choirs before she went to Nashville to record and tour with her gospel-singing engagements.

June Hunt would sing, Brother Criswell announced, a song that her father loved so well. It was about Jesus. "I shall know him," it went, "by the print of the nails in his hand." June is a tall, good-looking blonde, and she sang with poise and warmth, clear-eyed and smiling without a break in her voice. Brother Criswell read scripture. "Great and noble father," he intoned, "teach us to number our days . . . The grass withereth, the flower fadeth. . . ."

H. L. Hunt knew only too well that grass withereth, but he tried to forestall the aging process as long as he could. He developed a keen interest in what enabled other men to live beyond the usual life span. When items appeared in the newspapers about some Methuselah holding forth in some far corner of the world, Hunt would have his secretary call the Associated Press, or even the character in question, to see if there might be more details he could pick up.

In September, 1972, Rena Pederson of *The Dallas Morning News* went to the Hunt home to interview him at breakfast. Hunt sat munching grapes, pecans, dates, and apricots. He also had before him an array of fruit juices and bouillon. All of a sudden, he dropped to the floor on all fours and began crawling about. "I'm a crank about creeping!" he cried, rounding the antique dining table on his hands and knees.

"Don't go too fast," Mrs. Hunt cautioned.

"Yes, please slow down," the *News* photographer begged. "I want to get your picture."

"They never can keep up with me," he cackled, returning to the table. "Yahoo!" he whooped, and ordered a date for everyone. He bit into a pecan and declared, "I used to be the world's Number One softshell pecan grower. I suppose I still am. I eat them instead of meat."

To reporter Pederson's amazement, the billionaire barraged her with health food tidbits. Avoid white bread and white sugar. He recommended his own bread of cracked wheat and honey. He grew most of his own vegetables in a three-acre garden at the side of the mansion. Ate them raw as possible and salt free. He handed her literature: pamphlets on health, a mimeographed Bible verse, and an article he had written about the benefits of creeping.

"I have lots of money," he laughed, "so they call me the 'Billionaire Health Crank.' Heh Heh Heh."

At that time, a little more than two years ago, Hunt was convinced he had a good chance to live as long as the world record-holder, a Russian the Soviets claim was 167. He liked to compare himself to the Hunzakuts of the Himalayas, who played polo into their 100th year.

Frank Tolbert, *The Dallas Morning News* columnist and author, once put Hunt onto buying a Mexican border ranch because of the curative power of its springs. Tolbert claims to be the first writer Hunt ever consented to see. This was back in 1948, when Hunt was as reclusive as Howard Hughes. Tolbert didn't do too badly by him, so Hunt trusted him and was open to most of the other journalists who began beating a path to his door. Anyway, one day Hunt got all excited over Tolbert's tales about an old resort ranch at Indian Hot Springs, on the Rio Grande about 125 miles downstream from El Paso. There was a spring on the place called Geronimo Springs, which the old-timers out there likened to a fountain of youth. It revived an old feller's interest in sex and exorcised sores and such. The Vanderbilts once used it as a spa, and Pancho Villa used to dip in it to rid himself of gonorrhea. Hunt bought the retreat, and you rarely saw him without his old leather valise which contained bottled mineral water from its healing springs. Along with the water he usually had some of his bread, made of wheat from the Panhandle soil of Deaf Smith County.

One summer day a few years back, Hunt showed up in Judge Tom Neely's general store out at Sierra Blanca, near Fort Bliss. He had just returned from his hot springs, so he passed his water bottle and bread to the men about and joined them in a game of checkers, at which he was mightily skilled. Judge Neely, who is the Roy Bean of Hudspeth County, was complaining about a foot ailment, when to his surprise the world's richest man got up from the checker board and got down on his knees and pulled off Neely's boots and socks. "He started rubbing my feet," the judge said. "At first I felt bad about it, a man like that on his knees rubbing my old feet, but then I felt good about it and it did make me feel a lot better."

Dr. James Draper, the young associate pastor, followed Dr. Criswell. He said a prayer for Hunt and his survivors, and then, to my astonishment, called (in what I thought was a very pointed way) for some of the Hunts who had not accepted Christ to do so. I know that preachers grab you when they can get your attention, but at your father's funeral? He was obviously aiming at someone among the older children, all of whom are grown and quite competent to come to God in their own fashion. It didn't help matters much when he extended the invitation to the rest of us who might be beyond the fold.

Dr. Criswell came back to announce that the last hymn that H. L. Hunt had heard was one that had been broadcast on television a Sunday or so before, and that Beverly Terrell, a close friend of the Hunts, was going to sing it. She dedicated the song not to a man who was wealthy, but to the God who made the wealth of this world. "Voices of a million angels," she sang, "could not express my gratitude . . . All that I am and ever hope to be . . . I owe it all to thee, God . . . "

Sidney Latham, Hunt's long-time friend and personal attorney, a retired vice-president of the Hunt Oil Company, delivered the eulogy. He described Hunt as one of the finest Christians he had ever known. Hunt's faith was, he said, in keeping with the faith and nobility of the company and of the family who founded it.

He said something I liked. "Hunt," he said, "moved in and about the timberlines of life where the timid fear to venture." Sure, Latham said, Hunt had his faults. He was all too human, the old lawyer ventured, and certainly, he added, Hunt was one of the most misunderstood men who ever drew public comment. He described his old colleague as a patriot who proved that the American Way would work, but that in all candor, after all the millions were made, signed, sealed, and delivered, that the greatest happiness Hunt had had was the Sunday night he joined the church. "He said it was the best and biggest trade he had ever made," Latham said, raising his voice. "He said he had traded the here for the hereafter, and he was pleased."

What did Hunt have here? Certainly America's largest private fortune. And, some said, a divided family fighting over it—the children of the dead wife versus the children of the living wife. There were signs of struggle even before the old man's death, hidden beneath a confusing tangle of lawsuits and investigations, both private and public, that involved not only the Hunts and their employees, but of all things, Watergate-ridden Richard Nixon, his attorneys-general, John Connally, Senator James Eastland, Israel's Golda Meir, and the Arab terrorists Al Fatah.

The intrigue surfaced routinely enough four years ago, when a suburban Dallas policeman stopped Jon Joseph Kelly for running a stop sign. Kelly, a 25-year-old Houston man, identified himself as a private detective. The patrolman noticed a tape recorder in Kelly's back seat. "When I asked him if he was working on a divorce case," the policeman later recalled, "he stepped on the gas and took off. If he hadn't panicked, I wouldn't have hauled him in and none of this would have come out.''

What came out was this:

The FBI discovered that Kelly and a sidekick, Patrick McCann, had placed wiretaps in the homes of four Hunt Oil executives, among them Paul Rothermel, H. L. Hunt's chief security man. Rothermel, a former FBI man and an attorney, claimed that in 1969 he had persuaded Hunt to change his will to the greater benefit of the second Mrs. Hunt and her children. Since then, odd things had been happening, and Rothermel believed that the older Hunt sons were behind it. Kelly and McCann, however, remained mute—until they got three years in prison. Then they fingered two of the older Hunt sons, Nelson Bunker and W. Herbert Hunt, as the plotters and paymasters. Nelson and Herbert were indicted on wiretapping charges, but only after a curiously long time lag. They have since admitted that they ordered ''legal investigations'' of Rothermel and the other executives, but not wiretaps. They contend their motive was not to spy on their father's will-making, but to trace millions of dollars which were allegedly siphoned off into dummy companies. They backed up their charges with a suit against Rothermel and two other company officials. Since then Kelly has sued Nelson and W. Herbert Hunt, complaining they ruined his reputation and career. The Rothermels have retaliated with a suit against the Hunts, Mrs. Rothermel claiming the operatives interfered with her work as a psychiatrist's aide by eavesdropping on her patients.

That's the private war.

Publicly, three federal grand juries have returned indictments against nine men, including the two Hunt boys. Meanwhile, for almost a year, a fourth federal grand jury in Dallas has been investigating the three-year time lag in getting the wiretap indictments against the Hunt brothers. Hunt sources allege that President Nixon and his men promised Nelson Bunker and his brother immunity from prosecution if the Hunts would give the FBI a list of Al Fatah agents in the United States. Nelson Bunker, because of his attempts to keep Hunt oil fields from being nationalized by Libya, felt himself a target for assassination, and therefore kept a close count of Al Fatah agents in this country. Nelson Bunker and his father met President Nixon at the celebrated barbecue at John Connally's Floresville ranch in the autumn of 1972. Soon after, Nelson Bunker huddled with Richard Kleindienst, then the new boss of the Justice Department, at the plantation of Mississippi Senator James Eastland. Hunt sources claim Nelson Bunker came through for the FBI, and that the information helped foil a plot against Golda Meir when she visited New York in March of 1973. The indictments against Nelson Bunker and his brother went through anyway. In April, Kleindienst fell to Watergate. The next month Libya's Colonel Qadhafi confiscated the Hunt holdings in the Arabian desert.

Nelson Bunker Hunt is said to feel betrayed, and that's putting it mildly. At one time Libya was his happy hunting ground. He negotiated Hunt Oil's vast holdings there, wined and dined the inauguration of the new empire, and had high friends all over the Arab World. But then, because of his country's friendship toward Israel and their own growing nationalism, the Arabs turned against him. Nixon let him down. And then, two days after the burial of his father, he learned that the old man had bequeathed him a

stunner. The will gave Mrs. Hunt 100 per cent of the patriarch's stock in Hunt Oil, distributing to Nelson Bunker and the other nine children and their families the rest of the estate. True to his fashion, the old man kept it all in the family, with Ruth's offspring seemingly getting the upper hand. Ray Hunt, the oldest son of the second set, was named as sole executor. And to insure compliance, H. L. stipulated that any beneficiary who challenged the will in any form would be cut off without a cent.

To top it off, more indictments are on the way, which are said to incriminate Watergate figures, as well as some prominent Texans within and without the Hunt empire.

Few Godfathers, whether Irish or Italian, political or criminal, have left progeny with such a bounty of brains and ability. Nelson Bunker is an aggressive go-getter with many of his father's talents. Politically, he is a chip off the old genus Betula, a Birch not for bending, and has been almost as active as H. L. in backing Robert Welch and George Wallace. In 1973, he and Herbert, who himself is no slouch at real estate development, were reported to have cornered the market on silver bullion. They are now said to be trying to do the same thing with America's beet refining. Bunker is supposed to have more racehorses than any other breeder in the country, as well as some of the best Charolais in the cattle business.

Lamar Hunt, of course, is probably better known than any of the boys because he took his father's gaming instincts and love of sport and patiently turned the losing Dallas Texans into the winning Kansas City Chiefs. Lamar and his brother-in-law, Al G. Hill, put World Championship Tennis on tour, and Lamar helped kick life into the North American Soccer League with Kyle Rote, Jr., and the Dallas Tornado. The stepbrother and fifth son, Ray Lee Hunt, the executor of the will, is showing the same savvy with his dealings in downtown Dallas. Ray is also the angel of the new magazine, *D*.

As for the five daughters, June with her singing career is the most visible, but the others all married well, and each is as individual as the brothers. Margaret married Al Hill, the sportsman and banker; Caroline married Hugo Schoellkopf, scion of one of Dallas' first families; Helen married Randall Kreiling, a dashing young mover from Peoria who is already making his mark in Dallas; and Swanee married a quiet but brilliant young preacher, Mark Meeks.

Those children, along with 25 grandchildren and five great-grandchildren, are the sum of H. L. Hunt as a family man and provider—his private behest.

He went public in only one way really, and that was in his products—which included his political philosophy. William F. Buckley probably has never opened a can of HLH corn, but the old man's political gumbo he tasted and found lacking. Buckley says politics was the least of H. L. Hunt's talents, that his books were silly and that Hunt did more harm than good to the conservative movement. In a column published shortly after Hunt's death, fellow Texan Buckley declared that Hunt had left ''capitalism a bad name, not, goodness knows, by frenzies of extravagance, but by his eccentric understanding of public affairs, his yahoo bigotry and his appallingly bad manners.''

Yet Hunt was hardly a conservative, at least not as that term is used in American politics, and never claimed to be. I'm not quite sure how Hunt bothered Buckley. He made me nervous all right, but in some of the same ways that Buckley does. If Hunt had had his way, Senator Joe McCarthy would have purged every "pinko" and "subversive" from the roll call of American patriotism. Douglas MacArthur would have been president rather than Dwight Eisenhower, and we would have gotten out of the United Nations long ago and bombed the beJesus out of Russia and Red China—to deter their nuclear capacity before it matched our own. Hunt in 1966 told *Playboy* Magazine that the Air Force's General George C. Kenney had had such a plan back in 1950, and Hunt wished we had used it.

Hunt called himself a "constructive." A conservative, he argued, tended to put a weight around the neck of liberty. He defined liberty as "freedom for the individual to do whatever he likes consistent with organized society and good taste." The word, "conservative," he went on, "denotes mossback, reactionary, and old-fogeyism."

This smacks to me of classic liberalism, and I said as much on a Dallas television show a few years back. Hunt was intrigued by my calling him a liberal, and he asked me for a copy of my remarks. If they offended him, it never reached me. I couched my argument in this context: the terms "liberal" and "conservative" came to be used late in the 18th and early in the 19th century, out of the froth of the French Revolution and Napoleon's rise and fall. The liberal believed first of all in the independence and autonomy of the individual, answering only to his conscience. A free individual, the liberal believed, had an unlimited capacity for self-development and improvement. In personal freedom, man could create on this earth near-perfect conditions. Unconstrained man, giving full play to his personality! A nice definition of H. L. Hunt. But the liberal wasn't an anarchist. One man's self-expression could not impinge on the freedom of other men, and this fits nicely into Hunt's qualifications about "organized society and good taste" in his description of a "constructive." Liberals, however, were not to be confused with democrats. Liberals came to distrust the common man, because they feared his ignorance; they suspected he could be manipulated by despots. Liberals opposed universal vote, limiting suffrage to the propertied classes. And this nicely defines "Alpaca," Hunt's model republic. Hunt's utopia was not unlike Plato's *Republic*. If Hunt's was oligarchical and built upon mammon, Plato's was a communistic aristocracy built upon a pathological passion for order that was self-defeating.

Neither old theorist could influence anyone to take his advice. Plato thought for a while he might persuade Dionysus II, the ruler of Syracuse, to put his ideas into actual practice, but it was an unhappy wedding of the philosopher and the king. Twenty-three hundred years later, Hunt was just as pushy with his programs to Presidents Eisenhower, Kennedy, Johnson, and Nixon; but Booth Mooney, who was Hunt's man in Washington, admitted that "it is not of record that any of them solicited the counsel so freely offered . . . ." It was Lyndon Johnson that Hunt especially liked. But as Mooney has written, "Advise as the old gentleman might, it was of no use. Johnson never gave the slightest sign of paying any attention to the snowstorm of memoranda from Dallas, which for a time descended on the White House at the rate of four or five a week."

Other Americans did listen. For six years in the 1950s,

Hunt had Dan Smoot on radio and television with Facts Forum, a public affairs program which was finally replaced by Life Line. Hunt saw Life Line as a kind of Voice of America in the heart of the heart of the country; at its peak a few years ago Life Line was carried by 531 radio stations and heard by an estimated five million Americans. The guiding principle of Life Line is anti-communism, and it is delivered in fire and brimstone sermons about the evils of everything that has transpired since Sherman rode through Georgia and Roosevelt sold out at Yalta. The sum of it seems to have given form to some of the heart of darkness and fear of change that is in us all. The foe is everywhere, subversive and conspiratorial, and the instinct is to stack rifles in the basement and vote against minorities and long-hairs and the welfare state.

There is, however, one truth we should accept from H. L. Hunt, without reservation: you can't *buy* friends, domestic or foreign. He knew that long before he was rich, and so he never tried. The one thing you *can* buy, most of the time, is power, even political power and even in a republic. And that, ironically or not so ironically, H. L. Hunt did *not* do, either. And that's the beauty of the man for me. His mouth always got in the way of his money, and turned the right people off.

Hunt himself did not seem to suffer from all that hate and fear and trembling that he supported. He was altogether himself in an age of cover and cosmetics. He had more deer about Mount Vernon than dogs, and his bark was worse than his bite, unless you were a radish or a ravishing woman. We forget that he was not always old and wispy-haired and hyped on greens and granola. You could catch him each year at the State Fair, manning a modest booth displaying his HLH products, handing out a goodwill bag which contained one of his paperback books—perhaps *Alpaca*—along with a packet of "freedom talks" from Life Line, as well as a free sample of "GASTRO-MAGIC," his special brand of relief from heartburn and indigestion.

Some have painted him as sinister, the right-wing capitalist who conveniently left town the day JFK was killed in Dallas, but I can't let my paranoia run away in that direction either. I don't think Hunt conspired to kill the president anymore than I think Nelson Rockefeller is in league with Henry Kissinger to turn us over to the communists. Which means, I guess, that I give H. L. Hunt more credit than he gave Rocky and the rest of us.

Dr. Criswell returned to his pulpit. "Worthy, noble father," he cried, his voice breaking, "sentimental about his home and children, good to them beyond compare. Especially to the child who was not well. Oh yes, I often referred to him as Mr. Golden Heart."

And on he went, describing Hunt as a man too big for one life, a man wise as Solomon. "Haroldson Lafayette Hunt, living giant with gentle touch . . . au revoir, auf wieder-sehn, till we meet again. . . ."

An hour later Hunt was buried, in private ceremonies, beside the grave of his first wife in Hillcrest Memorial Park in north Dallas.

*—March 1975*

# HOW WE PLAY THE GAME

I t's a pretty far piece from the Duke of Wellington's remark that the Battle of Waterloo was won on the playing field of Eton to Darrell Royal saying that "a coach likes to have a lot of those trained pigs who'll grin and jump right in the slop for him." In Texas, sports are ends in themselves. Nobody takes their sports more seriously than the computer geniuses of the Dallas Cowboys, where the last joke was heard circa 1967 (the person who cracked it was immediately traded). Gary Cartwright, who had covered the Cowboys in their younger days and coined the term "Doomsday Defense," went with the team to Miami for Super Bowl X. In "The Ultimate Game," Cartwright was less interested in the game (which the Cowboys happened to lose, 21–17) than in how the veterans got their tired and broken bodies into the breach once more. Baseball by tradition is more nostalgic than football; Paul Burka's "At Play in the Fields of the Lord" is a true fan's notes about a very special baseball park with a cliff in center field, the kind of endearing touch that today's commercial approach would eliminate—which, sadly, it did.

It's hard to believe that the simple communication between man and fish that is the art of angling could be commercialized, but Gene Lyons points out in "Bass Fishing in America" that at least parts of the sport have become big business (as a footnote, Tommy Martin didn't win the 1976 Bass Angler of the Year title, Oklahoma's Jim Houston did). On the other hand, while they clearly have their interesting points, pit bulldog fighting and shark fishing don't have much potential for commercial exploitation. Gary Cartwright's "Leroy's Revenge" stays with a dead-game dog to the bitter end, and Stephen Harrigan's "Pray for Sharks" ventures out in the Gulf with the special fishermen whose passions are kindled by a triangular fin cutting the water.

For another kind of sportsman, the only competition that counts is the competition with one's self. "Water Log" is Beverly Lowry's account of why she swims a mile a day, and what she thinks about while she does. Finally, Gregory Curtis manages to put all sports in perspective with "The Old Indoorsman," which is about as far from Tom Landry and the Dallas Cowboys as one could get and still have a sporting chance of staying a Texan.

116

*Illustrated by Justin Carroll*

# THE ULTIMATE GAME

by Gary Cartwright

---

*All Bicentennial celebrations should be
called off; Super Bowl X said it all.*

---

My first image of Super Bowl X was a traffic jam around an airplane painted by either Captain America or the fourth-grade class at Eanes School. Someone told me to sit back with the niggers—two hundred years into the great experiment, nigger is a euphemism for *player*.

My second image was an overfed man with a television camera backing down the aisle of the Cowboys' inbound flight taking film of Too Tall Jones. It was a tight fit for both men. Too Tall wore a maroon leather suit patched with yellows and browns, and a black cowboy hat. He was compelled to stoop as he moved from cabin to cabin. If this airship were full of Too Tall Joneses, as it will be someday, it would not fly.

The airplane that flew the Cowboys to Miami turned out to be one of two Braniff Bicentennial ships painted by Alexander Calder, "the father of kinetic art": the other Calder plane would return the team to Dallas a week later, richer and wiser. The name Braniff does not appear on the ship—only the giant signature CALDER. Streaks of red and blue on white suggested that we were ascending to the galaxy of Super Week aboard God's own Comet.

At the Fort Lauderdale airport were more TV cameras, a band, fans cheering and waving banners, and a police motorcycle escort waiting to convoy the Cowboys to the Galt Ocean Mile Hotel where they would camp during the final week of preparation for Super Bowl X. Champagne, steak, and lobster salad had been served in flight, and now more champagne was waiting as the team fought its way into the lobby, paling in the glare of lights. The owner of the hotel welcomed the Cowboys and invited them for a cruise aboard his 96-foot yacht. He wore a blue cowboy hat with the white block letter D, as did room clerks, bellhops, waitresses, lifeguards, chambermaids, and everyone else. A

*Gary Cartwright, author of books and numerous articles, recently won the Texas Institute of Letters award for journalism. He is a contributing editor of* Texas Monthly.

woman seated at a table sold copies of Roger Staubach's life story.

Staubach himself maneuvered among the hand-held microphones and poised note pads, saying yes he was glad to be here, and no he didn't think his Pittsburgh counterpart, Terry Bradshaw, was all that dumb. In this most over-covered of all sporting events, Staubach would be the most overcovered Dallas Cowboy, a task he accepted with grace and skill.

Lugging a computer printout thick as the Pittsburgh telephone book, Tom Landry signed two autographs for every one yard of lobby captured. Alicia Landry, his wife for 26 years, clung fearfully to a backgammon set. "I brought it along so that Tom can get his mind off the game for a few minutes," Alicia told a woman gossip columnist in a mink-trimmed cowboy hat. "He always beats me." This was Alicia's birthday—she didn't know it yet, but her husband had wired ahead and ordered a dozen long-stem roses for their $95-a-day suite at the Galt.

Texas E. Schramm, the Cowboys' president and the man who put together much of what was to happen this week, shook hands with a couple from New Jersey who told him they had been faithful Dallas Cowboy followers since 1966. Schramm was pleased but not surprised. Even before they became the Cinderella team of Super Bowl X, the Cowboys were probably the most popular team in the NFL—at least among the masses, those who believe that a football field is 24 inches across and sells cars. A onetime *Los Angeles Times* copy boy and *Austin American-Statesman* sportswriter, Schramm still oversees the Cowboys' weekly newspaper—circulation 20,000, including 15,000 from outside the Metroplex, of whom 5000 are from out of state.

The Cowboy chairman, Clint Murchison, Jr., hadn't arrived from Spanish Cay, his private island in the Bahamas, but he was represented by Bedford Wynne, one of the club's original board members. Bedford stalked into the lobby in his new blue cowboy boots, waved to the crowd, and shattered a full quart of J&B on the floor. "The only full one you've ever seen me drop," he reminded me. Bedford might be thought of as the Bicentennial Man—affluent, undeterred, a pioneer who knows his time will come. Over the years Bedford has invested in such enterprises as microwave ovens, a water-distilling plant, and a record album commemorating Freddy Steinmark, the UT football player killed by cancer. They say he lost a bundle in an enterprise that sold non-nicotine cigarettes. Bravos they were called. Bravos smelled and tasted like burning lettuce leaves, which in fact they were. Toots Shor once threw two sportsmen out of his saloon for lighting up a Bravo. Lately, Bedford has been making mysterious trips to Egypt, and frequently drops names like Sadat and Hussein. Egypt, so I read, is preparing to market lettuce cigarettes, though this could be a coincidence.

With the precision of a well-drilled two-minute offense, the Cowboys staff had set up headquarters and opened the hospitality room, which would remain open around the clock and serve as a watering station and hangout place for coaches, media, family, and friends. Before the week ended, Dallas' entire 44-member administrative staff would be on the scene, everyone from Kay Lang, the former Ice Follies chorus girl who started out with Tex Schramm and the Rams and has been the Cowboy ticket manager since the club was organized, on down to Radar, an impish black man with a goatee who is Dallas' "electronics coach"— a euphemism for he who keeps the movie projectors working. The hospitality room would also become a collecting place for the usual number of walk-ons—Boots Garland, onetime Cowboy "speed coach," a freelance adventurer who teaches athletes how to run and who once won $4000 hanging for two hours off a bridge in Mississippi; Jungle Jamey, pro football's best-known gate crasher, who once showed up at the Cowboy camp carrying a white rabbit and a ten-pound smoked buffalo shank; and finally, Willie Nelson, Jerry Jeff Walker, and assorted Austin musicians and crazies.

"Don't you think Super Bowl X is the quintessence of the Bicentennial celebration?" the woman gossip columnist with the mink-trimmed cowboy hat asked me. "I haven't met you. I'm Pat Byrd . . . B-Y-R-D . . . as in Senator Byrd, my ex-husband. Yes, he just threw his hat into the ring. That same Senator Byrd."

I told Pat Byrd that I wouldn't be surprised, then slipped out the back door of the hospitality room and walked down to the ocean. It had been seven years since I had traveled with the Cowboys, and I was trying to sort out my feelings. I remembered the first time the Cowboys had come to Miami, the 1965 Runner-up Bowl. There had been a lot of bellyaching about curfews and the players' wives not being allowed to fly with the team. Except for the night before Super X, there would be no curfew this week for the Cowboys. Wives came and went as they pleased.

The Cowboys were young then, in '65. The Runner-up Bowl was the team's first taste of anything resembling success, and though the opposing Baltimore Colts cursed their fate and referred to the event acidly as the "Leftover Bowl," it was that once-in-a-lifetime for Dallas, the coming of age. The Colts did most of their hard work in the nightspots of the Gold Coast, but Landry whipped his team every step. Predictably, the Colts humiliated the Cowboys. Ah, '65—Perkins, Meredith, Clarke, Lilly, Andrie,

Jordan, Edwards, Neely, Pugh, Green, Renfro. And the first really class crop of rookies, players like Craig Morton, Bob Hayes, Danny Reeves, Pete Gent. I'd never seen a rookie get beat around worse than Gent, or hang in tougher. Hayes got tough when Red Hickey threatened to send him home to momma. On the team plane flying back from New York—the game in which Dallas staked its claim to the much-despised Runner-up Bowl—Hayes had his first glass of champagne. Also his second, and his fifth and sixth. No one in the organization—certainly not Landry—had ever heard a player break into "Darktown Strutters Ball" over the intercom of a team charter.

The heroes of '65 are mostly gone now, gone to other teams, gone to TV, gone to literature, gone to fat business arrangements with concerns owned by Murchison or men of his class, gone into that peaceful oblivion of small-town America where every kid knows that the tall guy with the big shoulders once played for the Dallas Cowboys. There are still a few who carry on—Jordan, Edwards, Neely, Pugh, Renfro. Reeves and Cornell Green now work in the organization. That is what remains constant—the organization: Murchison, Schramm, Landry, Gil Brandt, Kay Lang. *They* are the Dallas Cowboys. The rest of it came from Rent-a-Jock. It hadn't changed. *Spread your seeds thick, lads, the harvest is short.* Nothing had changed at all.

From the niggers' wing of the Galt came the sounds of laughter and the smell of funny cigarettes. Definitely not lettuce.

Quintessence or not, nobody ever said Super Bowl X was egalitarian. "The sports spectacular of the century," as Tex Schramm liked to call it, was a great gathering of the elite—bankers, brokers, publishers, corporate executives, politicians, network moguls, celebrities, something like 2000 media people, and your accidental gadfly, like the New York cab driver who had been saving ten years for this trip and would blow it all by Sunday without ever seeing the game.

One evening in the Cowboys hospitality room—as we were listening to Clint Murchison, Jr., and Senator John Tower harmonizing on "Beautiful, Beautiful Texas"—Tex Schramm remarked: "This is the prestige event, the place to be if you're anybody." Raquel Welch might as not pop up at the NFL press room. Juice and Broadway Joe and Hornung, Phyllis and Irv and Brent, Jurgy and Jenke, Jimmy the Greek, Smashie, all the Main Men were there.

The face value of a ticket was $20, but one didn't just walk off the street and purchase a ticket. What it came down to was who you knew: this was it, the payoff. In Dallas and Pittsburgh, where the largest allocations of tickets went (13,000 each), you had to be a season ticket holder even to be considered for admission to Super Bowl X. More than a thousand Dallas season ticket holders camped all night in SMU's Moody Coliseum, hoping to be among the elite. The Cowboys could have sold out two or maybe three times their allotted tickets. One Dallas corporate executive advertised that he would fly any four people to Miami in exchange for four tickets. Hundreds and maybe thousands of counterfeit tickets were sold. Jimmy the Greek complained that he could secure only 89 tickets, and CBS Executive Bill Brendle, a specialist in these matters, was forced to trade eight on the 50 yard line for 24 in the end zone— otherwise CBS would have been entertaining sixteen most unhappy guests. Something like 5000 innocents signed on for a travel agency package deal, complete with air fare and hotel but without, they discovered too late, tickets to the game.

On the other hand Willie Nelson and his band arrived unannounced six hours before the game and were able to secure eleven seats, through the good offices of Bedford Wynne. Willie sat on the 50, a few seats down from Clint.

Ten years ago when the ''First AFL-NFL World Championship Game'' (the name Super Bowl was coined later) was played in the Los Angeles Coliseum, more than 20,000 tickets went begging. The value of Super Bowl I was incalculable to pro football, however: it signaled the end of a costly eight-year war between the NFL and the upstart American Football League, sealed the terms of the two leagues' merger, pried open the purses of the sports-hungry TV networks, and, if you will, put the niggers in their place. No longer could they use one league to bid for their service against the other. Inevitably this led to the labor movement. According to Schramm, player salaries have about quadrupled, while ticket prices, TV contracts, and other sources of revenue funneled through an ingenious arm called NFL Properties has merely tripled. All in all, niggering ain't a bad life. Figure that O. J. Simpson makes $350,000—the O. J. Simpson of 30 years ago, Steve Van Buren, made $15,000, or $1000 less than the playoffs' bonus paid to every member of the losing team of Super Bowl X.

It's staggering to realize that 75 million Americans, and another 55 million in foreign countries, watched live TV coverage of this Super Bowl. Who would have believed it? Pete Rozelle and Tex Shramm, that's who. When the NFL defied tradition and moved west with the first major league franchises in 1946, Schramm was a pioneer of the new wave. As general manager of the Los Angeles Rams, Schramm was the papa-dad of the modern scouting system. Schramm gave Pete Rozelle his first job in pro football, and when Schramm moved on to CBS and then to the newly formed Dallas Cowboys, he was influential in persuading some of the NFL mossbacks to accept Fast Pete as a compromise commissioner.

''For years,'' Schramm reminded me, ''the league had been controlled by Bert Bell and his friends. It was basically a struggle between the haves [i.e., New York, Chicago, Baltimore, Philadelphia] and the have-nots [Los Angeles and San Francisco]. TV revenue was very small and very selective in those days, but you didn't have to be a genius to see that the boom was coming. Pete was young, energetic, he understood merchandising, he understood TV, he stayed on top of things. Most important, he wasn't a threat to either side.''

Having harnessed the monster tube, the task now is to control it. It is the nature of TV to want more. Like some faded flower trying on her old wedding dress, Super Bowl X bulged at every seam, leaving the observer to wonder what they would do next—shoot the players out of cannons? The oracle of television has completely taken over. The Landrys and Don Shulas still draw the x's and o's, but TV calls the time-outs, changes the rules, educates the public to what it needs and what it needs to understand, blueprints the season, primes the pump, and brings the Too Tall Joneses out of ancestral swamps. If the Players Association ever decides to boycott the Super Bowl, television would show it anyway, starring Tony Orlando and Joe Garagiola.

After a week of debauchery, watching the Super Bowl is almost as tough as playing it. Anybody with any sense wanted to be home with the old TV. It was uncomfortably cold in Miami, and watching Super Bowl X from an upper deck in the Orange Bowl was like curling up with a good postage stamp. There were a lot of things going on, but without the end zone camera, stop action, and instant replay, no one could say just what they were. We didn't see the fashion show. Or watch Phyllis, Irv, and Brent, the stars of the game, chitchat at the Palm Bay Club with Namath, Hornung, and Hugh O'Brian, or watch them board their yacht for the trip down Biscayne Bay to the stadium, or see how they conquered the last ten blocks by helicopter. As Phyllis, Irv, and Brent were escorted from their landing spot on the 50 yard line, the best of us were caught in a traffic jam on IH 95. A friend watched as dozens of vehicles were abandoned on the shoulder of IH 95. Liberated occupants tumbled down the grassy slope toward the stadium, binoculars beating wildly and thermos jugs sloshing. Only it was the wrong stadium: the Orange Bowl was still three miles down the pike. After many hours of suffering and deprivation, a privileged few retreated to the CBS hospitality room in Miami Beach, where they sipped medicinal remedies and watched a videotape of the day on a seven-foot TV screen.

That's when I felt like I'd seen the Super Bowl,'' my friend told me.

In his curious, perceptive way, Duane Thomas said it best. When they asked him back at Super Bowl V how it felt to play in the ultimate game, Thomas posed his own question: ''If it's the ultimate game, why are they playing it again next year?''

'Cause CBS says so.

I knew it was Press Day at the Galt when I stepped out on my balcony to sniff some sea breeze and a woman two balconies down took my picture. A day before, when the media had inundated the Pittsburgh headquarters, defensive tackle Ernie Holmes had finally complained to Dallas sports editor Blackie Sherrod, ''You guys in the press make us sound like them iguala bears always up in the top of trees eating juicy leaves.'' As defending champions, the Steelers and their followers had been through it and were understandably blasé. Neither Holmes nor defensive end Dwight White blinked an eye when a midget in a yellow Pittsburgh hard hat with a blinking black light asked for a favor: would Holmes and White each kindly lift him by a leg and shake him in the air. They did.

By some unexplained, arbitrary choice made at NFL headquarters, the Steelers were quartered much nearer the Everglades than the ocean and Gold Coast—in a land-locked resort called Miami Lakes Inn, where the only bar in the hotel was off limits and there was a curfew every night. Linebacker Jack Lambert expressed the sentiments of the team when he said they all prayed that a shark would take off both of Roger Staubach's legs.

But now it was the Cowboys' turn, and the Galt swarmed with writers and TV and radio men eager to hear firsthand about the shotgun offense or the flex defense or how Dallas liked to banjo the ends and loop the gaps and frigate the quibits, and why Cliff Harris wore a fireman's helmet with a flashing red light, and how Randy White ate the heads off toads, and how a team with twelve rookies could make it to the Super Bowl, and how was the pressure?

Fine, thank you. The pressure was just fine. While a crew from Channel 8 in Dallas set up equipment on the beach, Harvey (Too Mean) Martin lolled under an umbrella with his arms around two Oriental nifties in bikinis. Too Mean wore a golf cap, aviator shades, and a T-shirt with the message GOOD & PLENTY across the chest. Bob Lilly was gone, but the Doomsday Defense flourished, in excellent hands. Too Tall and Too Mean were the perfect pair of ends.

When the camera was ready, Channel 8 sports director Verne Lundquist called Too Mean away from his idling. Too Tall was already in position with a hand mike. All year Too Tall had played the straight man, but today the roles reversed. While Lundquist stood back, Too Tall interviewed Too Mean on the application of the flex defense, then he socked him with the big one.

"I came up a year behind you and watched you grow into your position of defensive right end," Too Tall said eloquently. "Tell our audience, how does it feel playing defensive right end knowing there's a legend at defensive left end?"

Stretched out on a sunchair, rookie linebacker Thomas Henderson was finding it difficult to stay awake and answer questions at the same time. Henderson, less than a year out of tiny Langston College, had been out most of the night with one of the Pointer Sisters and therefore slept through Landry's morning meeting. Henderson, one gathers, will eventually join the 45 or 50 other ex-Cowboys who populate more tolerant rosters around the league.

A reporter asked Clint Longley, Dallas' young backup quarterback, if he was one of the three NFL quarterbacks rumored to be homosexual. "No," Clint said with a twinkle, "but I'm sure Roger is."

Landry shaded his eyes from the poolside reflection and spoke into a battery of microphones, explaining just one more time why, if Staubach is so smart, Landry calls all the plays. "If Roger calls the plays, he can do it about as well as I can," Landry says in his flat Sunday school manner. "He obviously knows what we're going to do. But the coaches don't. When we call the plays from the sidelines, we know exactly what is going to be run and we can look at the point of attack against the kind of defense that is being used and know exactly whether this play is a good one and whether we should continue using it. A quarterback can waste three or four calls that way." The interviewers tossed knowing glances at their sound men, pleased and begging for Landry's approval. Even after sixteen years and three Super Bowls, the misconception of Landry as a stoic who lives in a white box and pulls the wings off pretty insects persists. You wouldn't want to engage Tom in a long cocktail conversation, but as Dan Jenkins pointed out, Steeler coach Chuck Noll makes Landry sound like Don Rickles. Landry's impenetrable Gandhi image—like Lombardi's volatile impersonations of Hitler—has certain voodooistic advantages that the Cowboy staff makes no attempt to dispel. On the contrary, their inside joke is that the Tom Landry you see agonizing on the sidelines is, in fact, a professional actor named Rocky Romance. The real Tom Landry lurks under a hood, scribbling messages in Sanskrit.

A New York-based writer wants to know if Landry enjoyed Pete Gent's 1973 best-selling novel, *North Dallas 40*, portraying the Cowboys as a seething mutation of dope fiends, paranoiacs, fruits, cretins, and homicidal maniacs—managed by direct descendants of Daddy Warbucks and Genghis C. Khan. Landry replies mildly that he doesn't read that sort of book, but is halfway through *The Rise and Fall of Richard Nixon*.

"Jee-*sus*," wails a voice behind a palm tree. It is Peter Gent, alive and well and covering it for *Sport* magazine. Gent made a half-million dollars and a lasting place in the mythology of football with his novel, but he didn't always handle fame and fortune as well as friends wished. Last time I saw Gent, about one year ago, he carried several loaded guns and believed that the CIA and the Mafia were neck and neck in the race to bring about his end. Today, Peter looks trim, confident, and as comfortable as could be expected under the circumstances.

Gent has driven 35 miles from Miami to interview his ex-teammates, but now he can't think of a single question worth asking. I tell him I feel the same way. "The next time someone comes up to me and says: '*Well, whataya think?*' I'm moving to Canada," I tell Peter.

"Both quarterbacks [Staubach and Bradshaw] claim to be in solid with the Almighty," Gent says. "I'm not sure how that works in the rule book. Maybe God changes sides at halftime."

Press Day is getting out of hand. In their panic to determine just what's going on here, the ladies and gentlemen of the media are stepping over each other. In the lobby, several dozen drunk fans are staging an impromptu pep rally.

"Just how dumb is Bradshaw?"

"What did he say?"

"Watch out. You're stepping over my cable."

". . . against your basic odd defense . . ."

"Up yours, turkey."

"What did he say? He looks older than his picture."

After a while veteran linebackers Dave Edwards and D. D. Lewis slip discreetly through the kitchen door and out a side entrance of the hotel. They've had it. The ears can't take anymore, and the tongue is going fast. Fuzzy Edwards' hair is a lot longer than I remembered, and he's losing it in front. Fuzzy has been a fixture at strongside linebacker since 1965, Dallas' first winning season. He is the silent, lethal type, seldom spectacular, but absolutely professional. He has slowed a half-step, but so what. For something more than 200 consecutive games Fuzzy has stomped and been stomped on, and he still enjoys football. Cowboy followers are certain that the club is phasing him out—but they were saying the same thing last year when the Cowboys didn't even make the playoffs. In camp last summer Landry acknowledged that this was the best group of rookie linebackers he'd coached, then he said, "It's going to take a pretty good effort by someone to beat Dave out. The challengers come and go, and when the dust clears there's Edwards doing his job."

A biplane towing a streamer advertising jock-itch powder circles low over the Atlantic and I think of a question.

"Are you surprised to be at the Super Bowl?" I ask.

"Naw," Fuzzy laughed. "Not any more than I'm surprised to be anywhere. When I first came here in 1962 [as a free agent] I wasn't suppose to make the team."

"How can they keep writing that we didn't expect to be here?" D. D. Lewis asked. "There are 25 teams who didn't expect to be here. Pittsburgh is the only team that really thought they'd be here."

Both Lewis and Edwards thought this was the most enjoyable year they'd spent with the Cowboys. The energizing influence of twelve rookies had a lot to do with it. Landry had always bent, however slowly, with the times—it was the secret of his success—but this year he was bending faster, and good, strange things were happening.

"But don't believe that bull about Landry being relaxed at the Super Bowl," D. D. warned. "He wasn't very relaxed chewing ass this morning, and he ran us nearly to death yesterday afternoon and will probably do it again today."

"It's like Renfro said this morning," Fuzzy added. "We didn't come down here to throw in our jocks."

How else can you say it. The National Football League's Tenth Annual Gala was obscene. Roman Number X. Obscene. Not vulgar, understand, not wicked, and especially not offensive to the spirit of the Bicentennial which it may in fact have been; it was obscene in the sense of self-glorification.

More than half of the invited guests to the Friday night party were media people, some top echelon. Three thousand invitations were issued, and nobody knows how many got in with counterfeit tickets. They picked the perfect spot—Hialeah, the spot Gatsby would have picked. Old-time elegance. Well-guarded gates and long driveways through towering palms, uniformly spaced and all precisely the same height and girth. Gaily striped tents that dispensed an astonishing variety of beverages and roving waiters with silver trays of pretty things on toast. A clubhouse buffet featuring several tons of sand crab and wide columns of prime tenderloin. A choice of domestic wines. A swinging Forties band inside, and outside rising like an apparition in front of the storied Hialeah clubhouse, the 300-member ensemble of Up with People singing about how we are "Two Hundred Years and Just a Baby."

And, yes, a full moon hung over Miami. God how the heart ached to see Red Grange's mud-splattered ghost plowing through the flamingos. Just once.

Landry blushed and posed with his arm almost around Phyllis George. Alicia gabbed with old friends, including Father Dudley, the priest who has been sitting on the Giants' bench praying for the lads since back when they still folded helmets in their hip pockets. Rozelle talked to Lamar Hunt, whom he once considered a fly-by-night multimillionaire, and to Paul Hornung, whom he once suspended for gambling on his own team, and to politicians who expressed continuing self-interest in the NFL. Dick Fincher, who owns one of the biggest Olds agencies in Miami or anywhere else and was once married to Gloria DeHaven was there, and George Owen, who was once married to Mo Dean. Gil Brandt, the Dallas superscout (his ex-wife is now Mrs. Clint Murchison, Jr.), gave me a fountain pen with a retractable window pumping the virtues of being a Cowboy.

I asked Gil a tough question. I asked him to think back over all the players he had scouted and signed for the Cowboys—what was his most satisfying accomplishment? Gil thought for a long time, then gave me one-two: (1) turning up the fact that Staubach had attended New Mexico Military Institute and was therefore eligible for the draft a year sooner than anyone else realized; (2) maintaining relationships with an assistant basketball coach at Michigan State who put him on to Pete Gent.

Phyllis George was telling the Jenkinses how her daddy used to try on her Miss America crown, and how when they'd go to a restaurant in Denton he'd run in first and shout, "Here she comes." Dan and June Jenkins were joining Phyllis and her parents later at the Raquel Welch show. The guy in the dark glasses who looked like a witless Al Pacino, the one who had been around all week, was chatting with a couple of high rollers from Dallas who should have recognized that he was what they call a "ten percenter"—a bounty hunter for the IRS. Irene, the first known sportswriter's groupie, was there, drinking strawberry daiquiris. An Atlanta sportswriter I hadn't seen in years reminded me of the time I got into a so-called fight with Norm Van Brocklin in Birmingham. I reminded Lamar Hunt of the time his older brother tried to bribe me to write nice things about Lamar's first football team, and Lamar recalled one of Jenkins' great lines: "*The man of a thousand tackles—E. J. Holub—Dallas Times Herald—December 11, 1962.*" Cornell Green, the ex-Cowboy headhunter who now scouts for the team and is therefore privy to these functions of the flesh, spotted Gent and swung him around like a broom; and though it was a gesture of goodwill, the flash of cold terror in Peter's eyes told me he wasn't altogether comfortable in his new profession.

And there was old Doc Bailey, bless his heart. He remembered the time we caught salmon off the coast of Astoria, and I remembered the time he got me a Dexedrine prescription in Portland. Joe Bailey was one of Washington, D.C.'s best-known heart specialists and a longtime running mate of Clint Murchison, Jr.—Doc's son Jody is now business manager of the Cowboys. Doc Bailey, Bob Thompson, and Irv Davidson, the lobbyist who worked for Caribbean dictators, were the backbone of the Chicken Club: a loose collection of ne'er-do-wells that is mostly dormant now, having experienced the ravages of age and too many slugs of Scotch down the old pipe, but back in the early Sixties they were the nemeses of the Rozelles and Schramms. Their most infamous stunt was helping former Redskin owner George Preston Marshall celebrate High School Band Day at D.C. Stadium. They helped by seeding the field with chicken feed and providing 5000 live and hungry chickens who would be set free just as the assembled bands were forming WELCOME. The plot was foiled by a guard someone forgot to bribe. George Preston Marshall is long gone—but so is the Chicken Club. The Rozelles and Schramms have football now, and it's so sanitary you can eat off it.

"God, we used to give Pete Rozelle fits," Doc Bailey chuckled.

"I think I'll go ask Pete whatever happened to our application for a franchise in Santa Fe," I said. "Remember? Bob Thompson had a government contract to build an underground nuclear stadium if he could land an NFL franchise. We were going to call ourselves the Sante Fe Nuclear Holocausts."

"That's right. Our colors were ash and yellow. Whatever happened to that application?"

Fast Pete. He stood there like a ramrod in a Ken Doll suit, smiling through ice, saying the right thing and moving on, doing his job. Pete was a salesman who believed in his product: Pete would have sold tickets to the French Revolution—but only if he believed in it.

Sure his parties were obscene. So are mine. I love obscene parties.

I don't know if they showed it on TV, but the Coral Gables High School band did a fine pregame enactment of Kent State. Berserk gunmen wasted fat tuba players and drummers who toppled and lay like wooden soldiers as the gunmen continued to rampage. Splendid theater.

My other indelible recollection of Super Bowl X happened during the actual playing of the football game. It was that split second before Bradshaw released the bomb that blew the Cinderella team back to the pumpkin patch: D.D. Lewis, blitzing from Bradshaw's blind side, got one hand on the Pittsburgh quarterback, and a split second after that, when it no longer mattered, Cliff Harris made Bradshaw disappear for good. Game of inches, right?

Afterwards, I dropped by the Dallas dressing room. I wanted to get D.D. Lewis' game jersey to take home as a souvenir, but he had already given it to Willie Nelson's sister. I read the next morning there was a lot of weeping and tearing of hair in the Dallas dressing room, but I saw none. The Cowboys accepted their defeat as one of those twin possibilities when two good teams play.

"I don't know what happened on the blitz," D.D. Lewis was telling reporters. "I got my left hand on him [Bradshaw] but he didn't budge. Cliff got tripped or he would have been there sooner. I was sure we would force a fumble. Instead, it was a touchdown."

A Pittsburgh reporter in search of praise asked D.D. what he thought of the Steelers, and D.D. said they were a pack of hot dogs. "Especially Lambert," D.D. said. "All that Mickey Mouse shit . . . intimidating. If he's all-pro, Lee Roy Jordan is all-world. But don't make me sound bitter. As the black knight said, my business is my pleasure."

"And what is your pleasure?" the reporter asked.

"None of your business," D.D. smiled.

In the training room Golden Richards was being treated for several broken ribs. Richards is a frail, gentle, soft-spoken Mormon kid from Salt Lake City, and also the fastest man on the team. The Steelers elected to defend him by punching him in the ribs everytime he came across the line of scrimmage. Golden pointed this out to the officials, but they never called a penalty. Golden said he had no complaints. Neither did Tom Landry. "What they were doing to Richards was a judgment call," Landry said. "They just elected not to call it."

A long season had ended; in maybe a few cases, long careers had ended. Cliff Harris still had the Pro Bowl to endure, but the main thing on his mind just then was the team's postgame party that night at the Galt. He asked if it was true that Willie and Jerry Jeff and those guys would be there. I said I didn't know. Jerry Jeff Walker had stayed up all night, picking and singing in the NFL hospitality room; his wife Susan observed the occasion by giving Jerry Jeff's Super Bowl ticket to a bus driver. Willie Nelson and his troop arrived after an all-night flight from Jerkwater, Tennessee, looking like they'd crawled out of a Goodwill box.

Outside the dressing room door, Willie leaned up against a steel girder, his Dallas Cowboy stocking cap pulled down over his ears and his eyes painted by Alexander Calder.

Willie was a longtime Cowboy fan: he went back to Don Meredith, who was a longtime Willie Nelson fan and used to mystify even the best of them by trotting into the huddle and singing "Hello, Walls."

Willie, Jerry Jeff, Jimmy Buffet, Billy C., and some other excellent musicians arrived as the party was starting to run down. To the great delight of the players and the bewilderment of the Cowboy establishment—who must have thought the Bolsheviks had landed in Fort Lauderdale —this group of gypsy outlaws replaced the standard hotel band. "The day is saved," publicity man Doug Todd grinned. Not to mention the night. Even some of the assistant coaches were on the dance floors. It was the first time I'd seen a losing team at a victory party. Tom Landry, Jr., a young Dallas attorney, told Willie Nelson how much he admired his work.

Willie thanked young Tom and inquired about his father.

"He's gone up to his room," Tommy said. "He's looking at the game film."

Slumping into his seat on the team bus headed back for the airport, Ralph Neely couldn't stop thinking about inflation. The six-foot-six Cowboy tackle had closed out his eleventh season with a $16,000 bonus check, but now it didn't seem like so much money, not when you considered that his chassis had all that mileage and no warranty.

"I'll tell you what causes inflation," he told Dr. Marvin Knight, who sat with his wife in the seat just in front. "Credit cards. Get rid of credit cards, inflation goes with it."

"That's probably the fact of it," Doc Knight agreed. Doc Knight, who had plastered and patched and wired together the Cowboys for sixteen years, recalled that when he interned at Walter Reed those many years ago, he established his credit by (1) borrowing money; (2) paying it back with interest. "That's the way it works in this country," Mrs. Knight said. "The only way to establish credit is borrow money."

"Another thing that keeps prices up," Dr. Knight told Neely, "pilfering . . . shoplifting. Ten per cent of the stock on the shelves is pilfered. The cost is passed on to you know who."

Neely was silent for a time, watching the winter erosion of the beaches and yachts frozen by foreclosures, condominiums that went unrented at the height of the tourist season, and old ladies in torn stockings waiting on concrete benches. Neely had thought about taking a short vacation, but changed his mind. Tomorrow or the next day he'd be back at his winter job, selling computer service for one of Clint Murchison's companies. Amazing the amount of data you could put on a little piece of tape. All of a sudden it made him feel small. And old. And expendable. He tapped Doc Knight's shoulder: "In a couple of weeks I think I'll come in for a complete checkup. Just to see how the old body's holding up."

I looked at my official Super Bowl X watch, opened my Super Bowl briefcase, and took out my Super Bowl program. I wanted to read the winning essay in the NFL Charities' $25,000 scholarship contest. The subject was the NFL's role in American history, and though it had been argued by good authority that the league had no role in American history, Anna Leider, the contest winner, thought otherwise. "Football," she wrote, "is a mirror of America."

Anna pointed out that the people of this nation (like the NFL) overcame enormous odds in their expansion west, forming an orderly, law-abiding society, freeing themselves of prejudice, and representing many distant regions. She did not mention drugs, labor disputes, rampant commercialism, or media hype. She did not mention that it took the NFL a quarter of a century (from 1921 to 1946) to move west of Chicago, or that even then, it went kicking and screaming; or that as recently as ten years ago black players were subject to quotas, and in some cities (Dallas, for example) found it almost impossible to locate good housing near their place of business; or how the cardinal rule is still *don't get caught*. But Anna's main point seemed well taken: whatever Super Bowl X was, it was us. There was no pretense, no attempt to gloss it over. What other league in what other nation would open itself to such scrutiny, and say—proudly, no less—this is how we are. This is America, 200 years down the road.

*—March 1976*

*Illustrated by Tom Ballenger*

# BASS FISHING IN AMERICA

by Gene Lyons

*Got $10,000, hair on your chest, and lots of time?*
*That might help you catch a bass, but don't bet on it.*

Under the right circumstances any fool can catch a bass. So what's all the fuss about: why are there specially designed bass boats, professional bass fishermen competing on several tournament circuits, slick bass magazines, even unofficial bass-catching uniforms? Why are hundreds of thousands of bass-crazed zealots on their way to replacing golf nuts and tennis bores as objects of bewilderment to their more normally constituted brethren? Because, you see, circumstances are rarely—indeed, almost never—right.

Until quite recently nobody worried about that very much. Bass fishing used to be thought of as a humble avocation pursued mostly by old men and little boys—persons with lots of free time. Either the fish were biting or they weren't. No big deal either way.

Not anymore. The almost legendary finickiness of the largemouth bass is becoming as important to the mythology of the New South as magnolia blossoms and mint juleps were to the Old. The bass boom is a sure sign that leisure time and folding money are within the grasp of Everyman on this side of the Mason-Dixon line. Men whose fathers struggled to scrape a living out of the red soil have found their life's challenge in landing a lunker. If bass were easy to catch, then Ray Scott wouldn't be a millionaire, Tommy Martin would still be making commercial loans in Nacogdoches, and nobody would have heard of Marvin Baker or Ricky Clunn.

Who are they? Well, if you're a bassin' man who follows the pro tournament circuit, you already know, in which case I'm very surprised you got beyond the part where I said any fool could catch one; or else it is news to you that Ray Scott is the Hugh Hefner of bass fishing, its number one organizer and merchandiser, and that Tommy Martin, Marvin Baker, and Ricky Clunn are professional bass fishermen, the best

Gene Lyons is a freelance writer and contributing editor of Texas Monthly. He has written for The Nation, The New York Times, Harper's, and other magazines.

hawg busters, as bass experts are called, in the state of Texas.

In the last ten years or so, bass fishing has been transformed from a pastime involving earthworms, minnows, and plastic bobbers into a certifiable American craze, complete with a technology and mystique every bit as complicated, arcane, and expensive as that of sports car racing or Alpine skiing. It is possible to earn upwards of $50,000 a year in prize money and endorsements just for catching fish, not to mention a shot at a syndicated television show. The sport has its own jargon, fan magazines, and legendary figures, and an entire industry has grown up to support it. About all it hasn't got at this point are groupies, and judging from a couple of spectators I saw recently at the Bass Angler Sportsman Society (BASS) Tennessee Invitational, it won't be long now. So if your kid prefers to take his exercise sitting down, take heart: he may grow up to be a sports hero yet.

Much more likely, of course, is that he will become a weekend participant and fan, in which case you are well advised to begin planning his financial future immediately. The way things are going, the average basser will soon be spending more per pound for his fish fries than it would cost to have Iranian caviar flown in direct from the Caspian Sea by chartered jet. A true devotee should expect to lay out somewhere in the vicinity of $10,000 just to equip himself to the point where his friends won't snicker behind his back when he comes out to play. For starters, there is the boat. One does not fish for bass in just anything that will stay afloat. If you're serious about catching bass, you'll want a bass boat ($5000 and up), which is equipped with more underwater devices than a World War II submarine and is just about as practical for catching anything other than bass—but then no self-respecting bassin' man would even consider fishing for another species. Next there's the unofficial uniform: the well-dressed basser resembles nothing so much as a vacationing fighter pilot in his bright polyester jump suit (preferably yellow or red), dotted with tournament patches resembling Strategic Air Command insignia. He also needs aviator sunglasses and a long-billed cap with an adjustable plastic sweatband. Throw in the usual fishing gear, annual dues to one of the several organizations for bass fishermen, and enough ready cash to haul everything around the countryside in search of *Micropterus salmoides*, and you're ready to begin.

Until very recently (future scholars will probably fix the date in 1968 with the first issue of Ray Scott's *Bass Master* magazine, published in Montgomery, Alabama), styles and trends in the piscatorial arts used to be set by New York-based publications like *Field & Stream* and *Outdoor Life*, which catered, with occasional exceptions, to regional tastes of Northeasterners. Now your average Yankee fisherman, the type who is always talking about "matching the hatch" and buys his equipment from L. L. Bean or Abercrombie & Fitch, regards the largemouth bass as an undiscriminating aquatic lout who hangs around murky, lily-padded water instead of gin-clear streams or pools. A bass is the kind of fish that would pass up a Mayfly or an exquisitely tied and artfully presented Royal Coachman in favor of some unspeakable lump of crudity like a bullfrog or a salamander. Worse, it has scales. If a bass should accidentally be taken, the best thing to do is throw it up on the bank to rot so that it doesn't stunt the growth of more useful fish. The kind of man who would deliberately angle for bass would pass up scotch in favor of beer or even wear double-knit suits and white shoes.

Exactly. Bassin' men tend to be Southern men, white Southern men to be a bit more specific, and in general they don't anymore care what non-bassers think of their passion than Cale Yarborough worries about the image stock car racing has on the French Riviera. Although bass are found in almost every state as well as in Mexico and Canada, and have for many years been the most popular American game fish, true bass idolatry is a Southern phenomenon. In Texas, the real hotbeds of zeal lie in that part of the state geographically and culturally closest to the Deep South—east of a diagonal between Houston and Fort Worth. Providentially, that is where most of the state's freshwater lakes are.

Your typical Northern fisherman tends to be an amateur environmentalist; he hikes and camps out and thinks the government ought to be more aggressive about protecting whatever rivers might have escaped the ravages of Consolidated Edison and its ilk. One has but to observe the Dallas Firefighters Bass Club on a hot July afternoon, drawn into a primordial beer-drinking ring on the shores of Lake Sam Rayburn, to realize that if there is one thing bass fishing is *not* about it's a Return to Nature. The men hunker inside a circle made by their machines: boats, campers, heavy-duty pickups, mechanized life-support systems that are probably costing them as much as their home mortgages. The sound of air conditioners and the whine of outboards from a nearby marina drown out whatever birds or insects might otherwise be audible. As usual, the bass aren't doing squat; nobody is catching anything. The conversation runs heavily to equipment. The average devotee is about as likely to be a member of the Sierra Club or the Audubon Society as he is to be a Hindu. Next to an efficient state program of stocking and managing public waters for the optimum number of lunker bass, all he asks of government is good access roads, fully equipped boat docks, paved launching ramps, and ample parking space for his car and trailer.

In his relationship to his prey, the bass fisherman is more combative than anything else. It is clear from the rhetoric of articles and advertisements directed toward cultists that the largemouth bass is to be regarded as a he-man fish—a rampant predator who to reach trophy size must survive heavy odds in an underwater free enterprise system that makes Melvin Munn's *Lifeline* philosophy sound like parlor socialism. A big bass is called a hawg or a lunker, macho terms whose sexual connotations are matched only by a "honey hole," which is a place one knows to be frequented by lunkers, and a secret to be shared, if at all, only with one's most trusted companions. Bassers regard the object of their quest as no beast to be tampered with; one acquaintance of mine, upon being chided for using a 25-pound test line where 8 or 10 pounds would be more sporting, growled, "If you want to be kind to fish, get yourself an aquarium."

The growth and development of contemporary bass fishing is both a cause and a result of three closely related phenomena. One has already been mentioned —the economic growth of the South to the point that the term "leisure industry" no longer means something like swatting flies in a hammock. The other two are the building of dams and subsequent creation of sprawling freshwater impoundments like Lake Sam Rayburn and Toledo Bend Reservoir in East Texas; and the spontaneous generation of somebody like Ray Scott, a New South entrepreneur of the kind that Izaak Walton could never have imagined.

Ray Scott is the founder and president of BASS and the publisher of *Bass Master*, a professionally designed special-interest magazine that is mailed out bimonthly to each of the club's 262,000 members, most of them in the South. A membership in BASS costs $10 annually and judging from Scott's imitators (among them magazines like *Southern Lunker* and *Fisherman's Digest*, the latter the official publication of the Poor Boy Bass Association, headquartered in Tulsa), the enterprise is turning over a lot more than just subscription money. In a recent copy of *Bass Master*, which featured national rankings of tournament professionals alongside full-color layouts of largemouth bass in provocative poses, 54 of the 128 pages were devoted to full-page ads for bassing paraphernalia, a fair amount of which Scott, like his precursor Hefner, sells himself. All in all it is the coziest marketing deal since Tom Sawyer's arrangement for white-washing Aunt Polly's fence. You send Scott $10 and he sends you advertisements for his own enterprises. The editorial content of the magazine runs to pieces like UNDERSTANDING GRAPHITE FISHING RODS, together with fan mag features on tournament pros like ROLAND MARTIN: 1975 BASS ANGLER-OF-THE-YEAR and JIMMY HUSTLE: BASSER-ON-THE-GO. In many cases the articles are virtually indistinguishable from the ads. One feature lists the top 24 tournament fishermen and tells what they prefer in the way of rod, reel, line, lures, boat, motor, accessories, and lakes. Since most of the pros are sponsored and salaried at least in part by the manufacturers whose products they tout and since Scott and BASS sponsor the most prestigious tournament circuit (and the only one *Bass Master* reports) the whole thing is a merchandiser's dream.

What all are they selling? To start with there are bass

boats, lavish rigs custom designed and really practical only for catching bass on large lakes. Typically they are equipped with an outboard motor anywhere in size from 85 to 175 horsepower that will do 40 to 70 mph, although one Houston basser I spotted on Toledo Bend had a 385-horsepower V-8 with chrome exhausts. These boats retail for between $5000 and $8000 and with accessories can go much higher. Most come with trailers, electric trolling motors with six forward and six reverse speeds to eliminate paddling, sonar devices for reading lake bottoms and locating fish, padded swivel seats, AstroTurf carpeting, electric-powered anchor winches, aerated live wells for storing the catch, and gauges to measure the water's temperature, oxygen content, and light intensity at any given depth. Some boats have two, even three, depth gauges along the sixteen- to twenty-foot length of the vessel to detect drop-offs. Many fishermen have installed CB radios. In addition, there are rods and reels (at upwards of $150 to $200 each), of which fewer than three or four for different fishing conditions is considered insufficient, not to mention lures and assorted gadgets for measuring, weighing, handling, and fileting the catch. Live bait like night-crawlers and minnows are considered beneath the dignity of the serious basser. In Scott's BASS tournaments such bait is illegal, and contestants are limited to ten pounds of artificial lures.

Despite all this stuff the average Joe Bob's chances of climbing into his rig on Saturday morning and returning with a string of lunkers varies somewhere between slim and none—even though, as I said at the beginning, sometimes it is almost impossible *not* to catch the dumb brutes. When they are feeding in shallow water they will fight to impale themselves on your hook the way adolescent young women once struggled over a pair of Elvis Presley's undershorts. But when they are not shallow and/or not feeding, locating and enticing them onto your line can be as fruitless as offering your own jockeys with you in them to the same girls. Zip. Nada. Hours of work casting and retrieving and nothing to show for it but a headache and a sore wrist.

Before I tell you about my fishing trip with Tommy Martin, who just may be the best bass fisherman in Texas, I suppose I should confess that I can only rarely be persuaded to fish for bass on purpose. Catfish are my preferred quarry. Not only are catfish bigger than bass, but they are much better to eat and a whole lot simpler to catch. Contrary to outdoor magazine propaganda, this is not because the largemouth bass is a clever and worthy adversary. The "wily Mr. Bass" of fishing rhetoric is only slightly more capable of guile than an earthworm. He ranks on the intellectual continuum about midway between a chicken and a potted geranium. Anybody who could be outwitted by a bass probably still believes that Rose Mary Woods erased those eighteen and a half minutes of tape while she was answering the telephone.

A few personal examples may suffice: the first, and until fairly recently the largest, bass I ever caught managed to hook, play, and all but land itself entirely without human assistance of any kind. I'd found an abandoned fishing pole buried deep in a closet at my apartment. I bought a purple plastic bream worm to go with it, the kind of bait that is designed less to catch fish than to separate little kids who don't like to touch real worms from their Popsicle money—

about twenty cents worth of it as I recall. I was 25 myself, but having been raised in northern New Jersey, where the rivers do not exactly teem with edible aquatic life, I was an easy mark. After twenty minutes or so of desultory casting in a Virginia farm pond convinced me that there were no fish in it I left the rod lying on the dock and walked off. Imagine my surprise when I returned the next morning to discover not only that the wind had blown my line into the water but also that the bait had been "inhaled," as they say in *Bass Master*, by a two-pound largemouth who by the time I found it was exhausted from trying to swim away with the dock. Ever the sportsman, I carefully untangled the line and braced myself for one of those tail-walking, gill-shaking displays of fighting spirit I'd so often read about in the barbershop. It just lay there on its side. I took it up to the house, cleaned it with the aid of my *Joy of Cooking*, and ate it for lunch. Expecting something vastly different from the despised Friday night frozen fish sticks of my youth, I was not so much surprised as disappointed: poached, a bass tastes remarkably like a spider web.

Most of my subsequent catches have been of the same variety. I have taken ole bucketmouth on minnows while trying for catfish or crappie, on crickets while looking for bream, and on worms while just idly potting around. My kid caught a two-pounder when he was four years old at high noon off the bank of the Arkansas River in downtown Little Rock on a jig. He'd gotten his line snarled while I was teaching him to cast. So it isn't cunning that makes bass hard to catch; it's inconsistency. Go to the deep water, find the bottom, and you've found the catfish 95 per cent of the time. Bass, on the other hand, move all over the fool place depending upon approximately 732 variables that only a computer could calculate, but which depend, or so I gather from reading about it, upon air and water temperature, oxygen content, availability of food and cover, barometric pressure, light, cloud cover, sunspots, the moon, Venus, the Dow Jones Industrial Average, and for all I know, Dave Kingman's ratio of strikeouts to home runs.

Given my ambivalence, the reader can imagine how I felt showing up at dawn on Toledo Bend Reservoir on the Texas-Louisiana border to keep a fishing appointment with Tommy Martin, who is the only Texan ever to have won the BASS Master's Classic, a tournament of the top 25 competitors on Ray Scott's circuit that is the closest thing to the Super Bowl of competitive bass fishing. That was in 1974, a year in which he also placed first in the Arkansas Invitational, making him the only person on the tour ever to have won the Classic and a second BASS tourney in the same year. Martin is fourth on the all-time BASS list of money winners with a total of almost $25,000. In 1974 his earnings from prize money alone (including winnings on a now defunct tournament circuit) came to $28,000. Though I am both scoffer and skeptic where the largemouth bass is concerned, it was hard to discount that kind of record. Deep down I figured Tommy Martin must know a whole lot about bass fishing, and what I feared was that I secretly wanted to learn it. One should never trifle with the elemental passions; men have thrown their lives away for bass.

Martin himself is a case in point. Six years ago he was 29 and an office manager for a Nacogdoches commercial lending company. In addition to a salary that made it possible for him to live quite comfortably, Martin had a company car for his personal use, insurance, hospitalization, and a retirement plan—all the trappings that entice most of us to sell ourselves to bureaucracies and stay put. One thing he didn't have was enough time for fishing. So he threw it all over and became a fishing guide, first on Lake Sam Rayburn and more recently on Toledo Bend, where he operates out of the Harborlights Marina, about five miles outside the crossroads hamlet of Milam and around sixty miles east of the nearest town of any size, which is Lufkin.

A fishing guide can pursue bass just about any time the inclination strikes him, which had better be pretty often, because even at $60 a day, he is not getting rich very fast. Then there is the cost of his equipment and the number of days that the weather is too lousy or there is too much competition from hunting or football and nobody calls. Those are the days Martin tries out new techniques, searches for new locations, or, believe it or not, fishes for fun. Asked how often he does that, Martin, a carefully composed man who gives the impression that he misses very little and keeps a lot to himself, acts surprised. "All the time," he says. During the warm months he is often on the water twenty or thirty days running for anywhere between eight and twelve hours at a time. For that reason I am inclined to doubt it when another guide confides in me, while Martin brings the boat around, that "I love fishing. Tommy's in it for the money."

It would take a genuine grouch or a real adult, of whom I have known two in my life, both female elementary school principals, not to get a certain charge out of taking a bass boat over the hump and whipping through a heavily timbered lake like Toledo Bend at dawn on a summer morning. I don't own a jump suit and Martin prefers cut-off jeans, but there is something about the two-man hunting team setting out in the gray half light that excites the urge to dress in costume and give the thumbs-up signal to other bassers as we pass them. Had we come upon a cheap aluminum flatboat like mine back home with a couple of wimps catfishing, I doubt that I could have resisted hooting in derision. For this Saturday morning anyway, I was more than a mere fisherman, I was a bassin' man, and with Martin nearby, I could even pretend that I knew what I was doing.

Although he is no doubt aware that his livelihood depends upon it, such childishness would probably embarrass or irritate Martin. On the water he is a professional; as in every form of human endeavor I know anything about, the difference between success and mediocrity in bass fishing is the ability to concentrate. Tournament bass fishing, Martin says, is roughly 80 per cent skill and 20 per cent luck. If we were fishing a tournament here, he would expect to catch the tournament limit of ten fish and more, culling the smaller ones and bringing in the ten heaviest to be weighed, which is how tournament winners are determined. The luck comes in the occasional big fish that can make the difference between being in or out of the money. And even that is not entirely up to fortune, Martin says; there are ways of locating and fishing for the big ones.

I am skeptical. *Nobody* catches a limit of anything with me in the boat. I talk too much, fidget, get bored. Sometimes I wonder if fish can smell my breath, my underarms. There are acquaintances of mine who would sooner go whitewater canoeing with a Saint Bernard puppy than angling with me. By the time the sun is high enough to cast a shadow, my predawn euphoria is gone. I have driven halfway across Texas to sit in the sun and put the curse on

a perfectly decent fellow whose only fault seems to be his over-confidence.

All the while Martin is crawling his plastic worm across the bottom in seventeen to twenty-five feet of water along submerged creek channels and drop-offs that he locates by consulting his depth finder. Anybody who uses anything but plastic worms this time of year, he says, is wasting his time. Cast and retrieve: for me the operation is repetitious, mesmerizing; for Martin it is not. He is cool and systematic. After fifteen or twenty minutes at one spot he cranks up the motor and we move to another. "If they aren't in here by now, they won't be," he says, squinting at the lingering cloud cover. "We'll try a little shallower." At the third or fourth spot he catches his first bass, a two-pounder. In the next couple of hours he will boat fourteen fish, all between two and three and a half pounds. Astonishingly enough I catch four myself after some instructions on how to set the hook properly with a plastic worm. The fish give a quick tap and they are gone; I am missing more strikes than a one-eyed umpire with a cataract. Martin, however, can give instructions, answer my questions fully and politely, and still seem to have the most sentient part of his mind down there on the end of that line, creeping over stumps and weed beds in the murk of seventeen feet of muddy water, just waiting for a lunker bass to make his ravenous charge.

In spite of his choosing to live where he does, Martin is not a rural type at all. A native of Texas City, when he got strapped for cash last winter he went back for a few weeks and got a job installing industrial insulation. What he admires most are people who know how to *do things* and live by their native wit. After beginning tentatively so he won't risk offending a client, he discusses his admiration for Muhammad Ali as a man who knows how to make the best of what he's got. In his spare time Martin plays pool and Ping-Pong. I had the distinct impression that one might take a game or two from him at first but would be ill-advised to put any money on repeating. Of his decision to give up the security of his office job for guiding and tournament fishing he is matter-of-fact. Anybody who really wants to can put together a living, he thinks. The only way to fail is to lack imagination; nobody has to do something he doesn't like. Although he has been offered a job by a friend in the salvage business at $40,000 a year, he says he prefers to keep fishing as long as he can make around half that, which is just about what he averages. Asked about retirement, he shrugs: "I think about it once in a while, but I see lots of old dudes around sixty-five or seventy out here guiding."

Not much figuring is required to determine that a guide charging $60 a day would have to fish virtually every day of the year in order to gross $20,000, let alone show a profit after expenses. That is where the tournament circuit comes in, although not quite in the way one might imagine. Although the winner's check for one BASS event might be in the vicinity of $5000, depending upon the number of contestants entered, a competitor fishing in all six tournaments qualifying him for the Classic would barely make back his expenses each year even if he could count upon placing first at least once each year. With 200 to 250 entrants in each tournament and prize money dropping rapidly from the top (second place brings less than $2000), the odds are very great against having a year like Martin's in 1974. Even Bill Dance of Memphis, the television sportsman who is second on the BASS list of all-time money winners, has not won a tournament since 1970, although he enters nearly all of them and is one of the legendary figures I spoke of earlier. In order to compete, a man like Tommy Martin has to take off from his regular guiding business for a week or ten days, drive as far away as Virginia or Florida with boat in tow, put himself up in a motel, and pay the $250 entry fee. If he had to foot the bill himself, fishing tournaments would make no economic sense at all. Even though Martin is having a very good year from the standpoint of consistency and is, as of this writing, fourth in Classic "points" among all contestants (which I will explain momentarily) he has won under $2500 in prize money, a sum that comes nowhere near matching his expenses.

But Tommy Martin doesn't pay his own expenses. The Rebel lure people do that, besides paying him a retainer as a consultant in equipment design. His boat and trailer are provided by Bass Cat boats, his depth finders by the Ray Jefferson Company, and so on. The only items of fishing equipment Martin owns that he paid for himself are a couple of reels. As long as he can stay ahead of the crowd as one of the top 25 or 30 competitors on the BASS circuit, Martin can afford to fish for a living. For the ordinary fisherman, though, there are no such benefits. What he looks forward to is the company of similarly minded men who view a tournament more as a fraternal gathering and an opportunity to keep up-to-date on the latest techniques than as a sporting event. It is the chance to meet and talk with fellow bass fanatics, plus the possibility of drawing one of the stars as a fishing partner, that motivates the vast majority of anglers who enter BASS tournaments without having a prayer of winning.

Besides the economic impact of *Bass Master*, the excellent press coverage and the $25,000 top prize for winning the annual BASS Classic, Martin and other pros like to fish Ray Scott's tournaments because they are well run and honest. Cheating at local or club tournaments is a fast way to make off with anything from trophies and bragging rights to several thousand dollars. The organizers of one-shot competitions offering exorbitant prize money are often suspected of chicanery, apparently for good reason. A fishing tournament is very easy to fix. Martin claims he has seen fish weighed at some tournaments that look as if they had been frozen for at least a year. Doubtless there is more than one lunker out there which has been weighed almost as often as a butcher's thumb. Commoner and more difficult to detect, however, are shady practices like contestants pooling their catch or staking out wire-mesh baskets of fish in hidden coves to be gathered when nobody is looking. One competitor has been banished for life from the BASS circuit for the latter tactic and another suspended for not reporting him. The winners of all BASS events are now routinely given polygraph tests as an added protection.

In order to get a firsthand look at the pros in action, I traveled to Gainesboro, Tennessee, about 75 miles east of Nashville, for the Tennessee Invitational, the fifth of six BASS events leading up to the 1976 Classic. By this time my successful trip with Martin had gotten me started on a mild case of bass fever, and I was ready not only to recant my previous heresies, but also to wonder about the manifold possibilities in combining a dual career of freelance writing and tournament fishing. I already

had a typewriter, I reasoned; all I needed was a bass rig. Then came Cordell Hull Reservoir.

By the fifth tournament of the year, BASS is having some difficulty in attracting a full field of 250 contestants. Only the top 25 point winners from the preliminary tournaments will qualify for the Classic, held each October on a "mystery lake" that is not announced until just before the event. The contestants themselves are airborne in a chartered plane before they are told where they are going. About fifteen of those spots are already locked up by men who have done well in the earlier meets. Tommy Martin, for example, was in third place with 154 points going into Cordell Hull. With points awarded on the basis of 50 for first, 49 for second, and so on, Martin had averaged a twelfth place finish for the first four tournaments. Only 14 points behind the leader, Martin was (and still is) very much in contention for the BASS Angler-of-the-Year award given the top qualifier. Other Texans in contention—Marvin Baker of Broaddus and Rick Clunn of Montgomery, ranked twenty-sixth and fortieth respectively—needed to do well here to have a shot at qualifying for the Classic. Persons much further down in the standings than Clunn had little chance, barring a miracle finish. Accordingly, the BASS staff writers had pulled out the rhetorical stops in a heated display of icthyo-porn that lured contestants from 26 states to Cordell Hull, which "starts producing bass by the wagonloads in July," and where "the weather is always nice—it's only the bass that get hot in July in Tennessee."

Now anybody who is capable of taking that last claim on face value deserves anything he gets, and for the tournament week he got it. Afternoon temperatures hovered between 95 and 100 degrees, which is about what the thirteen Texas entrants could have expected had they chosen to stay home—but what about the lone entries from Vermont and Minnesota? To make matters worse, the two dams upstream picked that time to flood the impoundment with millions of gallons of water at 45 degrees, creating water conditions more suitable for muskellunge or salmon than bass. The meeting of cold water and hot air produced a surface fog so dense in places that it looked as if the heavens had opened up a cascade of dry ice. On the first day of the three-day event, not one entrant caught his limit of ten fish. Junior Samples of *Hee Haw* fame did what most contestants with his bank account would have done and went home to Georgia. Tommy Martin weighed in one keeper at two pounds three ounces. Only Rick Clunn, who guides on Lake Conroe when he isn't tournament fishing, seemed to have things figured out. Whatever Clunn was doing out there brought in eight fish weighing in at more than seventeen pounds and put him so far ahead that many of the sportswriters were prepared to concede him the championship.

Unfortunately for Clunn, however, his technique quit working the next day. He managed one two-pounder in ten hours of fishing, but no one else did much better, so he retained the lead. Martin, battling a fever and headache as well as the heat, caught no keepers at all. Some of the fishermen began to complain that there were hardly any fish in the lake, that the site had been badly chosen. A rumor circulated that Ray Scott was privately peeved; he had ventured his opinion, so the story went, that there were more good bass in one acre of Toledo Bend than in all of Cordell Hull. But Scott showed no sign of distemper at the weigh-ins, where, resplendent in a white jump suit with BASS insignia, white cowboy hat, sunglasses, and open-toed sandals, he kept up a nonstop carnival pitch for the several hundred fans who sat sweltering in open bleachers. "Here comes Roland Martin, folks, of Broken Arrow, Oklahoma. Now this here is *some kinda* fisherman. Winner of eight BASS tournaments, 1975 BASS Angler-of-the-Year award. Say howdy to the folks, Roland. What you got there? . . . Two fish? Boy, I tell you. It's tough out there. The day Roland Martin catches two fish, that's a tough day. Tell the folks what you got 'em on, Roland."

It gets even tougher on the third day. The weigh-in is conducted in a parking lot adjacent to the marina. As fishermen pull in they are given plastic bags for their catch, which they fill with water as well as fish. Extra points are awarded if the fish is alive; all fish are dipped in a solution to prevent their being infected, then dumped in a tank. They are returned to the lake as soon as possible. The BASS motto is "Don't Kill Your Catch." But today fewer than half the contestants bother to weigh in at all. Boat after boat comes in empty. Those who do have something to weigh come up the steps from the marina to the scales trying not to look foolish with one, two, at best, four fish. Tommy Martin gets skunked again. He has driven sixteen hours to get here, scouted the lake for three days, fished for three more, and caught one fish large enough to keep. He has a cold. It is now 6 p.m. Friday. He is due back in Texas to take a client fishing at 5 a.m. Sunday. His car is blocked in and he can't leave. I figure he has got to be sick of fishing, that he will stay in Nashville, take in the Grand Ole Opry, and call in sick. "Shoot no," he says. "That's just the way it goes sometimes."

Scott's patter goes on: "Ladies and gentlemen, here comes Woo Daves from Virginia. Woo entered one tournament on his home lake last year and won it. Lotta people thought it was a fluke, but this year ole Woo's doing all our BASS tournaments and showin' 'em how. That's a nice fish there, Woo. Tell 'em what you caught him on." Woo explains he got that big one with this Little Scooper lure, which he produces from his pocket and dangles in front of Scott for the crowd's inspection. "Yes-sir," Scott replies, "I believe I'm gonna get me one of them little dudes." A TV cameraman standing next to me who says he used to fish the BASS tournaments back when the entry fee was just $100 spits on the ground. "Hell," he says, "that boy hasn't had that damn bait out of his tackle box in two months. He works for the people that make 'em."

In the end Rick Clunn does not hang on. He comes in with less than four pounds on the last day and is edged out by Wade Reed of Zwolle, Louisiana, just across Toledo Bend from Tommy Martin's place. Reed works on an oil rig in the Gulf of Mexico and drives 400 miles to get home so he can live on the lake. He caught the fish that took him over the top on a dollar lure his wife picked up off a bargain table at K-Mart the evening before. Everybody gets a big laugh out of that. Clunn comes in second, pays for his trip, moves closer to a Classic spot with 49 points, and gets a good chance to push Glastron boats to the sportswriters. It's good for his guide business back in Texas, he says, because people will hire a celebrity even if they don't know whether he can guide.

Had he won, Tommy Martin would have been able to replace his 1974 Ford station wagon, which now has over 80,000 miles on it from hauling a boat all over the South. That will have to wait. Had the tournament produced a mess of lunkers, a contestant named Ledbetter tells me, the owner of the Roaring River Marina where the weigh-in was held, "would have had to beat the bass fishermen off with a stick." But with none of the professionals catching a limit in three days of trying and the winning total reaching only 23 pounds, he is probably in for some hard times. Marinas have been bankrupted by bad tournaments like this one.

As for me, I am considerably chastened by the experience and am rethinking my decision to turn pro. I spent most of my time in Tennessee holed up in a motel room with the flu, eating aspirin, wondering if I'd survive until the weigh-in and half hoping I wouldn't. Flying home over the route I know Tommy Martin is driving, I am weak, unsteady on my legs, and much disillusioned. I am halfheartedly browsing through a copy of *Outdoor Life* when I encounter a beautifully illustrated piece on how to drive largemouth bass wild with a new kind of tandem spinner arrangement rigged with a trailer hook. On the page facing the text an enormous lunker is shown zooming from behind a submerged stump with its mouth open wide enough to swallow a Houston telephone directory, gills flared and a fanatic gleam of mingled rage and hunger in its eyes. It is going to bust that tandem spinner so hard it might just pull the fisherman overboard. Astonishingly, almost against my will, I feel my throat start to get dry. My chest begins to tighten and a wild, unwanted thought begins to dominate my senses. I can barely whisper it to myself: *I want to go fishing. I want to catch an eight-pound bass.*

*—October 1976*

# AT PLAY IN THE FIELDS OF THE LORD

## by Paul Burka

*College baseball just isn't the same game you see on TV;
at Clark Field it never tried to be.*

The big first baseman watched the curve ball break across the plate and knew he was out. He even started to leave the plate, and news reports recorded that he smiled when the umpire gave him a reprieve.

The assembled 5000 partisans at Clark Field on The University of Texas campus voiced their displeasure, some looking nervously at the short right field fence an inviting 300 feet away. The menacing figure in the batter's box had a reputation as something of a slugger, and this was no time to give him a second chance, not after Texas had rallied to tie the game at 6-6 in the ninth inning. But at least the wind was blowing in. . . .

On the mound the Texas pitcher grimly resolved to throw a fast ball past the hitter. It was a poor choice. The batter, who once had worn the uniform of Columbia University but now wore the better known pin stripes of another New York team, judged it perfectly and propelled what the *Los Angeles Times* was later to call "without a shadow of a doubt, the longest home run ever hit by man since the beginning of baseball." Lou Gehrig's bat, which only six months earlier had led the New York Yankees to a four game sweep of the 1928 World Series, had done it again, and the Yankees beat the Texas Longhorns, 8-6.

The ball Gehrig hit soared out of Clark Field over the center field fence, cut a triangle over a street intersection, and finally came to earth more than 600 feet away. Its landing site was halfway up a hill in the spacious front lawn of a fraternity house; legend has it that the ball was still going up when the hill got in the way.

The house and hill are gone now, bulldozed to provide landscaping for Lyndon Johnson's library. Next year Clark Field itself will be fed to the unsentimental earth-movers to make room for a fine arts center, and with its demise

*Paul Burka is a Rice University graduate, an attorney, and a senior editor of* Texas Monthly. *He won the National Bridge Open Pairs Championship in 1970.*

will die not only the last link to The Home Run, but also the most singular athletic playing field in the State of Texas. The Astrodome? Anybody can build a domed stadium; all that takes is money. Clark Field took genius.

The modern ball park is built for symmetry, favoring neither lefthanded nor righthanded batters. This achieves a statistical perfection of sorts but eliminates one of the most appealing aspects of baseball: the living, breathing presence of the physical setting as a dominant factor in the game. All the electronic gadgetry of the Astrodome scoreboard is essentially irrelevant to what happens on the field. But the wall at Fenway Park, the weird rectangular dimensions of the old Polo Grounds with its Little League foul lines and endless center field, the concave right field wall at Ebbetts Field in Brooklyn, and the brick-like infield at Forbes Field in Pittsburgh—these were an integral part of the game; they changed the way the game on the field was played.

Clark Field is not a modern ball park. Symmetry plays no role in its dimensions, which extend 350 feet to the left field wall, 401 feet to deepest center, and angle sharply in to only 300 feet at the right field foul pole. The profile, deep in left and center, short in right, vaguely suggests Yankee Stadium, but there the comparison ends. Clark Field is different from any other baseball park in the world. Some are larger, some smaller; some seat more, some less; some have lights, some don't—but all are flat. Clark Field is split-level. Other ball parks are divided into infield and outfield; Clark Field is divided into lowlands and uplands.

The dividing line is a 12-foot cliff which sits absurdly in the middle of the outfield. It begins in right center field, angles sharply across center field, and slopes gently down to the left field line where it tapers to little more than an incline. The plateau is 53 feet wide in straightaway center field, 60 feet wide at its widest point, a mere 18 feet wide in left center, and broadens out again to 31 feet at the foul line. Any ball hit on the cliff is in play, although when the collegiate district playoffs were held at Clark Field in 1970, this particular ground rule was a little more than the NCAA could take. Balls hit on the cliff were decreed to be automatic doubles, but Texas won the playoffs anyway.

No one knows exactly why the cliff was left there. Part of the slope was blasted away to provide rock which eventually served to build up the home plate and grandstand area. Perhaps it was too expensive to remove the rest of the cliff, or perhaps someone decided it was picturesque, but whatever the reason, the cliff has plagued visiting teams for 47 years. Texas outfielders are naturally more familiar with the terrain; they often scale the walls like lizards to hold enemy batters to doubles and triples, while Texas batters usually have time to circle the bases before opposing outfielders solve the mysteries of the cliff. A former Texas coach is said to have developed a practice routine of blindfolding his outfielders and timing their ascent to the plateau.

The cliff has contributed to some unusual baseball moments. Two years ago a Texas pitcher was working on a no-hitter late in the game when an opposing batter lofted a deep fly to left field. The Texas left fielder scurried up the slope, tapped his glove confidently, and watched helplessly from his perch as the ball fell just short of the incline on level ground.

Last year the cliff helped a Texas batter attain the dubious distinction of doubling into a double play. With men on first and second, he drove the ball to deep center. The runners stayed close to their bases, not knowing whether the ball would be caught. The enemy center fielder judged the rebound off the limestone perfectly, and the runners tried to make up for lost time. When the confusion ended, Texas had too many men on third base, and two of them were out.

The cliff produced a rare type of home run several years ago. A ball hit over the center fielder's head appeared destined for higher ground. The left fielder charged up the path to the plateau, intent on holding the batter to a triple. The center fielder went back to the base of the cliff and leaped for the ball. The shortstop raced into center awaiting a relay, and the third baseman covered his base hopefully. They all guessed wrong. The ball hit the top of the bluff, evading the desperate leap of the center fielder, and ricocheted into left field. The closest person to the ball was the runner as he rounded second.

Just as the Boston Red Sox have filled their lineup with right-handed power hitters to take advantage of the short left field wall at Fenway Park, Texas baseball teams have been shaped by the character of Clark Field. The short right field fence means that left-handed batters who can pull the ball are always in demand. Right-handed batters must not only overcome the handicap of a deep left field, but also face a fence that is abnormally high because of the cliff— so Texas right-handed batters are usually line-drive hitters. A promising catcher named Bill Berryhill completed three good years at Texas in 1973 but had the misfortune to be right-handed; he had a talent for hitting solid blows that were caught just short of the cliff. If the dimensions of the field had been reversed, he'd hold every Texas home run record.

Clark Field has been a good home for the Longhorns. They have won nine straight Southwest Conference championships, and have won or tied for the SWC title 48 times in 58 years. The cliff has helped, of course, but so have the players: through the years Texas has sent numerous players to the major leagues, including Pinky Higgins, Grady Hatton, Randy Jackson, Murray Wall, and most recently, Chicago Cub pitcher Burt Hooten. Bobby Layne led Texas to four straight conference championships but chose pro football. The next Texas player to reach the major leagues will probably be David Chalk, who has a chance to win the starting shortstop job for the California Angels this spring.

Future Texas major league prospects will play in a $2 million stadium under construction in East Austin more than a mile from the main campus. It will have a seating capacity of more than 5000, plus an artificial playing surface, lights for night baseball, and an electric scoreboard. The field will be one of the premier college baseball stadiums in the nation, comparable to new parks at Southern California and Arizona State, the schools Texas annually contests for the College World Series championship in Omaha, Nebraska. Like all the new ball parks, it strives for symmetry: 400 feet to deep center, 375 down the power alleys, 340 to left, 325 to right (to compensate for prevailing winds blowing in from right field). But it will not have a cliff.

To those who love Clark Field and the game that is played there, the new field is a giant antiseptic mistake. College baseball is an imperfect game; that is its beauty and the key to its enjoyment. Place it in a major league setting and it becomes an awkward parody. In the major leagues, a ground ball to the shortstop is an out, but in college ball, even a pop-up carries an element of doubt. The appeal of college baseball is that the players have talent but not perfection. They are capable of astounding accomplishment and unbelievable mistakes; they are, in short, just like ourselves. It is a game all of us can understand.

The major league game is different. It is beyond our ability to play. We can appreciate it as an art form, but as a sport it can be unbearably dull and predictable. Even the gap between the best player and the worst appears minuscule until it is viewed over the whole season.

Baseball is a marvelously conceived sport, and the college game takes advantage of its best aspects. Baseball is the only team sport played without a clock; no lead is ever completely safe and no game utterly lost. Relief pitching specialists have all but obliterated the late inning rally in the major leagues, but skills aren't so specialized on the college level. Last year the pivotal game of the College World Series saw Minnesota's all-American pitcher holding a one-hit, fifteen-strikeout, seven-run lead over Southern California in the ninth inning only to lose 8-7. Nothing like that has happened in the professional World Series since 1929.

Baseball also isolates its participants better than any other sport. It is impossible to assess the individual performances of football players without sophisticated motion picture equipment, but baseball strips the contestants of their anonymity, putting their skills on display on both offense and defense for all to see. College baseball adds the element of intimacy: because the ball parks are smaller than major league stadiums and spectators sit much closer to the playing field, the onlooker is part of the game to an extent not possible at a major league park. You can spot the third baseman's fatal mistake as he takes his eye off the ball, and you know before he does that the ball is past him. You can watch Burt Hooten in complete control, baffling opposing batters with an unusual pitch called a knuckle curve, but you're close enough to know that the dreaded pitch is not a strike, and that major league hitters wouldn't be swinging at pitches that college hitters are missing by a foot. And if you watch closely, you may begin to understand what a wide range of skills the game of baseball demands of those who would play it, and how difficult and subtle this game really is.

This is what college baseball is all about: relaxing in the awakening spring, watching a great sport being played by real people. Somehow the cliff seems an appropriate, even necessary part of the scene. It tells us, more eloquently than his 600 foot home run did, that Lou Gehrig was out of place here. It is something that could never be part of a professional stadium, something that reminds us that even at a school which has won the championship 48 times in 58 years, what is going on is only a game.

*—April 1974*

**134**

*Illustrated by Pat Foss and George Toomer*

# PRAY FOR SHARKS

## by Stephen Harrigan

*If you don't, nobody else will.*

I'm a Corpus boy. Like most people who grow up on the coast I was in a position to develop an early attitude toward sharks. Sometimes I would come across the remains of one hoisted onto the "shark hanging post" at Bob Hall Pier, its mouth torn apart from two or three hours of fighting a hook, its body covered with gaff scars and encircled with ropes and chains and marked in chalk with its length, weight, and species.

Even as I watched it hang there like a punching bag, surrounded by its grinning captors, it was difficult for me to be sensitive to anything but the awesomeness of that creature. I did not ask myself, as I am prone to do now, what purpose was being served by the death of this shark. I just stared. Even in death the fish's features seemed still attuned to blind menace, and like most observers I assumed that the shark had died by its own karma. It simply got what it deserved.

For a boy who wanted above all else to have a cunning, benevolent dolphin for a friend, who would leave the room when someone assaulted my ears with the word "porpoise," who rode the Port Aransas ferry back and forth to watch those clever mammals cartwheeling in the ship channel, the shark was allowed only a grudging place in my personal ecology. In the underwater morality play that I imagined ran continuously in the murky bays and lagoons of Corpus Christi, the shark was the inevitable villain, a constant threat to the dolphins' warm-blooded Never-Never Land.

Though they shared the same environment, though they shared very nearly the same bodies, the shark seemed to me a dolphin stripped of all resonance and humour, like a grandfather clock whose works had been removed but which still was diabolically able to tell time. I was stunned for days when I opened my new Time-Life book *The Sea* to find a picture of a shark tearing flesh from a dead dolphin. There had never been a plainer, eerier contrast: the dolphin's per-

*Stephen Harrigan, a contributing editor of* Texas Monthly, *has written for several publications. He is editor of* Lucille, *a poetry magazine, and a Paisano Fellow.*

manent smile, subtly altered in death, made me think of the way Marlon Brando always looked just before he was about to cry. The shark, on the other hand, was a dead-ringer for Broderick Crawford, and there was a look of such profound and aggravating disinterest on its face that I was brought almost to tears. How could the Natural Order of Things take such sinister form?

For a long time the shark remained my counter-totem. As far as I was concerned the more death that could be wrought upon those creatures the better. Then one day I was on Padre Island gazing down at the body of a five- or six-foot shark that had obviously washed ashore long before I came across it. It was so bleached and bloated that, except for a persistently fierce-looking set of jaws, it might have been a tuna. A man in a polka-dot railroad cap walked up and automatically kicked the shark in the gills the way he might kick the tires on a used car. "That's a shark, boy!" he pronounced. "I know," I said, suddenly realizing that, though I did not yet love sharks, I could see when they were being ill-served. And it became evident, as the man pried open the fish's mouth with a stick, that I must make some accommodation with those rows of teeth or be forever aligned with this bumpkin who was guffawing down the shark's throat.

And there is of course much about sharks to be appreciated, much that is pesteringly beautiful, that cannot be sentimentalized. No other animal is so exactly what it appears to be. By human standards the shark is ludicrously primitive; but judged by its own needs, and by its own evolution toward meeting them, it is flawless. Nothing about the shark is peripheral: it exists to subsist, and is masterful at it.

The shark is unaware of and unreliant upon anything its senses do not interpret as food; so it does not attack out of nobility or nastiness or confusion or boredom. The shark's only motive is *ingestion*: it abhors the vacuum that its own constant hunger maintains. Open the stomachs of enough sharks and you will find, besides maybe the chilling sight of human remains, everything from Vichy water to reindeer.

There are 34 species of sharks that inhabit Texas coastal waters. This is the conclusion of Dr. Donald Wohlschlag, who has been keeping count as he leafs through a zoological key to local marine life. Through his window I can see past the Port Aransas dunes out to the Gulf—a gray Gulf today, all its denizens securely tucked in. Wohlschlag is an ichthyologist and ecologist here at the University of Texas' Institute of Marine Science, an idyllic laboratory/learning complex peopled mostly by tanned and bearded graduate students.

Wohlschlag himself is a rotund man with small eyes that crinkle up gleefully whenever the talk turns from fish to human folly. Sharks are really a little out of his line—he's busy right now constructing a tank to monitor the metabolisms of pinfish and mullet—but he is ready to share both his literature and his opinions on the subject.

"Sharks are always super-nasty things in Grade B movies. We only listen to the propaganda. Did you know that at least half of the shark species aren't bad to eat at all?"

Scanning Wohlschlag's list, I'm pleasantly surprised to find that it includes the biggest of all fish, the whale shark, an animal that reaches a known length of 50 feet but which does not use its bulk to do damage to any form of life larger than plankton and small fish. In feeding, the animal creates a suction with its mouth and draws its food toward it, and fortunately for divers who have swum about whale sharks making a nuisance of themselves, its gullet is too small to accommodate them.

But there is another leviathan out there, this one so outrageously gruesome that it seems to have acquired its appearance not from nature but from the images of human nightmare. "The white, gliding ghostliness of repose in that creature," was how Melville saw the great white shark, a fish that is not so much a fish as it is a twenty-foot cartilaginous void shoving itself through the ocean, ready to devour very nearly anything it encounters. It is a great white shark that lunges upward to imbibe the swimming woman on the cover of Peter Benchley's novel *Jaws*, and though the proportions in that picture are exaggerated, it would be difficult to improve upon the natural grim reaper visage of the animal. Even the beast's scientific name, *Carcharodon carcharias*, cannot be spoken without hearing the whisper of crunching bone. Great whites tend to be scarce, especially in this part of the world. The only confirmed sightings I've been able to unearth occurred near Port Aransas in 1950, but there have doubtless been a modest amount since then.

Other species are more common. Tiger sharks, hammerheads, bull sharks, makos, lemons all thrive along the coast, and all are more than capable of eating you or your lunch.

Most of the sharks people lose sleep over belong to one genus, *Carcharias*, all of whose members resemble the Revised Standard Version of shark that rests in the public's imagination. An important exception is the hammerhead, from *Sphyrna*, a genus that includes a number of sharks with oddly proportioned heads. The hammerhead is the kind of fish you might expect to see surfacing from the ocean of another planet; Hieronymus Bosch could not have designed it better. While the heads of most sharks converge into respectable snouts, that of the hammerhead takes a wild,

lyrical leap just a step further into the grotesque. Its head ends as a kind of crossbar extending laterally on either side much further than seems reasonable. This endows the hammerhead with a kind of fixed propellor which can give the fish either a whimsical or exceedingly grim look, depending on how near you are to the toothy trap door underneath it.

All sharks, though, share the same basic physical characteristics. For one thing, their skeletons are made not of bone but of cartilage, and the flesh that covers this frame is studded with thousands of toothlike projections that give sharkskin the texture of very coarse sandpaper.

Sharks perceive their world through smell and sight and sound, but exactly what it is that these senses serve is something we can't know. Recent experiments have seemed to indicate that sharks do not experience what we know as "hunger." Whatever causes their legendary voraciousness, it is not simply an empty gut. More likely the creature is impelled to eat by an agitation that invades the totality of its body: a shark *is* hunger.

The photograph album that Paul Dirk hands me across the dining room table has a flowery print cover, the kind of album usually filled with out-of-focus shapshots of the family at Disneyland. But I am in the house of a shark fisherman, and so I am not surprised when I come upon dozens of photographs of dead and disemboweled sharks, some of which have been enlarged and are hanging in frames on the wall above a row of trophies.

"I only make 8x10s of fish that are over eleven feet long," Dirk explains.

Dirk is a big, courtly, deeply tanned man in his thirties who pours concrete for a living but whose joy in life is clearly the wresting of killer beasts out of the sea. Both of his fists put together would just about equal the size of the big Penn 16-aught reel that is fixed onto a 39-thread rod. He has almost $800 invested in this rig—even the hooks for shark fishing cost a dollar and a half apiece—and he has two back-up rigs in the garage.

Today is a miserable January day. Dirk is waiting for the middle of March, waiting for the water to reach 68 degrees so that the sand tigers and lemons, following the warmth, will move in closer to shore and start to feed near the oil rigs that are strung out in the Gulf, two to seven miles from shore. When the water reaches 72 degrees he knows it will begin to pull the hammers in, and at 75 degrees the tigers. He is erudite on these matters; his shelf-space that is not taken up by shark-fishing trophies is given over to a small library consisting exclusively of shark lore.

On the wall Dirk has a certificate of merit from the Corpus Christi Shark Association honoring him for the most sharks caught last year, but even for a pro it can be a tedious sport. It is not unusual for fishermen to camp out at the rig platforms for days at a time without a bite.

"You really got to put your hours in," he warns.

People still fish for sharks from the Bob Hall and Horace Caldwell piers, but most of the action off Padre Island has moved out into the deeper water, out to the rigs that hover on the horizon like an oncoming armada. Before the fishing began in earnest out there, the 100 members of the Shark Association would catch as few as five or six sharks a season. From the rigs that record can easily be beaten in a month.

Dirk points out a photograph of the record tiger shark he fought for five-and-half hours. It was 12′ 1″ long, weighed 1160 pounds, and contained 66 tiger shark pups that it was about to let loose upon the sea. In the photograph the fish is slung up by its lower jaw on the shark hanging post. Dirk, his hair a littler shorter, is standing beneath the dorsal fin as if it were an umbrella. Next to the great white, the tiger shark is the fiercest and is responsible for more human deaths than any other species. Dirk tells me that this particular shark tried to eat the rubber tires on the side of the platform as he hauled it up. Another tiger, a foot shorter than this one, attacked a hammerhead his wife Carolyn was hauling in and rendered it into the carnage shown in one of the 8x10s on the wall.

To catch a shark it is necessary to set the bait out about 500 yards from the platform, and since shark rigs are not exactly fly rods this must be done manually. On calm days Dirk and his colleagues board a rubber raft and paddle out with a big hunk of bonito or kingfish, set it in the water, and work their way back.

"Now when the water's rough you can't use a raft," Dirk says modestly. "That's when us hairy shark fishermen get out there."

What he means is that they swim it out. Dirk's own technique is to "hug the bait in close," doing a modified side-stroke designed to keep the fish out of the water, where the smell and sight and texture of it would seep to the nearest shark. Five hundred yards from the nearest shelter, with eight or ten pounds of a shark's favorite food cradled like a baby in his arms, Dirk becomes part of the public domain of carnivorous sea beasts. He leans back in his chair and relates a little too calmly several instances in which he has observed the famous fin zithering across the surface of the water.

"A lot of times you see them when they're not even there."

After a shark has been hooked, battled, hauled in, and allowed to expire, the rest is either afterglow or anticlimax, depending on who's doing the fishing. The beast is weighed, measured, photographed, maybe its stomach opened, its jaws cut out, and then it is buried in the dunes. Occasionally an unconscionable restaurant will buy the carcass to turn it into "red snapper," or the fisherman himself will make the effort to salvage the meat, but for the most part the shark dies not for what it yields but for what it does not. It dies for the sport it provides. Its own tenacity dooms it.

Paul Dirk opens the sliding door of his garage and the light pours in on the bags of concrete and bicycles and tools and all the standard accouterments of a suburban garage. But there, covering one wall, is something else. There must be twenty of them. Isolated from their owners, the jaws of these sharks do not seem particularly fierce. They crease in, some of them at the center, so that those rows of teeth and cartilage seem almost comically puckered. I run my hand over the teeth of the big tiger. They are not especially sharp, not as sharp as I would have expected, but there are phalanxes of them, and the jaw that holds them seems triggered like a bear trap.

I stand there in a peculiar state of awe. There is something missing in my understanding of this graveyard.

"What do you feel about sharks?" I ask, "I mean what is your *feeling* about sharks?"

"Well," Dirk says, indicating the set of jaws in which my hand is laid, "if you were gaffing that one there and you fell in with him you just know he'd chew you up in a second!"

On an August day in 1962, just about a year after a national study had concluded that the Texas coast was one of the few stretches of seashore free from fatal shark attacks, a 40-year-old Harlingen mechanic and German naval veteran named Hans Fix was surf fishing on Padre Island near Port Isabel. He had had some modest luck and had tied his stringer of fish to his belt so that they could remain in the water. The water came up to his waist, and, unless it was an exceptional day, it was fairly murky.

The shark hit him twice, both times on the right leg. Fix tried to beat it off with the only weapon at hand, his fishing rod. It might have done some good, because the shark did not attack again. His wife and two other fishermen, hearing his screams, entered the water and hauled him out. The lower part of his leg was badly mangled, and though he remained conscious and was able to describe the attack to his rescuers, he bled to death before he could be saved.

The attack on Fix is the only incontrovertible Texas shark fatality on record. There have certainly been others, but not many. It is probably true that the majority of shark attacks go unreported, since the whole point for the shark is the consumption of the evidence. But even taking that into account, Texas still remains a wonderful place not to be eaten by a shark.

Minor incidents, however, are common. One man recently stepped on a two-foot sandbar shark in the Packary Channel. The fish satisfied itself with a chomp at the offending foot and the man drove himself to the hospital. Coastal newspapers are full of the testimony of marooned fishermen who "fought off" or "swam with" or "saw the fins of" sharks on their way to shore. Surely most of these tales have grown in the telling, and surely many of the sharks who have kept a deathwatch over swimmers have turned out to be only inquisitive dolphins displaying their dorsal fins as they breached.

But it is still an undeniable and not entirely disagreeable fact that They Are Out There and that sooner or later a frequenter of salt water will see one.

When sharks attack human beings they do so out of the conviction that the potential victim is edible. The factors that contribute to this conclusion are unclear. There is hardly any doubt that it was Hans Fix's stringer of bleeding fish that attracted the shark which killed him. A shark can sense gore across miles of water, and its prowess in rushing to its source is almost magical. In the same way it can read noise. A swimmer splashing on top of the water attracts a shark's attention much more than the noiseless sauntering of a diver, and if a shark is attracted by noise, it is exalted when the noise becomes a thrashing panic.

Humankind is not the normal prey of sharks, but a shark is willing to waive that consideration if the signals it receives are familiar enough. Thus the first rule of shark avoidance: when in the water, do not behave like bait. Do not even associate with anything that can be construed as bait. If you are in the water and have caught or speared a fish, remove it or yourself at once. Avoid murky water. If a shark can't see you, it's likely to come in on instruments and its criteria for eating you will not be as strict.

And here's some wonderful advice from someone who is sitting at a desk 200 miles inland: if you see a shark, stay calm. Look him in the eye. Chances are he's not interested, but will readily become so once the scent of your terror wafts into his sinister nostrils and you begin to behave like a terrified and bite-sized kingfish. If the shark should attack, convince yourself that intelligence is on your side, and at last your college degree will be of some use. Then hit him on the nose, the famous One Vulnerable Spot, with the heaviest thing you can find, which will invariably be your hand, which will invariably end up in the shark's mouth, stationed as it is underneath the sensitive nose. From there on out it's all free-style.

Of course, the important thing to remember is that sharks rarely behave in any kind of predictable fashion. I have here on my desk an account of an attack on a boy in which the shark, a small great white, was so fixated in chewing on the poor kid's leg that three rescuers could not loosen its grip and had to haul the boy and the shark both onto the shore where the victim was finally pried loose and saved. The shark was left to suffocate on the beach.

This is an unusual case, but it brings to mind an interesting sidelight. Most sharks, once they have settled on their prey, are not interested in anything else. This does not mitigate the heroism of the people who have come to the rescue of shark-attack victims but it does help to explain the fact that they are still alive. In 85 per cent of shark attacks in which the original victim is aided by another person the rescuer comes away unharmed.

All of this, I sincerely hope, is academic. The chances of being maimed or killed by a shark in Texas waters are staggeringly small. If sharks had wit, if their intelligence operated on the same frequency as ours, they might realize that they face, individually and collectively, a far greater risk of death at our hands than we do at their teeth.

A dolphin arcs across the logo of the bank building in which the Corpus Christi Shark Association is holding its biweekly off-season meeting. The dolphin has been idealized in the cause of gracefulness, just as the hammerhead shark on the CCSA's own logo has been endowed with a spooky, tail-thrashing pose.

In the elevator, riding up to the meeting room, I find myself surrounded by six people wearing shark's-tooth necklaces. Paul Dirk is one of them, along with his wife and son. One necklace, swaying gently against the chest of its owner, consists of a single tooth that curves inward like a claw. For the duration of the ride it becomes an object of general admiration, and its owner certifies under questioning that it is indeed the tooth of a sand shark, *Odontaspis taurus*, a common enough species but one that is apparently not hooked with any regularity.

About 50 people have shown up by the time the meeting is to begin. They are a diverse group but there is some intangible link between them all, like the universal cartilage of their prey. There are old, weathered, astringent fishermen, young kids just out of high school with pointed cowboy hats and hair hanging lankly down to their shoulders, middle-aged men who look like pirates, women who are here obviously because of their husbands, and women who are clearly here on their own. A man and woman arrive wearing identical maroon slacks, pink-checkered shirts, and white shoes and belts.

The conversation is about boats and weights and monofilament. I talk for a while with someone named Dan who does his fishing off a boat, farther into the gulf. He maintains that the sharks that wander near the rigs are sick, or lame, or lazy, or spawning. A boat gives him the opportunity to go after the lively ones, and after mako, the one shark that behaves like a big-game fish, leaping beautifully in its harassment, a fish for which Ernest Hemingway once held the Atlantic record.

Carolyn Dirk is not the kind of woman whose hobby you would expect to involve momentous battles with gargantuan sharks. She is in fact so demure and polite that when she says, in answer to a question, "I have an 8-7 tiger and an 8-2 hammer," it seems that she is revealing the contents of a bridge hand rather than reciting the measurements of two monsters for whose death she has been the agent. Obvious questions are in order: for example, how did she get involved in this?

"Oh, my sister and I met some shark fishermen, and then I met Paul and we got married and I started fishing too. But I'd never fished, for *anything!* I sure enjoy it, though.

"You know, it may sound dumb, but if you're going to go out there and fish that hard you want some glory for it, and the glory is getting up in front of the club and getting a trophy."

The president of the club, who appears to be in his early twenties and has a faintly collegiate air, calls the meeting to order. He opens his briefcase and a bumper-sticker comes into view. It says "Pray for Sharks." The meeting is informal but orderly. The first topic is back dues. There is a proposal that members must pay up before they are eligible to receive a trophy. This is only fair, and the amendment passes unanimously, the hands going up one at a time, cautiously.

"Okay, another problem," says the president. "You know those little sharks we have on our trophies? Remember how last time the supplier didn't have enough of them so we had to put those little men on? Well, I want you to know the sharks are on the way."

"What do we do with the little men, then?"

"That's up to you. Here's the other thing: what about the patches. Do y'all feel satisfied with the way the club patches are?"

There is general agreement that the club patches are ugly.

"Not that the hammerhead isn't as good a fish to put on there as any other," someone explains, "it's just that the people didn't draw it too well. I had one and I threw it away. I mean it was *that* ugly!"

The meeting continues at this pitch. It is hard not to think of the sharks that are swimming tonight in the dark, moonless water three blocks from here, magnificently alert to the slightest shudders of change in their environment, but totally isolated from any awareness of the bureaucracy that is meeting to ritualize and reduce them.

Is it that unawareness, I wonder, that gives even a hooked and dying shark the upper hand? Though it will fight to the end of its strength, though it will gnaw at whatever is available even in the shallows of its own death, the shark radiates indifference. *It does not care one way or the other*, and a shark fisherman must eventually contend with that.

The rest of the meeting is taken up by a discussion of whether or not the women should be allotted a separate competition category for "most fish caught by a woman." The proponents—all female—argue that this would give them a chance at a trophy, one that is not automatically snapped up by people like Paul Dirk. The men, by and large, don't go for it. They see no reason why a woman cannot fish with the same expertise as a man.

"Ninety per cent of it is luck," Dirk told me at his house earlier. "Once you get the bait on the hook, it's just luck."

The crisis subsides and the motion is tabled. The meeting draws to a close. Things are sluggish in the off-season, and there is an air of restlessness. Someone announces that there is a contest going on for trout and redfish. But nobody can get too thrilled about hauling in a two-pound trout, not when they're used to throwing back anything under six feet.

Forgive this small irony. I've had to come to Galveston's Sea-Arama to get a decent, close-up view of a live shark. Except for a few sand sharks, hardly larger than the mullet that drift in the swells on the beach, my first-hand experiences have been with dead or dying sharks, sharks out of their element, their grace subverted into obstinate fury.

Adjacent to the arena in which the dolphins are playing baseball with a man in a pirate suit there is a huge tank full of big saltwater fishes which lumber about morosely in the green water, skirting the circumference of a giant fishbowl dotted with viewing windows. There are groupers here, and sea turtles, and gars, and sawfish, and a lone leopard seal who cavorts among them, flaunting his warm-bloodedness.

And there are sharks. Five or six of them, swimming to the liquid strains of "Some Enchanted Evening" as it reaches them through the Muzak system. As a junior ichthyologist I am able to determine that these are either lemon or bull sharks, though I will not know for sure that they are the latter until I go home and look them up in a book. The largest is maybe six feet, a beautiful coal gray on top, modulating below to the color of the water. A remora swims steadily with it, attached to the shark's underside by the suction cup on the top of its head.

What strikes me most about these sharks is their corporeality. They seem full-bodied, completed. They even seem to have an emotional dimension: those huge pectoral fins that hold them on course are endearing somehow. When one of them soars close to the window, that impossibly rough shark skin looks like velvet, and the shark itself, rather than appearing as a menacing mass of gristle, seems upholstered and comfortable.

Even the fatalistic shark grin is withdrawn, replaced with a look of consternation on some individuals, on others with a look of pensive brooding. I make a point of staring into the eyes of every fish that skirts by my window. The grouper's eyes are a lovely, cloudy blue, like the photographs of the earth taken from far away in space; those of the gars are old and wrinkled and patient; but the eyes of the sharks are incredibly rigid, black on white, like the glass eyes in a taxidermist's drawer.

Soon Vicki The Lovely Mermaid drops in from the top of the tank. She does a few cartwheels and begins to swim past the windows in the shark-infested water. The sharks do not eat her. They seem rather to congregate on the opposite end of the tank, making an effort to avoid her.

Watching her waving to the people on the other side of the glass I am struck by a phrase I have recently encountered. "Pray for Sharks." And I do just that, because it is suddenly apparent that, for all their savagery and stalwart breeding, sharks are in trouble. Somebody is after them. Somebody, eventually, is going to try and take them away from us. Sharks are just too mean to be left alone.

I know it takes courage to swim in a tank of sharks and sawfish and turtles whose beaks could pry her arm off, but when Vicki swims by my window I just can't bring myself to wave back.

*—May 1975*

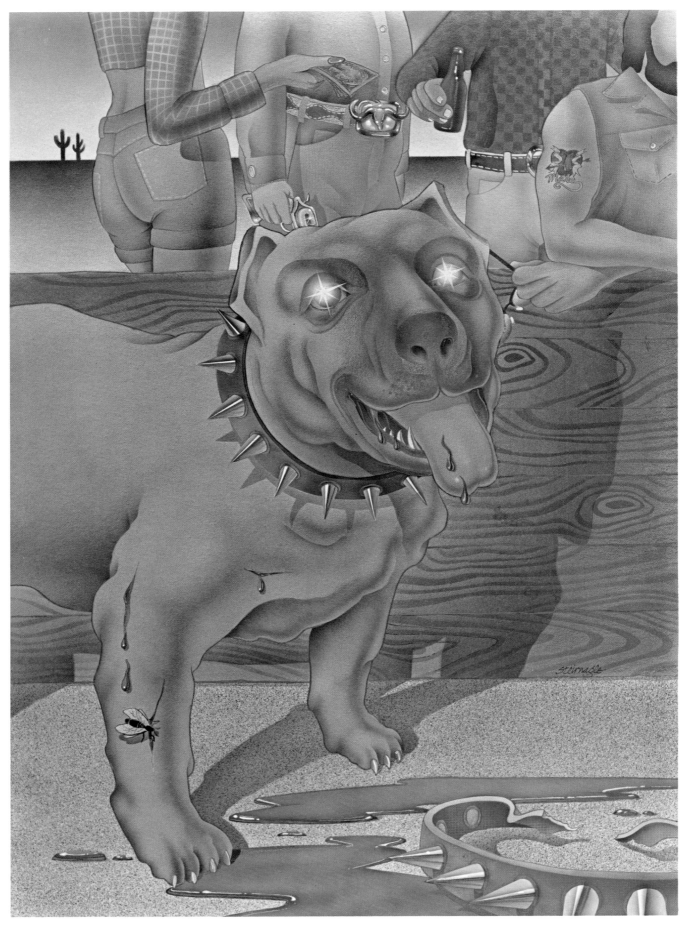

**140**

# LEROY'S REVENGE

## by Gary Cartwright

---

### *Animal lovers, don't read this.*

---

Otis Crater was late for the fanciers' organizational meeting at the Cherokee Lounge for good reason. He had just stabbed a U-Totem attendant following a discussion of the economic impact of a five-cent price increase on a six-pack of beer.

Crater kicked open the lounge door and bounced off the wall, scattering a table of Arabs who had made the mistake of thinking the Cherokee was a hangout for University of Texas exchange students. Crater carried the remnants of a six-pack under one arm and cradled his baby pit bulldog, Princess, under the other. He looked like a crazed, bloody scarecrow.

"That sorry bastard started it," Crater told those already gathered for the meeting. "I had turned my back to leave when he came at me with a butcher knife. He tore open my right side. Daddy was out in the truck with Princess and a load of cedar. I said: 'Don't ask me why right now, just give me your knife.'"

"Did you kill the sorry bastard?" Stout asked.

"I don't know," Crater said, as though he hadn't considered the question until now. "I 'spect I made him a Christian. Daddy told me, 'You're a goddamn fool springing a knife on a man when you can't even see straight. You're liable to cut yourself as him.' I think I got myself in the thigh."

Crater and his family are cedar choppers, a profession they have followed for a hundred years or longer. *Cedar chopper* has become a generic term, like *redneck*, almost without precise meaning. But there are still real people among the evergreen hills, spring-fed creeks, and wild backroads west of Austin who earn their keep by clearing stands of scrub cedar for land developers. Their wages are the wood they cut in a day. They drive broken-down pickup trucks, deal in cash, preach self-reliance, and maintain a fundamental faith in the use of physical force.

*Gary Cartwright, contributing editor of* Texas Monthly, *is the author of two books, a screenplay, and many articles.*

Thus, an increase in the price of a six-pack is of genuine concern. One could well imagine Crater's old daddy embellishing the story for the domino players, who would nod approval and observe that Otis was a good boy, if inclined to be a little hot-headed on occasion. "Heh, heh," his daddy would say, "I taught him better. First slash, he missed by eight inches and cut his ownself in the leg."

Stout, a telephone company lineman, had summoned the fanciers to call to their attention an ad in *Pit Dog Report,* an earthy, nearly illiterate "Mag. of reading and not to many picturs" published in Mesquite and circulated nationally.

The ad read:

> OPEN TO MATCH
> any time . . . any where
> BULLY, male, 54 lb.
> A DEAD GAME DOG!

Parties interested could contact Mr. Maynard at a post office box in Phoenix, Arizona. It wasn't necessary to mention that challengers lacking the proper securities need not respond. They had all heard of Mr. Maynard and his legendary beast, Bully. Mr. Maynard was the Max Hirsch of pit bulldog breeding, and Bully was Man O' War. Bully had every quality a fighting dog can have—gameness, biting power, talent, stamina, bloodline. As the saying goes, a dead game dog.

"We're gonna get it *on!*" Stout declared, cackling and slamming the magazine on the table.

"He's crazy as a mudsucking hen," Crater said, addressing the table. J.K., a professional breeder who works with his daddy, ran the tip of a frog sticker under his walnut fingernails and said nothing. Annabelle, a girl with an Oklahoma Dust Bowl face who lives with J.K., was practically sitting in J.K.'s lap, which was as far away as she could get from Stout.

"I got fifteen hundred bucks," Stout said. "That leaves fifteen hundred for the rest of you."

Crater looked down at Princess, who was chewing on his foot. "What are we gonna use for a dog?" he inquired. "I'm afraid Princess here is a shade might young. Boudreaux's dead . . . Tombstone's dead . . . and that dark brindle of J.K.'s wouldn't make a good lunch for a beast like Bully."

"Tell him," Stout said. Then J.K. related what fate had brought their way.

It seemed that J.K.'s daddy knew a driver who knew a dispatcher who had a brother in El Paso who had a dog named Leroy. Leroy was so god-awful bad nobody in El Paso would speak his name, but for a price his owner was willing to loan him out. J.K. and his daddy had taken a pretty game dog named Romeo out to El Paso where Leroy had had him for high tea.

But that wasn't all. J.K.'s daddy noticed that one of Leroy's toes had been cut off—cut clean, not like in a fight, but like a man had taken a chisel and cleaved the toe with a blow from a mallet.

Crater looked around the Cherokee and whistled. Stout yelled for some beer. They had all heard the story, how you never saw a genuine *Maynard* dog with a full set of toes. This was the result of a legendary training technique peculiar to the Maynard kennel. On a pup's first birthday, Mr. Maynard drops him in the pit with an older, experienced dog. As soon as the animals hit in the center of the pit and get a good hold, Mr. Maynard cleaves off one of the pup's toes. If the pup lets go his hold, if he loses heart and whines and slobbers, Maynard cleaves open his head and goes about his business. But if the pup holds on, if he keeps on fighting, Maynard has found a new beast to ward off the wolves of his trade. Any time you see a three-toed dog, move over.

"You trying to tell us Leroy is one of old man Maynard's stock?" Crater asked.

"I'm trying to tell you Leroy is the son of Bully!" Stout cackled, banging his giant fist on the table. "Only the sainted Doctor Maynard don't know it. He thinks Leroy is dead somewhere out in California."

"He won't for long," Crater said. "Don't you think old man Maynard won't recognize his own work?"

"Me and daddy cut off a toe on his other foot," J.K. admitted. "Then I dyed him brindle."

"Hell," Stout said. "You seen a thousand pit bulls. After a few fights, who knows the difference?"

Crater had to laugh. Leroy, son of Bully. Even his own daddy wouldn't know him.

"That's still a lot of money," he said, tumbling Princess with his other boot. "How do we know he can take him?"

"That's just a chance we have to take," Annabelle said, flinching as Stout grabbed her knee. Stout was leaning forward, grinning like a berserk grizzly bear. His shirttail was out, and you could see the bulge of a .38-Super pushed down into his jeans.

P it bulldogs. Killers, yes. For two thousand years or longer, pit bulldogs have been bred for a single purpose—to fight. To fight to the death, if necessary. To attack anything with four legs. They do not defend, understand. They are worthless as watchdogs unless the intruder happens to be another dog, or a lion or an elephant. No, they attack. That's their only number. They were bred that way—short neck, tremendously powerful

body and legs, an undershot jaw capable of applying 740 pounds of pressure per square inch (compared to a German shepherd's 45 or 50), a nose set back so they can hang on and breath at the same time. The symbol of Winston Churchill and the English-speaking race.

The American Kennel Club refuses to register the breed. In its well-stocked library in New York, which includes such titles as *The Dog in Action*, *Spine of the Dog*, and *Canine Madness*, there are a few references to the pit bulldog, or *American* pit bull terrier as they call it, careful to distinguish this non-dog from such registered breeds as the ordinary bull terrier, or the Staffordshire bull terrier.

Pure pit bulldogs are descendants of the old English mastiff, which Caesar greatly admired and brought back to Rome after his invasion of England in 55 B.C. Years before the Roman invasion, peasants kept mastiffs, or *tiedogs* as they were called—after the Anglo-Saxon practice of keeping mastiffs tied by day and letting them run loose at night. It was a practical method of regulating populations of wolves and other predators. Nobility, clergy, and other public-spirited citizens enjoyed dog fights and bequeathed legacies so that the common folk might be entertained on holidays.

Common folk are still entertained by the sport, especially throughout the South, the Southwest, and Southern and Central California, but also in Rhode Island, Massachusetts, Ohio, Illinois, Wisconsin, and most likely everywhere else. *Fanciers*, as they call themselves after the old English tradition, gather on Sunday mornings, in the thickets or bayous, along river bottoms or arroyos, in grape arbors, in junk yards, under railroad trestles. They bring their dogs and their wages and plenty of wine and beer and knives and guns, and they have one hell of a time.

Until recently, the fanciers bothered no one except each other, which was by free choice. Then, in the post-Watergate doldrums, newspapers in Dallas, Fort Worth, San Diego, and Chicago joined forces with the *New York Times* in exposing and deploring the sport, which they customarily refer to as a "practice." Boxing and auto racing are sport.

"This metropolitan area has more active dog fighting than any other region nationally," an investigative reporter wrote in the *Dallas Morning News*. Not only that, the story continued, but prostitutes and gamblers are rumored to congregate around the pits.

Almost every state has a law against dog fighting, but the sport is so clandestine that enforcement is nearly impossible. A vice squad detective for the Los Angeles sheriff's department told the *New York Times* that his department knew when and where the fights were being held, but they couldn't get on the property to obtain evidence. Dog fighting is a Class A misdemeanor in Texas and can cost you $2000 and a year in jail; the catch is you can't prosecute without a witness. There is not a pit bulldog breeder alive willing to testify against a fellow fancier.

But now that pit bulldog fighting has become an *issue*, all that may change. The *Dallas Morning News* (which supports the death penalty and Manifest Destiny and longs to invade Indo-China) published an editorial titled "Despicable 'Game,'" the final paragraph of which I quote:

"Every effort should be made to stop these fights. Quite simply, they are inhumane and appalling to any thinking citizen. Such senseless mayhem should not be tolerated in our midst."

Noble sentiments, but if history has taught us anything, it's that one man's mayhem, senseless or otherwise, is certain to be another's calling. Fanciers—like other individualists or subcultures—consider themselves to be a special breed, a class apart from what, to their point of view, are the drones of mainstream society. Fanciers care for their animals fanatically, certainly as conscientiously as most football coaches or generals treat their charges. Preservation of the bloodline is every fancier's solemn duty and privilege. When an insurance man advertised "White Cavalier (Pit) Bull Terriers" in the *Austin American-Statesman*, Crater and Stout called on the gentleman, pointing out that he was attempting to pass off lemons as oranges, and promising to break his spinal column if the ad ever reappeared, which it did not. The American Kennel Club should take note, if not of the method, at least of the diligence.

Otis Crater's jaded old daddy had reached an age where he'd lost interest in most dog fights, but he couldn't resist this one; there he was in Stout's house trailer, spitting Garrett's snuff juice into a paper cup and recalling the morning in Dripping Springs when the legendary Black Jack Jr. went nearly two hours before turning Marvin Tilford's Big Red.

The match ended when Marvin Tilford's dog *turned*, or gave up. Big Red knew when he'd had enough, but Marvin was so humiliated (and broke) that he didn't show up for a year. Big Red was later drowned by a boar coon who got him by the back of the neck in the South San Gabriel River.

"He should of never gone in water," Crater's old daddy pontificated as he rocked slowly and watched Princess chew on his boot. "Men and dogs belong on ground. Birds belong in air. Fish belong in water. When a creation starts believing they invented how things are, they forgot how things are."

"Hey, daddy," Crater interrupted. "Tell 'em about the deputy sheriff."

"That's another story," the old man snorted, dabbing his gums with a frayed matchstick. "We was going pretty good when the deputy called and asked me how things was going. 'Pretty good,' I said. 'The dogs been fighting twenty minutes and the people seventeen.'"

Watching Princess tumble around the floor of Stout's trailer, you wouldn't take her for a killer. She's no larger than a football, this furry little alligator with sad eyes and a wrinkled face, chewing mindlessly, somehow reminiscent of J. Edgar Hoover. According to procedure, Crater had already clipped her ears, which now looked like two raw navels. They were adequate for hearing, but impossible to bite down on.

Princess was fun to play with—the trouble was she didn't like to stop. She was playing with a big black poodle one afternoon when someone noticed that the poodle was no longer playing, or moving: the illusion of movement was caused by the steady jerking motion of Princess' head. Shortly following life's final measure of response, Princess dropped the black curly mess on the lawn and trotted over to examine a rose bush.

Before he got Princess, Crater traveled with a big brindle pit bulldog named Boudreaux. Crater was managing an Austin tavern when Boudreaux tore into a German shepherd three times his size. In the ten seconds or so it took Crater

to separate them with his hickory wedge, Boudreaux ripped out the shepherd's chest.

You could already hear the yelps and groans of men and animals down at the creek bottom when Stout arrived, carrying a package wrapped in brown paper.

"I guess you heard Claxon got stabbed," Stout said.

"I heard he got some new marks," Crater said. "What happened?"

"In the bathroom at the Cherokee. Claxon called this dude a Meskin. The dude was a Indian. Hell, I could tell right away he wasn't no Meskin."

"How's he doing?"

"He's about half dead and half proud," Stout said, and his laugh sounded over-oiled, hollow, and obligatory. He tore away the brown paper and held up a framed, hand-lettered scroll. There were tears in his eyes. The scroll was a poem, written by his mama, Toots; her first poem since Stout's daddy was shot to death by three blacks who hijacked his tiny grocery and market. Toots watched her husband die as she fired off several rounds at the fleeing killers. Austin police captured two of the hijackers, and the third, so it's said, was captured by Stout's vigilantes and is now fertilizing a worthy crop in a cedar chopper's garden. Who knows?

Stout turned his head so that the others wouldn't see the tears, and he looked for a place to hang the scroll. He selected a spot on the wall next to a poster of Pancho Villa enjoying a smoke under a mesquite tree.

Toots' poem went like this:

*The clock of life is*
*wound but once*
*And no man has the power*
*to tell just when the hands*
*will stop.*
*At late or early hour.*
*Now is the only time we own,*
*live, love, toil with a mill;*
*Place no faith*
*in tomorrow for*
*The clock may then*
*be still.*

There was silence throughout the trailer as Otis Crater read the words of Toots' poem aloud, but Stout excused himself and slipped outside. He kept his back to the trailer and his head down, following the fossilized debris of an ancient riverbed. He stopped in front of an oak almost as wide as himself and took something from a homemade cabinet nailed to the tree trunk. It was a package of sunflower seeds. His short knotted arms stretched for a low-hanging branch, and he filled a bird feeder with sunflower seeds.

Judging from the license plates of the campers and trucks scattered throughout the woods, the fanciers had come from as far away as California, Mexico, Florida, and even Canada. It was a young crowd, mostly in their twenties and thirties, a mixed bag of long-hairs, cedar choppers, and high-risk investors, with a few blacks and chicanos and some transients from a Houston motorcycle gang thrown in.

There were some women and enough children to make it look like a club picnic. A skinny kid named Tarlton, who stole ten-speed bikes for a living, passed out beer in paper cups. Tarlton wore a homemade T-shirt with a picture of Snoopy dragging a dead cat by the tail. There was no mistaking Mr. Maynard. He was the tall, lean, silver-haired man in a blue jumpsuit and wraparound shades standing by his Winnebago talking to J.K.'s daddy. You'd figure him for a bomber pilot in World War II, but he was just another dog soldier a long way from home. The cold scars in Maynard's eyes reached back to quarrels too horrible to translate: it had been a long time since he found it necessary to look tough or talk big.

There were a dozen bulldogs chained to heavy iron stakes around the perimeter of the clearing, but there was also no mistaking which one was Bully. While the other beasts were whimpering and sniffing blood and straining at their chains for some action, Bully relaxed on his haunches, observing the scene with sad, patient eyes.

Mr. Maynard and J.K.'s daddy talked and shared a drink, not at all interested in the fight in progress or the other fanciers clumped around the hay bales that formed the pit walls. A spotted cur owned by two black kids was trying to survive the jaws of one of Marvin Tilford's pups. The match was hopelessly one-sided, which meant there was hardly any betting, and the crowd was restless.

"Why don't you do the fair thing and give that leopard of yours a rest," Marvin told the black kids. They conferred in whispers, then picked up their pet and paid off. The bet was $50.

That's how most dog fights end, with a humiliated owner "doing the fair thing," picking up and paying off. Dogs are frequently wounded and occasionally killed, but only in serious challenges where the stakes are high and the owners' reputations well traveled. Even then an owner will usually do the fair thing when his beast is clearly outclassed, greatly preferring a healthy animal to an over-exercised ego.

"Dogs that are the best performers aren't necessarily the best dogs," Mr. Maynard told me as we drank Scotch in his Winnebago. He knew that I was a writer. He even helped me with my notes, spelling out names, and carefully considering dates. He was only anxious that the sport not get a bad name.

"People talk about pure Maynards as they do about Picassos," I observed.

"It's an art," he said.

"How do you do it? What's your secret?"

"No secret," he smiled. "I just breed best to best. Now, knowing what *is* best, that's a gift. I can't tell you about that any more than Sugar Ray could tell you how he boxed. The best performers aren't necessarily the best dogs, that's just one quality. You look for everything from performance to pedigree to conformation to the way a dog holds his head when he pees. 'Course, gameness is everything in a fighting dog, and you're not gonna know that until you see him scratch for the first time. I've heard it said that if fanciers had millions of dollars like horse people we could come up with the perfect fighting dog, but I haven't heard anyone claim they've come up with the perfect race horse yet."

I asked him about the familiar story, how he tested a pup by cleaving off one of its toes, then cleaved its head if the dog wasn't game enough to suit Maynard standards.

"Naw," he said, pouring two more drinks. "That's an old story. I did it once or twice when I was getting started. I'm a businessman. A man growing corn doesn't burn his

fields because a few ears aren't sweet. I raise dogs, I don't kill them. *Best to best*, that's the secret of a Maynard dog."

"Some people think this is a cruel sport," I said, understating this position as much as I dared.

"I guess it's cruel as anything else in life," he said, after considering the question from all sides. "These dogs only have one purpose in life, that's to fight." Fanciers are not long on philosophy. They accept what they do with the same lack of introspection that they accept war and General Motors. Their sport is part of their life.

The October sun came through the Winnebago window, overexposing the pastiche of fanciers around the hay bales. From the swell of the crowd it sounded like a hell of a fight, then I realized it was Crater and Stout doing the cat number.

The cat number is traditional at dog fights, much like clowns at a circus or halftime bands at football games. What they do is throw live cats—which they buy for 50 cents a head from the city pound—to assorted dogs who aren't fighting that day but who need exercise, self-confidence, and a show of affection. J.K. and his daddy use cats for training. Some handlers claim you shouldn't run a dog, but J.K.'s daddy runs all of his beasts, using a homemade device consisting of an axle and crosspole on which he can leash one dog and one cat. The leashes are measured so the dog can chase the cat till doomsday and never catch up, which he usually will attempt to do. If a dog has worked well, J.K.'s daddy will toss him a reward—the cat of his recent ordeal. A cat who has had a run-in with a pit bulldog is something out of a wax museum—a statue frozen in terror, eyes wide with disbelief, front claws arched, fangs bared in a silly, final grin.

Several wax museum cats lay in the grass around the hay bales. Marvin Tilford's little boy walked by, swinging a dead cat by the tail.

It was a few minutes after 2 p.m. when Stout and Annabelle brought Leroy down from the trailer. They had changed his name to Tag. If he made it through the day, he would be Leroy again. He would return triumphantly to El Paso, but for now he was Tag, a dog with no past and an unenviable future. Tag looked more like a walking anthill of petrified Jello than any animal that might come to mind. He had so much scar tissue that you couldn't tell what part was the original dog. J.K.'s dye job was blatantly atrocious; it looked as if Leroy had been tie-dyed.

"He wants Cajun Rules," J.K.'s daddy told Marvin Tilford, who by previous agreement would referee the match.

"Yessir," Marvin said.

"He says, if you see a turn, call it. But let them maneuver. Don't let the handlers push their dogs out of corner. Check the handlers . . . make 'em roll up both sleeves, and make sure they taste their dog's drinks. No sponges . . . no towels . . . all the handler can take in the pit is his dog's drink and a fan to fan him."

"Yessir," Marvin said.

When the handlers had carried the dogs to the pit, Mr. Maynard walked over and examined Leroy's teeth.

"Nice animal," he said. "Good head." If he thought the markings curious, or observed the stubs of two toes, one so recently cleaved the skin hadn't grown back, he didn't let on.

"Let's roll," he told Marvin.

Both dogs scratched hard out of their corners, and Bully took the lead, going low, forcing Leroy to bite around the nubs of gristle that had once been ears. Christ, he *was* strong. But there was no doubt Leroy was his daddy's boy; he just kept coming. "It's gonna be a long afternoon," Crater said. Unless you have more money than you can possibly afford riding on the outcome, a dog fight is about as interesting as a college wrestling match: the beasts hit, lock on, and hold fast, in endless repetition. The fight quickly settles into a test of strength, endurance, and gameness. Even the blood takes on a surrealistic quality after a while, like ghost shadows in a hall of mirrors.

After 45 minutes—when Marvin Tilford called the first pick up and broke the dogs apart by forcing his hickory wedge between their jaws and twisting counterclockwise—it was still impossible to say who was top dog.

While the handlers were cooling off their animals, Crater and I walked down by the old Indian mound. You could feel the excitement bouncing off the limestone walls of the creekbed: it wasn't watching the dogs that did it, it was *being there*, experiencing an almost-vanished culture of blood rites and a close familiarity with death.

Then we caught sight of Annabelle, coming out from behind some bushes, buttoning her pants.

"Damn," she said, "I'm so nervous I almost wet my britches."

"You think Mr. Maynard knows something?"

She shook her head: "I'd hate to find out. Old men like him can be real bad customers."

"He didn't say nothing when he looked at Leroy's teeth."

"That's not what worries me," Annabelle said. "Wait till his beast gets off on the acid."

"What's that suppose to mean?" Crater asked, squinting into the sun.

"Ask Stout."

"I'm asking you."

"We rubbed Leroy's chest with acid," Annabelle said. "Very shortly now Leroy's daddy's gonna take his first trip on LSD."

Crater watched the light hit and fracture off the creek walls.

"Oh, me," he sighed. "I get this awful feeling the center's not holding." Crater walked to his truck and got his gun. One of the fascinating things about Crater and his friends is the way they use the language. They are not educated, but they are amazingly literate.

At the second pick up an hour later, both dogs were bloody but strong. Bully's handler whispered something to Mr. Maynard, but Mr. Maynard shook his head and the handler told Marvin: "Let 'em roll." Leroy was bleeding from the chest and from the stifle of his left rear leg.

The battle was into its third hour when J.K. told his daddy: "His leg is starting to pump blood."

"I can't help that," his daddy said.

"He's making you like it, Leroy. You better eat!" Annabelle hollered out suddenly. At the name *Leroy*, both Stout and Crater felt for their guns, but Mr. Maynard didn't blink.

"Work him, *Tag*!" J.K. yelled.

Bully was clearly the top dog now. Leroy was losing blood and weakening noticeably, but Bully was zonked far past the limitations of fatigue and mere dogdom. The ploy of the LSD was backfiring. The hair and blood in Bully's mouth told him that he was a 60-ton gorilla at the Captain's Table reciting compound fractions in a tongue not previously heard on this planet. "Stand back," he said in his strange tongue. "This one will be for keeps." He took Leroy down by the front leg and chewed on the stifle, shaking hard, lifting Leroy off the ground and working him against the pit wall.

"Goddamn it, Marvin," Stout hollered, "keep 'em off the wall!" Marvin moved in with his hickory wedge, but before he could break the beasts Bully shook Leroy so hard he snapped off his hold and flew halfway across the pit. Then, by God, Leroy was on him, tearing at the soft part of his throat. This time Marvin called a pick up, which was the proper thing to do. Marvin had to help the handler restrain Bully and drag him back to his corner.

"Jesus, he's pumping," said Tarlton, the bicycle thief. "Don't let 'em roll again."

Marvin looked at Mr. Maynard, then at J.K. "You want to roll again?" he asked. J.K. answered by releasing his beast, who lunged straight at Bully and got him by the eye.

"No more pick ups," Mr. Maynard said quietly. "Let 'em roll."

"Let 'em roll," J.K. agreed.

So that would be it—one of the dogs would have to die or quit, and it wasn't difficult to project which it would be.

Three hours and fifty-eight minutes into the match, it happened. Bully was going for the chest, boring in like a jackhammer, when suddenly Leroy got a leg and flipped him easy as you turn a pancake. There was a wailing sound like echoes colliding, then Bully's eyes froze over. He lay still as Leroy tore out his throat. Leroy relaxed his hold, sniffed his dead opponent, then limped over and licked J.K.'s hand.

"If that don't beat all!" Otis Crater's old daddy said as they stood over the corpse of the late, great Bully. "It's like his old heart just give out on him."

J.K.'s daddy nodded, "Looks like he busted apart inside."

"That's just what happened," Mr. Maynard agreed.

"If that don't beat all!" Otis Crater's old daddy said again.

Mr. Maynard walked over to his Winnebago and returned with a .44 magnum and a sheaf of $100 bills. "Here's what I owe you," he told J.K.'s daddy.

Mr. Maynard turned the cold scars of his eyes on Stout, then on the others, taking his time.

"I don't know what you little bastards did to my dog," he said, "but you're the ones that have to live with it."

He walked over to Leroy, patted Leroy's head, then raised his .44 magnum to Leroy's head and blew it off. No one moved or spoke a word.

"If you boys ever get to Phoenix," he said, looking each of them over one more time, "look me up."

*—August 1975*

What to do if lost.

Recognizing edible indoor plants.

Calling an elk.

Survival indoorsmanship.

Stalking the indoor cat.

Communing with the great indoors.

*Illustrated by Tom Ballenger*

# THE OLD INDOORSMAN

## by Gregory Curtis

---

*A few survival tips from a man who knows.*

---

The modern world has lost respect for indoorsmen. Their lives are considered humdrum, confined, lacking in excitement, and yet the opposite is true. The adventures of the greatest indoorsmen would make even a novel of manners seem tame. What has been lost are the basic skills. Formerly they were handed down from one generation to the next, but the modern world—with its emphasis on camping, backpacking, nature walks, and getting back to the land—is leaving us empty when we once were full, ignorant when our knowledge was once sublime. My evidence? Consider Boy Scouts scraping sticks together in the dead of night in the vain hope of lighting fires. This is the heritage we leave our children. My hope is that the following hints will not only preserve valuable indoor traditions but also start those who heed its message down the proper indoor path.

**What to do if lost.**

Do *not* move around. Stay where you are and let them find you. Meanwhile, check all cupboards and refrigerators to see if you have enough food. Make sure water is still running from the taps. In winter place an extra blanket on the bed. Find a good book to read. You may be in for a long wait.

**Following and interpreting a trail.**

A trail is made up of tracks someone or ones left behind. A purse on the sofa, empty glasses in the living room, a pair of stockings on the hall rug, a shirt carelessly tossed against a closet door—these are tracks that together make a trail.

A trail can be interpreted by determining where it leads and trying to deduce why it led there. Often interpreting a trail is an enjoyable intellectual challenge. For practice, assume the trail mentioned above led to a pile of large floor pillows and try to deduce why. Fun, isn't it?

*Gregory Curtis, a member of the original* Texas Monthly *staff, is the magazine's executive editor.*

**Recognizing edible indoor plants.**

Anything green you cannot sit in, lie upon, or shatter is a plant. Inedible plants are stuffed, along with handfuls of dirt, into round pots. Edible plants are wrapped in plastic or tin.

**Calling an elk.**

Elks seldom come indoors but when they do they enjoy an occasional call. Early afternoon is a good time. By then an elk has been up and about for awhile, the morning foraging is over, and it has nothing more to do until bedtime. Speaking with an elk can be a trial, but his loud voice shouldn't, in itself, make him socially unacceptable.

**Survival indoorsmanship.**

Many indoorsmen like to test their skill by living for a week or more using only the things that can be conveniently put into an average-sized house. All the cupboards and freezers must be filled beforehand, since there's no going to the grocery store again during the week. The bathroom must be cleaned, the beds freshly made, the carpets vacuumed. Clothes must be picked up at the laundry, the electric, gas, and telephone bills must be paid, the lawn must be mowed if it's a summer survival week or the snow shoveled if it's in winter. After that, one must close all doors and windows and simply make do. It's hard, but that's the whole point!

**Stalking the indoor cat.**

The best time to stalk a cat is when it's asleep. Sit quietly watching television or thumbing through a magazine until the cat closes its eyes and doesn't move for several minutes. Now get out of your chair and tiptoe stealthily toward the animal. If it should hear you and wake up, look quickly at the ceiling as if searching for cobwebs and whistle innocently until the animal goes back to sleep. The cat has been successfully stalked when you are close enough to touch it with both hands. Now what? You should have decided that before you began stalking.

**Where to find dry wood after a rain.**

The best wood for burning is that round kind about two feet long, smooth on each end, with the bark still on it. In the fall this kind of wood collects in neat piles in garages and roofed porches where it is protected from the weather. Many experienced indoorsmen keep a small pile of this kind of wood next to the fireplace where it will stay dry in all but rather strange circumstances.

**Finding north.**

Telephone your Bureau of Roads or local equivalent body, tell them your address, and ask this question: "When I'm standing at my front door facing the road, which direction is to my right?" If the reply is "north," your problem is solved. If the reply is "south," you can assume that north will be on your *left*. If the reply is "east" or "west," you have a problem. This problem probably lies very deep and you must search elsewhere for the answer. Finding north will not help you.

**Communing with the great indoors.**

This is a subject that must be treated with caution because it is possible to get overly romantic. Yet, stop for a moment to consider the scope and variety of creation the modern indoors represents—the complex lattice of pipes carrying heat, water, gas, air conditioning; the perfect symmetry of linoleum; the hum, crackle, and hiss of FM stereo imperfectly tuned; the solid, staid respectability of a couch; the willing prostration of a carpet. No human intelligence could have conceived these things and during silent contemplation of their wonder we can sometimes hear them whisper hints of who their maker might be.

*—April 1977*

# WATER LOG

## by Beverly Lowry

---

## *The aloneness of the long-distance swimmer.*

---

We define ourselves in all kinds of ways. Ask me who I am and I may name any one of several names, all determined either by what I actually do in the world or how I see myself going about in it. I could start with woman . . . writer . . . wife. I could make a list, provide you an ordering that would tell you how I see myself, from which you could draw whatever interpretation seemed to follow.

But sometimes we are too strict on ourselves. Sometimes we leave off calling ourselves by the very thing we like best to do, the thing we may pursue with the most diligence. Without officially being labeled a critic, however often I go, whatever expertise I have developed, could I without apologies easily call myself moviegoer? Without blush a daydreamer . . . however overlong I sit staring out of windows at nothing? In comparison, woman, wife, and writer are easy to say. But ask me what name I give myself and somewhere not too far down the line, oh, maybe sixth or so, will be this answer: swimmer. Though I enter no races, vie for no medals, clock no sprints, though it is late to be still calling myself this, when competitive swimmers are often too old at eighteen, though no one seeks me out to swim in any group, still . . .

You may see me in winter, defying whatever virus is prevalent, with unseasonably wet hair streaming from my scarf. My skin will be steamy red from the change of temperature, from cold outside into warm indoor pool, then back again into cold. A faint trace of chlorine will linger and my eyes may well be raccoon-ringed from goggles pulled tight as protection against chemicals. About my ears you may detect a faint whiff of alcohol: dropped in after workouts, it helps ward off fungus, or swimmer's ear. My hair has a year-round glossy patina—like doll's hair, beauticians remark—and at the tips a certain incurable

*Beverly Lowry is the author of* Come Back, Lolly Ray *and several short stories. She teaches creative writing at the University of Houston. Her most recent novel,* Emma Blue, *will be published this year.*

yellow dryness. Regular doses of cod-liver oil help curb, but don't control, the dry skin that results from this perpetual oversoaking in bleachy pools. My pectorals flex to an amazing hardness; my upper arms are muscular and sturdy; my shoulders athletic. My thighs and back are strong; my lung capacity and overall stamina excellent. Much of what I am—much of how I look, of how this physical thing I live in operates—is attributable to this activity I pursue.

Miles each week, back and forth along painted lines. Nowhere to get to, no score to record, no victory to claim, no loss to mourn. No partner to receive from and no opponent to bounce skills off of; in effect, no game, no win, no outward sign of *return*. Only this inner traveling, straight and strong, back and forth and back and forth, in sunlight watching glittery bubbles go by, as one hand comes through, pulling its share of water behind, and then the other, seeing the shadow going slightly ahead, along the line painted on the bottom of the pool. On and on until the end . . . the goal, which is never arbitrary. You always know where you will be arriving, long before you begin.

I am constantly surprised at myself, that I do it and keep on doing it, that somewhere along the way, over the years I have not said, Enough, time to try something new. But after a while any routine, I suspect, becomes blood and bone deep, difficult to separate from self; becomes a *need*. At this point, to stop would be to rearrange my life; would be, in fact, probably more difficult than to keep on. And, who knows, perhaps by now I've even lost the knack of how. Also, there is this other factor, often downplayed by swimmers, runners, weight-pressers—those of us who push, pull, stroke, kick, lift, strain, and keep on—that underneath, we are supreme egoists. And that this literally dead-end attention to bodily pursuits is but one way of feeding ourselves. In that case . . . stop? Stop? Not a chance.

In the winter, of course, the shadow on the bottom of the pool disappears as, surrounded by perspiring windows, with an overhang of steam heavy in the air, I swim indoors. And wait out those cool months for a weather change, when

I can take to the outdoor pool and resume that cooler—to me more natural—swim. On one occasion, however, over-anxious, I pressed too hard for this first spring encounter and dove too soon, in the process lowering my body temperature until I had no feeling in my legs or lower body. There was a terrible dizzying burning in my head, and I had no sense of heat or cold at all. Afterwards, I had to get someone to tell me how hot my bathwater was, to see if I was about to scald myself. It took an hour of hot soaking to return my system to normal, and even then I shivered. Yet I flinch at being called a zealot. I skip a day now and then to prove who is in control of what. Prove to whom?

One mile in a 50-meter pool is 32 lengths. In a 25-yard pool it is 72. Back and forth along the line. One mile a day in approximately 30 minutes is what I do, give or take a minute or so this side or that; my clocking is imprecise, not down to seconds. Yet time is always a factor; if I swim the distance in 28 minutes, I know it all right, and will allow myself afterwards privately to boast. If in 31, I am glum and disappointed, inwardly scolding. This 28/31 time is no Olympic record certainly and yet it's not dragging either; it is above all the result of a strong and steady, time-bracketed *push*. For the duration, nonstop.

My routine is three-quarters freestyle, one-quarter breaststroke and backstroke, plus, when I will take the time or feel the urge, a session with the kickboard. Back and forth along the line, seeing little, hearing less, saying nothing, with even the familiar push of gravity lessened, buoyant, at home in the water, and unafraid: as at ease as if born there, as natural as breathing. To a swimmer, the water is altogether gentle and inviting, not treacherous, no threat. Along the way I solve problems; rearrange the furniture of my life; change beginnings, endings, swap paragraphs; check invention against life; re-create confrontations, allowing them to come out in my favor. With every stroke as I go, all this calculating notwithstanding, I reestablish where I am, which lap. Seven-seven-seven. Eight-eight-eight. Concentrating, I always know. Only when I change pools abruptly, say from a 50 meter to a 25 yarder, is my concentration broken enough that I sometimes lose track of the count.

I have never learned to do flip turns, but I do reverse directions as quickly as possible. Coming to a bank, I touch it with fingertips and, without coming up for breath, push off again, not stopping, never touching bottom, keeping the rhythm, maintaining the solid steady rolling flow, two kicks to a stroke, breathe on the right side: kick stroke kick, kick stroke kick, breathe, back and forth along the painted line, rhythm, rhythm, keeping on.

There is the secret to going for distances. It sounds too simple but there it is: not stopping. It is how to build stamina. It is how to paint rooms, build fences, finish novels. When you are tired, you keep on. When bored, you don't stop. The goal is far beyond and you are fixed on it. You must decide ahead of time what the stopping point will be, and then go for it. When you get there, if it is far enough, then stop. If you simply cannot get there, then you take one more stroke in that direction and then, unless paralyzed by exhaustion, you take maybe one more. And another. There must be horizons, of course, and the distance must not be so great that you cannot keep up a strong push to get there, and you do not set up so great a distance that *how far* becomes the whole point. (I could, for instance, go farther than one mile. I have done two, on occasion, and not felt the difference that much. Also, if I swam only freestyle, instead of alternating with the other strokes, I could decrease my time. But just as pure distance is not all, neither is pure speed, though both interact and contribute. You must find your own goal.)

And there must be this before starting: a will for distance, commitment to it, a capacity for not stopping. This may be a measurable factor, I don't know, possibly detectable in blood pressure or gland secretions. At any rate, you can see glimpses of it in the eyes of long-distance runners too, their focal point not close up on trees and cars passing by, but set off in distances, on getting there. Others, less patient, operate on quicker returns, on day-day-day schedules, or perhaps even minute-minute-minute, while the long distancer tends to have a solid, waiting year-year-year kind of rhythm and timing. A vision reaching so far ahead it may finally come back on top of itself and turn into a kind of meditation. It is a way of reaching the spirit and recharging the psyche through the body, honorably and gratifyingly, if inescapably alone.

Except for, and I mention this with great hesitation, the audience. Those admirers applauding in your imagination, as you keep on and on, back and forth. Your fans. The dream: what I call swimming for the ages. Today I am Diana Nyad, conquering Superior. Tomorrow I am going for gold. Often I am an Olympiad manqué, admired for her stamina, her rhythm, her stroke. (My God, the voices say, what that girl might have done!) Imagination: it may in fact be the greatest motivator; what pushes me with the hardest thrust, and makes me leave my books and go to the pool . . . then, once there, may be what finally convinces me to leave the side of the pool and the dread I sometimes cling to there—thinking of the time ahead, those 28/31 back-and-forth minutes—and go on in.

I believe the capacity for distance does not come so easily to the young. At an early age—say from five on—swimming is a heart-bursting kind of activity. (If, that is, you are to take it seriously enough to call yourself swimmer; if it is something you see yourself doing in the world.) How can you tell if you're going fast enough? A swimming coach has said to me, if it hurts. If your chest is in such pain you feel your heart is about to explode, you're doing it right. At the Olympics this year, a back stroker said he knows his timing is on, not by his stroke or how it compares with other competitors, but if he's gritting his teeth so hard his jaw aches. Watch a swim team work out and you will see them sprinting, lap after lap, chop-chopping back and forth, their bodies arched high to encounter the least possible resistance from the water and facilitate the rapid turnover of strokes. We solitary swimmers, on the other hand, take longer, deeper strokes, pulling hard and steady without the chop and arch, greeting the water as it comes instead of fighting to overcome it, hoping that the overall, long-distance view will in the end be more sustaining. Banking on *in the long run*, we are committed to the belief that how long we hold on will matter . . . trying all the while to forget what some fool said about the overview, that in the long run you're dead.

Yet there is no nostalgia here and no self-pity. I myself have raced, life-guarded, and taught swimming. I even once swam a ballet—*Swan Lake* no less—in a three-foot-deep plastic pool in New York City's Coliseum; doing watery pirouettes over the IND 59th Street express stop; smiling and flutter kicking, feet low, head high, to Tchaikovsky. Distancing is all that I do now and, even then, have not been at it that long: I was almost up to the notorious over-thirty before I ever began.

There is one last thing I am adamant on: that this routine is no victory of discipline over self. You won't hear me selling willpower or self-control. Swimming is simply what I do, a part of my life, a plain activity satisfying a plain need, as much as sleeping, woven that deep into the fabric of my days. Speak of physical fitness and watch my eyes glaze over. Ask me about blood pumping and heartbeats and I can only tell you mine does. If there were no spiritual advantage, no psychic flash, I would not do it; what has none offers me no interest at all. One-two-three calisthenics, roll for the thighs, lean for the midsection are not for

me, no matter what condition the Royal Canadian Air Force is in. There I find no style, no beauty, no culmination: no one mile's end to reach. The vision is too short, too rooted in the here and now, in that take-it-off-quick, minute-minute-minute kind of pursuit. Obviously, that's a matter of personal style, pure and simple. And probably, of glands.

On the contrary, I consider what I do to be an indulgence I often feel embarrassed to admit. My impulse, rather than being something of discipline is, I swear, practically hedonistic. By what feeds *me* am I here naming myself. That eternal, arrogant I. How many times by now I have repeated it here, telling my story so presumptuously, dragging on about *me*? But, if a thing is so gratifying in every way and so pleasurable and rewarding (not to mention being so approved of) would an egoist not be a fool to deny herself? And it is only after understanding that, that this back and forth along painted lines can assume its true value, that inner traveling, that endless self-nourishing: for me.

*—January 1977*

# STATESMEN AND STATESWOMEN

Somehow the words "Texas" and "politician" are just meant for each other. There's a certain wheeler-dealer style about Texas politicians, which Jim Fallows measures in "Fiendly Persuasion." But the days are long gone when Lyndon Johnson believed he had to drink bourbon and wear cowboy boots when in his heart he yearned for Scotch and English suits. Texas is an urban state, and the heirs of LBJ like Barbara Jordan and Lloyd Bentsen are urban people. Perhaps Dolph Briscoe will be the last Texas governor with truly rural roots and a ranch that's not a weekend hobby. Griffin Smith, jr., who with Jim Fallows went on to pen speeches for President Carter, examines the strange career of Governor Briscoe in "Why Does Dolph Briscoe Want To Be Governor?" It would be hard to find a greater contrast to Briscoe than Barbara Jordan, and William Broyles' "The Making of Barbara Jordan" is a story not only of a brilliant politician but of a determined woman overcoming the heritage of segregation.

All politicians want to be loved, and Larry L. King's "Body Politics" deals with those times when that desire for affection goes beyond just getting votes. On the other hand, expecting them to be more upright than most of us are seems, as King points out, a bit unfair. Jim Fallows' "Turning the Other Chic" talks about another of our shortcomings: how easily some politicians go in and out of public favor like hemlines. In the political arena personality is both shield and weapon, and nothing tests a politician's personality more than a good floor fight. Paul Burka's "So Close, So Far" is an intimate account of one such battle. The Texans almost win, but against great odds are defeated by two votes. Still, LBJ would have been proud: they played the game his way.

# FIENDLY PERSUASION

## by James Fallows

*All those pious candidates say they're against old-style politics, but we'd be better off if they knew how to operate like LBJ.*

After five years of work, any number of aborted lawsuits, and many thousand words of controversy, the Big Book about Lyndon Johnson has finally appeared. Doris Kearns, the Harvard scholar who became the president's confessor, has published *Lyndon Johnson and the American Dream*, to the consternation of the Johnson family and the titillation of the publishing world.

Anyone who has not by now heard the story-behind-the-story of this book has simply not been paying adequate attention to the book chat pages of the local paper. Kearns was a young White House fellow, on leave from Harvard, when she first caught Johnson's eye nine years ago. When he returned to the ranch, she became his confidante, recipient not only of his dreams and childhood recollections (which are fodder for a good deal of half-baked Freudianism in this book), but also of the firsthand details of his political career that no other biographer will ever get, at least not from Johnson himself. She was a "Harvard," a representative of the Eastern academic world Johnson so mistrusted; but, perhaps for that very reason, Johnson seemed to think that if he could win her over, she would be his best hope for a sympathetic reading of his personal and political history.

Like many Big Books—like, indeed its subject himself—*Lyndon Johnson* is both tremendously rich and terribly flawed. Kearns' psychohistorical explorations of Johnson's character are sure to attract attention, but they are by far the least persuasive portions of the book. When writing about political affairs, she has a fine sense of nuance and subtlety, but each pronouncement about the oedipal complex or castration fears is made in a club-footed manner. Kearns also seems undecided about who she is really writing to—the academic audience, which insists on endless and unnecessary citations to Richard Hofstadter and Louis Hartz, or the general reading public, which really could not care less about these demonstrations that Kearns has done the required reading in

*James Fallows is a former associate editor of* Texas Monthly *and has written for several magazines. He is President Jimmy Carter's chief speechwriter.*

Am Civ 102.

Having said that, I must add something else, which is that I could hardly put the book down, and doubt that anyone with more than a passing interest in Johnson will be able to either. For one thing, its details and documents about the political life are as rich as anything that has appeared in several years. Perhaps more significantly, it raises a question with immediate application to the strange developments in national politics this year—namely, about the value of an old-style politician.

What Kearns finally has to say about Lyndon Johnson is that he was a pure "politician," of a sort that has recently gone out of fashion. Unlike FDR, he was not a great political orator; unlike John Kennedy in the years after the Bay of Pigs, he was not a skilled political administrator. He was, instead, a masterful political persuader. Face-to-face with constituents, legislators, supplicants, kings, he knew how to wheedle, compromise, listen, persuade. "All his life," Kearns says, "Johnson retained the belief that any problem could be solved by personal force. He believed he could make a friend of anyone—Nikita Khrushchev, Ho Chi Minh, Charles De Gaulle—if only he could sit alone with him in a room and talk. Indeed, there were few who could resist the influence of his personal presence. He possessed a wholly intuitive and profound capacity to see into other men's natures. His greatest gift of leadership was the ability to understand, persuade, and subdue..."

This sounds uncomplicated, but how rare a gift it is. The best courtroom lawyers are not the thousands who have mastered the technical minutiae of the law but the dozens who can read a jury's mind and then choose the one appropriate argument from the many possibilities. What makes Edward Bennett Williams different from the drudge down the street is that gift of understanding and persuasion, and that is what made Lyndon Johnson special too. Ordinary politicians know how to overpower their opponents, but the masters know how to do the job more gently. "Johnson understood," Kearns says, "that the most important decision each Senator made, often obscurely, was what kind of Senator he wanted to be: whether he wanted to be a national leader in education, a regional leader in civil rights, a social magnate in Washington, an agent of the oil industry, a wheel horse for the party, a President of the United States. . . . As Johnson's mental portraits of his colleagues became more complete, his political touch became finer.''

Even during the happiest days of Johnson's reign, of course, there was something less than total public enthusiasm for the virtuosity of this ''Johnson treatment.'' By 1965 we had already passed the era in which to call a politician a ''Great Compromiser'' was to bestow an unquestioned honor. But in the eleven years since Johnson had a willing Congress enacting his Great Society, popular attitudes toward wheeler-dealer politicians have grown increasingly more hostile. Like most other aspects of ''back room politics,'' the Johnson treatment is now widely suspect as a blot on clean government and the democratic way. Apart from appearing in public in the company of Richard Nixon, there are few more damaging steps a candidate could take in 1976 than to speak approvingly of compromise and persuasion.

Half of the presidential candidates we have had to choose from, the half who are from Washington, have been outdoing one another with demonstrations that they have not been tainted by the pitfalls of compromise and politics. The other half—Jerry and Ronnie of California, plus Jimmy Carter—positively glow with the holiness of their ''new politics,'' no-compromise approach to things. Perhaps this is understandable in the case of Jerry Brown, who has little else to run on, but the Exceptional Piety Award must go to Jimmy Carter for his comments about this question just a few months back. Robert MacNeil of the Public Broadcasting System asked Carter ''Do you have any weaknesses, Governor?''

''A lot of them. Yes.''

''What are they?''

''Well, I think perhaps . . . I'm too demanding on other people. I'm pretty rigid. . . . I have never been able to compromise enough to accommodate, you know, those who feel differently from me. . . . If I go down, I go down in flames, and I don't compromise away my position in a back room. And this is incompatible with politics, and may very well be a problem. It's certainly a weakness, politically speaking.''

If there were the slightest inkling that Carter actually believed what he was saying, this would not be such a bad statement at all. It would mean that he recognized the value of compromise and negotiation and was sorry he lacked those skills. But, of course, Carter meant just the opposite; the exchange might as well have gone, ''Do you have any weaknesses, Governor?'' ''Yes, I'm too generous.'' What ''fault'' could sound more wonderful than this one? ''Pretty rigid''? Hooray for the new politics! ''Never been able to compromise''? We'll have an honest man in Washington. What, a weary nation asks itself, could be better for us than this new voice of candid, four-square dealings?

Well, a lot of things could be better—starting with a candidate who would admit less grudgingly than Carter that the old-fashioned tools of traditional politics are useful and necessary tools which should not be indiscriminately scorned. Many things have gone wrong in the Johnson and Nixon eras, and many politicians were to blame for them. But it was not ''politics'' or ''compromise'' that lay behind the difficulties—as Lyndon Johnson's record demonstrates.

In recounting Johnson's accomplishments, Doris Kearns makes clear that essentially similar political skills could be applied toward quite dissimilar ends. The first category of ends is that of nuts-and-bolts, functional politics—the steps that must be taken to keep the wheels of government turning. In one of several transcripts of Johnson's White House phone calls (does this sound familiar?), Kearns reports a conversation between Johnson and Roy Wilkins of the NAACP. Long before he picked up the phone, Johnson had decided to make a certain appointment, for which he wanted Wilkins' approval. Over the phone, Wilkins got the Johnson treatment, and by the time the call was over Wilkins was pleading with the President for the appointment that Johnson had intended to make all along. Later Johnson used a similar approach on the senators who had to pass on the nomination. If Johnson could keep pulling these coups off, so much the better. He got what he wanted, and no one really lost.

This sort of functional politicking might also include the more familiar sorts of logrolling, as Kearns illustrates with a talk between Everett Dirksen and LBJ. Dirksen, the Senate Minority Leader, wants a public-works project for Illinois; Johnson, the President, wants Republicans to come on board with one of his bills. A deal is struck, both sides ending up with less than they hoped for but more than they feared they might get. As long as there are different interests to be represented, deals like this must always be made.

If horse trading were all there was to politics, Everett Dirksen would be remembered as a great man. He was quite as good as Johnson at making deals in his own favor. But Dirksen will always be remembered as a hack, and Johnson as something both better and worse than that, because there was no horizon that drew Dirksen on, apart from the dealing itself. You can't tell the difference between a compromiser and a hack by the kinds of tools they use, but rather by what they want to do with them. Dirksen was essentially a quartermaster for his constituents and a few special interests, while Johnson had his own complicated ideas of how he could do ''good'' for his country and the world. Even at his worst, he was never a hack.

When he was trying to do ''good,'' Johnson exemplified the second category of political goals—genuine ''leadership'' of the country. In 1957, Johnson was more responsible than any other person for getting a civil rights bill through the Congress. Toward that end there was no bit of chicanery or back room skill he was embarrassed to use. He told Southerners that the bill was the only way to keep uppity niggers in line. He groaned with Northerners about those nasty bigots of the South. He discussed with his associates the effect the bill would have on his chances for the presidency three years later. He kept dozens of balls in the air, wore different faces at different times, dissembled and concealed. It was the Johnson treatment in all its questionable glory, but it got the job done. He did what President Eisenhower was not and President Kennedy would not be able to do.

In the first happy months after the 1964 election, Johnson had a set of similar achievements, engineering the Great Society. As best he could, Johnson also tried to exercise a kind of moral leadership upon the country. ''I knew that as President I couldn't make people *want* to integrate their schools or open their doors to blacks,'' he told Doris Kearns, ''but I could make them feel guilty for not doing it.''

Leadership like this looked fine as long as Johnson was

espousing causes history has endorsed. But he felt it just as important to exert his leadership in another direction, the one that led toward Viet Nam, and the harvest of that leadership was a bitter one indeed. Johnson used many of his old skills when he took the nation to war, which suggests a third category of their application.

By this point in our history, the many reasons for the failure of Johnson's war policy are known to all who care. (They are known largely because of David Halberstam's *The Best and the Brightest*, which does a better job than Kearns of connecting the peculiarities of Johnson's character with the deterioration of his career.) But amidst all these morals and lessons, there is one point quite easily forgotten. While some of Johnson's difficulties reflected the failure of his normal abilities (he could not understand the Vietnamese the way he could most Americans; he let himself be trapped by the "experts," a peril he had avoided in his domestic politicking), at least one part of the tragedy was due to Johnson's success. In the early days of the war, when Johnson felt he had to fight but hoped it would end quickly, he decided to keep the cost of the war a secret. Congress was eager to enact the Great Society; they might have lost their nerve had they known what the war would cost. They would have backed off, Johnson knew, and his plans to do good would be ruined. So he made sure they didn't know. The figures were concealed. Johnson was sure it would all turn out right in the end, because it always had. "When his leadership had proved effective," Kearns says, "Johnson had been praised by the very Senate on which he had practiced his deceptions. The country, then, would also reward the President for 'pulling off,' as he described it, 'both the war in Viet Nam and the Great Society at home,' even if he hadn't told them everything at the time."

All the tricks worked—and yet, although and because they had worked, he was driven from office, the economy was crippled, and the war continued to grow.

And there the story ends, at least so far as LBJ is concerned. He made his error and he paid his price. But the story does not really end there, because of the way these events have entered the conventional wisdom. Johnson was never able to explain himself to the nation; every time he tried, he took on the wheedling, pious tone which made him a TV personality almost as loathsome as Nixon. (Doris Kearns does not exactly explain this failure—perhaps no one can—but she gives a remarkable illustration of how it worked. While helping Johnson prepare *The Vantage Point*, she tried to bring some chapters to life by including Johnson's earthy stories about his colleagues—the stories which reveal his intelligence and skill. He would have none of it. " 'God damn it, I can't say this'—pointing to a barbed comment on Wilbur Mills—'get it out right now, why he may be Speaker of the House someday. And for Christ's sake, get that vulgar language of mine out of there. What do you think this is, the tale of an uneducated cowboy? It's a presidential memoir, damn it, and I've got to come out looking like a statesman, not some backwoods politician.' ")

So when the policies went down, everything that Johnson stood for went down with them. As Nixon and Agnew took his place, their very different shortcomings were lumped indiscriminately with his, and compromise politics began to seem odious at best, indictable at worst. Johnson's failure denied us the chance to understand the lesson of the lecture he gave Doris Kearns, a lecture that, to me, is worth the price of the book:

"A lot of people have written a lot of nonsense about my private meetings with senators. That is because most of the writing is done by intellectuals, who can never imagine me, a graduate from poor little San Marcos, engaged in actual debate with words and with arguments, yet debating is what those sessions were all about.

"But the Harvards, they picture it, instead, as a back-alley job with me holding the guy by the collar, twisting his arm behind his back, dangling a carrot in front of his nose, and holding a club over his head. It's a pretty amazing sight when you think about it. I'd have to be some sort of acrobatic genius to carry it off, and the senator in question, well, he'd have to be pretty weak and pretty meek to be simply standing there like a paralyzed idiot.

"But you see they never take the time to think about what really goes on in those one-on-one sessions because they have never been involved in persuading anyone to do anything. They're just like a pack of nuns who've convinced themselves that sex is dirty and ugly and low-down and forced because *they* can never have it. And because they can never have it, they see it all as rape instead of seduction and they miss the elaborate preparation that goes on before the act is finally done."

There is, of course, more than a little oversimplification in Johnson's view, but the basic point raises an important question: why is there so little honor for his profession these days, so little recognition that, if politics can be abused, it is the abuse we should change, and not the tool itself? I think there are two reasons, which— already powerful when Johnson was in office—have grown all the more important as the years have passed.

The first is the profound contempt for majority rule which runs through many recent political developments, and which, in its turn, offers nothing but contempt for those who compromise and negotiate to bring the majority around. Most of our grand democratic principles seem to have very few supporters when they actually go into effect. For quite a while it has been apparent that almost no one really believes in "free speech," not when the speech in question is insulting to your side. Most of the debates that take place about "free speech" are really about what kind of speech should be restricted.

"Democracy" is a similarly disturbing principle. Any sane man will have his doubts about the wisdom of majority opinion, but that skepticism is quite different from the contempt for the majority that crops up more and more these days.

Consider the records of two movements which, all things considered, I would classify as necessary and even healthy for the country—the campaign to save the environment and the movement to end the war. Despite their many logical appeals, both groups found themselves hopelessly outnumbered until very late in the game. Their answer was simply to tell the other side that it was wrong. Herbert Marcuse was rolled out to say that only the "false consciousness" of the poor duped majority kept it from seeing the truth. "Consumers" had been fooled by slick advertising into wanting bigger cars, more extravagant houses, and other products that Barry Commoner might have deemed excessive.

There was something to these points, but they led very

quickly to a breathtaking contempt for the complexities of human motivation. Why bother to reason with someone if you know his enlightenment can't compare to yours? No legislator could long survive with such a contemptuous attitude; you cannot persuade someone if your starting premise is that all his ideas are wrong. To persuade you must first *listen*, and you will never listen if you dismiss your opponent's objections out of hand. You also cannot preach a simple theory of false consciousness if you have spent much time talking to the people about whom you are pronouncing. In the untainted simplemindedness of its view, the "false consciousness" approach is like a view of the world in which one need look no further than the United States for the cause of any event, be it good or bad. People are starving in Africa? Well, says the left, it must be because of us. Western Europe has not yet succumbed to the commies? Well, says the right, that's because of us too.

Politicians, even the bad ones, indulge in such simplifications only at their peril. That is the redeeming side of Jimmy Carter's talk about "love." For all its power to nauseate, the phrase at least suggests some basic understanding for the range of human variety and the need to accommodate to it. Jerry Brown's divine-wind-of-enlightenment position, on the other hand, is the distillation of every brash reformer's arrogance.

The second reason for the low esteem in which politics is held is one of professional dividing lines, of the different sorts of institutionalized ambitions set loose in the world. Consider a scale of occupational motivations running across the white-collar professions. On one extreme we have the salesman and the politician, whose job is openly to ask other people for support. They can't be shy or coy or proud about it: they have to try to persuade, just as Lyndon Johnson did. You can't last long in such a calling if you close your ears to those who disagree; in order to persuade, you must first understand.

On the other extreme, we have those who (as LBJ put it) never have to persuade anyone of anything—or at least not very often. The exalted physician is the classic example. However kind he may be, people come to him only as supplicants, and he speaks to them with the voice of resonant authority. Professors, writers, and others of the ilk are in the same boat. They don't have to *listen* to the other side because they can pronounce rather than persuade. There are "politics" in these professions, no doubt—but the politics is usually such a seamy, backstairs business that no one can treat it respectably. In-house politics is a dirty little game in most professional worlds: consequently anyone who actually makes his living this way can hardly merit respect. If you are really good, the thinking goes, you won't have to scramble; people will come to you with offers. This is why the intellectual community was so delighted by Walter Mondale's withdrawal from the presidential race. By pulling out he said, in effect, that anyone who is willing to run for president doesn't deserve the job. Oh joyous confirmation of all existing prejudice! We happy, enlightened few deserve to run the country—but of course we won't demean ourselves to try. This may be why Garry Wills wrote a piece in *Harper's* several months ago called "In Praise of Compost Heaps." These creatures may be useful, the tone said, but they certainly are beneath respect.

This is not, of course, a sudden new development. When Teddy Roosevelt decided to enter politics nearly a century ago, his respectable relatives were aghast. A Roosevelt of New York rubbing shoulders with Boss Tweed? The thought was appalling. But by the time he had his own White House to run, politics had become "respectable" among the intellectual professions again—as it does, in the main, during Democratic administrations, and as it does, most of all, during those of aristocrat-celebrities like FDR and JFK. Lyndon Johnson, who knew better than anyone else that he was no aristocrat, drew many talented people to his administration, especially during the first few years, but too few were, like Kearns, willing to buck the tide of chic.

Lest a paean to politicians get out of hand, I will readily admit that politicians have made some terrible blunders in these last few years. So if "politics" is not to blame for the war, Nixon, Agnew, etcetera, what is?

Rather than a defect of politics, the trouble seems to me to lie with the presidency. A familiar—no, a boring—idea, you may say, but it is still an important one. Eugene McCarthy used to say that Lyndon Johnson would have made a great prime minister, though he made a disastrous president. The difference was the system. In a parliamentary body he could not, finally, cause a national disaster. The worst that could go wrong with one of his bills is that it would fail, and he would lose face. He could not cover up a war in the Congress—nor could he afford to let himself be cut off from dissent and bad news, the way he did as President. As soon as he stopped listening, he would lose his magic.

But when he was President, all the limits were off. He could cover up the war, for who would hold him back? Certainly he would not restrain himself; the Kearns book makes clear that Johnson believed with equal certainty in two things—the importance of "helping" people through the Great Society, and the need to stop communist aggression and thereby keep peace in the world. He was not duped into the latter by devious advisers (although he later let himself be sheltered from the truth, and although his insecurity about needing to appear "tough" also played its role). He believed the war was necessary, according to Kearns, to the very end of his days. The two causes, war and Great Society, seemed equally important and necessary, equally deserving of his most sophisticated guiles.

Nor could the Senate hold him back; there were none of the grappling hooks that might have been used against a prime minister. Nor could Johnson's own assistants in the White House. In the best of the Johnson-hands' reminiscences, *The Twilight of the Presidency*, George Reedy explained the theory of White House "courtiers." No one wants to bring the bad news to the President, so it never gets there. And even though those in the inner circle could see that things were going wrong, too few were willing to resign.

Saying this does not exactly solve our problems, because there is no simple answer to the abuses of presidential power. But it does suggest a different emphasis for this year's campaign. I cannot summon up much enthusiasm for a man who promises to be pure. I could for one who recognized the dangers of the job he hopes to fill.

*—July 1976*

The governor's office. *Photography by Andy Sieverman*

# WHY DOES DOLPH BRISCOE WANT TO BE GOVERNOR?

## by Griffin Smith, jr.

---

### *You remember Dolph Briscoe, don't you?*

---

It was a brisk cloudless Halloween afternoon; the kind of autumn day that redeems six months of unsparing Texas summer; football weather. Inside Austin's suburban Hilton Inn, Governor Dolph Briscoe had chosen the Tenth Annual Texas Conference on Tourist Development as the occasion for a rare public appearance. To a round of applause led by his wife Janey, he saluted the state's Coca-Cola bottlers, whom he awarded a Special Citation of Merit for their distinctive contribution to tourism: giving away a package of discount vacation coupons with every case of Cokes. There were other prizes, a speech, handshakes all around.

Outside, the Hilton's marquee announced in foot-high letters:

NOW APPEARING
THE TOTAL STRANGERS

Another Briscoe anecdote was born.

The sign was not a prank, the Hilton's management protested later with a hint of dudgeon: there really *is* a group called the Total Strangers, an easy-listening dance band performing nightly in the hotel's pub. Just a coincidence.

But a provocative coincidence, nevertheless. Somewhere, no doubt, there are other officeholders as reclusive, as secretive as Dolph Briscoe—a comatose ward-captain in the Bronx, perhaps, or a furtive county clerk in the wilds of Idaho. But are there any equal in stature to the chief executive of the third largest state?

It was not supposed to be that way. Briscoe, after all, once sought the governorship on a promise to throw open his doors to the public every two weeks, so that "anyone who wants to complain, make suggestions, or just talk to

*Griffin Smith, jr., is a former senior editor of* Texas Monthly *and an attorney. He is currently serving as a speechwriter to President Jimmy Carter.*

the governor will be welcome." Try that today. For all practical purposes the Invisible Man of South Texas is unique among the country's leading political figures. His low profile, and the lengths he has gone to protect it, have made him an enigma to many and a joke to others.

A joke. Aggie jokes; Briscoe jokes. Who could have foreseen it? There was a time when ridicule would have ranked near the bottom of any list of problems Dolph Briscoe might reasonably have expected to encounter. Five or ten years ago he was the First Citizen of Uvalde: a respected banker, a civic leader, the largest individual landholder in all Texas, one of its largest bank stockholders. He was a millionaire ten, twenty, some said even forty times over. He had pioneered chain-clearing techniques that helped turn the family's rough open brush country into extraordinary pasture-land; he traded in livestock and land across a half-dozen South Texas counties. He was a gentleman, soft-spoken but possessed of a razor-sharp business sense; the only son of a two-fisted rough-and-tumble rancher (also named Dolph Briscoe) who had settled in Uvalde, with less fortune and no fame, in 1914. He was president of the Texas and Southwestern Cattle Raisers Association, president of the Texas State Chamber of Commerce, a Boy Scout leader, chairman or trustee of half a dozen livestock groups, Laredo's Mr. South Texas, an Outstanding Young Texan, a Jaycee, a Lion. He was fondly remembered by his colleagues in the Legislature, where he had built a reputation during four terms in the 1950s as a leader—"a progressive, thoughtful, energetic man." He had everything; or almost everything. And on the January day in 1968 when he announced for governor from the steps of John Nance Garner's house, there were citywide celebrations: the stores closed and the schools let out. The *Houston Chronicle*'s senior political reporter observed that "many who follow politics closely praise him as the man"—in the crowded field of six major candidates—"who probably would make the best governor." Though he finished a poor fourth in 1968, he projected a convincing image of ability; four years later he won the nomination comfortably. Uvaldeans turned out to cheer as he rode through downtown in a "Dolph and Janey Day" parade.

If the governorship was intended to be the capstone of this glittering career, things took an unexpected turn. His reputation in 1976 bears scant resemblance to the one which carried him into office. His performance has been increasingly marred by doubts: doubts of those who must work with him, doubts of those who watch his behavior month-to-month. Concludes one prominent West Texas conservative: "Briscoe had every opportunity to be a *great* governor. He blew it."

How? And why?

The picture of Briscoe that emerges after three years in office is of an inaccessible, ill-informed, and largely inactive man, guided by the strong hand of his wife and sheltered from all but ceremonial contact with the outside world by an apprehensive, amateurish palace guard. It is a peculiar, and disturbing, portrait.

"He really is something of a ghost," says an aide to Lieutenant Governor Bill Hobby. No one outside Briscoe's innermost circle of advisers is kept regularly informed of his whereabouts; his predecessors' custom of issuing a travel itinerary has been discontinued, apparently because curious reporters might use it to intercept him for a few moments of impromptu questioning. Routine signings that other governors traditionally held in their formal public office adjacent to the Capitol newsroom are now held, unannounced and usually unreported, in his more secluded private chambers.

Most politicians *want* to be in the public eye as much as possible; Briscoe's extreme inaccessibility is one of the most striking facts about him. He has gone as long as eight weeks without a speech or formal public appearance of any sort. When he does appear in public it is usually a hermetic affair in which he is ushered to the head table, waits his turn to speak, and then either engages in a few moments of perfunctory handshakes or is whisked away before the program is finished. There is rarely any serious human contact.

The amount of time he spends in Austin, and what he does while he is there, are subjects he seems determined to shroud in obscurity. His aides have dismissed questions about his customary office hours as "insulting" and have declined to answer them. He himself has admitted he keeps no list of appointments, saying that he learns of his daily business agenda from "informal notes" passed to him by his secretary and "usually discarded at the end of the day." If a corporation ran its headquarters with the same haphazard unaccountability, it would be out of business in six months.

Lee Jones, a Capitol correspondent for the Associated Press, recently tried to tally Briscoe's absences from Austin by checking the flight logs of the airplane which the state makes available to its governors. The first obstacle was Briscoe himself, who tried to stymie Jones' inquiry by contending that the logs of his state-owned aircraft were secret and confidential information the public had no right to see. An opinion by Attorney General John Hill, based on the state's Open Records Law, made short shrift of that peculiar

claim, leaving Capitol observers to wonder how anyone could have been so politically and legally naive as to suggest it in the first place.

The answer is that Briscoe may have been acting out of desperation: the logs were as damaging as everyone expected. They showed the governor had gone to Uvalde for at least a portion of 135 days during the first ten months of 1975, including 64 non-holiday weekdays and at least one eight-day period during the last legislative session. That was a minimum: any additional trips he might have made in his own personal Lockheed could not be verified from the state plane logs.

In addition, when long-time Capitol newsman Stuart Long checked the state payroll records for "acting governors" who serve when a governor is out of the state, he found that Briscoe had been absent, not just from Austin but from Texas, on an average of one day every two weeks during Fiscal 1975.

Despite the evidence, Briscoe's executive assistant Ken Clapp continues to insist with a straight face that the governor usually leaves Austin "after work on Friday evenings" and returns "early on Monday mornings." In truth, not only does Briscoe seldom keep such hours, for him to spend as many as five consecutive days in Austin is the exception, not the rule. Last December, for example, he spent a total of seven days in the capital city.

Briscoe's friends uniformly report that he seems happier, "more himself," when he is away from Austin at the ranch. Lyndon Johnson did much of the work of his presidency at home in the Hill Country, so the real question is not whether Briscoe spends an inordinate amount of time in and around Uvalde, but whether he is attending to state business while he is there. The evidence is that he is not. Only three airplane logs showed members of the governor's staff joining him for the flights, reinforcing speculation that his attention to official duties in Uvalde might be minimal. A caretaker at one of Briscoe's Uvalde-area ranches told the *Dallas Times Herald* that the governor sometimes disconnects the telephones when he is there. The governor himself is evasive about his work habits away from Austin. When the Associated Press submitted a written question asking "what sort of communications and other facilities are available at Uvalde to enable [you] to keep in touch and do [your] job as governor," Briscoe curtly returned their inquiry unanswered.

A public official should be judged in more important ways than the number of press conferences he holds. But Briscoe's relations with the press have promoted his reputation as a phantom more by his own choice than by theirs. He has gone out of his way to promise regular news conferences and then repeatedly broken his own pledge. On November 10, 1972, shortly after his election, Briscoe promised reporters he would meet with them regularly before the inauguration to discuss his legislative plans; he then virtually disappeared until January. By May 1973, four months into his first term and deep in the midst of the legislative session, he had not called a single conference strictly devoted to answering newsmen's questions. At the beginning of the 1975 legislative session, he volunteered the promise to meet with reporters once a week; by April, he had gone five consecutive weeks without doing so. When he called in reporters to announce his opposition to the proposed constitution in October, 61 days had passed since his last "weekly" press conference. Challenged by reporters, the governor responded that, well, he might just have press conferences every 61 days instead.

Politicians commonly have friction with the press, but not in the way Briscoe does. The point is not so much that he tries so hard to avoid reporters, as that he makes gratuitous promises of cooperation which he then does not keep.

Most of the encounters which the governor's aides describe as "press conferences" are actually situations in which a few stray reporters have caught him in a hallway. As the governor wound up his speech to the Texas Research League last November, reporters for major Texas dailies whispered a request to this writer to join them at a door which seemed to be his most likely exit. "You don't even need to have any questions," one of them said. "We just need some more linebackers. If we can block the door he'll stop and talk to us for a minute, but if there are just a few of us he slips right on by."

Some of the governor's absences have been downright baffling. In the weeks after his election, he remained in seclusion in Uvalde, not merely avoiding the press but also denying audiences to senators who tried to visit him. The first week of 1973 came; the Legislature came; but still, no Briscoe. He had scarcely begun to assemble a staff. House members joked openly about the "mystery man," going so far as to ask whether the Speaker had formed a committee to "go find Briscoe and let him know we're down here." Two years later his behavior was even odder. A long-standing Capitol tradition calls for both houses of the Legislature to send a ceremonial delegation to the governor on the opening day of the session. The governor is expected to greet them politely, and they are expected to return and inform their colleagues that the governor has, indeed, greeted them politely. It is one of those ritual civilities of politics, symbolic of the separate but shared exercise of power: a gentlemen's courtesy that politicians ordinarily enjoy. In 1975 Briscoe was inexplicably missing. Recalls a high-ranking Senate employee: "We sent five dignitaries, headed by [elderly East Texas Senator A. M.] Aikin. A few minutes later Aikin came back, and the Senate asked for his report. He said, 'We went to the governor's office and it was locked. We found an aide who let us in the back door. He wasn't there.' "

There are those who believe the governor is simply following in the footsteps of his distant relative Andrew Briscoe, who, having been elected to the 1836 Convention that produced the Texas Declaration of Independence, arrived nine days late for the signing. But for most people in the Capitol, the jokes have begun to wear thin. If the governor of Texas were nothing more than a figurehead, an American counterpart of the British monarch, Briscoe's absenteeism could be dismissed as a harmless eccentricity. Instead he is an essential cog in the governmental machinery whether he wants to be or not. Regardless of whether a governor is liberal or conservative, public business cannot satisfactorily go on without him; the chief executive's attitude affects state government in hundreds of ways, shaping decisions others must make even in areas over which he holds no direct administrative responsibility. His appointees to boards and commissions often want to know if he supports or opposes controversial policies before they make an ir-

revocable decision; legislators want to know if he plans to veto a bill before they expend their political capital trying to pass it. Because the governor does so much to set the tone of public affairs, even other statewide-elected officials need to know what he thinks.

Briscoe's odd behavior has consequently impeded the conduct of state business in ways far more significant than his failure to greet A. M. Aikin's entourage. One example is the experience of Forrest Smith, a tax attorney for Mobil Oil who served as Chairman of the Texas Youth Council (the state agency that oversees correctional facilities for delinquent children). He wrote the governor in January 1975 requesting an "urgent meeting" to discuss legislative matters affecting the Council. Not only did he never get the meeting, his letter was never acknowledged. Three or four follow-up calls to Briscoe's office were never returned. Smith—a Dallas conservative leader of some renown and a devoted Briscoe supporter who once personally introduced the governor as "a born-again Christian" at the First Baptist Church—is plainly puzzled by the experience. "I have no knowledge that he ever saw my letter or knew I called," he says, "although I assume the messages did get through." When Smith's term expired in October 1975 the governor appointed someone else to fill the vacancy without any comment or explanation to him. Smith, who says he feels no rancor about the experience but seems to be a glutton for punishment, then wrote Briscoe a letter pledging support in the future. That was never acknowledged either.

Legislators have been particularly critical of Briscoe's unwillingness to make his wishes known in time to affect the legislative process. In an example that could be multiplied many times over, one Houston representative wrote Briscoe a note two months before the 1975 session began, describing a pair of simple housekeeping bills and asking whether "you have objection to either bill, if they pass together." He never heard another word. Under John Connally, Preston Smith, or any other Texas governor in memory, that sort of thing simply would not have happened.

An elected state official who was considering what he regarded as an "extremely significant" change in policy affecting the state's revenues repeatedly sought Briscoe's opinion on the controversial step. "For ninety days I left messages asking him to call me, but he never did," the official says. "So finally I just went ahead on my own. If he were a *governor* he'd not only *want* to be consulted, he'd *expect* to be. I don't think he even cared." Legislative leaders including former Speaker of the House Price Daniel, Jr., and current Speaker Bill Clayton freely acknowledge that Briscoe has ignored important calls or letters; they are at a loss to explain why. One former state official, a friend of many governors, says, "I could pick up the phone and call Connally and get him—or he'd call me back. I could call Preston Smith and get him. But Briscoe? Impossible. It's disturbing."*

Joe Allbritton of Houston, one of the nation's most influential businessmen, was exasperated by his chronic difficulties in reaching the governor while serving as chairman of the Offshore Terminal Commission. General James Cross, who as the Commission's Executive Director noti-

---

*This man, like so many others, was willing to speak frankly on the condition that his name not be used. Few people in politics can risk having adverse judgments of the governor quoted. Some are personally dependent on his presence in office; others, on his good will. Any governor holds a great deal of power over things other people need or want. Consequently much of what you will read in this story is from knowledgeable people whose names have been withheld. It has to be that way.

fied Briscoe's office "numerous" times that Allbritton needed to see him or consult with him over the phone, says that during a period of two and a half years "I was unable ever to get in touch with the governor himself" on Allbritton's behalf. While this was happening, the Commission was engaged in ticklish discussions about whether to recommend public or private ownership of the offshore superport.

Briscoe's own department heads sometimes have difficulty seeing him. According to one, requests for interviews on "matters of paramount importance ordinarily take five or six days to arrange (although there are rare instances where Briscoe has granted an interview almost immediately). Decisions on other matters requiring the governor's answer or approval may take up to three months. He adds: "We [Briscoe's department heads] have urged more 'cabinet meetings' because we *need* to know what direction he wants us to move in."

Virtually every politician has an innermost group of trusted political advisers through whom outsiders develop a path of circuitous access. Roosevelt had his "kitchen cabinet," Wilson had Colonel Edward House, LBJ had the informal "Texas Mafia." By contrast Briscoe is a remarkable—one is even tempted to say unique—loner. Two months of interviews among politically attuned Texans, including statewide officeholders, could not produce a single person who felt he could say with any assurance who Briscoe listens to. The politicians are as mystified as everyone else.

On frequent occasions in Austin, Washington, and elsewhere, Briscoe's personal demeanor has conveyed the impression that he is curiously detached from his work. "He seemed unfamiliar with the issue" is a recurring phrase time after time in news reports of his press encounters. At one point last session, when he was asked about the school finance plan he had earlier labeled his "first priority," it became painfully obvious that the governor was unaware a House committee had rejected most of his proposal two days before. A state legislator standing near Briscoe at a reception in May 1973 realized with mounting horror that the governor had failed even to recognize Education Commissioner J. W. Edgar. "How," he shook his head sadly later, "can he solve school finance if he doesn't even know the Commissioner of Education?" Another oversight had occurred earlier that year: several weeks into the 1973 session that saw a major fight over Briscoe's marijuana and drug legislation, officials of the State Program on Drug Abuse, a division of the governor's own office, were shocked to discover that he was ignorant of their existence.

While Briscoe stays deep in the background of his own administration, matters which need attention languish. By mid-January, the governor's Energy Advisory Council (directed by law to formulate a state energy policy) had still not been called together for the regular meeting that was due in November 1975. Having pronounced himself an implacable foe of special sessions, Briscoe dithered for weeks in 1973 trying to avoid calling one that was plainly inevitable: the reduction of the speed limit to 55 mph in order for Texas to continue receiving federal highway funds. He finally called it for December 18, disrupting Christmas holiday plans for legislators and staff alike. He is notoriously slow in making appointments to state boards and commissions—one of the most significant powers a Texas governor has. A search of the Secretary of State's register of appoint-

ments on December 1 showed dozens of vacancies, including some boards on which *all* the members' terms had expired. One advisory council had 29 vacancies. Some divisions of the governor's own office, like the Texas Film Commission, are under "acting" leadership more than twenty months after the previous director left.

Capitol observers are still incredulous about some of Briscoe's protracted delays, like the nomination of Jim Wallace to a new district judgeship in Harris County. Wallace, a highly popular state senator who had sponsored Briscoe's drug bill, had been checked out with everyone who mattered—including the local bar association, the Trial Lawyers Association, the defense attorneys, his Senate colleagues, and Briscoe's own informal committee of Houston lawyers—and had received top marks from everyone. Even before the 1973 Legislature departed, it was widely understood around the Capitol that Wallace was in line for the job. "Well," recalls a lobbyist from Houston, "Briscoe fiddled around with that appointment, and he *fiddled* around, and folks started going to see him. Finally Bill Hobby went to see him. He said, 'Governor, you remember back when we were setting up this seat, everybody agreed that Jim Wallace ought to have it? Well, you know, Jim's term is coming to an end, and I think you ought to go ahead and appoint him and get the uncertainty out of the way, because otherwise he's going to have to run for the Legislature again.' "

Months later, in 1975, Briscoe did appoint Wallace; but not until the uncertain senator had been forced to seek, and win, the Senate seat again. A special election costing $37,000 had to be called to replace him.

The situation prevailing on the State Banking Board is perhaps the most scandalous example of all. Charged with the responsibility of awarding new state bank charters—which are much-sought-after and potentially lucrative pieces of paper—the three-man board consists of two state officials and one layman who is appointed by the governor. Lay member James L. Lindsey's term expired in January 1973, and Briscoe still has not named a successor. Under the law he continues to serve until the governor does so. Lindsey, who could win Senate confirmation without much trouble, says he "indicated to Briscoe soon after he took the governorship that I would like to be reappointed," but he has heard nothing from the governor one way or another since that time. Because the other two members have a tendency to disagree about whether to grant new charters (Banking Commissioner Robert Stewart being more likely to frown on them than State Treasurer Jesse James), Lindsey has occupied the awkward position of a "holdover" swing vote for three years.

The failure of a banker-governor to act on such a crucial nomination to the Banking Board has caused extensive concern in financial circles. After Briscoe told newsmen at his last press conference in December that he had not given any consideration to the matter "lately," *Dallas Morning News* reporter Sam Kinch, Jr., suggested that the prolonged delay might be "about to set a record for a holdover appointment." Briscoe's response, in its entirety, was: "What is the record?"

The results of Briscoe's procrastination usually make no political sense. A case in point is the Joint Interim Surface Mining Operations Study Committee, created by the 1973 Legislature to investigate strip mining and present a report to the 1975 Legislature which would, thus informed, enact appropriate laws on the subject. The committee was to consist of three senators, three House members, and five "lay citizens" appointed by the governor. The legislators were ready to begin work when the session ended in mid-1973, and there was no real controversy about who the other members were supposed to be. Recalls a lawyer who followed the committee's work: "It was one of those situations where the two protagonists—industry and the ecologists—agreed the study needed to be done, and had pretty much agreed beforehand on who ought to be appointed. Well, Briscoe just sat on his appointments—which were necessary before the committee could meet. Everybody was telling him about once a week, 'Now goddamit Dolph, we don't really so much care *who*, just appoint *somebody* and let us get started.' " Why the delay? Senator Max Sherman of Amarillo, the committee's chairman, says, "A lot of people tried to get him [Briscoe] to move, and he didn't. That's about all anybody knows." Briscoe finally made his appointments on May 31, 1974, and by the time the legislators were finished with the Constitutional Convention in late July, only five months remained for them to complete the eighteen-month project.

With a sigh, the lawyer adds, "That's what he does with everything. He sits on it *forever*, until you absolutely despair that anything is ever gonna happen, and then he finally does it."

Visitors who manage to gain an audience with Briscoe often find the experience strangely unproductive. Several leading advocates of the proposed new constitution, who had been trying for weeks to win his support for the document, were finally allowed to meet with him on the day before he announced his opposition. Among those present were Attorney General Hill, Speaker Clayton, retired Supreme Court Chief Justice Robert Calvert, and state Representative Ronald Earle. "He greeted us all warmly," one participant remembers. "He said, 'I wanted you gentlemen to have the chance to discuss the constitution with me before I make my decision *public*,' or words to that effect. We discussed one aspect that we thought he might disagree with, and then someone said, 'Could you tell us any other concerns you might have?' Well, he just smiled and said, 'Oh, no. I couldn't do *that*.' So we had a little guessing game, talking about various articles. He just sat there, not saying anything, never asking any questions at all. The conversation kept lapsing. Finally we thanked him and left."

Advisory groups that have worked on a nonpartisan basis with Texas governors for decades complain that he, unlike his predecessors, does not follow up on his agreements. "After we talked to Briscoe," said an officer of one, "it was just like we'd never been there. It all disappeared."

"Nothing happened"; that is the recurring complaint of those who deal with Briscoe personally. What frustrates them is not his reluctance to give commitments—that is a common ploy among politicians—but his lack of interest in discussing issues and his unreliability about following through on whatever commitments he does make. It is rare to find anyone who claims to have had a penetrating discussion with him about anything, including (especially) matters about which he has been outspoken, like school finance and constitutional revision. What is he doing? His behavior is not devious, not the fancy skating of a skilled political operator. It is the indifferent behavior of someone who seems to care about next-to-nothing.

Among those whose work brings them into regular contact with the governor's office, there is virtually unanimous agreement that many of Briscoe's worst problems can be traced to his selection of staff.

From the beginning, Briscoe chose amateurs to run his administration. The Sharpstown Scandal did more than help elect him in 1972: it reinforced his own instinctive, homespun mistrust of political "types," while at the same time making that mistrust seem entirely appropriate in the eyes of the public. Briscoe, who saw himself as a non-politician, came to power at precisely the time when non-politicians were becoming fashionable; and far from perceiving that there might be hidden risks in carrying that approach too far, he gloried in it. "Politics," he told the bemused Legislature in his first address, "is not a game, and I will not play it."

In the interval between his election and his inauguration he made only half-hearted efforts to persuade experienced state capitol hands like Jim Oliver to stay on; he shut himself off completely from old acquaintances like Walter Richter, a former state senator who headed the State Program on Drug Abuse, leaving them utterly uncertain whether they were supposed to remain or not. Eventually he surrounded himself with innocents: two lawyers with no substantial political experience, a school administrator, the pampered son of a small-town mayor. Only his press secretary, former LBJ man Bob Hardesty, knew any political ropes. The result was chaos: for while there may be something to be said for talented amateurs, there is nothing to be said for untalented ones.

"His organization," says former Speaker Price Daniel, Jr., "is as poor as any I've ever seen. It borders on incompetence." That is an attitude which, quite honestly, few knowledgeable people seem willing to dispute.

"Not only does he [Briscoe] not deal with people directly," says a nonpartisan observer who has been in active contact with state government for years, "he doesn't have a *staff* capable of dealing directly. Preston Smith picked good people and gave them some leeway. Briscoe's staff doesn't get anything done." Says another: "The thing about Preston Smith was, at least he knew a lot about state government. Briscoe doesn't. And Smith at least surrounded himself with some people who were pretty good; Briscoe has surrounded himself with idiots. They may be real bright in whatever it is they did before they came to the Capitol, but they don't know a thing about state government. It's frightening how stupid those people are."

Both of these men had voted for Briscoe in 1972.

Shortly before Briscoe came out against the proposed new constitution last October, one of his top assistants called to discuss the document with a high-ranking aide to Lieutenant Governor Hobby. "We really like the Executive Article," he confided, "and we're gonna support that. But we just can't go along with that Legislative Article at all." Came the astonished reply: "But they're the same thing! You know, 'Proposition One: Executive and Legislative.' " "You're kidding," said the governor's man.

Briscoe's eventual opposition was based, he said, on a lengthy legal memorandum prepared by his aides. Over the

163

course of two legislative sessions, Briscoe's legal advisers have acquired a widespread reputation for strange, off-the-wall, alarmist interpretations of things that come their way —the mark, legislators believe, of the amateur who is unsure of himself. The reasons Briscoe eventually gave for his opposition to the constitution did nothing to dispel that view. One provision would have increased from one to 14 the number of courts available to hear appeals in criminal cases, and the number of criminal appellate judges from five to 42; Briscoe, amazingly, said he could not see how the criminal court reforms "could do anything but slow the process of justice." He castigated another key provision allowing for annual legislative sessions, although the previous year he had endorsed a constitutional amendment which would have created them. He denounced as inadequate a provision enabling governors to have budget execution authority, although he himself had asked for precisely that power, in precisely those terms, the year before. (The popular liberal notion that the governor was acting as a cat's paw for Houston industrialist George Brown and other conservative business critics of constitutional reform is emphatically disputed by the document's leading supporters, who are convinced the decision was home-grown. "There is no evidence," says Price Daniel, Jr., "that he was influenced by anyone outside his staff.")

Acting on staff advice, Briscoe vetoed a rider to the 1975 appropriations bill which gave University of Texas regents the power to authorize construction projects without Coordinating Board approval. His action took a favorite toy (and a powerful political weapon) away from influential representatives of the political establishment among the UT regents and gave it to Briscoe's friends on the Coordinating Board. "Those riders have been in the bills for sixteen years," says former regent Frank Erwin. "He doesn't have any power to 'veto' them; there's a line of cases going back to 1911 that establishes that. Everybody knew it but his people. They don't know the first thing about the legislative process." In mid-December, the state Supreme Court unanimously found Briscoe's attempted veto unconstitutional.

There is a distinct Keystone Kops ambience to the governor's office. When Briscoe vetoed one House member's bill, he gave reasons which applied to a *different* bill. Roy Coffee, Jr., Briscoe's legislative liaison man in 1973, so infuriated legislators with his flagrant lobbying that he was ejected from the floors of both Houses, an unprecedented action in modern Texas politics. The legislative sponsor of a bill that Briscoe had expressly endorsed in his 1975 "State of the State" speech was thunderstruck to discover that members of the governor's staff were going around bad-mouthing it to other legislators. On one memorable occasion, the governor called a press conference to sign a bill he did not have. Remembers a Senate employee mirthfully: "Everybody arrived in the governor's office—reporters, cameras, dignitaries, the whole bit—and Briscoe said to an aide, 'Where's the bill?' 'I dunno; I thought *you* had it.' And so on, all the way around his staff." A belated search uncovered the fact that it was still in the possession of legislative clerical personnel who were preparing it for signature. Such a staff goof would have been inconceivable with Briscoe's predecessors.

The examples, large and small, can be multiplied. The small ones are the most inexplicable. When a group of

school children raised the money to build a greenhouse stocked with state flowers, they wrote each state's governor asking for seeds. A Briscoe aide wrote back, "Governor Briscoe regrets that we are not properly staffed to gather bluebonnet plants for distribution"—despite the fact that the Texas Highway Department has plenty of bluebonnet seeds which it scatters along the medians.

Middle-level employees who brought some Capitol experience to the Briscoe administration have left, frustrated by the unprofessional atmosphere. Says one, a veteran of three decades of staff work for politicians ranging from conservative to semi-liberal: "All new governors have problems; that's not unusual. But they [Briscoe's people] didn't seem to want to learn, or take advice. They seemed to be afraid and suspicious of the press and anyone who had been around the Capitol before. It's not my job to set policy; I'm just a professional, and I want to do a good job carrying it out once somebody sets it. It wasn't that I disagreed with the policy at all; it's that there *wasn't* any policy."

Politicians deal with each other's staffs all the time, and the experience does not ordinarily produce ill feelings; that is what makes Briscoe's staff operation unusual. Politicians who want to work with the governor's office go away shaking their heads. "Briscoe's people are bothered by the vicissitudes of their responsibilities; it *upsets* them to have to *do* things. I nearly had fistfights with those sons-of-bitches when I went to talk to them," grouses one state representative who doesn't lose his temper easily.

The frustration is not confined to legislators. Heavyweight conservative lobbyists, including Searcy Bracewell of Houston, have had persistent difficulty with the governor's organization. Says a fellow lawyer who has watched Bracewell's efforts: "He can't get Briscoe on the phone, he can't get him to *move*, and so he does what everybody does—he calls Bob Hardesty or [Secretary of State] Mark White, the two people up there who know what they're doing. It's now gotten to the point, however, that you can't get Hardesty or White. The line's too *long*. Because nobody talks to The Man, and the guy has surrounded himself with clonkheads."

Without exception, the most hair-curling criticisms are reserved for George Lowrance, a young San Antonio attorney who is in the key position of handling the governor's appointments to state boards and commissions. Everything is fine as soon as we clear it with your senator, Lowrance tells prospective nominees, who know as well as he does that the custom of senatorial courtesy allows a senator to block confirmation of any objectionable gubernatorial appointee living in his district. Lowrance then calls the senator and says something on the order of: We've *talked* to Mr. Soand-so, and we're ready to appoint him to such and such. Do you have any objection? If the nomination then falls through, the disappointed nominee knows good and well why, and the senator catches hell. This technique deprives the senator of any graceful way to forestall a nomination. It is another illustration of the way Briscoe's operation flouts the usual civilities of politics. Says one veteran senator: "Preston [Smith] used to do this kind of thing every now and then; it was his way of punishing a senator for something. Briscoe's people do it as a matter of course."

The obvious question is, Why does Briscoe tolerate this kind of staff? The answer is, Because the only thing he really wants them to do, they do well. They protect his image.

Not only do they shield him from the politicians, the press, and an inquiring public, they also produce a blizzard of paper designed to give the appearance of activity where there is none. For all their lack of political skill, they know exactly how to flimflam the press. Announcements of Briscoe's official nominations and other ceremonial doings are issued periodically, complete with quotes he never said; these find their way in due course to the state's daily and weekly newspapers, where, presto! he appears as *busy*. The system has been perfected to the point where he could be dead, and no one might know for weeks.

One key image is always put forth in Briscoe's speeches: that he is a decisive, firm, and forthright man. It is a rare address that does not contain at least one "*I firmly believe*," and the incidence of phrases like "I strongly believe" and "I feel very strongly" is usually high enough to take on the aura of cliche. His listeners are reminded of the "tasks" and "decisions that must be made," requiring "all my energies" for such "pressing duties." Like the Dr Pepper crate that John Tower's aides conceal behind a podium so that he can stand on it and look taller, Briscoe's speeches represent a well-devised effort to obscure the impolitic truth about him. Firmness: it says so right here. The average voter who knows almost nothing about state government except what he reads in the papers or sees in a ten-second TV clip can be satisfactorily hoodwinked by that kind of talk, in precisely the same way he fails to pick up the fact that John Tower is five feet six inches tall.

Briscoe's staff members have successfully promoted this flattering image of their man, but otherwise the governor's effort to turn his office over to political amateurs has been a failure of awesome proportions. What began back in 1972 as a voguish attempt to portray himself as a leader who was independent of all those . . . well . . . *nasty* political forces that had disgraced Texas soon went awry; you cannot conduct an essentially political job by relying on people who are aggressively proud of their ignorance about things political. Beginning early in 1973, the accumulating avalanche of failures—staff failures—produced in the members of the Briscoe administration not a recognition that something might be wrong with *them*, but rather the firm belief that something was wrong with everybody else—all those tricky politicians out there who were laying traps, the political system itself. Says one state representative: "They react like you're trying to put something over on them any time you want to discuss anything. You have to strain to convince them you're being honest. They act like some country bumpkins who've come to town and think everybody they meet is trying to sell them the Congress Avenue Bridge; they've got that 'ain't no flies on me' attitude." Every failure reinforced the garrison syndrome that now dominates the Briscoe inner circle.

The conventional wisdom in state government today is to yearn for the return of "real politicians" to the governor's office. Memories are short; the answer is not so simple. It is easy, today, to forget the sinister mood that hung over the Capitol during the time when Briscoe's most expertly "political" rival, Ben Barnes, was Lieutenant Governor: a mood (as those who knew it will remember) of deception and intrigue and spyings and knifings and things-are-not-what-they-seem which emanated not from Barnes personally but from the clique that surrounded him. When the *Texas*

*Observer* headlined Barnes' fall with DING-DONG THE WITCH IS DEAD, Capitol employees shared a sense of relief that was more than ideological. Briscoe's staff is incompetent, but they do not deliberately generate an atmosphere of intimidation and fear. They are just part of the joke.

Briscoe's foremost amateur—the person who, all things considered, is perhaps the ablest and certainly the most influential figure in his administration—is his wife, Janey. A bright woman who holds a masters' degree in education, she enjoys being First Lady visibly more than her husband enjoys being governor. As a beauty queen at the University of Texas in the Forties, the daughter of an Austin grocer, she found and married the soft-spoken rancher's son from Uvalde. Her relationship to him soon transcended the usual devotions of a political spouse. When he became a state representative in the 1950s, she often sat beside him on the floor of the House. More recently, former members of the governor's staff tell of seeing her sitting cross-legged on the floor of his office, opening his mail; it is widely believed that she answers much of it. She has her own department in the governor's office called the First Lady's Volunteer Program, complete with its own letterhead and five employees. The extent to which she hovers over him at public gatherings has become a familiar anecdote around the Capitol; "she protects him," says an old-line lobbyist, "like she's afraid he's going to explode." They are so inseparable that on one rare occasion when she was forced to leave his side for a few minutes—when he was ushered into the Oval Office to discuss energy policy with Richard Nixon while she waited outside—the *Houston Chronicle* considered the fact newsworthy enough to warrant a separate article headlined WHITE HOUSE SPLITS UP THE BRISCOES.

Her obvious devotion to her husband is never more evident than during his speeches. She will sit on the dais, turned at whatever angle is required to let her face him directly, and watch transfixed. Connoisseurs of this phenomenon say that on occasion as long as eleven minutes have gone by without her looking away. She nods gently when he is about to make a good point. Often she leads the applause; during his addresses to the Legislature, she has repeatedly interrupted him with clapping that gradually spread to the rest of the audience.

A Republican official who came down from Washington to attend Nelson Rockefeller's White House Conference on Domestic Policy Issues in Austin last November found Janey's performance during her husband's address hard to take. "It was sort of creepy, really. It looked more like a mother watching her child get an award at a high school assembly than any sort of husband-wife relationship I've ever seen." As a matter of fact, she has sometimes startled men in the macho world of Texas politics by referring to Dolph as "our boy."

Her conduct has given rise to the pervasive rumor that Janey wears the pants around the governor's office. That point of view got its quintessential nationwide airing in a 1975 *Newsweek* article captioned "Boss Lady"; it suggested that Janey "is really the governor of Texas—her husband, Dolph, just happens to have his name on the door." It made Dolph furious. Bristling, but all the while keeping a fixed smile on his face, he told reporters that most Texans, including himself, don't read *Newsweek*, "and those that do probably don't pay any attention to it, like I don't. I have no further comment.'' Reporters have never seen him as upset about anything else.

Nevertheless, the popular idea that Janey controls Dolph like a puppet is false. While she obviously guides his behavior in public, and while she does audit his conferences, and while she helps him make up his mind on many things, she does not take command of his official meetings nearly as much as Capitol legend has it. There is no incontrovertible evidence that she actually runs the show. What she *does* do is make him nervous: a domineering woman with strong opinions about state government, she conveys the appearance of sitting in judgment on his performance. "When you catch him without her, he's relaxed,'' says an Austin political consultant. "When he's *with* her, it's like he's watching his step so she won't jump on him later.'' To the extent that Briscoe is insecure with his responsibilities, his wife's constant presence is at best a mixed blessing.

The news media, in their fascination with the Janey phenomenon, have looked through the wrong end of the telescope. She is exactly what he has insisted she is: his "partner.'' And the most significant thing about their partnership is not that Janey wields so much influence, but that Dolph wields so little. How can a man seek a position of power, achieve it, and then ignore it? Or if Dolph is not doing that, what is he doing? The question is far more intriguing than Janey's role, which after all has been quite perceptively explored by Shakespeare in *Macbeth*.

If the strange crew that occupy Briscoe's office were in fact carrying out some sort of conscious program, no matter how ill-conducted, one could at least feel there was some useful purpose to what is going on. But they aren't; and there isn't.

The Briscoe administration's program—or what would be the administration's program if it had one—can best be viewed as a pyramid. At the broad base are his ghostwritten speeches, which recite problems, priorities, and things that need to be done, all carefully spelled out to buttress the necessary appearance of activity. The best of them are excellent. His two "State of the State'' addresses in 1973 and 1975 were cogent, occasionally eloquent, explorations of Texas' condition. During the ensuing legislative sessions, however, his administration ignored or mishandled most of what he had said and backtracked on much of the rest. That, then, is the middle of the pyramid: what his staff actually does.

After Briscoe called for action to import water to the High Plains, including passage of water development bonds, his staff was so unconcerned about the necessary legislation that they dumped the entire matter, including the selection of a sponsor, into the lap of Lieutenant Governor Hobby. A legislator carrying a bill to permit the admission of oral confessions into evidence (one of the key planks in the governor's anticrime package) asked Briscoe aides for help in passing it but could recall nothing to indicate they had actually done so. With great fanfare in his 1975 address, the governor announced the creation of a special toll-free long distance telephone assistance service called TEX-HELP, the aim of which was "to make government more available and more open'' to anyone "who needs assistance or information involving state government.'' The toll-free

number is 800-292-9600 but unless you live in Austin you won't find it in your local telephone book.

Quite apart from the question of whether Briscoe's administration has selected the right goals is the question of whether they have pursued them in a way calculated to achieve results. Consider the 1975 session's dominant issue: school finance. At the end of the previous session, Briscoe hired respected educational consultant Richard Hooker, who worked for eighteen months and produced a school finance plan that was theoretically admirable but politically unrealistic. As submitted to the legislators, it entailed substantial tax increases at the local level and it was geared, in the words of one top education expert, "to walk all over the TSTA'' [the Texas State Teachers Association, whose political muscle is legendary]. Having thus misread the politics of the 1975 Legislature, the governor's people then proceeded to refuse any compromises—"which would have helped a lot at several points,'' says the expert. "It was obvious very early that the bill was going nowhere in the House, yet no effort was made to modify it to meet the objections and try to salvage something.'' The governor himself, who had been extremely supportive of school finance reform in his pre-session speeches, failed to assemble the legislative leadership for a personal selling-job that might have rescued his otherwise doomed bill. The version that finally passed was hastily put together in the Senate during the last two weeks of the session, and though the governor was by then willing to compromise, very little of his original proposal was left.

The real question is what Briscoe himself has wanted done. That, then, is the pyramid's tiny tip: the issues in which he as an individual, not as an "administration,'' has taken a direct, discernible personal interest. What does he himself really want to do?

The answer given by many who have observed and worked with him most closely is, virtually nothing. "I really don't know of a single piece of legislation he's taken a personal interest in,'' said former Speaker Daniel. "No new taxes,'' said current Speaker Clayton, "but that's all I can think of.'' Although Briscoe is popularly regarded as a conservative, his personal political "program'' is not so much conservative as it is *reactive*.

What does he react *to*? Politicians who have dealt with him agree on two things:

• He resists anything that he interprets as diminishing the power of the governor's office, regardless of how trivial it may be; and

• If he is ever directly confronted over something, even by accident, he fights hard to avoid losing.

The result has been that a high proportion of the issues in which he has involved himself personally have not been ones that he chose, but rather ones that were thrust upon him by others. Trying to discern a program in all this is impossible; there is none.

The three major displays of gubernatorial arm-twisting in the last session came on the Coordinating Board bill and the confirmation of his appointees Walter Sterling and Hilmar Moore. In the confirmation cases, two of his long-time personal friends were opposed by Senate liberals; he generated a ferocious counterattack to put the liberals down. In the other case, he expanded the power of the Coordinating Board (dominated by his own appointees and chaired by his close friend Harry Provence) against the indignant opposition of the University of Texas regents.

Anything that erodes executive power is likely to meet his personal opposition; he is more interested in *keeping* power than in *using* it. A provision in the new constitution that would have made gubernatorial appointments expire after February 1 of odd-numbered years, thereby eliminating "midnight" appointments by an outgoing governor, was regarded as a plot hatched in Bill Hobby's office to snatch away Dolph's rightful future powers. An uncontroversial bill revising the rules governing emergency medical leaves for penitentiary inmates—which had the support of prison officials and the Board of Pardons and Paroles—was vetoed; it had taken away the governor's existing (but practically never used) authority to countermand those leaves.

If there is anything that characterizes Briscoe's relations with the rest of state government, it is this petty insistence on preserving abstract power. At times it seems that not only does he not want to do anything himself, he does not want anyone *else* to do anything. There are those who see the hand of Janey in all this, protecting her husband from imagined threats to his authority; others see the hand of his staff, unable to distinguish between power that matters and power that doesn't. But the truth may be that Dolph himself, the soft-spoken son of that two-fisted rancher, is behind it: proving to any doubters that he is not some weak-kneed Milquetoast who lets others get the best of him. Remember those speeches: he is a man of firmness.

Insofar as Briscoe has a personal program, this idea of *forbidding* things is its dominant motif. Forbidding people to take away his power, forbidding them to get the best of him; and above all . . . forbidding any new taxes. That is the one continuing policy year-in-year-out which elicits his whole-hearted enthusiasm. It is the sole irrefutable accomplishment of his three years of office. One illustration will suffice to show the depth of Briscoe's attachment to this, his single monument:

Texas has never imposed a tax on refineries; legal authorities agree this could be done, and one state (New Hampshire) has already done so. The tax would get passed along to the customers who buy the refineries' products, of course, but because so much of the nation's petroleum is refined in Texas, a majority of those customers are out-of-state; thus, whatever share of the tax *they* pay, Texas gets to keep, free and clear. It is, all things considered, a nifty way to skim off for the benefit of home folks some revenue from the petroleum that passes through or from our state. A refinery tax is potentially a huge moneymaker: the Legislative Budget Board has estimated that a rate of a penny a gallon would yield a billion dollars per biennium—about the same as a state income tax. During the 1975 session, Speaker Clayton, Lieutenant Governor Hobby, and House Ways & Means Chairman Joe Wyatt brought up the idea of a refinery tax with Briscoe. Clayton inquired whether the governor would consider signing one if another existing source of revenue, like the sales tax, were reduced by an equivalent sum—an exchange that would actually *lighten* the tax burden Texans must carry. Briscoe said no because it would be—that's right—a "new" tax.

The shibboleth, No New Taxes, and its corollary, Cut Back Government, call to mind California Governor Jerry Brown. The controversy between traditional liberals and traditional conservatives today has essentially degenerated into little more than a dispute over who should get the government's money. Though Briscoe's more sophisticated Austin critics may not want to believe it, both he and Brown are in touch with a genuine, and rising, public desire to restrain government's apparently limitless growth, a desire that may be the coming thing in contemporary politics. The difference is that Briscoe's understanding stops with the crabbed assumption that the best government governs least, while Brown perceives that even the best government has limits to what it can accomplish. Briscoe concludes "it is not the duty or function of government to solve all the problems that exist in today's society"; Brown concludes "there are problems that *cannot* be solved. . . . There may be no solution other than acceptance." One philosophy reflects unconsidered dogma; the other, the experience of the past 40 years of American life. Briscoe is satisfied to cut back the number of problems that government should feel a responsibility to help solve; Brown is sobered by the realization that when government tries to solve problems it may be powerless to succeed. Given the complexity of the times, Brown's view has the ring of truth and Briscoe's, though superficially similar, is merely an archaism.

Another difference, of course, is that Brown is trying to act on his discovery, while Briscoe is largely just talking about it. Neither on taxes nor on controlling governmental growth has Briscoe faced the issues directly. He has not been tested on his tax pledge because the state's anticipated deficits in 1973 and 1975 were unexpectedly cancelled by a windfall of extra oil and gas tax dollars produced by the higher petroleum prices, by federal revenue sharing and social services reimbursement, and by inflationary increases in sales tax revenue: none of which he had anything to do with. His idea of forestalling a future tax increase by squirreling away part of the plump 1975 surplus into a working capital reserve account came to naught because legislators instinctively hate to leave money lying around on the table unless they are absolutely forced to, and Briscoe, true to form, failed to roll up his sleeves and play the tough politics required to force them. As a result, state fiscal experts anticipate "a tax bill of unprecedented size"—that means, around a billion dollars—in 1977.

Briscoe's attempts to control governmental growth have largely consisted of cutting back the number of employees in the various branches of the governor's office from 510 to 336, a plan that sounds like a good start until one notices that many of them have simply been shifted to other slots in state government. The Comprehensive Health Planning Unit, for example, was moved from the governor's office to the Department of Health last year. Many former employees of the governor's defunct Office of Information Services, a computer-coordinating bureau, now work for Comptroller Bob Bullock, who estimates that 95 per cent of the original group are still on the state payroll somewhere. Bullock says he has even received letters from the governor's top aides asking him to hire people they are trying to unload.

Briscoe's hiring freeze has produced some queer results. For example, it has prevented the replacement of many departing employees whose salaries are paid by federal grants instead of state taxes (some sections of the governor's office are more than 90 per cent supported by federal money). While this technique is at least saving *some* tax money, even if it isn't *state* tax money, its usefulness as a means of reducing the federal budget is akin to Lyndon Johnson's thrifty penchant for turning off the White House lights. And because federally salaried positions carry a 15 to 20 per cent bonus payment directly to the state for overhead expenses, each new vacancy takes more money away from the people who remain to carry on the operation. The *reductio ad absurdum* of all this was reached when the growing shortage of full-time secretarial and clerical personnel forced some departments to hire part-time "Kelly-Girl"-type assistants, who hour-for-hour are more expensive than the employees they have been brought in to replace. The upshot, admits Briscoe's budget director Dicky Travis, is that the actual cost of running the governor's office has gone up, not down.

No wonder, then, that morale among the surviving employees has been plummeting for months. By January, surreptitious job-hunting was widespread.

Briscoe's meat-cleaver attack on governmental growth shows how simplistic his understanding of the state's entrenched bureaucracy really is. Whatever governor eventually does prune down its size will succeed only by first using his personal leadership to win broad public support for the inevitably bitter and protracted fight. Though the Texas electorate may soon be skeptical enough of big government to grant that support, Briscoe has shown no inclination to invoke the governor's personal leadership for that battle or for anything else.

It should go without saying that Briscoe should be judged on the (basically conservative) things he *wants* to do, rather than on the (basically liberal) things his most vocal critics would *prefer* him to do. But you do not secure a niche in the pantheon of conservatism by botching conservative goals.

To stand back and contemplate the ongoing fiasco that is the Briscoe administration is to find oneself asking how such a remarkable political phenomenon could occur. 1972 is easy to explain: Sharpstown: a broke, liberal woman for a runoff opponent; a fluke. But what about 1974? Not why did Briscoe defeat Farenthold; that is easy. But why did he have no other opponent? Not Hobby, not Hill, not Armstrong, no one. If Briscoe and his people were so hopelessly overwhelmed by their job that the office was in a permanent condition of collapse, why did the conservative business interests—whose political clout is great and who after all can no longer enjoy the luxury of a government that does nothing—not find someone to take Briscoe's place?

The answer is that although the discontent with Briscoe runs wide among conservatives, it does not run deep: he *was* safe on taxes, and he *was* safely in office keeping out some liberal who, in the business community's eyes, would have been worse. Since a second term has traditionally been automatic for Texas governors, the effort to unseat him would have been prodigious, and it might have failed. Why bother? They could live with him; and at least he was, in his idiosyncratic way, predictable. "Predictability is very important for business," says one lobbyist. "Briscoe is a no-motion guy, which is an indentifiable result, and you can predict and go forward based on that result. That far outweighs the down side of no access when you need him."

So they kept him; they kept the man who wasn't theirs, who was a front man for nobody; the man who drove them up the wall, predictably. He was a fluke, but he was a *useful* fluke. And when he gave his fund-raising dinners they

turned out by the hundreds, more than had ever turned out for anyone in Texas before; and they told him *Dolph, you're great.*

But as soon as he was gone they laughed at him; laughed at their accidental good luck to have someone like that around: not just what we'd have wanted, you know; pretty weird in fact; but safe, that's the main thing, safe. Tell him he's great; he'll never catch on.

Whatever Dolph Briscoe's muse may be, the cumulative effect of his behavior has been to deny him, as governor, the unequivocal respect that had come his way spontaneously in private life. Can he not know that? A poignant reminder of the change was the celebrated "Orville Drall" caper last legislative session, in which a simulated press release from a fictitious state representative of that name announced the introduction of a resolution declaring Dolph Briscoe legally dead. Yes indeed: everyone got a good laugh over *that* one, including (they say) the governor himself; but when he was alone with his thoughts that night, what then? Did his memory roam back to Uvalde; and those first parades; and what it had all meant then, so long ago?

Why does Dolph Briscoe want to be governor? Years ago, he himself gave this answer: "You just go through life one time. I think you should try to do everything you can, serve wherever you can." A man does not, however, pursue something as hard-to-get as the governorship merely to fulfill Duty's abstract call; he seeks it for some reason. And the unavoidable fact about Briscoe is that none of the traditional reasons men go into politics seem to apply to him.

Executive command? He does not relish it in the manner of a Roosevelt, a Kennedy, a Johnson; his lackadaisical attitude toward his own appointments suggests he does not relish it at all.

A program? He has none, save for a small handful of taboos, of *don'ts*, of forbidden things like No New Taxes; after three years he has yet to develop and work for a coherent set of legislative enactments.

The pomp and ceremony of the office? He seems indifferent to it. He is feted at his speeches, to be sure, but he often drives away in a red Ford, not the official Lincoln Continental limousine. He seldom socializes at the mansion, rarely has parties at which he, the governor, could bask in adulation. When critics call him another Preston Smith, they could not be further from the truth. The two men are profoundly unlike: Preston loved the usufructs and fanfare of the governorship, reveled in them as much as Dolph ignores them. Briscoe is, in the currently fashionable language of the political science fraternity, a classic "passive-negative" executive. Not only does he not *do* anything, he seems to have no fun not doing it.

Money? Not a chance. A $65,000 salary is not exactly opulence for a multimillionaire, and if there is anything the Briscoes didn't need, it was another house. Besides, as their old friend Zeke Zbranek opined, "Ol' Dolph had a pretty good car when he came." And the idea of pilfering from the public purse is abhorrent to what everyone agrees is Briscoe's scrupulous personal honesty. Whatever else Dolph Briscoe may be, he is not a crook.

Political kingfishery? He has shown no interest in securing a place as a party boss, as, say, Shivers did; the State Democratic Executive Committee, which he controls, is down to one secretary and is deep in debt.

Cronyism? Analysts of the Texas governorship have remarked that the most noticeable characteristic of the state's chief executives since Reconstruction is that they have been front men for other interests. (As someone once remarked of Ben Barnes, the young state representative from De Leon whom the Connally-Johnson Democratic establishment groomed to preserve their control of the Capitol until Sharpstown and Briscoe upset their plans: "They interviewed a lot of people for the job, and Ben Barnes got it.") Briscoe, by contrast, is not just another front man for corporate business interests; they are frustrated by him personally, even though they are not especially unhappy at what he does. He is a fascinating anomaly in modern Texas politics.

It is not hard to discern definite personal reasons, however, that induced him to put a gubernatorial construction on Duty's call. His father's deathbed wish was for young Dolph to become governor. Friends remember the older man as a "backwoods Joe Kennedy" who bred his son from childhood for that office, and the father's influence is so strong today, 22 years after his death, that Dolph still puts Jr. after his own name. Beyond that, of course, there was the prestige of the office itself. The Texas governorship has been the terminal political achievement of those who hold it, a kind of pinnacle in itself; to Price Daniel in 1958, it was worth leaving the U.S. Senate for. In Texas the governorship is *something*.

It has prestige, and Briscoe has always gone after the prestige spot—an objective that has less to do with any specific set of goals than with the luster of the position attained, rather like being the titular chairman of a charity fund drive. Precisely: First of the Bankers, First of the Ranchers, and finally First of All the Texans. The crown of a career.

Then too, there is Janey. Not only does she have an abiding interest in things political, she also has plainly drawn vicarious pleasure from her husband's lifelong ascent in status and esteem—which (alas) was taking place in the relative obscurity of a small South Texas town. For Janey, who grew up a salt-of-the-earth social-climbing family surrounded by, but not part of, Austin's tantalizing political and social whirl, marrying Dolph was marrying up. And getting Dolph elected governor was the great escape: a ticket out of Uvalde and back to her hometown in triumph —not merely a ticket of admission to that world she had seen as a child, but admission at the very top of it, able to ordain what that world would be.

All of these things doubtless motivated Dolph to run for governor; but are they enough? Does a shy, aloof rancher really leave the wild solitude of the place he loves and endure two statewide political campaigns and the vexations of Austin in order to please his wife, add another feather to his cap, and lay to rest the ghost of his father? There must be more. What is it? "The reason," said a former state official as he turned in his swivel chair and gazed for a long time outside his window, "is that he enjoys the power."

The *power*?

The power. "He enjoys the power that sets him apart. The lofty pedestal. Being above the crowd, able to deal with people as you please with no accountability. That kind of power. Not the other kind."

He saw my puzzlement. "Let me tell you a story," he said. "Dolph and I were friends back in the Fifties. I admired him, and when he retired from the Legislature because his father had died, I wrote him a letter regretting it, telling him how sorry I was to see him leaving public life and how I hoped he'd be able to come back some day. We kept up a good personal relationship for years after that; I used to go down to Catarina [Briscoe's ranch headquarters] and fish with him. Naturally, when he became governor we didn't see as much of each other. But one day I was cleaning out some papers in my office and I ran across a copy of that old letter. I decided to send it to him, along with a little note about the old days and how he *had* come back after all—not just come back, but come back as governor. Dolph never acknowledged it at all."

He was not angry. He was hurt; you could tell the difference easily in his eyes. You understood he knew the note was unimportant by itself; you understood without his saying so that it had been meant to say, *Dolph, we were together long enough ago for these pages to turn yellow, and I am still your friend*. There are tokens that pass between men as affirmations of friendship. This was one.

There is nothing unique about this type of story. Kind personal notes from men as prominent as two former governors have gone unanswered. The more one looks, the more one finds that the distinguishing mark of his relations with the political and social world of Texas has been to emphasize that he is set apart—to do things that remind others he is dealing with them as he pleases. Many of his most inscrutable actions can be explained, at least in part, as a way of saying two things to other people: "I Don't Need You," and "Whether You Like It or Not, *You* Have to Wait on *Me* Now." That represents the exercise of power in a very special sense.

It helps explain his failure to greet the legislative delegations on the first day of each session; politics, for all its infighting, is soothed by a network of ritual courtesies among politicians, which are precisely the things Briscoe spurns. It helps explain the unanswered inquiries from legislators asking if he has any objection to their bills. It helps explain the appointments that go unfilled while impatient committees and agencies cool their heels. It helps explain his chilliness toward people who offer him advice, especially old friends; and the phenomenon, often noted, that he subsequently goes out of his way to show he is ignoring it. It helps explain his indifference to almost everything the Legislature does except those that challenge his supremacy or dilute the power of his office.

It helps explain, too, why he would assemble the Capitol press corps for an announcement of his intention to have weekly press conferences and then let 61 days elapse without one. He knows they will arrive incensed, knows someone will stand up and ask, fuming, "Governor, since you said you'd see us every week, why . . . "—but you can finish the question yourself, as he could. Ah, the press; they are all so *predictable*; they perform on cue, his cue, turn on the lights and watch them go nuts. It's been eight weeks or so, shall we invite them back for another show? Let's do. Meanwhile they never catch on; they just chase him around to Rocksprings and line up their friends to block the doors, where he can smile politely as though nothing is wrong and give a few nonresponsive answers. There's nothing they can do about it, and it's fun to watch.

The contrast between Briscoe's unvarying politeness in

**169**

person and his passive rudeness when he is safely cloistered away from human contact has left many of those who deal with him confused. They begin by telling you what a ''nice man'' the governor is, but if you visit long enough they finally confide some chilling personal story which contradicts that—some strange sad puzzling recollection over which their memory eventually trips, which they offer to you uncomfortably, tentatively, apologetically, in the form of a confession. ''Although he didn't acknowledge my letter pledging my future cooperation,'' said a bewildered Forrest Smith months after Briscoe had deposed him from the Texas Youth Council, ''I assume he did get it and appreciates it.'' ''I don't know what the situation is,'' said a former governor who had written two personal notes. ''I never heard anything again, but everything is friendly whenever I see him.'' Did you ask him about the letters in person? ''Yes. . . . He was friendly, but unresponsive.''

Unanswered letters from ordinary citizens could be passed off as bad staff work; letters from prominent people, old friends, former governors, no. Forrest Smith's story of letters ignored and phone calls unanswered was in the newspapers; a staff that could shield a governor from knowledge of *that* would have to be dealing with a man who could not read. No, he knew; and he made his choices.

*He enjoys the power*. Yes: the power to make people worry about him, to *need* to know what he thinks, to beseech him a bit; the power to ignore those who think they know the answers; the power to ignore his friends. For all these reasons, his behavior on the proposed new constitution was utterly predictable. Not merely that he opposed it, but that he waited so long to say so. In the same way that he had dozed through the Constitutional Convention of 1974—resisting every invitation to participate until, on third reading of the Legislative Article he abruptly produced a list of surprise objections that forced everyone to stop and change things according to his demands—Briscoe concealed his opposition to the constitution until the last possible moment. He had a right to take whatever position he chose, and there were adequate reasons for him to oppose it; but no one can read his statement without realizing that he did not give those good reasons, nor even particularly care what they were. He was against it regardless of the reasons—partly, at least, because Hobby, Hill, Armstrong, Daniel, Calvert, Hutchison, and all the rest had banded together for it. He set them up for the fall; for two years he said things that sounded like endorsements of constitutional revision, set up applause lines for it in his speeches, sounded like he was for it but never quite said so. He let them all climb out on a limb, from which precarious perch they regularly reminded him that new state constitutions do not pass these days, anywhere, unless the governor puts his full weight behind them. They climbed without him, and three weeks before election day he sawed the limb off. Immediately, just like those press conferences, the howl went up. One legislator fired off a three-page letter, dismantling the governor's arguments as though he were picking wings off flies, and drawing himself up to full height to huff: ''Your statement is . . . a personal affront to the Legislature and every member elected to serve in the House and Senate.''

Exactly so, just what it was intended to be. The constitution failed, you see; without *his* support, it failed. They thought they knew so much: but in the end, *they* needed *him*.

**B**riscoe's behavior ultimately reveals why he wanted to be governor. It is the behavior of a man who had everything which should have conferred the undisputed highest status—vast wealth, award after award, more land than perhaps any other Texan—but who still was not quite part of the inner circle of the Texas political and social establishment. He was everything in Uvalde, but in a sense that just made things worse: knowing that your position has begun to lose its luster when you get past San Antonio, and that by the time you get to Houston and Dallas, where the movers and shakers are, you are just a very rich, very nice South Texas rancher. The contrast was inescapable. Status, after all, is not a matter of hobnobbing with the rich and powerful, which Briscoe could do any time he chose, but rather of the subtle way the rich and powerful hobnob with *you*: whether they regard you as one of them. As much as Briscoe was admired by those people, it never quite occurred to them that he *was* one of them. And he knew it.

Worse still, he knew he was *real* landed gentry, someone who came by his land rightly, who had it *before* he entered politics: not like the Connallys and the Johnsons and the rest who got theirs afterwards. As landholders they were the imitators; he was authentic. They were parvenus, but they captured the status that eluded him.

For him, the governorship was a way to clinch that last full measure of respect. It is the one position that is by definition, unambiguously, the First Citizen of Texas; and whoever occupies it has pre-eminence. Briscoe's lingering hope that establishment circles would somehow recognize his achievements and anoint him voluntarily had begun to fade in 1962, when Connally received the nod, and was dashed for good in 1968, when he felt his turn had come and they followed Locke and Carr and Hill and Smith instead. That was the moment of truth, the end of his most fundamental illusion, and it came as a terrible shock. From then on he knew he could count on no one but himself, that he would have to get the governorship and that last full measure of respect entirely on his own. He is a different man now than he was in 1968; more than any other reason, that is why. ''They may not think I belong at the top,'' his attitude became, ''but if I ever get there they are going to have to come to me.'' People who think like that usually do not get to be governor; but 1972, as luck would have it, was an unusual year.

Briscoe ascended to the governorship with certain profoundly anti-establishment feelings: anti the politicians, anti the conservative business establishment's leaders (but not its goals), anti the people for whom the social whirl was everything. What part Janey may have had in shaping these feelings—who can say? The administration in which she plays such a leading role, however, manifests them pervasively, starting with the staff of amateurs that surround the governor. The choice of a complete unknown like Calvin Guest as chairman of the State Democratic Executive Committee has emphatically reminded the political establishment that they no longer control the game. Searcy Bracewell's calls go unreturned; political appointments go to Uvaldeans who pose no latent threat of put-down. If there is any social power in Austin greater than the power to decide who is invited to the governor's mansion, it is the power to decide who is *not* invited there. Under the Briscoes not only are the parties few and far between, but also old personal friends in Austin—friends close enough to have made regular annual visits to Catarina for years before Dolph and Janey moved to town—remain coldly and inexplicably uninvited inside the mansion's door. To invite the social establishment would be to risk the chance their acceptance might still be withheld, somehow, in spite of everything; to invite plain old friends would be an admission that you were still, somehow, no better than their equals. It is lonely at the top.

The Texas establishment had no icon more venerated than the late Miss Ima Hogg. She was especially fond of the state's fine governor's mansion, lavishing upon it many notable antique furnishings. Shortly after the Briscoes had won the Democratic nomination in 1972, she telephoned an offer to help with anything that needed to be done during their term in that stately antebellum building where she had lived as a child. Her offer was made "kindly, not being bossy at all," in the words of someone who knew her well. It was brusquely rejected by Janey, who afterwards remarked to another of Miss Ima's friends, "Someone had better tell that old woman she can't run this mansion forever." No small thing, when you think of it; no small thing for a grocer's daughter: the power to ignore Miss Ima.

The attitudes the Briscoes brought with them were amplified by the rapid deterioration of the first administration. As things began to go wrong—because they were amateurs, because they were in over their heads, because the *work* of the governorship had changed so drastically since Dolph last saw it in the Fifties—they responded by mistrusting the politicians with whom they had to deal, especially the ones who tried to tell them something was wrong: politics was not a game and he would not play it. Briscoe's steady shift in sympathy toward conservatives is partly due to the fact that after a while no one but conservatives tried to be nice to him; and even *they* did so, by and large, not because they liked him or thought he was a good governor, but because he was useful. His usefulness kept them from getting rid of him, but it could not keep them from laughing at him. The governorship, once the very thing that was supposed to secure the respect he craved, instead became a mechanism to destroy it.

In the end, Dolph and Janey used the governorship to prove they didn't need anyone else. We grow up thinking politics moves in that great purposeful sweep recorded in the civics texts, but politicians learn differently; they learn about the things that don't fit together, and the empty spaces. The governorship of Texas is, for a while, one of those empty spaces, a hollow place where two vulnerable human beings are doing an extraordinary dance to music that only they can hear. The rest of state government—the other state officials, the bureaucracy—for the most part restrain the impulse to be introspective about what they see; they regard the dancers as simply part of the setting, as

something to be tolerated or circumvented in the course of getting their own jobs done. The dance cannot go on forever, but while it lasts, it is Dolph and Janey against the world.

The irony is this: forty years ago, Dolph Briscoe could have had all the respect he wanted and, with a little luck, a successful governorship as well. There was a time when it would have worked; when he was a child, listening to his father, it would have worked. The myth that linked status to the ownership of land was secure. But Texas would not stand still. Dallas, Houston, aerospace, big oil, insurance, and all the rest elbowed their way into power and status until the myth gave way: there were people in Texas with power and status who did not care, really did not care, that they had no ranch. It came by degrees, but it came.

Lloyd Bentsen, another ambitious member of the South Texas landed gentry, figured all that out and moved to Houston; by contrast, when a friend of Briscoe's suggested that he might be smart to buy a home in River Oaks before the '68 campaign—not to pull up stakes from South Texas, but to bolster his contacts in that political and economic center—Briscoe was not interested. He stayed in Catarina, taking his measure of the state from those vast isolated brush country acres. The land: the myth: it was all supposed to work without anything else, the ultimate prestige was supposed to come without anything else; this was *Texas*. You can stand on the terrace of Houston's Alley Theater any evening, looking at the lights of the highrise buildings like Shell and Pennzoil and Tenneco and Bank of the Southwest and H L & P, buildings that crowd together until Louisiana Street and Milam Street look like Manhattan's corner of Wall and Nassau; and you can see why it didn't come. Forty years ago it could have, but not now.

What has moved Briscoe as governor is, in some atavistic sense rooted deep in two centuries of Texas soil, a rancher's rejection of this highrise aristocracy and all the other intruders on that cherished myth of the power of the land. By being governor he restores (as he sees it) the proper order to things, an order that without him is untuned; it is a holding action at best, but there is not much more that any governor *could* do to stop the changes remaking Texas.

There are echoes in all this of *Giant*, reminders of the gulf between what mattered in the old Texas and what matters in the new. Among Briscoe's potential successors not one truly belongs to that old Texas where the central myth was constructed from the land. Though several were born in small towns, they are all, in a real sense, urban, and they have all made their separate peace with what Texas has become. Dolph and Janey are quite likely the last of a kind; and their strange statehouse dance, whatever it may mean to them, is for the memory of that simpler Texas a kind of contorted requiem.

*—February 1976*

171

# So Close, So Far

## by Paul Burka

*A freshman congressman from New Braunfels almost convinced Congress to deregulate natural gas—but almost doesn't count.*

S am Rayburn couldn't do it, even though he was Speaker of the House for 17 years. Neither could Lyndon Johnson. Senators Russell Long and Bob Kerr, the two best friends the oil and gas industry ever had, failed too. And so, in the end, did Robert C. Krueger, although for a brief, tantalizing moment, victory was in his grasp.

For most of the Fifties and Sixties, Rayburn, Johnson, Long, and Kerr had tried to persuade Congress to deregulate the wellhead price of natural gas; and despite their accumulated years of experience and seniority, they had gotten absolutely nowhere. On a bitterly cold Washington morning this February, with the temperature languishing near fifteen degrees and an ill wind whipping off the Potomac, the latest leader of the deregulation forces brought his case before the House Democratic Caucus. Bob Krueger was as unlikely a successor to Rayburn and Johnson as could be imagined, except that he too is from Texas. Together Mister Sam and and LBJ amassed almost three-quarters of a century in Washington; Krueger is a freshman congressman with no political background. Rayburn and Johnson were hardscrabble; Krueger is a rich man's son. They were not exactly intellectuals; he is a former Shakespeare professor with a doctorate from Oxford. They knew the petroleum business backwards and forwards; a year ago all Krueger knew was that the stuff came out of the ground. Politically Rayburn and Johnson were masters at the art of compromise, at going along to get along; Krueger is something of a purist.

Yet Krueger came agonizingly close to succeeding where his legendary predecessors had failed. Narrowly defeated in committee, he took advantage of an obscure procedural rule to get his deregulation proposal to the floor. After several hours of intense and acrimonious debate, he won the first test vote by a comfortable 48-vote margin, and for the

*Paul Burka is a Rice University graduate, an attorney, and a senior editor of* Texas Monthly. *He won the National Bridge Open Pairs Championship in 1970.*

next two days he kept on winning, until, stunningly, his support evaporated at the crucial moment. The battle had all the elements of a classic political drama: desperately close votes, intense lobbying campaigns, endless behind-the-scenes intrigue, last-minute revelations by the press, and a Young Turk challenging the system. It is the stuff of which movies are made and novels written, and for a few minutes on the last afternoon, as the scoreboard clock on the wall of the House chamber blinked its way from 15:00 down toward zero and the vote stood tied at 196-all, the tension in the huge room was almost insupportable.

The fight over deregulation dates back to the late spring of 1954. Less than a month after the Supreme Court had ruled that separate but equal is "inherently unequal," the Court handed down an opinion in *Phillips v. Wisconsin* that would also influence the course of American history. Unlike the school desegregation case, however, the *Phillips* decision hardly created a stir outside the petroleum industry. So the Federal Power Commission would regulate the wellhead price of natural gas; so what? Wasn't the country swimming in natural gas? Didn't wildcatters curse their luck when they found gas instead of oil? Some oilmen even thought so little of natural gas that they contemptuously burned it on the spot rather than accept the meager prices offered by the giant pipeline companies—in some cases, no more than a penny or two per thousand cubic feet.

The immediate effect of FPC regulation was to change the structure of the natural gas industry. The commission controlled only the price of gas produced and sold to interstate pipelines; gas destined for intrastate consumption was unregulated. This two-tiered market, as it is known, didn't really make much difference as long as natural gas remained plentiful. Gas sold for about the same price in both the interstate and intrastate markets. But in the late Sixties, the supply situation changed dramatically. Demand kept going up, but production leveled off, then started to decline. The intrastate price began to rise, but the FPC kept the lid on interstate prices to protect customers at the other end of the pipeline.

It is customary in the gas industry for producers to sign long-term contracts with pipeline companies, usually for twenty years at fixed prices. The escalating price of natural gas reflects not the cost of *all* gas, but the cost of newly discovered gas, much of which is recovered by increasingly costly methods. New intrastate gas that had been selling at the wellhead for 12 to 16 cents per thousand cubic feet in the late Sixties climbed rapidly over 20 cents, 50 cents, a dollar, and, unbelievably, over two dollars, while the FPC grudgingly raised the interstate price to 52 cents. It was small wonder that producers didn't even bother to explore for gas unless they had an outlet to an intrastate pipeline. Those who did drill refused to sell new gas finds to interstate suppliers and dealt instead with intrastate companies. The intrastate market today is therefore glutted with gas, while the interstate pipelines must survive on production from old fields which are slowly playing out.

No one likes the two-tier market. Northerners have low prices which won't mean a thing when there's no gas to buy. Texans generally (customers of Coastal State's Lo-Vaca Gathering Company being the notable exception) have all the gas they want but have to pay four times as much as anyone else to get it. Even the FPC, in an uncharacteristic move for a regulatory body, asked Congress to revoke the agency's jurisdiction over natural gas prices. The problem is that no one can agree on how to get rid of the current system. The industry, rallying behind the banner of free enterprise, argues for deregulation; they claim higher prices will give producers more incentive to drill and will mean more gas for everyone. But northern liberals, who proliferated in Congress after the Watergate-influenced elections of 1974, view the industry with attitudes ranging from suspicion to outright hostility. Some believe that producers are deliberately holding back gas and are falsifying reserves in an effort to scare Congress into eliminating price controls. Others argue just the opposite: our gas reserves are so depleted, they say, the increased production is impossible, regardless of price—so the only effect of raising the price will be to line the industry's pockets for no purpose. One thing is certain. Neither group of liberals is about to loosen price controls and transfer billions of dollars from consumers to gas producers. Instead, they want the FPC to regulate *intrastate* gas as well as interstate, so that all the gas that's currently going to Texans can be redistributed across the country.

That is the rather complex background of the fight over deregulation which took shape in the House Commerce Committee last fall and culminated on the floor during the first week of February. At first it appeared that deregulation had no chance. It is virtually impossible for a bill to survive a hostile committee, and Commerce was hostile from top to bottom. Chairman Harley Staggers of West Virginia and powerful subcommittee chairmen John Dingell of Michigan and John Moss of California were sworn enemies of the oil and gas industry. In the unlikely event they wavered, some of the more strident freshman liberals, men like Toby Moffett of Connecticut and Andy Maguire of New Jersey, were around to shore up their determination. So was Houston Congressman Bob Eckhardt, and that spelled very bad news for supporters of deregulation. Eckhardt's casual air and slightly disheveled appearance belie a brilliant legislative mind; he is one of the few liberals in the House who understands how the petroleum industry works. He fought the industry in the Texas Legislature for years, without success of course, and finally managed to escape to Congress in 1967. "I was so happy to get away from Austin," he recalls, "because I wouldn't have to fight the oil and gas lobby any more. And then I got to Washington, and you know what? I found they'd gotten here first."

Deregulation had its supporters, of course, but there was no one to carry the ball. Outnumbered 29 to 14, Republicans could do little more than wring their hands and cast their votes. On the Democratic side, northern antigas industry liberals had a heavy majority. Except for Eckhardt, Krueger was the only Democrat on the committee from a major producing state—and he was just a freshman. True, he had made something of a name for himself in an earlier battle over decontrolling oil prices, but there he had had Dingell's help in subcommittee. This time the leadership was firmly aligned against him. Still, it had to be Krueger; there was no one else.

A few months earlier no one would have been more surprised that he would be leading the fight for deregulation than Krueger himself. When he arrived in Washington to represent the vast 21st Congressional district—it extends from New Braunfels on the east to the Big Bend on the west, and north almost to Abilene, an area larger than Pennsylvania—Krueger had his eye on the Agriculture Committee. But another Texas freshman wanted that seat, former State Senator Jack Hightower of Vernon. Seniority, of course, was equal, but ties are broken alphabetically. So Krueger had to look elsewhere. He decided that energy might be interesting and opted for Commerce.

With the help of Bill White, a twenty-year-old Harvard undergraduate from San Antonio whom Krueger hired as a $400-a-month intern, the new congressman didn't remain a neophyte for long. Like most Texas congressmen, he learned the gospel as preached by the oil and gas companies—except that Krueger managed to make it palatable by interjecting a quote or two from Shakespeare along the way. The Bard of Stratford has many remarkable accomplishments far too numerous to recount here, but not the least of these was lulling northern liberals into thinking that Bob Krueger represented not just the 21st District of Texas, but reasonable men everywhere. For the first time since the Arab embargo, debate over energy policy took place in a relatively calm and rational atmosphere, thanks in no small part to the polished style of the former university professor. An Oxford man a tool of the oil companies? Impossible. (Well, not so impossible, it turned out later. But that's getting ahead of our story.)

By the time the Commerce Committee was ready to take up natural gas legislation, Krueger had already proved himself a force to be reckoned with. His proposal for decontrolling oil prices had lost by only one vote (22-21) in the full committee and had come within eleven votes of adoption on the floor. Staggers and Dingell weren't about to risk a repeat performance on natural gas, so they carefully prepared a narrow bill with only one purpose: to let interstate pipelines buy intrastate gas in emergencies for up to eighteen months. (Current law limits these "spot" purchases to 60 days.)

The Dingell bill was a clever maneuver. It gave congressmen an easy chance to look as though they were doing something to increase gas supplies, when in fact they were only paving the way for interstate pipelines to raid the intrastate market. It was, as one oil and gas lobbyist lamented, "exactly the kind of bill the House loves," a simplistic short-term approach to a complex long-range problem. The bill was so narrowly drawn, in fact, that Krueger couldn't even use it as a vehicle for his long-range deregulation amendment—which is exactly what Dingell intended. ("We crafted that bill to keep you out," one of Dingell's allies warned Krueger.) Sure enough, when Krueger offered his amendment in subcommittee, Dingell—who as author of the bill and chairman of the hearing was both player and referee—ruled it out of order and nongermane. Krueger tried again in the full committee, but Staggers merely reiterated Dingell's previous ruling. Finally Krueger resorted to a short-term deregulation amendment, more as a test of strength than as a viable proposal; surprisingly, it came close but lost on a tie vote. With no other obstacles in the way, the committee sent the original bill on its way to the floor. The entire episode was an object lesson in the power of the committee system, and Dingell made certain that Krueger got the point. "Even if you'd won on the deregulation amendment," the twenty-year veteran told the freshman, "we'd never have let the bill out of committee." Round One to Dingell.

The most surprising thing about Round Two is that it happened at all. When Krueger lost in the Commerce Committee, natural gas deregulation was written off as dead. But it turned out that the fight was just beginning.

Krueger's new lease on life began, of all places, in the House Rules Committee, a much vilified body better known for performing last rites than resuscitation. The committee acts as a giant funnel—or bottleneck—through which all legislation must pass before it gets to the floor. Theoretically Rules only determines the sequence and procedure for debate, but as more than one frustrated congressman has learned, the power to schedule carries with it the power not to schedule. For years Southern Democrats used Rules as a last line of defense to kill liberal bills that somehow managed to escape one of the substantive committees. Finally President Kennedy and Sam Rayburn broke the committee's near-absolute power in 1961 by persuading the House to go along with their plan to pack the membership. Nevertheless, southerners clung tenaciously to the chairmanship and the disappearing remnants of the committee's power for eleven years. Then Mississippian William Colmer retired and Indiana's Ray Madden, now 84 and the oldest member of Congress, took over.

Under Madden the committee's reputation has deteriorated to the point where it is now regarded mainly as the closest thing Washington can offer to the circus. His colleagues openly joke that the chairman is actively senile. When not humming idly during committee meetings, he departs from the business at hand to ramble at length on subjects like the Bank Panic of 1907. Not surprisingly, committee sessions often degenerate into shouting matches.

But John Dingell hasn't spent twenty years in Congress for nothing. He knew that Rules still holds the power of life and death over legislation, even if the committee hasn't tried to exercise it lately. He also knew that Speaker of the House Carl Albert has tremendous influence with the committee, and that Albert is from Oklahoma, which just happens to be a major gas producing state. In order to nail the coffin shut on deregulation, Dingell and Staggers tried to get their bill designated as "emergency" legislation—which would mean *no* amendments could be offered on the floor. It didn't work. Instead, Corpus Christi Congressman John Young proposed a rule declaring Krueger's long-term deregulation amendment germane, and Albert interceded on Krueger's behalf. On December 12, the Rules Committee voted 12-4 with Young, and Krueger was suddenly very much alive. True, the rule would still have to be voted upon by the entire House, but any chance was better than none at all.

Now the maneuvering began in earnest. That was the perfect situation for the very special talents of Congressman Charles Wilson of Lufkin, one of the most baffling figures in Texas politics. Wilson, who has not undeservedly acquired a reputation as a good time Charlie in both Austin and Washington, has been an enigma almost from the day he arrived in the Texas Legislature as a 25-year-old state representative in 1961. He was reputed to be a moderate liberal but somehow wound up sponsoring the state's first sales tax for conservative Governor Price Daniel. It passed, and Wilson has defied classification ever since. No one has ever accused him of being a great legislative technician—obstreperous State Senator Bill Moore once groused that Wilson has never read a bill in his life; for his part Wilson says only that he's read as many as Moore has—but as a strategist and as a pure political animal Wilson has few equals. He has Lyndon Johnson's uncanny knack of knowing exactly the right way to approach other politicians—an instinct which came in very handy when the House was trying to repeal the oil depletion allowance in 1974. When the depletion debate started, Congress was awash with hatred for the entire oil industry; Wilson waded in and managed to persuade his colleagues that independent producers should be treated differently than the multinational energy corporations known as the majors. Today this proposition ranks alongside mom and apple pie in the congressional pantheon of American institutions, and it was Charlie Wilson who put it there. What makes this accomplishment so startling is that Wilson became accepted as an expert on oil and gas matters without being on a committee that deals with them. In Congress, such things just don't happen.

Together Wilson and Krueger made a formidable team: while Krueger patiently explained the details of his amendment to his colleagues one by one, Wilson mapped out the strategy. Krueger had already decided that deregulation should be sold not simply as a solution to the energy crisis, but also as a benefit to consumers, an approach Wilson endorsed with enthusiasm. He put together a coalition of gas users, groups like the National Cotton Council, the American Paper Institute, the Society of the Plastics Industry, the Aluminum Association, and, irresistibly, the International Association of Ice Cream Manufacturers. They were joined by every agricultural lobby known to man: the International Apple Institute, the milk producers, the corn growers, the National Broiler Council, the corn refiners, the wheat growers, and on and on. Any industry that depended upon natural gas was brought in to hear Wilson's basic theme: ultimately the supply of gas is more important than the price, and only deregulation could bring about increased supplies by restoring the incentive to drill. It is better, Wilson argued, to go to a job at a factory paying $1.70 for gas than to be unemployed and paying 52 cents for gas at home.

Wilson's office on the fifth floor of the Longworth Building became a command center. Krueger, very much an intellectual purist, was convinced he could win on the merits alone, but Wilson knew better. Staff aide Candy Shy maintained a thick file of tally sheets, rating members from 1 (certain FOR) to 5 (certain AGAINST), then, as the vote on the rule neared, from 1 to 7. The first head count showed 137 firm votes for deregulation, with another 149 of the 435 congressmen listed as possible. Eventually even seven categories weren't enough; the final list, marked in ten different colors, looked like a road map, with lines and circles everywhere.

Wilson kept a tight rein on the lobbying effort and orchestrated it brilliantly. He made it clear to the big oil companies that their help wasn't wanted and concentrated instead on selling the idea that deregulation would benefit independents, who drill most of the new wells. (What Wilson didn't say was that although independents drill 80 per cent of all new wells, they find only 50 per cent of the new gas.) He rounded up independents not just from Texas, but from California, Colorado, even New York, and matched them with potential votes. Anyone who showed up wearing cowboy boots and diamond rings was politely sent off to talk strictly to Texas congressmen and otherwise kept out of sight. Meanwhile farmer groups worked Midwest and border-state delegations, and industrial users called labor-oriented congressmen like Fred Rooney of Pennsylvania to warn that if deregulation failed, plants like Bethlehem Steel would have to lay off workers because of natural gas shortages.

Slowly, gradually, the balance began to tip in favor of deregulation. By this time Dingell and Staggers wished they had never produced a bill at all. The projected shortages of the winter had failed to materialize and there was no need for an emergency bill. First they made an abortive attempt to kill their own bill; then Dingell and all the other Commerce subcommittee chairmen met with Krueger in the Speaker's office one week before the House would vote on the deregulation rule. All pleaded with Krueger to pull his amendment down out of respect for the committee system. "You're going to be around for a long time," they told the freshman. "You've got to learn to have respect for House traditions." But Krueger stood firm: hadn't Dingell already warned him that Staggers would never let a deregulation bill out of committee? "I'm just following your political advice," Krueger told Dingell.

The vote on the Krueger rule was scheduled for the afternoon of February 3, a Tuesday. That morning House Democrats caucused in the chamber. Krueger's strategy was evident from his opening statement: "I have a simple story of one who wants his case heard." He was determined not to argue the merits prematurely, but to stick to procedure, and above all, to show the proper deference toward the seniority system; Bob Krueger wasn't about to get labeled an uppity freshman. He stressed over and over how he was blocked from presenting his amendment in committee, but always softened his narrative with phrases like, "I understand the Chairman's prerogatives and I understand that he acted correctly." It was an intelligent, well-thought-out

battle plan, for if Wilson's count was correct, Krueger's job was not to win votes but to avoid losing them.

Dingell counterattacked in a burst of outrage. He accused the Speaker and the Rules Committee of flouting the committee system and warned that the Krueger amendment had never undergone hearings or careful scrutiny. Staggers chimed in with a plea to "let it happen the orderly way." Krueger's side seemed to have the better of the argument, though, and most of the Democrats had tired of the debate and were chatting aimlessly when, at the very end, Eckhardt got up to speak against the rule.

"The trouble with this process," Eckhardt began in his soft drawl, "is that it's just like the Texas Legislature." The buzz of conversation stopped; comparisons with the Texas Legislature are not taken lightly. "There's virtually no committee action," he continued. "A bill springs full-blown from the lobby and makes it to the floor in the identical form. What's wrong with this is that it polarizes debate —you're either for the bill or against. There's no opportunity to compromise. Give us a chance to hammer out a solution between men of good faith. That's what the committee system is for." It was a compelling argument, but it fell on too many deaf ears. Dingell had erred badly by attacking the Speaker; he forced northern liberals (majority leader Tip O'Neill was one) who were against deregulation into voting for the rule to avoid embarrassing Carl Albert. Furthermore, Staggers was the wrong person to defend the integrity of the committee system; he is neither a powerful nor a popular chairman. When the vote on the rule was taken several hours later, it was surprisingly lopsided: 231 for, 183 against. Round Two to Krueger.

Facing a 48-vote deficit, opponents of deregulation could only play for time while friendly lobbyists mounted a counterattack. For the next three days Capitol Hill swarmed with representatives of consumer groups and the AFL-CIO, who were unmoved by Wilson's argument that less gas meant fewer jobs. Even actor Paul Newman showed up to announce his opposition to deregulation. (Unimpressed, Wilson noted that as a child he'd watched Gene Autry for 25 cents, but Butch Cassidy cost $3; maybe we ought to deregulate gas and regulate movie prices instead.)

Meanwhile, the Dingell forces adopted a three-pronged strategy in floor debate. The younger liberals protested that deregulation would cost consumers anywhere from $5 billion to $20 billion. "Regulation is the only thing which keeps this concentrated industry from dictating prices and decimating consumers," Andy Maguire warned. Richard Ottinger of New York called deregulation a "congressionally donated windfall." Their emotional arguments were balanced by the hard-nosed speeches of John Moss, who as chairman of Commerce's oversight subcommittee had discovered that some producers were holding back gas in hopes of profiting from deregulation.

Most of the burden of stopping Krueger, however, fell on Bob Eckhardt. For three days Eckhardt stood before the House, leading the direct assault on the bill, offering amendment after narrow amendment—all designed not to kill the bill, but to plant the suspicion that, in Dingell's words, "the Krueger amendment is an ambiguous piece of legislation with many internal defects." Most of Eckhardt's changes were minuscule—one merely changed the word "ceiling" to "ceilings"—but cumulatively they began to suggest that this proposal would benefit from a trip through the usual committee process. "I do think that if the Krueger bill should by some strange quirk of conscience on the part of the House become law, it should be written in a way that will work," the man who is reputed to be the best technical legislator in the entire Congress lectured his colleagues. By Wednesday afternoon, Eckhardt was clearly out-maneuvering his younger opponent. On one occasion Krueger was ready to accept a proposed Eckhardt amendment but wily Jake Pickle of Austin leaped up to continue the fight.

It was on Wednesday afternoon, too, that the fight turned deadly serious, with the mysterious appearance in the press gallery of an unsigned statement detailing Krueger's campaign contributions from the oil and gas industry. The next morning the *Washington Post* published a story headlined OIL INTERESTS AID KRUEGER'S DRIVE. The article pointed out that Krueger had run up a massive campaign debt by spending more money in his 1974 race than any other congressman; that he had to raise $200,000 in the last half of 1975 to balance the books by the December 31 deadline; and that he collected more than $50,000 from the petroleum industry. The paper was careful to point out that there was no evidence of any wrongdoing, but the story had made its point: Krueger's posture as a rational man, committed only to the more logical side, was irreparably damaged.

As Thursday morning turned into Thursday afternoon, the strategies of both sides remained unchanged. Opponents of deregulation continued their delaying tactics as labor lobbyists blanketed the Capitol. Krueger, still calm and deferential, continued to lace his arguments with factual evidence while Wilson ceaselessly navigated the floor, working to hold the coalition together. It was widely assumed by both sides that the outcome would be determined after the weekend, that no final vote would come until Monday. The House would debate an amendment by Neal Smith of Iowa for a few more hours but would recess for the weekend before taking a vote.

Everyone knew the Smith amendment would be the crucial test. It was really Dingell's proposal, but he had fallen into disfavor by attacking the Speaker during the caucus, so Smith—a moderate Democrat with no particular expertise in energy—was chosen as the front man. The amendment was a last-gasp attempt to stop Krueger by offering something to everyone: it deregulated independent producers, but put all majors, including those in the intrastate market, under regulation.

Suddenly, at 3:27 p.m., Dingell rose and called for an end to debate and an immediate vote on the Smith amendment. The move caught Krueger and Wilson by surprise. They didn't know—perhaps they should have guessed—that Dingell thought *he* now had the upper hand. They agreed to the motion, and immediately the bells announcing a record vote began to sound throughout the Capitol and the three House office buildings across Independence Avenue. Once more the concealed electronic scoreboard flashed into view above the gallery facing the House, and the twin clocks on the side walls began their countdown from 15:00. Members jockeyed for positions around the five doors to the chamber, ready to buttonhole any arriving member whose vote might be in doubt. Slowly the giant room filled with congressmen, and the running tally on the scoreboard began to mount. With four minutes to go barely half the

members had voted, and Krueger led 116–112. As the clocks blinked into the final minute, Krueger led by eight votes, then seven, then five, then, at 0:00, none. It was a tie, 196–196. Theoretically Smith had lost—but this scoreboard was operated not by the National Football League or some other literal-minded organization, but by the House of Representatives. One or two congressmen wandered in late and voted after the deadline. Several announced their votes from the floor and were not recorded electronically. A growing clump—a hundred, a hundred and twenty—huddled around the Speaker's desk: what was going on? Finally the end of voting was announced—and the score stood at 204 for Smith, 202 against, 26 absent—most of them committed to Krueger. Liberal Democrats erupted into cheers, answered by victorious shouts from union and consumer lobbyists in the hallways outside the chamber. One vote, one person switching, was all Krueger had missed by. And one person did switch. Republican Millicent Fenwick of New Jersey . . . but she switched the wrong way, from nay to yea, making the official tally 205–201. Round Three to Dingell.

No one expects the Smith amendment to become law; it shows so little understanding of how the gas industry actually works that the Commerce Committee staff has called a leading oil and gas lobbyist for help in unsnarling its complications. Even if the bill somehow emerges from a conference committee (the Senate has already passed a deregulation bill) and goes to the White House, a presidential veto is certain. Krueger and Wilson hope that the Senate deregulation bill will be adopted by a conference committee, but that too is unlikely; Dingell will control the House conferees by at least a six to five margin. It looks as though deregulation is dead for the session, but then it looked that way once before.

Why did Krueger lose? One thing is certain: the bulk of the votes for the Smith amendment were against Krueger from the start. (Remember, Wilson's first head count showed 149 firmly opposed to deregulation.) These were congressmen who hated Big Oil, who refused to believe that gas couldn't be produced profitably at regulated prices, who would never consider total deregulation unless Congress first passed a windfall profits tax. They were congressmen who resented producing states like Texas that have been siphoning off industries and people and jobs from their section of the country, mainly thanks to cheap energy, and they didn't want to hear any Texas solutions to the energy crisis. Only six Democrats from states east of the Mississippi and north of the Mason-Dixon line voted with Krueger against Smith. (One of them was Charlie Wilson's target Fred Rooney.)

As for the others, many of them found the Smith amendment too attractive to resist. They didn't care about the mechanics—all they knew was that it let them vote for deregulation and against the majors, a combination too appealing to pass up.

These (plus a warm winter) were the substantive reasons for Krueger's defeat, but a far more interesting topic of discussion in Washington after the vote were the tactical issues: how crucial were the absent members, what difference did the *Washington Post* story make, and did Krueger blow it by getting outmaneuvered?

Most supporters of deregulation, including Krueger,

blame the loss on absenteeism—specifically, on Republicans whom the White House had guaranteed would be on hand to vote. The charge is indisputable, but it raises an even more interesting question: how did Dingell know the absentees were gone when Krueger and Wilson didn't?

As for the *Post* story, it is hard to believe the article was not decisive; after all, if it affected just two congressmen, it made the difference. Even Krueger admits that the story changed one vote (probably liberal Republican Margaret Heckler of Massachusetts). One former administrative assistant to a northern liberal Democrat guesses that the story may have changed as many as eighteen votes—an estimate Krueger and other members of the Texas delegation scoff at. Even if it didn't decide the outcome, however, what the article did do was change the momentum of the debate; it put Krueger on the defensive. One oil and gas lobbyist says that Krueger agreed to Dingell's motion to vote on Thursday afternoon because he was worried about additional stories over the weekend.

In the end, his inexperience and naiveté cost him dearly: faced with the Dingell motion and feeling the pressure of the *Post* article, he lost his poise and made a bad decision. Talking to Krueger, one senses his frustration at having come so close, his bitterness at the *Post* article, his feeling of betrayal by the absentees and the advisors who told him to move ahead with the vote on Thursday. A friend described Krueger as ''crushed'' by his defeat and ''really singed'' by the *Post* story. The picture that emerges is not without irony: the Shakespearean scholar learning the lesson of Caesar's wife.

*—April 1976*

# BODY POLITICS

by Larry L. King

*There may be strange bedfellows in Washington these days,
but no stranger than anywhere else.*

I was lunching with politicians in Washington recently when somebody asked—apropos of the sensationalized "sex scandals" preoccupying the media, the governed, and certainly the quaking pro-pols themselves—why only Democrats had been discovered in the exercise of carnal freedoms. While I attempted to frame a response touching on the ideological, the answer came: "Well, there's no fun in getting a little piece of elephant."

Amidst the laughter, someone told of a new "campaign button" being worn by particularly well-endowed congressional secretaries: "I type 74 words per minute." There was much joshing about firing well-turned young lovelies and hiring old crones in corrective shoes. Someone repeated the joke circulating in Capitol Hill cloakrooms: "When they caught Wayne Hays and John Young they said I couldn't sleep with my secretary. Then they caught Allan Howe and Joe Waggonner and told me I couldn't sleep with prostitutes. That only leaves my wife—and *she's* always got a headache." More yuks and chortles as everyone ordered fresh drinks.

Well, now, I fancy to enjoy a joke as much as the next man. But under the cover of giggles more appropriate to errant schoolboys convened behind the barn, our statesmen —and others—are begging serious questions having more to do with honesty and individual freedom and the workaday realities than with mere rolls in the hay or a knee-jerk morality.

We of the media, particularly, may be guilty of sins even larger than those who attempt to joke away the subject. We are springing to our microphones and typewriters to tell of hot tails—pun definitely intended—on the Potomac as though Antony and Cleopatra spent their time playing backgammon when Octavia and Ptolemy Dionysus happened not to be looking. We tell it so straight-faced you'd think our jaws were numbed by novocaine, even though our cheeks are so full of tongue we're in danger of strangling.

*Larry L. King, a contributing editor of* Texas Monthly, *has authored several books and innumerable articles. He lives and writes in New York City.*

Politicians, including Republicans, have been running carnal fevers outside their home beds since the first hairy tribe elected a leader on about the 103rd ballot in some lightless, airless cave. So have members of the media, not to mention doctors, lawyers, plumbers, housewives, carpenters, feminists, and you name it. Even such a pious parson as Rev. Billy James Hargis, the Oklahoma pulpit pounder, had occasion a few months ago to plead that the Devil made him do it. The sad thing is that poor ol' Billy James probably believes that, when all he was doing is what comes naturally.

The sex drive is among our more basic instincts, even ranking ahead of the need for Coca-Cola or peanut butter. If nature had not so willed, no species would survive. We simply would be too indifferent to procreate and would bumble around eating grass or drilling oil wells or joining the Jaycees past the point of no return. Sex feels so good because its primary function in nature's order is to perpetuate not only the beautiful but also the ugly, and that's why rattlesnakes and giant turtles and sand crabs and fat congressmen get that wonderful urge the same as peacocks and cuddly pussycats and beautiful blondes and handsome dudes like me.

Nature knew it must bribe us with an overwhelming instinct to make sexual music together so the earth would not remain a lifeless rock. Whether you believe that evolution brought light in its timeless and tireless work, or that God in His earliest effort said, "Let there be light," *something* brought light long before the Pedernales Electric Co-op or West Texas Utilities Company. With light came heat, without which no life might exist. In time the great hot lump of earth cooled, and the moisture in its atmosphere fell as rain, and water gathered and pooled, and the winds came and helped the rain wear away the cold stone. This formed thin coatings of soil, which eventually toddled its way downhill into the water. There the sun kissed this new mixture toward the end of bringing forth original life: microscopic, tiny, jellylike floating cells. These linked together and multiplied themselves and grew the instinct to keep on doing it.

The surface waters began to get overcrowded, and just floating around like little bits of jelly became boring. So some of these cells went off and decided to become fishes and underwater plants. Then the pioneers of *those* bold groups got washed upon the shore and lay around in the sunshine and opted to turn into snakes and dinosaurs and weird-looking clumsy birds. Finally, those who got tired of living under rocks and such and who wanted to cuddle, decided to turn into warm-blooded mammals. The minute that decision was made, it was inevitable that one day we'd have Miami Beach and massage parlors, and that one day Wayne Hays could not keep his hands off Elizabeth Ray, even if it meant paying her out of tax funds.

Now, the point is that no matter what these original little cells decided to become, they fought against great odds. They had to overcome Ice Ages and Stone Ages and the big 'uns always trying to eat the little 'uns. They caught chills and fevers and everything but city buses. It rained on 'em and hailed on 'em and things growled at 'em in the dark. They had to grow their own gills or wings or whatever. All this, now, with all manner of ugly species thrashing about making faces and otherwise threatening them. Yet, no matter how howling or hairy were the enemies in pursuit, and no matter if nature's creatures had to creep or crawl or fly away from danger, enough of each species paused to get it on sexually that just about everything but the dumbass dinosaur survived. Against such irrepressible instincts, what's a poor politician gonna do?

Things worked swimmingly well until Man came along to superimpose "civilization" on nature's order. Until Man decided to govern sexual conduct, a baboon or a turtle (within the confines of certain loose processes of natural selection) could pretty much kiss and cuddle who he wanted to so long as a stronger baboon or a meaner turtle didn't object. Man, however, discovered early that anything as good as sex needed to be rationed and made difficult or else people would have too much fun. They'd loll around in the shade cooing and touching when they ought to be up killing whales or inventing the spinning wheel or taking Dale Carnegie courses. The kings and the pharaohs and other precinct bosses fretted that if people made love rather than war, then there would be no booty to claim and fewer excuses to levy taxes. So they devised laws, some of which they credited to God, to get everybody out of bed and up and doing. These laws said that people could make love only under such restricted conditions as pleased the state. The young or unmarried would not be permitted to do it at all, the married could do it only to each other, and *nobody* should do it except to make babies. If a boy wanted to cuddle a boy, or a girl wanted to cuddle a girl, they ran the risk of jail—to say nothing of the worst possible social contaminations. If you had some for sale, the fruit of your commerce was a trip to the pokey. There were even laws saying that under certain conditions you couldn't *give* sex away, or accept it, even in a fair swap. They finally hit on the notion that if you showed too much imagination and discovered especially exotic ways to do it, well, then, they'd reserve you a jail cell for that, too.

All these anti-love laws haven't worked, of course. All they've done is make people sneak around and lie and cheat and go crazy and kill each other—or, like poor old Wayne Hays, take overdoses of sleeping pills. It sure was simpler when we were floating around on the water as itsy-bitsy cells and reproducing ourselves while the sun smiled on us.

We are considering here more than sex and no less than personal freedom. Most people do not really believe in personal freedom even though they think they do. While almost any American is quick to claim it as a birthright, many fewer are willing to extend it to others. We may give love to a child or a spouse or a neighbor, but in the matter of their free choices we tend to become policemen of the spirit and censors of the soul. We tell them "don't" more than we tell them "do." We tell them "no" more than we tell them "yes." It is no accident that we are so shaped and formed: the Ten Commandments, no matter their worth, are stated in the negative; more laws are written to prohibit people than to set people free. Richard Nixon once told an interviewer that people were like children. That is the basic presumption of the state, whether its agents label themselves liberal or conservative or lay claim to any of the various ideological isms. The state and its agents and allied institutions are collectively almost certain to repress, even when attempting benign acts. Example: that welfare law which, under the guise of assisting needy families, threatens to withhold benefits from poor mothers and their dependent children should a nonworking man live in the house. "We will allow you the freedom to eat marginally," the state says, "but don't let me catch you doing any *loving* around here."

Our politicians are quick to proclaim that we are the freest and richest people in the history of man. That is probably true, and we are surely freer than the Russians and the Cubans and richer than the Hottentots, but before we are smitten with paroxysms of pride, we would do well to remember just how far we have to go. This free society can put you in jail for smoking the wrong substance or for spitting on the sidewalk or for thousands of other reasons. This freest government in the recorded history of man is licensed to kill you, to take your money, to lock you up, to restrict your freedom of movement and your social preferences. Now you'd think with all *that* power the state wouldn't demand the right to dictate how you may make love, and with whom, and under what conditions. But it does, old pal. It does.

Your government will even go so far as to *entrap* you should you be overpowered by sexual instincts outside the limited permissions it has granted. Congressman Howe of Utah and Congressman Waggonner of Louisiana are far from the first men to fall prey to the state's bogus nooky salespersons. And since the slimy idea first hatched in some lilliputian official brain, prostitutes have been enticed to sell themselves—and then have been hustled off to jail by the same undercover creeps who entrapped them.

If diddling is so all-fired evil that we must discourage it through law, then why in the name of reason would the authorities attempt to *encourage* men or women to break that law? In this time of record crime are the jails so empty that clients must be solicited to fill them? Are we so desperate for new victims that we must create our own? Why have we become so miserable in spirit that if all the repressive laws on the books will not naturally suffice to land our neighbor in jail, then we must get him there with trickery? These are serious questions and they cannot be erased by giggling at jokes about "sex in Washington."

**179**

I have been waiting for one thoughtful and honest and humane man to rise in Congress and say—without pious preambles invoking the flag or claiming improbably pure institutional instincts—''Enough of this crap.'' No one has. No one is likely to. This is because they know that Americans are two-faced about sex, that although a high percentage of hanky-panky goes on among all socioeconomic groupings, the society prefers to live a lie and force others to live their sex lives as lies. So our public men are intimidated and cowed and afraid to speak out—not for the first time, either.

When poor Congressman Howe was entrapped in Utah, the press skewered him without paying the slightest attention to his constitutional rights of due process or the presumption of innocence. His political colleagues and church colleagues instantly turned into sharks. They demanded his resignation and his head. It was a panic reaction and panic there should have been: but the panic was for all the wrong reasons and misdirected as to source.

There should have been panic because a presumably free citizen of the Republic (no matter whether he happened to be a congressman, oilman, or mechanic) could have his freedom and rights so lightly held that the state would: (1) grubbily attempt to entrap him; (2) release to the press, before he'd had his day in court, a transcript of what he'd supposedly said; and (3) tardily admit, after the damage had been done, *that it had no transcript of actual worth but had concocted one on the basis of what its entrapping and self-serving agents claimed to have transpired*. Nixon lost the presidency for trying to hoke-up tapes, but at least he *had* some. The Utah police didn't. I have not heard a politician or a churchman or any of Congressman Howe's critics express the slightest indignation over these crimes—and that is what they are.

His story that he had been lured to the scene by an invitation from unnamed constituents to a party originally sounded weaker than 3.2 beer. But if the authorities would go so far as to release a bogus transcript, then who's to say he may not be telling the truth? Did someone want to ruin him politically, or did the cops panic when they found they'd netted a congressman in their tawdry game—and *then* concoct their fake record to cover themselves? Either way, their guilt is the greater—no matter that Congressman Howe was later convicted for trying to spend his twenty dollars illegally.

District of Columbia police were guilty of equally shoddy practices in the case of Congressman Waggonner. First, they entrapped him with a bogus prostitute. When they discovered they'd bagged a congressman in a town run by congressmen—rather than some poor powerless government clerk—they let him go and then covered it up until somebody tipped off the press during the current hysteria. Joe Waggonner could have bought the services of every streetwalker in Washington and still would have done less damage to freedom and justice than did the police.

I'm no pal of any of these particular pols, and certainly not of Wayne Hays. I think he richly deserves his designation as ''the meanest man in Congress.'' That, however, does not detract from his constitutional rights; nor should it make him fair game for crucifixion. Among the intimacies the press revealed was that Hays, while making it with Liz, kept one eye on her bedroom digital clock. How Hays does it or at what speed is no business of yours or mine, even if you *think* we may have paid for his hurried fun from our

tax monies—as Ms. Ray claims we did, and as Mr. Hays insists we did not. And even if we did, so what? Politicians have hired drones since time immemorial for reasons other than their typing speed, most of the time to pay off political debts, and no one, not even the *Washington Post*, raises much of a stink about that. Yet the employee performs no useful work, and how is that different from Elizabeth Ray?

The answer, of course, is not at all—though certain feminists would have you believe that the crucial difference is that the delicate Ms. Ray was exploited. No sooner had the story broken than some women writers started trumpeting their denunciations of the Washington scene under headlines such as the one that appeared in the *Village Voice*: WAYNE HAYS MUST GO. Well, maybe she was exploited, though personally I've always felt that any person—man, woman, or politician—had the option of refusing to whore. Ms. Ray, who reportedly approached the *Washington Post* as a woman scorned (after her friend Wayne Hays advised she would be most unwelcome at his wedding reception), was suddenly so eager to attain justice that she continued to perform her debilitating special nightwork—while, with her consent, reporters skulked about to eavesdrop. When the story crashed into the front pages, she just happened to have hot from the publishers her trashy book about Sex in Washington and held press conferences as far away as London; within a week her book winked and blinked from stores all over America. It is a classic case of coincidence, I guess we are supposed to believe. If Ms. Ray was exploited as she claimed, then she's by now gained parity with Wayne Hays in the exploitation department. And among *her* victims, of course, are those women on Capitol Hill who've been giving us taxpayers our money's worth all along—a fact that should have been noted by the outraged women writers as they vented their wrath upon Wayne Hays and his male colleagues.

Sure, they do some hanky-pankying in Washington, and the same applies in the Texas Legislature. A beloved former governor, who has prayed more than one pious public prayer, periodically used to call a sorority house at the University of Texas to establish trysts with a lovely lady I much admire myself. And a former lieutenant governor notoriously got around. But all this is as true of the private sector as it is in government. Politicians—provided they finance their own romances—are no more and no less ''guilty'' than the rest of us. The politician, however, is more vulnerable to the public mood. There are not enough of you out there to vote me out of my job as a freelance writer even should I kiss a goat, but your congressman's scalp is there for the taking should you want it. Since the sex scandals exploded, a United States senator from Virginia has been accused of offering to help a female constituent in exchange for her sexual favors. The senator's name made the papers before the *Washington Post* investigated and found his accuser to be a demented lady with a troubled history of telling many improbable tales. Should someone else, however— looking to be a cover girl or the author of the next sexsational book—name almost any public figure, he'll be in hot water from his home bed to his hometown even if wholly innocent. Such people, as with the rest of us, are entitled to their full protections and rights and legal assumptions. They will not, of course, receive them because more people are less rational about sex than any other subject.

*—September 1976*

# TURNING THE OTHER CHIC

## by James Fallows

---

### *In politics as in dress, what's in today may be out tomorrow.*

---

Along with "voter apathy" and "campaign rhetoric," there is one other horror sure to be condemned as we reach primary time this month. That is "personality politics"—the phrase used by candidates who are ugly or boring or shifty-eyed to denounce their golden-haired opposition.

Fair enough. But there is another kind of "personality politics" that has absolutely run amok this year. It is the kind which is aimed not at the personality of the candidate so much as at that of the voter.

A historical illustration: in the springtime of 1968, I was working on a college newspaper, joining in the vast generational effort to unseat the reigning President of the United States. Until the time of the New Hampshire primary, this crusade made for great fellow-feeling among students. We would trudge up to New Hampshire to work for Gene Mc-Carthy, or write editorials, or at a minimum think good thoughts about him as we lazed about the pinball halls. McCarthy "won" in New Hampshire, and all of a sudden there was trouble. From out of nowhere, Robert Kennedy appeared, ready to push McCarthy out of the race. At this point a great moral scimitar came sweeping through our previously united troops.

Bobby, of course, was "opportunistic" and "ruthless" for having sat it out while McCarthy took the risks; but the real target of these denunciations was not him so much as any student who would dare support him. Whenever someone spoke up for Kennedy at an editorial meeting, everyone else was given an instant insight into his soul. Here was someone—we were convinced—who had probably cheated to get into college. The mark of opportunism was upon him as much as on Bobby. No doubt he'd stab you in the back if it stood in the way of his admission to medical school or his promotion to assistant vice president in charge of sales.

There was, of course, another side to the story. The Ken-

*James Fallows is a former associate editor of* Texas Monthly. *He is President Carter's chief speechwriter.*

nedy people looked on McCarthy as a dog in the manger. Obviously he couldn't win, but he wouldn't step aside for Bobby, who could. McCarthy was unrealistic, a poetic poseur—and everyone who clung to him was marked with the same insolence of the mediocre. They bore chips on their shoulders against those who moved more swiftly in the race for life's rewards.

It was a vicious little arrangement, and it ended only under far more vicious circumstances, when Robert Kennedy was killed. This alone enabled the bitter enemies to join together once again.

College emotions, you may say. During those uncertain adolescent years, everything from your choice of classes to the particular shirt you wear is freighted with revelations about your inner soul. Surely this sort of thing would never happen to adults.

No? Consider the case of Jimmy Carter in the 1976 primaries. I should make clear right now that I am beating no drum for Carter. As this is written, campaigning has barely begun in Texas, and—like, I suspect, most other voters—I have little clear sense of where Carter, or the other candidates, stand on several important issues. Neither Carter, nor anyone else, has yet won my vote.

I do know enough, though, to smell a rat in the way Carter has been treated by his opponents and the press. Unlike any of the other serious candidates (I exclude George Wallace) Carter has suddenly run into a barrage of debunking articles. Their purpose has not been merely to show that Scoop Jackson, for example, would make a better president than Carter, but rather that Carter is beyond the pale of serious consideration. He is Out, not In. By the implications of "personality politics," anyone who supports him may also be excluded from the company of reasonable men.

The essential ingredient in this campaign has been the portrayal of Carter as a con man. P. T. Barnum with good teeth. Thesis: Carter is a huckster. Corollary: if you're for him you've been conned. In the April issue of *Esquire*,

Helen Dudar expressed this sentiment rather delicately and impressionistically. After traveling with the Carter campaign, she said, you "wake up a day or two later to find yourself invaded by an unconquerable sense of disquiet. The Carter afterimage is how I have come to think of it, and the impression is not exclusive with me. I kept calling up colleagues who had spent time with Carter and had written fondly of him . . . and had subsequently developed similar unease."

A far blunter accusation came from Reg Murphy, who was editor of the *Atlanta Constitution* when Carter was governor of Georgia. In an article last February in the *New Republic* entitled "The New Jimmy Carter," he said that "to Georgians, the idea of Carter as a presidential candidate is hilarious.... He has so little popularity left at home that they all thought his public support would hurt rather than help, even though he was still in office. But plastic surgeons have made him a national figure. The boys in the bus haven't had a chance to look into his background and administration yet. When they do they won't be quite as tempted to produce a papier-mâché mask because political campaigns aren't covered that way anymore—thank goodness."

The real Sunday Punch, however, was delivered by the March issue of *Harper's*, with an article by Stephen Brill. The title was a charming portent of the subtle reasoning that lay inside: "Jimmy Carter's Pathetic Lies." Brill's point was that Carter had done things in Georgia that he was not trumpeting to the heavens during his presidential campaign. He had said nice things about Lester Maddox when Maddox was his lieutenant governor. He was a nuclear engineer, not a "nuclear physicist" as he claimed to be—and he was a wealthy peanut broker, rather than the salt-of-the-earth peanut farmer that his ads portrayed. He said different things to one audience than he did to another. "His is the most sincerely insincere, politically antipolitical, and slickly unslick campaign of the year. Using an image that is a hybrid of honest, simple Abe Lincoln and charming, idealistic John Kennedy, he has packaged himself to take the idol-seekers for a long ride."

About the content of the article, there will be more to say in a moment. In terms of delivering the votes, the impact of magazines like these should not be exaggerated. (One political manager used to speak with scorn of trends that "are sweeping the country, from the Atlantic . . . to *Harper's*.") If forced to choose, Carter would probably hold onto his endorsement from Greg Allman rather than win glowing praise from the editors in New York.

Still the magazines do exert an influence—an indirect one, most often exercised through the other levels of the press. TV news, in particular, often acts as a kind of *Reader's Digest* of what the magazines have been printing. Whenever candidates appear on the Sunday talk shows, most of the interviewers' questions have been cribbed from magazine and newspaper reports. When Jimmy Carter appeared on *Face the Nation*, for example, the line of questioning followed Stephen Brill's argument with remarkable precision. Later, when Tom Snyder interviewed him on the *Tomorrow* program, the article itself was introduced into evidence, and Carter discussed its charges. Apart from the legendary unwillingness of television to do its own research, there is another reason for this ripple effect. No less than other people, political reporters—for both newspapers

and TV—hate to be caught off base. No one wants to be the person who goes down in history as saying that Muskie is sure to win the nomination, or that Wallace will trounce Carter in the Florida primary. Ceaselessly tramping from town to town with the candidates, the reporters have almost no time to conduct investigations of their own, so when an apparently authoritative sign appears, such as Brill's article, they can protect themselves by incorporating a little bit of its analysis into their own.

(As it turned out, this particular article had an even more direct effect on the campaign. In the weeks before the Florida primary, Henry Jackson's troops handed out reprints of Brill's piece wherever liberal voters were gathered, hoping that the accusation—that Carter was a "phony liberal"—would win them over. For their part, the Carter men were using reprints of one of Brill's earlier efforts, a *New York* article with the self-explanatory title "Wallace Lies," to discredit the Alabama governor.)

Similar patterns of "personality politics" have affected some of the other candidates. Until quite recently, Gerald Ford's greatest obstacle was the fashionable judgment that he was a clumsy buffoon, and that no one who was serious about important things could be serious about him. Even among some of Scoop Jackson's diehard supporters, you will find a pose of knowing cynicism rather than the evangelistic devotion of the Carter stalwarts. Scoop may be boring, his people say: he may be a little stupid, but he's the only one who can save us from the Georgia Cracker. Perhaps the most fascinating illustration of personality politics has turned up in several recent opinion polls. As the people of Massachusetts, say, or Florida have gone to the polls, some of the news services have tried to get an early feel for the trends by asking people as they come from the polling place who got their vote. Time and again, these surveys have turned out to be wrong; they have underestimated the strength of George Wallace. Many people who will vote for Wallace, in there alone with the ballot, will not tell anyone they did—not even an anonymous poll-taker they will never see again. Of all the candidates, Carter's predicament is unique primarily because of the catch-22 nature of the charge against him. You're either for him or against him, and if you're for him you're a sucker. Any argument in his defense only demonstrates more fully how brainwashed you have been.

T he interesting thing about these fashions is their instability. In politics as in couture, what is chic today may be ridiculous tomorrow. Look at the Nehru jacket. Look at the McGovern campaign. This brings us to the first small sign that the Carter tide is turning, the March 22 issue of *New York* magazine.

The essential function of magazines like *New York*, it has long seemed to me, is the declaration of attitudes. In a majority of cases you need not read a single word of an article's text to get the most important message. You read the headlines, you look at the pictures, and you've got what you came for. You know what's In and Out. A few recent headlines from *New York* give the idea: "The Who—Still the Best Band in Rock." "And Heeeeere's TV's Hottest New Comedy Star!" "The Most Important Film Director since Bergman." "Options, the Hottest Game in Town." "35 New Players in the Power Game." A glance at other regional magazines, this one being no exception, would yield a similar harvest.

*New York*'s contribution to the Carter debate was an article by Richard Reeves. It suggested—aha!—that it was Brill and the others who might be working the con: "Washington is in a small panic over 'Wee Jimmy.' The titans of old Washington, led by Reston, Averell Harriman, and Hubert Humphrey, seem ready to take to the streets of Georgetown. Why? Mark Shields, the Dr. Johnson of Duke Zeibert's, summed it up: 'The problem is that no one in Washington owns a piece of Jimmy Carter.' "

As it turns out, I thought the article was quite good, but the quality really didn't matter. The point was the declaration: Jimmy Carter is OK. You guys knocking him may be wearing the Nehru jackets.

The reason for mentioning these trends is not that they've done an injustice to Jimmy Carter—if they have, that's his worry—but that they do an injustice to those of us who are trying to make up our minds. I have never considered myself a prominent racist, for example, but I find the accusations about Carter's closet racism extremely unenlightening. So what if he made a separate peace with Lester Maddox, or wrote placating letters to George Wallace? Teddy Kennedy sat on a platform with Wallace and no one has been yelling racist at him. All of these points need to be weighed, of course, when considering Carter—or, for that matter, Kennedy—but they are shocking only if you had previously assumed that the candidate was an absolutely perfect human being. Maybe Carter believes that about himself; Stephen Brill accuses him of trying to plant that belief in his audience's mind. If that is so, and if he keeps it up, then Carter is a fool and deserves to lose.

Perfection, however, is not what I'm looking for in a presidential candidate. The question I want answered about Carter is whether, on balance, he'll do a better job than the other candidates who are available. The fashionable line on Carter et al. has not helped us make much progress toward this decision. I have already had one too many discussions along these lines: Carter is imperfect, and Scoop has done a good job for Israel. Or, Carter is imperfect, and Hubert will stick up for the poor. Or, Carter is imperfect, and Udall is honest. The imperfections of all the candidates are certainly worth consideration—Carter's deviousness, Jackson's diehard support of the war in Viet Nam, Hubert's mental fatigue, et cetera. So are their relative strengths. With all the elements in view, we can try to figure out who will be the strongest candidate and the best president. The problem with the analysis spawned by personality politics, whether favorable or unfavorable, is that it doesn't provide much help with these questions. Its main motivation is to stay one jump ahead of ridicule. This may be a fine pursuit for fashion designers, but it is a hell of a way to choose a president.

*—May 1976*

Barbara Jordan, 1965. *Photography by The Houston Post Co*.

# THE MAKING OF BARBARA JORDAN

## by William Broyles

### I looked over Jordan, and what did I see?

At night Dowling Street is one of the toughest streets in Houston. From its ramshackle bars and flophouses bursts a surging stream of sex and energy that can easily explode into violence. But during the day Dowling is one of the main thoroughfares of the Third Ward, the cultural and intellectual heart of black Houston. Black artist Edsel Cramer has lived at the corner of Dowling and Wheeler for 25 years. To this brick bungalow, nestled amid convenience stores and bars, Barbara Jordan came in the spring of 1973 to sit for a portrait. She was just beginning her first session as a member of the U.S. Congress, and her former colleagues in the Texas Senate, still flush with affection for her, had decided on the unprecedented step of commissioning her portrait to hang in the Texas Capitol alongside portraits of Davy Crockett, Sam Houston, Lyndon Johnson, and Jefferson Davis. She made six visits to Cramer's studio, always arriving precisely on time and staying exactly two hours.

Cramer has spent years studying the faces of his subjects, searching out the planes and angles, the subtleties of bone structure and coloring, that define appearance and character. He did the same with Jordan, isolating the elements of her face and putting them back together on canvas. "Studying her up close you see exactly how intense she is," Cramer remembers. "There are fine lines etched around her eyes, the sort of lines that mean stress, hard work, and determination. Her head is like a bull's head; across her brow is a lump of bone that stands out like the forehead of a bull. That look of bull-like strength is part of her character. But the most impressive thing about her is she is simply so big —both in size and personality. I just couldn't paint normal scale no matter how hard I tried, even though I prefer to keep the scale of my paintings down. But her painting just kept coming out too big; I couldn't help but make her larger than life."

*William Broyles has been* Texas Monthly's *editor since the magazine's inception. He won a 1977 Penney-Missouri Award for his article on Barbara Jordan.*

Cramer seemed to consider this some professional failure on his part, as though his hand had failed to restrain his brush. If it's some consolation, Barbara Jordan's images have always had a way of becoming larger than life. For example, here are some verbal portraits painted of her lately by journalists and other politicians: "a genius"; "a hero"; "the best politician of this century"; "the salvation of American politics"; "a mythic figure"; "the main inspiration for a troubled time"; "a woman of high destiny"; "a cross between Lyndon Johnson and Mahatma Gandhi." Her reception at the Democratic National Convention in New York City this summer dwarfed that of every other politician, with the possible exception of Jimmy Carter. A legitimate American hero like John Glenn was given short shrift by a crowd eager for her magic, like an audience impatient with preliminaries and ready for the main event. When her filmed introduction began, and her disembodied voice was heard saying, "If there are any patriots left in this country, then I am one," the convention roared into life. This was the woman whose eloquent speech ("My faith in the Constitution is whole, it is complete, it is total") for the impeachment of Richard Nixon elevated that grave process to the level of a national rite. To a country wracked with the longest war in its history, torn by racial division, unsure of its institutions and its future, she furnished clear hope. A Southern woman from the race of slaves, she dramatically affirmed, in spite of slavery, civil war, and segregation, her faith in our original ideals. She inspires the belief that one day the burden of race may be set aside. The first black state senator since 1882, the first black congresswoman from the South, now bandied about as possibly a U.S. senator, and—who knows?—perhaps the first black president, she has established her place as the symbolic trailblazer of Texas politics.

On the other hand, she says she does not want to be a symbol, the first black this or the first black that. She wants to be seen for her performance on the playing field. "I am neither a black politician nor a female politician," she says.

"Just a politician. A professional politician." But no amount of insisting that's all she is seems to work. People don't want to see her as a politician. If she were white, perhaps then they would. Then the ambition would shine clearly through the rhetoric; then the opportunism in her political alliances would be obvious; then she, not John Connally, would be seen as the true heir to Lyndon Johnson's wheeling and dealing skills. To a good politician the symbolism of Jordan's position—being Southern, black, and female—would be prime political capital, not to be risked on quixotic causes, but to be invested wisely for political ends. Among the greatest of political ends, of course, is personal advancement. And not only does Jordan continually remind people she is a politician, she also doesn't make a big secret about wanting to go places. For those who believe her symbolic position as a black woman with power imposes the grave responsibility to consider issues over advancement, this personal ambition does not always sit well. "I have watched Barbara Jordan for almost ten years," says one critic. "And I have yet to see any evidence she is interested in anything beyond the advancement of Barbara Jordan."

Now politicians have been accused of sacrificing principle to ambition and expediency since long before Julius Caesar. In Jordan's case this accusation is made mostly by whites—and a few black militants—who think she isn't doing enough for liberal causes or her people. On the other hand, even her most skeptical black constituents seem to applaud not only her performance but also her ambition. They say they are tired of political kamikaze pilots who crash and burn against the warships of the establishment. They want someone who can hold his own with the toughest movers and shakers, someone with staying power. Barbara Jordan has staying power. Although they can point to few concrete examples, they continue to believe she is using the establishment, and not the other way around. This gap between what she says she is and how she is perceived is a paradox; almost everything about Barbara Jordan is. That's what being larger than life is all about. Her personality ranges from frosty, devastating dignity to warm, humorous folksiness. Her distinctive voice seems without root or place. Personal details about her are few and closely guarded. Much of her time seems spent in rehearsal for some future role, but only she knows what it might be.

## GONNA BE SOMEBODY

The best place to begin understanding Barbara Jordan is with a brief tour of black Houston. The primary black neighborhoods are Third Ward and Fifth Ward. Barbara Jordan had her portrait painted in Third Ward, which is just west of the University of Houston and southeast of downtown. Fifth Ward is north of the Ship Channel, northeast of downtown. Until the Elysian Viaduct was built in 1955, Fifth Ward was connected only tenuously to Houston. It was the poorer neighborhood, the brawn to Third Ward's brains. Like black communities in every Southern town, it was built and owned primarily by whites, who expected at the bare minimum a 20 per cent return on the block after block of shotgun houses (so called because you could fire a shotgun through the front door and hit everything in the house). Since the city fathers proceeded on the dubious assumption that blacks paid no taxes—and since until 1945 fewer than 5 per cent of the city's blacks were registered to vote—paved streets, street lights, sewers, and other municipal services were slow coming.

Even the cramped poverty of black Houston shone like a beacon for the rural blacks of East Texas and West Louisiana. From 84,000 blacks in 1940, it grew to more than 350,000 in the seventies, more blacks than Atlanta, more than New Orleans, the largest black population in the South. There are more blacks in Houston today than the entire 1940 population of the city. The old black neighborhoods were steadily swallowed up into the larger boundaries of the expanding black city. And as Houston grew by annexing the white suburbs that surrounded it, blacks took over virtually the entire east side of old Houston. From well north of Fifth Ward, threading across the Ship Channel and warehouse district to Third Ward, then spreading south to Sunnyside and beyond, black Houston stands like a large expanding hourglass in the center of Houston, cutting the city north to south and separating the more prosperous west side from the industrial east side, the port, and the chemical plants of the Ship Channel.

Even though some black leaders worry about a loss of community identity amid such growth, black Houston has at least as much center to it as white Houston does. The old neighborhoods of Fifth and Third Ward still provide the character. Texas Southern University, the black newspaper, and most business and professional offices are in Third Ward. The black elite lives there, in the former mansions of the Cullens and the Weingartens along MacGregor Bayou; so does the black middle class, mostly in the abandoned Jewish neighborhoods just east of Main Street and north of Hermann Park. Still, there has not been in Houston the sort of second- and third-generation inherited black wealth which has dominated black communities in Atlanta and New Orleans. Black Houston has been a more open place, just as white Houston has. That is true of Fifth Ward as well, which remains the grass-roots heart of the black community. The labor unions are there, as are the largest and most fundamentalist black churches, the largest black funeral parlors, and the wealthiest blacks like Mack Hannah and Don Robey. Wheatley, the Fifth Ward high school, usually wins in football and basketball; Yates, the Third Ward high school, usually excels in academics and debate. Fifth Ward is a poorer and tougher place.

Barbara Jordan is from Fifth Ward. A few years after her birth in 1936, her father, B. M. Jordan, became a Baptist minister. To help support his family he kept his job as a warehouseman. When Barbara was in her teens, the family moved to Campbell Street, just east of Lockwood near the corner of Campbell and Erastus; she and her mother still live there. Most of the houses on the street are shotgun shacks, house after identical house about sixteen feet wide and five feet apart, each constructed with a center door, a small porch, and a window to either side. Since the houses are so small, a good deal of the life on Campbell Street occurs in front yards. Everybody knows everything about their neighbors; it is a small-town feeling that much of white America, with its air conditioning and fixed-glass windows, has unwittingly let slip away. Immediately behind the houses across the street is the vast expanse of the main Houston freight yard, where thousands of trailer trucks and hundreds of railroad cars are constantly in motion, supplying Houston's booming commerce. But Campbell Street, with its corner bar, Lou's Beauty Nook, and the Tornado Motel, might as well be light years away from that cosmopolitan prosperity.

The distinctive qualities of Barbara Jordan—her speaking ability, her ambition, her charisma, and, of course, her size—all developed early. Reverend Jordan's churches were solidly missionary and fundamentalist, the churches that for 300 years had promised black Americans salvation from a world of tears and travail. On Sundays, Barbara and her two older sisters would get up behind their father after his sermon and sing gospel music, the old-fashioned kind where they clapped and swayed and affirmed the joyous promise of their religion. The father prided himself on speaking correctly, in full, rounded, unaccented tones. To him correct speech was a mark of good breeding and class, and he insisted his daughters speak correctly. The common assumption that Jordan developed her speaking style at Boston University Law School could not be more wrong. "She had it in the cradle," says Tom Freeman, her debate coach at Texas Southern University (TSU). "She did get a little JFK cadence in her voice from Boston," says her old friend Andrew Jefferson, a former state district judge and a talented politician. "Those of us who knew her well noticed a little extra when she came back from Boston—a sort of embellishment, a little frosting on the cake." So far as Jordan herself is concerned, "I don't have an accent. I just talk like me. I have talked this way as long as I can remember."

Jordan's attitude is disingenuous, at the least, since her voice is much of her image. It underscores her aloofness and dignity, it lifts her beyond region, it masks any fuzzy thinking or lowly ambition, and it scares hell out of people. On hearing it for the first time, one awed young woman said, "I turned on my television set and thought I was listening to God." It sounds, as Congressman Andrew Young of Georgia says, "like the heavens have opened up." The religious parallels are apt, because the voice is an evangelical voice, a voice designed to bring to the fold the presence of the Lord. For that voice, for much of her ambition, and for her exacting standards of excellence, she can thank her father.

Reverend Jordan wanted his three daughters to become music teachers; two did. In a segregated society, being a music teacher was one of the best ambitions a young black woman could have, and Reverend Jordan insisted on the best. "I would come home with five A's and a B," Barbara Jordan told Molly Ivins of the *Texas Observer*, "and my father would say, 'Why do you have a B?'" She wanted to please her father, to meet and even exceed his standards; but she wanted to be more than a music teacher. "I always wanted to be something unusual," she says, "I would never be content with being run of the mill, I was thinking about being a pharmacist, but then I asked myself, 'Whoever heard of an outstanding pharmacist?'" When she was in the tenth grade at Phillis Wheatley High School, a Chicago lawyer named Edith Sampson addressed the Career Day assembly. Sampson was crisp, competent, confident. Then and there, Barbara Jordan decided that was what she was going to be. At first, her father told a teacher who encouraged this ambition to "stay out of his family's affairs": that the law was no profession for a woman. But he came to encourage her "to do whatever I thought I could." (Reverend Jordan died in 1972, the day after he

attended his daughter's Governor for a Day ceremonies in Austin.)

If anyone who knew her as a girl remembers Barbara Jordan having any doubts about herself, they aren't letting on. "She has always been, even as a little girl, very sure of herself," says Mary Justice York, who has known her since the third grade. "We knew from the very beginning she would do something different from the rest of us. She has always been large. . . . In those days, the kids who were the leaders were usually slim and pretty, with nice, long hair and pretty brown skin . . . but Barbara—it wasn't that she tried to be the leader or strove for it—we just recognized her." A. C. Herald, who was her homeroom teacher at Wheatley, remembers that "she had, even then, such an amazing sense of self." She had a weight problem, she wasn't attractive—"My mother says not to make me pretty," she told her portrait painter—but she was smart, and above all, she had boundless ambition and belief in herself. Apparently the sight of an overweight young black girl (she entered TSU at 16) going about the normal business of growing up in the Fifth Ward with this doomsday voice, this fierce sense of dignity, this tenacious idea of herself and her future, didn't seem strange. When people who knew her then are asked if she didn't seem a little, well, phony, with that voice and everything, their response is consistently some variation of: "No, not really. She was just Barbara. That's just how she was. We always knew she was gonna be somebody."

At TSU she was everywhere; she wanted to get to the top of everything. She ran for freshman class president, and lost to Andrew Jefferson; she ran for student body president, and lost by six votes. Finally, she was elected editor of the yearbook. But she really shined in debate, where she was the only woman. Her freshman year, Tom Freeman, the debate coach, told her she wasn't able to speak extemporaneously, and so kept her from doing refutations. "She went on to become one of the best debaters at refutation I have ever had," Freeman recalls. "I think when I told her she wasn't good at it that it really challenged her." While she was at TSU the debate team was spectacular. They toured the country, beating everyone, including Harvard. They integrated the Baylor Forensic Tournament and won the first three years they competed. From TSU, Jordan went on to Boston University Law School, where she was the only woman in her class.

At this point a certain perspective might be helpful. Until she went north with the TSU debate team, Barbara Jordan had lived *completely* in the segregated society of black Houston. Even when the debate team integrated the regional meet in Waco, they couldn't stay at the hotel with the other teams. Instead they were put up at all-black Paul Quinn College. The city Barbara Jordan left to attend Boston University in 1956 had segregated taxis, restaurants and lunch counters, restrooms, hospital wards, swimming pools, churches, labor unions, and schools; the handful of black policemen could not arrest whites or eat in the segregated city cafeteria; blacks could not vote in the Democratic primary—the only election in one-party Texas that mattered—until 1944. In 1956, black Houston was a separate city of 200,000 people. Its leading citizens were small businessmen and the leaders of the segregated institutions—the ministers, the educators, the union officials. These men also served as ambassadors to the white society—they lobbied to get a road paved or a library built. In such a society, if you were young, gifted, and ambitious, you had to become aware, in a way no white could really understand, of the limits on your ambitions. You could rise only so far. You had to stay in the black society since the great opportunities of the larger white world were closed. That was what ''knowing your place'' meant.

The accepted current view of this system, as expressed by the Supreme Court, is that it created a ''badge of inferiority''; the white society's claim that separate could be equal was false: separate was inherently unequal. But the vast effort to dismantle this system has obscured certain of its more positive elements. For example, today many Houston blacks believe their schools have lost something crucial. ''Give us back our black principals and teachers,'' they say. ''The new white teachers don't understand our children, they don't enforce discipline or values, they don't make them learn.'' When Barbara Jordan was at Wheatley High School they taught *pride*. ''They taught us dignity,'' says one of her contemporaries. The segregated black society was ironically a breeding ground of the very fundamental values white Americans were coming to question. Houston blacks were pro-military, pro-education, and in their own way, pro-American. ''I can still get goose bumps when I hear the Star Spangled Banner,'' says Jordan, who is fond of reciting the Pledge of Allegiance in her speeches. While blacks most likely burned with a common rage at the humiliation of segregation, they also made the best of things within it. And they were proud of their schools, proud of their athletic teams, proud of their churches, proud of themselves.

Barbara Jordan, for one, has never given the slightest indication she feels ''a badge of inferiority'' because she went to Wheatley and TSU, or because she grew up in a segregated society. In fact, there must be few pleasures sweeter than going to a debate tournament and beating all the teams you aren't good enough to stay in the same hotel with. And when TSU traveled north and beat the best debate teams America had to offer, that must have dispelled any doubts she might have had about just how good she was. But ability was one thing; ambition was another. Satchel Paige was one of the best pitchers who ever lived, but he only got to play in the major leagues in the twilight of his career. Barbara Jordan was to become the Jackie Robinson of Texas politics, but it would not be easy. When she returned home with her law degree from Boston University in 1959, the first black to win elective office in Houston since Reconstruction had been on the school board for less than a year. The system of segregation was still in effect (after political meetings, if she and her white allies wanted to eat or drink in public together, they would have had to go to black Houston). It's one thing to play in the black leagues when that's all it seems can be done. But Barbara Jordan had supreme self-confidence, she had a boundless capacity for hard work, and she had her eye on bigger things.

# JUST BARBARA

**W**hen she returned to Houston, Jordan started her law office on the dining room table of the house on Campbell Street. She also started doing nuts and bolts political work with the Harris County Democrats. This coalition of labor minorities

and white liberals was the mainspring of Houston liberal politics. It had its own office, its own leaders and candidates, and its own platforms; in almost every respect it was a separate political party. The struggles with the Johnson wing of the Democratic party were pitched battles. The liberals had great heart, tremendous esprit, high principles —and they almost always lost. With remarkable resilience they would get up to fight again. Since they openly courted blacks, they were the only place for an ambitious black office seeker like Barbara Jordan to start, just as debate was the place to make her mark at TSU. In the 1960 Kennedy presidential campaign she stuffed envelopes and licked stamps, went on to set up systems to identify block and precinct workers, then was asked to speak at a small rally when the scheduled speaker didn't show up.

If there is anything Jordan has never wasted, it is an opportunity to speak. Soon she was as prominent in the Harris County Democrats as she had been at TSU. She became vice-chairman; she helped screen candidates; she seemed in every respect a committed liberal. When the Connally-backed black political organization set out to keep the endorsement of the Harris County Council of Organizations (HCCO, the key black political group) from going to liberal Don Yarborough in the 1962 Democratic gubernatorial primary, Jordan went to bat for him. Some members of the HCCO still remember her speech that day, although the Connally blacks did succeed in blocking Yarborough's endorsement. By then she was running on her own. She borrowed money for her filing fee and persuaded Al Wickliff (who had himself run unsuccessfully for the Legislature and who had managed Mrs. Charles White's successful campaign to be the first black on the school board) to be her campaign manager. The only problem was that blacks made up less than 20 per cent of Houston's electorate, and all state representatives had to run countywide. White ran for reelection that same year, got 34 per cent of the white vote, and won with a plurality; Jordan got 23 per cent of the white vote and came in third.

As she took stock of her defeat, in a subtle but significant way, she crossed the Rubicon, from black politician to politician. Principles weren't worth much if you had no power. A black might win election to the Houston School Board, but its politics were byzantine and unrelated to most everything else. But it seemed unlikely that a black, strictly with liberal support, could win a countywide race. What Barbara Jordan had to do, in practical political terms, was expand her base. She had to keep her original black and liberal allies, but she had to find more. She decided to leave the friendly womb of liberal, black Houston and venture forth into the heartland of her opposition. In her own words: ''It was clear then that if I was to win . . . I had to persuade the monied and politically influential interests either to support me or to remain neutral.'' In 1964 she increased her white vote by 50 per cent, but that, along with her now customary 97 per cent of the black vote, was still not enough. And, in the wake of her second defeat, Governor John Connally vetoed her nomination to serve on the State Democratic Executive Committee, on the grounds it wasn't ready for a black.

And so, her efforts to court the establishment had been unsuccessful; her law practice was barely off the ground because of her political efforts; and ahead seemed to lie only an endless series of losing campaigns. Barbara Jordan contemplated her future. Again, in her words: "I considered abandoning the dream of a public career in Texas and moving to some section of the country where a black woman candidate was less likely to be considered a novelty. I didn't *want* to do this. I am a Texan; my roots are in Texas. To leave would be a cop-out. So I stayed." This story, of course, has a fairy tale ending. The next year the Voting Rights Act extended the franchise, and the "one man one vote" Supreme Court decisions led to the equalization in population of legislative districts. And there, in the twinkling of an eye, was not only 25 per cent more registered black voters, but also a brand-new Texas Senate district almost 50 per cent black. Barbara Jordan had been out front first, she had worked hard, and that seat was *hers*.

She won 66 per cent of the vote in the primary (including 34 per cent of the white vote) and brushed aside a token Republican opponent to become the first black to serve in the Texas Senate since 1882. When she was elected, the civil rights movement was splintering into separatists, militants, and moderates. The vestiges of segregation were everywhere. Yet this first black state senator had not a single item in her platform designed specifically to benefit blacks. She came out for traditional bread-and-butter liberal and union issues like the minimum wage, fair labor practices, and better teacher salaries. She also strongly supported limits on oyster dredging, and played political expediency with welfare, calling for its expansion on the one hand and getting cheats off the welfare rolls on the other. It was a solid, traditional political platform. It was also a pale reflection of her extraordinary rhetoric and presence. Because of her charisma, she led people to expect that she would set things right, and they didn't have oyster dredging in mind.

But black issues did not go without their champion in 1966. A young black businessman named Curtis Graves was elected to the Texas House of Representatives the same year. Graves was a vocal black activist who had been arrested in a Houston sit-in demonstration in 1961. When Graves got to the Legislature, he made clear he was a black man interested in black issues, and woe betide white racists. As the sixties continued to unfold, Graves started talking of "honkies" and the "oppressors"; he began building a coalition with the New Left and with hippies; he called Viet Nam a racist war. The contrast with Jordan could not have been more direct. Graves was passionate and impulsive, she was aloof and calculating; he was angry, she was conciliatory; he made whites feel personally guilty for the sins of segregation, she emphasized common problems; he would have nothing to do with the establishment, she courted it. While he made herculean efforts to become an effective day-to-day politician, Graves' real ambition was to make the transition from civil rights activist to politician with principles intact: same strategy, different tactics.

Looking back from the perspective of the mid-seventies, it seems obvious that Jordan's approach made more sense. At the time, however, it was not so clear. The changes most affecting the lives of blacks were being inspired by black activists, not black politicians. These blacks—mainly students and young ministers—were the new leaders of black Houston. They could point to concrete accomplishment; blacks who worked within the system came back with their hands empty. Quiet voices didn't get action. Loud voices did. In 1960, the year after Jordan returned from Boston,

the sit-ins began, and continued until 1962, the year she made her first race for the Legislature; lunch counters were integrated, and some firms began hiring black employees. Three years later, the focus switched to the slow pace of school desegregation. Ten thousand blacks led by Reverend Bill Lawson marched on the school board; there was a school boycott. Black Houston seemed up in arms.

Through this epic period in black Houston's history Barbara Jordan ran for office. She was a member of the NAACP, the most conservative civil rights organization. She took part in no sit-ins, marched in no demonstrations, carried no signs. And although there were fewer than 30 black lawyers in town, she did not volunteer to defend any of the jailed protesters. In spite of the practical effects of the attacks on the system, she never wavered in her burning desire to find a place in it. And as the sixties wore on, she attacked black power and made no bones about her intentions to continue working with the white establishment. For someone of her age and ambition, this behavior might well have earned the epithet Uncle Tom. But it did not, in part because of the sheer power of her rhetoric, but also because as a woman and lawyer she was not expected to be a fighter. Just as her childhood friends had accepted her uniqueness ten years before, so the leading civil rights leaders of black Houston—some her former TSU classmates—accepted her uniqueness in the sixties. She was "just Barbara," and she had her own role to play.

It was not a "black" role. Barbara Jordan can count votes; to achieve power she would have to expand, not jeopardize, her white support. The "black" issue she has most consistently fought for is voting rights. When she filed in the State Senate race she brought along the black dentist whose law suit in 1944 had won blacks the right to vote in the Democratic primary. She made a rare display of calling in her political chips to prevent the Texas Senate from considering a bill to restrict the franchise by compounding the difficulties of voter registration. She took the same risk in Congress when she went against both the Texas establishment and the congressional black establishment—the two normal sources of her strength—in her successful effort to expand certain provisions of the Voting Rights Act to cover Texas. The blacks were against expansion on the grounds it would jeopardize the Act being renewed for the South; in this case, contrary to the accepted stereotype, they were timid and she was bold. She considers the Voting Rights expansion her most significant legislative accomplishment. The franchise is her sort of issue; its exercise is decorous, restrained, impersonal—but effective. It is the cornerstone of the system she believes in. She wasn't raised to rebel or to make a scene; she didn't learn that at home, and she didn't learn it at Wheatley. And, as far as she knew, most blacks were as uncomfortable with those methods as she was. But the militants paved the way for her. They made her seem moderate, respectable, and safe. As Everett Collier of the *Houston Chronicle* says, "Barbara worked to prevent any violence or radicalism that would cause trouble." And there could be no more pure political tightrope artistry than the ability to make a Collier think she is keeping the blacks in line, while making a Reverend Lawson think she is manipulating the establishment.

"The civil rights movement," says Lawson, the leader of the school boycott, "brought to prominence a different sort of person than Barbara. The civil rights leaders were angry, passionate, impulsive people who drew attention to an ancient wrong in a dramatic way. In the language of the Olympics, they were the dash men; for the long haul you need distance runners. Barbara is a distance runner. It's simply not her style to get out with a sign, or to be disruptive. It is no accident that the impulsive and eloquent voices of the civil rights movement did not make the transition to positions of power and responsibility. Those sorts of positions belong to people like Barbara, people with a purpose but also with the ability to hold their own in political infighting with the establishment's best.''

And so, when the clash between Graves and Jordan came in 1972, it would be Jordan who would win. After the census of 1970, Houston was redistricted; a new congressional district, the 18th, was drawn for Jordan. She had, however, left Graves the impression he would get her senate district when she moved up. Instead, it was cannibalized into other districts, making it virtually impossible for a black to win. Graves held her responsible for losing it. It was the last straw in what he took to be a long string of compromises and deals with the establishment. He decided to oppose her for Congress. Jordan had worked hard on labor issues, and had the unions sewed up. She also had the financial backing of the Houston establishment. Graves was the underdog; labor unions threw him out of endorsement meetings, he had no money, his old friends didn't seem to mind that the richest blacks and whites were backing Jordan—her money men were old black conservative Mack Hannah and white Houston booster Gail Whitcomb. Those were the sort of people Graves and his allies had always fought, but his allies seemed to be slipping away. The hippies and the New Left radicals he had courted were little help.

Graves then did the only thing he could: he attacked. He called Jordan a ''tool'' and raged about ''an open attempt to buy the 18th district'' as she sat tight-lipped on the same platform. This was his case, which has been the standard case against Jordan: ''The congressman from this new district must be someone who owes his allegiance to the people who are in the district and not to the corrupt politicians who have brought our state to shame and ridicule. If you are looking for someone who goes along to get along, one who plays politics with your lives, one who is long on speaking but short on delivering services, then don't vote for Curtis Graves.'' As his position became more desperate, some of his supporters began spreading rumors about Jordan's sex life. It was a tough campaign, an unprecedented battle between two prominent black politicians. Jordan never attacked Graves, and simply repeated that the issue was ''who can get things done, who is more effective.'' She received 80 per cent of the vote. Graves got 13 per cent, and left Texas for good.

Why did she win? There are several answers, but the most important is she was simply a better politician. She had carried water for key supporters like labor unions, she had gathered new supporters among the Houston establishment, and she had protected her base in the black community by appealing to its abiding conservative instincts. Although Graves played an important role in the protest movements of the sixties, he didn't know, as another black politician said, ''when it was time to put his dashiki in the closet, stop raising hell, and start getting things done.'' The politician with a low civil rights profile beat the militant. In the words of Reverend Lawson, who is also a friend of

Graves: ''She had a vision back in the sixties. Most of us couldn't see it. She saw beyond conflict to the enduring institutions, and she saw that most people, even black people, wanted to believe in them, if only they could be made to work. Within those institutions she saw that people like Sam Rayburn and Lyndon Johnson got more done. So she wed her philosophy and purpose to their practical skills. But she kept her purpose. The rest of the civil rights movement is far behind her in making that transition.''

# THE HEIR OF LBJ

The transition from the civil rights movement to Johnson-Rayburn politician was actually not that difficult a transition for Barbara Jordan to make. She had never really been in the civil rights movement. She had always, from her days at TSU, been in politics. Johnson-Rayburn politics were the politics of the bigtime campus operator writ large, and the first opportunity Jordan had to practice them since her student days was when she arrived in the Texas Senate in 1967. As a freshman, she had to earn the support—in student terms—of the seniors. ''The Texas Senate was touted as the state's most exclusive club,'' she wrote in *Atlantic Monthly*. ''To be effective I had to get inside the club, not just inside the chamber. I singled out the most influential and powerful members and determined to gain their respect.'' Barbara Jordan was the perfect freshman to integrate the school: she was bright, she did her homework, she had great talent; she also loved the institution, gave deference to its elders, and made them feel that it—and they—were the most important things in her life.

Since no black face had been seen in the Senate chamber since 1882, and since that body had its share of unreconstructed Southerners, there still was a certain period of adjustment. Back then it was traditional for Claude Wild, Sr., the Humble Oil lobbyist, to give a little dinner dance for the Senate before the session began. Wild thought he had a bit of a problem, so he called Don Kennard, a liberal senator from Fort Worth who was rumored to know a few blacks personally. Kennard tells the story: ''Don,'' Wild said, ''I've got a little dilemma with Senator Jordan.'' ''What's that?'' Kennard asked. ''Well, it's about [late Dallas Senator George] Parkhouse and Mrs. Parkhouse, not to mention some others. What if Senator Jordan brings along a big black man from Houston? How will everybody react? What if her date tries to dance with Mrs. Parkhouse? What then?''

''They were breaking new ground, and no one knew what would happen,'' Kennard recalls. ''So my wife and I invited Barbara to go to the dinner with us. Within three minutes after she arrived she had charmed everyone and was the center of the stage. Just by being so gracious and charming she literally compelled even the biggest racists to be gracious and charming too. It started that night, really. She obviously respected them and didn't make them feel evil or guilty. And they had never been confronted with an intelligent, imposing, witty black person before; so they warmed to her. I know it sounds silly looking at it all from ten years later. But those were different times. She was the first, and she ended up beating all of us at our game.''

The game, of course, was politics. Jordan studied the Senate's procedure so closely that within weeks she was recognized as one of its leading parliamentarians, not above using, as she puts it, "the trickers' tricks." Among politicians political skill is respected apart from ideology, and Jordan quickly demonstrated that she had great technical skills. She only spoke when she knew what she wanted, she didn't preach or harangue, she concentrated on a few subjects and became the Senate expert on them. She never embarrassed a fellow senator; she always gave the impression she understood his own political situation and left him room for self-respect. She shattered stereotypes about blacks: to racists she wasn't shiftless and dumb and she didn't smell bad; to guilt-ridden liberals, who believed that all blacks would be liberal, pure-of-heart, and anti-establishment, she proved to be a hard-nosed politician who gave no hint she had suffered under segregation.

She also shrewdly combined her exacting and aloof sense of dignity with warm good humor. Since it softens the abrasiveness of conflict, humor is among the most valuable political skills. Few politicians appreciate a somber ideologue, even if he is on their side. Jordan came to the Senate as a female and a black, an inevitable damper for the club's easy sexual and racial humor. It didn't work out that way. "There have always been jokes told on the floor of the Senate," Kennard recalls. "Sexual, racial, good taste, bad taste. No one would have ever thought of including Mrs. Colson [a previous female senator]; no one would have ever thought of *not* including Barbara. She had a superb sense of humor and could even top old Parkhouse when she wanted to. We'd clean it up a little bit for her, because she just required by God respect. I'm sure the antics of the Senate frustrated her, seemed too frivolous. But she never let on. She put up with it, participated in it, and she used it." (Extemporaneous political humor doesn't always translate very well, but here are two examples: Senator Chet Brooks, addressing Jordan: "Senator, the only thing missing in this portrait is your voice; without your voice, it just isn't you." Jordan, in reply: "Senator, these walls have been needing a touch of color, and when my painting hangs amid the august people on the walls of this chamber, believe me, it's gonna talk." Reporter: "Senator Jordan, congratulations on your election to Congress." Jordan: "Thank you, but that's premature. I still have a Republican opponent in the fall, but since none of you seem to know who he is, I'm not about to tell you his name.") She was, in short, one of the boys. She would joke with them, drink with them, stay up late, play the guitar and sing songs with them. But there was something at the center she always held back. In both her personal and her political life, there was no way to assume you knew her, or to take her for granted.

"Even though Barbara was with us on almost every crucial issue," said one liberal senator, "somehow you never could *assume* she would be. If you had a real good bill, you know, that did everything right, that had in it all the sort of things she had been supporting, you still couldn't just check off her vote on your scorecard. You had to go see her, reason with her, make her understand what you wanted to do. The same was true of her personal contacts. While she had the easy banter and could be one of the boys, few politicians felt they really knew her. If they tried to get too close, she would cut them off cold. Land Commissioner Bob Armstrong recalls one occasion, when he was in the Legislature: "It was one of those parties Charlie Wilson used to give. Barbara was there, and she and I stayed up almost all night—laughing, joking, telling stories, playing the guitar, and singing songs. It was one of the happiest nights I've spent. I really felt I knew her—she was like my sister. The next day or so I ran into her in the Capitol and went rushing up, and—nothing. She was polite, but everything I thought was there between us just wasn't. I don't regret that experience we had together. I was just surprised."

Now some politicians are committed people, as are some friends. Many committed Texas liberals and conservatives believe that if someone is against you on one issue of principle, then he is automatically against you on all issues of principle; that he is, in short, either a friend or an enemy. If a man is your enemy on civil rights, so this sort of absolutist political approach goes, then he will be your enemy on environmental matters, gun control, education, taxation, labor issues. Jordan's, however, was not a seamless fabric of political ideology. She approached one at a time, and she took her allies where she found them.

In her three regular sessions she introduced more than 150 bills and resolutions, about half of which were the apolitical meat and potatoes of legislation, from creating a new court and establishing a new medical school, to closing off the street that ran through TSU and setting safety standards for people who go into manholes. But the rest were solidly liberal: extending the minimum wage to cover non-unionized farmworkers and domestics; a fair labor practices act; pollution control; a whole range of workmen's compensation acts (her specialty); equal rights and anti-discrimination. She fought for liquor by the drink and against extending the sales tax. But she insisted on not being taken for granted, and she had the charisma to make that insistence stick. She always ended up in the corral, but damned if she didn't have to be rounded up every time.

In the Senate, then, her political techniques were the same ones she would later perfect in Congress: deference to leadership, loyalty to the institution, hard work, humor, an unwillingness to be typecast, all wrapped up in the power and mystery of her personality and topped off with that old standby, her voice—which could either create an easy intimacy or intimidate, seemingly at will. At the end of her first session, her colleagues unanimously passed an unprecedented resolution expressing the Senate's "warmest regard and affection. . . . She has earned the esteem and respect of her fellow citizens by the dignified manner in which she conducts herself . . . and because of her sincerity, her genuine concern for others, and her forceful speaking ability, she has been a credit to her state as well as her race." The 30 men then rose and gave her two standing ovations. To call a militant like Curtis Graves a "credit to his race" in the emotion-charged years of the late sixties would have been patronizing and unthinkable; he would have been outraged. Barbara Jordan was pleased. "I have not been treated with any more respect by any group of men anywhere," she said, apparently unambiguously; when she left in 1972 she said, "Nothing that can happen in my lifetime will equal the memories I have of my years of service in this chamber."

The dazzling show she was putting on for her fellow senators caught the eye of the protean godfather of Texas politics, Lyndon Johnson. It was not a good time for the president. The prodigious outpouring of Great Society and civil rights programs was behind him, and the Viet Nam War, no matter how much he wheeled and dealed and plotted and planned, steadily kept pulling him beneath the political waves. His protégé in Texas, John Connally, didn't care about the Great Society and in fact had done some impressive foot dragging on antipoverty programs and civil rights. This pained Johnson deeply. To LBJ, these programs were more than just legislative accomplishments; they were his legacy, they were what would go beside his name in the history books. All the political operating in the world wasn't worth a damn if you didn't do something with it. So far as Johnson could tell, both Connally and his protégé Ben Barnes had inherited his skills but none of his heart.

Barbara Jordan was different. She had many of the qualities Johnson admired: she had a deep respect for legislative bodies and the legislative process, she was uncomfortable with ideologues, and she had great humor and political skills. She admired and recognized what a political accomplishment the Great Society programs were, how much arm twisting and cajoling and convincing and political chips they had used up. But she also knew what they meant to real people. She told him the Voting Rights Act had been crucial in getting her elected. His Texas cronies didn't appreciate that, and other prominent blacks didn't appreciate what he had done either—they just kept yelling "More! More! More!" or encouraging separatism, riots, God knows what. When black riots swept Washington and other cities after the assassination of Martin Luther King, Johnson took it personally. "Don't they realize what I've done for them?" he would ask. Barbara Jordan realized what he had done, and told him so. After he had renounced his reelection campaign because of the war, she went to the 1968 Democratic Convention in Chicago, announced she would support him over anyone should he change his mind and openly fought to keep the Texas delegation solidly behind the plank endorsing LBJ's Viet Nam policy. In the King Lear fantasies of his final year, with John Connally a Republican, Barnes' political career in ruins, and Nixon dismantling the Great Society, she was the one child who never wavered, who kept his legacy and promised to carry it on. When he died, she said simply, "He was my political mentor and my friend. I loved him and I shall miss him."

LBJ was a great help to her. He opened establishment doors, attended her fund raisers, touted her to influential politicians and businessmen, helped get her a seat on the Judiciary Committee when she went to Congress. John Connally, however, was another story. She had spoken passionately against his gubernatorial campaign in 1962; he had vetoed her for a place on the State Democratic Executive Committee in 1964. But beyond those earlier clashes was a fierce clash of egos. Connally maddened Jordan by simply ignoring her. She was the star attraction of the 1967 Senate, but he acted as if she didn't exist. They both had LBJ's backroom magic, but Connally had Lyndon's poorboy materialism and she had Lyndon's New Deal heart. Blended together, they made a pretty good LBJ. But like half-siblings, she and Connally were fated to clash.

When Connally led the Texas delegation to the Democratic Convention in 1968, Jordan announced from the beginning that she would not support him as a favorite son. She was for Humphrey. Then Connally changed his mind and wanted to lead the delegation into the Humphrey camp. Jordan then changed *her* mind and wouldn't go along (she

did end up supporting Humphrey). Whatever Connally wanted, she opposed. In 1972, when one of Connally's key political operatives, UT Regents Chairman Frank Erwin, Jr., sent her a $1000 campaign contribution as a peace offering, she sent it back. However, she did testify as a character witness at Connally's bribery trial, for some or all of these reasons: because it put the Houston establishment even deeper in her debt; because beneath the deepest of differences politicians share a basic mutual protection society so far as prison is concerned; and because—less likely—as a lawyer she believed her testimony would help him get a fair trial. At the trial, she testified, "As far as I know from my personal experience, he has a good reputation for honesty." When asked if she had any political differences with Connally, she replied, "I have had spectacular . . . ." At that point the prosecution objected, and she was not allowed to finish. Full circle on irony: he helped keep her off the State Democratic Executive Committee in 1964; she helped keep him out of prison in 1975.

From LBJ to Connally the line of succession went, until Jordan came along, to Ben Barnes. Barnes was a real comer, the major star—Jordan had a supporting role then—of late sixties Texas politics. He was the youngest Speaker ever of the Texas House of Representatives, and in 1968, when he was 30, he was elected lieutenant governor by carrying *every* county in Texas. Barnes and Jordan were both natural politicians, and they got along well. They understood each other. Jordan knew what Barnes was up to, and he knew that while she was in the full flights of her oratory on the Senate floor he could catch her eye from the podium, wink, and she would wink back. They almost never agreed on issues, but they had one thing in common: towering ambition. In the spring of 1971, he helped her carve out a congressional seat for herself; she gave him the impression she would support him for governor. She made it, he didn't.

# THE REVENGE OF AUNT JEMIMA

The election of Barbara Jordan to Congress in 1972 continued an undeniable personal achievement. She had come home from the East at 23, a black lawyer with few prospects in a segregated society. She was returning to the East at 36, a U.S. Representative and the protégée of the former president of the United States. Her traditional approach to politics had been overwhelmingly vindicated against a black militant. Her ambition, her intelligence, her sense of personal destiny, her voice, and her charisma—combined with her shrewd political skills and her penchant for hard work—would make the Congress her personal national stage. But while Jordan has tirelessly sought office, she has not so obviously sought acclaim. She has consistently gone after power, but recognition came to her. She worked hard to get where she is, but she became a celebrity almost effortlessly. Before taking a final look at her personal and political achievements, the real and symbolic sources of her national appeal, and the reasons she seems to strike such a deep chord in America, it would be wise to reconsider just how she got there.

Barbara Jordan brushes aside high-flown descriptions of her symbolic significance and insists she is just "a practical politician." In judging politicians, means are often as important as ends: how a politician reaches his goals can be as important as the goals themselves. Jordan's means have been the classic politics of her mentor, Lyndon Johnson; some of her liberal critics call her "a black LBJ." Those politics can be characterized in many ways, but above all they are the art of the possible: the practical craft of knowing how things work, what buttons to push, who has power and who doesn't. Such a politician is popularly known as "someone who can get things done." The reduction of politics to the level of the practical makes good, hard-nosed sense in most cases; there are times, however, when it backfires.

Being practical means avoiding unnecessary risks. The line between political prudence and political timidity is very thin; the danger lies in settling for less than you might have gained had you fought harder. When Barbara Jordan used good old political horse trading to create a congressional seat she could win, somehow her old Senate seat got lost in the process. "Either that was part of the deal with Barnes or she just felt she had to give something up to get something, but it wasn't necessary," recalls a former Senate colleague. "If she had used her muscle to keep the Senate seat for blacks, she could have had both. They would have cratered. That's exactly the sort of thing they are most afraid of her about. But she didn't make a peep." "It just wasn't in the game plan," says Jordan. Safe, practical politics. The result: while each state senator represents about 400,000 people, there is no black state senator for Houston's 350,000 blacks, which is the rough equivalent of dividing up Fort Worth to be represented by Dallas, Abilene, and Wichita Falls.

Being practical also means knowing where the power is and cultivating it. The trap here is confusing the trappings of power for power itself. When Jordan let Barnes believe she would support him for governor, she confused his power in the state Capitol, which was near absolute, with his power in the state, which had dissipated in the wake of the Sharpstown scandal. (Barnes seemed "clean," but he was then the state's most prominent wheeler-dealer politician, and the political mood was "throw the rascals out.") Both conservative and liberal political outsiders smelled blood. Frances Farenthold was the liberal candidate for governor. To Jordan, Farenthold must have seemed a political lightweight: she was only a state representative, she didn't understand how practical power worked, she was, in short, yet another quixotic, maverick liberal doomed to defeat. But when Jordan went to the Harris County Democrats endorsement caucus, she got a surprise. It was a heated meeting. The liberals were disillusioned with Jordan. They wanted to know where *she* stood on the governor's race; they wouldn't stay neutral in her congressional race with Graves unless she endorsed Farenthold. For an excruciating moment, the chickens were home to roost. Then Jordan made her choice: without naming Farenthold, she pledged to support the candidate of the Harris County Democrats. No one knows what she told Barnes, who got 17 per cent of the vote and came in third. Farenthold made the runoff, losing finally to Dolph Briscoe, another outsider.

Being practical means playing the game with the people in power. In the intraparty squabbles of Texas Democrats, Jordan customarily comes down on the side of the "ins," which means the conservatives. "Party issues are power is-sues," says one committed liberal. "Barbara's devotion to the conservatives means she keeps the party's power on the side of the people who oppose her legislative goals. She's been vice-chairman of the State Democratic Executive Committee for four years, and as far as I know she's never attended a meeting. That means blacks and liberals really have *no* voice, which is how the conservatives want it. She doesn't seem to care that her inaction means important issues like voter registration and party finances are in the hands of conservatives. In party politics, she is truly a token. They use her, and she gets nothing for blacks or liberals in return."

Being practical is making the most of what you've got. The most immediately obvious thing Jordan has is being black. What should have been an obstacle she has turned into an asset. One longtime liberal recalls that no one even thought to scrutinize Jordan's intentions or character when she first became active in liberal politics. "I had no idea she would turn out an establishment Democrat," he groused. "Back then we didn't question the motives of blacks. It didn't occur to us that one of them might be using us for her own ambitions. It sounds naive, but then we thought, well, blacks were better, more pure and honest, than white politicians, that they had a cause bigger than themselves. If she had been white, we would have seen her as just another ambitious politician." The source of white admiration for Barbara Jordan, this theory goes, is akin to the admiration white audiences had for an entertainer like Al Hibbler, a blind black pianist. Hibbler was good, but the applause was out of proportion to his performance, because white people were so proud of him for overcoming his handicaps. "Barbara makes it easy for mossbacks to like her," says one white political reporter. "They get buddy-buddy with her and in one fell swoop they can convince themselves they aren't sexist or racist." Admiring Barbara Jordan, in other words, solves the problem of how to deal with all these blacks and women clamoring for recognition. "Black politicians who try to follow Barbara's footsteps are doomed to failure," says one black politician who has tried. "The establishment only needs one black to be cozy with, and she's it."

Being practical also means trading off today's issues for power tomorrow. It means, for example, going with the establishment on energy to get their support on other issues. A better example, however, was Jordan's support for the plank in the 1968 Democratic platform praising President Johnson's Viet Nam policy. As early as 1966 Jordan had been opposed to the Viet Nam War, but in Chicago she rigorously defended it. Why? Here's what she told the *Wall Street Journal*: "That plank probably resulted in further killing and dying, but I felt it was important for Texans to be supportive of their man." These values—that supporting "their man" is more important than killing and dying—are odious. They are an extreme example of how the Rayburn-Johnson practical politics can function as moral blinders, blocking out conscience by political expediency. These values of "Texans supporting their man" may well also have contributed to her decision to testify for John Connally.

Now no one seriously wants politicians to be "impractical," and no doubt subjecting the careers of other ambitious politicians to similar scrutiny would yield at least as many, and probably more, lapses, missteps, errors in judgment. Such performance is disturbing in Jordan's case, however, because in spite of her protestation that she is only a politician, she is universally thought to stand for something more. In her behalf, her supporters say, as Reverend Lawson did, that she *has* tied Rayburn-Johnson techniques to higher purpose. Further testimony comes from black State Representative Mickey Leland, whose Houston district includes Jordan's home: "Barbara uses the system for blacks; it doesn't use her." But Andrew Jefferson says it best: "Barbara will listen to the establishment about their problems, and she'll take the time to understand divestiture and the natural gas shortage. She won't oppose them just because they are the establishment. But when it comes down to some long-standing demand, some long-standing principle, she can be counted on to help the establishment understand it just as she tried to understand their energy problems. She gets her leverage that way, and she's not afraid to use it."

The central dilemma about Barbara Jordan is that while almost everyone *believes* she has this central core beyond politics, this ultimate devotion to long-standing principles, no one really knows what it is. No one can point to many long-standing principles she has made the establishment recognize. Given her constituency, she should be expected to vote liberal, and she does: she rolls up 80, 90, 100 per cent scores on all the tallies kept by black, liberal, feminist, and environmentalist groups. She votes virtually down the line with the Black Caucus on black issues, although she will occasionally oppose them on energy. In Texas she did work for the minimum wage, workmen's compensation, fair labor practice, antidiscrimination. In Washington she passed the Voting Rights Act expansion and extension. But these voting records and these legislative accomplishments are simply straight liberal politics; they are not the core. The remark is, "Well, they're part of it, but they're not *it*."

What "it" is, is of course the mystery. The same aura that surrounded her as a young girl surrounds her as a mature politician. That elusive quality of being beyond definition, of being "just Barbara," defies the analysis of skeptical adult observers just as it defied the analysis of teenagers. More than anything else, this accepted inevitability of her greatness is her biggest asset. "Barbara has that rare mental capacity to have a master plan for her life, a sense of high destiny," says Reverend Lawson. "Gandhi had that. Martin Luther King had that. John Kennedy I believe had that. When you have it, other people can sense it. It's both a knowledge of how much only you can do and how little time you have to live to do it in. I suspect it's what makes her work so hard, drive herself so much. It's a destiny not so much for herself, but for a people; not black people, but a whole coalition of suffering, yearning people. I can't define it, and she might not be able to, but I am sure she understands what it is."

One of the most important reasons she inspires such hope is because she is a Southerner, and understands as well as anyone the significance of the New South. While she may rigorously avoid being typecast as a black, female, or liberal politician, she takes pains to insist she is a Texan and a Southern one. "I am a Texan," she wrote. "My roots are there . . . 'Texan' frequently evokes images of conservatism, oil, gas, racism, callousness. In my judgment, the myths should be debunked, or at the least, should include

the prevalent strains of reasonableness, compassion, and decency." Her friends say she is really only comfortable with Southerners, including blacks like Georgia's Andrew Young but also some of the most reactionary members of Congress. Jordan says she has a "very good relationship with old, establishment white conservatives. Maybe I have a natural affinity for Southerners because I am a Southerner." Part of the reason, of course, is her application of the same charm, deference, and humor she used on the same sorts of men in the Texas Senate.

Barbara Jordan's rapport with white Southerners is also testament to the basic political change in the South since the Voting Rights Act of 1965. Representative Andrew Young of Georgia, the influential Atlanta black who has thrown in his chips with Jimmy Carter, describes the process: "It used to be Southern politics was just 'nigger' politics, who would 'outnigger' the other—then you registered 10 to 15 per cent in the community and folks would start saying 'nigra' and then you get 35 to 40 per cent registered and it's amazing how quickly they learned to say 'neegrow' and now that we've got 50, 60, 70 per cent of the black votes registered in the South, everybody's proud to be associated with their black brothers and sisters." That is the language Jordan understands. Although blacks are only 20 per cent of the voting-age population of the South, that still makes them the largest cohesive voting bloc, except on those increasingly rare occasions when whites vote together. It is not rare for candidates to get more than 90 per cent of the black vote; in political arithmetic, that means with only 40 per cent of the white vote the election is won. In urban areas where blacks are more than 20 per cent, the arithmetic is even better. The result is a Fred Hofheinz or a Jimmy Carter, a Barbara Jordan or an Andrew Young.

But beyond politics, back in the nooks and crannies of a society's most basic psyche, the South has made an even more fundamental change. Blacks now openly talk about preferring the South to the North, of feeling a greater trust and understanding for their fellow white Southerners than for even the most bleeding-heart Northern liberal. Black support for Jimmy Carter is of course one manifestation of that trust, but it goes deeper. Black voices make this point best. This is Eddie Bernice Johnson, a black state legislator from Dallas: "In the North, racism has had a facade, a pretense that it didn't exist. People wanted to think that nothing was wrong, that everything was okay and the problem was somewhere else. They didn't want to admit they had it too, and if you don't admit the problem, you can't deal with it. In the South whites are trying to deal with it; the ones that have dealt with it have been through something, and you can generally trust them down the line." And Reverend Lawson: "The South has always depended on the power that brings the harvest and the seasons, something bigger than one's self and one's strivings. That condition reminds us of our common humanity beneath the shadow of larger forces; it breeds a basic compassion and a basic religiosity, an esteem for others even when you don't particularly like them. In addition, white families in the South have always depended on blacks. Black mammies raised their children and taught them manners, black men tilled their cotton and built their houses. Martin Luther King called it a web of mutuality, a binding of the two races together. That isn't true in the North; the black is a newcomer there, and by and large he isn't wanted. Even

George Wallace is somehow more aware of the humanity of blacks than is the average white in Grosse Point.''

The symbolic dimension of Barbara Jordan's achievement is to link the troubled past with a hopeful future, to bridge from a segregated society to an unsegregated one. She has been called Aunt Jemima by both her friends and her enemies, and, although she doesn't like it, the metaphor is apt. In appearance she conjures up the common memories of a culture—she is every black maid, black cook, black mammy. She comes to us direct from *Gone with the Wind* or *Uncle Tom's Cabin*, an enduring stereotype of the black women who lived closest with whites, who sustained the web of mutuality. The awesomeness of her presence is rooted in her explicit destruction of that image, as if every black mammy and Aunt Jemima had risen up with their rolling pins to take over the world.

The final mystery about Barbara Jordan is, what next? One of 435 United States Representatives can only do so much, no matter how great her political skills or symbolic import. Carter had her on his list of vice-presidential possibilities (and rejected her, Carter sources say, not because she was black but because, like Carter, she was from the South), and she is mentioned as a possible attorney general or Supreme Court justice should Carter win. For her part, she considers the Supreme Court a place to retire to. The U.S. Senate? Perhaps. Four years ago she dismissed the idea with incredulity: ''Barbara Jordan run for senator? A black woman run for the U.S. Senate in Texas?'' Today she knows those old barriers are falling and is now open to the possibility, perhaps against John Tower in 1978. But ultimately, as one friend says, ''all she really wants to do is be president.'' And brothers, that *will* be the day.

*—October 1976*

# LIVING WITH LAWS AND OUTLAWS

In the early days Texas had no law, and a good many of its most distinguished citizens weren't too pleased when law arrived. A hundred and fifty or so years later, some Texans still follow that dubious tradition. For every Leon Jaworski, there's a Fred Carrasco, the murderous chieftain of a vast dope empire who became a folk figure after barricading himself and his hostages in the library at Huntsville prison. Gregory Curtis' "The Strange Power of Fred Carrasco" not only chronicled Carrasco's career in crime, but it also illustrated how thin was the dividing line between Carrasco and the men who tried to bring him to justice. Another Curtis story in this section is "The Girl, the Con Man, and the Massage Parlor King," a comprehensive account of a murder so mundane in its venality, so heartbreaking in its result, and so intriguing in its investigation that it transcends mere crime writing.

Of the detectives who track down criminals none is more interesting than a scholarly doctor who solves cases with a scalpel. "Ah, Sweet Mystery of Death" is Al Reinert's profile of Joseph Jachimczyk, the Harris County coroner who proved Texas' first known case of arsenic poisoning. But no detective anywhere can hold a candle to Jay J. Armes, the dead-end kid who overcame a childhood accident to become, in his words, one of the greatest detectives of all time. Gary Cartwright went to Armes' headquarters in El Paso to write a glowing account of his exploits; his story, "Is Jay J. Armes for Real?" didn't exactly turn out that way.

The true spirit of early Texas really shines through best in "Busting out of Mexico," Jan Reid's account of the daring raid three Texans mounted to free American prisoners from the Piedras Negras jail. Why did they do it? For a little money that barely covered expenses, but also, because it was there. Like the first Texans, that was just how they were.

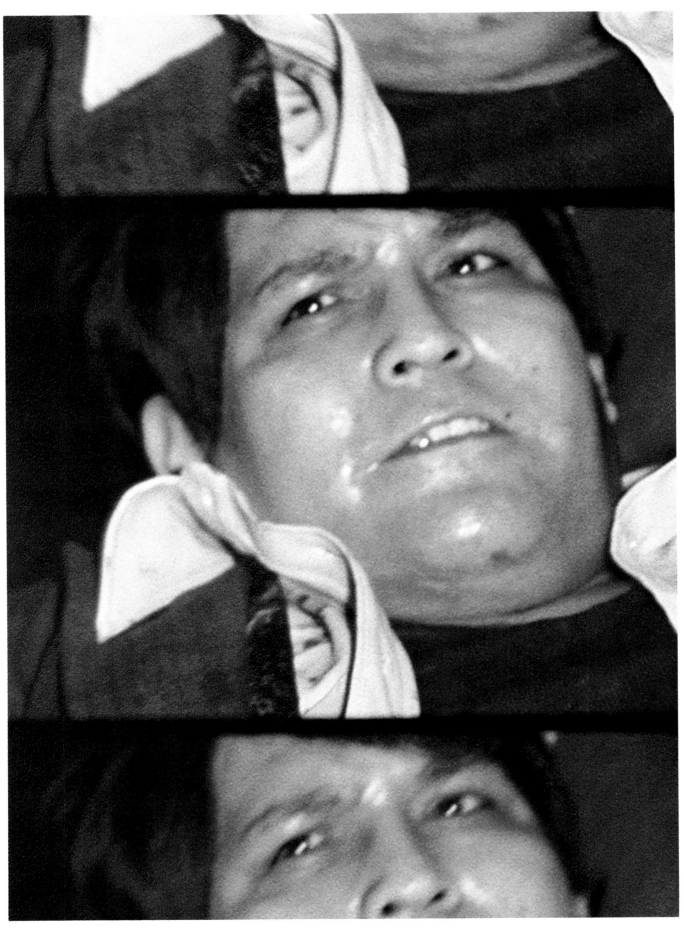

Fred Carrasco. *Film courtesy of KENS-TV, San Antonio*

# THE STRANGE POWER OF FRED CARRASCO

## by Gregory Curtis

*The evil men do lives after them, and in unexpected places.*

About noon on the day after Fred Carrasco seized ten hostages and garrisoned himself in the library of the Huntsville prison unit known as The Walls, a lean and lighthaired male citizen, 29 years old, left Austin for the San Antonio offices of James Gillespie, Carrasco's lawyer. The latest news across the AP wire was that Carrasco had demanded additional weapons and body armor by three o'clock or he would kill his hostages. The citizen had reason to believe that phone contact might be made between Gillespie in his San Antonio office, Governor Dolph Briscoe in his Austin office, and Carrasco in the prison library. The citizen wanted to sit in Gillespie's office and listen during these calls.

He left for San Antonio with some reluctance but was spurred on by something more than idle curiosity. Last March, after Carrasco had been sent to Huntsville, the citizen had spent a long month running around San Antonio trying to piece together the story of Fred's life. The project was a grim one. Fred had left a bloody trail from San Antonio to Nuevo Laredo to Guadalajara and back to San Antonio again. Estimates about the number of men Fred had either killed or ordered killed ranged from a high of 57 to a *low* of 40. His first was when he was eighteen; a young girl lured a man out of a San Antonio dance hall and Fred shot him. Antonio de la Garza, who would later be a lieutenant in Fred's heroin smuggling operations, witnessed the killing. That was in 1958. In September of 1971, Fred had de la Garza killed. He chose another lieutenant, Pete Guzman, for the job. Guzman not only killed de la Garza but also mutilated his pregnant wife. About a year later, after Guzman had started bragging that Fred was now taking orders from him, he was found in a ditch in Mexico dead from 45 bullet wounds. Many of Fred's killings were like that—murders of gang warfare, murders in response to real or

*Gregory Curtis, a member of the original* Texas Monthly *staff and a former senior editor, is the magazine's executive editor.*

imagined affronts, murders of discipline within the gang—and no amount of friendship or service was insurance against Fred's blood lust: the murdered de la Garza had known and worked with Fred for fifteen years.

Fred served two years for the dance hall murder and was paroled in 1961, but in April of 1962 he received eight years for possession and sale of heroin. After serving five years of that sentence he was paroled in 1967 and returned to San Antonio. For the next five years he and his gang, who called themselves the Dons, dealt in increasingly large amounts of heroin while Fred, now a fugitive for violating his parole, split his time between San Antonio and Nuevo Laredo. His presence on the border ultimately caused open warfare as Fred tried to expand his power over two older Nuevo Laredo gangs, the Gaytans and the Reyes-Prunedas. The fighting became so violent and so open that in the spring of 1972 the Mexican government sent squadrons of federal troops into the city. The rival gangs were, by this time, either arrested or dead or in exhausted disarray, and by fall the fighting was over.

Fred found himself caught between what was left of the two older gangs and the *federales*, and he got into further trouble with the Mexican underworld when a member of his gang got arrested and started spilling trade secrets to the authorities. Fred moved on to Guadalajara where the final sequence of events that culminated in the Huntsville siege really began and where Fred's only redeeming quality, his devotion to his wife, first became publicly apparent.

What happened in Guadalajara was that Fred and assorted gang and family members were arrested on September 20, 1972, with 213 pounds of heroin and enough guns for a whole army of bandidos. Fred's wife Rosa was also captured in this haul, but Fred had no respect for any man who would let his wife languish in jail. He held a shard of glass against his throat for five hours until lawyers negotiated her release. Fred had good reason for wanting her out. His half-brother, Robert Zamorra Gomez, was found dead in his

**199**

cell hanging by the neck from his own belt, even though that belt had been confiscated when Zamorra was booked. Fred accused prison officials of murder.

In December Fred escaped. Four confederates from San Antonio drove to Guadalajara with bribe money and Fred made it through the gate hidden in a laundry truck. He headed straight to San Antonio. He was convinced that he had been cheated by his gang while he was in jail, that his authority was threatened, and he knew only one way to deal with that situation. He started killing again. On March 10 he walked into an ice house where Gilbert Escobedo was drinking. Escobedo, formerly sort of a treasurer for the gang, had held back $80,000 from a heroin deal while Fred was in jail. Fred drew two pistols and used them both.

On April 8 he ordered Agapito Ruiz and Roy Castano to take him for a drive. They rode in the front seat while Fred and at least one other person, Joe Richard Garcez, a young dealer who had carried the money down to Guadalajara to bribe Fred's way out of jail, rode in the back. The police had been following Agapito very closely and had even gone so far as to place an electronic beeper on his car. Agapito discovered the device and took it to his attorneys, who returned it to the police. But Fred thought he had turned informant. As they drove along an obscure road south of the city, Fred pulled out a gun and shot them both.

Afterward Fred ate a steak dinner, but the killings had made Joe Richard sick. He had to leave the table to vomit in the men's room and was still sick the next morning. A Viet Nam veteran with decorations for bravery, he had gotten into the dope traffic for the money and the excitement. He liked to spend lavishly on his friends and maintained several women in their own apartments. But these killings were too much for him. He mentioned them to friends with horror.

Joe Richard always worked with David Garcia, a friend since childhood. On June 8, on another lonely road south of the city, Fred shot them both. They had been talking too freely about the Ruiz-Castano killings and about leaving the gang because of them. That made five murders in less than four months.

Stories began to circulate that Fred had a death list of twelve names and was going down it one by one. His name began appearing frequently in local papers and his capture became a cause célèbre with the San Antonio police. They finally surrounded him, along with Rosa and two others, at the El Tejas motel on July 21, 1973, after 12,000 manhours on the case. Although Fred drew his pistol when he saw the police, he never got off a shot. He was wounded three times, but managed to run about twenty yards before finally going down. He cursed and spat at the officers who pulled him up and sat him in a chair to wait for an ambulance. When it arrived, Rosa and Fred threw themselves at one another. Rosa clutched Fred, huge diamond rings flashing on her fingers, and kissed him with elaborate passion. Behind her she could feel the arc lights of television filmmakers and hear the clicking shutters of newspaper cameras. She kissed her husband an extra moment, then wheeled and, while the cameras rolled, shot everyone the finger.

Many wondered why Fred hadn't been killed that night. He had openly vowed that he wouldn't be taken alive and that he would kill as many police as he could before going down himself. In the weeks following the capture many came to wish that he had indeed been killed. Fred became surrounded by a labyrinth of plots and counter-plots that

finally split the San Antonio police department into opposing factions, cast suspicion on the mayor's office, and wrecked careers built through long years. Fred started the ball rolling in the ambulance that took him away from the scene of his capture. He told the two officers who were guarding him that cops had committed the Ruiz-Castano murders and he had a witness who could prove it.

The citizen could not quite bring himself to wish that Fred had been killed the night of his capture, but he would not have wept over it either. Tracing the story of Fred's life had been grim, frightening, and unrewarding. Even now, as he made for San Antonio where he hoped to be privileged to at least one corner of the triangular conversation between Carrasco and the governor and the lawyer Gillespie, the citizen went only out of some feeling of obligation to the work he'd done on Carrasco in the past. He was, in a sense, Fred's hostage too.

Last March when he had first met Gillespie, the citizen had come away from the meeting not completely sure what he'd seen. He had been told of Gillespie's reputation as an extremely able criminal defense attorney, particularly in the federal courts, who got his share of important cases in San Antonio and throughout South Texas. He had, for instance, defended South Texas political boss Archer Parr. But except for his voice, which was as deep and lulling and pleased with itself as Everett Dirksen's, and except for the titles in the bookshelves which rose to the ceiling behind his desk, titles which indicated an interest in psychology (*The Mask of Insanity*) as well as in the techniques of his profession (*How to Win Criminal Cases by Establishing Reasonable "Doubt"*), nothing else about Gillespie even hinted at the kind of self-assurance the citizen had assumed would go with Gillespie's reputation. He was taut, as if his nerves had been stretched into a jangling network just below his sallow skin. He swallowed occasionally from a plastic bottle of antacid; he complained about high blood pressure. The skin on his face hung in swollen folds. Looking to be in his late forties, of medium height and build with thinning, wiry black hair, Gillespie peered at the citizen through thick lenses in black plastic frames and complained that his eyesight wasn't getting any better either. All in all he had the sunken and frantic air of a man for whom events were getting badly out of hand.

His large desk, which he sat behind throughout the meeting, was overrun with messy files stacked several feet high, piles of open mail spilling over one another, thick brown case reports, crumpled cigarette packages, desk-top calendars and little desk-top figurines, pens, pipes, and encrusted ashtrays lying indiscriminately on top of everything. This effusion spilled over into the office where available spaces on couches and along the walls were taken with more piles of paper and more thick files; every bit of looked like it would, if let loose, flow out over the office floor and possibly overwhelm the world. Almost as if to buttress the walls against such a possibility, they were completely covered with myriad framed documents that at one time or another had been presented to Gillespie: everything from his law school diploma to his military commission to his membership in TWA's Ambassador Club, perhaps 50 in all. The citizen sat down in a chair in front of the desk and began the interview in utter amazement.

Gillespie talked rather distantly about Fred, as if he were

not sure what attitude to take toward his client. On one point, however, he wanted no mistakes: "You know it's a funny thing about Fred"—he stopped to puff a cigarette, a pause that let the echoes of his voice settle over both of them—"in all the many conferences I had with Fred, he never mentioned narcotics to me. *Never*. Not once."

That disclaimer left Gillespie with only one anecdote from all his many conferences with Fred, an anecdote of Fred's passion for his wife. The lawyer and his client were conferring in the Corpus Christi jail after Gillespie had won a change of venue motion which had moved the trial away from San Antonio. Fred wanted to plead guilty to assault to murder and accept a life sentence; in return for that plea all charges against Rosa would be dropped. Gillespie advised Fred against pleading guilty. The important charges against him—murder, assault to murder a police officer—turned out to hang by very slender threads of evidence; and the evidence against Rosa, who was charged with assault on a police officer, was contradictory. But after Guadalajara, Fred did not want to bear the shame of having his wife go to jail a second time. Lucky for Rosa. When Gillespie repeated that he thought Fred *and* Rosa would win their cases, Fred said, "Can you promise me in writing that Rosy will go free?"

"Of course," Gillespie told the citizen, "Fred knew very well that was something no reputable lawyer could ever sign." Gillespie swiveled his chair halfway around and turned his head back to look over his right shoulder at the citizen.

Still, a written promise to Fred from his lawyer would have had the binding effect in Fred's eyes of a blood oath. No reputable lawyer who knew what was good for him would sign such a thing. So Gillespie said, "No, Fred, you know I can't promise you in writing. But it looks so . . . ."

"Then I will plead guilty," Fred said. "I will take life. I will take life upon life. Rosy must go free." Carrasco knew that Gillespie's own marriage had ended in bile; he leaned closer to his lawyer: "Jimmy, someday if you're lucky, you will meet a woman you'll die for. For Rosy I would die."

The Romantic touches a deep nerve in Gillespie's soul; even as he told the story to the citizen, tears appeared in his failing eyes.

"That sounds like a moving moment," the citizen said lamely.

"Oh, it was. Well, you can see the way I am now. And it was very emotional then. Tears—" Gillespie's hands jerked to his eyes and his fingers trailed down his cheeks along the paths of his tears. "—I was sitting there, overcome, and Fred put his arm around me and you know what he said? He said, 'Look now who comforts who.'"

This time, arriving about 2:30, half an hour before Fred's next deadline, the citizen found Gillespie's office more orderly than it had been during that earlier meeting. The stacks of files and papers strewn about the room were gone and the heap on the desk had diminished, although it certainly hadn't vanished completely. Gillespie himself, in a wrinkled shortsleeved white shirt and a thin black tie and shapeless aqua-blue trousers, was obviously feeling the pressure of the situation. He was very pale, he was distracted, his wiry hair stuck out here and there at odd angles; and every time he wanted a cigarette, which was often, he had to search across his desk and through his pockets before he found his pack and then had to search some more to find

his lighter. His shoulders and chest sagged and strained so hard against his too-tight shirt that he looked from the waist up like a sack of grain.

The citizen sat down in the same chair across from Gillespie's desk. Gillespie told him, "You can sit here as long as you like, but if I get a confidential call from the Governor I may ask you to step outside."

"Well." The citizen shrugged. They would cross that bridge when they came to it.

Two other lawyers, Alfonso E. Alonzo and Steve Takas, both associates of Gillespie's, were also in the office. Neither one said much at first. Alonzo, a swarthy and handsome man about 40, dressed in burgundy, sat to the left of the citizen near the side of Gillespie's desk. Takas sat on one of the couches against the back wall. He was younger than either of the other two—round-faced, brown-eyed, ambitious.

With Gillespie understandably distracted and looking at the phone expectantly every few seconds, and with Alonzo and Takas in the room, themselves simply observers too, the citizen found that he really hadn't anything to say to anyone. When all was said and done there was nothing to do but sit and wait for the phone to ring and link them all with the prison library in Huntsville.

A desultory conversation ensued with Alonzo grinning slightly to himself and Takas sitting on the couch with his feet resting on a chair and Gillespie searching for cigarettes and casting yearning glances toward the phone. "Is the Walls a high security unit?" the citizen asked Gillespie out of desperation.

"No. I think it's just medium."

"That's right," Alonzo piped in. "No guns allowed except in the library."

Then one of the lawyers proposed that a certain friend's ex-wife, a woman all three men knew to be a problem, be offered to Fred in exchange for all his hostages. "She'll start bitching about community property," the lawyer said, "saying this gun is mine, that gun is mine, and Fred will surrender just to get rid of her."

They laughed, but not very easily, since the clock was coming closer to three. The citizen had moved to Takas' couch against the wall. The lawyers had, for some reason, started talking about attention to detail. Gillespie said, "Wherever I go on a case I always find out all there is to know about the prosecutor. Everything. What he likes to eat, where he went to school, what his marriage is like, what his weaknesses are, his strong points, everything."

Takas, who had been a prosecutor in San Antonio before going into private practice, innocently asked, "Did you find out all that about me?"

"I sure as hell did," Gillespie said.

"Oh." Takas puffed on a cigarette. He glanced at the citizen and then snorted. "Funny time to be finding all this out," he said.

It was almost three and the phone still hadn't rung when Joe Conant and Manuel Ortiz walked into the office. Conant is a federal prosecutor who had obtained indictments against Fred for conspiring to sell heroin while he was awaiting trial in the Bexar County jail. Ortiz, a local police narcotics agent, dapper and slight of build, not far from retirement, had done important work that led to Fred's capture. He was one of the San Antonio policemen

Fred had accused of murder. The other was Sergeant Bill Weilbacher.

When the story of the accusations hit the San Antonio papers, no one really understood why Fred had singled out Ortiz; but it was obvious why he had singled out Weilbacher. During his 24 years on the force, Weilbacher had developed a thorough and widespread network of informants whose information he digested with his own native intelligence and street savvy. His conclusions were nearly always accurate.

He and Fred were natural antagonists. Both were bigger than life, both had reputations of being the most cunning and toughest men in their respective worlds, both had inspired individual legends. Though San Antonio is the tenth largest city in the country, it is literally true that the place was not big enough for both of them.

Weilbacher is an imposing figure, to say the least. He stands about six feet tall and weighs 300 pounds. Nearly all that weight is in his shoulders, chest, and stomach; he moves around on his legs like some great Idaho potato on toothpicks. His face is narrow with a thin nose and eyes set close together, a high forehead, and thin, curly hair combed straight back. Folds of flesh hang from his jowls and below his chin so that he seems to have no neck. His jackets hang over his great bulk like circus tents and his ties do not hang straight down but rest on his belly, moulding themselves on its hills and dales. He chews his fingernails, squints his eyes into narrow slits as he talks, and, since his glances can pierce through a man like a needle through an insect, it is apparent that Weilbacher does not maintain his informants' loyalty with sympathy and kind words.

Weilbacher was in Guadalajara when Fred was put in prison there, and he marched over to the jail wanting to see Fred. But among Fred's effects when he was arrested was a Xerox copy of one of Weilbacher's secret reports about Fred and his gang. The Mexican authorities knew only that Weilbacher's name was on the report and, not wanting to take any chances, they threw him in jail with Fred. There Weilbacher saw Fred weep over the death of his brother. When Weilbacher got back to San Antonio, he told Fred's parents that he had seen their son shedding tears. Fred considered this a devastating insult.

Although it was information from Weilbacher's sources that led to Fred's capture, the immediate publicity went to another San Antonio cop, Lieutenant Dave Flores. Flores was the one who shot Carrasco during the capture. Mayor Charles Becker took the opportunity to honor Flores with a plaque; police department wags said he should have been awarded a practice target.

Flores went to see Carrasco in jail. Fred was not at first particularly receptive to the Lieutenant, but that reluctance faded when Fred realized that Flores was ready to investigate Fred's charges against Weilbacher and Ortiz. Flores asked Fred to produce his witness.

Flores lives deep in South San Antonio. It is a predominantly Mexican area, different from the west side *barrio* in that small pockets of white ethnic groups—Poles and other Eastern Europeans—control much of the area's political power. From the South Side to a position of respect in downtown San Antonio is a very long road, but one Flores had decided to travel as far as it would take him. He would not be content, like Weilbacher, with reputation; Flores wanted rank.

Along the way Flores had made one very powerful friend, San Antonio wheeler-dealer and land developer Morris Jaffe. Jaffe cultivated Flores and his family, let them use his lake house on weekends; and Flores returned the friendship even though Jaffe is not the sort police usually meet and greet socially. Jaffe bought the remains of Billie Sol Estes' financial empire in 1962 for $7 million, subsequently developed uranium interests, and later promoted an immensely successful shopping center in San Antonio. But he also has had some questionable business associates. He owned an interest in the insurance firm Cohen, Kerwin, and White. Cohen has convictions for mail fraud. Kerwin, whose real name was Leroy Silverstein, had convictions for fraud and income tax evasion. Kerwin had had long associations with organized crime; and when he was murdered—executed, in all probability, by a mob enforcer—in Canada in late 1970, his briefcase contained documents disclosing various Mafia-connected swindling schemes. These have become known as the Kerwin papers. The firm Cohen, Kerwin, and White insured for $15 million an Oklahoma rancher named Mullendore who was later mysteriously murdered. Jaffe is also acquainted with Carlos Marcello, the Louisiana underworld boss whose days in power number back to the era of Huey Long. Marcello owns land not far from New Orleans that Jaffe has tried to buy. San Antonio police think that Fred sold some of his heroin to Marcello's organization.

Morris Jaffe is also very close friends with the present mayor, Charles Becker. Becker is the scion of a wealthy family whose money comes from the Handy Andy chain of grocery stores. He has never really gotten along with police since his younger days when he used to like racing his sports car around the streets of the city. Jaffe had introduced Flores to Mayor Becker. The three of them, acting independently, decided they would investigate Fred's charges.

But Fred wasn't willing to produce his witness, the man who was supposed to implicate Ortiz and Weilbacher, without getting something in return. First he asked for safety for his family and for the witness' family. When Flores agreed to that, Fred said that he would reveal the identity of the witness only after Flores had performed one more task. When Fred was in jail in Guadalajara his two remaining half-brothers were robbed by men who entered their homes flashing badges and claiming they were officers executing search warrants. They then proceeded to strip the two houses of all the money and drugs they could find. And they seemed to know just where to look for what they wanted, finding loot beneath stairwells and behind pipes. When Flores got a confession for those robberies from two addicts and police characters, Fred finally produced his witness, a 26-year-old narcotics peddler named Daniel Jaramillo.

Flores met with Jaramillo and tape-recorded his story, then took the tape to the mayor's residence. Jaramillo said he had been riding in a car with Ruiz and Castano when another car pulled up behind them. Suddenly a shot burst through the car and killed Ruiz who was sitting in the front seat. Castano, who was driving, jumped from the car; Jaramillo jumped out on the other side, leapt a wire fence and hid in the darkness. Castano was not so fortunate, according to the story; he was shot where he lay in the middle of the road. The mysterious car circled his body and its occupants pumped him full of bullets. Jaramillo said he heard the dying Castano shout two names: Weilbacher and Ortiz.

Unfortunately for Flores, Becker, and Jaffe, reporters from the *Light*, one of San Antonio's two dailies, had gotten wind of the investigation about a week earlier and they, too, heard Jaramillo's tape. The next morning, a Sunday, the *Light* ran a headline in red ink that said, "Witness Says Cops Killed 2."

The story didn't mention the names Jaramillo said he had heard, but by Monday everyone around the courthouse and in the police department knew who had been named. Ortiz was dazed by the news. But Weilbacher did not take kindly to being paraded publicly as a murderer.

The story had broken on a Sunday. Both the mayor and Flores had said the witness was in protective custody in a secret location. The investigation was proceeding, they said. The *Light* was calling for a swift resolution. All that lasted two days. On Tuesday Jaramillo, the secret witness, and five other men were arrested in a motel room with ten pounds of heroin. The investigation was suddenly at a halt. "Good God, that's all we needed," the mayor said when reporters told him about the arrest. Having composed himself, he described it as "a reversal of the highest order." It turned out that the witness hadn't been in protective custody at all. Since his name was never mentioned in the papers, Flores had decided to let him run free.

The same day Jaramillo was arrested, Weilbacher identified himself publicly as one of the officers mentioned, proclaimed his innocence, and said he would cooperate fully with any investigative body. The next day he stood in the same room with Jaramillo, who didn't recognize him. The grand jury, after a two-week hearing, reported there was not a "scintilla of evidence" against the two officers. It was the right verdict, but one that while clearing Weilbacher and Ortiz would condemn Flores. After the smoke cleared both Weilbacher and Flores were reassigned duties. Flores is back in uniform performing essentially clerical tasks. Weilbacher, not quite as autonomous as he was, still prowls his old territory.

Becker and Jaffe continue as before. Their power is above such reversals.

When Ortiz and Conant walked into Gillespie's office just before three, the citizen considered the stage set for the governor's call. On hand would be Carrasco's defender, his prosecutor, and one of the police who had captured him.

Conant, the prosecutor, walked to one of the few sections of wall that was not covered with Gillespie's diplomas and opened the door of a hidden cabinet, reached for the bottle of bourbon, and poured it into a plastic champagne glass until the glass was full. Then he sat down in the chair across from Gillespie's desk in the middle of the room, took a drink, set the glass on the edge of Gillespie's desk and said, "I'm hurtin'. I'm really hurtin'."

Conant is a big man. He has longish blond hair, a thick face, thick shoulders, a thick girth—an ex-football player now somewhat beyond his playing weight. Looking at Ortiz and Conant, if someone said one was a lawyer and one was a cop and asked you to name which was which, you would have said Conant was the cop.

"I'm really hurting," he said again. "It's as much my fault as anybody else's that that son of a bitch is in Huntsville. Did you know that my sister-in-law, my own brother's wife, the same last name as me, works in that library? The same last name as me, now. She was visiting her sick grandfather and he took a turn for the worse. She decided to stay an extra day. She works that same shift. If it wasn't for her grandfather she would be in there with Fred right now." He paused significantly, and held up one admonishing finger: "The same last name as me." The whole idea galled Conant so much he took another slug of his bourbon. Then he turned to look at the citizen who was sitting with his arms resting straight out across the back of the sofa. No expression passed between them and, without any real pause, Conant turned back to Gillespie. The citizen could only assume that Conant wanted to gauge his reaction to that speech and perhaps check to see if he were taking notes or using a recorder. But it wasn't until Conant finished that the citizen understood the reason for that pause. "I came *that* close," he said, holding his thumb and forefinger a sliver of light apart, "to driving down to Huntsville and walking out in that courtyard in front of the library—armed—and calling Fred down."

Gillespie began, "It's a good thing you . . ."

"Maybe I'll still do it. My very own name, now. Remember that."

"Don't go down there," Gillespie said. "Fred is very fast. He would kill you."

"Maybe he would," Conant said. He took a drink and tilted his head like he was once again considering the possibilities. "Or maybe the others would get me *after* I got Fred."

The citizen tried to watch all this with absolute calm. Except in a movie theater he had never heard anyone talk even half-seriously about a duel with guns.

But Conant suddenly changed the subject: "Jimmy," he asked Gillespie, "where's Rosa?"

"I don't know. I don't have any idea."

That was the first hint of why Conant and Ortiz had come there in the first place. Officially at least, Rosa was not yet wanted for aiding Fred in getting the guns; officially, government planes were in wait to whisk her to Huntsville, where she might be of some use during the negotiations with Fred. In any event, they wanted Rosa and the trail had led to Gillespie since the car she was thought to be driving was registered to his law office. Evidently Carrasco had given Gillespie money to buy Rosa the car as a Christmas present. Gillespie had bought the car, registered it, and then Rosa had picked it up but never bothered to change the registration to her name. Ortiz and Conant asked some close, quick questions, returning now and then to ask the same question a second time, and in a few minutes were satisfied that Gillespie didn't know where Rosa was. Three o'clock had long passed.

"Do you think anything's happened?" someone asked.

"No," Gillespie said. "They are supposed to call me *immediately* if anything happens." Gillespie, in addition to the obvious strains and worries of the moment, was also annoyed that another attorney who had had some dealings with Carrasco, Ruben Montemayor, had arrived in Huntsville a few hours after Fred took over and was now acting as the conduit through which Carrasco and prison negotiators were speaking. Montemayor was thereby getting considerable publicity in the newspaper stories about the event. They generally labeled him "Carrasco's attorney." Montemayor's publicity backfired somewhat when he volunteered to go the library to talk with Fred. Fred's answer to that suggestion was, "If he comes, I will kill him." Gillespie hoped for that phone call with the governor not only because he was genuinely concerned about what might happen in Huntsville, but also because it would have been he, not Montemayor, who had done the negotiating when it really counted. Earlier he had instructed his secretary to "take Ruben off the list of people to call when I'm out of town."

Since the three o'clock deadline was the third one Fred had let pass that day and since there had been no news at all from the prison, the immediate crisis apparently had subsided. Strangely, the release of that tension made the citizen feel a little like a hostage himself. There had been no phone call, no new information about Fred; and now he was stuck far from the door in an office filled with swirl and sputter and braggadocio.

Conant drained the last drops of his bourbon from the plastic champagne glass. He held it up empty. "You want some more?" Alonzo said, the devil in his eyes. "I'll get you some more."

"That's exactly right," Conant said. He handed the glass to Alonzo, who walked past him to the rear of the office where the concealed liquor cabinet was. "You should get me a drink the way I beat you in court. And I'll say something else—" he looked around the room at everyone but Alonzo "—if he pees in that glass instead of pouring me bourbon, I'll shoot him right on the spot and that's a promise." He held his arms outstretched, palms up, shrugging. "Now you're all watching. Did he pee in my glass? No? All right then. I guess I won't have to shoot him." He forced a few chuckles as Alonzo, unruffled, handed the refilled glass back to him.

"I'm still thinking of going down to Huntsville," Conant said. He pulled out a black gun that looked a little like a Luger with a thick long barrel. It was all black in his pudgy white hand.

Everybody looked at the gun which Conant proudly held. Then Gillespie pulled a .25 caliber pistol from a drawer in his desk and showed it to Conant and then Ortiz pulled out his silver revolver and began exhibiting it. A gaggle of technical data about each weapon filled the air.

It was so odd. At the same time Carrasco and two confederates were waving guns in the faces of their hostages in the prison library, three men in this lawyer's office were waving guns in the air and boasting about who was fastest, the best shot, which gun was the most lethal. The citizen felt uncomfortable, less uncomfortable certainly than he would have felt in the prison library just then, but uncomfortable still as gun barrels from time to time were inadvertently pointed in his direction. A death in the prison library would be called a murder; a death in this office under these circumstances would be called an accident.

After a while, Conant and Ortiz left and then Alonzo left. Takas began regaling the citizen with funny stories which he acted out waving his arms and changing his voice. Gillespie nervously smoked. About 6:30 the phone rang. Gillespie answered. "Yes, *sir*, I'll hold for the governor," he said.

Takas and the citizen sat up straight. The citizen felt his palm turn clammy as he readied his pen.

"Yes, Governor, this is James Gillespie . . . Yes sir . . . No, you may *not* kick me right in the ass, governor . . ."

Takas and the citizen looked at each other in confusion. Gillespie started laughing for the first time that day. It was Alonzo who was calling.

"Oh, God damn," Takas said.

The citizen agreed: *God damn*.

—*October 1974*

204

# BUSTING OUT OF MEXICO

## by Jan Reid

---

### *It couldn't happen this way in a million years—but it did.*

---

When the American inmates at Piedras Negras talked to Blake Davis, they sometimes caught themselves staring at the jagged, reddened scar that underlined the ridge of his jaw. Blake Davis was ebullient, powerfully built, well liked by the other Americans. Even in moments of discouragement he somehow managed a rueful smile. "Next week" was always the time of Blake's anticipated departure from the Piedras Negras jail. He always had a scam.

Blake did not mind talking about his scar. He said he'd been arrested near Saltillo and charged with transporting 175 pounds of marijuana. For three weeks, Blake said, he was strapped naked to a bed while *federales* interrogated him, until finally he signed a Spanish confession he could not read. While he was in prison at Saltillo, Blake claimed he bribed a warden for $2000, but when the tunneling started the warden alerted the guards. Blake said he unwisely cried foul; the warden referred the matter to Mexican inmates who set upon Blake with crude knives and razor blades. Hence the scar. Blake's tale of horror did not rate him special privileges in the Piedras Negras seniority system. When he was transferred there in August 1975, like all other new arrivals he took a seat on the floor.

When a Mexican attorney arranged his transfer from Saltillo, Blake thought he was destined for a federal prison in Piedras Negras called Penal. But Mexican officials claimed Penal was overcrowded, and they blamed Americans for a November 1974 breakout in which 24 prisoners tunneled to freedom. Blake Davis was thus assigned to the Piedras Negras municipal jail. Inside the jail were five cells for men, one cell for women, and a drunk tank, each of which measured eight feet by nine. The windowless cells contained four bunks, a toilet, a water faucet, and from six to twelve sweating, panting, claustrophobic prisoners. Mexican national inmates were eventually transferred to Penal. but the

*Jan Reid is a contributing editor of* Texas Monthly *and author of* The Improbable Rise of Redneck Rock.

Americans waited for enough seniority to occupy one of the bunks. When they moved around their cells they shuffled. They never breathed fresh air, never saw the sky. The lights of the jail were never turned off, so their only concept of day and night came from the jail kitchen, which provided gruel in the morning, soup at noon, beans and tortillas at dinner. The Americans depended upon friends to bring them vitamins and food. After a few months their teeth began to decay and their hair began to thin. They passed the time playing scrabble, backgammon, studying Spanish. Two or three performed yoga and isometric exercises. Though the Americans inside hated and feared Mexican cops, they had a certain empathy for the jail guards, who were poor men working for five or six dollars a day and were helpless to do anything about the crowded conditions of the jail. The guards also seemed to understand that the Americans were under severe mental and emotional stress, prisoners of a foreign government and a foreign system of justice. Certain liberties were in order. Hard drugs could be smuggled past the guards, and the Mexican fink assigned to each cell containing Americans often operated a marijuana concession. Sometimes the guards allowed women to join the men in their bunks or in the privacy of the shower room. But now and then the powder-keg tension of the jail would explode. Some American would faint, his skin would turn the shade of alabaster, and the other Americans would start shouting angry demands for medical attention.

Except for weekenders in the drunk tank, all the American inmates were alleged narcotics violators. Under terms of the Mexican Napoleonic Code, any felony suspect caught red-handed, *in flagrante delicto*, can be held, interrogated, and denied access to an attorney for three days. If, after six days, a magistrate concludes that evidence warrants a trial, and the maximum sentence of the alleged offense is more than two years, a suspect can be held up to a year before he is tried. Even if a suspect proves in an *amparo* court of grievance that his Mexican constitutional rights have been

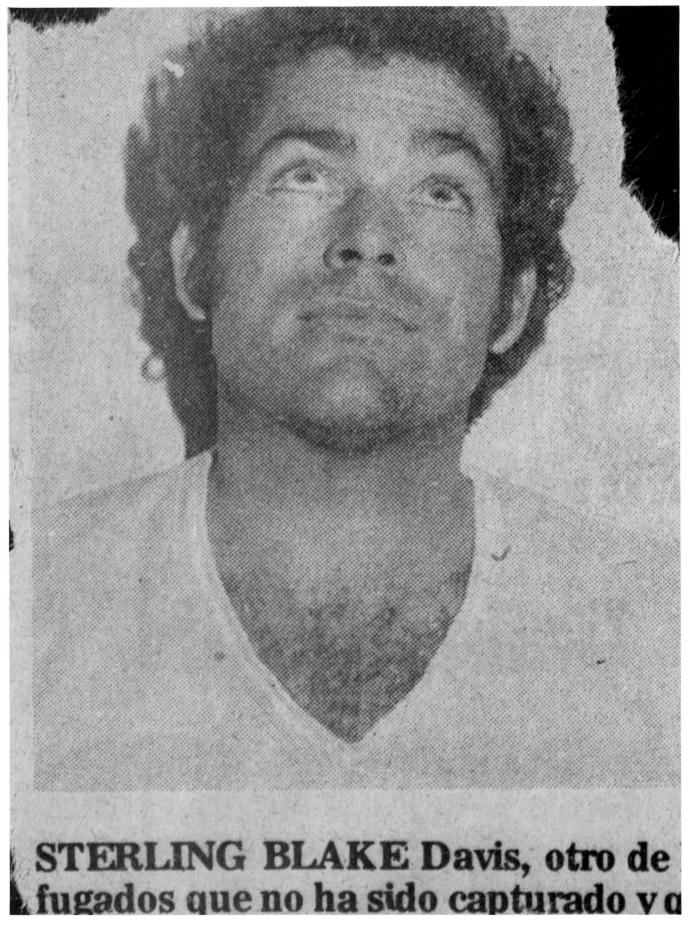

**STERLING BLAKE Davis, otro de**
**fugados que no ha sido capturado y q**

Blake Davis. *Photograph from Piedras Negras newspaper* Zócalo

violated, the charges against him still stand. In January 1975 the Mexican government enacted a law that denied narcotics suspects any kind of release on bond. From the standpoint of the Americans in the Piedras Negras jail, Mexican law was a stacked deck. Only Davis had actually been convicted, but the rest of the Americans never talked about waiting for trial. They always said they were waiting for sentencing.

Blake Davis and the other Americans knew that a California congressman named Pete Stark was spearheading a House subcommittee hearing on the fate of 600 Americans in Mexican jails, but they placed very little trust in the United States government. The U.S. Drug Enforcement Agency (DEA) trains Mexican narcs, analyzes Mexican confiscations in its Dallas laboratories, stuffs American dollars into the Mexican control agencies at the rate of $14 million per year. Operation Cooperation, American officials like to say, is designed to disrupt the guns-for-heroin trade. But the American inmates claimed the barber-shirted *federales* busted any American they possibly could, by whatever methods, while their DEA benefactors applauded. It was no longer easy for American prisoners to buy their way out of Mexican jail. One of the American inmates at Piedras Negras theorized that nothing had really changed: the favors of Mexican *mordida* still went to the highest bidder—the United States government.

Once a month U.S. consular officials came to the jail; one of those callers was Leonard Walentynowicz, the administrator who represented the State Department at the congressional hearings. But the American inmates were in no mood to wait on Washington. Every prisoner had a plan. One considered smuggling in hydrochloric acid on visitors' day to weaken the bars of the shower room. Another wanted to blow a small hole in the roof. Another pinned his hopes on a brother-in-law who worked for the CIA. The most dubious scheme involved advance payment to the Mexican secret police, who would then assist the escapees through a shower room window.

Blake Davis was king of the freedom schemers. For six months his father in Dallas had been trying to finance a Piedras Negras jailbreak. Every twelve hours, at six o'clock, the inmates were taken from their cells into the corridor for a *lista*. While the guards called roll, counted heads, and inspected the cells for signs of tunneling, the American inmates exchanged notes. They slept with their clothes easily accessible and tried to raise money through friends on the outside. Tuesday and Wednesday were the most likely nights, for there was less drunk traffic at the jail. Inevitably, the rumors reached the ears of the Mexican guards. One day in January an American tough recruited by Blake's father signed the visitors' register, submitted to a frisk by the guards, and came back to Blake's cell. The American whispered through the bars that the jailbreak was on. Some of the American inmates altered their sleeping habits so they would always be awake in the hours after midnight. But when the American returned to Piedras Negras, he passed word the next visitors' day that the break was no longer possible: armed guards were now circling the block and maintaining a lookout on the roof of the jail. Some of the inmates grew tired of constant anticipation. Everytime the Coke machine noisily dispensed a ten-ounce bottle they wondered if commandos had broken down the door. After two months of breakout rumors, the guards also

tired of hearing them. A new *comandante* ordered a search of the prisoners' possessions, but told the warden that the guard on the roof was no longer necessary.

Blake Davis remained optimistic, for the alternative to optimism was exceedingly grim. He had lost 25 pounds during his incarceration. His body was covered with boils, and a cyst at the base of his spine was seeping pus. Poison from an abscessed tooth descended with his saliva and gave him a stomach ache. Blake Davis had served only two years of a ten-year sentence. He did not think he could survive eight more years in a Mexican jail.

In the late forties Sterling Blake Davis, Sr., introduced the limp-wristed flair of Liberace to the macho world of pro wrestling. While his old Houston crony, Gorgeous George Wagner, made a fortune with the routine on California TV, Dizzy Davis sported colorful, hand-sewn robes and dispensed flowers in the smoky arenas of Texas and Mexico. Sometimes called Gardenia Davis, he was a better wrestler than Wagner.

Davis' luck since those days had been a carousel ride. By 1972 he owned a large home on the east shore of Dallas' Lake Ray Hubbard, but his health was failing, and he was only 58. One of his sons seemed to be adjusting nicely to middle-class adulthood. The other, Sterling Blake, Jr., nicknamed Cooter, was doing time in a federal penitentiary for possessing 770 pounds of marijuana in Arizona.

The old man would soon be in a heap of trouble himself. In November 1973 he was named in a thirteen-count federal fraud indictment and was tried in February 1974 in the Dallas courtroom of Judge Sarah T. Hughes. Testimony in that trial portrayed Davis as a shuck and jive artist who convinced 70 customers that bullfrog farming was the wave of the future. One investor testified that Davis falsely claimed to own a 650-acre frog farm in Arkansas, from which in a single year Rice University research scientists bought 9000 bullfrogs—at $16 a frog. Frog distributors came from as far as Iowa and Florida to testify that Davis and two other men sold them a $3000 package of goods that included two portable swimming pools with inefficient filters, a few frogs, an instruction manual, and a piece of vibrating sheet metal called an automatic feeder. The instruction manual said bullfrogs could be taught to feed in captivity if they were offered a fare of bouncing maggots, and then rabbit food, on the vibrating sheet metal. One distributor said he hung a rotting armadillo over the feeder to keep the frogs supplied with maggots. Another testified that his wife watched for signs of progress with binoculars from a nearby tree. Most said they eventually set the starving frogs free.

At the trial Davis contended the feeder worked perfectly for some of his more prosperous clients, but the court remained unconvinced. "Now I heard the evidence and I don't think the feeder is working," Judge Hughes replied. After the jury found Davis guilty on ten counts, Hughes told him, "You are one of the best con artists that has appeared before me." She ordered him to make restitution to his former customers, fined him $10,000, and sentenced him to five years, followed by five more years probation.

Davis, who carries the long vertical scar of open-heart surgery, pled ill health. After studying the doctors' affidavits, in May 1974 Hughes probated the remainder of Davis' five-year sentence. That very same month Davis' son Blake, paroled by then on his Arizona pot conviction, was arrested 150 miles deep in Mexico and charged with possession of marijuana. Sterling Davis felt like a man accursed.

To pay his legal fees Davis had to sell most of the two acres he owned on Lake Ray Hubbard. His probation officer vetoed a couple of ideas for new employment. Finally Davis offered his services to the administrator of a non-credit educational institute in Dallas, explaining that in the frog farm episode he had been a mere management consultant deceived by the two salesmen. Davis convinced the administrator he had valid degrees in psychology and experience as an industrial psychologist. At the institute Davis tutored night students on meditation techniques allegedly developed by long-lived Andean Indians. To avoid incurring the legal wrath of the TM organization, Davis called his course Transcendental Relaxation. In January 1975 he applied for a state license to practice clinical psychology. The board of examiners informed him that before he could take the qualifying exam, two years of experience supervised by a licensed psychologist were required. Davis found a psychologist who would sponsor him. Extremely secretive about his personal finances, Davis somehow put his hands on enough money to furnish an office on Northwest Highway with a $1500 stereo that played soothing music and a vibrating chair which gave the person sitting in it a massage.

At the same time, Davis was trying to get his son out of jail. He pursued embassy channels to no avail and developed a very low regard for Mexican attorneys. To his surprise, however, he learned that if nobody was hurt, and no property damaged, there was no law against jailbreak in Mexico. After Blake was transferred to Piedras Negras, Davis started looking for ways to raise money, including efforts to involve friends and families of the inmates. He put out a feeler which moved through an underground of Dallas bars, drive-ins, and all-night restaurants. It was not a very attractive offer. The jailbreakers stood an excellent chance of getting killed, and if they were captured by the Mexicans, they were as good as dead. If they killed any Mexicans while freeing the inmates, the American government would probably extradite them. The money Davis offered was insufficient to attract mob professionals. Davis thus interviewed a long line of maniacs and scoundrels. One group Davis rejected wanted to storm across with enough explosives to start a war. He advanced money to another gang of small-time heavies who bought guns and an El Camino pickup, then partied until the money ran out in San Antonio. Davis had high hopes for the assault team that approached his son inside the jail, but they were frightened off at the last moment by the beefed-up security. He had begun to wonder if jailbreaks happened only in the movies.

At his Northwest Highway office on Monday, February 16, Davis gazed across his desk at another prospective jailbreaker. The man did not look like much of a commando. He had an enormous belly, and when he opened his mouth there was a dark gap where his two front teeth should have been.

Don Fielden was a Marine without a mission, a truckdriver without a rig. After moving to Dallas from the northeast Texas town of Gladewater, Fielden had dropped out of Woodrow Wilson High School and joined the Marine Corps in 1966. Assigned to the infantry during boot camp at San Diego, he underwent field radio training at Camp Pendleton and drew orders to join the First Marine Division in Viet Nam. "They'd been telling us all along that this was a police action," he recalled much later. "They instilled that thought so deep in my mind I expected to go over there and use a .45 and a nightstick. Patrol the streets. The first night I was in Da Nang, they shelled the hell out of us. I thought, man, I ain't never seen a cop go through this shit."

Fielden explored the Vietnamese countryside by helicopter and combat patrol. "I was able to condition my mind to where it was like I was back home squirrel hunting," he said. "Except these squirrels were shooting back. I don't have bad dreams about killing people over there. I'm not ashamed of it. It was a job my country told me to do." Fielden helped ward off enemy attacks during construction of the air base at Phu Bai, then took his R&R leave in Japan. Nineteen days before he was scheduled to rotate back to the States, he was pulling radio watch in a sandbagged bunker near the DMZ. After finishing his watch, Fielden stood at the door of an unfortified wall and gazed longingly at the two-man privy positioned a few yards away. He paused in the doorway to monitor a radio message; at that moment a stray communist rocket scored a direct hit on the two-holer. Shrapnel gouged a chunk out of Fielden's shoulder and nearly severed his right leg below the knee.

At the U.S. Naval Hospital in Corpus Christi, Fielden worked in the Marine liaison office and extended his enlistment for a year. He soon learned that antiwar sentiment was running deep; even some of the sailors at Corpus Christi treated him like a murderer of children. On his first leave he found that things were no better in Dallas. Fielden's favorite times during that period were spent in the company of other convalescent Marines at a bar called the Town Pump. But there was scant future in the Marine Corps for a sergeant with a chronically aching leg. Fielden was severed from active duty in 1970 with a purple heart but no disability pension. In 1972 he received his honorable discharge in the mail.

Back in Dallas, Fielden sometimes told people that the hideous scar on his calf was the result of a motorcycle accident. He bought a Corvette and entertained new acquaintances with his jovial banter. But he was drinking heavily, and his weight pushed far past 200. The father of two children, he soon would be able to report he had been divorced three times.

Fielden was becoming a tough character in a tough town. The Marines had trained him to function in a world of total violence, where the ethic of work was survival. No civilian experience matched the overcharged excitement of Viet Nam, but he didn't stop looking. He drove a truck and moonlighted for a collection agency that fronted as a nightclub janitorial service.

On the night of March 3, 1975, the freeway driving habits of a Dallas municipal employee so outraged Fielden that he fired off a couple of shots from his pistol—clean misses—while Dallas Cowboy flanker Golden Richards witnessed the incident driving in an adjacent lane. The grand jury no-billed Fielden when nobody chose to testify.

Fielden was relatively happy as a long-haul truckdriver. He liked his life on the road; trading truckstop stories about bears and tourists reminded him of the masculine camaraderie of the Marine Corps geedunk beer halls. But then on December 23, 1975, Fielden returned from a trip and parked his truck on the lot of his Dallas employer.

When he returned the next day his boss told him, "We can't use you anymore. You're fired."

"Merry Christmas," Fielden said to himself.

Fielden was not making it on the outside; he remained a casualty of the Viet Nam War. As a teenaged recruit Fielden never questioned the Marine Corps line. He labored torturously for contemptuous drill instructors who told him he would "never make a pimple on a Marine's ass." Fielden had proved himself a Marine at home in the barracks and overseas under fire. Now he was failing in a world that did not care if he had made the Marines. Out of work, out of family, running out of money, Fielden was desperate for drastic changes in his life. During the day he wasn't doing much of anything. At night he hung out in north Dallas trucker bars and discos—the world in which Sterling Davis' jailbreak offer was circulating. A friend explained the situation and gave him the doctor's phone number. On February 16, 1976, Fielden kept an appointment in the blue and silver office building on Northwest Highway.

Fielden had a very stonefaced way of listening to people. His chin jutted out and his mouth turned down: characteristics shared by the Marine Corps mascot, the bulldog. In the office Fielden listened as Sterling Davis recounted the story of his troubled efforts to free his son. Davis said that he'd studied in Mexico; a diploma on the office wall indicated he earned his PhD from the University of Mexico in 1951. Fielden did not speak Spanish, and he asked Davis to provide him with the Spanish equivalent of "get your hands up" and other key phrases. The doctor stammered and changed the subject.

Fielden earned his high school equivalency certificate during his tour in the Marines. He respected men with superior education. He did not respect men who feigned academic credentials. Fielden pegged the old man as a con, and he had scant compassion for busted dope dealers. But he said he would free the doctor's son for $5000 and expenses, reimbursed afterward. It was a job, a mission, almost like the Marines. In a dull civilian world, where he did not quite fit, it was a chance to rejoin the action. You can take the man out of the war but you can't always take the war out of the man.

Fielden spent most of the third week of February in Eagle Pass, reconnoitering his combat patrol into Mexico. Fielden was pleased by some of the things he saw. The Piedras Negras jail was only three blocks from the Mexican tollgates at the International Bridge. On visitors' day he took Blake Davis some food and called him by the family nickname Cooter. Blake knew immediately why Fielden was there. Fielden thought the jail looked like the set of an Old West movie. The cells were locked with hasps and chains that could be cut with heavy-duty bolt cutters. But the jail sat far back on its lot, adjoined on both sides by the walls of buildings that extended to the street. When Fielden stepped out of the Piedras Negras jail, he was looking at the rectangular dimensions of a trap. If he had been a history buff, he might have reflected that Emiliano Zapata rode into a similar Mexican trap. Reluctantly, Fielden concluded he would need another man.

Mike Hill was broke and he was looking for trouble, if trouble would get him out of Dallas. Hill had been scraping a living off the streets of Dallas since he was thirteen years old, and at 32 all he had to show for it was a Chevy StepVan painted reflective silver. He spent part of the winter of 1976 sleeping in his van.

The son of alcoholic parents, Hill stopped going to school when he started living alone in a deserted fire station. He subsisted at first on a diet of soda pop and bread, then stole a bicycle so he could take a delivery job. During the rest of his teens Hill's residence alternated between the homes of friends and the state reformatory at Gatesville. Hill always ran away from Gatesville. He couldn't stand the feeling of confinement.

In 1965 Hill was convicted of burglary but his sentence was probated. Over the next decade he was jailed and hauled before grand juries on an assortment of charges but was never indicted. A marriage produced two daughters before it ended in divorce. He bought used cars wholesale, then sold them through the classifieds. He ran a wrecker service that rousted him out of bed at all times of the night. Then in 1972 Hill discovered marijuana. When it wasn't feeding his paranoia, a marijuana high dulled the sharp edges of Mike Hill's world. He sold his business, motorcycled to Florida, and returned to exploit the Dallas towaway ordinance. A fleet of independent wrecker operators hauled cars away from private property posted with warning signs, then delivered the cars to a lot leased by Hill. Hill paid the drivers $25, then charged the owners of the impounded autos $43 in cash. Perfectly legal. Ensuring order at Hill's lot were snarling dogs and a gang of shotgun-toting cronies. In May 1975 an ad department employee of the *Dallas Morning News* detailed the treatment in a memo to reporter Dave McNeely, who went to the lot with newsroom comrade Dan Watson. Gruff and burly, McNeely is the kind of reporter who once got into a fistfight as a result of his questions. He does not scare easily, but Mike Hill frightened him.

The reporters' story placed Hill in the center of a storm of bad publicity, but worse news was yet to come. Hill's drivers towed away the car of Dallas Mayor Pro Tem Adlene Harrison. One driver tried to remove the car of Dallas undercover narcotics agents who were parked at a closed filling station observing a progressive country nightclub on Cedar Springs. The narcs ordered the wrecker driver away, and the driver called Hill. When Hill arrived at the site in his van, the narcs radioed a vice-squad officer for assistance. The ensuing argument ended, inevitably, in Hill's arrest. In Hill's van, Dallas officers told reporters after the incident, were a loaded derringer, a loaded pistol, a dagger, a shotgun, and two baseball bats. Adlene Harrison proposed a new tow-away ordinance to the city council, and a misdemeanor gun conviction was added to Mike Hill's growing Dallas Police Department record.

Through it all, Hill remained eminently likable. A blond mustache concealed a beer-bottle scar, the bridge of his nose was enlarged by numerous fractures, and there was something tense and hard about his eyes, but when Hill laughed he was handsome. He was a good storyteller, and women found him attractive. He stood nearly six feet and was muscular, with only a little flab above his belt. He had an odd, slouching stride, shoulders hulking forward as he walked. Mike Hill was a familiar Texas character: the tough guy good old boy. When he drove his van into the lot of a favorite hangout the last week of February, he wasn't necessarily up to no good. He was just passing through. A friend who also knew Don Fielden stuck his head in Hill's van and grinned. "Hey boy. You wanta go to Mexico?"

Hill was intrigued; the whole idea seemed so, well, *bizarre*. Besides, he needed money badly and an expense-paid trip to Mexico sounded like a vacation. The two men arranged to meet on Saturday night, February 28, at the Denny's on Industrial Boulevard. By this time Fielden was desperate for a partner. Few men had been interested in the deal before Hill: the risks were mortal and the take-home pay was only $2500. That night Hill listened to Fielden's story and studied his plans for the breakout while Fielden drew pencil sketches on paper napkins. Fielden kept emphasizing, "It's not against the law, as long as you don't hurt anybody it's not against the law." Hill avoided making a commitment for a while, but when Fielden said he wanted to leave on Monday, Hill replied, "What's wrong with tonight?" Fielden said he had to get some traveling money together and agreed to leave the next day.

Driving south in Fielden's Ford they quickly got on each other's nerves. Hill was a coffee freak, so every few miles Fielden had to stop at a cafe. Hill's legs were numb from the frigid gale of Fielden's air conditioner. Fielden wanted to talk about the break; Hill wanted to watch the passing countryside and think about getting laid in Mexico. Hill asked Fielden how much money he had raised, and his partner muttered, "A hundred dollars." Hill thought: a hundred dollars? I thought I was getting in on a big-time deal. In the car were Fielden's sawed-off shotgun and Hill's twelve-gauge pump. As they drove farther south it became more apparent that Fielden intended to stage the raid without any further delay.

"Uh," Hill said, "I thought we were just gonna go down there and kinda look at it."

The next morning, March 1, Fielden and Hill paid nickel tolls at Eagle Pass and walked the International Bridge across the Rio Grande, on that day a shallow, muddy stream that swirled against the steep bank on the Mexican side. Hill had always been enchanted by the culture of Mexico. He liked the food, the music, the brown-eyed raven-haired women. Hill was excited as he passed the Mexican customs inspector and his sign that read *TERMINANTEMENTE PROHIBIDA: La importación de armas y cartuchos . . .*

Hill's stomach convulsed with fear when he saw the jail. It was too well guarded, too far back from the street. Back in the Eagle Pass motel room, they considered diverting the Mexican cops' attention with fires or explosions, but whenever Fielden started talking too intently about the break, Hill rolled a joint and smoked it. On Tuesday, March 2, they watched the jail from a tamale stand and inspected the streets in the vicinity, attracting a following of shine-boys, pimps, and guides. Everything still looked wrong to Hill. The street in front of the jail ran one way in the right direction, but the road was extremely narrow. Cops stood in front of the jail. Hill and Fielden weren't even sure Blake Davis was still in the Piedras Negras jail.

Returning to the motel, Hill talked by phone to Sterling Davis for the first time. The doctor in Dallas "sounded real positive about not sending anybody any money," and he only presumed that his son had not been moved. Fielden wanted to stage the break while he still had money to pay the motel bill. At midnight Hill put on his gloves and drove

the Ford across the bridge, but as Fielden inspected the sawed-off double-barrel, Hill continued to argue strenuously against going through with it. Hill said he didn't even know what Blake Davis looked like. If Fielden got killed, was Hill supposed to run in the jail yelling which one of you guys did we come after?

The argument was interrupted when a Piedras Negras patrol unit pulled up behind the Ford and turned its flashing lights on. Twisting around to see if the cops got out with pistols drawn, Fielden reached for the door handle and warned, "We're gonna have to take 'em out . . ."

"Wait a minute," Hill cried, grabbing for Fielden's arm as one of the cops got out of the car. "Let's see what he wants, and then we'll kill him."

As the Mexican cop approached, Hill extended a hand toward him and said, "*Señor*, which way to Boys Town?"

The cop's gaze focused on Hill's grimy glove. "Ah, *señor*," he said. "Follow me."

Trailing the patrol unit, Hill fell far enough back that Fielden was able to ditch the guns in some bushes. In the bordello Hill and Fielden thanked the cops and went into one of the bars. Hill only had $20, but he was so happy he bought one of the whores several drinks.

Wednesday was visitors' day at the Piedras Negras jail. A guard frisked Fielden and Hill and unlocked the door which led back to the prisoners. A stocky man with curly hair greeted Fielden from the first cell. Fielden stood shoulder-to-shoulder with other visitors outside the bars as he whispered instructions to Blake Davis. Hoping to gain some insight into the man he was going to rescue, Hill spoke briefly with Blake, but he wanted badly to get out of that jail. Hill was convinced that the purpose of their visit was transparently obvious to the guards; compared to the other visitors, they looked like gangsters. And Hill had spent enough time in American jails to react emotionally to the horror of this one. The odor in the jail was appalling. The visitors were panting and drenched with sweat. Recalling the expressions of the prisoners' faces, Hill later remarked, "Have you ever seen a drowning dog?"

In the motel room Hill and Fielden argued again. Hill wanted a third man in the car with a walkie-talkie. "I've got to get this deal done," Fielden finally exploded. "I never took a deal that I didn't do. All I want is somebody to watch my back. I'll do it."

"Your back!" Hill cried. "I'm thinking about my butt, I'm thinking about my whole damn body!"

Fielden drove when they crossed the bridge after midnight. As they headed for the brush where they had stashed the guns, Hill was talking fast and furiously. They'd been hanging around the jail for three days; the Mexican cops had to know something was up. They didn't have enough gasoline money to get back to Dallas. "I don't wanta do it tonight," Hill said. "My karma's not right."

Fielden was more confident, but their lack of money worried him, as did Hill's queasiness. Fielden knew from his combat training that in an operation like this, both men needed conviction, if not total confidence. Hill's reluctance could get them both killed. After they retrieved the guns they came upon the same cops who had stopped them the night before. This time Fielden got out of the car. "Well, we're through in Boys Town," he told the cops. "How do we get out of here?"

The next morning a friend wired Fielden $50. They paid

the motel bill, gassed up the Ford, and headed back to Dallas. On the way they had a flat. Fielden was disgusted, uncertain he could ever count on Hill. But he had no other partner in mind; in hiring Hill he felt he'd already scraped the bottom of the barrel. Hill told Fielden he would proceed with the breakout only if they could recruit a third man and if they had enough money for their expenses. Fielden assigned Hill the task of finding the third man. As a token of good faith, Hill said he could probably raise the money if Fielden could not.

On Saturday, March 6, Hill met Sterling Davis for the first time in the office on Northwest Highway. Hill was impressed by the verbal assurance of the craggy-faced man, but something about the office made Hill think the doctor "hadn't been there too long." Davis showed Hill a photocopy of a check for $5000, but again refused to advance any expense money.

Hill proceeded with marked ambivalence. In the presence of Fielden, he offered the lookout job to a hulking friend. But something—perhaps affection, perhaps doubts about the man's reliability—made Hill ask his friend after Fielden was gone: "You remember those wetbacks you took on with a ball bat? They paid me two thousand dollars to get you across the border." The friend quickly withdrew. With him removed from the picture, Hill next offered the job to Billy Blackwell, a stocky eighteen-year-old with shoulder-length brown hair who had previously worked for Hill in the wrecker business. Blackwell now mowed lawns for a living and said he could not read or write. Billy lived with a teen-aged brother but he ran with a tough older crowd. To Blackwell, Mike Hill was a figure to admire, to emulate. Hill often teased his young protégé. "Stick with me, Billy, and we'll go places," he joked. "Let's you and me rob a bank." Billy laughed at the banter and always tagged along; Mike hadn't gotten him in trouble yet. Hill was willing to trust his life to the eighteen-year-old. He knew that Billy Blackwell's loyalty was absolute.

Having fulfilled his responsibility of hiring a third man, Hill again stalled. By now both men had begun to feel some sense of personal obligation to the Piedras Negras inmates, but Hill would have welcomed a development that took him off the hook. "I was trying to stay alive as long as I could," he later explained. He called Fielden and asked if he had been able to raise the money. Sounding dejected, Fielden said he had exhausted all his possibilities. Hill regretted his offer to raise the money himself. He considered telling Fielden that his monetary well had dried up too, but he hated to lie his way out of a commitment. He kept remembering his visit to the jail—how it looked, the drowning-dog expression on the prisoners' faces. So instead he lied to raise the money. He told a business creditor that repossession of a tractor-trailer rig in Mexico was worth $10,000 to himself and another man. With considerable misgivings, the creditor loaned Hill $1000, using the silver van for collateral, and said he was also willing to extend enough money on a separate loan to put Hill back in the used-car business. The offer provided Hill with a monetary out; he could pay his bills now without Sterling Davis' money. But Hill had become intrigued by another possibility. An electric-haired American in the cell next to Blake's had gotten word to Fielden that he would pay equal money if he came out too. Fielden at first intended to bring out only those two men. Hill wanted to free all the prisoners. If every freed Ameri-

can voluntarily came up with $5000, they were talking about a potential haul of more than 50 grand. Though Hill was more cautious than Fielden, he craved adventure, too. All those factors tipped the balance in favor of Hill's participation. He borrowed a spare for Fielden's Ford, walkie-talkies, new gloves, and blue ski masks with red insets on the faces. Hill was not an educated man, but he understood guerrilla psychology. They would go across in dark clothing, relying on the element of surprise. Mexican cops did not often encounter men with shotguns and ski masks.

On Wednesday morning, March 10, Hill phoned Blackwell and said, "Get your clothes together, Billy. We're going." Hill smoked a joint as he waited for his partners, and when Fielden's Ford pulled up outside the metal prefab apartment Hill looked out and saw a man with sandy razor-cut hair. That's not Billy, Hill thought, then remembered that Blackwell had been instructed to wear a short-hair wig.

Hill had described the project to Billy in extremely vague terms. He suspected that his young friend thought they were actually going down to repossess a truck. As they drove south, Hill tried to impress Blackwell with the seriousness of the situation. "Billy, what it boils down to is we're going to war down there, actually."

Billy swallowed hard. "Well Mike, don't you think I need a gun?"

In Waco Fielden bought a bottle of scotch. Hill knew he had to be straight when he crossed the Rio Grande, but in the meantime he and Billy were passing joints. As darkness fell and they passed through San Antonio, tension in the Ford began to build. "Why don't you quit smoking?" Fielden finally said.

Hill thought about it for a minute and said, "Well, hell, you're drinking."

They checked into the Holly Inn in Eagle Pass and watched TV until it went off. Billy got extremely quiet when Hill and Fielden pulled out the guns and ski masks. Fielden briefed Blackwell on each of the five checkpoints, and shortly after 2 a.m., Thursday, March 11, Billy wrapped his jacket around the walkie-talkie and began his lonely walk across the International Bridge.

Hill and Fielden gassed up the Ford and returned to the motel, where Hill stashed the rest of his money, about $400, in his shaving kit. He didn't want the Mexican cops to have it. Near the bridge again they tried to raise Billy, but a Mexican CB operator broke in over them. Finally Billy called from the vicinity of the jail: "*Ringo, this is Sam. There's a bunch of activity over here now. Cars coming in and out.*"

"OK. We'll call you back in ten minutes."

Waiting at the border, Hill took a couple of swallows from Fielden's bottle of scotch. A few yards away two Eagle Pass patrolmen were conducting some kind of investigation. Hill and Fielden pretended to study a map, and the cops drove away after giving them a long look. The cops circled the block, circled the block again. Hill got out and went over to the patrol car. "We been trying to read that map for an hour," he told the cops. "How do you get to Boys Town?"

The cops laughed, gave Hill directions, and drove away. In the car Hill and Fielden were unable to raise Blackwell. "They must've got Billy," Hill finally said. "Let's go on across." Crossing the bridge, Hill swallowed a tablet of speed.

Fielden's intelligence report anticipated three Mexican cops at the border, one in the small park behind the tollgates and three at the jail. At the border Hill saw at least six uniformed officers, all impressively armed with chromed sidepieces. After clearing Mexican customs, Hill turned off the plaza and tried to circle through the maze of narrow streets to the jail. Very quickly they were lost. A carload of Mexican youths pulled up beside them. Hill and Fielden knew that the street in front of the jail led to the bordello. *"Pinoche, pinoche,"* Hill cried. The Mexican youths laughed and motioned for the Ford to follow.

After tipping their guides a dollar, Hill and Fielden at last raised Billy. *"Six of the cops just left,"* he radioed. *"There shouldn't be but three in there now."*

They picked up Billy a block from the jail, and Hill parked the Ford one parking space away from the jail lot. "If you have any second thoughts, if your karma's not right . . ." Fielden began, but Hill was putting on his ski mask, too.

On the sidewalk Hill did a double take as he passed the car parked in front of the Ford. "Don't freak out," he whispered to Fielden, "but there's a cop asleep in that car."

Fielden froze.

"What? Where?"

Headlights fell upon them from behind. Fielden concealed the sawed-off with his bulk and turned his face away; Hill stuffed the pump in a long flower pot on a wall, ripped his mask off, and turned to face the approaching motorists. Just another carload of horny American boys, Hill sighed to himself with relief. He put his ski mask back on and stared across the street. In the police auto pound he saw cars with all the doors flung open. Paranoid flash: they'd been set up, cops were lying down behind the seats! Fielden forged ahead with the tense determination of a Marine about to plant the flag at Iwo Jima. Hill followed at a trotting walk, searching the rooftops for soldiers with rifles. When Fielden grabbed the handle of the jail door, for the first time Hill was absolutely certain this deal was going down.

Fielden had been studying a Spanish dictionary, but he was still not certain how to say "get your hands up." *"Palmo asente!"* he yelled as he burst through the door; when he saw the inside of the jail, he thought god *damn*, we're gonna have to teach that boy to count. Through Hill's mind sped an image from a favorite movie: Newman and Redford, Cassidy and Sundance, running toward a lethal hail.

Behind two counters five guards and five police officers were interrogating an eighteen-year-old Mexican girl who'd been jailed on drug charges but claimed membership in *Liga 23 de Septiembre*, the cop-killing terrorists of the Sierra Madres. When Fielden and Hill ran through the door the disbelieving cops froze for an instant, then scattered in ten different directions.

"Freeze!" Fielden bellowed, and gave one cop a whack with the shotgun when he proved reluctant to surrender his pistol. Hill vaulted across the counter, and the Mexican stenographer fell out of his chair in front of him. Fielden looked up after relieving the first cop of his gun and saw that two more had their pistols drawn and aimed. "Huh uh," Fielden warned, and the force of the sawed-off twin barrels won out: two more pistols dropped to the floor. Staring at the bore of Hill's twelve-gauge, two cops raised their hands;

as if he were bailing water, a third tried to dislodge his pistol from his holster. Then Hill saw the M-1 propped against the wall. Easing toward the rifle, Hill glimpsed the toe of a man's shoe just behind him. He yelled and wheeled his twelve-gauge around. The cop reeled back in terrified surrender. Mike Hill had come very, very close to committing murder.

The element of surprise had worked. They had subdued the cops without firing a shot, which was essential if they had any hope of escaping death, capture, or at best, extradition. Fielden hurried to the barred door which led back to the cells and popped the chain with the bolt cutters. While Hill watched the cops, Fielden encountered the unarmed guard who tended the cells and a Chicano prisoner who was outside his cell when the shouting started. Fielden ran to the first cell and weighed down on the handles of the bolt cutters. But this chain broke the jaws of the bolt cutters. Fielden looked helplessly through the bars at Blake Davis. Davis groaned, "Oh, shit."

"Get the keys," one of the inmates recommended. "How do you say keys in Spanish?" Fielden snapped. *"Llave,"* the inmates clamored. *"La llave."*

What were they saying? Yobby? The Chicano inmate lashed the unarmed guard with the broken chain. The guard finally got the message when Fielden held the sawed-off to his head. Fielden walked the guard to a desk in the front office, then came back and unlocked Blake Davis' cell.

Hill started herding the cops down the corridor toward the cells. The eighteen-year-old girl looked at Hill and said, "Me too?"

For all Hill knew the girl was a cop. "You too, baby. You better move."

"Me too?" the girl said again.

Hill raised the shotgun to the girl's eye level and she followed the cops down the hall. Blake came out front and Hill handed him the Mexican M-1. While Blake watched the cops, Fielden unlocked the two remaining cells containing American men. One imprisoned Frenchman opted for the security of his cell, but the Mexican nationals were extremely willing to share the fruits of American labor. One of the American inmates ran around to the back and pried a weakened bar until the women were able to wriggle free. At least two dozen inmates were soon milling in the corridor, shushing each other and trying to contain their excitement. "Nobody goes out before us," Fielden ordered. "There's a man out there who'll cut you in two."

The Chicano who had attacked the guard broke for the front. Blake shouted a warning and leveled the M-1, but the Chicano reached Hill, who'd been pacing nervously and exhorting Fielden to hurry up. In the confusion, Hill forgot to snip the phone wire. The Chicano asked Hill if he had any more guns. Hill noticed the man had blood on his head. He handed over a Mexican pistol, and the Chicano kicked open an office door, revealing two *federales* who had been interrogating his wife before the jailbreak started. Since then they had been hiding quietly. The Chicano proceeded to pistol whip the *federales* noisily.

"Who was that?" Hill asked Blake, who had followed the Chicano up the hall.

"He's all right," Blake replied, then returned to the back. Suddenly Billy's voice came from the walkie-talkie: *"Mike, you got two coming through the door."*

Heart pounding, Hill crouched behind the counter and

waited. The Mexican cops never arrived; opening the door they'd seen an American inmate carrying a carbine. "Billy, where are they?" Hill finally blurted into his walkie-talkie.
*"I don't know, man. They left."*

Inside, Fielden herded the cops into a rear corridor but he couldn't get the dead-bolt lock to slide. He rounded up Blake and his hirsute friend who had promised money and led the procession out into the office. One of the American men asked Fielden to take the women but Fielden shook his head. Fielden told the Americans to turn right at the sidewalk, right again at the first corner. "When you hit water you know you're at the river."

Hill was jumping up and down, trying to let Fielden know he was caught up in the crowd. One of the American girls grabbed Hill's arm but he pried her fingers loose and joined Fielden, Blake, and his hairy monied friend in the front ranks. They ran to the Ford as the escapees sprinted. As the five men pulled away from the curb, the Mexican cops were already filtering back into the front office of the jail. The driver of a garbage truck pulled out in front of them. "Punch it!" Fielden yelled. "They're trying to block us in." "Calm down!" Hill yelled. "That guy's just trying to turn around." Hill had been in Mexico eight minutes, and the blurring rush of his amphetamine was really coming on. After what seemed like an eternity, they circled the plaza and reached the tollgate. Hill groaned and kept his foot away from the accelerator as the driver of a red station wagon chatted amiably with the customs toll-taker. Finally the station wagon moved on. Hill grinned at the Mexican official and handed him a quarter. Twelve cents would have sufficed.

As they crossed the bridge Fielden leaned forward and Blake started heaving incriminating evidence toward the river. Hill thought one of the guns bounced off the bridge, and Fielden looked back and saw one of the ski masks lying on the walkway. Everybody in the car was jabbering. Looming above the roof of the U.S. customs station was the neon sign of Texaco, and beyond that, Sears. "We're home," Hill was saying. "We're clean, just stay calm, we're gonna make it, we're doing it, god damn, we're home . . ."

The U.S. customs inspector was an old man. "Are you all American citizens?" he asked routinely. "Did you bring anything back from Mexico?"

When his editor called, *Dallas Times Herald* reporter Robert Montemayor was dressed to play tennis. A Texas Tech graduate and a cousin of the late Fred Carrasco's trusted attorney Ruben Montemayor, Robert joined the *Herald* staff in hopes of specializing in reporting Mexican-American news. Tennis could wait. After nine months, Montemayor finally had a South Texas assignment.

On Friday, March 12, at the Maverick County jail, Montemayor talked to a Piedras Negras escapee detained on an outstanding U.S. warrant. The man sent Montemayor to the motel room of one of five escapees who'd been arrested in Eagle Pass and then released. They talked for two hours at the motel, and after midnight the escapee urgently requested a ride out of Eagle Pass for himself and his wife. He told Montemayor that Maverick County officers had warned that *federales* were in town looking for escapees. On Saturday Montemayor interviewed the *comandante* of the jail,

then picked up his photographer and passengers and headed north. On the road Montemayor pressed the escapee for information about the breakout team. "They'll be reading your newspaper," the escapee finally hinted. In San Antonio Montemayor gave the escapee his Dallas phone number and reminded him, "You owe me a favor."

Montemayor's indebted passenger forwarded the reporter's phone number to Blake, who was staying at a Dallas Rodeway Inn only one block from the Mexican consulate. On Sunday, March 14, Blake called Montemayor and said he was sitting beside the two men who had pulled off the Piedras Negras jailbreak. He answered a few of Montemayor's questions but did not name Fielden or Hill, then said he had to turn himself over to federal marshals and would get back in touch in three or four days. Sterling Davis came to the motel happily shaking hands. Davis said there might be some movie money in this; one of his patients would draft an outline. Enthused, Blake mentioned that he'd been thinking about feeding some information to a *Times Herald* reporter. Sterling Davis was aghast. He pointed out that he was still on probation from the fraud conviction. Moviemakers fictionalized. Newspaper reporters named names.

Billy Blackwell took his $500 and went back to mowing lawns. Hill refitted his van with carpet, Naugahyde upholstery with a Lone Star flag motif, and a decorative American flag on the rear panel. Fielden, aware that Maverick County officers had found his sawed-off shotgun and the Mexican M-1 in weeds ten feet from the river, and suspicious of Davis' Hollywood negotiations, told his story to his Dallas lawyer, Ernie Kuehne. Blake had served 14 months of his three-year U.S. sentence on the Arizona pot conviction. Since then he had served 23 months behind Mexican bars. Surely the federal authorities would agree that was punishment enough. When Blake turned himself over to the marshals, he confidently expected to be interrogated and freed after a few days. Instead the marshals charged him with parole violation and remanded him to the federal reformatory at El Reno, Oklahoma.

Robert Montemayor still did not know the name of the escapee who had called him. The escapee he'd driven to San Antonio came by for some clippings one day and asked Montemayor if Sterling had called him. Sterling? The Mexicans had first identified the escapee Blake Davis as Sterling Blake. Montemayor ran a check of area prisons and located Blake in the Dallas County jail, but it was a week before he was able to reach Blake at El Reno. Blake detailed his experiences by phone, then referred the reporter to his father for more information. At first Sterling Davis denied any knowledge of the matter. But twice during April, Davis granted Montemayor interviews in his office.

Montemayor noted that the doctor's 1951 University of Mexico diploma was written in English. "I'm smiling at you, Robert," Davis told the young reporter. "You'll never know if a word of this is true." Davis claimed he had spent $70,000 trying to free his son from Mexican prison. Montemayor applied a pencil to the doctor's figures and observed they totaled only $40,000. By now *Times Herald* investigative reporter Hugh Aynesworth was working with Montemayor on the jailbreak story. Up to this point Davis had not revealed Fielden's name, but two days before the article was to appear, he referred Montemayor to Kuehne, who in turn gave the reporters his client's name. Aynesworth, who has a huge list of sources, quickly gathered information on Fielden, and when he told Kuehne the story was about to go to press, the lawyer called his client and said it looked like now was the time to talk.

Mike Hill was flabbergasted when he saw the copyrighted, joint byline story in the May 9 *Times Herald*. Hill had scarcely kept his role in the jailbreak secret; among friends he talked of little else. But glaring from the front page of the Sunday paper was a photograph of Fielden under the headline: DALLAS MAN EXECUTED JAIL BREAKOUT. Fielden was described in the lead paragraph as ''a former Marine sergeant turned soldier of fortune.'' In the story Fielden, apparently caught up in the drama of his own role, referred to Hill as ''the backup man'' and called Billy ''a west Dallas punk.''

The next day Hill decided to share the spotlight; he appeared on the Channel 4 evening news wearing a ski mask and wielding a shotgun. In colorful detail he described the experience of standing down the Mexican guards. Sterling Davis confirmed his role in the break to UPI and consented to an interview by Montemayor and two television reporters. But the media party did not last long. The same Monday Hill appeared on TV, U.S. customs officials were in Kuehne's office looking for Fielden. The next night at a north Dallas singles bar called the Number Three Lift, Kuehne and Fielden charted a course of action. They would cooperate fully, cop the best possible plea, and peddle the story for all it was worth. On Thursday, May 13, Fielden was charged with illegal exportation of the sawed-off shotgun and released on bond. Hill, who was not part of the bargain and had not been consulted about it, underwent the same process the next day. The following Tuesday, Fielden, Hill, the elder Davis, and Cooter were summoned before the federal grand jury in San Antonio.

The Piedras Negras jailbreak was flaring into an international incident. Mexican officials called Fielden and Hill common criminals and decried their heroes' reception by the American press. The Mexican government initiated extradition proceedings against the American escapees. Wary of more American raids, penal authorities busily transferred prisoners and tightened security at all Mexican jails. In the past, U.S. embassy and consular officials had fielded allegations of Mexican abuse of American prisoners. Now the issue graduated from their hands. Out of Secretary of State Henry Kissinger's mid-June negotiations with Mexican President Luis Echeverría came proposals for a U.S.-Mexico prisoner exchange. In late June Gerald Ford signed a military assistance bill Congress had amended to commit the force and authority of the presidency to the investigation of prisoner abuse. Kissinger would submit a personal report to Congress; Ford would negotiate directly with the Mexican president.

To Mike Hill it seemed the world was spinning on his axis. Heads of state were probably talking about him. Yet Hill was broke again, and he was in the worst trouble of his life. One June night at White Rock Lake Fielden told Hill that he'd already cut his deal; it was every man for himself. Hill had been told by his lawyer to keep his mouth shut, but everybody else was talking. Once again Hill likened his predicament to scenes from his favorite movies. *The Getaway. The Missouri Breaks*. Paranoia overwhelmed him.

Maybe he was an unwitting pawn on a huge conspiratorial chessboard. He was absolutely certain his old comrades were dealing him out of the movie game. Hill fired his lawyer and consented to an interview by Dan Rather. *Sixty Minutes* wouldn't talk to him in Dallas; Hill had to go to Eagle Pass, where he nervously answered Rather's questions with his back to the Rio Grande and Piedras Negras. Hill summoned a press conference the morning of June 28. He told reporters that he deserved equal blame or credit for the break, then he hitched a ride toward his arraignment in Del Rio, where he intended to plead not guilty.

In San Antonio that night Hill told me there would have been wholesale changes if he had commanded the Piedras Negras operation. ''Namely, I wouldn't have used Chubby,'' Hill said of his former partner. Examining his motives, Hill said, ''I've got a whole lot of potential. I can make a lot of money. Five thousand dollars don't turn me on enough to make me wanta go die for it. I can make five thousand dollars in a little while, just working, doing what I do. I don't know why I did it. But in the end I don't think the money had anything to do with it. I'll say this: if I ran for president I know seventeen people who'd vote for me.''

In Del Rio the federal indictments rained down. The original indictments against Fielden and Hill were superseded by a new four-count bill that named Hill on all counts, Sterling Davis on three, Billy Blackwell on two. Mentioned on three counts but *indicted* only for conspiracy, Fielden copped his plea. When Hill arrived in Del Rio he was looking at a maximum sentence of two years; when he left he was looking at as many as 22. Hill bitterly contended he was being prosecuted under pressure from the Mexican government. ''If we'd killed anybody, the Americans would have taken us right back across that border, and I wouldn't have blamed them a bit. We don't have the right to go over there and kill anybody. I'd feel the same way if they'd come over and done something like that, if they'd killed anybody. But it was a peaceful kind of deal and the Mexicans don't have any right to be mad, because nobody got hurt. They oughta be thankful for what they've got. That's the main mistake people make; they ain't ever thankful for what they got left. They just cuss everybody for what happened to them. They don't think about how bad it could have been.''

In Dallas Hill delivered Blackwell to U.S. marshals on June 30, then learned the judge in Del Rio wanted a $25,000 cash bond. Billy was in jail three days before the bond was reduced. When we talked over supper one night, Hill glumly said he had twenty cents to his name. ''I'm not working because I can't keep my mind on it,'' he said. ''And the way things are going, it looks like I oughta take a little vacation. It may be a long time before I get another chance.''

Ernie Kuehne is hopeful that Fielden will serve no more than a year. Endeavors to capitalize on Fielden's exploit had proved taxing but fruitful. Austin public relations executive Neal Spelce listened to Fielden's story and told Kuehne he believed they'd been scooped fictionally by the Charles Bronson movie *Breakout*. Fielden made a couple of promotional trips to Los Angeles and finally sold his story rights to Mustang Productions, a company owned in part by former Dallas City Councilman Charles Terrell. Kuehne said the deal might run well into six figures; of course, given the uncertainties of the movie business, it might amount to very little. On the advice of Kuehne, who dislikes Dan

Rather, Fielden declined a *Sixty Minutes* interview, but after the plea was copped in Del Rio, he went public with a new image. He bought a new suit and had his hair styled. Kuehne portrayed his client as a figure larger than life, a patriotic veteran who, except for one wild act of valor, had a clean criminal record.

"Let him shoot his best shot," Fielden said of Hill's erratic efforts to crowd into the limelight. Asked for a personal reading of his former partner in arms, Fielden told me, "I wouldn't go out partying with him, drinking or anything. I'm not saying I'm better than anybody else, but we're coming from two different places. I like to feel I have a little class. I basically hired the man to do a job. He did his job, and he was paid for it."

Fielden delved into his motives at the time of the break. "No one should be treated the way those prisoners were being treated. But the number one reason was the money. If somebody had said, 'Well, I can't give you any money, but would you please do it,' I would have said, 'Up your ass.'

"I really didn't think I was doing anything wrong," he continued. "If I'd known, going in, that I was going to be breaking the laws of this country—Mexico I didn't care about—I wouldn't have done it. But since I found out that I did break the law, I'll have to pay for it. That's the American way, isn't it?"

But surely Fielden understood that even American prisons were no picnic ground?

"Now I won't go in liking it," Fielden said. "But the last thing I want is to owe this country anything. This country's been good to me. If I owe it a year or two or five out of my life, well, I can't run away. I'd be losing too much."

Mike Hill was convinced that Fielden's view of Hill as a hireling rather than a partner was costing Hill money. Had Blake's electric-haired friend kept his promise to reward his rescuers? Had the other prisoners shown their gratitude to the man the *Times Herald* had portrayed as the leader of the jailbreak? If so, none of the money had found its way to Hill.

Billy Blackwell mowed his lawns in a daze, wide-eyed with fright. In El Reno, Blake Davis talked to nobody and hoped for an early release on parole. The world of Sterling Davis had been crumbling for some time. On May 12 he was forced to withdraw his application for a state psychologist's license. On July 9 the Mexican consul in Dallas, Javier Escobar, announced that the National University in Mexico City categorically denied ever having granted Sterling Davis a degree. On July 12 Judge Sarah T. Hughes scheduled a hearing to discuss revocation of the discredited doctor's probation.

Subpoenaed as a possible witness but unaccompanied by Kuehne, Fielden sat on the rear bench of Hughes' courtroom in a new suit. "This pretrial release program is all right," he said companionably. "They'll send you to trade school if you wanta go. They keep trying to get me a job, and I tell them, man, I've got a job." A job promoting Don Fielden. Hugh Aynesworth, whom Fielden considers "an OK dude," shook his hand and took a seat beside him. Hill came in wearing a cowboy hat, accompanied by an attorney who wore a cowboy hat. Then Sterling Davis entered the courtroom, walking slowly and carefully, a gaunt but broad-shouldered figure in a gray suit.

Judge Hughes said they would not discuss particulars of the Piedras Negras jailbreak, since Davis was charged in connection with that in another federal court. However, U.S. attorneys charged that in November 1975 and February 1976 Davis violated terms of his probation by leaving the country without permission. They claimed that at the time Davis was telling Robert Montemayor and two television reporters he had spent $70,000 trying to free his son, he had paid only $225 of his $16,000 restitution obligations and retired only $200 of his $10,000 fine.

On the stand Davis said one of the violations was the result of a misunderstanding on his part. To him Eagle Pass and Piedras Negras were one and the same. On one occasion he asked his probation officer if he could go to Eagle Pass to take Thanksgiving leftovers to his son. He attributed the $70,000 figure to a misunderstanding by Montemayor: he had told the young reporter about a woman in California who claimed to have squandered $70,000 trying to free her son, but he never claimed that himself. ("The conversations are on tape," Aynesworth said later.) When he quoted that figure to the television reporters, he was trying to enhance his movie negotiations; indeed, he had warned the reporters that he would not be telling the truth. In order to meet the monetary demands of his probation, Davis said that in the past few weeks he had borrowed $3000 on his life insurance policy, $2000 from his son, $1000 from his mother-in-law. After the trial in Del Rio the $2500 he had used to post bond would be forwarded. He was prepared to sign over his movie contract rights . . .

"What is this movie?" Judge Hughes interrupted. "I want to know more about it."

"When all this came out in the newspapers," Davis explained in a soft, deep voice, "people descended from everywhere. Movie and book people. Most were, pardon the expression, fly-by-nighters. But Warner Brothers advanced me a thousand dollars on a movie contract. The Warner Brothers people were here in town last week. They're supposed to start shooting in September."

Davis continued that he was not a rich man. A thousand-dollar advance is not much assurance in the movie business, and Davis' attorney conceded the letter agreement was rather loosely written. After the frog farm trial he had trouble finding work. Just when he was getting on his feet, he had to hire a full-time nurse for his invalid mother-in-law.

"How much did you pay the nurse?" the U.S. attorney asked.

"Eleven dollars a day," Davis replied.

"How did you afford that?"

Davis started to answer, then winced and closed his eyes. If the long moment of silence was a con, it was a brilliant performance. "I was working then," Davis finally said, "teaching. Sometimes the students asked for counseling."

Davis' attorney reminded the court of the doctor's heart and diabetic conditions and then played his trump cards. The attorney entered as evidence two letters which indicated the $5000 that financed the breakout was raised by friends of Blake and forwarded to the doctor by a Tucson attorney.

Judge Hughes recessed the hearing pending disposition of the September 21 trial in Del Rio, where the elder Davis, Hill, and Blackwell would face the charges of international gunrunning. Fielden's sentencing was set the same day in the same courtroom. Kuehne insisted that the terms of Fielden's deal did not include turning state's evidence, but by pleading guilty Fielden has waived his Fifth Amendment rights. If subpoenaed, Fielden would have no choice but to testify against his former comrades.

Mike Hill cut Fielden a baleful look as he left the courtroom. As Sterling Davis moved slowly toward the elevators, he nodded to reporters and Fielden. The smile on his face was inscrutably kind. In the hallway Fielden stood talking to the U.S. customs agents who had conducted the Piedras Negras investigation. For a man bound for the penitentiary, Fielden looked remarkably happy. His rounded cheeks seemed on the verge of explosive laughter. As a part of some publicity hustle, he was going to Scotland to dive in search of the Loch Ness monster. Don Fielden. Soldier of Hollywood fortune.

Four hundred and twenty-five miles away the Rio Grande was raging. Rain had been falling at Eagle Pass and Piedras Negras for nearly two weeks: maddening rain, ten or fifteen brief showers a day. Knowledgeable residents of Eagle Pass claimed the American escapees had picked the worst spot to swim the river. As the river sweeps around the International Bridge abutments it deepens and forms strong undertows. When the American escapees splashed into the water the morning of March 11 the Rio Grande was running shallow. Four months later the flooding river churned violently and frothed with heavy debris; only the strongest swimmer could have stayed alive in that current beneath the bridge.

Across the river, the Piedras Negras municipal jail was a bristling fortress braced for attack. More armed guards, more heavy steel bars. It was no place for gringos to go sightseeing. A khaki-uniformed police officer gripped his carbine sling and squinted malevolently at three American visitors who seemed excessively interested in the barred door and corridor back to the cells. When the suspicious-looking Americans hurriedly drove away, three guards ran outside to record the license number. Too late, the Mexicans had learned to be careful. In the coffin-like cells of Piedras Negras jail, two new American prisoners waited for someone to come rescue them.

*—September 1976*

# THE GIRL, THE CON MAN, AND THE MASSAGE PARLOR KING

by Gregory Curtis

*How a murder was conceived, committed, solved, and prosecuted.*

I first met Sam Corey during a time that must now seem like the high point of his life. His massage parlor in San Antonio, the Tokyo House, was doing well, so well in fact, that he had expanded to Irving and was engaged in a legal fight to open parlors in Dallas. At the same time he was running for mayor of San Antonio. His campaign had no importance politically and its main effect was that it produced a great amount of publicity for Sam. He adopted the slogan, ''Let's put the nitty gritty before the city,'' had several masseuses run for city council on the same ticket with him, and promised voters that, if elected, he would hire a girl in hot pants to chauffeur the mayoral limousine. Sam also took a stand on such genuine issues as the completion of a freeway running through town and construction of a domed stadium. He even, in his first press release, claimed that in order to finance his campaign he would mortgage everything he owned and live in poverty, just as he had ''successfully lived in the days of monastic existence as a Brother of Mary.'' All this, the whole campaign, was a mixture of hokum and bombast, of a need to be taken seriously combined with a perverse delight in acting not at all serious. Sam wanted to be mayor and had a few ideas, not many but a few, of things that needed to be done in San Antonio. But apparently, the real reason he wanted to be mayor was not so much to get things done as to cruise around town in a limousine driven by a girl in hot pants. Sam assumed the voters of San Antonio would find this idea endearing.

I found it, if not exactly endearing, at least intriguing and went to San Antonio to write a story about Sam, his massage parlors, and his political shenanigans. Never has a reporter had a more willing subject. When I returned a few days later with a photographer, Sam, who weighed over 300 pounds at that time, immediately agreed to my suggestion

*Gregory Curtis, a member of the original* Texas Monthly *staff and a former senior editor, is the magazine's executive editor.*

that he pose getting a massage. He stripped off the tentlike dark blue suit that he had worn especially for this session. Then, in only a pair of voluminous white boxer shorts that began at his rib cage and extended in yards of billowing white cotton below his knees, Sam crawled up on a massage table and lay there, giggling as foolishly as a baby in its crib, while a team of his masseuses kneaded his ponderous belly and rubbed his stubby legs and the photographer circled the scene clicking off shot after shot.

The candidate for mayor lying on the massage table, moaning in lugubrious pleasure, seemed incapable then of anything beyond low foolishness. But while Sam was busy posing for my photographer, two men were waiting for him in his office. One of them was Dr. Charles Guilliam, and he and his associate were there to sell Sam a credit-card service for his massage parlors. This Dr. Guilliam was neither a psychologist as he claimed nor was his name Guilliam. He was Claudius James Giesick, a 26-year-old rip-off artist, con man, and pathological liar, who less than a year later would take his bride of a few weeks, a young masseuse Giesick had insured for $351,000, to a lonely road outside New Orleans and push her under a speeding automobile. Her skull and hips were brutally crushed, and yet she lingered for nine hours before she died. After a five-day trial, a New Orleans jury took only twenty minutes to decide that Sam Corey was the man who drove the car. Whatever cause far in the past or deep in their psyches made Corey and Giesick capable of conceiving and carrying out such a scheme, the direct series of events that led to the murder began when Sam, rosy-skinned from his massage and full of himself from being the center of attention for most of the afternoon, pulled his blue suit back over his boxer shorts and went into his office to talk about credit cards with this man posing as Dr. Guilliam.

I have seen Sam only twice since then. Once was a casual visit at the Tokyo House several months before the murder; the second was at Angola State Prison in Louisiana where

Sam now waits on death row. Giesick, who testified against Sam in return for a lesser sentence, is serving his 21 years in another part of the same prison.

Angola is deep in the backwoods of Louisiana, not far from the southwest corner of Mississippi. The road that leads to the prison curves past ramshackle cabins, a logging mill, and a single tiny settlement grown up around a service station, before it dead-ends abruptly at the prison gate. Inside, the prison is all cement floors and pale green walls; my first impression was that life there would be rather like life locked inside a high school lavatory. A Cajun guard led me through barred doors that he opened and locked behind us and down a short hallway and through another set of doors to death row. The guard motioned me into a long, narrow V-shaped room with nothing in it but two metal folding chairs. After a few minutes, another guard brought Sam in. He was handcuffed to a thick leather belt which went around his waist and buckled in back. As the guard unlocked the handcuffs and unbuckled the belt, Sam looked over at me. He had not known until the guard had come to get him that I was coming to visit, and the news had obviously cheered him up.

Sam has always maintained his innocence. Just before my visit Giesick had told reporters that he had lied on the stand and related a completely different account of his wife's murder, one that didn't implicate Sam at all. Giesick's changing stories had given Sam new hope that he might be released and spared the electric chair. Seeing me now, Sam immediately assumed that I had come to help him. The look in his eyes as he gazed toward me was positively beatific. "Greg, I can't believe it," he said. "It's *won*derful to see you."

"It's good to see you, too, Sam," I said, but I was feeling more than a little uncomfortable. Sam assumed I was there to write what he called the real story, but I had no way of knowing whether the real story as I saw it would help Sam or not. I tried to mention this a few times but my small warnings were washed away by the torrent of Sam's enthusiasm for seeing me and his desperate hope for himself.

He looked miserable. He had lost, he told me, more than 150 pounds and now weighed 185. Instead of looking trim, however, he looked deflated. Skin hung in slack folds about his surprisingly small frame. His eyes were deep, black holes in a rather large head. He wore a T-shirt, blue-black gabardine slacks, no socks, and black brogans that were now, since he'd lost so much weight, far too large for him.

He smoked a small pipe with a curved stem. He would light it, take a few puffs, let it go out, then light it again. He kept all his burnt matches in a neat pile beside him so as not to litter the bare floor of the room we were locked in. Frequently as we talked Sam would rise from his chair, shamble over to the guard who was sitting just outside the door, and explain to him the important nuance of something he had been telling me. "No kidding," the guard would say patiently and I could tell that he had had to listen to Sam's story many times. Then Sam would shamble back to his chair and, distracted now, fiddling with his pipe, ask me, "Where *were* we? What were we talking about?"

He stuck to the same story he told at the trial, that when the girl was run over he was in his motel room with a prostitute named Linda whom he had met outside a massage parlor on Canal Street earlier that afternoon. Linda has never turned up and that, to say the least, put a crimp in his defense. Sam says he said good-bye to her in the parking lot of a Holiday Inn and hasn't seen her since. "I'd never have been with her at all," he told me, "if I'd known I was going to have to explain to the whole *world* what I was doing."

A television blared in the background. At one point, Archie and Edith singing "Those Were the Days" echoed down the cellblock. "It's two o'clock," Sam said. "*All in the Family*." He went on to say how bored he was, that it wouldn't be so bad except for the boredom. He gets out of his nine-by-twelve cell only one hour every day so he can take a shower.

"If any good has come of this," he told me, "it's that this whole experience has brought me closer to God." He receives literature and letters from the members of the Full Gospel Business Men's Fellowship. He keeps a small altar in his cell, and a priest regularly hears his confession. Otherwise he is a debilitated man, desperate for the sympathy of anyone, pleading his innocence while the weight of his sentence pushes him farther and farther out of touch with reality. Just before I watched him get locked in his handcuff belt and led away toward his cell, he said to me, "But you know the *worst* thing about this?" And without waiting for me to reply, he answered his own question, "It's ruined a perfectly beautiful city for me. New Orleans. I'll never go back there again."

But later, driving back to New Orleans from the prison, I remembered one moment with Sam different from the rest. He was telling me how he'd met Linda outside the massage parlor. He'd given her some money to wait for him while he had his massage. "I had a very good massage," he said. And his whole countenance, until then very serious and businesslike, changed completely. A wicked gleam appeared in his eye and, smiling and flushed, pleased with himself and giving me conspiratorial winks, he said, "I got a local there, too."

I knew what a "local" was. That is massage parlor jargon for a masseuse masturbating her client. But I didn't understand why this moment remained so vividly in my mind or why it seemed so revealing of Sam or what it had to do with murder.

Patricia Ann Albanowski, the masseuse who would be run over and killed early one foggy morning in New Orleans, was a girl who pursued love. She grew up in New Jersey, but in September 1972, when she was 24, she left her parent's home and moved to Dallas. She had come halfway across the country after a dark and handsome pharmaceuticals salesman named Roger. She had a broad flat face with rather thick features which she tried to cover with too much make-up. On the other hand, she had long, slender legs, graceful movements, pretty strawberry blond hair, and a pleasant, if slightly goofy, disposition. Roger indulged her for a while.

They may or may not have been married. Trish later told neighbors different stories. Sometimes she said that she had never been married, other times that she had, and still other times that she had been married twice. Whatever their legal status, she moved in with Roger in a large apartment complex in suburban Richardson. She worked at various jobs, in a food-processing plant for a while, in a carpet company. One day she came home to discover that Roger had moved out. About the only thing he left behind was the message that she could find the mailbox key in the manager's office.

Whether for lack of money or lack of inclination, Trish didn't return home, leave Dallas, or even move out of the apartment. She still had her job at the carpet company but was so alone and friendless that she was forced, since she couldn't afford the apartment by herself, to advertise for a roommate in the newspaper.

Luckily, a girl who turned out to be pleasant and dependable answered the ad. When she came to see the apartment for the first time, Trish, instead of telling her potential roommate about the rent or the living arrangements or asking her any question about who she was or what she did, immediately began talking about Roger. She didn't call him by name but said that a guy had just moved out and left her all alone and that he had been in pharmaceuticals and now she was very sad. Trish talked on and on and her potential roommate didn't know what to say. She thought it odd enough to have a few second thoughts before finally moving in. But the explanation was simple enough—Trish didn't have anyone else she could talk to.

The roommate soon discovered about Trish what her neighbors and her succession of bosses always discovered, too. She was a cheerful, good-hearted, sweet girl, but hare-brained and empty-headed, someone so bewildered by the world around her she seemed to be living in a fog. She could not hold on to a job. Eventually even her boss at the carpet company, a man who liked her personally more than many people did, finally had to let her go. He could afford only one girl in his office, and Trish, despite her best intentions, had an aggravating tendency to work at her desk all day and leave everything more confused than when she started. Around the apartment complex she became an object of pity. Her neighbors told each other they felt sorry for her. They also agreed that she was a little strange, an impression that was most strongly reinforced when Trish was trying hardest to make friends. She would knock on someone's door and start talking to them on and on in a vague and confused ramble; she would lurk behind the floor-to-ceiling window at the front of her apartment and make what she hoped were funny faces at the people walking by; and she would stand at her kitchen windows with the curtains only inches apart and stare, sometimes for more than an hour, into the identical kitchen window of the identical apartment next door.

She made no secret about what she wanted, although it was obvious to everyone anyway. She wanted a husband or, lacking that, a man. She attended mass regularly, knew how to keep her apartment clean, liked trying to fix it up to look nice, could cook some, and enjoyed playing with children. But these wifely qualities didn't seem to appeal to the men she attracted. They came and went, a long string of them after Roger left, and none of them stayed with her for very long. Some were unsavory; one threatened to disfigure her and she lived the next weeks in extreme terror.

In the fall of 1973, about a year since she had come to Texas and nine months since Roger had left, she told the managers of the apartment complex that she was going to take a second job. That came as no surprise in itself since, needing money badly, she had recently sold some of her furniture to people at the complex for absurd prices—$30 for a nearly new console television. She told her neighbors, depending on her mood, that she was working as a model or as a hostess in a club. In the summer she lost her job at the carpet company, and after a brief stint at a food-processing company, she fell back on her new work for her total support. The only person who knew what she was really doing was a bachelor who lived in the apartment complex. She gave him a book of matches from her new place of employment: the Geisha House of Massage. Trish was neither a model nor a hostess but a masseuse. She began to keep very late hours and frequently arrived home with different men. When the bachelor asked her about one of the men he'd seen leaving her apartment, she replied, "Oh, him. He's a client." And the bachelor assumed she meant him to know exactly what she had implied.

Dallas had an ordinance that prohibited masseurs or masseuses from massaging anyone of the opposite sex, as did many of the suburban towns surrounding the city. Massage parlor operators tried to have the law declared unconstitutional by the courts, but while they were fighting that legal battle, which they were never able to win, they established their businesses in unincorporated county areas in the environs of Dallas. The first to arrive was Sam Corey, who opened his Tokyo House on a street just west of Irving, which is in turn just west of Dallas. Neighbors protested, not wanting what they took to be a den of prostitution in their midst, but their pleas to officials and picket lines outside Sam Corey's door weren't able to force Sam to close. On the contrary, the business looked so successful that a man named Jim Floyd opened a competing massage parlor of his own and named it the Geisha House. His first location was just outside Irving not far from Sam Corey's place. He soon opened a second parlor southeast of Dallas near Seagoville.

The Irving parlor may have been somewhat better, but the Seagoville parlor, the only one still operating, is merely a mobile home on cement blocks at the side of a highway access road. Inside two bored masseuses pass the time between customers by playing solitaire. They are surrounded by cheap furniture, dirty carpet, dismal wood paneling, overflowing ashtrays, empty soft drink cans, and half-empty cups of coffee so old the coffee looks solid. Trish worked here. She also worked in the Irving parlor. Whatever it seemed like to her, to anyone else it would seem like a place, even among massage parlors, where one would go only at the very end of the line.

About the time Trish started working full-time for the Geisha House, a man in his late twenties who said he was Dr. Guilliam, a clinical psychologist, became a regular customer of massage parlors in the Dallas area. He was a few inches shorter than Trish and had let himself get just slightly on the pudgy side, but he had a pleasant, open face, an easy and friendly way of talking, and always seemed to have plenty of money. Trish was still unabashedly looking for a man. All the other masseuses knew it; they thought she should have been smart enough to know that a massage parlor was the wrong place to look. Still, Trish wasn't shy about saying that she wished she could see something more of Dr. Guilliam.

Trish got a call one afternoon from another masseuse who had gone to a meeting with their boss Jim Floyd. She said Floyd was sending a man over and Trish was to give him a complimentary massage. The man turned out to be Dr. Guilliam. He took an immediate interest in her. They spent a long time together that first meeting. He seemed to understand her loneliness. He talked about his work and the money he made from it. She made love with him. After that he kept coming around to see her and, right from the start, began asking her to marry him.

At first she said yes, but then she changed her mind. He was nice and all that, but she didn't have any strong feelings for him and there were certain things about him that worried her. It turned out that his name wasn't really Guilliam but Claudius James Giesick. He told her he used Guilliam because he had helped apprehend some gold smugglers and, as protection from reprisals, the federal government had given him a new identity. He said he really was a psychologist; however, he didn't have an office, and he would disappear suddenly only to turn up again later. Trish had already had too much experience with disappearing men. Still Giesick-Guilliam kept coming around to see her.

Giesick, despite his glib and friendly manner, didn't seem to have many more friends than she had. The only one she knew about was Sam Corey, the owner of the rival massage parlor in Irving. Giesick had brought Corey with him several times and when Trish decided that she didn't want to marry Giesick after all, it was Corey who interceded and convinced her that she should. He said that Giesick really loved her and had enough money to take good care of her. She agreed a second time to marry him. At least it would be better than working at the Geisha House.

Nevertheless, Trish didn't feel completely comfortable with her decision. She went to see her former boss at the carpet company and talked to him about it. He said the man sounded a little suspect and gently asked her if she thought it was a good idea to marry someone she knew so little about. Neighbors at the apartments would occasionally ask her the same thing, but she took these questions as criticisms of her and responded by defending her decision. Only to her bachelor acquaintance did she say that she didn't love Giesick but that he was nice to her and made a lot of money and that was why she was going through with it.

Giesick told Trish that he had been married twice before. Once was to a former Miss Texas who, along with their child, had been killed in a hit-and-run accident. He had been married another time and divorced. That prevented them from being married in the Catholic church as Trish would have liked. It turned out, however, that Sam Corey had once been a novitiate in the Brotherhood of Mary and had now become a pastor in something called the Calvary Grace Christian Church of Faith. His motive in becoming a pastor was no more high-minded than the wish to escape police harassment of his massage parlors. He wanted to claim massage as a religious rite in his church, a rite whose practice would be protected under the Constitution. He had even taken steps to change the name of his business from Tokyo House of Massage to Tokyo House Massage Temple. Even so, Sam Corey had the legal right to perform marriages, and his old affiliation with the Catholic church made him seem to Trish something closer to a real priest than an ordinary minister. On January 2, 1974, he performed the ceremony in Trish's apartment. Only Sam Corey, Giesick, and Trish were there, although two other names were falsely added to the marriage license as witnesses. After the ceremony, Trish called her parents in New Jersey. "Hi, Mom," she said. "This is Mrs. Giesick." The new couple set up housekeeping in the apartment where Trish had been living since she came to Texas.

Before they were married, Giesick had promised that he would buy her a $100,000 house in Richardson and a yacht and take her on a long honeymoon trip. But after the marriage, the first thing her husband bought was life insurance. Losing one wife in an accident had taught him a lesson, he said. He wanted to be prepared in case, God forbid, anything should happen to either of them.

Their marriage had taken place on a Wednesday. The following Friday her husband had an insurance agent call on them at the apartment. The next Monday Giesick bought a $50,000 policy with a double-indemnity clause that covered both him and Trish. It seemed like a rather large policy to her, but her husband was a man who made lots of money and should know how much insurance to buy. When she signed the forms, she wrote "Patricia Ann" and was about to add her maiden name, Albanowski. She got as far as the "A" when she realized her mistake. She drew two lines through the letter and wrote "Giesick" after it.

Then her husband left town on what he told her was a business trip. He gave her a number where he could be reached but it turned out to be the number of an answering service. Trish desperately called Sam Corey and finally managed to reach her husband through him. Giesick told her he would be back by the weekend and she should start checking with travel agencies because they were going to take that trip he'd promised her. They would go to Florida, the Caribbean, home to New Jersey, perhaps to South America. When he reappeared that weekend he was sporting a new dark blue Chevrolet Monte Carlo with a black vinyl roof. He also presented Trish with a St. Bernard puppy as a wedding present.

Sunday afternoon, January 13, her new husband drove Trish out to the Dallas-Fort Worth Airport, which had just opened that day. They were leaving for New Orleans and he thought it would be a good idea to buy more insurance for the trip. He took her to the Tele-Trip insurance booth and asked specifically for the $300,000 annual policy. The woman in the booth explained that $200,000 of the coverage would be on vehicles, common carriers, and scheduled airlines, but the remaining $100,000 would only cover common carriers and scheduled airlines. Giesick immediately asked if that extra $100,000 covered automobile travel. The woman in the booth told him it didn't and Giesick said that he definitely was not interested in the additional coverage. The woman wrote out a $200,000 policy for Patricia Ann Giesick with Dr. Claudius Giesick as the beneficiary.

It was late in the evening before they were ready to leave. They planned to go to New Orleans first and from there to Florida where they would see Disneyworld and catch a boat for a Caribbean cruise. Trish insisted, although it was getting a little late, on taking the puppy down to the apartment of her bachelor acquaintance so she could say good-bye and let his young son, whom she had always liked, play with the puppy. When she introduced the two men, Giesick, normally so glib and outgoing, was coolly polite, remained in the background, and said very little. It was after nine o'clock by the time they left, but Trish now insisted on showing the puppy and saying good-bye to two girls who lived in a neighboring apartment. Again Giesick stayed quietly in the background. But when the visit dragged on, he interrupted, on this midwinter night, with, "Come on, Trish. Let's get going before it gets hot."

The vague unease about Giesick that had bothered Trish before their marriage did not go away. If she had hoped that his strange behavior would change on the trip, she was disappointed. They arrived in New Orleans on Monday afternoon and the first thing Giesick did was disappear again. He told her the car, new as it was, was having transmission problems and he needed to see about having it fixed. Their motel was an isolated Ramada Inn far away from the center of the city on a road called Chef Menteur Highway. This road had once been the major thoroughfare entering New Orleans from the east, but when a new interstate opened, traffic on Chef Menteur dropped off drastically. The Ramada Inn and the Quality Inn next to it survived only because several large plants nearby brought in business. A few blocks away there was a shopping center with a grocery store, a service station, and a few small shops, but nothing that was very entertaining. Left alone in the motel, Trish had nowhere to go and nothing to do but play with the puppy.

Giesick didn't come back to their motel room for more than two hours. He said that he'd had to hitchhike from the dealer where he'd left the car. He acted very restless and upset. They watched television in their room for a while, but still he was restless. About 9:30 p.m. he suggested that they go walk along the highway for a while so they could talk things over. Trish said all right, although she was tired from the long drive from Dallas. It wasn't a pretty or quiet or easy place to walk. Cars and trucks, noisy and belching exhaust, rumbled past. Their wheels frequently spit gravel that had spread onto the asphalt from the narrow shoulders. It was dark and Trish and her husband stumbled along the side of the road. They couldn't really talk—it seemed like a car or truck went by every second—and Trish was soon ready to go back to the motel. But her husband seemed determined to stay out there. They walked up and down the same stretch of road several times before Giesick finally agreed to return to their room.

But he didn't stay there. He said the puppy needed walking and left her, almost exhausted, alone again in the room. Perhaps a half hour later he came back. He said he'd found a pretty bayou just on the other side of the shopping center down the highway and wanted to show it to her. Reluctantly, tired as she was, Trish agreed to go. They walked the four or five blocks to the shopping center and another hundred yards up a street called Michoud Boulevard. It led past the shopping center to a low four-lane bridge spanning the bayou and on to a new and now, since it was nearly midnight, quiet residential area.

In the parking lot of a service station near the bridge a Chevrolet Monte Carlo, the same year but a different color from the one she and her husband had driven to New Orleans, was parked alone. A police car, lights on and motor running, had stopped next to the Monte Carlo and a patrolman was shining his flashlight into it. They had hardly gotten to the bridge before her husband wanted to take her back to the room again. But once there, he said he needed some time by himself to think things over and went out walking once again. Trish went to bed and her husband didn't return for several hours.

They slept so late that it was after one o'clock the next afternoon when Trish, alone, wandered into the motel lobby and asked if there was a good place to eat nearby, a place close enough to walk because their car was still in the shop.

The only place, other than the motel restaurant, was a combination bar and restaurant across the street. She ate there and went back to her room. Her husband was gone again—he had said he was going to hitchhike to the dealer to see about the car—and she had nothing to do. She spent the time waiting in the room or playing with the puppy on the small lawn just outside their door. Once the phone rang and she answered it, thinking it must be her husband. "Hello," she said, but whoever was on the other end of the line hung up without saying anything. It could have been a wrong number, but the phone rang several more times that afternoon and each time the same thing happened. She was alone in a strange city, stuck in an isolated motel, married to a man she had known only a month, and now strange phone calls plagued her dull and lonely afternoon.

Her husband returned about six o'clock with the news that their car still wasn't ready. They sent out for some pizza and spent the evening watching television or, rather, she watched television. Giesick was even more restless than the night before. He took the puppy out for several walks and other times went out by himself. He told her something had come up in his business and he was going to have to catch a plane the next day for a quick trip. He asked her to take some of his clothes to the desk clerk to see if they could be cleaned in time. Then he went out again because, he said, he needed to be by himself and think. She glumly gathered up her husband's dirty clothes.

It was just before 10:30 p.m. when she took the clothes to the desk clerk. Trish was despondent. She talked to the clerk a little and tried to make a joke about all that had gone wrong since they'd come here on their honeymoon. The brief conversation made her even sadder and, back in the room, she called her mother in New Jersey. Trish talked with her for half an hour. She told her about their difficulties with the car and said her husband was acting so strangely that she had begun to worry about something else—all that insurance Giesick had bought for her.

When her husband returned from his walk, it was well after midnight. Trish didn't want to be alone in the room anymore, but she was apprehensive about seeing him as well. For the first time, however, he was more like the way he'd been before they were married, more solicitous of her, filled with plans for what they would do together in the future. And he had seen something he wanted to show her. Down on the bayou they'd visited last night was a small family of ducks. They were right there near the edge of the road. The two of them could walk down there, discuss their future together on the way, and then watch the ducks on the bayou.

That wasn't much of an evening's entertainment for a honeymoon, but at least it was something. Trish put on a pair of old blue jeans, a red-and-blue striped cotton jersey, and a heavy white sweater. Outside it was slightly chilly and there was a thick fog. Giesick had a flashlight which helped them see their way, but even with its light, it was very easy to stumble and impossible to see very far ahead.

Still, Trish was feeling excited. The combination of cool, damp fog and her husband's better attitude helped pick her out of her doldrums and she found the walk down the highway to the intersection and then down Michoud Boulevard more interesting than it had been the night before. With her new enthusiasm, she kept pointing out various things they passed to her husband and kept wanting to stop and examine trees and street signs and store windows more closely. He indulged her for a while but seemed determined that they should get to the place along the bayou near the bridge where he'd seen the ducks. They walked under the overhead lights along the short bridge. The fog, illuminated beneath the lights, was a shimmering, golden mist. Just across the bridge they walked down a short terrace to the bayou's edge. The grass, wet from the fog, was slippery. It was very quiet, the water making no sound, no one out but the two of them, no lights on in the houses nearby, and, except for an occasional car, no traffic on the boulevard. They spent several minutes down by the edge of the water until finally, when they were somewhat chilled, they began to climb the few slippery steps back up the terrace. During the climb a souped-up car with very loud mufflers drove by. The car was dark-colored and the driver looked very young. By the time they had reached the top, no longer than a few seconds, the car was out of sight, its mufflers a low moan resonating deep in the fog.

Her husband had fallen slightly behind and Trish waited on the sidewalk for a moment with her back to him. Then she started across the street. She had taken only a few steps when hands shoved hard against her back at the same time something tripped her. She sprawled face down on the street. She turned on her side and tried to push herself up on one arm to see what had happened. But a car traveling at high speed came at her out of the fog. One front tire hit her head; a rear tire, her hips. The car drove completely over her and kept on. She tried to lift herself on one arm again, then fell back against the pavement. If she saw anything before losing consciousness, it was her husband coming tentatively toward her.

Young Ricky Mock had just dropped his friend off at home. He was driving back down Michoud Boulevard, his loud mufflers roaring in the quiet night, when he saw the accident. A woman lay bleeding in the road. A man knelt over her. The man flagged Mock down and asked him to call for help. Mock gunned his '73 Dodge down Michoud, the car's mufflers roaring louder now, and turned right on Chef Menteur. Eight minutes later there were five patrol cars and an ambulance on the scene.

As ambulance attendants administered to the woman, the man walked over and sat on the curb. He had blood on his hands. An officer named Henderson came over to ask if he was hurt. "No," he said, "but she's hurt bad." Henderson asked him if he could describe the vehicle that had hit his wife. "I think it was a four door, a late model," the man said. "There was only one person in it and he was dark. I really don't know what kind of car it was." Henderson asked if he'd seen which direction the car took when it reached the highway. "No, I didn't," the man said. "The car never slowed down. In fact, after it hit my wife it picked up speed."

The ambulance was leaving by then and the investigating officers, Henderson and his partner Lesage, put the man into one of the patrol cars which would take him to the hospital. Henderson and Lesage stayed behind to take measurements and inspect the scene for whatever additional evidence they could find. The man had given his name as Claudius J. Giesick, Jr. He said he had driven with his wife to the bridge and now his car was parked in the supermarket park-

ing lot nearby. The officers walked over and inspected his car—a 1974 silver-blue Monte Carlo with a black vinyl top. It had no license plates. There was nothing else to help them, no skidmarks, no gouges in the road, no mud samples or other physical evidence of any kind, and no witnesses except Giesick. Henderson and Lesage went on to Methodist Hospital to question him some more.

When they arrived, they saw Giesick in the parking lot outside the emergency room talking with a short, but very heavyset man. The heavyset man had his back to the officers. Giesick waved and walked up to meet them. The heavyset man, even as Giesick walked away, didn't turn around but stood exactly where he was and kept his back to the officers.

Giesick had apparently regained some of his composure. When the officers asked him if he could remember anything else that might help them in their investigation, Giesick said he remembered more about the car. "It was dark," he said. "I believe it was a late model. After it hit my wife, I think it took a right at the highway. And I remember one more thing. It had loud mufflers." He explained that just before the accident he and his wife were standing near the bridge looking at the water. They were getting ready to go back to their car in the supermarket parking lot when she said, "Let's race back to the car," and started to run across the street. She didn't see the car coming which by then was only a few yards away. It didn't have its lights on. It swerved to try to avoid her but it was too late. The car knocked her to the ground, ran over her, and never slowed down.

The officers took down where Giesick was staying and then left the hospital to join in the search for the hit-and-run car. They stopped numerous cars that night but to no avail.

At 1 p.m. on January 16, a priest at the hospital contacted Lesage to say that Patricia Ann Giesick had passed away at eleven that morning. The officer then tried to call Giesick at his hotel and, since Giesick wasn't in, left a message for him to come to the district station at 11 p.m. when Lesage came on duty. Instead of coming to the station, Giesick called. He said he was already back in Dallas and left a number where he could be reached.

By now the death was in the news. Reporters called it "New Orleans' first traffic fatality of the new year."

The next afternoon Henderson went to the Ramada Inn where the Giesicks had stayed. Giesick had registered under the name of Charles J. Guilliam. At the time of the accident he explained this by saying he didn't want anyone to know where he and his wife were staying on their honeymoon. Henderson now learned that Giesick had paid his bill with a credit card issued to Dr. Charles Guilliam. The motel clerk had checked the card and found that it was valid. Giesick told the clerk Guilliam was a good friend who had given him the use of the card as a wedding present. Giesick had signed Dr. Guilliam's name to the bill and then signed his own name below it. Henderson and Lesage turned in their report with the recommendation that Homicide Division question Giesick further and make a more detailed investigation of the accident.

That job fell to Detective John Dillmann, a young, intense, extremely serious investigator with the general size and build of a college halfback. He began by reviewing Henderson and Lesage's report and interviewing them personally. Dillmann shared their doubts about Giesick but became especially determined in his task after reading a letter the New Orleans Police Department received about ten days after the accident. It was written on behalf of Trish's mother by her lawyer. From this letter and from telephone conversations with Mrs. Albanowski, Dillman learned that Patricia had called home only a few hours before her death and said she was worried about the large amount of insurance on her. She had also complained about their car still being in the shop. But Giesick, when he talked with Mrs. Albanowski after Patricia's death, at first said they had driven to the scene of the accident. When Mrs. Albanowski questioned him about the car being in the shop, he had changed his story to say they'd walked. She didn't know how much insurance money was involved, but she was extremely concerned that Patricia's death might not have been accidental.

It is one thing to suspect, as Dillmann already did, that this accident was really a murder. That suspicion combined with his immediate sympathy for Patricia's parents made Dillmann very determined about his investigation. But it is another thing, sympathy aside, to find whether those suspicions are true, and still another to develop the evidence to prove those suspicions in court. Dillmann began with very little solid information. He knew two names, Giesick and Guilliam, knew from motel records when Patricia and her husband arrived in New Orleans, and knew from Mrs. Albanowski her daughter's address in Richardson, the date she and Giesick had married, and the make of their car.

Beginning with the car, he canvassed Chevrolet dealers in the vicinity of the motel and discovered the one where Giesick, using the name Dr. Charles Giesick, had taken his Monte Carlo on January 14, the day he and Patricia arrived in New Orleans. Giesick claimed the car had transmission problems, but the mechanics found nothing wrong with the transmission. They made a few minor repairs and called Giesick. He picked up the Monte Carlo shortly after 5 p.m. the next day. Yet, Dillmann noted, later that night Patricia had complained to her mother that their new car was still in the shop.

Dillmann returned to his desk at the station and soon received a call from a representative of the Farmers Insurance Group who wanted to talk to the officer investigating the accident. One of Farmers agents had just contacted the home office. This agent had sold the Giesicks a $50,000 policy with a double-indemnity clause and Giesick had recently registered a claim to collect the $100,000 for Patricia's death. This information confirmed Mrs. Albanowski's statements about the large amount of insurance on her daughter.

Dillmann had been assigned to the case on a Tuesday. The following Saturday, February 2, he flew to Dallas hoping to question Giesick. Unfortunately, Giesick had disappeared, but Dillmann took the opportunity to interview Patricia's neighbors. He learned that she had come to Texas about a year and a half earlier and had known Giesick only a short time before marrying him. She had worked at several jobs, and according to one neighbor, had recently been working as a masseuse in "one of Sam Corey's places."

Dillmann was unfamiliar with this name and ran a routine check on it. Corey turned out to be well known to the Dallas and San Antonio vice squads because he owned massage parlors in both places. He lived in San Antonio but flew to Dallas almost daily. His only real trouble with the law,

however, was recent. Although free on bail, he was under indictment in Dallas County for the theft of some massage tables from another parlor. On Monday morning, checking with the Bureau of Vital Statistics, Dillmann learned from the Giesicks' marriage license, much to his surprise, that the presiding pastor had been the "Rt. Rev. Dr. Samuel C. Corey" of the Southwest Calvary Grace Christian Church, a church not registered in Dallas County.

Still, assuming Corey was actually ordained, there was nothing wrong with performing what appeared to be a legal marriage. Corey's involvement was peculiar and suspicious, but certainly not yet incriminating. For that matter, the same might be said, with only slightly less justification, about Giesick. But that afternoon Dillmann received a call from a representative of the Mutual of Omaha Insurance Company. They had written a $200,000 accident policy on Patricia Giesick. The insurance official suggested that he take Dillmann to the Dallas-Fort Worth Airport so he could interview the employees who had sold the insurance to the Giesicks. These interviews, which Dillmann conducted during most of the following day, revealed that Corey was involved in aspects of the case rather less religious than the rites of holy matrimony.

Dillmann talked with four employees of the Tele-Trip Company, a branch of Mutual of Omaha, which had issued the $200,000 policy on Patricia. From their statements he learned that two men had first come to the Love Field booth on January 10. One of the men was identified from a photograph as Corey; Dillmann had no photograph of Giesick, but the second man had identified himself by name and he matched Giesick's general physical description. When they first approached the booth, Giesick was holding a brochure that explained the various types of policies available. He asked about one called Plan C. Corey then prompted Giesick to ask about hit-and-run. After Giesick had asked, Corey again prompted him to say that he was interested because a friend had been involved in such an accident and the insurance company hadn't paid. Again, Giesick followed the prompting. Then he asked several more questions, all having to do with hit-and-run coverage and all prompted by Corey. He said he was interested in this coverage because he was planning a trip to Africa where the roads were very narrow and he wanted to be sure he was covered.

Two days later, on January 12, the two men returned and again asked about Plan C. This time Giesick was particularly interested in an additional rider of $100,000 that could be added to that plan to bring its total value to $300,000. On his earlier visit he had left the definite impression that the coverage was for him; now he said it was for his wife. He returned the following afternoon with her and asked specifically for the $300,000 policy. When he learned that the $100,000 rider didn't cover accidents involving private automobiles, he said he didn't want it after all and bought the $200,000 coverage in his wife's name with himself as beneficiary.

Dillmann, at the end of a week's investigation, now had a choice. One option was to fly to San Antonio and question Corey about the marriage and his trips to the insurance counter. But Dillmann, like a halfback, favored end runs over plunges through the center of the line. Obviously Corey was, in some strange way, linked to Patricia's death. But he still had nothing that linked Corey directly with the events in New Orleans. And he thought he was more likely to find that in New Orleans than in San Antonio.

Back in New Orleans he returned to the Ramada Inn on Chef Menteur. He talked to two desk clerks, the manager, a waitress in the restaurant, and a maid. They had all seen Corey with Giesick the morning after the accident and identified him from a photograph. According to their statements, Giesick had returned from the hospital about 10 a.m. that day. He was covered with blood and a little later gave his clothes to a clerk to send to the laundry. About 11 a.m. he entered the motel dining room with Corey, whom these witnesses, like the Tele-Trip personnel, all described as heavyset and very shabbily dressed. A few minutes later a priest from the hospital phoned to tell Giesick his wife had died. Giesick talked with the priest for several minutes and then left the motel with Corey.

Late in the afternoon one of the clerks went back to Giesick's room to tell him his clothes wouldn't be back from the cleaners until the next day. Corey was with Giesick in the room. The two of them were packing suitcases into a maroon car with a white roof. Giesick said he'd pick up his clothes later and asked if he could leave his Monte Carlo in the motel lot until he came back for his clothes. The clerk nodded but when she looked for the car the next day, it was gone.

Two days later, on Friday, January 18, Corey appeared at the Ramada Inn again and asked for Giesick's clothing. The police had requested the motel staff to notify them if anyone should come by to pick up this cleaning. The manager stalled Corey by saying he'd have to wait a few minutes as the clothes weren't back from the cleaners. Corey, suddenly very nervous, didn't wait. He got back in his car and sped out of the parking lot so fast that his rear wheels spun up a sheet of gravel. He stopped in the parking lot of the motel next door where he talked to a man waiting in a late-model blue car. The two men then drove off toward town.

The last person Dillmann interviewed was a maid who had seen Corey when he came back for Giesick's clothes. She said he was the same man she had seen walking across the street toward the Quality Inn next door the day before the accident. Dillmann walked straight next door and, from the motel register, discovered that Corey had checked in about 2 a.m. on January 15, about 24 hours before the accident. Not only had Corey been in New Orleans when Patricia was killed, but he also had been staying right next door.

The same night clerk who had checked Corey into the motel, a young student with the unfortunate name E.J. Swindler, had seen Corey the next night around two o'clock, only about fifteen minutes before the accident. Corey had come into the lobby asking for a place where he could buy aspirin. Swindler had no idea where to suggest at that late hour, but Corey came back about 25 minutes later to tell Swindler he'd managed to find an open doughnut shop down the highway where he'd made his purchase. Swindler said Corey was in a happy, expansive mood and seemed very pleased with himself.

Dillmann also noted that one of the calls Corey made from his room was to the residence of a Dr. Charles Guilliam at an address on Tuxford Drive in San Antonio. And, exploring one final nuance, Dillmann checked back with the Ramada Inn to see if they had rooms available on the night

of January 15. They had. Even though Corey knew the bride and groom well enough to have married them, he stayed out of sight in an adjoining motel.

Whatever Dillmann may have suspected at this point, all he could *prove* was that they were both in New Orleans on the night of Patricia's death. He had yet to talk with either Corey or Giesick to see how they would explain their actions; nor had he talked with this Dr. Guilliam to see where, if anywhere, he fit in. And he could not identify the murder weapon. Had it been Corey's car, or Giesick's or Guilliam's?—had he, by the way, been in New Orleans, too?—or had the weapon been some other car entirely?

A week later, Giesick was arrested in San Antonio on an old charge of passing worthless checks. That was enough for Dillmann to catch a plane in the hope of getting to San Antonio and interviewing Giesick before he got out of jail. And the way he'd gotten arrested was the first sign that, while Dillmann was trying to crack the case from the outside, the case might be cracking from the inside, too.

Giesick had contacted a San Antonio police detective with a story that he had spent the last two years keeping out of sight because his life was under constant threat from a criminal named Zent. Now, Giesick said, his wife had been killed in an accident down in New Orleans and the police from there might be making some inquiries about him. Would the detective tell New Orleans that Giesick had disappeared because he was a police informer in San Antonio? The request was so strange that the detective simply ran a computer check on Giesick, discovered the warrant, and arrested him. Dillmann wasn't sure, either, what Giesick was trying to do except throw up a smoke screen to hide himself from inquiries out of New Orleans. And Dillmann didn't get to ask Giesick what he was up to. By the time his plane landed in San Antonio, Giesick had been released on bond—posted by Sam Corey.

Dillmann had arrived in San Antonio early Sunday morning, February 17. Although thwarted in seeing Giesick, he asked Corey to come to the police station at 10 a.m. and took a formal statement from him. Much of what Corey said was untrue. He "emphatically and positively" denied knowing whether Patricia had worked in a massage parlor; he said he had seen Giesick only one time since his marriage and that was in Richardson; he claimed he had first heard of the accident when Patricia's mother called him at his massage parlor in San Antonio on the morning of January 16 and that he talked with Giesick long distance later that day; he said he had not been in New Orleans for several months; and he said that, although he had just posted bond for Giesick, he didn't know his address.

Then, having watched calmly while Corey lied to him at every turn, Dillmann drove out to the Tuxford Street address of Dr. James Guilliam. A woman in her middle twenties with long, straight blond hair came to the door, said she was Dr. Guilliam's wife, and that he was out of town where he couldn't be reached by phone. She claimed her husband was a consulting psychologist and a business associate of Giesick's. The only contact he had with Sam Corey was an occasional visit to his parlor for a massage. No, she had no pictures of her husband to show Dillmann. She became very nervous and insisted that her husband answer any more questions personally. As Dillmann left the house, he noticed a small detail that led him closer to what he had already begun to suspect—that Guilliam and Giesick were the same person. Patricia's neighbors in Richardson had told him that Giesick had given his wife a St. Bernard puppy. There were several St. Bernard puppies in the Guilliams' yard.

That growing suspicion was confirmed later that evening. Sitting in his motel room, Dillmann got a call from a San Antonio police officer who had known Giesick for six years. Giesick had asked the officer not to tell the New Orleans police he was now using the name Guilliam. This was, Dillmann thought, an obvious attempt to continue the confusion that Giesick's double identity had created during all the investigation. It also meant that Giesick was getting more and more worried about Dillmann finding him and was taking greater chances to try to prevent it. The San Antonio officer told Dillmann that Giesick was living on Tuxford Street with his wife Kathi, a woman with long, blond hair. She was the same woman Giesick had been married to for the six years the officer had known them. He didn't think they had ever been divorced although Giesick now was asking him to say that they had been divorced for several years.

Dillmann went to the Bexar County Bureau of Vital Statistics and found that Giesick had married Katherine Kiser in September 1969. There was no record of their ever being divorced. He talked with several neighbors near the Tuxford Street house who, from the mug shot taken when Giesick was arrested, identified him as their neighbor Dr. Charles Guilliam. Dillmann tried again to interview the blond woman he now knew to be Kathi Giesick, but she wouldn't talk at all without a lawyer.

That evening, February 18, after Dillmann had been working on the case for three weeks, he got to interview Giesick at last. It was Giesick, finally, who contacted Dillmann and, while he refused to come to police headquarters, agreed to meet at Sam Corey's massage parlor. During the interview Giesick claimed he was working with retarded school children in Dallas and had degrees from universities in Brazil, Germany, and Mexico. None of this turned out to be true. Giesick also volunteered, and subsequent checking confirmed, that he had been married four times: once from 1966 to 1967, which ended in divorce; once in California, a marriage that was annulled after three days; once to Katherine in 1969; and then, bigamously, to Patricia. His version of the accident was essentially the same story he told New Orleans police: he and Patricia had gone out by the bayou to look at ducks and she raced into the street where she was hit by a speeding car. Then, he said, the evening after the hit-and-run he'd flown to Houston and on to Dallas. He didn't mention seeing Sam Corey until the night of January 17 when he flew to San Antonio. Toward the end of the interview Giesick began acting extremely nervous, insisting that he had to catch a plane to Dallas and didn't have time to talk any longer. Dillmann pressed on. If he'd flown from New Orleans, what happened to his car? Well, he'd flown back to get it and on the way had stopped at the Ramada Inn to pick up his clothes. And yet, Dillmann knew, it was Corey who had tried unsuccessfully to pick up Giesick's clothes. Why had he listed himself as a widower on his marriage license? Giesick said he'd lied about that to Patricia and was simply keeping up the lie. After that Giesick insisted on leaving to catch his plane.

Dillmann himself then flew to Dallas, where he told police what he'd found, particularly the new information that Giesick was already married when he married Patricia. They had a justice of the peace issue a warrant for Giesick on charges of bigamy. On February 22 San Antonio police arrested him in front of his house on Tuxford as he tried to flee in his Monte Carlo. Dillmann had thought this car was possibly the one that killed Patricia, but a thorough examination by the police lab found nothing that could prove the car had hit anyone.

Although disappointed—after all the time he'd spent on the investigation, the best case he could make against Giesick was bigamy, not murder—Dillmann returned to New Orleans and tried, in the hope he could find additional evidence, to discover more about Giesick's and Corey's activities while they were in New Orleans. He learned that Giesick, far from losing all means of transportation when he took his Monte Carlo in for repairs, had immediately rented another Monte Carlo from Avis. In fact, Avis had come to the dealership to pick him up. At two o'clock that night, exactly 24 hours before the accident, Giesick and Corey appeared at the Avis rental desk at the New Orleans airport where Giesick exchanged his rented Monte Carlo for another one that was identical except for color. He gave no reason for wanting to exchange cars and the attendant, when he checked the returned car, found nothing wrong with it. Dillmann was now disappointed to learn that the second Monte Carlo was out of the state and he would be forced to wait for its return before inspecting it.

He conducted several more interviews. A guard at the hospital had seen Corey there shortly after the accident. The doctor who treated Patricia said she had tire marks on the left side of her head and left shoulder. If she had been hit running across the street, as Giesick had claimed, she would have been struck around her waist and hips and thrown clear rather than run over. And Dillmann found Ricky Mock, the first person on the scene. When he heard the loud mufflers on Mock's car, Dillmann deduced that this was the car with loud mufflers Giesick had described as the hit-and-run car.

At this point he was stalled in his investigation until the Avis car turned up; but he managed to make some progress anyway with the unwitting help of Giesick and Corey. They were beginning to show more strain under the pressure of Dillmann's dogged pursuit. Corey resorted to a private polygraph examiner he had once employed to screen girls who worked in his massage parlor. Apparently Corey thought he knew enough about polygraphs to be able to beat the test. Instead the test showed deception or guilt when Corey answered no to the questions "Do you know who killed Patricia Giesick?" and "Do you know who was driving the car that struck Patricia Giesick?" Corey then pleaded with the examiner not to let the New Orleans police know the full results of the tests.

The examiner, of course, was legally obligated not to conceal possible evidence, and when Dillmann learned of the test he flew back to San Antonio. The examiner said he had concluded from the test that Corey was involved in Patricia's death or at least had knowledge that Giesick planned to take her life. Dillmann went straight to the Tokyo House where he told Corey that, because of his knowledge of Giesick's plans, he should voluntarily come to New Orleans and give a statement to police. Corey denied having any knowledge, but Dillmann told him what he'd just learned from the polygraph examiner. Flushed and nervous, Corey called the examiner, who confirmed that Dillmann was telling the truth. Corey then became mysteriously ill, complaining of severe pains in his chest. He said he would think about coming to New Orleans and tell Dillmann his decision the next day. But when Dillmann returned to the Tokyo House, the receptionist said Mr. Corey had suffered a stroke. Further questions were referred to Corey's lawyer, William Miller. Dillmann had no luck that day trying to contact Miller.

Unless Corey agreed to go voluntarily, Dillmann had no way of forcing him, so he returned to New Orleans himself and waited—waited for the Avis car to turn up, waited for something to break in San Antonio. Three weeks passed and nothing happened. But during that time Corey and Giesick were apparently feeling the heat of the investigation more and more. They must have met together in fear but not yet, judging from the plan that resulted, in mistrust. The first Sunday in May Giesick met in a Denny's with a San Antonio police detective and regaled him with a tale about the night of Patricia's death. The detective called Dillmann who in turn called Giesick so he could repeat the story.

It was the wildest and most desperate story yet. Giesick said he was ready to surrender himself in New Orleans and plead guilty to conspiring to kill his wife. Giesick said Sam Corey wasn't involved in this conspiracy, and, on the contrary, had been the one who prevented him from carrying out his plans. Giesick said he had met a "hippie" he knew only as Ronnie in Dallas. They had conspired to take Patricia to New Orleans where Giesick was supposed to beat her over the head with a rock and Ronnie would run over her with a truck to make her murder look like an accident. Corey learned of the conspiracy, came to New Orleans, and talked him out of it. Then he and Patricia went out walking by the bayou. He told her of his former plans. She became hysterical and ran into the street where, completely by accident, she was run over. Although he had planned to kill her, her death was purely coincidental. Giesick added that now he knew he was a habitual liar but was under psychiatric treatment and thought he was making progress. He was willing to confess to conspiracy now because he believed he was emotionally unable to serve the long prison sentence that would certainly follow a murder conviction. He repeated that Sam Corey was never involved in the conspiracy. Dillmann was somewhat less than greatly moved by Giesick's tender emotional condition. He assumed since Giesick had been so careful to exclude Corey from guilt, that Giesick was making his confession because of pressure from Corey.

Two days later Giesick called Dillmann again. The pressure had finally produced a break between the conspirators. Giesick said there had been an attempt on his life by, he believed, Sam Corey. He wanted to know, if he came to New Orleans, confessed everything, and agreed to cooperate, would he be granted a lesser charge than murder. Dillmann consulted the district attorney's office and called Giesick back to say his cooperation would be taken into account but if he came to New Orleans he would be arrested. Giesick declined to come. "I'd rather take my chances with Sam Corey," he said. But the break was final. Two days later Giesick's attorney was in the DA's office trying to work a deal to get Giesick a reduced charge in return for testifying against Corey.

On May 13 the Avis car, the one Giesick had rented at the airport the night before the murder, arrived back in New Orleans. A thorough inspection revealed two nine-inch strands of human hair wrapped around and embedded in a spot of grease on a tie rod near the right front tire. Dillmann sent these hairs to the FBI Crime Lab. In order to obtain samples of Patricia's hair to compare with those on the car, Dillmann went to New Jersey where she had been buried near her parents' home, obtained a court order, and had her body exhumed. He took samples of her hair and sent them to the FBI. Hair, unlike fingerprints, does not have enough unique characteristics for one to say with certainty that it comes from a particular person. But there are some fifteen different traits by which hairs can be compared, among them color, texture, oil, type of scales, and various others. The hairs on the car, which had been crushed and ripped from the scalp as they would have been in an accident, matched Patricia's hair in all fifteen characteristics. Dillmann had found the murder weapon.

On June 6, 1974, Dillmann told an Orleans Parish grand jury what he'd learned of Patricia Albanowski Giesick's death. After listening to four hours of testimony, they returned indictments against Jim Giesick and Sam Corey for murder in the second degree.

But the conduct of the trial changed many things. The maximum penalty in Louisiana for second-degree murder is life in prison. Sam Corey now awaits his execution on death row.

Ralph Whalen, the man who prosecuted Sam Corey, joined the Orleans Parish District Attorney's staff in 1971, immediately after graduating from the Tulane law school. He didn't seem like one of that school's most promising graduates. Not especially enamored of study, he had finished in the middle of his class and took a job with the DA as much from default as from choice. He spent his first week observing the trials in progress. That Friday afternoon, riding a crowded rush-hour bus home, he began to cry. The spectacle of defendants and victims and police and tales of horrible crimes and men and women hauled off to jail had overwhelmed him. He wasn't sure he was doing the right thing. Perhaps his deepest sympathies were opposed to the very office he was now serving. Hadn't he seen people go to jail that very week for smoking marijuana, an act he wasn't sure should be a crime at all?

The following Monday, however, he was given a handful of case files, a pat on the back, and the instructions that it was time for him to get in there and start prosecuting. The moment he stepped into a courtroom as a lawyer with a case to win, those tears became a relic of a past life. The courtroom battle intrigued and inspired him; he lost his doubts about whether the defendants he prosecuted deserved jail; and he became so skillful so quickly that by the time the Corey case came along—the most publicized criminal case in New Orleans since Clay Shaw—the newspapers were referring to Whalen as "the Whacker," and he had decided that a prosecutor's job was his life's calling.

Whalen found himself matched against a lawyer whose reputation was as old and established as Whalen's was new and promising. Irvin Dymond, the most famous criminal lawyer in New Orleans, the man who had defended Clay Shaw, had taken Corey's case. While Whalen was short, trim, neatly dressed, and aggressive and intense in the courtroom, Dymond had a calmer style, slower, and, in appearance at least, not at all flamboyant. About 30 years older than Whalen, Dymond had not only the benefit of longer experience in the courts but also a marvelous deep voice and a talent for a sonorous and compelling oratory that is seldom found outside the South. William Miller, Corey's San Antonio lawyer, also helped with his defense. He had, strangely enough, first been Giesick's lawyer. When Giesick abandoned him for C. David Evans, a well-known San Antonio attorney and former state legislator, Corey went to Miller. Dymond's responsibilities were to try the case while Miller's were research and investigation, a separation of duties that did not prevent the two lawyers from publicly disagreeing about the progress and direction of the defense.

The prosecution's case, despite all the evidence Dillmann had compiled, was weakened by the lack of witnesses to the crime. There had been two people, a man and a woman, in a car in the parking lot where Giesick had left his Monte Carlo. Officers at the scene questioned them and discovered that, though they were both married, they weren't married to each other. Both the man and the woman denied seeing anything. They pleaded with the officers not to take their names and the officers acceded. The prosecution could establish only that Giesick was present at the scene, but not what he did there; it could establish Corey's whereabouts before and immediately after the murder, but had no evidence that placed him precisely at the scene. The DA's office had no doubts that these were the guilty men, but juries were unpredictable. They might not convict without some direct evidence or testimony about exactly what happened that night. The events on Michoud Boulevard remained a large spot of white canvas at the center of an otherwise convincing painting.

At the same time, Giesick's attorneys had been trying to make a deal for a reduced sentence in return for their client's testimony against Corey. Giesick could be the eyewitness the prosecution needed. David Evans, Giesick's attorney, also added another bit of pressure. He said he would fight extradition from Texas every step of the way. It was unlikely that, in the end, the Texas courts would refuse to extradite Giesick, but such legal maneuvering would tie things up in Texas for at least a year, perhaps longer. Eventually, the DA, who had come to believe that Corey was the instigator and mastermind of the plot, agreed to let Giesick plead guilty to manslaughter. Giesick surrendered himself and agreed to testify against Corey.

The case finally came to trial on November 6, almost ten months after Patricia's death. It had been scheduled once before, but Irvin Dymond, saying that he'd not had time to prepare his case properly, asked Whalen if he would agree to a continuance. Whalen agreed, but as the November 6 date approached, found that he was the one now not ready to go to trial. In the last ten months, important witnesses had moved or changed jobs and Whalen couldn't find some of them. He asked Dymond if he would agree to another continuance, but Dymond, thinking he had Whalen on the ropes, refused and insisted on going to trial. When the trial opened and Giesick and Corey stood stonily ignoring one another before the bar, Whalen shocked everyone by announcing that he was dropping the charges of second-degree murder against Sam Corey. A moment later he added,

"Your honor, it is the state's position that a charge of first-degree murder more accurately reflects the crime and we intend to seek such an indictment." Corey walked out of the courtroom a free man only to have Dillmann arrest him once again.

Whalen, forced into a corner, had spent some time consulting the law books. Louisiana had recently revised its laws concerning the death penalty to comply with Supreme Court decisions. The result was a special and specific category of crimes that were defined as first-degree murder. That offense carried a mandatory death penalty. Part of the statute stated that murder is in the first degree "when the offender has specific intent to commit murder and has received anything of value for committing the murder." The Louisiana lawmakers probably had murder for hire in mind in writing that passage, but Whalen saw no reason why it couldn't be applied to Corey's case. Wasn't the state contending that his motive was more than $300,000 in insurance money? Would not obtaining that money be receiving something "of value for committing the murder"? One day after the second-degree murder charge was dropped, the same grand jury again heard Dillmann's testimony and returned a first-degree murder indictment against Sam Corey.

When the trial began late in April 1975, the prosecution began with the testimony of a pathologist who had performed the autopsy on Patricia. Then Whalen put Giesick on the stand to tell how he and Sam Corey had plotted murder.

Whalen had warned the jury in his opening statement that he had made a deal with Giesick whom he described as "a killer, a murderer . . . a man about as bad as they come." Though this might have seemed at the time like undermining his own witness, it was Whalen's attempt to lessen the effect of evidence the defense would surely introduce about Giesick's character. He had been diagnosed by a psychiatrist as a pathological liar with a lifelong history of anti-social behavior. He had threatened the life of the father of one of his former wives. He had been indicted for writing bad checks. He posed as a doctor of psychology. He had made much of his living for the past ten years by confidence games and insurance rip-offs, an occupation that had forced him to adopt a double identity. Under cross-examination by Dymond, he freely described a method he used to steal cars from airport parking lots. Everything he had, as he would also admit on the stand, he'd gotten by cheating someone. And the defense witnesses, the majority of them, were people called to discredit Giesick with testimony about actions he wouldn't admit so readily. A masseuse said he had suggested murdering her husband for insurance money. Another masseuse, one who had bought Sam Corey's parlor in Irving, said she'd hired Giesick as a psychologist to help two of her employees who were having emotional problems. Giesick treated them by prescribing frequent sexual intercourse with him. Later he propositioned the woman's fourteen-year-old daughter. Other witnesses testified to similar behavior.

Still, for a person as thoroughly bad as he was shown to be, Giesick made a good witness. He has an easy-going, soft-spoken manner and a glib tongue that, treacherous as it is, can also be charming. He does not, on first impression, seem like a killer or even, when he tries hard, which he did on the stand, like a liar. And in the end the jury chose to believe him.

The tale Giesick told on the stand was not so much of violence, although it was violent, and certainly not one of cleverness, but of remarkable coldness, callousness, and cynicism. Giesick, using the name Guilliam, had met Sam Corey when he came to the Tokyo House in San Antonio to sell him a credit card service that day I was winding up my story. After that they saw each other occasionally and twice happened to run into each other's cars. (These accidents had all the earmarks of insurance frauds.) Around November 1973, while they were eating in a restaurant in San Antonio, Corey first brought up the possibility of Giesick marrying a girl and the two of them killing her for insurance money. Corey said he knew that Giesick was wanted for a bad check charge and threatened to turn him in unless he went along with the plan. Their conversation lasted about an hour and a half and at the end of that time Giesick had agreed to the idea.

He began frequenting massage parlors in San Antonio and Dallas looking for a girl. Before long he found Patricia and married her. She was the perfect victim. She was lonely, gullible, down on her luck, and desperate for both money and affection. He began insuring her. On at least one occasion Corey provided the money for the premium.

After the marriage, Giesick drove with Patricia to New Orleans and checked into the Ramada Inn on Chef Menteur. He immediately took his car to the shop for unneeded repairs and from there called his wife Kathi in San Antonio who told him where Corey was staying. Giesick rented a Monte Carlo from Avis and met Corey at his Holiday Inn. Then Giesick drove back to the parking lot at the intersection of Chef Menteur and Michoud where he parked his rented car. He walked the rest of the way back to the motel. The plan was to make Patricia think they had no car. This would confine her to the motel most of the time and force her to walk across the highway to the small bar and restaurant if she wanted to eat. They originally thought this might provide an occasion for her to have an "accident."

That night Giesick took the St. Bernard puppy out for a walk as an excuse to meet Corey. Corey signaled from his car by flashing his lights. They discussed possible locations and the mechanics of the crime. Then Giesick went back in, got Patricia, and walked her up and down Chef Menteur. Corey was on the road driving a Buick he and Giesick had stolen from Love Field in Dallas. But the traffic was too heavy to risk anything then.

Giesick took Patricia back to their room, took the dog out for another walk, and met with Corey again. They decided to try again that night on Michoud Boulevard near the bridge over the bayou. Giesick went back to the room and talked Patricia into coming outside with him once again. As they walked up Michoud toward the bridge, Giesick noticed a police car by his parked rental car. An officer was shining a flashlight inside. Giesick panicked a little, took Patricia back to their room, told her he needed time to think by himself, and, outside, told Corey the police had spotted his car. They both got in the rental car, Corey driving, and went to the airport where they exchanged that car for another one using the phony excuse about transmission trouble. On the way back, Corey checked out of his motel and moved to the Quality Inn next door to the Ramada Inn where Giesick and Patricia were staying.

The following afternoon Giesick picked up his car at the dealership and spent the rest of the afternoon and evening driving Patricia around and watching television in their room. (Patricia, however, later that night told her mother and a desk clerk that their car was still in the garage. The defense never questioned Giesick about this discrepancy.) Giesick took the dog out several times that night and met with Corey. Corey whispered through the door of his motel room, and Giesick stood facing away from him so Patricia if she should happen to wander outside, wouldn't see him talking with anyone. They agreed on a time and place.

After midnight Giesick drove Patricia to Michoud Boulevard. (Here again his testimony conflicts with Patricia's comments about their car.) They walked across the short bridge and down to the edge of the bayou. Corey drove past, made a U-turn, and parked in front of the first house in the block after the bridge. He signaled with his parking lights that he was ready.

Giesick and Patricia walked up to the road. He stopped by a small tree. Holding his flashlight behind his back, he signaled three times. Corey signaled with his lights and then started toward them. Giesick waited for the right moment, grabbed Patricia, and shoved her and tripped her at the same time. Corey ran her down and kept on going. Some time later, after the police and ambulance had arrived, Corey drove by the scene again. Giesick concluded his testimony by saying that he met Sam Corey on the roof of the hospital as Patricia lay unconscious below. "Don't worry about it," Corey said. "She's not going to live. Everything's fine. We're home free."

The rest of the prosecution's case was designed either to augment or corroborate Giesick's testimony. Whalen knew that Giesick's psychiatrist would testify for the defense that the prosecution's star witness was a pathological liar. But Whalen, by taking special courses and with a certain amount of study on his own, had learned rudiments of psychiatric theory and practice and how they applied to the law. He knew that the psychiatrist would also admit, as he later did during Whalen's cross-examination, that the testimony of a pathological liar could be believed if it was corroborated.

Whalen called Kathi Giesick to the stand and she testified about calls Corey and Giesick had made to her from New Orleans. Ricky Mock testified about discovering the accident after dropping his friend at home. Dillmann described what he'd discovered during his investigation. A criminologist from the FBI testified that the hair found on the rented Monte Carlo matched Patricia's hair. A guard at the hospital swore that after Patricia was brought in, he saw Corey at the hospital parking lot behind the wheel of a Monte Carlo. He was positive in his identification because a friend drove a car just like it "with the small windows behind the large windows." Employees of Tele-Trip, the Ramada Inn, and Avis all testified to the same information about Giesick and Corey that they'd provided Dillmann during his investigation. And Mrs. Albanowski, Patricia's mother, told the grim story of her daughter's funeral. Giesick, accompanied by Sam Corey, arrived somewhat late. Corey was dressed in a black suit and clerical collar. Mourners assumed he was a priest, and at a dinner after the burial, he strolled around accepting small donations to say prayers for Patricia's soul.

Whalen had another witness whom he could not decide what to do with. He wanted to wait to put this witness on the stand during his rebuttal to the defense, when the testimony would have the most impact. But he was worried that Dymond might put on no defense at all, simply rest his case, and proceed directly to final arguments. If that happened, this witness's testimony would never get before the jury, and it was, Whalen felt, the testimony that topped off the case he had so carefully built. Finally Whalen, holding his breath like a gambler who tosses his last chips into the pot and waits for the cards to fall, kept his witness back and rested his case.

Corey's attorneys had a continuing disagreement about whether to put Corey on the stand. This argument became so heated that they once came to words in the hallway outside the courtroom. Dymond, however, as the attorney responsible for trying the case, prevailed and the defense, instead of resting immediately, called several witnesses, including Corey. Whalen began to breathe somewhat easier.

First a series of masseuses told the stories about Giesick mentioned earlier. Their testimony, while hardly flattering about Giesick, did little damage to the prosecutor's case. Whalen asked each one of them whether they knew anything of the events on Michoud Boulevard around 2 a.m. on January 16, 1974. They all answered that they did not.

Then Dymond called Sam Corey and asked him three questions: had he killed Patricia; had he conspired with anyone to kill her; and had he conspired with Jim Giesick to kill her? To all three questions Corey answered, "No, sir, I did not." Dymond turned his witness over to Whalen.

Corey then weighed more than 300 pounds. He overflowed the witness chair, where he sat sunk in an extremely disheveled suit, wearing old scruffy shoes worn way down at the heels, and nervously popping mints in his mouth as he testified. He frequently mumbled in answer to Whalen's questions, many times answering that he couldn't recall where he'd been at a particular time or what he was doing. Whalen asked about the statement Corey had made for Dillmann when he denied being in New Orleans at the time of the murder. Corey was forced to admit he had lied then. Corey repeated his new story that he had come to New Orleans to patch up a lovers' quarrel between Patricia and Jim and had spent the night of the murder with a prostitute named Linda whom he had met in front of a massage parlor. Regardless of how many contradictions and unexplainable circumstances Whalen was able to reveal between Corey's story and all the other testimony—and there were many—here was where he made Corey look the worst.

"At that massage parlor," Whalen asked, "did you get a local?"

"Yes, sir."

"And what is a local, Mr. Corey?"

The would-be priest, the supposed minister, the man who solicited donations from mourners at the funeral of the girl he was now accused of murdering, glumly replied, "The genitals are massaged." If Corey's former priestly and ministerial poses had provoked any sympathy from the jury, this testimony destroyed it.

Then Whalen presented his rebuttal case. There were several witnesses but the last was the one Whalen had held back: E. J. Swindler, the desk clerk at the Holiday Inn whom Corey had asked for aspirin just before the time of the murder and who had seen Corey again about 25 minutes later when he returned to the motel lobby. Swindler's testimony placed Corey out of his room near the time of the

murder, Linda or no Linda.

After closing arguments—Dymond's eloquent and moving; Whalen's, powerful and persuasive—the jury retired to deliberate. The trial had lasted five days, but the jury returned in only twenty minutes with their decision.

Sam Corey was sentenced to death and Jim Giesick to 21 years in prison, the maximum punishment in Louisiana for manslaughter. But the story doesn't end there. As this is written Irvin Dymond is working on Sam Corey's appeal, and Giesick has, in interviews with reporters and from other forums, claimed he lied on the stand. He now says the real killer wasn't Sam at all but his wife Kathi in league with a man desperately in love with her, the mysterious hippie named Ronnie. The precise reason why his love should have driven Ronnie to murder his beloved's husband's other wife is a little complicated to explain. There is no evidence, however, to support this new version of the story.

In prison Giesick spends most of his time making plastic knickknacks which he sends to people along with an exorbitant bill. And he writes nasty letters. "Do try to write soon—Killer" was the way one to his wife ended. "Your secretary sounds nice. Does she have any life insurance?" was the postscript of a letter to Whalen. He is smug and unremorseful, and when I talked with him in prison, he maintained a rather breezy attitude about all that has happened. He has lost weight, has neatly styled and perfectly combed hair, and the day I saw him he wore a gray T-shirt with "Jim" printed in fancy letters over his heart.

During the trial Giesick's mental instability received considerable attention. There was the testimony of his psychiatrist, his psychiatric discharge from the service, the history and habits of his life. But it seems to me now that Corey is the one with far worse delusions.

After our prison interview I kept seeing the way Sam's face looked—happy, conspiratorial, self-satisfied—when he told me he'd gotten a local in the massage parlor he visited the afternoon before the murder. For a while I assumed this was a new and private detail that, for some reason, he had decided to tell me, perhaps as a way of establishing a masculine rapport between us. But when I read the transcript of the trial and talked with people who had seen Sam testify, I discovered that it was one of the most public details in the case. Didn't Sam know how low and sleazy this testimony had made his appear? And yet he couldn't restrain himself from telling me. I could still see the way his face looked then—red, happy, his eyes alive with pleasure, and his whole body shaking with glee.

The crime itself, of course, reveals certain dark streams of the mind that lead directly into a psychological thicket: the gross, unattractive man brings a younger, handsomer, sweeter-talking man under his control; it is a woman they decide to kill; the marriage has an extremely voyeuristic aspect with the older man performing the ceremony and hovering unseen around the couple on their honeymoon; the actual killing requires their mutual cooperation complete with signaled contact in the night; rather than violate their victim's body with a bullet or knife they choose simply to crush her; the older man has religious delusions; and the older man, it turns out, was rejected by his mother early in life and raised by an aunt.

I can do nothing more with that thicket than to say it's

there. I do not know a clear path through it. But I do believe I now understand the look on Sam's face when he told me about the local. It was the face, surely, that E. J. Swindler saw when Sam, self-satisfied and gleeful, just back from killing Patricia, walked into the motel lobby to share with someone, however partially, his moment of greatest pleasure.

*—July 1976*

# AH, SWEET MYSTERY OF DEATH

## by Al Reinert

*These men know a secret: Dead men DO tell tales.*

An early morning squall line, steel-gray and intimidating, moved north from Galveston at about the same speed the car traveled south from Houston. They met just as the car exited the freeway. "This Choate Road is a favorite dumping ground for some damn reason," said Thomason. "There's a lot of bodies picked up down here." The rain began falling in dense, melancholy sheets.

After two miles of overgrown grassfields, Thomason turned into a narrow private road posted: Exxon Co. USA, Do Not Enter. Four cars were already there—three Plymouths painted in hard, spare colors, and a patrol unit from the Harris County Sheriff's Office. A half-dozen men were gathered at the road's edge, clad in bright yellow raincoats with "Sheriff's Dept." stenciled across the back. Thomason parked his car, muttered hollow blasphemies at the weather gods and stepped into the downpour. "What's the matter, J.C.?" greeted a yellow figure. "Can't they afford to buy raincoats for you folks?"

Thomason swore back and joined the group at roadside, staring toward the body discovered that dawn by an Exxon employee on his way to work. It lay six feet away, curled to one side as if rolled from a waiting car, a notion further supported by the bent, broken grass between it and the pavement. The sheriff's men had not yet disturbed it. They are instructed not to touch anything until Thomason, or some other investigator from the Harris County Medical Examiner, is on the scene.

Determinedly trying to ignore the rain, the men now set about their business. Thomason fetched his Instamatic and photographed the body from each of the four compass points. He was joined by a sheriff's photographer who took many more pictures with a much better camera.

The body was that of a man past middle age, white hair

*Al Reinert is a contributing editor of* Texas Monthly *and has written for several other magazines. He is completing a book for Harcourt Brace Jovanovich.*

cut short and stubbly, dressed in a beige nylon shirt, cheap brown cotton pants, and plain black shoes. "Those look like army shoes," suggested an officer. "Nope," said another, "army shoes just got four holes for the laces." "Shit, you can't tell anymore," responded the first, "they keep changing uniforms so fast you can't keep up with 'em."

There was blood on the man's face, a scarcely discernible hole in his left cheek and another, more obvious hole in the top of his head, from which small pieces of brain tissue were slowly seeping. "Looks like he got shot in the face and it came out there," said Klevenhagen, the senior homicide detective from the sheriff's office. Everyone seemed to agree but Thomason, who wiped his glasses and said nothing.

By now the rain, having accomplished its morbid visitation, had passed over, and three more Plymouths had appeared. A dozen sheriff's investigators fanned out along the roadway searching for shell casings, bloodstains, random artifacts of unknown specification. Ten feet from the body, an empty fifth of Windsor Canadian merited a small conference, much speculation, and a roll of film. It was picked up gingerly, finger in neck, and carried to one of the Plymouths before anyone realized the grass beneath it was dry and far too withered for it to have been deposited as recently as the body. The bottle was thrown away. Nothing else of any significance was found.

The body car arrived from the funeral home notified by the dispatcher, and the mortician and his assistant emerged. The mortician wore a white shirt, wide muted tie, double-knit slacks, and matched patent leather shoes and belt. He had a razor-cut hair style and looked very effete. He and his assistant donned surgical gloves and withdrew a stretcher from the body car. They were the only people who would actually handle the body. Klevenhagen turned to Thomason. "We ready to turn him over, my man?" Thomason nodded yes.

The body was rolled onto its back. The legs kept their

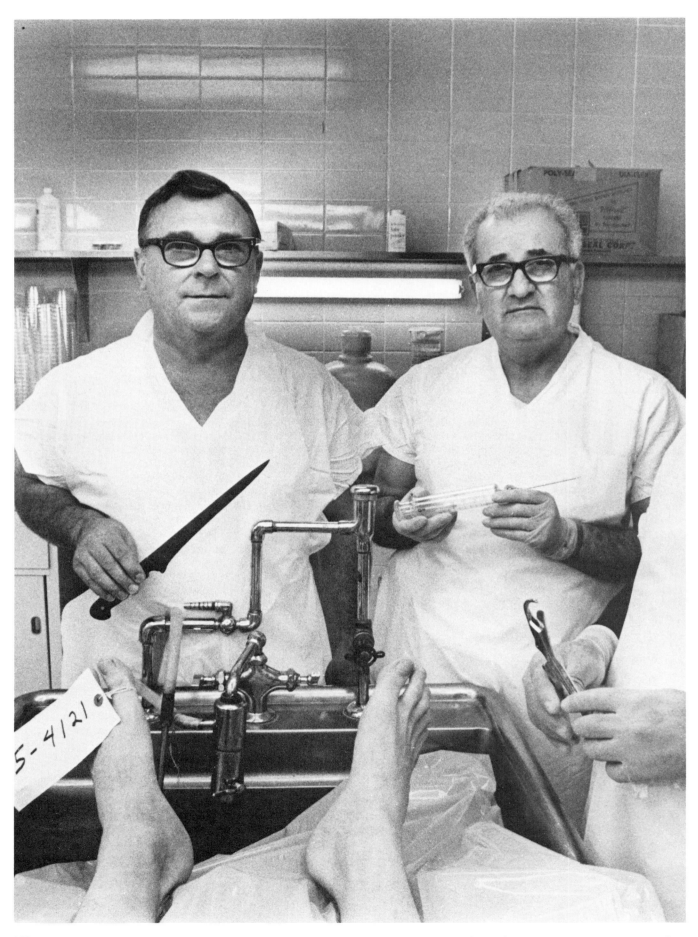

Jachimczyk (left), Gutierrez. *Photography by Joe Baraban*

awkwardly angular pose, one arm poked stiffly up at the wet sky. The flesh was discolored to a grayish purple except for a clay white portion of the face that had pressed against the ground. Ants paraded in and out of the ears and nostrils. "How long, my man?" asked Klevenhagen. Five or six hours, guessed Thomason.

"That looks like another wound there," said an investigator, pointing to the oddly upthrust left arm. They knelt to examine a little black hole in the bicep, carefully measured its location, noted it down, photographed it. "Must've been shot a couple times," observed the investigator. "What do you think?" he asked Thomason, who responded with an ambiguous shrug. "Can't really tell till we get him in and clean him up a bit."

The two morticians rifled the dead man's pockets, producing a small penknife, a checkbook, two neatly folded dollar bills, and a pack of Camels. It was all handed to Thomason. He conferred briefly with the sheriff's men, traded information, then prepared to leave while the morticians loaded the body. Two investigators were pulling up patches of bloodied grass where the body had lain.

During the long trip back to the morgue, Thomason grumbled to himself, half aloud and semi-bitterly, ". . . wanta stand around in the goddam rain and gape . . . can't tell nothing anyway till he's stripped down and cleaned up," he muttered. "Might've been shot twenty times for all you can tell out there . . ." His clothes were thoroughly soaked, stuck to his skin and uncomfortable, a condition which transformed his normally placid disposition into assorted ills and aggravations. He disliked these undermanned weekend shifts and the frequent journeys to distant outbacks in the country. He disliked paperwork, bickering morticians, defense lawyers, prima donna cops, slow drivers, and rain.

He liked his job. Before joining the medical examiner's staff, J.C. Thomason had been an investigator on the Houston police force and then with the district attorney's office, 25 years all told, enough that he eventually had regular weekday hours with leisurely lunches, and holidays off. He occasionally wondered why he gave it up.

By the time he entered the parking lot at Ben Taub Hospital, the body car was already standing empty beside the elevator landing for the county morgue. Thomason pushed the button for the basement, where the morticians were in the prep room undressing the body. They stuffed the clothing into a paper sack, first calling out sizes and labels to Jay Evans, the sheriff's office homicide detective assigned to the case. When the body was stripped the morticians lifted it off their stretcher and placed it in one of the morgue trays, thus passing official custodianship to the morgue.

Mateo, one of the dieners (morgue assistants), logged in the body, hand-lettered the case number on a white card, and dropped it on the dead man's chest. He stepped back to allow Thomason, wielding the Instamatic again, to photograph the newly christened corpse. It was now officially number 75-3786, the only reality it would own unless, and until, positive identification was forthcoming from fingerprints or next-of-kin. The checkbook found in his pocket might or might not prove helpful in this regard, a question Evans had already begun trying to answer. Mateo printed the i.d. number on a manila tag and slipped it over the right big toe. Then he weighed, measured, and finger-printed 75-3786 and began to wash it down with damp sterile rags.

"Well, what do we have here?" Jachimczyk cheerfully inquired as he ambled into the prep room. "Hello, Doc," greeted Evans, who summarized where the body was found and what was known about it. "Do you want him done today," asked Jachimczyk, "or can it wait till tomorrow morning?" Evans said he'd prefer it that day if at all possible. Jachimczyk nodded agreeably, then left to read Thomason's report and prepare for the autopsy. He had performed four autopsies already that morning. It was eleven o'clock.

75-3786 was wheeled down to the autopsy room where Lee Roy, the other diener on duty, was laying out the equipment. He assembled the specimen containers, sharpened the knives, snapped fresh Bard-Parker blades in the scalpel handles. The plastic handles were heavy and palm-sized, unlike surgical handles, and were designed for comfortable use during the lengthy autopsy, rather than for the tedious work of surgery. Lee Roy placed the knives and scalpels on a wooden carving board.

Jachimczyk stood behind the board, depressed the foot pedal activating a tape recorder, read the case number into the microphone mounted before him, and proceeded to dictate his official autopsy report. "The body is that of a well-developed, well-nourished, moderately obese, elderly Caucasian male," he intoned. "It weighed 188 pounds and measured 66 inches in length." He proceeded to describe 75-3786's external appearance in scrupulous detail, often pausing while scars were measured and precisely mapped. "Is that a bruise on the lip there?" he wondered aloud at one point, walking around to look more closely. "Sure enough is," he announced, sounding almost surprised. He returned to his position, stepped on the pedal and spoke into the microphone. "There is a small bruise on the left lower lip, approximately one-half inch in length with a slight superficial cut and moderate hemorrhaging."

He then moved to examine the bullet wounds. There were two in the left arm, the one in the bicep and another behind that in the tricep muscle, with a dark purple ring surrounding the rent itself. This was a "contact wound," the ring caused by powder burns from a gun fired less than twenty inches away. Jachimczyk described them to the tape recorder, calling the contact wound an "entrance wound" and the bicep wound an "exit-type wound." "The wound admitted a probe through the musculature, and did not involve the underlying bone," he recorded.

Turning to the head wounds, he decided that the perforation in the left cheek was also an entry wound. After shaving the area around the hole in the top of the head he determined that this, too, was an entry wound. He inserted a segment of supple aluminum wire and probed for the bullet, unsuccessfully. "Somewhere in there," mused Jachimczyk, "there ought to be a couple of bullets."

He went about his work with casual efficiency, almost with grace, the way every fine craftsman pursues his skill with what seems to be ease and simplicity. Jachimczyk had performed over 20,000 autopsies in his career, and the subjects, or objects, of that labor had long since lost their purchase on his sensibility. They had become just so many numbered cases and bloodless puzzles, the inevitable bookends of irrelevant lives. Their individuality for Jachimczyk lay in the riddles they posed to the scalpel of his science, the clues they offered to the wit of his craft. 75-3786, aptly named, was merely the latest in a series of small but answerable mysteries. "Sometimes you don't have any witnesses, no clues, nothing but questions," said Jachimczyk. "But the answers are right here if you look for them. This dead body tells us. It can tell us what happened to it."

They now began the formal autopsy. The spinal canal was tapped with a giant syringe and enough pink spinal fluid drawn off to accommodate the various routine chemical analyses. Then the scalp was slit from ear to ear across the crown of the head and the skin pulled back to reveal the calvarium, the skullcap. Lee Roy plugged in the Stryker Saw, a nonrotating vibrating saw shaped like a drill and developed originally for cutting off casts. Pressure-sensitive, it can saw cleanly through cast or bone without savaging vulnerable underlying tissue. Thirty years earlier, when Jachimczyk was first learning how to do autopsies, he had had to use a hacksaw.

Quickly and easily, amid a faint spray of bone dust, the Stryker sawed the skull in a neat quarter-circle. Removing the calvarium, Jachimczyk gently pushed his little finger into the wound in the now-exposed brain, probing again for the bullet track, again fruitlessly. He carefully removed the brain and placed it on the carving board, washed it and the skullcap with slow-running water. Once washed, the skullcap seemed almost artificial, nearly white and smoothly curved with a modest puncture to the left of center, perfectly round on the outside but beveled and jagged on the inside. "Thirty-eight?" asked Evans, who was watching from a discreet and satisfying distance. "No, I think it's smaller than that," answererd Jachimczyk.

Evans walked over and produced a .38 caliber bullet from his pistol belt. "Here, try it." Jachimczyk tested the bullet against the hole, found it much too large. "I think it's probably a 32, or maybe a 25." "Want to try a 25?" suggested Evans. "Do you have one of those too?" Evans drew a small pistol from his shoulder holster, unloaded it, and handed over a .25 shell. "This man comes prepared," deadpanned Jachimczyk. The fit was perfect. Jachimczyk placed the skullcap on a table with the cartridge end sticking straight out like a brass peg, and the bullet head protruding exactly through the opening. "We ought to take a picture of that," he realized, and Thomason once more supplied his Instamatic for that purpose. "You know," said Jachimczyk, "that's really kind of pretty."

He returned to the brain which still rested sullen and strange on the carving board. Rinsed down, it was light tan and coruscated and looked like a deflated walnut. Jachimczyk surveyed the glands and nerve ends for possible signs of damage or violence, found none and reported this fact to the tape recorder. There was only the one small, terribly final bullet hole.

He took up a knife and began to section the brain, lopping off thin, even slices as if he were carving a roast. The interior showed white with minute red dots. The dots were blood vessels in cross-section, meaning there was blood pooled in the brain at the time of death, which only happens when death is traumatic and fiercely abrupt. There were thick, dark, almost black clots of blood in the left frontal lobe, "caused by massive hemorrhage secondary to the bullet wound." Jachimczyk picked cautiously through the brain slices until, from one of the edges, he retrieved a flattened, mangled, once-lethal clump of lead. "By darn!" he exclaimed, "it's a 22, a mashed-up 22. Boy, it's really smashed." Evans peered over at the fragment. "Looks like it might be one of those new 22 magnums," he said. "Maybe so," Jachimczyk agreed, "maybe we'll find some more of it. A lot of it is missing." He started sifting through the mutilated brain some more.

Lee Roy meantime had been searching in the vicinity of the left jaw for the second bullet, to no avail. He wheeled 75-3786 outside to the X-ray machine and shot some pictures of the area. Jachimczyk occupied himself dissecting the neck organs, which Lee Roy had previously removed. They revealed no evidence of hemorrhage and the hyoid, a fragile wishbone-shaped bone at the base of the tongue that is almost always snapped when strangulation is attempted, was still intact. Jachimczyk dutifully informed his tape recorder of this news, then turned to peruse the X-rays. They betrayed a twisted piece of metal imbedded deep in the jawbone.

Guided by the X-rays, they had little trouble recovering the second bullet. "It's torn up almost as bad as the other one. They're gonna have a helluva time trying to do much with these," scowled Jachimczyk, referring to the ballistics experts at the police lab. He scratched a tiny, identifying J in the base of each fragment where the mark wouldn't obscure the remaining microscopic riflings on the tip, and dropped them into a small cardboard box.

Speaking again to the tape recorder, Jachimczyk characterized the bullets vaguely as "small caliber." Although he might speculate more precisely for his own benefit, he would not incorporate into his autopsy report anything to which he could not ultimately testify beyond a reasonable doubt. "They can weigh them over at the lab," he said. "They'll probably figure out what they are." Like most specialists, he resented unqualified intruders into his own field of expertise, so he too avoided venturing into another's domain.

Evans walked back into the autopsy room. He had by now confirmed the dead man's identity and had spoken to his ex-wife and an in-law who had been with him the night before. "He was pretty drunk when they saw him last," advised Evans. "We'll check that out," answered Jachimczyk. A blood-alcohol test is standard in all autopsies, as are drug and narcotics screens in all homicide cases.

Jachimczyk continued with the remainder of the autopsy. Mateo had already cut the Y in 75-3786, twin incisions from each shoulder which met at the solar plexus and then extended down to the bottom of the belly. The internal organs had been removed and placed in a tray next to the carving board, where Jachimczyk began to inspect them one at a time. It was doubtful that these would affect his finding on cause of death, that being grimly apparent, but they were still essential items in a complete and thorough autopsy. His certainties had been waylaid before, and he knew it could happen again. "Nothing is ever obvious," was his motto. "Always be suspicious."

He reached for the little rust-red engine that is the heart, weighed it, scrutinized it, dissected it, sought out whatever stray facts it could yield to him. "Oooh boy," he whistled, pointing to the tiny mounds of cholesterol plaque that gathered in the aorta and clogged the ventricle. "Here was a prime candidate for a coronary occlusion." In somewhat more clinical language, he confided the tangible secrets of

75-3786's heart to his tape machine, then moved on. "This fellow was a real smoker," he observed, "look at all that heavy black streaking throughout his lungs." Jachimczyk knew nothing of the Camels that were found in the man's pocket.

"Paragraph liver," he dictated, indirectly, to his typist. "The liver weighed one-nine-six-zero grams, the capsule was smooth and glistening. On section the cut surfaces revealed a homogeneous, relatively dry, tan-brown lobulated appearance. The gall bladder contained ten milliliters of green viscid bile. The mucosa was intact . . ."

In this fashion, progressing to the kidneys and spleen and stomach and elsewhere, he relentlessly explored the physical reality of 75-3786, recorded it all in prodigious detail. The body was reduced to so many paragraphs of dense terminology, preserved for the time when it might testify through Jachimczyk against its murderer. Two years and 3000 autopsies from now, when the case might conceivably go to trial, Jachimczyk could sit in the witness box, report in hand, and re-create the whole of it with remarkable exactitude. "You can always challenge an opinion," he said, "but you can't dispute a fact. This man was killed by a gunshot wound in the head and that's a fact that can't be avoided."

His own opinion was that a struggle had occurred, which accounted for the bruised lip and explained the paths of the bullets. The track through the arm traveled upward and back-to-front, as if the arm had been raised in protest or defense, and the shot was fired from extremely close range. The bullet that penetrated the arm, Jachimczyk felt, was the same one that struck the face and lodged in the jaw.

"The question," he proposed, "is whether the first bullet could have killed him. The answer is probably not." The question was important because, in that hypothetical future courtroom, the first bullet could be plausibly argued as self-defense, and the case tried as manslaughter. But if only the second shot would have been fatal, then it was murder.

"We've found the car," Evans announced excitedly as he hurriedly returned to the autopsy room. When the man was last seen alone, he was in his own car and intoxicated to the point of passing out. "It was abandoned in a shopping center off the Gulf Freeway."

"Looks like robbery," remarked Jachimczyk, to no one in particular. He had developed a kind of instinct where murder was concerned, had seen enough homicides to recognize the patterns and probabilities. The man had been drunk and alone late at night; he was found without a wallet. The likelihood was robbery. "There's not much that's unusual about this one," he said. "It's a fairly typical murder."

"I'll check back with you on the bullets," said Evans, rushing out the door.

"Keep me posted," called Jachimczyk. He ordinarily worked closely with the police, talked with them frequently while a case was in progress, and found this mutually helpful. He was also curious. An avid reader of murder mysteries and detective novels, as well as a friend to detectives and a solver of mysteries, Jachimczyk had a connoisseur's appreciation for nuance and subtlety.

Thomason came up to say that the man's brother was on the way down to claim the body. "They don't know he's been killed yet," he said. "They think it was a heart attack. They said they've been expecting it 'cause he's been having

a lot of heart problems."

Jachimczyk replied that he would wait and talk to the brother. Another of his bywords was: "There's nothing you can do to help dead people anymore, but you can still have some compassion for the families they left behind." Sometimes he told little white lies where he thought it might help. This case, however, didn't afford much room for that.

Lee Roy and Mateo by now finished closing up the body. The chest cavity was tacked back together, the scalp sutured into more or less normal shape. After the embalmer and then the mortician took their turns and added their skills, 75-3786 would appear to be a man who had succumbed peacefully and whole. Even the wound in his face would be invisible.

In 1956 the Texas Legislature created the office of County Medical Examiner, and required that every large metropolitan county find someone to fill it. The medical examiner was to assume the responsibility, previously defaulted to amateur coroners, of establishing cause of death in all cases covered by the statute, basically those involving violent or unattended deaths. Prior to the law, justices of the peace generally doubled as coroners in most places, and still do in many, regardless of their qualification for the work. The medical examiner, on the other hand, was expected to be a duly certified forensic pathologist, schooled in both law and the branch of medicine devoted to studying death.

In an effort to fill this new post, the Harris County Commissioners Court offered the job to Doctor Joseph Jachimczyk (pronounced ya-HIM-chick), assistant professor of legal medicine at Harvard School of Medicine. The $20,000 salary represented a step down for him, but Jachimczyk, the son of an immigrant iceman, felt subtly discriminated against at Harvard. Ivy League institutions, he wrote, "whether they like to admit it or not, are bound by musty tradition which does not ignore wealth and prestige." He accepted the offer to come to Houston.

At least one commissioner didn't want anyone to have the job. "How many deaths can be nailed down to something like poison?" Phil Sayers wanted to know. "If somebody is poisoned, so what? Is it worth it to the taxpayers to try and find out?" Jachimczyk got the job anyway.

Within a year of Sayers' futile outburst, the new coroner was called in as outside consultant after a man died strangely and inexplicably in the Houston Veterans Hospital. The man's week-long ailment had mystified VA doctors, but he'd already been buried and his death certificate, citing unknown gastric disorders, had been signed before Jachimczyk even entered the picture. He proved it to be Texas' first known case of arsenic poisoning. An excitable local columnist declared that it marked Houston's emergence into "the modern era of criminal investigation."

"Some places are still pretty primitive," says Jachimczyk, leading a visitor on a short tour of his very unprimitive morgue. "The sheriff or a JP or somebody'll come in, take a quick peek at the body and say 'Oh-ho, there's a hole there, musta been shot.' It's ridiculous."

Like most professionals trained in the hard sciences, Jachimczyk swears by the untainted, superior validity of empirical fact, and is convinced that the scientific method, properly applied, can subdue all problems and resolve all riddles. He embodies the philosophy etched in stone above the entrance to the morgue at the Yale University School of Medicine: *Hic Locus Ubi Mortuii Docent Vivos*—This is the place where the dead teach the living. When he lectures to police cadets, or law or medical students, he always enjoins them to "obey the one great commandment: rely primarily, and I hasten to emphasize this, on medical evidence and scientific findings." He once co-authored an article debunking the "myth," as he called it, that crimes of violence increase noticeably during the full moon, a myth that nonetheless has considerable currency in police departments and, ironically, in his own office.

He opens a large, airtight door and leads his visitor into the "cold room," a sort of walk-in vault kept at slightly above 40 degrees. "Except for weekends, we usually don't have to use it that much," says Jachimczyk. "We try to release a body within 24 hours of the time we get it, and we usually make it." The room seems bare and empty, with part of it given over to storage space. Off in one corner is a grim little pile of green plastic body bags containing shapeless bodies, the nameless remains of six young boys, the last of the 27 unearthed more than two years ago in the Houston homosexual mass murders. "I don't know if we'll ever identify them," he says, shaking his head. "We've got enough dental work on one of them, but we've never been able to match it up anywhere."

In a normal year lacking such a ghoulish windfall, only three or four of the more than 5000 bodies that pass through the morgue are impossible to identify. These few are buried in the county paupers' cemetery, beneath small brass plates with the simple engraving U, for unknown. One of the unknowns, however, is officially carried on state records as being buried at the county morgue, and has been for eleven years. "We call him Stubby," explains Jachimczyk, pointing out the padlocked freezer locker that contains the corpse. "I guess you could say we've grown kind of attached to him around here."

Stubby is a man's torso—headless, legless, and armless—with no identifying marks save a small cyst, that was found on a rural Fort Bend County roadside in 1964. "It was some kind of gangland-style killing; he was left there on purpose so the message would get out. We think that's why nobody's come forward to identify him, because they're afraid to. One of these days they will though, then we can take Stubby out and give him your proverbial Christian burial."

He relates all this rather matter-of-factly, casual almost, as though it were entirely reasonable to bury someone in your office refrigerator. But he says it also with a genial lilt to his voice, a gentle glimmer in his friendly hazel eyes. The lilt and the glimmer are always present, always threatening to change into unreserved laughter at the first good opportunity. Short and squat and fanciful, Jachimczyk seems altogether too good-natured, too gregarious, too boisterous and *alive* to do the work he does.

It seems contradictory to the visitor. Coroners were always supposed to be Sydney Greenstreet in deep shadow and three-quarter profile. Now along comes this Polish leprechaun with a marvelous sense of humor who plays boogie piano and collects tattoos. Actually (and contrary to some rumors) they're just photographs of tattoos. "There was one man who had a big arrow pointing down his spine to the anus, and inside the arrow it said 'foxhole.'" Then there was the woman with "sweet" and "sour" beneath her

breasts, and the other women with "Whitey's Property" and "Pay to Enter" tattooed just where you'd expect to find them. "Some of them are really imaginative," chortles Jachimczyk.

"They can also be very helpful for identification purposes," he adds, a little more soberly. "Many people have had their social security numbers tattooed on, sometimes their blood type, too. I think that's an awfully good idea. There have been proposals made to have everybody do it, but nothing ever happens with them, there's too much emotional opposition to it. It does make sense, though. At least the blood group."

Impish humor and barren proposition, the leprechaun and the scientist. These two sides are most apparent when Jachimczyk goes to court, wearing his shiny bow tie and resembling the jovial host of a Saturday morning kiddie show. No sooner is he installed in the witness stand, with the jury wondering who this nice man is, when the prosecutor asks his credentials and Jachimczyk unleashes a résumé that sounds like course work for a Nobel Prize. "You should never let him get that far," counsels a defense attorney who's been to trial with him. "Once he gets all that out about Harvard and Johns Hopkins and all those degrees, the jury'll believe anything he says. You should just stipulate that he's acceptable as an expert witness and leave it at that."

During his testimony, Jachimczyk explains himself lucidly and thoroughly, slowing up to elaborate on critical points, then rambling off into fascinating digressions while jurors and slow-thinking defense lawyers sit raptly attentive. His language is precise and formal, heavily salted with medical jargon, but his presentation is pure vaudeville. At the same time he's describing a bullet hole as "thirteen inches below the suprasternal notch and four inches to the left of the midline" he's sticking fingers in himself to indicate the wounds, twisting around to illustrate the track, generally contorting himself into some kind of Emmett Kelly parody. He's the ideal witness—a combination of good theater and effective testimony.

"Doc's just straight as an arrow," observes J.C. Thomason. "Me, I'm kind of inclined toward the prosecution, I guess, and I know some other doctors who lean that way a little. I've seen 'em almost cause mistrials leaning too far. But Jachimczyk won't give you an inch from telling it the way he sees it."

That's because he doesn't see himself as belonging among the authorities. Jachimczyk rather regards himself as a neutral observer of the fact—a Dick Tracy Rosetta Stone, an analytical tool to be employed by whatever parties might find it useful. "Our records are available to anyone who's legitimately involved in a case," he says. "I spend as much time talking to defense lawyers as I do prosecutors. We just present our findings and leave the interpretations to the judge and the jury.

"Actually, I'd probably prefer to see a hundred guys go free than to let some poor innocent slob go to jail because of a sloppy investigation." Jachimczyk considers this for a moment, considers his work in general, and then he remarks, "The greatest pleasure I get, I suppose, is when we have a case that to all outward appearance is murder and I prove it to be natural. That's really satisfying for me. You can get big headlines by showing that a natural was a murder, and catching whoever did it, but that's not as satisfying to me as the other way around. I don't like sending people to prison."

"There really isn't any practical laboratory test for marijuana," says Howard Hagan. "At least not from biological specimens. You can test from saliva, though, and I've read about a finger-tip test, too, but they'll only give results within 30 minutes from the time it's smoked. That isn't much help in the morgue."

The young chemist measures out 100 milliliters of half-normal sodium hydroxide and cants it into a solution that, three or four stages earlier, had been blood. "Most common drugs you can pick up easiest from liver tissue, but it depends on what you're looking for, what you've got available, lots of things. In a standard drug screen we'll test from blood, urine, liver, and stomach contents." He lights a cigarette and waits for the centrifuge to finish whipping the solution. "Cerebral spinal fluid will show about the same alcohol level as blood, but the test is a lot easier to do, so we use that. And this barb screen could be done other ways, but blood is the simplest."

When he's finished extracting and concentrating whatever barbiturates reside in the solution, Hagan passes it through the impressively futuristic, dial-festooned spectrophotometer. The machine bombards it with ultraviolet rays, then graphs the absorption pattern where the drug's chemical molecules thwart the rays at specific, individual wavelengths. Graph in hand, he turns to "look it up in Clarke," that being E. G. C. Clarke, *Isolation and Identification of Drugs*, a bulky, four-inch-thick tome containing the absorption graphs of every drug known to medical science.

Dr. Ethel Erickson, a pleasantly serene, matronly woman, enters the toxicology lab and asks, "Have you got anything on that young boy yet, Howard?" One of the two assistant medical examiners, she had performed an autopsy the day before on an unidentified youth thought to be in his late teens, whom she suspected was the victim of a drug overdose.

"No, it'll probably be a good while longer," replies Hagan. "There's still no i.d. on him either, is there?" The body had been discovered in a field, ten days dead already, badly decomposed, and almost totally dehydrated. "There was very little left that might have had any fluids," says Erickson, "and the brain maggots had pretty much eaten away everything there. But I did find two testes and I thought, well, if Howard can get a positive on testes he could really make a name for himself."

"I did a CO once on a piece of bone marrow," remembers Hagan, meaning a carbon monoxide test, "and it was awfully hard. This one isn't any easier."

Given the enormous variety of chemicals currently in fashion, postmortem testing for them requires breathtaking foresight on the part of the pathologist, as well as a high index of suspicion bolstered by a fertile imagination. "If you get one that's a possible freon, for example, you should stick a needle in the trachea and get an air sample right away," Erickson explains. "Once you open the body all the gas will escape, so if you've forgotten the air sample you need to pack the lungs right away. The lab can get enough from seepage to test with. But if you really forget and cut up the lungs and throw them out before you think to look for

freon, then the only thing you can do is get a big section of brain."

"And that's a pretty difficult test," interjects Hagan. Freon, the propellant in most aerosol sprays, is rapidly outstripping glue-sniffing as the preferred turn-on of lower-class mid-teens. "We've had them as young as twelve or thirteen," Erickson says. "It's gotten to where it's the first thing that comes to mind if I see a youngster with no traumatic injuries."

"It's just incredible some of the things people will take," offers Hagan. "They'll eat those roach pellets, those big white ones, then have cardiac arrest from the sodium fluoride. Some of them even drink the stuff from those five-day deodorant pads that have heavy nicotine base. And Drāno, they'll drink Drāno and char their whole esophagus."

"A lot of those are probably suicides," suggests Erickson. "That's the hardest part of this job, calling a death a suicide. Sometimes it just breaks your heart. I've had families come in for two- or three-hour talks, just absolutely refusing to believe that someone they loved could have committed suicide. It's as grueling as psychoanalysis.

"But the saddest thing," she reflects, "is that the biggest arguments are because of money. The beneficiaries have double indemnity clauses where enormous amounts are paid out for accidental deaths, or else they lose their insurance if it's ruled a suicide. That's when it gets really nasty."

"That's one of the things that surprised me about this job, the number of suicides," says Hagan, who's been on the morgue staff two years. "You never read about them, but there are as many people killing themselves as are getting killed. We must run a dozen trace metal tests a week around here."

In shooting deaths where suicide is a possible explanation, a trace metal test can determine whether the victim had recently handled a gun. The decedent's hands are sprayed with a chemical agent and observed under ultraviolet light, revealing by fluorescence the presence of any metallic particles, and the kind—and sometimes the shape—of the metal. Contrary to televised lore, one cannot tell if a person has fired a gun, only if he's held one.

Dr. Erickson walks next door to the investigators' office to see if any progress has been made in identifying the dead youth. "It's such a shame, he couldn't have been more than nineteen or twenty," she says. "And he seemed so healthy, he had perfect teeth!"

Two of Jachimczyk's investigators, Harry Hall and J. L. "Tooter" Turner, both seem to be deeply engrossed in their telephones. "How old was she?" Hall inquires of his phone. "Who found the body? Yeah . . . . When'd he last see his wife alive? . . . 8 p.m.? Was she in bed?" He's speaking to someone at the scene of a death—a policeman, mortician, ambulance driver, or whoever was there and knew enough to call it in.

Virtually all of the county's unattended deaths, or those occurring other than in hospitals or in the presence of physicians, are called into the morgue as soon as they've been reported. "No signs of any trauma?" asks Hall. "What kind of medical history she got? . . . Ask him, yeah. . . . Cardiac problems? Ask him who her doctor was . . . ." By grilling their witnesses over the phone, the investigators can decide if it's necessary to inspect the scene themselves. "Yeah, well, lemme go ahead and call Dr. Arnold and if he'll sign it you can go ahead and release it to the funeral home. I'll call you right back.''

If a death is a natural one, and a doctor is prepared to attest to that fact and sign the death certificate, then the body need never come to the morgue. Only those resulting from unnatural causes or violence, whether accidental, homicidal, or suicidal, are deposited there. And of these, only about half will require autopsies. As Jachimczyk puts it in his job description, ''Autopsies are done when it is necessary to distinguish between violent and natural deaths, not simply for the distinction between the various natural causes of death. If the cause and manner of death can be ascertained beyond a reasonable doubt without an autopsy, then an autopsy is not done.''

''Dr. Arnold, one of your patients has just passed away . . .'' Hall is on the phone again. Somewhere between 50 and 60 per cent of all cases can be dealt with over the phone. ''You were expecting her to die, then . . . this quick? . . . What kind of cardiac problems was she having? . . . You'll sign it coronary occlusion, then? . . . Thank you, Doctor.''

He hangs up and turns around to face Tooter Turner. ''He's gonna sign it,'' reports Hall. ''Said he just saw her yesterday, been treating her for two years. Didn't think it'd be that quick, though.''

''I wish that other doctor'd call back,'' replies Tooter. ''I'm gonna tell 'em to just bring it on in if he don't hurry up.'' Tooter is the genial, white-haired elder of the morgue, the senior employee with twenty years on the staff, and with twenty more running a funeral home prior to that. ''I've made all the really big ones,'' he says, ''the Texas City blow-up, the Gulf Hotel fire in '64, the New London School up in East Texas. I was at all of 'em.''

He says this in the same way that any old-timer might recall the landmarks of his life, partly regretful and partly proud, with a wispy affection for the days that were. He's friendly and relaxed and open and looks like someone's favorite uncle. He's also the Ahab of the Stubby saga, a man grimly obsessed with solving a mystery that for eleven years has been locked in a county morgue cooler at 40 degrees. ''For eleven years now, and you probably think I'm nuts, I've walked in here every day and checked that gauge. And if that needle's up past 42 I'm raising hell and gettin' it fixed straight off.''

When Stubby's torso was found in 1964 there was absolutely no way to identify it. The body's original height, weight, and age could be fairly closely approximated, but nothing more. All that was known was that a man, formerly about 5' 10", 160 pounds, and 50 years old, had somehow had his arms, legs, and head severed and the rest of him dropped by the side of the road. ''To me, and I may be wrong, it was a typical gangster killing,'' Tooter says. ''It's been the most interesting case since I've been here, and there've been some lulus in there.''

Shortly after the discovery, ''I got a crazy hunch, just an idea,'' he remembers. ''I ran down leads day and night, called all over the country, sent out more police flyers than any other case the county ever had.'' It did no good at all. Even when everyone else gave up on it, Tooter pursued the case zealously on his own time, on vacations, weekends, holidays. Unmarried and with few major distractions, he found himself devoting more and more of his attention to the case the farther it receded in time. He refused to allow the torso to be buried in the paupers' cemetery; instead he had it embalmed by a friendly mortician and filed a death certificate, listing place of burial as the Harris County Morgue. Then he locked Stubby in a cooler and pocketed the key.

''I still say that one of these days something'll happen,'' argues Tooter, sounding very convinced, if not necessarily convincing. ''And I'll say something else, the day after he's taken out of here and buried then somethin' sure'll turn up.'' He still checks out leads whenever he has any that need checking, still sends out flyers and reads the missing person bulletins, still stands ready to respond day or night to any calls regarding the Stubby investigation. The last caller, he very quietly admits, ''was five or six months ago.''

Once, almost a decade ago now, on a small stack of three-by-five cards, Tooter wrote down everything that was known about Stubby and the case. He wrapped a green rubber band around them and put the cards in his shirt pocket, where they've been ever since. ''I make sure I've got 'em with me every morning,'' he says. ''Can't ever be sure when I might need 'em.''

He pulls out the cards to hand them to a visitor, seems a little disappointed when the offer is ignored. ''I've laid in bed half the night many a time thinking over some of the leads in this case,'' says Tooter. ''I'm really sure that we'll turn something up soon. And I think that after I find out, then I'll be ready to retire I guess.''

*—November 1975*

# IS JAY J. ARMES FOR REAL?

## by Gary Cartwright

*He says he's the world's greatest private detective, but ...*

Jay J. Armes was running short on patience and long on doubt. He was slipping out of character. It was possible he had made a mistake. The self-proclaimed world's greatest private detective, and internationally famous investigator who liked to brag that he'd never accepted a case he didn't solve, fast on his way to becoming a legend, was stumbling through a television interview with a crew of Canadians who never seemed to be in the right place at the right time, or to have the right equipment, or to ask the right questions.

Jay Armes calculated that his time was worth $10,000 a day, which meant that the three-man crew from Toronto had gone through $15,000, on the house. Pretty much ignoring his suggestions, the Canadians had concentrated on what Armes called "Mickey Mouse shots" of the "Nairobi Village" menagerie in the backyard of his high-security El Paso home, and on his bulletproof, super-customed, chauffeur-driven 1975 Cadillac limousine.

Worse still, the Canadians were not from the Canadian Broadcasting Corporation, as Armes had led himself to believe, but from CTV, a smaller independent network. He had badly overestimated the value of this publicity.

The seeds of discord had been scattered unexpectedly the previous day, at a corner table of El Paso's Miguel Steak and Spirits where Jay Armes sat with his back to the wall regaling the Canadians and two American magazine writers with tales of his escapades, or "capers," as he called them.

He talked of the long helicopter search and dramatic rescue of Marlon Brando's son Christian from a remote Mexican seaside cave where the lad was being held by eight dangerous hippies; of the time he piloted his glider into Cuba and recovered $2 million of his client's "assets"; of the famous Mexican prison break, another helicopter caper which, he said, inspired the Charles Bronson movie *Break-*

*Gary Cartwright, author of books and numerous articles, recently won the Texas Institute of Letters award for journalism. He is a contributing editor of* Texas Monthly.

*out*; of the "Onion King Caper" in which a beautiful model shot her octogenarian husband, then turned a shotgun on herself because Armes wouldn't spend the night with her—all incredible adventures of a super-sleuth, adventures made more incredible by the fact that both of Jay Armes' hands had been blown off in a childhood dynamite accident.

He raised one of his gleaming steel hooks, signaling the waitress, still watching the faces around the table. Too much, they said in admiration: how did he do it? "I read the book," Armes replied enigmatically, "and I saw the play." That was one of his best lines.

At another table strategically positioned between his boss and the front door sat Jay Armes' chauffeur-bodyguard, Fred Marshall, a large, taciturn man who used to sell potato chips. You could not detect the .38 under the coat of his navy-blue uniform. When they traveled in the limousine, which was a sort of floating office, laboratory, and fortress, Fred kept what appeared to be a submachine gun near his right leg. Armes claimed there had been thirteen or fourteen—the number varied from interview to interview—attempts on his life, a figure that did not include the six or seven times he had been wounded in the line of duty. He lifted his pants leg and exhibited what appeared to be a small-caliber bullet wound through his calf.

Concealed on his left hip, under his immaculate, custom-tailored suit with epaulets and belted back, was a .38 Special; implanted in the base of the hook on his right arm was a .22 magnum. What's more, he told CTV producer Heinz Avigdor, he held a third-degree black belt in karate—and that was the point of the ensuing argument.

"I want to show you what a black belt does, besides hold your gi [karate regalia] up," he smiled at the producer. "Look, I've been in a lot of films, I know what I'm talking about. Do it my way, I'll show you what it's all about."

Armes had called ahead and cleared the plan with the Miguel manager. It would be a scene right out of *The Investigator*, a proposed television series which, according to

239

Jay J. Armes. *Photography by Anthony K. Roberts*

Armes, CBS would begin filming right here in El Paso, right here at the Miguel, in fact, on January 20. CBS planned a pilot film and 23 episodes, all of the stories adapted from Armes' personal files. Jay J. Armes, of course, would play the title role of Jay J. Armes.

This was the scenario Armes outlined for the CTV producer:

As soon as the Canadians had positioned their lights and camera, a telephone would ring. Armes would be paged. Fred would presumably go on eating his steak and chili. As Armes approached the lobby he would be confronted by a large Oriental who would grab him by the collar and say, "You've been pushing around the wrong people, Armes." Jay would project his thin smile, inform the Oriental that he was a man of peace, then flip the startled giant over his shoulder with a lightning-quick maneuver of his hooks. A second man would charge him with a pepper mill. Armes would deflect the blow with one of his steel hands, jump into the air, and paralyze the second assailant with a judo chop.

"Uh, Jay," producer Heinz Avigdor said feebly, "I think that is a bit dramatic for the purposes of our show. We're doing a documentary. I think perhaps a workout in your private exercise room, wearing your karate outfit, then some footage in your shooting range downstairs, and maybe a shot in your library. Something from real life, you see."

Jay Armes saw, all right: he saw that the producer was a fool.

"I'm offering you something from real life," he said, that edge of impatience returning to his voice.

"But, Jay, it's so . . . so staged," Avigdor argued. "W-5 isn't that sort of show."

"It's real," Armes snapped, and the pitch of his voice was much higher. "What you're talking about isn't real. There's nothing real about working out in a gym, with a body bag, wearing a stupid gi. This way, I'll be in a suit and tie in a public place doing my work, exactly like real life."

Avigdor protested that his crew didn't have the manpower or equipment for the scene Jay was suggesting. Jay sighed, adjusted his hooks to the fork and knife. he changed the subject abruptly: he began telling the two magazine writers about his secret code, and about his dissolvable stationery that you could stir in a glass of water and drink.

But the affront hung in his mind, and he began to speak of the amateurish approach of the Canadians, about how when *60 Minutes* comes to El Paso in a few weeks to do the Jay Armes story the CTV crew would be eating tin cans. He estimated that the *60 Minutes* segment would be worth $2 million in publicity, and would probably get him elected sheriff of El Paso County, a post he covets not for personal gain but in the interest of justice. "When I decided to run for sheriff," he said, "I telephoned my producer at CBS and he said, great, what can I do to help?" The producer's name was Leonard Freeman, and what he agreed to do, Armes continued, was to send the *60 Minutes* people to El Paso. The show would appear in January, a week before the election.

"Look," Armes told Avigdor, "I've tried to be patient with you guys. I wore the same suit two days in a row—I won't even look at this suit for at least a year now. I invited you into my home. I took time out from my work. I showed you around. I called my producer at CBS a little while ago, and, frankly, he advised me to blow you off."

Armes was smiling, but it wasn't his dark, boyish face and licorice-drop eyes that captured attention, it was those powerful, gleaming steel hooks. Each hook could apply 38 pounds of pressure per square inch, three times that of a normal hand. They were sensitive and deadly, these hooks, and he used them the way a surgeon uses his hands, picking rather than hacking, demonstrating, extracting, mesmerizing, proving precisely what it means for a man to turn a liability into an asset. Somewhere in those gestures was the message: I'll bet you couldn't do this. And yet what you saw was not an amazingly skilled man who could shoot and play tennis and paint and do pushups, what you saw was the dark bore of a .22 magnum inches from your forehead. It was rimmed with black powder and projected an even more deadly threat than the threat of the hooks—the threat of subconscious impulse, unchecked by distance or time—for the trigger mechanism of this weapon was connected by tiny wires to Armes' right biceps. The operation cost $50,000, Armes added, and was performed by a New York surgeon named Bechtol. Don't worry, he said, it has a fail-safe: it can't go off by accident.

"It can only be fired by my brain," Armes had told us. "It's like . . . let me put this right . . . like opening your mouth. Your brain can tell you to open your mouth, but it doesn't just fly open by itself."

That was the same day that Armes asked Avigdor and his two technicians why it was that "Canadians condone concubines." Armes said he had known many cases, especially among French Canadians, in which prominent men "kept concubines [sic] of fifteen and even twenty women."

I don't know if Armes noticed, but Heinz Avigdor's mouth dropped wide enough to accommodate a jack rabbit.

The first thing you see when you enter Jay Armes' office at 1717 Montana in El Paso is a mural on the wall at the end of the hallway. The mural depicts a man in a trench coat and hat, cradling the world in one arm. Painted on the face of the globe are all the cities where Jay Armes operates branch offices. On closer inspection, the man in the trench coat turns out to be Jay Armes. It is a self-portrait.

There are other Jay Armes paintings throughout the office, and throughout his home, mostly of long, graceful tigers springing at some prey off canvas.

The office has a jungle motif. The rooms are dimly lit in eerie reds and greens. "Psychological lighting," Armes says. Armes says he employs more than 2000 full-time agents—600 right here in El Paso—but the only employees visible are a secretary who sits in the front office, and the faithful bodyguard Fred, who lurks nearby.

Armes escorts the visitors to his crime lab. On a long table under the weird green light, laid out like organs in an autopsy, is a curious assortment of detective gimmicks— the latest touch-tone portable telephone, its range worldwide; a de-bugger that Armes values at $10,000; a Dick Tracy-like wristwatch recorder; a tranquilizer gun that shoots sleeping gas; many small bugging devices; and two microscopes. Armes says he can do a complete laboratory breakdown here. In addition to his mastery of chemistry, Armes says he has degrees in psychology and criminology from New York University, as well as the ability to speak seven languages, including thirty-three dialects of Chinese.

Photographs on the wall and in the fat scrapbook show

Armes in diving equipment, or playing with his lions and tigers, or firing on his pistol range. There is a photograph of his son, Jay Armes III, riding a pet lion. Jay III used to have a pet elephant, but a neighbor shot it with a crossbow. In a rear room with a coffee pot and copying machine, Armes points out several bullet holes in the window and door, the marks of that night when an assassin sprayed the building with a .45-caliber grease-gun.

Armes leads the visitors to his private office and sits at his desk, his back to 71 volumes of *Corpus Juris*. On the wall are the framed diplomas testifying that Jay J. Armes is a graduate of a number of detective academies, and a member of a number of detective associations. One of the academies is the Central Bureau of Investigation in Hollywood. Curiously, there is no diploma from NYU. But Armes tells a story about how his old mentor, Professor Max Falen, discovered Armes was working his way through NYU as a dishwasher. "He blew his stack," Jay says. "He said I was shortchanging criminology." Falen arranged for his prize student to receive a paid student assistantship and moved him into his own home. The years passed, poor Max Falen began hitting the bottle. NYU finally had to let him go. When Jay learned what fate had befallen his onetime friend and benefactor, he hired the professor and moved him to the Los Angeles bureau of The Investigators.

Although he graduated with honors at age nineteen, Jay Armes soon learned there were few openings for criminologists. That's when he decided to open his own detective agency.

"I wanted to clean up the image of the profession," he says. "In TV and the movies, private detectives are usually pictured as crooked ex-cops who keep a filing cabinet of booze and work both sides of the street." Jay pointed out that he did not smoke or drink (not even coffee), and was "deeply religious." Ten per cent of everything he makes goes to the Immanuel Baptist Church in El Paso. A secretary at the church later confirmed that Armes "attends regularly and gives generously."

Although Armes is seen regularly at church, at the El Paso Club and Empire Club, at the police station or courthouse, and cruising the streets in his black limo, he remains a mystery man to most citizens of El Paso. Most of what they know about him comes from recent articles in magazines like *People*, *Newsweek*, and *Atlantic*, or from national TV talk shows.

According to *Newsweek*, Armes "keeps a loaded submachine gun in his $37,000 Rolls Royce as protection against the next—and fourteenth—attempt on his life. He lives behind an electrified fence in a million-dollar mansion with a shooting range, a $90,000 gymnasium and a private menagerie, complete with leopards that prowl the grounds unchained at night. He is an expert on bugging, a skilled pilot, a deadly marksman and karate fighter and, perhaps, the best private eye in the country."

The article in *People* was similar, except for a couple of discrepancies. According to *People*, Armes earned his degrees in criminology and psychology from UCLA, not NYU. And they referred to him as "recently divorced."

"My wife went through the ceiling when she read that," Armes said. His wife Linda Chew is the daughter of a respected Chinese grocer. She is a handsome, soft-spoken woman who seems to accept her husband's chosen role with traditional stoicism. "When I leave home in the morning," Armes says, "she never knows if she will see me again."

Armes doesn't especially enjoy discussing his childhood in Ysleta. The Lower Valley, as it is called, was a mostly lower-class, predominantly Mexican-American area of small farms and run-down businesses and ancient Indian teachings. It's now part of El Paso, but it was another town when Armes grew up. As Armes tells it, he was born August 12, 1939, to Jay Sr. and Beatrice Armes. His parents were Italian and French. His father ran a grocery.

"I was a tough kid, like the sidewalk types of Chicago," he recalls. "I had to fight for what I thought was right. I was always at the head of the class, captain of the football team, a boxer, a basketball player, a star in track. Even after I lost my hands I still played all sports."

Armes remembers that he was about eleven when the accident happened. An older boy of about eighteen found some railroad torpedoes beside the track and brought them to Jay's house. The older boy stood back and told Jay to beat the torpedoes together. He did, and they blew his hands off just above the wrists. The accident hardly seemed to slow him down. He recalled holding down four jobs, and running a loan-shark operation across the street from the school. "I'd loan a quarter and get back fifty cents," he said, and the memory seemed to please him. "If someone was slow in paying, I'd kick ass."

What he says happened next is straight out of the Lana Turner saga. Jay was drinking a milk shake at the Hilton Plaza drugstore when a Hollywood casting director named Frank Windsor strolled over and said: "Hey, kid, you're pretty good with those mitts." The casting director offered Jay a part in a movie called *Am I Handicapped?*, starring Dana Andrews.

Jay was barely fifteen—he recalled that he had just started taking flying lessons—when he quit school and moved to Hollywood. The next few years are vague in his recollection, but they apparently weren't dull. He graduated from Hollywood High, landed roles in thirteen feature-length movies, studied one year (1959) at UCLA, moved to New York, did three years (or, as he sometimes remembers, six) at NYU, and returned to El Paso, a triumphant nineteen-year-old determined to change the image of his new profession. Somewhere in there he also graduated from the Central Bureau of Investigation in Hollywood.

Why El Paso, the visitor wonders? With that background, why go home again?

Jay says, "I am deeply religious. It says in the Bible that you will not prosper in your hometown. How could a carpenter's son become king of the Jews? Jesus had to go to Nazareth to be recognized."

Was he then trying to outdo Jesus?

"I was trying to see if this was a fact," he says. "And it is. I am recognized now all over the world more than I am in my hometown."

While the crew from CTV is setting up outside on Montana Street, I take another look around. There is something too deliberate about the way those crime-fighting gimmicks are laid out on that table under the green light in the lab, like toys under a Christmas tree. The holes from the .45 caliber grease-gun would be more impressive if they had smashed the glass or shattered the thin layer of wood instead of leaving clean, neat punctures. I glance through the Jay J. Armes Training Academy correspondence course, which can be had for $300. Sample question: "Eighty per cent of

people do not see accurately because:
(a) they have a stigmatism
(b) there is to much smog in the air
(c) because they do not pay attention
(d) because they usually just watch the ground.''

I wonder if the Central Bureau of Investigation was like this. Then something else catches my eye—the mural at the end of the hallway, the self-portrait. I didn't notice before, but Jay Armes has given himself blue eyes. And that's not a hook holding the world, it's a hand.

Fred, the ex-potato chip salesman, stands at attention, holding the rear door of the limo open for Jay Armes and his guests. There are a few rules you learn in Jay Armes' company: you do not smoke, you do not swear, and you do not open your own limousine door. A New York book editor who was in El Paso a few weeks earlier recalled the door ritual as his most vivid impression. Jay Armes always got out first, explaining that ''I'm armed. I can protect my friends.''

As the black limousine pulls silently into the traffic and winds past the refinery adjacent to IH 10, Armes reaches out with his hooks and activates the video tape camera buried in the trunk lid of the car. On the black-and-white screen we can see the CTV station wagon trailing us. Sometimes, Armes tells us, he uses the video tape gear to follow other people. ''While they're looking in their rearview mirror,'' he says, ''I'm right in front of them watching their every move.''

The limo is also equipped with a police siren, a yelper, and a public-address system, each of which he demonstrates. There is a front-seat telephone and a back-seat telephone with a different number, revolving license plates, and Jay Armes' crest on each door. You might suppose all these trappings would make it difficult to remain inconspicuous, but Jay has his methods. ''I read the book,'' he says, ''and I saw the play.'' Sometimes he uses a panel truck with Acme Plumbing on the side. Or the bronze Corvette with the Interpol sticker on the back. He even has a stand-in. Somewhere in El Paso there is another Jay J. Armes.

The limousine pulls off IH 10 and follows a narrow blacktop along rows of cheap houses, hotdog stands, and weed fields. This is not exactly your silk-stocking neighborhood.

Armes has been talking about his $50,000 fee for cracking a recent jewel robbery at the *UN Plaza* apartments in New York, and about a potential half-million dollar fee that he turned down on advice of his attorney. Working through his producer, Leonard Freeman, a national magazine that he is not at liberty to identify offered Armes that sum to locate Patty Hearst, which he boasted he could do in three weeks or less. ''The FBI called and said, hey Jay, how can you find her in three weeks? I said: 'cause I know my business.'' In return for its money, the magazine wanted Armes to guarantee an exclusive 30,000-word interview with the mysterious heiress, and that's when Armes pulled out. ''Even admitting to you now that I had her located,'' he said, ''could subject me to criminal prosecution. But I'll tell you this much, that's a damn lie about her being in school in Sacramento. I'm writing a book for Macmillan, maybe I'll tell the true story. The FBI actually put a tail on my book publisher, thought maybe he'd lead them to Patty Hearst. I'll say one more thing. I'll bet you $10,000 that Patty will never be convicted.''

Outside the eighteen-foot electrified fence that runs along the 8100 block of North Loop, Fred activates a small electronic box above his head and the gates swing open. He parks the car in front of Jay J. Armes' curious little mansion with its tall columns and flanking white stone lions.

A Rolls, a Corvette, and several other cars are parked in the driveway between the house and the tennis court. Gypsy, Armes' pet chimpanzee, screeches from her cage until Armes walks over and swaps her a piece of sugarless gum for a kiss. A pack of dogs hangs back, menacingly.

While the crew from CTV is hauling its equipment upstairs to the library, Armes conducts a tour of the Nairobi Village in the backyard. Armes stiffens when visitors refer to this as a ''zoo,'' and with good reason: this place is right out of a Tarzan movie, except that most of the animals are caged. There are thatched huts, exotic plants, narrow trails through high walls of bamboo, and a lighted artificial waterfall beside a man-made lake. Though the lake is not much larger than a hockey rink, there is what appears to be a high-powered speedboat anchored against the far bank. And on the bank nearest to the house, inside a corral of zebras and small horses, sits a twin-blade helicopter. This is the chopper, Armes reveals, that he uses most often. He can have it fueled and airborne in less than half an hour. He also says he owns a jet helicopter (it's presently in Houston), a Riley turbojet, and a Hughes 500.

In the heart of the jungle, a telephone rings. Armes opens a box on the side of a palm tree and talks to someone. Then the tour resumes.

''When I was a kid,'' Armes says, ''I couldn't even afford a good cat. I decided that when I got older and could afford it, I'd buy every animal I could find.'' So far he has found 22 different species, including a pair of black panthers from India, some miniature Tibetan horses that shrink with each generation, some ostriches, a West Texas puma, and a 400-pound Siberian tiger that roams the grounds at night, discouraging drop-in visitors. Many of his prize animals, he tells the visitors, are currently grazing on his 20,000-acre Three Rivers Ranch in New Mexico.

Armes opens the tiger cage and invites his guests inside. He smiles, having already detected the presence of fear in the tiger's movements. The tiger seems suddenly irritable. Armes talks to the tiger and strokes its head. The tiger rears back and Armes controls it with a skilled movement of his steel wrists.

Entering Jay Armes' mansion is yet another trip beyond the fringe: it is something like entering the living room of an eccentric aunt who just returned from the World's Fair. There is a feeling of incongruity, of massive accumulations of things that don't fit, passages that lead nowhere, bells that don't ring.

We wait in what I guess you would call the bar. The decor might be described as Neo-Earth in Upheaval. It was as though alien species had by some unexplained cataclysm been transposed to a common ground. Dark green water trickles from rocks and runs sluggishly along a concrete duct that divides the room. There are concrete palm trees, artificial flowers, and stuffed animals and birds. Two Japanese bridges span the duct, and the walls sag with fishnets, bright bulbs, African masks, and paintings of tigers. There is a piano in one corner, but Jay Armes does not volunteer to demonstrate that skill just now. Although neither Armes nor his wife Linda drink, the bar is well-stocked with Jack Daniels, Chivas Regal, Beefeater, and two varieties of beer on tap.

In an adjacent room, what appears to be a living coconut palm floats in a tub in the indoor swimming pool. Though the pool is small, it takes up most of the room. In one corner of the room, hidden behind a thatched bar, is a washer and dryer and a neat stack of freshly laundered children's clothes.

The room behind the swimming pool is Jay's exercise room. Steps lead down to his computerized target range in the basement. After his customary two-and-a-half hours sleep, Jay wakes around 4 a.m., dictates into his recorder, exercises with his karate instructor, practices on his target range, has a sauna and a shower, selects one of the suits with the epaulets from a closet that he estimates contains about 700 suits valued at $500 a pop, has a high-protein breakfast, and calls for Fred to bring the limousine around.

"Almost every day of my life," he says, "there is some violent or potentially violent incident. I have to stay in tip-top shape." His single vice is work. "The Lord has given us a brain," he says. "We only use one-tenth of ten per cent of it. The rest is dormant. That's because we are lazy. I try to use as much of my brain as I can." Armes claims that he personally worked on 200 cases last year, and that doesn't count the thousands of cases in the hands of his more than 2000 agents.

Like the other rooms, there is a disturbing incongruity to the exercise room. It's too neat, too formal. The equipment is the kind you would find at a reducing salon for middle-aged women. It's mostly the easy stuff that works for you.

Upstairs above the exercise room is the Armes' master bedroom. Scarlet O'Hara would have loved it. Flaming red carpet, flaming red fur spread, a lot of mirrors, and the ever-present eye of the security scanner. From the video screen beside his circular bed, Jay Armes can watch any point in or outside the house.

Armes is pacing like a cat: the CTV crew is still not ready in the library. He leads the two magazine writers downstairs again, to his shooting range where he demonstrates both the .38 and the .22 magnum.

"Yes," he says, "I have killed people. I don't want to talk about it. It's sad . . . no one has a monopoly on life. But it's like war. Sometimes you must take a life in the line of duty. I'm guarding some diamonds, say, my job is to protect my client's property. If someone gets in the way, maybe I'll have to kill him. But I don't like to talk about it."

Then he tells of a caper in which he rescued a fifteen-year-old girl runaway from an apartment somewhere in New Mexico. He kicked open the door and a hippie with a .32 shot him three times. The third bullet struck less than an inch from his heart. There was no time for the .38. Armes raised his right arm and killed the hippie with a single .22 slug square between the eyes. "Remind me to show you a picture of it when we get back to the office," he says. Bleeding like hell, Armes drove the runaway girl back to her parent's house in El Paso. Only then did he drive himself to the hospital.

"It's funny," he says, "but when I get shot, I seem to get super strength. I know the Lord is looking after me."

When the TV camera is finally in place, Armes goes up to the library and stands in front of a painting of a tiger which is actually a secret door to the children's room. On cue from Heinz Avigdor, Jay Armes shows off his gun collection, and tells a little story about each weapon. I had examined all this hardware earlier, so I excused myself and walked down to the bar where I telephoned a friend.

Through the fishnet and the porthole window I could get a closer look at Jay Armes' helicopter. From appearances, it hadn't been off the ground in years: its tires were deflated and hub-deep in hard ground, the blades were caked with dirt and grease, and the windows were covered with tape instead of glass. Armes had told us that the chopper had a brand-new engine. I wondered why he hadn't put glass in the windows.

I walked back upstairs and told Armes that I had to get back to town. I made up a lie about having dinner with my old college roommate.

"Say hello to Joe Shepard," Armes said with a thin smile.

"Is Jay J. Armes for real?" I asked Joe Shepard as we devoured the *grub du jour* of his favorite Juarez hangout.

"No way in hell," Joe said. At least that was his hunch. Like almost everyone else in El Paso, Shepard (as he calls himself) knew Jay J. Armes only by reputation. He was that mystery man in the black limo. You'd see that big sinister Cadillac glide up in front of the police station or the courthouse, Fred would pop out, look around, open the door, and Jay Armes would hustle up the steps, his head low and his hooks locked contemplatively behind his back. They had all read about Armes and seen him on TV talk shows. He lived behind that eighteen-foot electric fence way out on North Loop, in a poor section of town, in that white mansion with the never-land facade, next to the parked helicopter, next to the miniature lake. They had heard that wild animals roamed the estate.

Shepsy had heard, too, about the repeated attempts on Armes' life and had concluded: "El Paso must have the worst assassins in America. If I wanted to shoot Jay Armes I'd sit across the street from the courthouse for an hour or two."

Shepsy is a licensed private investigator. He showed me his card. License number A-01123-9. True, he didn't know Jay J. Armes, but he knew enough to dislike him.

"I don't want to sound like sour grapes," Shepsy said, ordering another round of tequila and beer, "but it's not that difficult to run a magic lantern show in this business. The more sophisticated a client is, the easier it is to take them. They seem to feel an obligation to understand what you're doing. The wife of Dr. —————— [he named an El Paso surgeon] hired me to shadow him—I could have worked her for $50,000 bucks, that's how sophisticated she wanted to be. But I didn't. I checked the doctor—there was nothing to it, so I dropped it.

"A good investigator will find out what a client wants to hear. After that, it's no problem to write a report. The hell of it is, there are a lot of poor people getting ripped off, too. You have no idea how many poor husbands or wives will take everything out of their savings and hire a private investigator. They feel trapped, they *don't* know what's going on in their lives. . . . I guess they believe it's like it is on television."

Shepsy is 43, the same age as Jay J. Armes, although

Armes claims to be 36. Shepsy has been frequently married, and his life is constantly in danger from his current wife, Jackie, a high-spirited free-lance nurse anesthetist who supports his unorthodox lifestyle and sometimes heaps his clothes on the back porch and burns them. Shepsy drives a red VW and has never owned a gun in his life.

"If I carried a gun," he said, "sooner or later someone would take it away and shoot me. If someone is going to shoot ol' Shepsy he's damn sure gonna have to bring his own gun."

None of Shepsy's wives, including the pretty incumbent, Jackie, could get it through their heads that he was really spending all those lonely nights perched in a tree watching bedroom windows through binoculars.

They had been married about four months when Jackie hired Jay J. Armes to check out Shepsy's story that he was flying to Albuquerque on business. She paid Armes $300—she's still got the check to prove it—and he reported back by telephone. The entire substance of his report was that one of his "operatives" followed Shepsy and, sure enough, Shepsy had driven to the airport. He made a couple of "mysterious phone calls," then boarded the flight for Albuquerque, exactly as he said. Case closed. Fee paid.

"Nobody followed me," Shepsy said. "Not in a New York minute. I wasn't anywhere close to the airport that night. I *drove* to Albuquerque with my clients."

Shepsy had heard all about those fantastic fees that Jay Armes commanded, but he was skeptical. Nobody in the business charges like that—not half a million, not $100,000, not even $10,000. Shepsy works for $15 an hour, or $150 a day, plus expenses. One of his larger cases popped up just that morning when a distraught father paid him $500 to prove that his daughter was dating a homosexual, which in fact she was. What a price to pay for truth.

But this was a border town; the rules were a little different. Nothing was just what it seemed. So was everything. For $50 you could have someone killed. Any Juarez cab driver could arrange it. Investigators knew the rules of operating in Mexico—speak the language and have the money. They all heard about the 25 grand Jay Armes got for rescuing Marlon Brando's son. They believed it. They didn't believe the part about the three-day helicopter search in which Jay Armes survived on water, chewing gum, and guts, but they all knew the trick of grabbing a kid. You hired a couple of *federales* or gunsels. The problem wasn't finding the kid, it was getting him out of the country.

I told Joe Shepard what Armes had said as I was leaving. He'd said: "Say hello to Joe Shepard." I don't know how he knew I was meeting Joe Shepard.

The next night I had dinner with Joe and Jackie and some of their friends, and the entire conversation was Jay J. Armes. It turned out that Jackie had gone to Ysleta High School with Linda Chew, Armes' wife. Jackie recalled that Linda was shy and obedient, a hard worker. Jackie's friend, Guillermina Reyes, hired Armes a few months ago to substantiate her contention that the business manager of Newark Hospital was embezzling funds. Mina had been fired from her receptionist job by the business manager, but the hospital board had agreed to hear her story and she needed some hard evidence.

"This was last August," Mina told me. "I hadn't heard of Jay J. Armes at the time—I picked him out of the phone book. I went to his office and told him my problem and he

said he would look into it for $1500. That shook me up. Then he said, how about $700? I apologized and said he was way out of my range, so he said, 'How much have you got?'"

Mina finally paid Armes $150, and several weeks later, Armes told her, "I checked it out. This guy is clean." That was the entire report. A few weeks later Mina and everyone else began hearing just how clean Ramirez was—the Newark business manager was arrested, charged with embezzling funds in the amount of some $21,000, and placed under $500,000 bond. Whatever the truth, Jay J. Armes hadn't exactly resembled the world's, or even El Paso's, greatest detective.

Brunson Moore, a lawyer and former El Paso JP, recalled a time when Armes had performed spectacularly in a domestic case involving a husband who thought his young wife was playing around. She was playing around all right—Armes gained entry into her apartment and produced some amazing movies. The wife's co-star turned out to be the pastor of one of El Paso's larger churches. The films were not admissible evidence, of course, but the pastor soon moved out of town.

Clarence Moyers, an attorney, had a Jay J. Armes story. This was a couple of years ago, when Moyers was getting a divorce. Jay Armes telephoned, very familiar, very friendly, saying, "Clarence, ol' buddy, I've been out of town and a terrible thing happened to you while I was gone."

"I had never spoken to Jay Armes," Moyers said, "but suddenly he's laying it on me how his agents didn't realize what great buddies we were, so they accepted an assignment from my ex-wife to do an investigation on me. Armes said he had a stack of pictures a foot deep. He said he was sitting there right then looking at one of me in a daisy chain. I asked him what a daisy chain was, and he told me. Well, I hadn't been in a daisy chain recently, but I was still worried. Then he got to the point: he said my ex-wife had paid his agents $300 cash, so if I'd put up another $300 he'd give me the pictures and return my ex-wife's money."

Moyers instructed Jay Armes what to do with his pictures and hung up. When he confronted his ex-wife later, she denied ever hiring Armes or one of Armes' agents.

There was a paradox here. Jay J. Armes' stories didn't check, yet the man was absolutely larger than life. He didn't support his flamboyant lifestyle by misleading poor receptionists or working both sides in domestic cases. The riddle of Jay Armes hung in some dark passageway; tracing it back was like looking in old encyclopedias for new discoveries. The city directory, for example, first took note of Jay J. Armes in 1957, when he should have been in California. Armes operated the Central Bureau of Investigation, named no doubt for the detective course he took in Hollywood. His office was in the Caples Building, an old seven-story warren of bail bondsmen, quicky finance companies, and ambulance chasers. "The Investigators" first appeared in 1963.

Joe Shepard nudged me with his elbow and motioned to follow him outside. We walked to a remote corner of the parking lot, and stood on a high ledge overlooking the lights of El Paso. Shepsy waited while a small aircraft passed overhead.

Then he said in a low voice, "The reason you're having trouble tracing Jay Armes is that's not his real name. He's really Julian Armas."

He pronounced it hool-*yon* are-*mas*.

Julian Armas was born August 12, 1932. His father was Pedro, not Jay Sr., and his mother was Beatriz. Pedro didn't own a grocery store as had been claimed, but he worked in one. He was a butcher at the P&N Grocery in Ysleta. "He worked hard and drank his beer," recalled Eddy Powell, who used to own the store. Like Professor Max Falen, Pedro had a drinking problem.

Pedro and Beatriz Armas and their five children were Mexican-Americans. Not Italians. Not French. Julian, a friend recalled, didn't speak English until he started to school.

Records in the El Paso County Courthouse show that Julian was nearly fourteen when he jabbed the railroad torpedoes with an ice pick and blew off both of his hands. A negligence suit filed against the Texas & Pacific Railroad on December 6, 1948, claimed 75 per cent disability and asked for $103,000 in damages, based on Julian's estimated total income for the next forty-six years. The case was dismissed. The way Armes, or Armas, tells it, he was awarded an $80,000 settlement, which he gave to his family. A lawyer connected with the case says Armas collected nothing.

"The boys didn't find the torpedoes beside the track," the lawyer said. "They broke into a section house. There was no evidence of negligence on the part of the railroad."

Margaret Caples Abraham recalled the day of the accident. It happened in the chicken yard behind her house. She was about seven at the time. It was her brother, Dickie Caples, who was with Julian. When Margaret and her family returned from a Saturday afternoon shopping trip, the boys were gone and the chickens were pecking on bits of flesh and small fingers. Dickie wasn't injured, but the trauma of that day still haunts him. Curiously, the Caples own the Caples Building where Jay J. Armes first started his detective business.

Van Turner helped Julian get fitted with his hooks. Van and Julian attended the same Catholic Church and were members of Boy Scout Troop 95. They also shared a paper route. Julian operated a motor scooter specially customed with two bolts instead of handle grips, and Van rode on the back.

"I never made any money from the paper route," Van Turner recalled. "I never knew what Jay did with the money. I felt sorry for him."

Van Turner remembered that the other kids helped Julian with his homework. After two years of high school, Julian split for California. "When he came home seven or eight years later," Turner said, "he had changed. He was always sort of a bully, but now he was very obnoxious."

"He came back with a different attitude," said Rudy Resendez, who also delivered newspapers with Julian Armas. Resendez is now principal of an elementary school in Ysleta. "It was like he had to prove himself. He was a strange person. Nobody could get close to him. He gave the impression that he was better than anyone else."

Old friends recalled well when he returned from California. Julian, or Jay J. Armes as he now called himself, drove an old, raggedy-topped Cadillac with a live lion in the back and a dummy telephone mounted to the dashboard. He would pull up beside the girls at the drive-in and pretend to be talking to some secret agent in some foreign land.

"He told stories about all the war movies he'd been in,"

recalled a doctor who asked that his name not be used. "He also told the story that he had lost his hands in the war. He had his hair cut very short. He wore a hat and sharp clothes. Yes, people in Ysleta were impressed at first."

"He had another wife back then. I don't remember her name, but I remember treating one of their daughters in the emergency room about 1962. Julian [the doctor used the Spanish pronunciation, hool-*yon*] said, 'Don't cry, honey, we'll watch our TV in the car on the way home.' He wanted everyone in the emergency room to understand that he had a television in his car."

The doctor, a one-time Golden Gloves champion and a Korean War veteran, was a few years older than Julian Armas, but he recalled that "he was very active, real smart, he had his finger in every pie. No, he never played football at Ysleta, but he was a pretty good touch football player, even without his hands. He had a competitive drive even before he lost his hands.

"There are many people in Ysleta who think of him as a phony, and by most standards perhaps he is, but I don't think so, because I understand the motive behind his behavior. I have respect for Julian. For most people, losing both hands would be the end of the show; for him, it was the beginning.

"The other things, the name change and claiming to be Italian, that's compensation . . . not only for his physical handicap, which is really an asset to him now, but for the psychological stigma of being a member of the much persecuted and chastized Mexican-American minority in Texas, which can be a problem even to the most intellectual of minds."

When you get down to it, the doctor said, Jay J. Armes isn't all that different from Julian Armas. He was always a braggart. He always demanded center stage. He always had a need to achieve, and a need to exaggerate his accomplishments. If he sold fifty newspapers, he would claim that the figure was two hundred. Even now, when he apparently has the wealth to live anywhere in the world, he built a fortress for himself located less than a mile from his place of origin. Why not one of the silk-stocking areas, you ask. Why not Coronado Hills, a section of El Paso that he openly admired?

The doctor's laugh was not sympathetic. He had a patient in the next room who manifested some of the same problems. This person had commissioned a sort of wood-carved Mount Rushmore in which his face appeared alongside Zapata, Villa, and Cortés. "The sine qua non," the doctor said, "is a departure from reality."

"Julian," he said, "lives here in the Lower Valley because these are the people he needs to impress. In a better part of town the rich gringos would just look on him as another crazy Mexican."

The Catholic church that Turner, Resendez, Julian Armas, and almost everyone else in Ysleta attended still stands, as it has since 1682. It was the first mission in Texas. From the Tigua Indian museum across the church grounds visitors can still hear recordings of the ancient ceremonial chants. Long before Europeans had crossed the Atlantic, the ancestry of these people—Julian Armas' forefathers—had perfected a civilization that the flock at the Immanuel Baptist Church might not yet comprehend. This was the heritage that Jay J. Armes denied.

Almost everyone I spoke with in Ysleta who was anywhere near Jay J. Armes' age, knew the story of Julian Armas. "He wasn't tough," a drunk Indian named Rachie told me, "but he was mean." Rachie recalled Julian's first job as a security officer—it was throwing Rachie and his friends out of the movie house where Julian worked. Rachie remembered how delightful it had been, shooting Julian in the head with chinaberries. Van Turner remembered the high school PE teacher made Julian take off his hooks when they played touch football. All of the old friends remembered that Julian liked to pinch the girls with his hooks. Or heat them red-hot in the popcorn machine at the movie house. One of his pleasures was heating up a 50 cent piece and throwing it to a younger kid. The doctor, Margie Luna, and several other eye-witnesses recounted the time he heated his hooks in the popcorn machine and grabbed Rosalie Stoltz by the arm. You can still see the burn scar 30 years later.

A few years ago when Jay J. Armes ran for justice of the peace, he failed to carry his home district of Ysleta. The prediction is he won't do much better running against Sheriff Mike Sullivan, who is also from Ysleta.

**M**ike Sullivan is half Irish and mostly Mexican. The people who know him think he's a pretty good man. Until very recently Jay Armes professed to think the same thing.

Sullivan made his department's criminal investigation division available to Armes, and helped Armes get appointed deputy constable last August, which is the reason Armes is permitted to wear a gun and maintain a siren and yelper on his limousine. Armes also claims to be one of three authorized Interpol agents working in the United States, but Sullivan has no knowledge of this.

Cynical talk has it that they are still friends, that Armes has volunteered his services as a stalking horse to ward off other potential candidates. Armes did this once before, in the JP race some years ago.

Whatever the motive, Armes sounds like a serious candidate. Lately, he has been speaking to labor and women's organizations, telling how he could find Jimmy Hoffa in a few days if the price were right, and spreading bad tales about his old mentor, Mike Sullivan. He called Sullivan a "figurehead" who allows prisoners to walk in and out of jail as though it were a resort motel, who permits his deputies to beat Farah picketers, who hires ex-cons and homosexuals, who gives his inmates amphetamines, which are "the same thing as tranquilizers, and also known as Darvon." But the most serious charge *was* serious, even by border-town standards. Armes accuses Sullivan of framing and even assassinating his enemies and credits several recent attempts on his own life to the Sheriff.

At the El Paso Club one afternoon when Armes was avoiding the crew from CTV, he struck up a conversation with a banker and an architect who were talking business at the next table. The El Paso Club is one of those phony-formal, itchy, squirmy private clubs frequented by movers and shakers, a place where you're embarrassed to cough unless someone winks first. So it was that everyone in the room (except Fred, who has having lobster salad at the next table) looked up when Jay Armes began to speak of Mike Sullivan as "the first dictator in the United States, except J. Edgar Hoover." He told the banker and the architect that Mike Sullivan was arranging small cells for his enemies, and when the cells got too small, he was arranging for them to be killed.

The banker puffed on his cigar and said, "I had no idea that situation existed." Then, as though the question naturally followed, he asked, "How's the TV series coming?"

Armes told them how his producer, Leonard Freeman, had leaned on *60 Minutes* to help him get elected.

"How is the media treating you?" the architect asked.

"I'm more worried about the press than anyone else," the banker said. "If they can do it to the president, they can do it to anyone."

"Don't be surprised if a bomb goes off and blows me up," Armes said. Then he shrugged with his hooks, smiled, and said, "But that's life."

On the street outside the El Paso Club, Armes stopped to campaign with three gnarled loafers eating pecans on the curb. They didn't seem very interested. "I don't vote," an old man in a World War I campaign hat said. "I'm eighty-one. To hell with it." Armes shook his head and walked toward his waiting limo. "Can you imagine what this country would be like if everyone had that attitude," he said sadly.

Mike Sullivan refused to talk about his differences with Armes, except to say, "I knew the kid since he used to deliver my paper in Ysleta. I liked the kid. I helped him in many ways. Then something happened and he turned against me." What happened was a disagreement over just how Jay Armes could use the El Paso Sheriff's facilities. In the beginning, Sullivan had authorized his criminal investigation division to cooperate with Armes, and together they had solved some cases. Armes got the money, Sullivan pointed out, and most of the credit. From Armes' standpoint, the biggest case involved the theft of some men's slacks stored in the Lee Way trucking terminal. "We broke the case," Sullivan said, "but the kid took the credit, and Lee Way was pleased. They hired him to check out a terminal in Oklahoma City where some TVs and stereos had been ripped off. I told him to go up there and work the same way he did here—work with the sheriff. Sure 'nuff, the goods were recovered. That led to even a bigger contract. He made better than a hundred grand off of that."

Then Armes became dissatisfied with Sullivan's criminal investigation division and started demanding the use of the patrol division as well. Getting Marlon Brando's son back from Mexico had been a good lesson. So had his authority as a deputy constable to serve subpoenas. Joe Shepard estimated that the right to serve subpoenas was worth at least $10,000 a year to a private investigator.

"He wanted our patrol cars for cover," said Captain S. J. Palos, one of Mike Sullivan's officers. "It was the same trick he pulled when he recovered Marlon Brando's kid. Brando's attorney already knew where the kid was. Jay Armes crossed the river, hired a couple of gunsels and got him out of Mexico. There was a similar child custody case here in El Paso. He got one of our marked patrol cars to park outside the residence. After that, all he had to do was knock on the door and say, 'I'm here for the kid. My backup is parked just outside.' The rest is automatic."

Captain Palos, a retired Army colonel, said, "Jay is not a scholar of evidence. We've had to reject several of his cases because the evidence just wasn't there. It appears to me that he lives in a type of fantasy world. He reads an adventure story, and a week later he tries to relive it."

"I liked the kid," Mike Sullivan repeated. "He came back from L.A. in an old Cadillac convertible with a dummy telephone, all fired up to be a private detective. I told him then, 'You do that work just like you do anything else: you take care of business, you do it by the book.' I said, 'You'll be living off human suffering, you had better stay on a straight line.'"

I asked Sheriff Sullivan about the submachine gun that Fred the bodyguard carries. Sullivan told me it was an M-1, hammed up to look like a submachine gun. A hype. Just like the helicopter at the side of the house. The same prop rusted years ago in front of Kessler Industries until Armes acquired it and had it shipped to his place.

Captain Palos had an explanation for Jay Armes' boast that he employs more than 2000 agents around the world, 600 of them in the El Paso office. There is an association of private detectives with about that number of members. They can all claim each other. "There are about 400,000 police officers in the United States," Palos said. "Sheriff Sullivan, as a member of the National Sheriffs Association, could claim all of them as agents. I seriously doubt if Jay's got two agents in El Paso, let alone 600. I have never seen them as long as I've been here. Put a pencil to it and figure up how much 600 full-time agents would cost a year."

I did, using the mythical poverty line as a pay base, but the figure was so ridiculous I threw it away.

If this were a real detective story it would now be time to confront the suspect, and with him the reader. It would be the place to pull in all the facts and discard all the red herrings and wrap the whole package with a red bow. But there won't be any neat red bows, because the true story of Jay J. Armes lies buried beneath the rubble of twisted stories, mistaken dates, and transposed facts: we may never know the true story, but it has little in common with what *Newsweek* and *People* and other periodicals printed, or with the B-grade plots and grand mystique that Armes projects for himself. The real story is of a Mexican-American kid from one of the most impoverished settlements in the United States, how he extracted himself from the wreckage of a crippling childhood accident and through the exercise of tenacity, courage, and wits became a moderately successful private investigator. There is more sympathy, drama, and human intrigue in that accomplishment than you're likely to find in any two or three normal studies of the human condition.

Who really understands the agony of Julian Armas? He wanted much more: he wanted the hands and blue eyes of his self-portrait, he wanted to be in the movies, he wanted his life to be *like* the movies. Maybe he didn't see the right movies. Maybe they didn't show them in Ysleta, or maybe he wasn't paying enough attention to see that the audience eventually woke to reality. What makes the story of Jay J. Armes, aka Julian Armas, so difficult to tell is precisely the Hollywood mentality in which nothing is what it seems, in which everything is an illusion.

There is no recourse then but to pare away the misstatements and exaggerations and attempt to fill in the blanks, but first I want to point out that I did not go to El Paso for the purpose of exposing Jay J. Armes. I had never heard of him until two days before I arrived, a bewildered guest, at his home. I hadn't read any of the magazine articles or seen him on any of the TV talk shows or even heard the mention of his name, although I soon discovered that half the kids in El Paso and even Austin knew him as that dude in the hooks who can do karate. The reader has discovered Armes the way I discovered him, and if the first part of this story overwhelms you, imagine what it did to me.

As the reader may have guessed, they never heard of Armes/Armas at UCLA. They never heard of Armes/Armas *or* Professor Max Falen at NYU. If this classic father figure, this teacher who first recognized his student's talents and took him into his own home, really is employed "as a sort of visiting fireman" in Armes' Los Angeles office, then he too has a serious handicap. Neither Falen nor the office is listed. Neither Falen nor Armes has a California detective's license.

The Federal Aeronautics Administration never issued a pilot's license to Armes or Armas. The Academy of Motion Pictures has no record of a film entitled *Am I Handicapped?*, starring Dana Andrews or anybody else. Old friends speculate that Armes may have made some technical films illustrating expert command of hooks, but no one knows for sure. He did appear in one episode of *Hawaii Five-0* as a heavy named Hookman, but some people who know Armes and have heard the sound track believe the voice is dubbed. Armes claims the Library of Congress selected that episode as the "best show ever on TV," an award the Library has never made or has any intention of making.

CBS isn't filming *The Investigator*, as the *El Paso Herald Post* reported on November 29. That film crew that everyone supposed to be from CBS was a crew from Chicago doing commercial work for a toy company. A spokesman at CBS acknowledged that the series was a hot project of producer Leonard Freeman. But Freeman, the man Armes was repeatedly calling while I was there, died almost two years ago. The dog-eared script on Armes' desk is owned by Lorimar Productions, but it is not an active project. It is one of hundreds of scripts mildewing in Hollywood.

There is a staff memo making the rounds at *60 Minutes* suggesting a story on Jay J. Armes, but no decision has been made. Whatever the decision, it won't help Armes to any election victory in January. The Democratic primary isn't until May, of course, and the general election is in November, as always. The wonder of it all is that apparently Armes himself is so wrapped up in his own myth that he doesn't realize what damage an investigative TV show like *60 Minutes* could do to him.

There was, to be sure, a dramatic Mexican jailbreak using a helicopter which inspired the Charles Bronson movie *Breakout*. The only authoritative account of it, *The 10-Second Jailbreak*, does not mention Jay J. Armes. Armes takes credit for this oversight: he claims that the pilot who got the publicity was a soldier of fortune from Jamaica whom Armes hired to take the heat off himself. Otherwise, Armes says he would be arrested the next time he put a foot over the border and be forced to serve out the remaining sixteen years of the sentence. Who knows?

Law officers in El Paso believe that Armes did bring Marlon Brando's kid out of Mexico, though they believe the circumstances were considerably less dramatic than the tale Armes spins. I saw a photograph of Armes and Brando, both exercising large smiles, but I also saw a photograph of

Armes and Miss Universe. I couldn't reach Brando for his version. The *UN Plaza* jewelry caper, which came after Armes' recent spate of publicity, appears genuine, but there is no way to check the other claims—the Interpol connection, the third-degree black belt in karate, the glider caper into Castro Cuba, or the friendship with Howard Hughes; for that matter, Armes could have easily said he was a CIA agent or a UFO carrot farmer.

As for the obvious question, where does Armes get all that money if he's not a big-time operator? I didn't see evidence of that much money. When you check the El Paso city tax records, Armes' "nine-acre estate" turns out to be 1.24 acres, although he does own 1.5 acres of adjacent property, as he claims. Most likely the net value of his estate is considerably less than the $1 million figure quoted in *Newsweek* (or the $1.2 million that he told me). The estimated replacement cost that appears on the city tax real estate card is about $50,000. Armes paid real estate taxes last year of $476.13.

Armes probably did earn a nice chunk for the Lee Way security job, and there is convincing evidence he collected on an $80,000 settlement from a bizarre law suit against the American owner of a Juarez radio station who hadn't paid Armes for his work in Mexico. Armes' friends trace a big part of his personal wealth to his friendship with an eccentric and reclusive multi-millionaire named Thomas Fortune Ryan, who has supposedly cut Armes in on some lucrative real estate deals. The Three Rivers Ranch on the backside of White Mountain in New Mexico, which Armes claimed to own, is in fact Thomas Fortune Ryan's reclusory, although Leavell Properties picked up a purchase option a few years ago.

It is true that Jay J. Armes drives around El Paso in the damnedest black limo you ever saw, armed to the teeth. That pistol in his hook is the real McCoy; I watched him fire it. So is the loaded .38 on his left hip. Fred's "submachine-gun" might technically qualify as a submachinegun: anyone with a knowledge of weapons can rig an M-1 with a paper clip and make it fully automatic.

Of all those incredible tales, at least two are fairly accurate, and they probably say more about our junk-commodity society, counterfeit-hero mentality, and burned-out consciences than all the fantasies and delusions of a poor boy from the Lower Valley.

The Ideal Toy Corp. is marketing a series of Jay J. Armes toys, designed along the line of the highly successful Evel Knievel series. "It's what we call our hero action figure," Herbert Sands, vice president of corporate marketing, told me. "Batman and Robin, Superman, that sort of hero, but like Evel Knievel, Jay Armes is a real live super hero doing what he really does." There will be Jay J. Armes dolls with little hooks for hands, Jay Armes T-shirts, a Jay Armes junior detective game. That film crew that the *El Paso Herald Post* reported was shooting "The Midget Caper" with Armes and Mike ("Mannix") Connors in November was in fact doing a trade film for Ideal toys.

And Macmillan Publishing Company of New York does have a contract for the Jay J. Armes story. I talked to Fred Honig, executive editor of the general books division, who got the idea for the book after reading the article in *Newsweek*. Honig immediately flew to El Paso and arranged the deal. He wouldn't confirm the price, but the contract I saw in El Paso revealed that Jay Armes would receive about $15,000 advance, and an extra-large break on royalties.

I asked Fred Honig for his impressions of Jay J. Armes.

He told me, "Here in New York we always think of someone from El Paso . . . in the wilds, you know . . . we think of them as being fairly unsophisticated . . . fairly unknowing of what's going on. But this man is fascinating. Very quick, very intelligent, able to grasp problems and solve them."

Yes, I thought, that sounds like Jay J. Armes.

*—January 1976*

# DEEP IN THE HEARTS OF TEXANS

Texans share with all Americans the common dilemmas of modern life. None of our writers has captured those dilemmas with more wit and insight than Prudence Mackintosh. Her "Crossing into Thirty" documents one of the classic passages of adult life, while "Pacem in Terrors" explores the painful, yet funny, sibling rivalries of childhood.

One of the revolutions of our time has been how women see their social roles. While feminism was getting most of the publicity, Gregory Curtis visited families who were returning to an older set of values. His "Retreat from Liberation" was one of the first stories about the backlash to feminism rooted both in a fundamentalist religious theory of the family and a 1970s appreciation of the power of sex.

Whenever women are seeking to redefine their roles, then naturally men end up thinking about theirs. Stephen Harrigan's "Paternity Suits" muses on his experience of becoming a father for the first time. When the social history of our time is written, surely the phenomenon of fathers assisting with the birth of their children will have an important place in affecting what future generations will be like.

Harrigan's other story in this section, "Six West," is a poignant visit to the children's cancer wing of M. D. Anderson Hospital, a visit that leaves the reader wondering at the random injustices of life. If the mysteries of cancer undermine our confidence in the omnipotence of doctors, then John Deaton's "Physician, Heal Thyself" helps show doctors as human beings with human weaknesses. Deaton developed a drug habit to help him through the intense strains of his medical training, and he tells, with forthright honesty, how it happened and how he broke it.

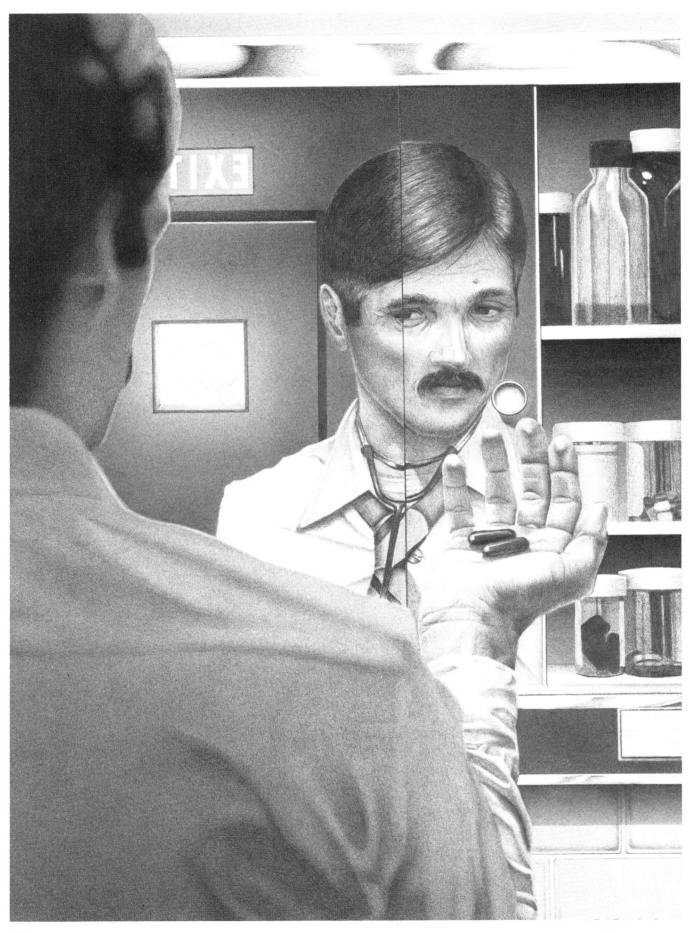

252

*Illustrated by Lonestar Studio/Stephen Durke*

# PHYSICIAN, HEAL THYSELF

## by John Deaton

---

## *The story of a doctor with a drug problem.*

I should have stopped taking them the first time I took two instead of one, three instead of two, four instead of three. I knew perfectly well about tolerance, the body's tendency to need more and more of a drug just to keep getting the same physiological effect; I saw it working on some of my patients. But I wasn't a patient, I was a doctor. It came as quite a shock to realize something I had learned in class applied to me.

Besides, taking pills is as American as apple pie. As a medical student I remember thinking I had finally arrived when I was able to sit down with a patient, take a history, do a physical examination, put down a list of possible causes of each symptom, and then prescribe a drug as treatment. It was all such a nice, neat package. Something for constipation? Okay. Something for sleep? All right. Something for nerves? I can fix you up. Something for the blues? Sure. Now, what else?

Fellow undergraduates at the University of Texas had told me they sometimes took pills to stay up all night before an exam. I was naive. Pills to keep you awake? Surely there was no such thing, and besides, I was so methodical in my study habits that I didn't need them. The same was true for medical school, but internship was different. By then I knew that there was such a thing as a pill to keep you awake; I also had discovered that I regularly had to stay on my feet practicing medicine for 24 to 36 consecutive hours.

At many hospitals the intern was through with emergency room duty after a block rotation of several weeks or a month. I interned at a city-county hospital in Texas for a year in the mid-Sixties, and since there were only eight interns and no residents, each of us pulled a 24-hour emergency room call every eighth day. I'd show up around 7:30 a.m., start clearing out the few patients left over from the night before, take care of new patients, and then be off

*John Deaton is a medical doctor turned freelance writer and medical editor. He is the author of five books. Deaton currently lives in Austin.*

to make the rounds on my own patients. The day nurse and technicians on duty when I got to the emergency room were able to handle most of the morning patients. But not everything. People came in with kidney stones, or heart attacks, or gunshot wounds. One morning a kid came in choking. I rushed into the ER; the mother was hysterical and wrestling with the nurse while the technician was trying to suction the child's throat. On impulse I swung the two-year-old into the air by his feet and hit him on the back, dislodging a large wad of bacon. I was writing a note on the chart when two orderlies wedged a lifeless form on a stretcher into the room. The man was not breathing. His eyes were closed, his mouth was open, and his face was the color of faded newsprint. I had to go outside and tell his family he was dead, but was interrupted by the wail of a siren and the arrival of three people who'd been injured in a car wreck. While I was examining them a woman arrived who'd given birth in a taxi en route to the emergency room.

After eight hours of this sort of chaos, the day shift left, to be replaced by a bright-eyed crew at 3 p.m. They wanted to get things rolling, and would call me from the wards, from the clinics, or even from surgery. One day during the course of an appendectomy I treated a case of strep throat and two women with urinary tract infections without ever leaving the side of the operating table. Evenings were busiest of all: people came in wanting treatment for fever, dizziness, gonorrhea, pyelonephritis, pneumonia, colds, rashes, pain, breathlessness, and headaches. The afternoon nurse and technician left at 11 p.m., to be replaced by a new crew, the third of my day. By that time of night I was desperately tired, a zombie who still had to smile and make competent, compassionate decisions on matters of life and death.

The police played a big part in night-time business. They might bring in a guy and request a shot of Thorazine to calm him down. That sounds easier than it was. A reluctant patient on his way to jail does not exactly roll over and dutifully offer his bum to the nurse; with shouts and screaming, he'd have to be fought into submission and might shit on the stretcher out of spite. The night passed while drunken men made phone calls, accident victims waited for x-rays, sirens in the distance announced the arrival of more business. I simply got tired. Grew surly. Around 2 or 3 a.m. my vision would blur and I had trouble keeping stitches straight and skin edges everted. But good job or poor, I never lacked for customers. Above the cacophony of ringing phones, laughing people, and groaning patients, I wanted to shout, "Hey, you guys! I'm a goddamned doctor, don't drive me into the ground! I can only do so much!" Of course I didn't complain. I kept going.

Across the hall from the emergency room was an intern's lounge, where the intern could sneak over to use the bathroom or to snatch a little rest if things quieted down after midnight. A sofa was right next to a little table with a phone where you could stretch out and maybe even go to sleep. I rarely slept though, because as soon as I'd get still the phone would ring. "I'm sorry to bother you, Dr. Deaton," the musical, accented voice of Mrs. Lopez would say, "but we have here a man who says he is short of breath. Police was taking him to jail and brought him by for you to check. And there is this woman here who wants for you to put her a check of her blood pressure, and I hear an ambulance. Can you come right over?"

I could have called out another intern to help, but *you* handled it when you were on duty, just like *he* handled it when it was his turn. I needed help, but I didn't need to call another intern for it. Along with the phone, the sofa, and the bathroom, the intern's lounge also contained a drug locker. And in the drug locker were lots and lots of drugs, including a selection of several different brands of pep pills.

*I was psychologically hooked from that initial geeze. It was as though nature had inadvertently neglected to supply my system with the required ingredients. Heroin was the missing chemical that made me a complete human being. Suddenly, all the soul-pain was gone. I felt right and light and aware and calm. There was an inner peace at the very core of my being. I was alive!*

Chic Eder, in *Ladies and Gentlemen—Lenny Bruce!!*

That pretty much describes my initial reaction to pep pills. It was about midnight, and I was tired, but the pill set me free! I became acutely aware of every part of myself. The very hairs on my arms emitted a pleasant sensation. My clothes felt good on my skin. My hands were perfect—steady and able. The pill gave me a new awareness of my own existence, of my own worth, of my own sense of *being*. Surely this was the way life should be. Pep pills, or speed, stimulate the sympathetic branch of the central nervous system, and produce what is known as the "fight or flight" response. The brain and spinal cord buzz with excitement. The heart beats faster, blood pressure goes up, goose bumps break out on the skin. Speed makes one feel alert, ready for anything. With this all-out reaction comes a glorious feeling of happiness. Under natural conditions this euphoria is the "laughter in the face of death" often noticed among soldiers just before a battle. My battle was in the emergency room, and five minutes after taking the speed I was the happiest conqueror on earth. I felt good, capable, strong, and energetic. I was trustworthy, loyal, helpful, friendly, courteous, kind, obedient, cheerful, thrifty, brave,

clean, and reverent. I was sensational.

All of a sudden with a pill on board I could not do enough for other people; it was my delight to serve them. Emergency room duty? No sweat! My coordination was better than O. J. Simpson's. Power surged into my tired legs; I felt it was the first fresh day of spring. Talk? When tired, I ordinarily clam up like a lizard, but release me with a pep pill and the sentences would spin out of my slack mouth and bring to the faces of my reassured patients smiles of gratitude that they were, after all, going to get what they had come to get: balm. I had plenty of balm, and I was the biggest balm of all.

The pills became a habit.

They were left in the intern's lounge by the drug detail men, left there not necessarily for the personal use of the physicians, but who was to know what you did with them? The drug locker was in the bathroom, so that you had an excuse to lock the door while you picked and chose among the pills. For my part, all I had to do was put a Preludin (similar to Dexedrine in its effects) on my tongue, scoop a handful of water from the lavatory, and swallow. The pill did the rest. Pooped, I'd duck into the lounge, pop a pepper, and zip out like Clark Kent become Superman. Nights on call I took peppers like a prescription, one every three to four hours as needed for energy.

Why didn't I see what was happening and stop the first time I needed two instead of one, or three instead of two, or four instead of three? The all too easy answer I gave myself was that I needed them to do my job. I was an achiever. Set a task and I could accomplish it. The end doesn't justify the means? You couldn't have proved it by me. I was asked for medicine, gave medicine, took it myself. We were all in this together, the patients and I, and I wanted to hold up my end of the bargain. At first taking pills bothered me, but I did not let my mind dwell on it; I took the pills because they were there and I needed them; I took them because I took them.

The bad thing about taking uppers is what the pharmacologists call post-stimulatory depression. After every high there is a low. The low with pep-ups came the next day: my eyes would redden from lack of sleep; my bowels would lock from constipation; my urine, yellow as that of a patient with jaundice, would reflect my lack of fluid intake. I'd wake up on a real downer, and to take the speed the following day seemed the only reasonable course.

Practicing medicine was not anything like I had imagined. For one thing, my patients did not always love me. Quite the contrary, I was the most tangible link in the sickness-treatment chain, and when recovery was not forthcoming, I was apt to be blamed. One day, bleary-eyed after a night on call, I was waiting outside the hospital for my wife to pick me up. A lady nearby was waiting for a bus. She saw me, and to my amazement, hurried over and started hacking at me with her purse. In between blows I ascertained that I had seen her last night; she was angry because I hadn't admitted her to the hospital. A hard blow to the face spun me around, and I balled my fists and prepared to attack. "Leave me alone!" I growled. She covered her retreat by spitting at me. "You doctors are all the same," she shouted, "full of shit!"

Many patients seemed to blame their problems on my lack of curative ability. They didn't want to lose weight on their own, they wanted fat-melting medicine. They didn't want to stop smoking, they wanted a magic cough syrup. They didn't want to eat right and drink plenty of fluids to prevent constipation, they wanted laxatives. And when the drugs didn't work, it was the doctor's fault. I went into medicine thinking it would be like football. I knew I wouldn't win every time, but I at least expected to move the ball, to kick well, to execute the fundamentals of the game. Instead, very often I had to sit on the bench and still take the blame for the team's loss. And then there was the problem of death. At the hospital, when someone died, I felt guilty. To avoid this feeling, I went to great lengths to save the life of every patient, even the terminally ill ones. Older doctors, even some of the interns, were able to take the loss of a patient in stride. They appeared calm and dignified, explained that everything possible had been done, and gave what comfort they could to the grieving relatives. I played this role myself, but hated it. In telling of a patient's death, I felt that I was admitting my own failure.

Pep pills changed my outlook. I had never been particularly gregarious, but with some speed in me I was the life of the party. Despite the dry mouth the pills caused, I could talk endlessly. I remember one time my in-laws were visiting. They had brought with them the driest, toughest roast beef in South Texas, and they couldn't understand why I preferred to sit talking and sipping Pepsi while they ate. It was my duty to get up for people; I felt they expected me to entertain them. I was lost without my peppers, and began to wonder which self was the real me—with pills or without? I decided I wasn't my true self until I had taken them. They were indeed the missing chemical that made me whole.

Who was doing this to me, and why? I knew I was in a trap, but getting out of it was something else. Still, I did. A few months after I'd gotten hooked, I weaned myself of speed. It wasn't a complete break, because I would still take pep pills now and again, but I no longer needed them to get through a night on call. The glow of confidence at quitting one habit blinded me to the onset of another.

A detail man had provided each of us with a generous selection of his company's sleeping pills. I went by the lounge one day to find my gift in the stack with the other interns'. It was like a Whitman's Sampler. Through the plastic lid shone capsules of Seconal, Amytal, and Tuinal; bright capsules of red, blue, and blue-and-red; gelatinous containers of secobarbital, amobarbital, and a mixture of these two barbiturates. I seriously doubted I'd ever need them, but took them home to the closet shelf, where they were waiting for me when I began to have trouble getting to sleep.

Stimulants caused insomnia, and I dreaded the weary, red-eyed day after. One way I avoided it was to take more speed; another course of action was to grab a sleeping pill. I was surprised to find, however, that even after I stopped the speed I still had trouble falling asleep. The hospital and what was happening there were in my blood, and I couldn't escape it even at home. I worried about patients. I fretted. I retraced my treatment and its effect, and worried some more. The worst thing was finally to fall asleep, then be awakened by a phone call from the medical or surgical ward. Someone's blood pressure was down, or his fever was up, or his pain was worse. Even if I didn't have to leave

the house I would lie there and worry about the patient. Toss and turn. A sleeping pill was a natural antidote, though I soon learned that if I took the Seconal late at night I faced the next day with a barbiturate hangover. Better to take the sleeping pill at bedtime on a regular basis, like a toddy. *One at bedtime, PRN sleep.* The kid doesn't smoke or drink, see, and he needs something, no, he *deserves* something to unwind. Besides, he's going to stop tomorrow, next week at the latest.

It should have worried me the first time I took two instead of one, three instead of two—well, here we go again. Tolerance occurs with many drugs, sleeping pills included. Actually, I did pause the first night I found myself reaching for a second sleeping pill. I remember it well. By now I had a bottle of the redbirds, and I got them out of the hall closet for a moment of scrutiny in the overhead light. In the bedroom slept my wife, blissfully as always. The bottle I was holding against the light was labeled *Seconal, 100 mg. caps.* I knew the little red capsule I held in my palm was 100 milligrams, but surely there had been some mistake. It looked so small, so absolutely tiny. Could it be only 50 milligrams? Yes! That was it, of course! In shipping or packaging the drugs a mix-up had occurred. These were only 50 milligrams, and you had to take two to get the effect of the 100 milligram size. So I took the second capsule. Tossed it off without another thought, because all I was doing was making up for somebody else's mistake.

I had always made good habits and stuck to them. Bad habits were easier to make. They warned us about drugs in medical school. The movie they summoned us to see during our sophomore year was promoted with the fanfare: "No medical student who has seen this film before graduation has ever gotten hooked on dope." The film, which featured a general practitioner who "gave in" one night and injected a dose of Demerol into his leg, made the following point: *Don't ever take that first injection!* Boy, I thought as we left that day, I'll never do that. And I didn't. I never did inject myself with anything or take what I considered "dope." I thanked my lucky stars for that, as night after night I bit the red curse. The number of pills I needed to get to sleep began increasing.

An old medical saying goes "Physician, heal thyself." As a medical student, I gloried in this admonition, because it meant that a doctor should practice what he preached. Who isn't repulsed by a fat doctor chiding an overweight patient? Or one that smokes telling someone else to quit? But with my dependence on pills I began to detect a cynical, leering message of mockery in *physician, heal thyself.* The words seemed to imply: *if you can. But you can't, you sonofabitch, can you? And if you can't heal yourself, how are you ever going to help anyone else?*

One night I vomited in my sleep and was too groggy to turn over; my wife saved my life by getting me on my stomach. The next morning I refused to look at the wretched red stains on the bedroom wall—but she insisted. She also demanded an explanation. Sadly, I took out my pills from all their hiding places, and we held services at the commode. Even flushing the Seconal down the toilet was a chore. They kept popping to the top of the swirling waters, kept floating to the surface for one more breath of life. Two or three days later I noticed some twitching in my legs. Suddenly, sitting quietly, I was startled by a series of jerks and twitches that ran the length of my body. I had a vague idea that this was related to my having gone cold turkey on the red men, but I didn't give it a lot of thought. The relative ease with which I quit the sleeping pills was deceptive.

Residency came; we returned to Galveston for three years of training in internal medicine. I was one of the lucky ones given military deferment, which let me finish my training as a specialist before I entered the service. A year passed, two. Patients lived or died. Some of them had a great effect on me. I presided over the death of a 22-year-old black woman with leukemia. She was the mother of six children, one almost every year since she was fourteen, and she was pregnant with a seventh. I worked her up when she was admitted to John Sealy, and the morning we went in to tell her what the bone-marrow test had revealed, that was the morning I fell in love with her. ''Mrs. Jones you have leukemia,'' the staff hematologist had boomed out, ''acute myeloblastic leukemia.''

''That's pretty bad, huh?'' Stella asked, turning to me. ''Is they a cure for it?''

''No,'' the staff man was quick to say. ''No cure.''

''Well, it's not for me I was worried. It was for my baby.''

''Why'd you talk to her like that?'' I asked the hematologist when the sentencing was over and we were outside the room. ''You've destroyed her hope.''

''She's in for a rough time, and there was no other way. We're going to need her cooperation.''

Stella did eventually deliver a healthy boy, but not until she had lost all her hair, developed foot drop and wrist drop, and almost died several times. After she left the hospital I followed her in the clinic. And then she was admitted for the last time. She died quietly, and since another resident was in charge of the women's ward, I didn't have to tell her relatives that she was gone. But who was to comfort me? I walked outside that afternoon and tried to take stock of myself. I was 27 years old and I was a physician. I had gotten good at it and was respected for my skills, but they weren't good enough to keep Stella from dying. I wanted out, but the only freedom I could find was in a bottle of red capsules.

I reported to the Armed Forces Examining Station in Houston for my pre-induction physical in 1966, a year ahead of schedule. After the examination, I filled in a form saying I would volunteer to serve in Viet Nam. I became convinced that I would die there. Even when I took sleeping pills, I twisted and turned in my fear. Sometimes my palms would sweat like sluices had broken loose in my wrists. The only consolation Viet Nam might offer was that with death would come sleep, blessed sleep, which would have been all right except for one thing: miserable as my life was, I didn't quite want to let go of it. It was my curse to dream the dreams of a hero, and sweat the sweat of a coward.

''You're taking it so good,'' said a friend who happened over the day I received word that I was assigned to Viet Nam. The friend didn't know about my support. That night I locked myself in the bathroom, let fall into my mouth six Seconals, and stuck my tongue out at the mirror. Looking at the tiny red coffins and then at the person in the mirror, I tried not to think about what had happened to me—or what

lay ahead. I waited impatiently for the sleepers to take hold, waited for the sweet zap I had grown to anticipate. It was a comforting electric jolt that zinged through my arms and legs to let the peripheral parts know that the red men had boarded ship and were about to shift me into low gear. Taking sleeping pills was a way of recharging my body, and my entire day was a crescendo that built up to the barbiturates. The downers slowed the same processes that the speed had stimulated. They cut down on my coordination, but eased my tensions, kept me from caring. They made me drowsy. They gave me sleep. I took them every night, and this meant carrying along a supply of sleepers when we visited relatives or went on vacation. I could no more have done without them than I could have done without water, or food, or rest. Sometimes when I gulped the small handful of capsules they would catch in my throat, and kick and scratch before descending further, as if refusing to do their rightful job. Then, I'd belch a cutting acid belch and in my moment of dyspepsia have deep self-illuminating thoughts. I learned to shrug off these moments of insight. The road to addiction is one of rationalization.

A barbiturate hangover is a terrible thing, and after drugging myself with 600 milligrams of secobarbital I came awake next morning with a hell of a one. My eyelids would be heavy, breakfast had no taste, voices and images came at me from a great distance. My hands were coated by thick gloves. My body belonged to someone else. My inhibitions were gone; I was grumpy and argumentative. What friends I had gave me funny looks. Some mornings I was ''sick'' and didn't go to work at all. I had lost my zeal for life, and would lie like a wounded hero on the davenport and beg my wife to come wait on me. She saw what was happening to me, what was happening to us, but it was a measure of my dependency on drugs that I would not let her help me.

I grew to hate myself.

Using as many sleeping pills as I used the year before I left for Viet Nam required a source of supply. I never stole them; I didn't have to. I ordered them by the bottle from a drug company that sent fliers to physicians. The drug supply house also carried sundries, so to show them that drugs weren't my only interest I'd order two tubes of Crest toothpaste, a bottle of aspirin, a roll of dental floss—and one thousand Seconal. I had the boxes containing the Crest, the aspirin, the dental floss, and the Seconal shipped to my mailbox at medical school. Getting the pills into the house past my wife was the hardest part, but that was no task for one becoming accomplished in the art of legerdemain. I was so secretive that I could carry a night's dosage of pills into the bathroom tucked under the waistband of my shorts and remove and pop them in the bat of an eye, even while my unknowing wife sat reading a book in the tub three feet away.

A drug habit is like smoking or overeating. Soon the main preoccupation is not how much fun it is, but how to get rid of it. Viet Nam was my answer. What awaited me there was a hasty resolution to my problem: if I did survive the year, one way or another I'd come home with the monkey off my back.

Six weeks out of internal medicine residency I found myself on a plane for Viet Nam. Majestic cumulus clouds stretched out between the 707 and the Pacific but my thoughts were on matters closer to earth. I had in my suitcase one bottle of barbiturates, and when they were gone that was it, over, finished. Someone across the aisle pulled out a copy of *Valley of the Dolls*. I did not ask to read it.

On Thanksgiving day, 1967, groggy as I was, I tried to listen to the annual University of Texas and Texas A&M game. It didn't matter that I was nauseated and hadn't eaten for two days, or that maggots and other insects roiled across the ceiling in such numbers that I was afraid they would soon spill off and fill the bed with the stink of their leavings. It didn't matter that I was 10,000 miles from College Station or that my hootch was so near the flight line I could barely hear the radio for the drone, then roar, then whistle, then pop, of the F-4 Phantom jets as they screamed into the sky on combat missions. It didn't matter that the broadcast over Armed Forces Radio was delayed, and that the game had already been played. What mattered was that I was the number-one Texas rooter of all time, and would give my yells to an empty room if necessary. At the very least, I had to find out who won.

I was destined to miss it. At the half, A&M led by a score of 3–0. I got out of bed, pulled on some pants, opened the door of the hootch to the bright clouds of midday, and fell to the sand after emitting what they later told me was the screech of a banshee. I had chosen cold turkey for Thanksgiving, and what it got me was an unexpected grand mal convulsion.

I woke up in the emergency room of the 12th USAF Hospital, Cam Ranh Bay, Republic of Viet Nam, where I was assigned as a staff internist. My rank was Captain, Medical Corps. My serial number was FV3166651. I woke up and cried in pain, because the nurse was shooting something into my arm. The monsoon rain on the tin roof of the infirmary sounded like a gravel truck skidding over a rock quarry. The Lysol smell of the emergency room was nothing compared to the packet of ammonia smelling salts someone had placed on my upper lip. My back was on fire, my vision was blurred and I felt like I had been smeared on an end run.

"John," the man kept saying, peering at me out of the shadows, "you had a convulsion. Yes, a grand mal. We brought you to the emergency room." He was the leader of a group of six holding me down. He was my chief of medicine, my boss, Major Monte Miller. "Have you been taking anything?" he wanted to know.

He would have to ask that.

My first thought a few moments earlier had been *Now you'll never get to be President of the United States*. My second thought had been *Now it'll all come out*. My third thought was the only one I was willing to verbalize. "Who," I asked through puffy lips, "won the A&M game?"

"The Aggies," someone said.

My spirits dropped to new lows.

"But you're a doctor, John," the chief of medicine told me when I spilled my story about the sleeping pills and how I had stopped taking them when my supply ran out. "Didn't you know that a convulsion could have killed you? The mortality rate for withdrawal convulsion from barbiturates must be twenty-five, thirty per cent. Didn't you think about that?" I shook my head. I had not. It was a measure of my degree of rationalization that I thought I could quit and get off scot-free.

Miller examined me, ordered weaning doses of secobarbital to be given during my hospital stay, then left. That first night, the monsoon rain still drumming down, was the worst. The elaborate wall of self-deception I had built around my life had fallen; I had lived with a lie and now that it was gone I felt naked. The next day a psychiatrist came, and he had to step gingerly to avoid the puddles of water that had flowed under the door from the storm's runoff.

"As far as I'm concerned," the psychiatrist said after hearing my story, "you're just another doctor with a drug problem. What matters is what happens a month or a year or five years from now. You'll have to watch it the rest of your life. And John, before you ever reach for another pill you had better think long and hard about what you're getting yourself into. See you."

*You're just another doctor with a drug problem.*

The words stung, and the more they came back to me the more they stung. I had never considered myself just another anything, but I concluded that the shrink was right. Big as my problem was to me, it was only my personal experience of something that happens all the time. How many doctors get hooked? Quite a few. One reason is that, like me, doctors grow so used to solving problems by giving pills that to use these same methods on themselves seems not only reasonable but desirable. Stopping the pills and convulsing were only the beginning of recovery. Waiting for me after I returned from Viet Nam was a year of duty treating military dependents at an air base in California. It was the hardest year of my life. I spent many sleepless nights, nights when, if they had been available, I probably would have taken sleeping pills. I didn't. In time I learned that for every bad night there follows a good one, and that sleep is a habit that can be cultivated by one who will make the effort. And I came to realize that even if pills can take you to nirvana, the world is always waiting for you when you get back.

Five years ago, two years and three jobs after I left the military, I decided that medical practice was not for me. We moved to Austin, where I have been able to teach part-time, write, and do medical editing. My wife has gone back to teaching school, and we share the housework and child rearing. I can make a passable meat loaf, and my slowly simmered pinto beans are the family's favorite dish. I hang out the clothes, jog, dole out lunch money to the kids, and have supper going by the time my hungry wife gets home from work. It is a selfish existence when one considers that I could be on the line seeing sick patients, but for me it is not only the right thing, it is the only thing to be doing.

I don't take pills any more, but I'll never forget the personal hell that using them brought me. The process of recovery has been a long one, and part of it has been a search and destroy mission through my past. "Where you going for your workup?" a flight surgeon asked me not long after the convulsion. He thought that the cause of my seizure was unknown and that a lengthy neurologic workup would be necessary. There would be no workup, but to tell him this I would have had to explain my addiction and withdrawal. Instead I answered vaguely and kept my secret. Nor have I told others, at least not many.

I had almost forgotten something Monte Miller said the day in late November 1967 when I checked out of the hospital and walked with him around to the medicine ward, Quonset 8, where I would be resuming my duties as an Air

Force physician. Miller was an over-grown boy in his late thirties, tall, balding, from Missouri. He seemed to sense my need for encouragement, for something that would sum up what had happened. We paused on the sidewalk outside the door to the ward, and my boss looked at me and grinned. He said, "John, some docs get so strung out on pills they never get off. But you had a convulsion and it shook the hell out of you. All things considered, it may just be the best thing that ever happened to you."

I nodded, not then fully able to comprehend the truth of what he said. Then Miller opened the door and we went inside and started making rounds.

*—June 1976*

# PATERNITY SUITS

## by Stephen Harrigan

---

*"The clothes I wore to the birth of my daughter were the same kind I had when I was seven and made a vow never to grow up."*

---

When we found out we were pregnant I went to the library and looked up "embryo" in the encyclopedia. There they were, the same old charts and acetate overlays of life in the womb, the little bug-eyed creatures with their vestigial gills and the indistinct appendages that would go on to become hands or flippers or hooves. I had, of course, seen these pictures before, but had always regarded them with the casual indifference of someone scanning the map of a country he never plans to visit.

But now the matter was close to home. One of these embryos was harbored in my wife's body. It would be very small now, I thought, smaller than a cocktail shrimp, almost an abstraction. Yet at that moment, as I gazed at a picture of an embryo in its cutaway uterus, whatever rational distance I may have felt suddenly dissipated. I was not a father-to-be but a father-in-fact, the parent of an organism that had already sprung into being and was now going about the process of assembling itself with an industriousness that was, for me, almost unbearably poignant. Deep in its mother's body, our embryo had its own concerns, its own integrity. It knew, in every one of its swarming cells, that its existence had been ordained.

That I was a father in any sense seemed an improbable thing to me. I was 28, but I did not feel I was old enough to have children. I had barely gotten used to being an adult. Long ago I had made a vow to myself that I would never grow up, and I looked back on that covenant now with nostalgia, half-believing I could still abide by its terms.

"Sue Ellen is pregnant," I would say, and our parents and relatives would startle us with the unreserved joy with which they received the news. We were finally making sense to them. This was, in its way, reassuring, but we were more comfortable with the mixed reactions of our contem-

*Stephen Harrigan, a contributing editor of* Texas Monthly, *has written for several publications. He is editor of* Lucille, *a poetry magazine, and a Paisano Fellow.*

poraries. A few of them sneered, offered their condolences, and made it plain that they held us in the same regard as they did people who keep Shetland ponies in their apartments. Most smiled sheepishly and suspended their reactions until they were sure congratulations were in order. Our friends who already had children of their own took the news with relief, as if every new baby brought into the world confirmed their situation.

The embryo nurtured its wild run-away substance in secret, and over the months our appreciation of it became quiescent. It was a thing we could not see that was rooted to us, that would change our lives forever once it ripened into an infant and came forth. The concept was so enormous it could strike us only at certain moments, and even then we could not assimilate it, only regard it with awe.

At some precise, yet arbitrary point the embryo officially became a fetus. As it made the transition I watched helplessly as Sue Ellen's hormones ran wild. One day she broke into tears for no apparent reason.

"I can't make pottery," she said.

"You've never tried to make pottery. You've never *wanted* to make pottery!"

"What's going to happen to me?" she wailed, in a melodramatic tone that was only half ironic, then she went into the kitchen where she ate an entire angel food cake.

The only thing that was sure to relieve her depression was the weekly episode of *The Pallisers* on public television. The series had 22 installments, enough to last until the end of her pregnancy.

"It's not a soap opera," she explained. "It's Trollope. Anthony Trollope."

By the eighth month it was time for us to gather up our blanket and two pillows and attend the first class of the workshop that would teach us the Lamaze method of prepared childbirth. The purpose of Lamaze is to enable women to have their babies with a maximum of awareness and a minimum of drugs. It sounded reasonable, enlightened, and it was certainly the thing to do, but after the first session we were both a little disillusioned, perhaps because our condition no longer seemed unique.

We were shown a movie, the standard scenario: the woman panting like a dog, the husband—the "coach"—saying, "Push, honey, push," the doctor announcing, "I can see its head," the baby coming in a great fluid rush and the whole thing degenerating in bathos.

Everyone in the audience was in tears when the lights went up, including the coaches. We all sniffled and smiled wanly, as if we were members of an encounter group in the afterglow of a collective primal scream.

"None of that ecstasy for me," Sue Ellen said on the way home. "Just give me a cesarean."

But of course we continued to attend. Each week we sat on the floor, propped against our pillows, and listened to our instructor. During her lectures she sucked on Wint-O-Green Life Savers, and we could hear the faint click they made against her teeth as she told us about dilation, effacement, mucus plugs, pudendals, episiotomies.

The sessions were explicit on the importance of the husband's role—we were indispensable for morale, for timing—but I felt that this emphasis was little more than a courtesy, a way to keep us from feeling irrelevant. Some coaches tried more than others to dominate the situation—"Might one be present," one of the husbands asked, making notes on a clipboard, "when one's wife has her enema administered?"—but most of us realized that our wives were going somewhere without us. Childbirth was a crucible we could not follow them into. We skirted around its edges and watched our women—sullen, inspired, beatific—being drawn into its center.

During the second half of each session, while the women lay on their backs on their pillows practicing the breathing that was to focus their attention off the pain of childbirth, we would squeeze their legs just above the knee to simulate a contraction. But they were beyond any impressions we could make on them. "Pant, blow," the instructor said, "pant, blow," as I looked down at my wife's face. She was looking up at the ceiling, panting, blowing, soaring somewhere far above the pain I was so earnestly inflicting upon her. When the exercise was over, I looked across the room at a dozen pregnant women lying belly up, their men kneeling at their sides, attending them like witless, devoted beasts, a little in awe of their own daring and fundamentally ignorant, despite the lectures and films, of the adventure they were going to undertake. In two months we would all be buying Wet Ones and nursing pads at the grocery store, following our wives about with collapsible bassinets and Port-a-cribs and dirty diaper bags stinking of ammonia. It better be worth it, I thought.

I found myself envying Sue Ellen that pain, though that was something I would not have told her, or any woman. Every night we trained together, like athletes, but when the event arrived at which we would be tested she alone would be on the field feeling the athlete's sweet, high-principled agony at the finish of the race. I would be there cheering, holding out the Gatorade.

It happened three weeks early, two days before our last Lamaze class. At 4:30 one morning I felt a soft pawing motion at my shoulder and rose up out of sleep to find Sue Ellen staring at me, a worried, resolute expression on her face.

"I have Bloody Show," she said.

"What kind of show?"

"Bloody," she said firmly.

We looked the term up in the glossary of our Lamaze pamphlet, since neither of us remembered exactly what it meant. Bloody Show was the evidence of a dissolved mucus plug, and it meant that birth could take place any time from a few hours to a week.

I suggested we go back to sleep. But about that time she had her first contraction. It was clearly a righteous, powerful pain. It seemed to swoop down from the ceiling and strike with a sudden, unanticipated blow deep in her abdomen. She doubled up with pain.

"Do your breathing," I said, very coachlike.

I got out my notebook and tried to time the contractions, but looking at my watch I remembered that the second hand had been broken since 1974. But I was able to tell that the pains were regular, and this indicated that Sue Ellen was not undergoing false labor. I called the obstetrician, who confirmed, with drowsy competence, that this was it, that a baby was about to be born. I wanted somebody to tell me it was false labor. I thought if I could have another two weeks or so I might be grown up enough to be a father.

But the mythical event was here. We packed a suitcase, something we should have done a month earlier. We put baby clothes in it and I thought, when we come home some little creature is going to be wearing these.

The contractions were five minutes apart by the time we got to the hospital. Sue Ellen had wisely skipped the first eight or nine hours of labor, taking it up instead very near its peak. They hauled her up in a wheelchair while I signed the papers in the lobby.

"They're prepping her," a nurse told me when I got to the maternity ward. "You can't go in for about twenty minutes."

Unlike that zealous husband in our class, I was not especially anxious to know what was going on in the prepping room, or whatever they called it. But I missed my wife intensely. My presence did not seem specious anymore. She needed me.

For twenty minutes I wandered around the hospital. I talked to a nurse who told me she had once written a script for *The High Chaparral*. I bought a sweetroll from a vending machine, scraped the icing off with my pocket-knife, and ate the rest without sensation, as an act of sustenance.

When at last I was admitted into the labor room I saw that things were happening very quickly. Sue Ellen was lying on her side, panting. I taped a picture of a hippopotamus to the wall. This was her "focal point," and she gazed at it dutifully, her eyes still wide with distress. I said, "Breathe, that's it, breathe," and, "This one's nearly over," and "You're really handling it well." Between contractions she drifted off into a shallow unconsciousness as I tried to make sense of what was going on. According to my calculations she was in the "transition" phase, in which the contractions were the longest and most painful.

The nurses came in and said, "Good Bloody Show!" and the OB came to the door as cheerful and composed as if he were the milkman. "Looks like we're going to have a baby this morning," he said. Sue Ellen took her eyes off the hippopotamus long enough to give him a dirty look. Her pain repelled all our ministrations—it had its own power that none of us could touch.

Soon I was standing in the delivery room in a green suit, holding up her shoulders while she bore down and began to push the baby out.

"Breathe, breathe," I said from behind the surgical mask, just like the fretful husband in the movie we had seen. "Push, push, that's it."

"How . . . how long?" she asked from some far outpost of consciousness.

"Oh," the OB said cheerfully, "not too long. Another few good pushes like that and it'll be all over." He looked around the room and swung back and forth in his swivel chair. I was afraid he was going to start whistling.

"Now, I could give you an epidural and it'd be over right away."

I watched the conflicting emotions playing on her face. What was this man offering her? No doubt at that moment she saw him as a tormentor, the devil himself offering with his anaesthetic surcease of pain in exchange for blessed awareness.

"No," she said, "I can do it."

Fifteen minutes later, we watched the baby's head emerge in the big mirror at the other end of the room.

"Push," we all said. I was drenched with sweat, I had no feeling in the ends of my fingers, and my awareness had strayed. Much to my annoyance, my mind would not stop repeating the jingle of a TV commercial I especially hated.

Get a Genie automatic
garage door picker-upper
and you'll never leave your car out
anymore.
'Cause a Genie automatic
garage door picker-upper
will open and close
your door.

I decided it was not worth the effort to dispel the jingle. I let it stay, thinking of it as a mantra.

Suddenly our daughter was there, wailing on her mother's stomach, clay-colored, streaked with the remains of her ruined home. I watched her. She was a refugee now. In the womb she had been a perfect citizen, with all the cognizance she needed. Now she was in our care, utterly dependent on the human reflexes of devotion. They took her footprints. Her mother looked at her in a way I had never seen her look

before. They handed her to me and I held her against the sweat-stained surgical gown and tried one last time to make that jingle go away.

"Does she have a name?" the doctor asked.

"Marjorie Rose," I said.

Afterward they put her in a glass crib in the nursery. She lay there placidly, her eyes open, registering no concern. Somebody had taped a yellow bow to her head.

That afternoon while Sue Ellen slept I went home to change my clothes and to walk the dog. The sense of dislocation on coming back to the house was keen. The dog followed closely at my heels, knowing some monumental change had occurred and fearing that she would be left out of it. I looked at the bloody clothes in the bathroom and for a moment the exaltation I was experiencing worked against me and I thought something dreadful had occurred. But I knew rationally that no one was dead and kept reminding myself that what I was feeling was probably joy.

I glanced at a full-length mirror and noticed that the clothes I had worn to the birth of my daughter—blue jeans, tennis shoes, a striped T-shirt—were the same kind of clothes I had worn when I was seven years old and had made that vow I would never grow up. Now here I was. I took a shower and rummaged in the closet for my good pair of corduroy pants.

May 16 in Austin was overcast, oppressively humid. I noticed this for her sake, and everything else I saw, the bare concrete parking garages, the revived gingerbread houses, the grove of live oaks in the park where the dog was running now off her leash, chasing the same squirrel she had been after for a year, I saw all of this through the baby's eyes as well as mine, as if I had never grown up and ceased noticing these things.

The dog chased the squirrel up a tree, wallowed around in the creek, and then ran back to me. We walked through the park together, two full-grown, natural beings. I thought of one of the terms in the Lamaze glossary—"effacement." Something had been effaced in me—those things I had just thrown off could as well have been an old skin. I was a man now, a father. In a few days the insurance people would begin calling ("Steve—hear ya had a baby—congratulations!") and we would be getting samples of baby soap in the mail, even a coupon for a free hamburger. But for now the world was dead calm—everything was effaced and waiting. I drove back to the hospital to rejoin my family.

—*December 1977*

*Illustrated by Mike Hicks*

# CROSSING INTO THIRTY

## by Prudence Mackintosh

*A woman's passage into her thirties may be eased by accomplishments unimagined at twenty.*

The peanut butter and jelly luncheons at my house are often accompanied by heated, irrational debates as to who is bigger, older, or faster. The dispute usually begins with the two-year-old, who rises in his chair, lowers his voice two octaves, and announces, "I'm big." With partially chewed bite still apparent as he speaks, the four-year-old picks up the gauntlet with "I'm bigger, and I'm older than you—I'm four."

The two-year-old, depending on how eager he is to return to his sandwich, will either persist absurdly with "I'm bigger!!" or acquiesce reluctantly with "Okay, shut up you dumb Bozo."

In late September, shortly after my birthday, I quashed one such debate and put the pecking order in its proper perspective. "I'm 30," I announced before the two-year-old could rise, "and I may not be the fastest anymore, but I'm still bigger than the two of you put together, so sit down and finish your lunch."

Thirty. It's a crisis time, according to the recent covers of at least two magazines. Divorce is rampant now among my contemporaries, and many of the marriages that remain intact are undergoing serious review. I've been spared that crisis. My husband's domestic talents predate any women's liberation jargon, and the only time I can recall that we had to "work" at our marriage was a brief period before I agreed to discard a superfluous suitcase full of shoes as we trekked across Europe on our honeymoon.

Thirty. There is a nagging suspicion that I am not really as "big" as I am supposed to be. In times of real emergency, such as the partial severing of a two-year-old's finger by a slammed door, or on viewing a hammer-gashed forehead, I still look around for the "real" mother to take charge. Surely I cannot be old enough to bear the responsibility.

*Prudence Mackintosh is a contributing editor of* Texas Monthly *and won a 1976 Penney-Missouri Award for her magazine work. She is completing a book for Doubleday.*

However, I have begun to note telltale signs of age. Physical signs among my female contemporaries are minimal—a thinning of the face and thickening of the thigh perhaps, but on the whole, they look younger and better than they did in our high school days. We are the high school class of '62, whose yearbook photographs with tight permanent waves and red lipstick look eighteen-going-on-forty-five. So now, it isn't *our* appearance so much as it is the fact that policemen have begun to look too young to be of much assistance these days. Young men and women interviewing my husband's law firm are cautiously beginning to put a "Mr." before his name, and quite frankly I'm beginning to yawn when they ask the same idealistic questions that I asked six years ago. "How much time does the firm allot to *pro bono* work?"

The clincher occurred last spring. My husband and I ventured onto the SMU campus to see an old friend's award-winning film, *Badlands*, at the USA Film Festival. After the showing, our film-maker friend was swamped by autograph seekers and aspiring student film-makers. Standing to one side of the celebrity with a look that said "I knew him when . . . ," I was approached by one young film student who asked, "Do you happen to know how old Mr. Malick is?"

"Yes," I smugly replied, "He's only 30."

"Thank God," the obviously relieved freshman responded, "that means I've got at least twelve years to make it big."

Stunned, I came home and tried desperately to recall what as an eighteen-year-old I thought I would have accomplished by my thirtieth birthday. At eighteen my roommates and I were performing some sort of balancing act that included the inanities of UT sorority life, a fairly heavy academic load, the slightly suspect University "Y," and an unwashed serape-clad beatnik named Dave, who saw it as his mission in life to save us from ourselves and our misguided cultural legacy. Knowing full well that we were pledged to seek "the good, the true, and the beautiful" at chapter meetings in secret basement rooms of the sorority house every Monday night, Dave delighted in showing up at our posh dormitory on his bicycle (a most unacceptable mode of transportation in the early Sixties) to offer us a ride to a scientology lecture. The summer after our freshman year, he sent us each postcards exhorting, "You are better than animals. Do not be satisfied with 'birth, reproduction, diversion, and death'." An appropriately heavy reading list followed, to which we responded with a postcard bearing small paw prints.

But we were serious students, even if our grade point averages occasionally belied the fact. We flaunted illegally obtained "stack passes" that enabled us to go into the musty carrels reserved for graduate students, and we flocked to Bergman movies at the Union.

Women's Liberation had not dawned, and we somehow saw no incongruity in running from a philosophy seminar on the nature of prejudice to a "Ten Most Beautiful" interview. Our most radical political involvement had something to do with the National Students' Association, and though we sat through heated debates and handed out leaflets, I can't even remember whether we were for it or against it. We lamely protested our fathers' demands that we take the "female insurance policy"—twelve hours of education courses—but our career goals were poorly defined, and no one pressed us to define them. Summers spent working in Washington in glorified secretarial positions called "summer internships" may have made us briefly consider life as the wife of an aspiring politician, but we did not seriously contemplate political careers for ourselves.

If we were ill-suited for money making careers, we were even less prepared for life as wife and mother. We smugly believed that anyone who could read could cook; our husbands have not forgotten the early days of ground meat in gray sauce that resulted. Never in my wildest dreams at eighteen would I have predicted that my age 30 accomplishments would include Beef Wellington or a loaf of homemade French bread.

We are 30 now. Oh Dirty Dave, where are you? I won't fault you if you're a sales representative for IBM. Although I reread Sterne's *Tristram Shandy* last year as Professor Eliosef said we should at 29, I'm a bit fuzzy on "appearance versus reality" and quite frankly the "objective correlative" has escaped me. I am not fluent in Spanish or French, and Book I of Bach's Preludes and Fugues collects dust on the piano. The summer of '66 that my husband and I spent in Europe will just have to do us for a while. We have two sons instead.

Our childless friends have been spear-carriers in the opera, have traveled through the South of France, or basked on the beaches of Dubrovnik more than once. They take impulse trips to Zihuatenejo. Their coffee tables are unmolested, and we are glad that we know them. It is soothing occasionally to dine at a candlelit table where there is no fear of two small streakers bounding through yelling, "Get me . . ."

But we do not envy their passing 30 and pondering, "Shall we have children or not?" In our twenties we pondered very little. We made art purchases impetuously, acquired an electric typewriter and a stereo, all of which we

now know we couldn't possibly have afforded then. Had we waited until 30 to make a decision about having children, I'm quite sure we would now debate it through menopause. We're glad we didn't wait.

The raising of children, at least our children, is not always a rational process. There are days when we are Spock, Ginott, Piaget, and Montessori all rolled into one, and on those days we have no doubts that our children will rise up and call us blessed. Just as frequently, however, it is simply a matter of coping. Only this week I have blotted bloody heads twice. My four-year-old is so inured to the sight of his brother's blood that he often waits until I'm off the telephone to announce casually, "Mom, Drew's blooding again. He said he wanted my hammer, so I gave it to him." I have also been thrown out of my favorite branch of the public library because my two-year-old insisted on shouting "Burger King" while his brother did body rolls the length of the main desk. Later the same day at the post office the two-year-old took a bite out of the damp sponge in a dish on the table because big brother said it was cake. And only a day later I was seen behind an industrial-sized mop at Safeway mopping an easily identified amber puddle because the two-year-old couldn't wait until I finished writing my check.

My doctor, who once regarded me as relaxed, cool, and unflappable, now gazes out the window as I recite the symptoms of what seems to me to be advanced stomach paralysis. His eyes glaze slightly, and I know that he no longer sees me as he begins, "Young mothers often have these complaints. In these times of stress and strain, we must not be ashamed to admit the effects of tension . . ."

The long bathtub "soaker," that last bastion of privacy that restores my physical and mental equanimity, has now been invaded by small boys who never knock and who will ax the door if it's locked. "Gee, Mom, I bet you were lonely in here all by yourself," they say. Leaning on the tub, they reject Mr. Rogers' Neighborhood theory that "Everybody's fancy, everybody's fine. Your body's fancy and so is mine." By their standards I am funny, not "fancy."

Though I take pride in their occasional civility toward neighbors or grandparents, I cannot regard them as my age 30 accomplishments; they are not finished. In fact, nothing much gets finished around here any more, and they have forced us to appreciate the processes of living rather than the finished results. Taking freshly baked bread from the oven is never quite as important anymore as deciding earlier who gets to "slug it when it gets all puffy."

Crayon on the dining room wall, Lincoln Logs in the instep, and perpetually-spilled milk are small prices to pay for the dimensions they add to our lives. To open my sleep-encrusted eyes to a soft pat on the arm and a small voice that says, "I gwad see you soo much, Mama," is far better than the jolt of an electric alarm clock. Who but a two-year-old notices the faint moon in the midmorning sky, or looks at birds hopping around our bird feeder and says, "Dance, Mom?" And who but a four-year-old hyperventilates twice in one afternoon trying to learn to whistle?

The self-knowledge that my children continually force on me is occasionally painful, but far less expensive than group encounters and analysis. Recently in a rare idle moment, I polished my fingernails, something I'm sure I haven't done in at least five years. My older son was irate.

"Mama," he yelled, "you'll have to get that stuff off right now."

"Why?" I asked, admiring the chic effect of "Cool Copper." "Haven't you ever seen a lady with nail polish before?"

"Yeah, but you're the lady who's supposed to help us dig those holes this afternoon."

They catch every hint of hypocrisy. "How come Daddy bought a new rake instead of finding the old one behind that junk in the storeroom? You always say that we can't have new stuff just because we've lost the old stuff."

Their profane utterances mirror our own and cause our backs to stiffen. "Goddamit, Daddy," the four-year-old shouts as his father oversteers a curve, "where did you learn to drive?" We're strong on "Aw, shucks" now.

Our children keep our egos remarkably trim. I am not much with a football, but on reaching my thirtieth birthday I do read stories with as many as three different voices, make up original lullabies, and bake creditable chocolate chip cookies. So what do they think I do best? "Wash dishes," the four-year-old replies without hesitation. I am not seriously wounded; he thinks his trial attorney father's forte is hedge-clipping.

Their admiration is at times unbounded. Sitting on the floor of a dressing room with amazing patience, the four-year-old watches as I desperately exhaust the sale racks in search of a long skirt. "Oh, Mama, if you wear that one, you'll have to be a queen, but if you get the blue one, I think you'll be a beautiful dancer lady." To his three-foot stature, I am not a short and slightly dumpy five feet four inches. He empties his piggy bank and says, "When I get some more money, I'll buy you dresses like Cher wears."

At this point I have few rivals for their affection. Talk of growing up and marrying some girl (other than the thirteen-year-old baby sitter who runs me a close second) always ends with some Oedipal remark about their being already married to me.

And despite my thirtieth birthday, there is strong opposition to my aging. A serious autumn conversation about how we all grow older like the leaves on the trees ended abruptly with the stamping of a small foot and the shaking of a finger, "You will never, never, never be an old lady. Never!"

Like Erica in Alison Lurie's recent novel *The War Between the Tates*, I too may come to view them in years ahead as "awful lodgers who pay no rent, whose leases cannot be terminated." In the meantime, I'm playing a pretty fair Cat Woman to their Batman and Robin. And for a 30-year-old with so little training, that's making it big.

*—November 1974*

# RETREAT FROM LIBERATION

## by Gregory Curtis

---

*Will the new trend in male-female roles be the old trend—dominant man, submissive wife, obedient kids?*

---

The audience was well-dressed, well-scrubbed, well-meaning, and well-heeled. They were all young couples, most of them about 35, sitting attentively in rows of folding chairs in the living room of a large house in Highland Park, that exclusive municipality in the heart of Dallas. The house belonged to Roy Coffee who, during Dolph Briscoe's first term, was the governor's liaison with the legislature. Having returned to Dallas to pursue his law practice, Coffee has been providing a space in his home for Tim Timmons to teach a "seminar" in what Timmons calls "God's game plan for family living."

Timmons' seminar is one of several that teach essentially the same game plan. These seminars are now being taught throughout the United States, but they have developed especially devoted followings in Dallas, where Timmons' and another important seminar are based. While similar in intent, the various seminars do differ in important ways. One seminar, for example, prescribes punishing the transgressions of young babies by spanking them with Popsicle sticks; another advocates having sex underneath the dining room table as a way to put romance back into marriage. But all of the approaches to family living are based on a fundamentalist religious belief called the doctrine of submission. Ignoring its teaching is supposedly against God's intent and produces tension in the marriage, unrest, breakdown of communication, divorce, and, worst of all, homosexual children.

According to this doctrine, submission means respectful, willing, and complete obedience. That obedience is based on a chain of command from God to the husband to the wife and finally to the children. All people must submit to God and God's will. The husband must also submit to his employer and to his government. The wife must submit to her husband. She must do his will in everything unless obeying his will would lead her to personal sin. If he wants

*Gregory Curtis, a member of the original* Texas Monthly *staff, is the magazine's executive editor.*

her to wife-swap, for example, she must refuse, since wife-swapping is a sin; but if he tells her not to go to Wednesday Bible class, she must not go since not going is hardly sinful but disobeying her husband is. Children, at the end of the chain of command, must be taught by their parents to submit to everyone above them in the hierarchy.

This sounds like a game plan created not so much by God as by an anti-feminist coach. But these seminars together form a movement that is definitely a *woman's* movement. Several of these seminars are given by women for women only. Although Timmons' seminar is designed for married couples, in most cases the couple has started coming because the wife has talked her husband into going with her. "I think women are so interested in this," Timmons told me, "because they can't get out of their lives like their husbands who can go spend the day at the office. So the women want to make the life they have the best it can possibly be."

Other women, women also wanting to make their lives the best they could possibly be, have involved themselves directly or sympathetically with some part of that wide range of organizations, actions, and attitudes that make up the woman's liberation movement—a movement founded on the conviction that the lives of women could be improved by social and political change. But for the women in the submission movement, the best possible life is one that requires no social or political change whatsoever.

They are women who, ten or fifteen years ago when they were in their twenties and making life choices, decided they wanted to lead a traditional family life, one very much like their parents had led. Then they watched while those traditional values were attacked, first during the sexual revolution and now by the woman's movement. While their own belief in traditional values was not changed, they found themselves needing to defend a way of life they had always assumed was above question.

They *want* to be wives, have kids, drive station wagons,

send their husbands off to work in the mornings, go to church on Sundays. They want those things because they also want to be "happy" and they believe the family life is not only what will make them happy but is happiness itself. Once they have a husband, a house, a family, they see no reason why their lives shouldn't be perfect. When imperfection inevitably creeps in, they think the fault is not with the institutions and values they have always believed in but with themselves for not living up to their goals. They look about for a personal solution, not a political one. The seminars are so appealing because they claim to identify the woman's mistake—not submitting to God's will—and then propose a solution—submitting to their husbands' will—which supposedly will create a perfect, happy family life. And, not to seem outmoded, some seminars promise all this and an erotic marital wonderland as well.

The word is rapidly spreading. Timmons not only conducts his weekly classes at Roy Coffee's house and a Wednesday morning prayer meeting at the Dallas Country Club, but also travels across the country giving a seminar in a different city practically every weekend. Recently he has taught in such widely spaced locations as Newport Beach, California; Portland, Oregon; Arlington, Virginia; Lincoln, Nebraska; and Little Rock, Arkansas. Another seminar is named Eve Reborn, a course devised and taught by Susan Key, the wife of a wealthy Dallas doctor and mother of three young children. In the last two years her Dallas lectures have drawn thousands of women, most of them well-to-do. A woman who went to Eve Reborn one morning as a favor to a friend was amazed to find herself in a crowd of 600. Susan Key has also taught in other Texas cities and her students have carried the message to such far-flung places as Paris and Singapore.

Two books, *The Total Woman* and *Fascinating Womanhood*, have spawned courses of their own, also given just to women. *The Total Woman* was the largest selling hardback book in the United States in 1974 and is still selling over 3500 copies a week. *Fascinating Womanhood* has sold over 400,000 copies since it was first published in 1965. Bantam books recently issued it in paperback and the mammoth first printing sold out in two and a half weeks. (Another seminar, Bill Gothard's Institute in Basic Youth Conflicts, seems to appeal equally to women and men. His scope, however, is much wider than the other seminars. Gothard discusses everything from breaking bad habits to making friends, to determining whether your job is the one God wants you to have, as well as the doctrine of submission. He first came to Dallas in 1969 when he spoke to 65 people in a conference room of the Republic National Bank Building. Last year in Dallas he drew 20,000 people to the Convention Center. His is the oldest of these seminars and the one whose success has inspired both Timmons and Key.)

The majority of these women are white, middle class, college-educated, which makes them women from the same social class that is carrying on the woman's liberation movement. What makes one group of women submit and another group of women from similar backgrounds rebel is a difficult question; but if there is something in common among the women who submit it is a fundamentalist religious belief. Which is not to say they are necessarily members of fundamentalist churches; the people in Roy Coffee's living room went to one of the large, socially prominent Methodist, Episcopal, or Presbyterian churches in Highland Park. But they do believe that in the Bible is found the solution to all life's problems and all the seminar teachers rely to a greater or lesser degree on scripture to support their ideas, even those leaders with the most explicit ideas about sex.

"Learning submission has made all the difference in our marriage," the wife of a real estate man told me. She was a tall, blonde woman, extremely intelligent and likeable, who had been an executive with a large corporation before she married. She had been successful, independent, competent. Now she was an active club woman, an organizer of events and meetings and charity balls. She lived in a large house on a quiet street not far from Highland Park. She told me that though her husband consulted her about family matters, once he made his decision, she obeyed him, even when that decision was contrary to her wishes or her good sense. If in a time of family financial crisis, she said, and this was an example used in one seminar, the husband decides to buy a speedboat instead of spending the money, say, on food, the wife must not berate him but pray thanking God for the speedboat.

"And if you just do it," the woman told me, "if you just go ahead and submit no matter how much you think you don't want to, it always turns out for the best." She told me a story from her own experience. Her husband was supposed to come home from work at four o'clock one spring afternoon to take her and her three daughters to the opening of Six Flags. She had the girls dressed in crisp spring dresses and waiting for their father on the front porch at four o'clock. Time passed, father did not come home, the girls began to grow restless. After about an hour the woman called her husband's office. A secretary told her he was with a client and would be home as soon as he could. The woman started to get angry. Her husband was habitually late and it was a vexing habit since she was organized and punctual herself. But she had learned in the seminars that she shouldn't get angry at her husband. She prayed to God, thanking him for making her husband late and asked Him for the strength to deal with this trial. Then she had her daughters pray with her, thanking God for making their father late.

In the meantime the weather changed. What had been a pretty spring day turned cold. Dark clouds moved in from the north. The woman sent the girls in to change from their dresses into warmer things. At nearly six o'clock, two hours late, the father finally came home. He was not met with any recriminations—his decision, after all, was not to be home when he said he would and that decision was not to be argued with—and in fact he was warmly welcomed. They all piled into the car and left for Six Flags. "And praise the Lord," the woman said, "the children who had gone out there at four o'clock all still had on light clothes. If he hadn't been late, the girls would have been out at Six Flags not dressed warmly enough for the weather."

I talked with another woman, this one in her mid-twenties. She was an artist and also helped her husband run his business as an illustrator. She was smart, confident, and appealing—beautiful in fact—and she believed in the doctrine of submission. I asked her whether following the doctrine had made her go against her natural inclinations

267

and if things had turned out better or worse for it. She told me that about a year ago she and her husband had taken a trip to Mexico with her husband's parents. She had been reluctant to go. She wasn't sure she liked Mexico in the first place and that made her even more hesitant to undertake this journey with her in-laws. Before she would go she made her husband agree to one rule: they must always have their own room, no sleeping in the same room with his parents. Once inside Mexico, however, there were some problems with reservations and one night, sure enough, they ended up having to share the same room in a hotel. She exploded. Her husband took her aside and told her he had agreed to the arrangement out of consideration for his parents' feelings. They had taken it as an affront that their son and his wife were so reluctant to share a room with them. He told her they *would* do it, that she wasn't to say any more about it, and that, if she was unhappy, she would let no one know. It was difficult but, believing that it was God's will for her always to obey her husband, she did what he wanted. "And you know, it worked out so great," she said. "We really got along together and I got to know his parents really well and my husband became a lot closer to his father, which was something he had always wanted to do. If I hadn't been submissive we would have missed out on all that."

I said, "Yes, but suppose the situation had been reversed. Suppose that the trip was with your parents and your husband said that he didn't want to sleep in the same room with them. You would have had to obey him and get another room. And then *he* would have missed out on gaining all the closeness you just described."

"I know," she said without a moment's pause, "but God rewards obedience. Somewhere else along the line we would gain, gain more, because of my being obedient." Then she added with great conviction, "I've had to take a lot of crap about all this from some women I know. They just don't understand."

The seminars that teach the doctrine of submission are not affiliated with any particular church or denomination. They are fundamentalist and the people who give them are Baptist, but they do not, as the faithful are quick to point out, employ the old hellfire and brimstone style of preaching. In fact they don't call what they do preaching at all. These people think of themselves as teachers. As one man said to me about Bill Gothard, "He is to Christian teaching what Billy Graham is to evangelism." And they are teaching much the same thing with virtually the same method. They all distribute thick loose-leaf notebooks with the outlines of their lectures separated into convenient sections by plastic dividers. Graduates are called alumni, the fee for taking the seminars is called tuition, and the course material—those large notebooks—is called the syllabus. Timmons takes 12 hours to teach his seminar; Bill Gothard takes 32.

This collegiate veneer is certainly one reason the seminars are so appealing to the thirtyish, upper-class, college-educated couples who come to Roy Coffee's house to hear Tim Timmons. But Timmons' popularity also lies in his easy-going, familiar manner. He is about 35, rotund, likeable, hard working, ambitious—in fact about as much like this audience as a Baptist minister is ever likely to be.

Timmons once worked for Campus Crusade for Christ and is a graduate of Dallas Theological Seminary. His seminars are sponsored by Christian Family Life, Inc., which he helped found two years ago. Presently he is called their Director of Communications. He illustrates his seminars with anecdotes from his own family and has enough showmanship to make those stories funny and interesting, at least up to a point. He has the lamentable habit of taking pot shots at "hippies" and Jews, and he is capable of making such statements as, "I like to speak to hostile audiences. I spoke to the Junior League. That's where a lot of libbers are, you know." Nevertheless he is the most progressive, or least regressive, of the seminar teachers. His interpretation of the doctrine of submission, though it still has the man dominant, also places great emphasis on the man's obligations. He will quote Ephesians 5:22–23— "Wives, submit yourselves unto your own husbands, as unto the Lord. For the husband is the head of the wife, even as Christ is the head of the church"—verses that are among the doctrine's most important scriptural basis. But he immediately refers to the 25th verse of that same chapter: "Husbands, love your wives, even as Christ also loved the church, and gave himself for it."

Timmons says the man's role in marriage is to exercise "headship." He is God's representative authority in the family and as such has the duty to guide the family and make what decisions are necessary. But he must also love his wife with the same kind of sacrificial love that Christ had for the church, and it is this sacrificial love that precludes the husband from using his power harmfully. The wife's role is that of "helpmate." She must obey her husband but, since man and woman are equal in God's love, hers is, according to Timmons, "not a status of inferiority but subordination."

Timmons knows his audience. His talk is seasoned with little vignettes from family life that, however corny, had everyone poking one another as they recognized themselves or their spouse: "For the wife the time from five to seven-thirty is known as The Pit. The kids are hanging around the kitchen whining 'What's for dinner? What's for dinner?' Then the King arrives. The King moves toward his throne with his paper in his hand. 'Hey, honey,' he shouts into the kitchen, 'what are we having?' She can barely hear him because of the kids but she calls back 'We're having meat loaf.' There's a long pause. The King says, 'Oh.' . . . After dinner the King retires to his other throne, in the boudoir suite. He turns on the TV and starts watching agent double-o-two and seeing how swift agent double-o-two is. And then he starts thinking 'I'm pretty swift, too.' It isn't too long before he's thinking he's even swifter than double-o-two. Meanwhile, the wife is bathing the kids, getting them ready for bed, taking them to the last potty run. About ten-thirty she staggers into the bedroom. He's gotten all juiced up and he has eyes only for her and he says 'Hey, honey, how about tonight?' And she says, 'How about tonight *what*?'"

His point, though, which he comes to a little later, is that one way for a man to love his wife as Christ loved the church is to help out around the house whenever he can. This may seem a small bone to throw to someone whose status is "not inferior but subordinate," but it is enough bone to make Timmons something of a liberal in the context of the rest of the movement.

His seminar used to include a discussion of sex, which seems a highly appropriate topic to be touched on sometime during a twelve-hour seminar on marriage. He wanted to show that the Bible had much to say about sex and that the Song of Solomon had specific instructions and comments on the dynamics of the act itself. This proved a little too strong for audiences who came expecting religious answers more than physical ones. His mention of women's breasts, even while quoting from scripture, was particularly upsetting.

Finally Susan Key (of Eve Reborn) and two others went to Tim—two others because the Bible says one should do this kind of thing in groups of three—and asked him to tone down this particular part of his ministry. He has. He still talks about intercourse being a "gift from God" and at one point exuberantly proclaims that he and his wife are "having a ball"; but sex is a subject that probably deserves somewhat more examination than that. Other seminars take the attitude that sex needn't be discussed in any detail because once the spiritual side of marriage is properly arranged the physical side will fall into place on its own accord. Can it be that simple? Tim Timmons on the Song of Solomon might not have been the answer either, but at least he wasn't taking sexual fulfillment for granted.

Sex, however, is what made *The Total Woman* the best selling book of last year. It was written by Marabel Morgan, 36, the wife of a Miami lawyer and, as the dust jacket describes her, "a former beauty queen." Her book, as I mentioned earlier, spawned Total Woman Classes which have been taught in virtually every large city. Marabel subscribes enthusiastically to the doctrine of submission, which she supports with several chapters of sorority house theology, but her book stresses the temporal rewards of submission more than the spiritual. The author quotes this testimonial from a graduate of one of her courses: "The Total Woman is in heaven—a beautiful suite overlooking the Atlantic Ocean in the heart of San Juan—new, gorgeous luggage in my closet, with the sweetest guy in the world as my companion. That course is powerful stuff! 'Nothing's too good for my honey!' Bob says."

Circumstances in her own marriage led Marabel to write her book. "I think in superlatives so naturally I expected that my marriage to Charlie Morgan would be the world's greatest." She quickly points out that her "knowledge of what that entailed was nil." She believed "in the all-American Cinderella story; marriage was ruffly curtains at the kitchen window, strawberries for breakfast, and lovin' all the time." During their courtship she and her husband Charlie had marvelous communication, so things looked very promising. "I understood his vibrations; we were on the same wavelength." Charlie used to study his law books in her apartment. During study breaks he would explain the cases he was working on and tell her his "dreams and fears." There must have been some static in the vibrations because she then says without the slightest pause, "I didn't understand most of what he said, but I hung on every word because I loved him." In spite of this perfect communication her marriage gradually turned sour: "Each evening, when Charlie walked into the front door after work, a cloud of gloom and tension floated in with him. . . . We were at each other for some unknown reason. . . . I thought back to our engagement period. How romantic Charlie had been! He was such a fabulous kisser, but now there were very few

kisses. . . . After a few short years of married life, I found myself sighing as we sat in front of the television set."

One night, after what was apparently the argument with her husband that remains most vividly in her mind, she ran upstairs crying. Charlie's final words had been, "From now on when I plan for us to go somewhere, I will tell you twenty minutes ahead of time. You'll have time to get ready, and we'll do without all this arguing!" Marabel says she "felt as if my little world was crumbling all around me. What disturbed me most at the moment was having only twenty minutes to prepare for any event." She should have been upset. Her little world *was* crumbling around her. That night, instead of leaving ruffles and strawberries behind, she decided to discover what she had to do to get them. Her search resulted in her concept of the Total Woman.

The Total Woman follows what Marabel calls the four A's. She Accepts her husband by thinking about his virtues and forgetting his faults; she Admires her husband and compliments his body even if at first it makes her "choke"; she Adapts to her husband by living according to his schedule and tastes rather than her own; and she Appreciates her husband by being grateful to him and for him.

And following this plan made her wishes come true! Much to Marabel's delight Charlie started buying her gifts—something he had never done before. He bought her a new refrigerator ("I wanted one without someone else's germs") and, though he had resisted her on this for years, he announced one morning that she could redecorate their house. Marabel "stopped squeezing the oranges and started squeezing him." The results so inspired her that she started telling her friends about her ideas which led to the Total Woman classes and book. After one of her early classes, one of Marabel's friends came back to the second meeting "radiant." Her husband had never given her a gift but that week he had showered her with "two nighties, two rose bushes, and a can opener."

After reading all that, it was a great surprise to find that her section on sex, one-fourth of the book, is, in its own way, not all that bad. Her basic attitude is positive and confident—"If your sex life isn't satisfying, you can do something about it today." Yet she is aware that old habits are not broken at the drop of a nightgown—"If you are suddenly overprepared for sex after months of denial, don't take it as a personal rebuff if he reacts with apparent disinterest, preoccupation, or suspicion. Perhaps he needs to trust you. Be prepared and patient." And she offers specific suggestions to keep things from becoming stale. They may not be things that appeal to *you* but Marabel believes part of the fun should be discovering your own games: "For an experiment I put on pink baby-doll pajamas and white boots after my bubble bath. . . . When I opened the door that night to greet Charlie . . . he took one look, dropped his briefcase on the doorstep, and chased me around the dining-room table. We were in stiches by the time he caught me." Or "One wife changes the sheets every few days while her husband is dressing for work. As she sprays the sheets with cologne, she purrs, 'Honey, hurry home tonight.'" She suggests books that deal with what she calls "the physical mechanics of sex," although she realizes that sex is as much an attitude as an act: "A woman's most important sex organ is her brain" and "Sex is an hour in bed at ten o'clock, super sex is the climax of an atmosphere that has been carefully set all day." And she is fully aware that the husband may need help and education too: "It is surprising how ignorant so many husbands are concerning their wives' sex lives."

In this section Marabel finally encourages Total Women to take some initiative and learn how to get something on their own. It may be impossible not to laugh at the thought of hundreds of thousands of American housewives in pink nightgowns and white boots lying in wait behind the front door for their husbands, but aren't people supposed to have a good time if they can? The key to the success of *The Total Woman* is that Marabel Morgan somehow realized that the average housewife wants to take part in the sexual revolution, too, but she wants to do it with her husband. Marabel took it upon her slim shoulders to show the housewife how.

Helen Andelin, author of *Fascinating Womanhood*, also wants to show housewives how to live. She sees the woman's role as making the male feel superior by herself becoming helpless and dependent. Over 300,000 women have taken her course from one of the several hundred women nationwide who have paid $12 to become certified teachers. In Houston, for instance, there are fifteen Fascinating Womanhood teachers holding regular classes.

Mrs. Andelin, a doctor's wife from Southern California, believes that being feminine is being a storybook version of a little girl. She advises a woman when buying clothes to "visit a shop for little girls and study their clothes. . . . There will be jumpers, pleated skirts, and baby doll yokes and lots of petticoats and pantaloons. Many of these styles are repeated in the women's sizes. You will not lack for ideas if you study what little children wear. . . . Ribbons and flowers add girlishness to hair styles, as do also barrettes and bands. . . . Childlikeness will make a man feel bigger, manlier, and more like the superior male. It is this feeling which makes the quality of childlikeness in woman so charming to men." This "childlikeness," she claims, is not the same as being childish. Just what the difference is she doesn't make quite clear except to say childishness is a "negative quality."

In addition to dress, she advises women to adopt childlikeness in manner, too. She believes women should develop a "childlike anger" which she defines as "sauciness": "There is no better school for learning childlike anger than watching the antics of little children, especially little girls who have been spoiled by too much loving. . . . When such a child is teased . . . she stamps her foot and shakes her curls and pouts. . . . One feels an irrestible longing to pick up such a child and hug it. . . . This is much the same feeling that a woman inspires in a man when she is adorably angry." While being adorably angry a woman may even threaten her husband, but only in an adorable way: "Your threats should be exaggerated as are those of little children who say, 'I'll never speak to you again,' or 'I won't do anything for you anymore,' or 'I'll tell my mother on you.'"

Helen Andelin confidently makes a list of masculine characteristics, things like skill in repairing a motor, deep pitched voice, heavy jaw, and says that they have suited the man for masculine tasks like "painting, repairing the furnace, fixing the roof, or handling the family finances." If the woman is "stuck" with any of these tasks she is to do them in a "feminine manner," in other words badly: "Women are supposed to be inferior in the masculine duties. If you are not, it is because you have taken on

unnatural capability." I should think a man married to such a woman, one who bungles about the house in barrettes and petticoats, would lead a very strange life.

I had hoped to be able to discuss Bill Gothard's Institute in Basic Youth Conflicts which, as I said before, is the largest seminar and the one whose success has precipitated the others. Unfortunately, people who have attended his sessions are asked not to discuss the course in any detail with an outsider nor to show anyone the course material Gothard hands out, because, as they say, it is so easy to misunderstand. I was also refused admittance to a seminar he was conducting in Fort Worth since it had been "booked up months in advance," but then was allowed to see him on the night after he had given his lecture on marriage, which is titled The Chain of Command. The "booked up" Convention Center was two-thirds full. I had a ten-minute interview with Gothard. When I asked him about the chain of command in marriage he replied that took him several hours to explain in the seminar, so we reached an immediate stand-off. Security at his seminars is tight because it costs $45 to enroll.

I have been saving Susan Key's Eve Reborn for last. Key has modeled her course after Bill Gothard's. Her publicity releases describe her as "the wife of a Dallas medical doctor and mother of three young children. Her lecture is based on God's principles revealed in Scripture for today's woman." Her strongest following is among women of means. When she gave her seminar at Highland Park Methodist Church, the most socially prominent Methodist church in Dallas, the main chapel filled to overflowing with women; many came to each of the three morning sessions 45 minutes early to get good seats.

Her family has lived in Dallas for several generations, and she was raised in the First Baptist Church listening to the legendary sermons of Dr. Criswell. She told me she had had a crisis in faith when, with babe in arms, she read about rioting in American cities during the late Sixties. "I wondered," she said, "what I was going to do when the rioters came to my door." That is an unlikely occurrence now, even if there were riots, since she lives far north of the central city in a huge new house which she has elegantly furnished. She was a successful interior decorator before she married and, judging by the evidence of her home, her success was no accident. She is willing to follow the doctrine of submission as far as it will go: "One time it led to the cross, you know." As we sat talking beside a glass wall that looked out over a golf course, she added, "Since there is no authority that is not ordained of God, we must submit to all earthly authority."

"But," I said, "you don't mean something like Hitler."

"Yes."

When giving her seminar she wears long dresses and enough expensive jewelry to make her imposing, but her voice in class is always a very soft monotone. She teaches the concepts of male headship and female helpmeet and believes that it is the woman's duty, not the man's, to place herself in submission: "If you want your husband to rule, you must first give him a kingdom." Failure to do this will prevent her husband's spiritual growth. "When a wife is putting pressure on a husband," she says, "God can't." God, according to Key, has given women "a unique capacity for submission and obedience and when this capacity is thwarted by rebellion and deceit, it becomes a capacity to destroy which begins to work within her heart and then sulks out to her intimate relationships, widens to her acquaintances, to society, and then into history.''

She discusses what to do about ''the other woman.'' The wife must never criticize her husband but must become even more submissive. The man will then ultimately see that the other woman is merely the counterfeit of the true woman he has at home. And she ends her course with a discussion of how love of money can prevent loving God. She believes that God knows ''when it is better to withhold money than to provide it,'' and that ''riches often inhibit spiritual growth'' and cause conceit, pride, and insomnia. Since she is so obviously well-heeled and wears the clothes and jewelry to prove it, this disparagement of wealth often falls on skeptical ears.

With the possible exception of Gothard's, hers is by far the most severe notion of the world among all teachers of submission. Her advice on child rearing shows this best of all. ''My aim in spanking is to break the will of rebellion against authority and to underscore that each of us is responsible for our actions, our reactions, and our attitudes. I apply the rod until they are prepared to agree with me. The spirit of rebellion may require a longer use of the rod than a bad reaction (biting or hitting in retaliation). The results of the rod are rarely visible for more than an hour or so. . . . My first indication that I need to correct behavior is usually my own disposition. When I begin to be cross with the children, and when the general noise and confusion begins to increase, I realize that I have been neglecting my responsibility. I issue warnings at a family council meeting and ask for suggestions from the children about what they think we should do to improve the situation. The next day, I begin to spank each one of them for every transgression. Over a period of the next three days, I may administer two spankings to the one who responds quickly, and as many as five each to the other two. We arrive at this situation about four times a year and our children are now five, six, and seven. . . . Ideally, I use a flexible branch from the willow trees in our yard.''

She also recommends using a Popsicle stick as a ''rod of correction'' on babies too young for willow. Before spanking the parent is supposed to get the child to admit what he did wrong: if he lies or won't admit guilt he is spanked until he does and then spanked for the original transgression.

Without arguing the pros and cons of spanking itself, surely five spankings in three days four times a year for

young children means that something *else* is wrong, something that spanking isn't correcting. One Christian man who uses this method told me he spanked one of his children whenever he wouldn't eat at the table. ''Of course,'' the man added offhandedly, ''he's taught himself to throw up at the table now, so I have to spank him for that, too.''

These extreme views of child rearing reveal most clearly the insidious side of the doctrine of submission. It is, in spite of its biblical basis and in spite of the sugar coating Tim Timmons or Marabel Morgan may put on it, still a doctrine that requires the subjugation of one human will beneath another. While a certain amount of submission may be necessary to make the world run, any doctrine that revels in submission makes me wary. After all, the Bible says, ''Do unto others . . .''

Still, it's difficult to argue with people who have, of their own free will, accepted submission fully and are happy with it. After Tim Timmons finished his talk at Roy Coffee's, I sat talking with a man and his wife who had attended the seminar several times. The man told me he had been brought up in Dallas in a comfortable family environment. He had returned to Dallas after attending the University of Texas and Stanford Business School. He was doing well. ''In business school they told me what to do—A, B, C—and I came back here and did A B C and it worked.'' And he knew very well why he kept coming to evenings like this: ''I never, and I tried, had a really deep relation with someone, I mean really talk with someone about the things that are important until I met this group of friends with a common interest in Christianity.'' His marriage, like that of many other couples I talked to, had fallen into a pattern of male headship and female submission before they had ever heard the terms. The husband wanted to go out in the world and provide for a family; the wife wanted to be provided for and take care of domestic responsibilities. The seminars led them to realize the patterns they were following, gave them a rationale for feeling comfortable with those patterns, and offered God's love as a higher existence those patterns could achieve. His wife said, ''We had a good marriage before, but now we love each other so much more.''

Well, if they are happy, they are happy. But at least two warnings seem to be in order: (1) Men, if your wives are submissive, be worthy of them; and (2) husbands and wives, relinquish your ways the moment vile spots appear on the tablecloth in front of family members.

*—June 1975*

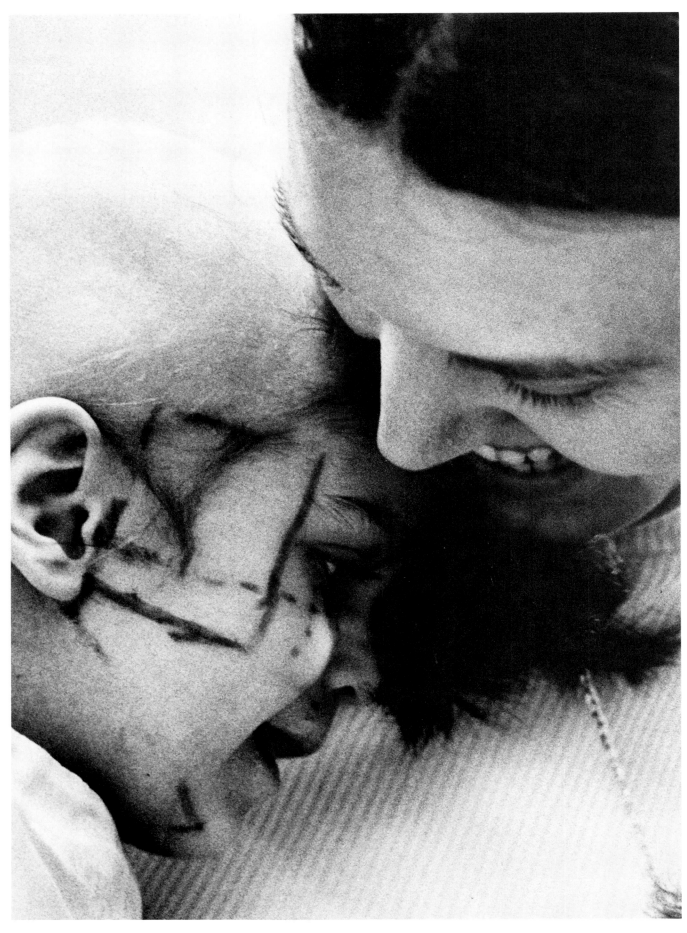

Child of Six West. *Photography by Tom Payne*

# SIX WEST

## by Stephen Harrigan

---

*Laughter and tragedy are uneasy companions in a children's cancer ward.*

---

This week it's not Tiny Tim or Vikki Carr or Pinky Hull, the ragtime piano player. This week it's supposed to be the Houston Rockets, at least *some* of the Houston Rockets, but even with that qualification things aren't looking too hopeful: two basketballs intended for demonstration purposes are lying about conspicuously idle, and it seems possible that this appointment might just have slipped the Rockets' mind. To take up some slack Katie Dixie abruptly hands me a basketball and asks me to show the children the art of dribbling.

Uh, this is how it's done, kids. I display the technique which failed me when the time came for the first cut on my high school B-team, a technique which doesn't seem too impressive now either—judging from the bland, almost autistic attention paid by the children to the ball bouncing clumsily off my fingertips. I wonder how many of them could be expected to be able to dribble a basketball. Not many. Maybe five or six of the fifteen or so kids assembled here look as though they're feeling well enough to try.

Who knows what kind of a fatalistic gloss cancer can impose on a child's mind? Are they brooding? Are they in pain? Or is it just the quiet tension that infects any group of children waiting for a party that puts this morose look into their eyes? After I end my demonstration a girl of about six semi-accidentally rolls the other basketball across the floor to the sole of my shoe—I return it with my foot. She rolls it back, trying to look distracted as nightclub entertainer Paul Clark comes in with his guitar and greets Katie Dixie with mock declarations of love to which she responds in her three-octave speaking voice. Then for a long time the girl and I roll the basketball monotonously back and forth without communicating in any other way. She has dark hair and a body as frail as a bird's, and she resists, quietly, any alteration in the pattern of our game.

This is Six West, the west wing of the sixth floor of the

*Stephen Harrigan is a contributing editor of* Texas Monthly *and has written for several other magazines.*

M.D. Anderson Hospital and Tumor Institute, one of the only three comprehensive cancer centers in the country and one of the prominent fixtures in that vast Disneyland-gone-sour known as the Texas Medical Center, where new hospitals seem to reproduce themselves as rapidly and unobtrusively as cells dividing. (Even now Anderson is cloning an extension of its present butterfly-shape off into a parking lot.)

And in this ward the children, the inpatients who are waiting for this party to begin, are all afflicted with cancer—a slight majority of them have leukemia, the rest have the disease in other, less prevalent forms. Some of them are dying of it, a few are being cured of it, and the rest hover with their parents in its shadow, not really knowing.

This is the high point of the week for the children on Six West and for their mothers who, through a hospital policy, live with their children on the floor during their stay (the median inpatient stay is about two weeks, but some are here for months). Every Wednesday at two in the afternoon Katie Dixie has somebody lined up—she calls up the agents of people who are in Houston in various stages of their fame and usually persuades them to come by and entertain. She's maybe 60 or so, it's hard to tell  since she's one of those people whose enthusiasm eclipses every other feature. It's she who is going to get these kids laughing today; she seems to know that that look they have in their eyes is not indifference, but merely a kind of reserve.

Katie Dixie is an Anderson volunteer, one of seven on the pediatric floor, and the coordinator of these "Pedi-Parties," which are now famous enough throughout the hospital to cause people to drift up from the other floors to check them out. After all, they could be having the Maimi Dolphins again, who showed up last week. (There's a picture circulating on the floor now from the *Washington Post*, which got it from the wire services, of Larry Csonka signing an autograph for a boy on the floor, with the boy's one leg carefully concealed below the frame.) Or it could be

Jimmy Durante, or Charlie Pride, or Carlos Mansanto, or the Oilers, or the Astros, or Pistle the Precious Parakeet. And those are just the most visible celebrities. She's brought in operas and string quartets and bell-ringing choirs and local entertainers like Paul Clark on a regular basis, with a lot of them asking to come back. At the moment she's booked two months ahead with people who have called *her* wanting to volunteer their talents.

The parties are held in the ward's kindergartenish day room (and indeed there keeps intruding a hazy resemblance between Katie Dixie and Miss Connie or whatever her name was on *Ding Dong School*). There is a huge Teddy bear and a popcorn popper and little geometrical plastic chairs that, for adults, are like sitting on suction cups. There is also a fairly decent stereo with a record collection that seems at least half-donated (who would *buy* a record by Sam the Sham and the Pharoahs for a children's cancer ward?). Maybe it's owing to the decor that not too many of the older children seem to have come down for the party—the pediatrics floor, which holds about 50 patients, accepts people up to fifteen years old, but most of the kids here seem less than ten.

The children who are here have their mothers with them, and a few have their fathers. Occasionally a father will stay with his child on the floor, but the great majority of resident parents are mothers. One boy, Mike (I'm changing the names of the kids, not because I think anybody would mind if I used them, but because I feel freer in talking about them that way), who's about nine and whose only hint of infirmity is a shunt on his left wrist, has an outgoing personality that matches the surface appearance of his health—the cut-up at the Cub Scout meeting.

"What are you doing?" he asks me with what passes for irony in pre-adolescents.

"Oh, not much."

But then what else is there to say? I'm here for the "human interest," feeding off it, feeling obligated to ask Mike cleverly-disguised questions about pain and innocence and death but not for one minute believing I'm actually going to do it. ("Jesus!" my friends say, "that must be a hard article to write!" And, yes, it's turning out that way, not because the sight of children and suffering is unbearable, as I'd originally assumed it would be, but because an honest reaction to it seems, for now, so out of reach. Sentimentality, cynicism, rage, humor, philosophy —all of them are such cheap shots and yet all of them seem essential.)

Paul Clark is tuning his guitar while the volunteers pass out little presents to the kids—soap bubbles, dolls, paperback copies of *Jonathan Livingston Seagull*. Most of them receive their gifts joylessly, as tribute. The Rockets have still not arrived, and it's beginning to look like they might not show at all. A girl is wheeled in on a cart; someone says her name is Marcy. There's no telling how old she is—she's as small as a baby and doesn't move, only lies on the cart attached to a plasma bottle. Her mother's hand never strays from the side of the cart.

"Let's see," says Katie Dixie, starting the party, Rockets or no Rockets, "who's new today?"

A boy named Bill is new today, and when his name is spoken he grins for the first time. His hair is vividly red and his face is so pale it seems that his hair cannibalizes the color in his skin.

"Your commercial is beautiful—you sound just like Nat King Cole," a woman tells Paul Clark, who has finished tuning and is now ready to begin his act, stretching his arms to free his hands and wrists from the cuffs of his sportcoat.

I'm about to take a seat in one of the plastic chairs when I notice someone has left a cup of punch there.

"That's all right, you can sit there," says Eddie, a boy whose face has been so narrowed and misaligned by disease that below his nose it is almost no face at all. He's been silent all the time I've been around him, morbidly silent, so that now his small gesture to make me feel at home seems an act of immense graciousness.

Paul Clark, by this time, is into the first few bars of "Gentle On My Mind." A girl named Adriana watches him from under her knit cap, her face swollen and impassive as an owl's. You can't tell what song she's hearing.

"The very young have remarkably strange concepts," says Dr. Jan van Eys, the head of the Anderson pediatrics department, using metronomic swiveling of his chair to emphasize points about a child's perception of reality. "What makes the biggest impression on you as a child is usually way out of proportion."

Van Eys is a tall man with soap-opera-gray hair and what must be a Dutch accent embroidering the edges of his speech. He's talking about how children in the hospital deal with their own pain and, frequently, with their own deaths.

"I think that we have here an adult concept of leukemia," he says, "the younger a child, the less his ability to look into the future. We over-interpret what the child thinks about it. The parents' attitude is far more important than the child's.

"Cancer has changed in children. Fifty years ago it was an acute, lethal disease. With chemotherapy we have a success story—we have changed cancer even for children who have leukemia."

Chemotherapy is the use of very toxic natural and synthetic drugs—cell-killing drugs—in combination with one another. Van Eys admits to having "grave misgivings" about using these drugs—the side effects are often powerful and often unknown. But the idea is to find the right combination so that the harmful effects of the drugs will cancel themselves out as much as possible without losing their power to kill cancer cells. Treatment for each patient is highly individualized, and experimental drugs are never administered unless the parents request them.

With chemotherapy, van Eys can claim a 95 per cent remission rate for leukemia. That's not a cure: remission is a suspension of symptoms that can last months or years, during which time the child is almost normal and has to come in only for periodic treatment. (Anderson handles hundreds of outpatients every day.) In only rare cases does a remission modulate into what are only cautiously referred to as "cures," continuous, complete, and unmaintained remission. Some other forms of cancer have more encouraging prognoses: Wilm's tumor, for example, a cancer of the kidneys, is now 60 to 70 per cent curable.

Chemotherapy is the preferred method of treatment at Anderson. The alternatives, radiotherapy and surgery, are a little cruder. There's evidence that radiation treatments can stunt growth, and surgery is a little too cruel a euphemism for what often is simple amputation.

"Mutilative surgery has to be taken into far greater consideration," says van Eys. "We reserve it for those cases for which we hold out a reasonable possibility of cure. Of course, there's a psychological element—a cure that is purely physiological is not a cure.

"The point is we can help almost every child with cancer. We can change the disease from acute to chronic, from horrible to bearable. The longer he's alive the better his chances.

With my—*cupped hand*
Round the—*tin can*

That's Paul Clark doing John Wayne doing "Gentle On My Mind."

So it turns out he's an impressionist as well as a singer, and he's not too bad at it either. He runs through the same song as it might be done by Dean Martin, Walter Brennan, and Paul Lynde. The kids don't get the impressions—but the whole thing is just weird enough to get them laughing, especially when they look up and see their mothers nearly howling, like they were trying to wring the most possible release out of every near-funny moment.

But the kids are seriously lost when Clark goes into a Nelson Eddy/Jeanette MacDonald number, an allusion that has a hard time taking root even among the parents, most of whom seem too young to appreciate it fully. Bill is beginning to look disgruntled again until Clark assumes his falsetto voice for the Jeanette MacDonald half of the duet, twisting his right maroon pants-leg suggestively and acting like a drag queen. That pulls back the attention.

Cheryl, a slight, Alice-in-Wonderlandish girl for whom today is the first day on the ward, is sitting between her parents, who look a little too heart-breakingly like the young couple in bank commercials who have their whole lives ahead of them. She keeps looking up at them and cueing herself nervously on their laughter. Chemotherapy has different side effects for different people: about half of the children here have lost their hair, leaving only a sort of down remaining on their heads; others are very pale, others thin, others slightly bloated in the face. Nearly all of them are equipped with shunts, devices inserted in their wrists to provide permanent access to their veins. The shunts are covered with something like white plaster and resemble the shiver guards that linebackers wear. But Cheryl has not yet been affected in any of those ways. She looks like the average leukemia-stricken little girl on *Marcus Welby, MD*, and she seems all the more vulnerable for it.

Clark breaks into "Zippadeedooda" about the time a nurse comes in and whispers to a tall, thin, hairless girl in white whose delicately elongated features make her look like a Preraphaelite angel.

"Want to come get your chemotherapy, honey? It won't take long."

She slips away quietly with the nurse, missing Clark's greatest child-pleaser, the Invisible Object in the Dixie Cup. Here is something a kid can latch onto: Clark holds a Dixie Cup in his hand in such a way that his index finger is available to thump it from underneath, creating a sound for the invisible object when it is caught there. He does it straight a couple of times, throwing it up and catching it with only modest body English. Then he throws it again,

watching it languidly defy gravity and physics until it makes its re-entry, to thunderous laughter. Clark gives the object to Eddie, who accepts it grudgingly and throws it back straight toward Clark, only by Clark's interpretation the thing is sailing over his head: he makes a dive for it and barely recovers it before it hits the ground. Eddie smiles for the first time—a shy grin from that atrophied mouth is a triumph for any number of people, as well as for him.

Clark then leads a sing-along in which very few of the children fail to take part. Marcy's mother leans down to the cart to make sure Marcy knows about it—it's her favorite song.

Oh tie a yellow ribbon
Round that old oak tree,
It's been three long years,
Do you still want me . . .

And the mothers are singing too, even those who don't speak English are humming or mouthing the lyrics, sharing the song, I suspect, as much with one another as with their children.

Margaret Buchorn is a social worker assigned to the pediatrics department at Anderson, a woman with broad expressive features set free to graze under what is no more than a functional haircut.

"The fact that parents can stay here," she is saying, "is of primary importance. A child's greatest fear is being left alone—separation anxiety."

At Six West the parent sleeps on a cot beside the child's bed, sharing a room and one bathroom with usually three other children and three mothers. But the overcrowding only occasionally erupts into bitterness: the mothers seem too preoccupied with concern for their children to pay much attention to their own situation, and that incredibly sharp focus is probably what gives them a fierce sort of solidarity with one another.

Later I sit in on one of Buchorn's Tuesday afternoon sessions for parents. There are about seven or eight mothers and two fathers, none of the same people I saw at the Pedi-Party. Everyone is gathered together in the same dayroom. One of the mothers constantly gets up to see whether it's her child that she hears crying.

There are a few people to be introduced: two babysitting volunteers, me, and a student nurse from Lebanon working on her master's degree. She's here to ask if there are any objections to her doing a study on their children, to gauge the reactions they have toward illness, fatal illness. She wants to find out the difference between children who have been told they're dying and those who have not.

To do this, she explains, she plans to show each kid four pictures and ask him or her to make up a story about them. The pictures are simple coloring-book drawings of scenes like a doctor whispering to a boy's parents outside his door, of a girl walking with a nurse toward a room that says "Intensive Care Unit" on the door.

And the parents look interested, a little stony-faced, but receptive in a strange way.

A woman who seems at least 50, wearing Levis, with a very strong, very weathered face, is the first to speak, asking if the parents get to find out what their children say about the pictures.

"Oh, yes, of course," says the graduate student, a little encouraged that her broaching the subject of death has not turned them against her.

"Well, I'd love to have her work with my son," the woman replies.

"Our child is blind," one of the fathers says. "Is your program adaptable? We'd like to have her participate, even though she doesn't like strangers at the moment."

She says that she'll have to give it some thought but, yes, it can probably be done. Then she leaves, as agreed, to give the parents a chance to make a decision without her presence.

"I think it's a pretty good idea," says Buchorn. "Sure it's going to bother the parents more than the kids—the whole ordeal bothers the parents instead of the kids."

The proposal is implicitly accepted and there is a silence. One woman is just back with her child after having been home for three months.

"Is it okay?" Margaret Buchorn asks her.

"Is what okay?"

"Your little girl."

"Oh. No, not really."

Another silence. Someone brings up the fact that some of the other wards, the adult wards, are going to be having parties and have invited the parents from Six West. No one shows much enthusiasm.

"Well, what do you do at these parties?" the woman in Levis asks.

"What you always do at adult parties," says Buchorn, "you play Bingo."

The parents agree that they get more out of the Pedi-Parties—a chance to be with their kids and to see them enjoying themselves; a party without their children just doesn't appeal to them. They seem helpless, tethered to the condition and moods of their kids for whatever form of peace they can find—yet they seem aware of that helplessness. It's an adult group of people, quiet, very accepting in a way that is not morbid.

("We have a lot of parents who become distraught and irrational," Buchorn, who has lost a child herself, told me earlier, "but most human beings do what they have to do. If they have any substance they manage to get through it.")

The two volunteers are then encouraged to talk about why they're here. Pat is here because she enjoys kids and her mother suggested that she do volunteer work—to baby-sit for the parents, if their children aren't too sick, so they can occasionally get away from the hospital for a couple of hours. She's a sixth grade language arts teacher.

Mike was reading the paper one day and saw that there was a need at Anderson for volunteers. "I'm not a teacher like Pat. I'm a businessman for IBM. I asked myself what am I doing to make a contribution with my existence? Not much."

They are both tacitly accepted, welcomed into the family, but not without some critical looks on the part of the parents, who seem concerned with looking for undercurrents of sentimentality and egotism in volunteers: they're not going to trust their kids to just anybody. But, once accepted, Mike and Pat are welcomed as warmly as that awesome collective of reserve will allow.

A woman says she feels sorry for the Spanish-speaking mothers (who consist of, at the moment, about half the mothers on the floor) because they can't really participate in meetings like this. Someone suggests that the volunteers could teach them English, but three or four of the women agree that they would rather learn Spanish instead.

Then there is some complaining about maintenance problems, the overcrowded conditions of the bathrooms, toilets that overflow.

"Well," says Margaret Buchorn, "the only thing y'all can do is just keep cussin' each other and bear with it."

Katie Dixie is now back in the room with the news that the Houston Rockets have made their appearance; or, *one* Houston Rocket, at least. Ed Ratliff, a guard, walks into the room looking not at all accustomed to this sort of thing. His eyes, which are a good foot higher than anyone else's in the room, dart about apprehensively, and his hands fidget nervously with a stack of soon-to-be autographed pennants.

"You're a tall one, aren't you?" says Katie Dixie, and introduces him to Paul Clark who, seeing that the top of his own head comes to about Ratliff's sternum, exaggerates his own lack of out-sized height by bending his knees and looking up at Ratliff with an awed look on his face. Ratliff responds good-naturedly. Heh-heh.

"Won't you have some punch, Mr. Ratliff?" Katie Dixie asks, determined to make him feel at home.

"Uh, no, ma'am. I can't stay long. I've got to, uh, go somewhere."

He eagerly steps out of the limelight and encourages Paul Clark to finish up his act, which his arrival has interrupted.

Marcy's mother comes up to tell Clark that her daughter wants to hear "Yellow Ribbon" again. He goes over to her cart and leans down close over her ear, above that body that is almost ethereal, and sings once more through her favorite song, making it into a talisman for her.

Now the whole darn bus is cheering,
And I can't believe I see
One hundred yellow ribbons
Round that old oak tree . . .

For a finale Clark sings a rather too-stirring version of "You'll Never Walk Alone," fairly shouting at the final "with faaaaaaaith in your heaaaaaaaart" and finishing with an apocalyptic crescendo from his guitar.

Which is, because there is no way to follow it, the official end of the party. Some of the kids, Mike and Bill among them, go up to Ed Ratliff to get an autographed Houston Rockets pennant. He's very shy about giving them out, kind, maybe not really aware how much someone like him means to them. Cheryl's parents talk her into having her picture taken with him.

Then someone hands him one of the neglected basketballs and he spins it, balancing it on the end of his index finger, grinning, in his element at last. Gwaaaaah! They've never seen such magic. He hands the ball to Eddie, who accepts it cynically, knowing it won't work for him, but he tries it and for a microsecond before the ball brushes off the tip of his finger it hovers there, balanced, rotating like a planet. Ed Ratliff tells him to try it once more, this time with a little more spin.

*—July 1974*

# PACEM IN TERRORS

## by Prudence Mackintosh

---

*All's fair in brotherly love and war, so ignore that bloody nose. Sibling rivalry is healthy.*

---

Last week it occurred to my two-year-old that his older brother does not have a divine right to the Zooper Looper that comes in the Cheerio box. And I think that means that things are going to get worse around here before they get better.

"Can't we just send him on back to heaven?" my four-year-old asks in disgust as he watches his younger brother dutifully shovel in the last bite of spinach, a prerequisite for the meager dessert that will now have to be shared. "I'll bet Gene Blakeney would give me his brother."

My firstborn was a little more than two years at his brother's birth. We did everything the books instructed to ease the jealousy. We read Ezra Jack Keats' *Peter's Chair*, a charmingly illustrated tale of a little boy who discovers that he really is too big for his baby bed and small chair and who finally agrees to help his father paint them pink for new baby sister Susie. We arranged for him to view the less than beautiful baby at the hospital, bought a toy helicopter for the baby to present his big brother on arrival at home, and for at least the first three months of his life we virtually ignored the newborn whenever big brother was present. The firstborn rewarded our efforts by demonstrating the inadequacies of his toilet training on the front sidewalk in the presence of five finicky neighbors.

My well-meaning pediatrician assured me that in three months my older boy would have no recollection of life without a brother. I took little comfort in that. Would he also have no recollection of what I regard as the halcyon days of my motherhood? Those were the days when he lolled in his playpen while I wrote piano melodies for Mother Goose rhymes about boys named Jack. Those were also the days when we made unnecessary trips to the grocery store just to collect smiles from sweet old ladies. There are few smiles for us at Safeway now. The stock

*Prudence Mackintosh is a contributing editor of* Texas Monthly *and winner of a 1976 Penney-Missouri Award.*

boy, who remembers that my kid is the one who pops wheelies with the grocery cart, stands guard over his precariously stacked cans of V-8. Halfway through the shopping list, I encounter innocent, fashionably dressed women and their pink, powdered first babies cooing over the Gerber's counter and wonder if they will fall from grace as I have. I feebly apologize when they find it necessary to lift their carts over my four-year-old, who has prostrated himself in the aisle in front of Captain Crunch with hopes of wearing down my nutritional scruples. The two-year-old who, under duress, still rides in the kiddie seat of the grocery cart, smiles coyly at sweet little ladies and then, well-tutored by his older brother, yells "Karate chop" when they try to chuck him under the chin. At the counter, I look up from my check writing to see that the four-year-old is climbing on top of the gum machine. "You'll fall," I say. "But I won't hurt myself," he replies, and he's right. He falls squarely on his soft brother, whose head it is that bangs into the grocery carts. Two children at the grocery store at 4 p.m. bring me to the realization that one child was none.

With a second son in tow, I am no longer the consistent, reasonable parent I intended to be. I shamelessly resort to bribery and/or spanking for expedience and am occasionally guilty of allowing my children to overdose themselves on wretched TV cartoons. Earlier this week, when they appeared barefoot for the fourth time in one cold day, I bounced their sneakers off the wall in uncontrolled rage. (I concur with a friend who says children should have their feet laminated until they are able to tie their own shoelaces.) My dentist says I'll need orthodontic treatment if I don't quit gritting my teeth.

Before my second son was born, a mother of two confessed to me that she had spent the better part of a day setting the kitchen timer to buzz at ten-minute intervals to enforce the peaceful sharing of a rusty cap pistol found in

277

the alley by her two boys. I distinctly remember murmuring, ''Ridiculous.'' I now beg her forgiveness. I have gone to far more absurd extremes to avoid confrontations, particularly before I've had my first cup of coffee in the morning. The sibling bickering can be set off by my carelessly dispensing different-colored chewable vitamins. ''I wanted the orange one. You always give him the orange one.'' I have learned to ask, ''Would someone please go get the newspaper?'' only if one child is still asleep, or if it is Monday or Thursday, when the milk cartons on the porch provide an equally important alternate chore. One slip-up on my part and the morning paper is shredded in the living room by two small helpers screaming, ''She said for me to bring it.'' ''No, my turn!'' If one of them perchance gets it to the table intact, it is often necessary to return it to the porch so that the other one can provide equal service.

Variations on the same rivalrous theme occur throughout the day. ''He flushed my potty,'' the two-year-old shrieks. Or at lunchtime, the four-year-old can always draw the two-year-old offsides with the primeval taunt, ''Nyah, nyah, nyah, nyah, nyah, nyah, I got the blue cup.'' If I hand him the red cup, it's the same tune, different color. The two-year-old responds by throwing his milk or spitting—crimes punishable by spanking at our house.

It is easy to fault the older child. He is more articulate, an adept con man, and he knows precisely which taunts will strike a responsive chord. He knows how to intone a question like, ''Want me to rip your arm off?'' so that his brother will say, ''Yes.'' He has traded his brother more apple slices for cookies than I care to remember. He creates clever games where he is the jumper and his brother is always the hurdle. He deliberately trips over his little brother's feet as a pretext for vengeance.

However, I have observed these boys long enough to know that the younger child is not guiltless. If the four-year-old fails to provoke a battle, I have seen the two-year-old climb out of his high-chair, pull up his shirt, and say, ''You can't get my tummy.'' This may elicit one or two playful pokes from big brother. However, if the two-year-old is foolish enough to run in for a third poke, he always gets a gut wrencher. The villain has full protection. ''He told me to do it, Mom.''

Doctors Benjamin Spock, Haim Ginott, Fitzhugh Dodson, and William E. Homan assure me that the scene is normal. Though Spock may be anathema in many homes, I still find solace in my battered volume. (It always flops open to those dog-eared pages which we read so frequently and nervously as novice parents: Infant bowel movements, varieties of.) Spock advised parents in his 1945 volume *The Common Sense Book of Baby and Child Care* to prepare the older child for the arrival of a sibling, to treat each child as an individual, to avoid comparison among siblings, to accept and mirror children's feelings, and to generally keep out of their fights. All of this advice is echoed in more recent popular volumes by pediatricians less tainted by politics.

I rather like Dr. William E. Homan (*Child Sense, A Pediatrician's Guide for Today's Families*) because he explodes the theory held by the others that it helps to prepare a child for the birth of a sibling. He and Dr. Fitzhugh Dodson (*How to Parent* and *How to Father*) use a similar analogy to help parents appreciate the first child's position when the second child arrives. Dodson writes in

*How to Parent*:

''Suppose that tomorrow your husband informs you of the following delightful bit of news. 'Dear,' he says, 'next week Roxanne my old girl friend will be joining us. Of course, I love you as much as I always have. And I will be with you on Mondays, Wednesdays, and Fridays. But on Tuesdays, Thursdays, and Saturdays I will be with her. Sundays we will put up for grabs.' Furthermore, when this rival actually comes to take up residence in your house, you discover that she does not intend to lift a finger to help you around the house. All she does is loll around all day, reading women's magazines and drinking milk punches. How would you feel about Roxanne?''

But Dr. Homan takes the analogy a step further by asking, ''Would it help much if your husband told you far in advance about his plans to bring the old girl home?'' And to mothers who say, ''Surely my twelve-year-old won't be jealous,'' Homan responds, ''Of course not. You wouldn't mind if the second woman your husband chose were twelve years younger than you, would you?''

Dr. Haim Ginott has been so overused, or perhaps misunderstood, by my contemporaries that I sometimes think I will defy all he stands for and slug the next mother who says, ''Do it with words, Jeremy,'' to the kid who just bloodied my kid's nose. Ginott's suggestions on nonviolence make good reading, but they require a verbal sophistication that just isn't practical for a four-year-old. For that matter, my two-year-old's verbal ability has grown phenomenally because of his brother's primitive teaching technique. ''If you call this hammer a wrench one more time, I'll crush your head with it.''

A skeptical friend warns me that I should use Ginott's ''draw-me-a-picture-to-show-me-how-you-feel-about-your-brother'' method only if I really want to know. Her own five-year-old's drawing made a medieval torture chamber look like a health spa. Frankly, the expression of feelings gets so free at my house that I'd like to see a little repression here and there.

Presuming that sibling rivalry is inevitable, these experts offer several specific suggestions for minimizing the fracases:

• Avoid referring to one child when reprimanding another. (''Your brother always puts his bike up without being told.'')

• As far as possible, encourage your children to develop their talents in different directions.

• Connive to see that each child operates within a group of his friends, not a group of his siblings.

• Try to spend some time each day with each child.

• Take one of your children's friends along on trips to take some of the pressure off you and reduce bickering.

• Interfere less. (''I have confidence that you can work out a solution that is fair to each of you.'')

• Use a ''time out'' technique when a fight starts. Send each child to a neutral, boring place for five minutes. The fighting thus will not be reinforced by parental attention and the parent avoids having to referee.

• Be moderate enough in temperament so that occasionally yelling, ''Quit, dammit!'' will effect a temporary cease-fire.

A fifth expert, Dr. Lee Salk (*What Every Child Would Like His Parents to Know*), does not accept the inevitability of sibling rivalry and insists that he has known cases where no jealousy exists. He suggests that spacing children three years apart virtually eliminates sibling rivalry in homes where the children are valued as individuals. My own childhood certainly doesn't bear this out.

Six years age difference between my brother and me did little to diminish the tormenting and the bickering. It only increased my disadvantage. The power an older child holds over a younger sibling is irresistible. Because I was so much younger and a girl (those were the days when boys were admonished, "We don't hit little girls"), the physical abuse was minimal. However, there was the match incident when I was five. We were planning an unauthorized wiener roast in the backyard. "Here, Prudence," my brother said, handing me a lighted match, "don't let this go out whatever you do. We need it to light the fire. I've got to go in the house to get the mustard." I dutifully took it, delighted to be trusted with such responsibility. "Turn it upside down," he yelled from the back door, "it won't burn so fast." I did, and the tears spilled down my cheeks not so much from the pain of my smoldering finger, but because I had let the match go out. He berated me accordingly, and, thanks to his eleven-year-old friends who gleefully witnessed the incident, the story followed me well into adolescence.

Though I could not appreciate it at the time, his tormenting was remarkably creative. He once offered to fix lunch for a little friend and me. "Deviled ham sandwiches and Seven-Up, coming up," he said, cheerily spreading Dash dogfood on slices of bread and dropping Alka Seltzer tablets in the glasses. He still recalls how the reticent little friend politely cleaned her plate.

I worshipped him—even when he called my eleven-year-old boy friend with the aerodynamically protruding ears "The Trans Eddie." He never fought a battle for me, but his very existence allowed me to say, "I'll tell my big brother on you." Though I can't explain it, I understand my two-year-old's need for a gut wrencher from his brother. "Why don't you just stay away from him?" I hear myself echoing my own mother's words. But, of course, I remember that being separated from my brother was the greatest punishment.

As this brother entered the rock perils of adolescence, I lost my "tattle tail" and became his staunchest defender. I was privy to all of his misdoings and was paid handsomely not to tell. The payoff wasn't nearly so important in cementing our closeness as the opportunity he offered me to be ten-and-a-half-going-on-sixteen. I knew his high school teachers by such irreverent, but appropriate, nicknames as Duckie, Mousie, or just Old Lady Walters. I sat patiently through poker games and on one occasion was served a beer at a local drive-in notorious for poor enforcement of the liquor laws. Like the childhood tormenting, his teenage rebellion was creative. I shudder to recall that he once fed laxatives to a goat and turned it loose in the high school over the weekend. Perhaps I played Little Missionary to his Prodigal Son simply because I knew I could never flaunt authority with such style.

My husband was an only child. His childhood storybooks have been saved for my sons. They bear no tug-of-war scars. An enormous bag of marbles—steelies, clearies, cat's eyes, aggies, etc., found by our sons in their grandmother's closet—reveals that their father was of the "greedy marbler" species, who had no brother to drop his hoarded treasures in the floor furnace. No wonder he finds what we now call the Cain and Abel Show at our house so unsettling.

The fact is, however, the rivalry has its redeeming features. In the midst of tension, tears, and raw nerves, we can also see glimmerings of affection, filial camaraderie, self-awareness, and even maturity.

Strange as it seems, it is this little brother who intervenes when the older son and I butt heads. "Make Mama happy? Give a kiss?" he says, melting the resolve I had mustered to spank.

Little brother, himself the worldly-wise second born with whom I have special rapport, cannot know what he missed or perhaps what he has been spared by getting a "used" mother. In a year or so we will read *I'll Fix Anthony* by Judith Viorst, a little brother's superb lament and fantasy about what he will do to his big brother when he is six. (For little girls with older brothers, I recommend Charlotte Zolotow's *Big Brother*, or for bossy big sisters, *Big Sister and Little Sister* by the same author.) My baby boy's position as second son allows him to be two-going-on-four. Because his brother told him he looked like a girl in the beautiful hand-me-down Lord Fauntleroy suits, he has worn blue jeans that hang low on his hips since he was eighteen months old. He was a twenty-two-month-old toilet prodigy, thanks to his brother's example. His first sentence was predictably, "Give a turn." The treasures I find in his pockets tell me that he has occasionally been permitted to dig with his brother's pirate gang in the forbidden alley. Only a second-born two-year-old goes around singing, "Popeye the sailorman, he lives in a garbage can." Though he is battered daily, he wakes from his nap—just as I did years ago—saying, "Where's my brother?"

How has a younger brother enhanced my older son's life? If I ask him what he thinks of his brother, I am likely to get a cryptic reply like, "Did you know that he eats the muscles out of his dolls?" We read Charlotte Zolotow's *If It Weren't For You*, a big brother's fantasy of what life would be like without a little brother. The older brother notes that the last slice of cake would always be his, and no one would ever say, "Set an example." He concludes, however, "I'd have to be alone with those grownups."

Without the second child, I might not have seen the beginning of a conscience so early in the first one. Contrition is not one of his strong points, but I have seen him cry when he has committed a deliberate act of violence such as shoving his brother, tricycle and all, head first into the street. "Are you crying because you know you'll be punished?" I ask. "No," he hiccups with sincere remorse, "he's my brother and I pushed him and a car could have hit him."

Occasionally when other children come to play, someone will accuse his little brother of foul play. I am amused to hear the four-year-old come to his sibling's defense: "He didn't kick you. He never kicks anyone unless I tell him to."

His nursery school teacher complains to me that on Fridays my older son refuses to join the story circle. He sits with face pressed to the sliding glass door that looks out on a playground because he knows Friday's the day his little brother is at ''baby school'' and will appear on the playground. ''Pssst, Drew,'' the older brother beckons with stage whispers until little Drew's nose is pressed against the glass door outside. ''Don't come over here. You have to go play with your baby friends.''

A giant helium-filled balloon that has given the two-year-old much pleasure gets popped as the two boys are dueling with my electric mixer beaters on a cold, rainy afternoon. I listen in amazement as my older son, instead of taunting, ''Nyah, nyah, crybaby,'' imparts the verities of life to his wailing brother. ''You know, Drew, every balloon has to pop. I never had one yet that didn't.''

*—February 1975*

# HIGH ROLLERS

Texas is famous for its rich and powerful oilmen and ranchers, but much of the state's power has passed into the hands of the lawyers, bankers, and businessmen who are much more astute in manipulating the complexities of the modern economy. For sheer concentration of power over the lives of everyday Texans, no single person or organization can compete with the giant Houston law firms that dominate the business life of our state. Griffin Smith, jr.'s "Empires of Paper" brings these lawyers into the light of day for the first time.

Naturally, one of these firms represented Oscar Wyatt in his rags-to-riches rise as head of the giant Coastal States Gas Corporation. Wyatt is one of the best examples of another Texas myth, the wheeler-dealer. Paul Burka's "Power Politics" explores in telling detail how Coastal States helped bring the energy crisis home to Texas, complete with blackouts in Austin and San Antonio and a darkened State Capitol building.

"Diamonds Aren't Forever" by Harry Hurt III amply illustrates the personal struggles that lie behind business success. His account of the battles within and without the Zale family as its giant diamond business foundered in stormy waters could have been a Shakespearean play.

The overwhelming size of Texas has been the source for many of its fortunes, now including the fortunes of the airline companies that enable us to get from one end of all that land to the other. So lucrative have been the air routes within the state that for years the two established airlines, Braniff and Texas International, waged a furious campaign against an upstart newcomer, Southwest Airlines, which planned on undercutting their prices by serving *only* Texas. That sort of competition would never happen in Indiana, and James Fallows' "The Great Airline War" is a full account of what happens when Texas companies take off the gloves and hit the mat.

*Illustrated by Tom Ballenger*

# DIAMONDS AREN'T FOREVER

## by Harry Hurt III

---

*How a penniless immigrant built the world's largest diamond empire from a tiny Wichita Falls store, and how the scandals and feuds of the next generation might turn it to dust.*

---

On a streaky blue morning in early 1976 Shearn Rovinsky curled up in the backseat of his car to die. Rovinsky had been a member of Zale Corporation's ruling family for seventeen years, a mathematical whiz recognized for his brilliance as the company's chief financial officer and number one money manager. He was fond of saying that he loved Zale as much as he loved his own life and family. But on this particular work day Shearn Rovinsky did not make the usual drive from his suburban Dallas home to the headquarters of the world's largest retail jeweler at Diamond Park. Instead, he waited until his wife had taken the children off to school, then closed his garage door, started his car, and climbed into the backseat, apparently hoping to succumb to the sweet sleep of carbon monoxide poisoning. In a suicide note left for Zale chairman Ben Lipshy, Rovinsky promised to "take the company's secrets . . . to the grave."

Ben Lipshy had already been in his office for nearly three hours when Shearn Rovinsky decided to kill himself. Famous for arriving at the building at 5:30 every morning, Lipshy had spent much of that time in consultation with his nephew, company president Donald Zale, the 43-year-old son of Zale's founder, Morris B. ("M.B.") Zale. The day before, Donny and Ben had confronted Rovinsky about some $600,000 found missing from the corporation's accounts after a week-long investigation prompted by a Rovinsky assistant. After several controversial meetings and much circumlocution, Rovinsky had finally been given 24 hours to come up with a satisfactory explanation for the missing money.

Now Rovinsky's time had just about run out, and he had not shown up at the Zale's Building. With M.B. out of town, Donny and Ben had to decide what to do. Ben kept dialing Rovinsky's home phone number and kept getting a busy signal. Then the maid answered and said no one was home.

Meanwhile, Ben Lipshy's son Bruce, the company's 35-year-old senior vice president, was engaging in some decision making of his own. The day before, Bruce had discovered that 26-year-old Shari Oliver, a svelt part-Indian "executive secretary" with whom he had been having an affair, had also been having an affair with the hapless Rovinsky. About 8:30 on the fateful morning of February 6, Bruce summoned Shari to his eighteenth-floor office.

According to her recollection of the meeting (Lipshy will not discuss it), the younger Lipshy lit into her the moment she came into the room.

"I know, baby, I know!" he shouted. His eyes were boiling—not with tears but with liquid rage.

"I don't understand," Shari answered.

"I know who your boyfriend is!" Bruce shouted. "And this morning we fired him."

Then according to Ms. Oliver, Bruce began to scream. "Just get out!" he yelled. "Tell your boss you have to be home with your baby. Anything. Just get out!"

Bursting into tears, Shari turned and ran out of the office. She frantically telephoned her embattled "boyfriend" to see if what Bruce had told her was really true.

But this time Rovinsky himself answered the phone. His suicide attempt had failed as miserably as his accounting acrobatics. Clumsily, luckily—some would later say, calculatingly—he had rolled up the windows on his car, creating an air bubble that kept him alive until his maid discovered him. Neither Rovinsky, nor the company's secrets, would make it so easily to the grave.

Meanwhile, back in the glittering Zale headquarters building, the tension mounted. There were guards everywhere, especially around the bookkeeping vault on the fourth floor, where no one was allowed in or out. Every employee in the building knew something was wrong, but no one was sure what it was. The initial rumor was that the company's chief financial officer had been caught with his hand in the till and had fled to Brazil. Then, around mid-

*Harry Hurt III is a Harvard graduate and an associate editor of* Texas Monthly. *His profiles of Texans for* Texas Monthly *include Ben Crenshaw and Leon Jaworski.*

morning, a more somber rumor arrived: Rovinsky had not flown off to Brazil; he had apparently committed suicide instead.

Up on the eighteenth floor, Donny, Ben, and Bruce and their legal and public-relations counsel prepared an urgent press release announcing that Sol Shearn Rovinsky had been fired for "violation of company policy." By the time that news came out, Shari Oliver and Rovinsky were on their way to her mother's home in Oklahoma, where they could get away from the crisis and where she could help prevent another suicide attempt.

As the day wore on, several other family members swung into action. While Shearn's wife, Linda Burk Rovinsky, grappled with a severe bout of anxiety, Ben Lipshy's daughter, Joy Burk, picked up the three youngest Rovinsky children at school and took them back to the Rovinsky house on Yamini. By the time the Rovinsky's eldest son Kirk, 16, arrived home, he found the house under the command of his uncle, Larry Burk, Joy's husband. According to Kirk's recollection, Burk informed him that his father had been caught stealing and that his whereabouts were unknown, but that he had probably killed himself. Then Burk told the boy that he, Burk, would be head of the household thenceforth, adding solemnly, "Your father's not part of the family anymore."

That, in the eyes of Shearn Rovinsky, was the unkindest cut in the whole affair; the blow which would ultimately compel him to attack his own family—one of the state's most powerful—in the harsh glare of the public limelight. But it was the family that would move first.

The next day, Bruce Lipshy personally filed charges of criminal theft against the still-missing Rovinsky with the Dallas County district attorney. Returning to Diamond Park to clean out Rovinsky's desk that afternoon, Bruce confided to a friend that "this is going to hurt us"—meaning, of course, the family members still in good standing—"as much as anyone."

That turned out to be one of the grossest understatements in the 53-year history of the company. For when he was finally brought to trial last fall, Rovinsky was acquitted of the theft charges. Worse, his attorneys, George Milner and Billy Ravkind, cleverly turned the tables and put the Zale Corporation on trial. They alleged that Rovinsky had taken the $600,000 as "secret compensation" for carrying out a whole series of multimillion-dollar tax evasion and secret payment schemes that permeated the company's recent history. In the course of the trial, many of these charges were substantiated in whole or in part by documentary evidence and by the admissions of top Zale Corporation officers and employees.

Suddenly, the house of Zale was rocked to its foundations. The company's stock plunged from $25 a share to less than $12. The IRS and the Securities and Exchange Commission (SEC), already aroused by Rovinsky's pretrial allegations, spurred on separate criminal and civil investigations, while three groups of outside shareholders pressed lawsuits aimed at removing the company's top management. The corporate family structure *Fortune* magazine once described as "nepotism that works" was threatened with virtual annihilation.

That threat is still pending. But the Rovinsky affair has not simply been diminished by its revelations of corporate misdeeds and amorality—those, by now, are fairly common stuff. Rather, the most interesting aspect of the story is the glimpse it has given of this exceedingly powerful Jewish family and the unique institution they have created.

Zale Corporation is not, as many still believe, just a chain of cheap jewelry stores. It is the world leader of its industry, a $650-million-a-year multinational conglomerate that owns a full line of jewelry houses from the discount level to the "carriage trade" level of its Corrigan's stores in Houston, its Lambert Brothers stores in New York, and its Bailey, Banks & Biddle stores in Philadelphia. Zale also owns 100 drugstores under the Skillern's name, the Karotkin furniture chain, newsstands at Dallas–Fort Worth airport, the Butler Shoe Company, the Cullum and Boren sporting goods chain, and the Sugermen military insignia and optical/electronics company of San Antonio; until recently, it also owned the Levine's department store chain. Zale has family, business, and political ties that run deep into the heart of the Texas establishment, linking it to such institutions as Republic of Texas, the state's second-largest bank holding company; Commercial Metals, one of the state's twenty largest corporations; and both major political parties. And despite being a "public" corporation it remains 50 per cent owned by the family and family friends who operate it, a corporate anachronism that has made millionaires of them all.

To understand the tragedy that has befallen the house of M.B. Zale, you must understand what it means to be a member of this family. Especially a member who, as the Yiddish phrase goes, knows the *emis*—the "real truth." The real truth about the Jewish merchant heritage and the small-town prescription drugstore beginnings. The real truth about the decision to go public and the drive for bigness. The real truth about the sort of pace and practices required to keep Zale Corporation the world's largest and most profitable retail jeweler.

As in so many great family stories, the *emis* begins and ends with the father, the family patriarch, Morris Bernard Zale, "Mister M.B." Physically, M.B. Zale is not a very imposing man: he is short and skinny, with dark bushy eyebrows, steady gray-green eyes, and enormous ears set on a balding, angular head, hardly the sort of figure one would expect to play godfather to a great dominion. But the range of his mind and the intensity of his energy are astounding. At the age of 76, he has been in "official" retirement for half a decade; his brother-in-law, Ben Lipshy, his son Donny, and, increasingly, his nephew Bruce Lipshy, have taken over the corporate family leadership—at least in title.

But there is no question that M.B. still passes on every major corporate and family decision. He still logs tens of thousands of miles in world travel each year; he still knows his business from top to bottom. Nearly every employee in his company, nearly every member of his family will stand hand on foot to please him, for despite his advancing years, Morris Zale is still *der mensh*—"the heavy."

Some time around 1905, Morris' father, Sam Zalessky, managed to immigrate to America, thanks to some money sent to him in the Russian-Polish border town of Shereshov by his wife's brother, Sam Kruger. Kruger had begun a budding jewelry business in Fort Worth and Sam Zalessky went to work for him in the family store. The jewelry business was a natural one for Jewish immigrant clans like the Krugers and Zalesskys. Excluded from many European countries and barred from owning property in others, Jews had traditionally gravitated toward portable professions and toward merchandise with high per-weight value. Diamonds and jewelry were more dependable and more widely negotiable than the fluctuating currencies of Europe. They were of incontrovertible worth and were easy to carry from place to place, small enough, in fact, to be smuggled out of a country in one's teeth. So just as they had become the continent's moneylenders, hoarders of gold and silver, Europe's Jews had also come to dominate the trade in precious gems. When they immigrated to America, they brought their acumen and expertise, even though they often had to leave their merchandise behind. Three years after coming to America, Zalessky had saved enough to send for Morris and his mother.

Morris was not yet eight years old when he first crossed the Atlantic on a ship crowded with huddling women in tattered old scarves and shawls and bearded men in high hats and dusty black coats. Had he been capable of grasping the history of the time, he would have known himself to be a part of the third and largest wave of Jewish immigrants to America, one of the lowly Eastern European Jews that even the Sephardic of the first wave and the German *doktors* and *meisters* of the second wave disdained and called "kikes."

If the Zalesskys had chosen to stay in the ghettos of old New York, Morris might well have been exposed to these internecine class distinctions at an early age and found his horizons limited accordingly. But after passing the dreaded medical tests on Ellis Island, Morris and his mother moved quickly through the pushcart-crowded streets and boarded a train for Texas.

Here, the Zalesskys would encounter their share of prejudice, but conditions were generally more benign than in the East and the class structure more flexible. There was also a considerable and fairly well-accepted Jewish presence in the state, particularly in the booming city of Dallas. In fact, by the late 1890s great families like the Titches, the Sangers, the Harrises, and the Goettingers had already forged lasting business ties with the gentile establishment and were conducting their own high-society affairs with as much lavishness as any *goyish* debutante ball in town. Among Jews themselves, the basic distinction was between city and country, between those who were still close to the rural rag-seller tradition and those who felt that their income and urbanity put them above and beyond the indignities of the past. If Dallas was the center of the new Jewish affluence, Fort Worth, where Morris' Uncle Sam Kruger had his store, was the "jumping-off place" for those who had yet to make their way. As Morris would recall years later when he recounted his life to University of Texas oral historians Floyd Brandt and Joe Frantz, "There was no place else to go."

For half a dozen years, young Morris went to school in Fort Worth and spent afternoons and weekends at his uncle's store. Then, at thirteen, he quit school and went to work full time. He soon became a traveling salesman, peddling his uncle's wares down the dirt roads and in the small towns of North Texas, places like Ranger, Brackenridge, and Burkburnett, villages light-years removed from Shereshov.

In 1922, the oil boom hit Graham, and Morris, by then a veteran salesman of 21, moved to town and opened a small drugstore that sold everything from potions and poultices to jewelry and Victrolas. These early days in Graham were the days of Prohibition, and the ambitious young merchant also engaged in the lucrative "prescription" liquor trade. Indeed, while men like Joseph Kennedy made their family fortunes bootlegging on the East Coast, Morris chipped away selling booze by the pint bottle; conveniently, there was a "prescribing" doctor in the office above the store.

The Ku Klux Klan, however, had come back strong in the twenties, and the new objects of its bigotry were not just blacks, but Catholics, Jews, and immigrants. As elsewhere, the Graham KKK had so cloaked its hatred in the robes of respectability that even the town's most prominent citizens were proud members. Law-abiding folk by day, by night they would burn crosses on the hill east of town. The message to an immigrant with a funny name and one of only two Jews in town was clear. But by this time, Morris had accumulated several debts and was forced to auction off all his merchandise before he could leave town. Fortunately, Uncle Sam Kruger was vacating an old storefront in Wichita Falls. Though he still made a small profit on his Graham venture, the experience would rankle him for many years to come.

Better days were soon at hand. On March 29, 1924, Morris took the small profit he had made in Graham and with his brother, William Zale, and Uncle Sam Kruger incorporated the first "Zale" jewelry store at the corner of Eighth Street and Ohio Avenue in Wichita Falls. It was the tiny flagship of what was destined to become a huge corporation.

Setting the style and substantive principles that would guide him into the future, Morris vigorously attacked his new business, spending virtually every waking minute in or around the store. For him, there was no separation of work and play. He lived and loved every aspect of his trade and insisted on knowing everything about every transaction. At the same time, he never succumbed to the "love of merchandise" for which he often castigated his uncle. Morris recognized that an interest in jewelry stores and an interest in what he sharply termed "museums" were not compatible: no matter how pretty it was, the merchandise had to be moved. Thrifty to the point of being penurious, Morris kept a tight rein on each expense. "This is not a business of genius, it is a business of detail," he said then and says again now. "We make pennies, not dollars."

Of course, it took more than penny pinching, toughminded merchandising, and blind energy to do the sort of things Morris Zale was beginning to do, and it was during these early days in Wichita Falls that he got the inspiration upon which the greatest share of his future success would rest—the idea of selling jewelry to modest-income customers.

At the time, most jewelry stores were like the ones owned by Morris' uncle. They were austere, formal places that invited only the so-called "quality people." To the common man, these stores were as forbidding in atmosphere and clientele as they were in price. But Morris Zale changed all that, starting with his uncle's old Wichita Falls location. He introduced into his jewelry store something of the atmosphere of his old drugstore back in Graham. Keeping the checkered tile floor swept but uncarpeted, he filled the cabinets and shelves not only with bracelets and gems but also with pots and pans, gifts, and specialty goods. Thanks to these "traffic items" and to services like watch and eyeglasses repair, the store became a place that could attract people for more than a once-in-a-lifetime purchase like a wedding ring.

Morris also did his best to make his customers feel wanted and needed regardless of their means. More, he helped enhance their means by selling his merchandise on liberally arranged terms of credit. Morris Zale was not the world's first credit jeweler—in fact, he claims to have learned the technique from the Chicago diamond suppliers—but, more than anyone else, he introduced and popularized the idea at a retail level. He and his brother would go out of their way to keep a customer, shaving the price, extending the due date, doing whatever they could to build up a broad-based and faithful clientele.

It was also during this period that Morris Zale began building an even greater commercial asset—his family. In 1924, he married Edna Lipshy, the dutiful daughter of another East European Jewish immigrant couple who were struggling to make a living selling vegetables from a push-cart in Wichita Falls.

From the outset, their union produced growth for the company and prosperity for the two families. Quick to recognize the genius of their brother-in-law, four of Edna's seven brothers and sisters soon went to work for Morris or married people who did; the only male sibling in the Lipshy family who did not enter the Zale business wound up in an insane asylum. Together, they expanded the sales force, while keeping the enterprise family controlled, something that would continue to pay inestimable dividends as the company and the family grew larger and larger. Asked years later to explain the reasons for his enormous financial success, Morris Zale would point proudly to his family and remark, "That's really the secret of it."

The Lipshy destined to go the farthest within the company ranks was Edna's younger brother, Ben, the current chairman. Ben began as a clerk and all-around errand boy in the Wichita Falls store in 1926 at sixteen. His starting salary was $16 a month; characteristically, Morris withheld part of the money so that the boy would not squander it all at once. Such precaution proved unnecessary. Ben soon showed himself to be no less thrifty and diligent than his brother-in-law. In fact, he made a point of working even longer and harder than Morris did, often arriving at the store at 4 and 5 o'clock in the morning. "Here was a fellow whose concentration on the job was extraordinary; and whose ability to get the work done with a minimum of discussion was and still is a rare talent," M.B. would remark years later with admiration.

Still, the two were as different as diamonds and gold. Though both displayed a special brilliance, Morris was talkative and personable and blessed with a great breadth of vision, while Ben was quiet and diffident, absorbed in detail. Morris was quick and decisive, Ben was slow and cautionary. They were, in short, wonderful complements to each other. Nonetheless, the true genius of the two was Morris, and Ben was fated to live out his life in M.B.'s shadow.

Ben and Bill Zale, Morris's younger brother, strengthened and broadened the Zale-Lipshy family ties by marrying a pair of loquacious Wichita Falls sisters, Udys and Sylvia Weinstein. Like other great family dynasties, the Zale-Lipshy clan grew tighter and more fiercely loyal as its founders struggled through life together. They cultivated few friends outside their kinship group, in part because of their time-consuming devotion to the family business and in part because a certain introversion was one of the widely shared family traits. Proudly iconoclastic, they set their own standards and style in everything they did. Education is one particularly ironic example. Though the family now contributes generously to support higher education, the first generation of the clan takes pride in the fact that none of them ever finished high school. The second generation, in turn, is proud that only three of their number ever finished college, a fact they delight in underscoring with the prideful reminder, "We don't always do everything by the book."

Morris' attention to this budding family and to his early clientele proved its worth with the onslaught of the Great Depression. After half a decade of steady growth and the addition of two more stores, the family business ran into a half decade of stagnation and a severe credit squeeze. But rather than call in the accounts and risk losing the clientele they had cultivated, the family joined together to economize at every level. Morris cut down on overhead, reduced his sales force, cut back salaries, and allowed his customers more time to settle their accounts. As a result, the house of Zale weathered the hard times and kept the foundation for second and third generations of jewelry customers and jewelry sellers. (Ironically, while Morris Zale recommended credit to his customers, he remained firm in his determination to avoid bank borrowing to finance his business. In fact, after leaving Graham in 1924, he borrowed only once—and that time only $10,000—until 1956, shortly before Zale's went public.)

When the Depression began to bottom out, Morris resumed expanding the family chain across North Texas and into southern Oklahoma. As a rule, he looked for what he then considered "medium-sized" cities and towns, places where the business was brisk but the competition was not too expensive. Bill Zale took on the management of Tulsa, and Ben Lipshy started store number four in Amarillo. The company opened store number six in Springfield, Missouri, then the farthest out-of-state venture; in 1937, Zale's opened its first Dallas store, which was number seven. World War II brought the chain more business than ever, much of it credit sales to departing servicemen, their brides and families. Zale's gained four more stores, completing the group company insiders refer to as "the first eleven."

In 1944, Zale's came to another crossroads. Until then, Zale's had been exclusively a discount jeweler. But the approaching end of the war promised to bring home flocks of marriageable servicemen and a new affluence. There were signs of an emerging petrochemical industry and a population boom in Texas and the Southwest. Morris Zale decided it was time to fill out the company's portfolio, so to speak, by moving into the high-priced jewelry lines. Conveniently, Leo Corrigan's fine jewelry store in Houston was for sale, and Zale's snatched it up.

By 1947, Morris and the family company were doing an annual business of about $10 million a year in three states. They had clearly outgrown Wichita Falls and were badly in need of a headquarters site serviced by a transportation network with arteries linking the chain's major outlets. The logical choice was Dallas. Morris found a home for the company in a two-story building on North Akard Street and led the family flock into comfortable and unostentatious North Dallas neighborhoods. He soon made fast friends with Fred Florence, the Jewish wunderkind of Republic

National Bank, and formed a lasting business relationship; in 1963 he joined the Republic board of directors.

Over the next ten years, Zale's grew nearly fourfold. By the late fifties, company sales had increased to $60 million per year; though this was just a fraction of the total industry sales and the Zale Corporation annual sales of the future, the company was already the world's largest retail jewelry chain. Morris always said that he had no "big plan," that each expansionary move was but a "step next door." But to continue his own metaphor, it did not take Morris long to acquire the whole block and then the whole neighborhood. In the years to come, he quickly took Zale's across the country and around the world, from the towns of North Texas to London, Switzerland, Belgium, Brazil, South Africa, Israel, India, Hong Kong, Tokyo, and Puerto Rico. Perhaps his greatest strength was his ability to adapt to change and reap profits from it. He was, for example, one of the first retailers in the country to computerize his operations, beginning in 1954 with an IBM 350 he saw at an exhibition in San Francisco. When commercial jet service was perfected, he quickly seized the opportunity to go global on a major scale. Later years saw the introduction of regular polygraph tests for employees and the installation of point-of-sale TV-screen computers to allow daily monitoring of business.

Of course, at no time did Morris think solely of business. Along with Ben Lipshy, who with his socially fervent wife, Udys, often acted as Zale's official public figurehead, Morris also devoted considerable time and money to civic and philanthropic activities. Though hardly a giver of Rockefeller proportions, he became a big contributor to and board member of Bishop College, a black college south of Dallas, and he gave generously to area hospitals. In 1951 he established the Zale Foundation, which has a current endowment of $5.5 million. The foundation has supported projects ranging from educational programs to train black ministers, doctors, and lawyers (Morris Zale's scholarship support, was, for example, one of the chief behind-the-scenes factors in the integration of the SMU student body in 1955) to programs that brought milk to starving children in India.

Morris Zale's liberalism has been shaped by continuing personal experience. "Being excluded from a lot of places sort of wakes you up," he told the two oral historians. "I'll tell you frankly that there are very few times that I had any feeling of being wanted in the gentile community. I mean by that socially." (This liberalism has conveniently found no contradiction in Zale's close working relationship with the South African diamond suppliers.)

Politically, Morris Zale has supported one candidate or another as much for business as for ideological reasons, something about which more will be said later. Two of the men he has most admired are Lyndon Johnson and John Connally, the first having hosted him at the LBJ Ranch and the second having spoken to the company's annual meeting. He has also "tolerated" company employees who engage in all sorts of fringe organizations, including some who were in the peace movements of World War II and the Viet Nam War. Though the top echelons of the company always were and still remain occupied by Jewish males, the company reports that about 15 to 20 per cent of its current employees and 33 per cent of new hirings are blacks and other minorities. Women, however, have not fared quite so well, a fact some attribute to attitudes of the Jewish males who

run the company. Traditionally, females have composed the vast majority of the direct sales force in the Zale's stores, but they are seldom found in top managerial or executive positions.

The very top positions are reserved for the family, but Morris always took pride in evaluating his relatives' abilities with cold objectivity, regardless of the repercussions. One good example came at still another company crossroads, the great reorganization of 1957, when Morris decided to take the company public and move up from president to the newly created post of chairman of the board. Instead of passing the presidency to brother and cofounder Bill, he gave the job to Ben Lipshy and kicked his brother upstairs. Despite all the single and double family ties, the decision created something of a family schism. According to company insiders, Bill Zale's opinions continued to be heard and often acted upon by the highest family councils, but he was no longer among the family power brokers. His sons, meanwhile, worked only briefly for the company, then left to pursue other careers and enjoy their considerable inheritances.

About the time of this schism two portentous young men joined the company ranks. One was Morris Zale's second son, Donny. An SMU graduate who did a brief stint at Texas A&M, Donny never displayed his old man's absorptive intelligence. But unlike some of his cousins and siblings, Donny always showed tremendous drive and seemed to have a crystal-clear vision of his corporate destiny. He began working in Wichita Falls store number one at the age of six and continued to work for his father on Saturdays and on afternoons after school when the family moved to Dallas. Short and stocky with a wide, rounded face, he had already developed a sharp and abrasive self-confidence and outward toughness by the time he joined the company full time in 1954. Though he twice failed the certified public accountant's examination, one of Donny's first major jobs was supervising the accounting department. His task: to set up the bookkeeping principles that would guide the company through the coming boom of the sixties. It was an assignment that would one day come back to haunt him.

The other ominous young figure to enter the corporate-family picture during the fifties was Sol Shearn Rovinsky. Also short and bespectacled, but with a lean, delicate build and crafty, arched eyebrows, Rovinsky was the opposite of Donny Zale in almost every way. The son of an executive with Southwestern Life Insurance Company, he had been a publicly acclaimed whiz kid. He had a photographic memory that had enabled him at the age of six to memorize the Gettysburg Address from a first reading. But his true gift was for numbers. Given a person's birth date, he could tell him on what day of the week he was born—*instantly*. These and other numerical talents won him recognition in *Ripley's Believe It or Not* before he was ten years old, but because of constant requests to perform, they also gave his personality something of a beating. By the age of seven, young Shearn was under doctors' orders not to display his talents without parental permission.

Rovinsky attended Highland Park High School in Dallas, where he was a classmate and casual acquaintance of Donald Zale. After graduating from the University of Texas, he did a brief stint as an officer aboard the aircraft carrier *Yorktown*, then joined the IRS as a special agent and went to school to get his CPA certificate. In 1958, Rovinsky married Linda Burk, the daughter of a successful Dallas blue-jeans manufacturer. Linda's brother Larry had recently married Joy Lipshy, Ben's daughter, and in short order, Linda made the appropriate connections for her new husband. In the fall of 1959, Shearn joined his former schoolmate Donny Zale in the company's accounting department. As time went on the Rovinsky's and the Lipshy family's offspring would have children the same ages, send them to the same private schools, and celebrate the traditional Jewish Seder in each other's homes.

Not too suprisingly, this cozy family relationship has been utterly destroyed by the recent allegations and counter-allegations. But remarkably enough, both Rovinsky and present and former Zale loyalists paint similar portraits of the company and its ruling family as they fought their way to power and prestige in the sixties and seventies.

Zale's struggle to modernize and grow—the period insiders refer to as the company's ''phase two'' of growth—actually begins with two critical executive decisions of the late fifties. The first was the move in 1957 to become a publicly held company. Oddly enough, the decision was not primarily motivated by the need to raise money from equity markets; in fact, the company was so underleveraged that it could easily have raised as much money from banks and other sources as it did from its stock offerings. Rather, the main reason for going public had to do with the family and with taxes. Morris Zale and the other senior members of the clan were advancing in years and could easily envision their fortunes—which already amounted to several million dollars apiece—being decimated by estate taxes. By converting their personal assets to corporation stock and keeping the majority of stock for themselves, the Zales and Lipshys could protect themselves and their descendants and still retain control over their company. Or so they thought. In reality, the decision to go public also brought with it a tremendous amount of exposure, since the corporate family opened itself and the company for the first time to the scrutiny of a host of regulatory agencies. The true implications of this decision wouldn't become apparent until almost two decades later when Zale and Shearn Rovinsky began their fight to the finish.

The second critical decision the Zale company leaders made in the late fifties was to begin cutting and polishing their own diamonds on a large scale. This decision meant they would have to broaden an already existing relationship on the international diamond Syndicate by gaining an invitation to participate in the Syndicate's diamond sales in London. By becoming the only retailer invited to the Syndicate sales, Zale gained an unprecedented privilege and potential. Zale could now acquire the raw materials of its product—the rough or uncut diamonds—directly from the people who mined them, thus eliminating entirely one middleman other retailers could not avoid. Much like today's major oil companies, Zale could add a measure of ''vertical integration'' to its operations by becoming involved in nearly all phases of its industry—from cutting and polishing the stones and manufacturing the jewelry to marketing and retailing.

Being invited to participate in the Syndicate sales also meant joining an elite and arcane fraternity unlike any other business organization in the world, with the possible excep-

tion of the OPEC cartel. The Syndicate consists solely of the seller, sometimes called the Central Selling Organization or CSO. This, in turn, is another name for the DeBeers Consolidated Mines of London and South Africa, which controls about 80 per cent of the world's rough diamonds. Sales are made exclusively on DeBeers' London exchange to some 250 approved buyers about ten times per year. In 1975, the total was 2.5 million carats for a gross of $7.5 billion. The other major world diamond suppliers are the Russians and the Angolans, but neither provides much competition for the South African cartel.

Transactions on the London exchange are based on blind trust. All sales are made in sealed parcels called ''sites.'' The buyer does not even see what he is getting until *after* his purchase is completed. Aside from applying for a certain type of assortment, he has almost no control over the shape or quality of the diamonds he gets. In most cases the seller simply quotes the weight and price; the buyer can take it or leave it. On large stones, however, DeBeers does leave some room for price negotiations.

The shipment and transaction of these diamonds is a matter of mystery and top security. Zale executives often say they do not know how diamonds are shipped and would not tell if they did. However, a company spokesman says that the bulk of the diamonds Zale receives are sent by registered mail, often to a low-profile addressee. For example, when Zale brought the massive 130-carat $1.3 million Light of Peace diamond into the country, it was mailed to M.B. Zale's granddaughter in New York.

Obviously, business of this sort could not be conducted for very long without high ethical standards. The buyer must feel confident he is not being systematically defrauded; the seller must fill his sites with a view toward the needs and capacities of the buyer. Both must maintain impeccable credit and credibility. The Yiddish phrase for these transactions—as well as for deals of trust on all levels of the diamond business—is the salutation ''*mazel und brucha*,'' which literally translates ''luck and blessing.'' More than a Semitic rendition of let the buyer beware, *mazel und brucha* is the industry expression for honor and integrity.

Closely connected with the Syndicate are world diamond trading markets in Antwerp, Belgium and Tel Aviv, Israel, where stones are bought and sold after being acquired on the London exchange. Both Israel and Belgium grant jewelers special tax advantages and minimal reporting requirements that some say amount to officially sanctioned black markets.

Blessed with its special rights of participation in these two special societies, Zale surged into the sixties with a force none of its competitors could hope to match. By the end of the decade, the corporation had expanded from 140 to over 1000 stores and increased its sales volume twelvefold. By 1975, the year before all the trouble hit, Zale had 1700 stores with sales of $607 million per year, and profits of $30 million. Gordon's Jewelers, its closest rival, had only 386 stores with annual sales of $197 million.

Thanks in part to some uncharacteristic skittishness on the part of its founder, the company also became a conglomerate. Worried that the development of the synthetic diamond would rip the bottom out of his jewelry business, M.B. decided in 1963 that the company should begin to diversify. The company's first acquisition was the Skillern's drugstore chain, a symbolic return to Morris Zale's commercial roots in Graham. Soon after, Zale acquired the Butler Shoe Company of Atlanta, the Cullum and Boren sporting goods chain, and the family-connected Levine's junior department store chain. Morris Zale began to think of his enterprise not as a jewelry business but as a pure retailing business, a company concerned with the movement of merchandise, regardless of whether that merchandise be 24-carat pendants, size 14 wash-and-wear dresses, high-heel shoes, double-stitched baseballs, or bottles of mouthwash. Most of these acquisitions proved successful with the exception of Levine's, which Zale managed to sell early this year after ten years of losses totaling nearly $7 million.

In the process, the mechanics of Zale's daily business became infinitely more complex. Zale had to be tuned to the fluctuating world price of gold, the politics of underdeveloped mineral-producing countries, women's fashions, the price of cotton and synthetics, military recruitment projections, trends in sports and leisure, and government food and drug regulations, to name but a few of its diverse considerations. Even the marketing of an ostensibly simple jewelry item like a five-stone diamond cluster ring became a major project. To make only five such rings for each jewelry store would require finding 25,000 diamonds of the same size and weight and color, a task roughly akin to finding 25,000 dollar bills with the same pattern of folds and wrinkles.

Still, selling jewelry was and is the company's true strength, and it was jewelry that formed the backbone for Zale's unprecedented growth in the sixties. While comprising only 62 per cent of all Zale's stores after diversification into nonjewelry retail lines, the jewelry division still accounted for 78 per cent of the total profit.

One of the secrets of Zale's success was its ability to keep innovating. For example, the company brought about a subtle but significant transformation in the basic design of the modern jewelry store by eliminating the long, unbroken glass cases, in which watches blended into bracelets which ran together with rings. Instead, Zale introduced "islands" of cases, which permitted the customer to focus on individual items rather than a glittering undifferentiated array.

Another key to Zale's growth was the company's ability to attract and train top personnel. "Zale's became the West Point of the jewelry business," recalls one successful former executive. "Anyone who wanted to get ahead in the jewelry business wanted to work for Zale's. We were the best, no question about it." Army after army of salesmen, store managers, and executives poured out of the Zale's training programs and filled the ranks not only of the mother company but also of the independent stores and chains around the country. "Probably one-third to one-half of the people you see running jewelry stores in San Antonio, Dallas, and Houston are graduates of Zale's," says one knowledgeable industry source. As one result, Zale's began to nurture the business that nurtured it: barely a billion-dollar-a-year industry in 1960, the U.S. jewelry trade had grown to $5 billion a year by the early seventies.

Much of this growth, of course, was buoyed by the general spread of affluence during those years; jewelry in general and male jewelry in particular became an affordable new luxury. But Zale's exploited this phenomenon with an aggressiveness and perspicacity that left its competitors in the dust. As this new affluence brought a flight to the suburbs, Zale's was quick to spot the trend and seize leasing space in the multiplying new suburban shopping centers. As

was and still is the case with other retailers in other industries needing shopping-center space, the company and the developer would often agree to an "exclusive" contract that prohibited leasing space in the same center to another jeweler. Many of Zale's slower-moving competitors found themselves trapped in the central city where they would often wither and die. (Levit's jewelers of Houston is currently suing Zale's and Gordon's jewelers, which also negotiated "exclusive" contracts, claiming that the contracts amounted to a violation of the antitrust laws and restraint of trade.)

Zale's also learned to use its size to great advantage. Being the world's largest retail jewelry chain, the company was often in a position virtually to name its price on large volumes of merchandise. This was especially true when, for one reason or another, a supplier had to unload his goods quickly. At times, Zale's would be cast in the role of savior, as recently when it picked up several million dollars' worth of Bulova watches. Other times, Zale's would be cast in the role of backbreaker.

But, like the military academy to which it was sometimes compared, Zale's was toughest when it came to its own people and its own internal practices. M.B. Zale's favorite saying is, "Our people are our greatest asset. We could lose everything tomorrow and build it all back if we still had our people." But the way M.B. treated his people was, to quote several present and former executives, "like Dr. Jekyll and Mr. Hyde."

On the one hand, M.B. made sure that he did not create a static organization. Although there was an unspoken consensus that the top positions were reserved for family, everyone always knew there was room to grow and a higher job to strive for. And if anyone had a personal problem, M. B. would attend to it as if the employee were a member of the family. This was particularly true when it came to personal financial problems. Over the years, he and Ben Lipshy made hundreds of thousands of dollars in interest-free loans from the corporate accounts to both family members and regular employees. One nonfamily executive, for example, was lent over $200,000 to cover a stock market loss. Others were lent ten, twenty, fifty, one hundred thousand dollars simply on their word. It is unclear how—if at all—some of these loans were finally paid back.

Salaries, on the other hand, were notoriously low and still are. "The company was built on the backs of the salesmen and the managers," says a veteran of the phase-two growth years. "They had a lot of people working for $15,000 to $20,000 who could have made $35,000 to $40,000 somewhere else."

To supplement its low salaries, the company made skillful use of its profit-sharing plan. Each store was assigned a sales goal and its manager was promised a certain percentage if the goal was met; the same system worked on up the organization chart to the top executive level. However, there was considerable flexibility in the way this program was actually administered. If, for example, a good man in a good location simply had an off year because of some extenuating circumstances, he would often get as much profit sharing as he had the year before. Conversely, a manager who turned in an exceptional record might get no more than the standard share with the assurance that "your year will be next year."

"The new people would get the pie-in-the-sky treatment," says one Zale's veteran. "M.B. would point to the senior people at the company and brag about how much profit sharing they had built up. And some of the people who had been with him for a long time really did make themselves millionaires or close to it. Once you'd been around for awhile and had built up a certain amount of profit sharing, it was harder than ever to leave."

Just as in the old Wichita Falls days, M.B. and Ben continued to work sixteen-hour days six and often seven days a week. Both zealously guarded their health, but their only major exercise consisted of taking early-morning walks, often as much for thinking as for stretching their legs. Habitually the first ones to arrive at work in the morning, they expected the same sort of singular devotion from their hirelings. Neither touched the typical time-consuming executive sport of golf. Indeed, on one occasion when M. B. learned that the manager of a North Texas store was a devotee of the game, he had the "golf shooter" fired at once.

M.B. was also tough when it came to executive perquisites, or perks. Despite its heavy national and international travel requirements, the company owns no private planes and no company cars. The company pays only for a tourist-class ticket for executives. If an individual wants to fly first class, he must pay the difference. M.B. and Ben, however, always fly tourist. Though their enormous stock holdings make the gesture purely symbolic, M.B. and Ben have always insisted on paying themselves very low salaries relative to their status and positions; the highest either has ever earned is $100,000 a year. The highest salary in the entire company today is only $110,000. This goes to Allen Ginsberg, the company's resident diamond expert.

"I know it sounds like a Jewish stereotype, but the Zales and the Lipshys have always been tight and they still are," says one former employee. "It's not that they're cheap, it's just that they happen to be extremely thrifty."

That, still, is an understatement. Even as the company's yearly volume swelled into the tens and then into the hundreds of millions, M.B. maintained his practice of checking every invoice the company paid. Though he eventually had to delegate some of the responsibility to others, M.B. will still make periodic invoice checks for a whole month at a time. "You used to get a personal call from M.B. if you so much as bought thirteen light bulbs instead of twelve," recalls one Zale veteran. "I know because that is exactly what happened to me. The boss wanted to know why I needed that extra bulb. When we would move into new stores, he would always remind me to buy used fixtures instead of new ones. 'You save five thousand dollars that way,' he'd always say."

Similarly, M.B. was never sentimental about closing stores that did not do well. "That's one of our great strengths," he has been quoted as saying. "The only thing we're sentimental about is cash."

This was particularly true at tax-paying time. Like all other forms of saving, saving on taxes was always a number one priority at Zale. And again, the impetus came from M. B. A citizen of the world, he has never been awed by the divine right of governments to exact tribute. This attitude has been traditional among Jewish jewelry merchants since before they moved the world jewelry trading center from Holland to Belgium in the wake of a decision by the Dutch to impose a tax on the industry.

One of his most ingenious tax-saving gestures was to develop a unique identity and structure for his rapidly modernizing corporation. The basic idea was consistent with Morris' vision of his company as being actually two things at once—a unified mother corporation and a loose confederation of independent and self-sustaining individual stores. With the help of a longtime family accountant named Joe Bock (one of Shearn Rovinsky's predecessors), Morris translated this vision into a legally convenient form known as "multiple corporations," a structure fairly rare among major retailers. While Sear's, Penney's, and McDonald's, though also composed of a multiplicity of individual outlets, were considered solely as unified corporations, Zale tried to get the best of both worlds. The first 11 stores and the company administration acted as a holding company for the other 1700 stores in the various merchandise chains, which were in turn organized into 1000-odd separately incorporated subsidiaries. At different times and under different circumstances, Zale was one or it was many.

The extra accounting work required to run such a multiple-corporation structure was considerable, which was why most other large retailers avoided it. But the possible tax savings this setup afforded were also considerable, and no one was better at exploiting these possibilities for tax-conscious Zale than the company's brilliant young chief financial officer, Shearn Rovinsky. Unfortunately for himself, the company, and the ruling family, Rovinsky's tax-saving schemes often crossed back and forth between the realms of the legal, the extralegal, and the illegal, a pattern of behavior that may ultimately be the undoing of them all.

The legal devices Rovinsky used were clever enough. For example, Rovinsky saved the company some $300,000 in property taxes by having the Dallas real estate upon which the Zale headquarters building sits purchased by the company's Puerto Rican subsidiary. Similarly, when Zale brought the Light of Peace diamond into the country, Rovinsky saved about $700,000 in U.S. entry taxes by having the diamond purchased by the Puerto Rican subsidiary. Both maneuvers were perfectly legal and brilliant uses of Zale's corporate structure and the special tax advantages that flow from Puerto Rico's status as a U.S. territory.

But Rovinsky also devised and maintained several highly questionable tax-saving and cash-payment schemes. One is the practice of paying many overseas employees—including Israeli executives—cash salaries so they can cheat on their foreign income taxes. The company has done this for years and, according to the trial testimony of Donald Zale, intends to continue it in the future. Why? Because in Zale's view, Israeli taxes are "too high," and direct payment is the only viable method of retaining "top people" in that country. Asked during Rovinsky's trial, "Does that tell us, Mr. Zale, that you would bend the rules when necessary to do your business?" Donny answered with a crisp, "Yes, sir."

The fund that Shearn Rovinsky set up to handle these and other curious transactions has come to be known as the "Belgian fund" because of its location in the benign tax climate of Antwerp. But proceeds from the fund were also used in the United States. During the Rovinsky trial, Zale admitted making some $25,000 in illegal political contributions to undisclosed U.S. politicians with money from the

Belgian fund. The company insisted the donations stopped in 1972. A ledger produced at the trial also showed that numerous withdrawals for unspecified purposes were subsequently made by M.B., Ben Lipshy, Donald, and Donald's brother Marvin, with the largest and latest withdrawal being $175,000 to Marvin in late 1975, just a few weeks before Rovinsky's demise.

Zale also admitted during the course of the Rovinsky court proceedings that the company's Sugerman division, a San Antonio-based military insignia supplier, made unspecified "gifts" of Zale merchandise to certain unnamed military post exchange buying agents in the late sixties and early seventies. The company said that upon discovering the "gifts," top management stopped them and made it known that anyone continuing the practice would be terminated. However, Rovinsky now claims that top management was in on it all along. He says that at Donald Zale's request he created a fictitious customer named "Sol Jackson" to whom the merchandise was billed. Donald Zale proposed the name Sol Jackson, Rovinsky says, because he knew that Rovinsky—whose full name is Sol Shearn—hated the name Sol.

Of course, neither the Belgian fund nor the "gifts" to the buying agents are terribly unusual in the corporate world, and the crisis at Zale would not be so severe had Rovinsky's projects ended there. But they did not. Instead, as he told the judge in his first trial, Rovinsky went on to devise a series of tax-evasion schemes, ranging from the simple under-reporting of inventory value to complex but improper deferments of profits. By far his most ingenious ploy was a tax "misallocation" scheme designed to save money on what was known as the surtax exemption. The essence of the scheme consisted of "switching" the profits of high-income stores—the "winners"—with the losses of poorly performing stores—the "losers"—to minimize the number of stores showing a profit of more than $25,000 in a year. Under the surtax provision the stores would be taxed at a reduced rate of 28 per cent, like a small business, instead of at the regular corporate rate of 48 per cent, which applied to stores with over $25,000 profit. The key to Rovinsky's scheme was moving the profits of stores which made over $25,000 a year into stores which suffered net losses. Some measure of the tax-saving potential of this plan can be gleaned from the knowledge that the actual profits of Zale's stores range from the $15,000-to-$20,000 level of its discount stores to the $250,000 level of its Corrigan's stores, a spread which leaves plenty of room for beneficial "misallocations." Eventually Rovinsky systematized his switching scheme with the help of the company computer.

About the basic outline of this "misallocation" plan there is relatively little substantial disagreement between Rovinsky and the ruling family. The dispute is over how extensively and with whose knowledge and authorization these schemes were conducted. Rovinsky claims that the practice began on a small scale way back in 1960 after a run-in with M. B. over the way the tax returns were being handled. According to Rovinsky, the old man in checking the returns had complained that Rovinsky had listed a recently acquired store as having been acquired at a taxable profit, which, because of the value of the store's inventory, was in fact the case. Rovinsky quotes M.B. as saying, " 'The way I look at this, this is one company. I don't understand why one of my stores has to show a profit when my Phoenix store is losing money. As smart as you are, you ought to be able to figure something out.' "

That summer, when Zale acquired a store in Canton, Ohio, at a profit, Rovinsky "moved the profit" into the Phoenix store.

"Canton, Ohio, was the first store where we buried the profits, and there were many more from 1960 through 1964," Rovinsky says. "Every time we made an acquisition, we made a profit. It was all examined in detail by M. B." In 1970, as the surtax exemption was being phased out by the government, Rovinsky reasoned—on the basis of his own IRS special agent experience—that government auditors would not give much attention to surtax matters and concluded the time therefore was ripe to use the computer for a refined company-wide "misallocation" scheme.

By this time, he says, Donny and Ben and several others had become party to the knowledge of what he was doing and smiled upon it and other schemes. Rovinsky claims when he first showed Donny his computerized version of the "misallocation" scheme, Donny noticed a Corrigan's store that usually made $250,000 profit had been listed at only $25,000 profit and told Rovinsky, "This is fine for tax purposes, but I need the *emis* to run this company." Henceforth, Rovinsky says, the company kept two sets of books: one for tax purposes, and another for running the company. The latter set, Rovinsky says, he and other family insiders called "the *emis*."

Aided by computer technology, switching the profits and losses of "winners" and "losers" became easy fun. "We didn't consider tax evasion a crime," Rovinsky recalls. "It was just a big game."

Rovinsky estimates the "misallocations" resulted in a total tax savings of $8 million. He says the total tax liability with penalties for that and other schemes he ran is about $50 million—conservatively. His allegations have received at least partial support from the testimony of his two assistants, Joe Underwood and Ronnie Hickerson, who admitted participating in the "misallocation" scheme since 1971, but said they did not report it to Donny and Ben because "that was Shearn's job." Neither man was fired. In addition, two former high-ranking executives of the company who did not become involved in Rovinsky's trial proceedings have said in interviews that "at least twenty" top people in the corporation were aware Rovinsky was falsifying the company's tax returns; there was, say these sources, a "standing joke" about which set of books the company would show when the tax men came.

Meanwhile, the corporation itself has admitted to $4 million in potential tax liability as a result of the "misallocation" scheme, a figure which admittedly covers only the last four years of Rovinsky's tenure. But while acknowledging an "underpayment" of taxes may have occurred, M.B., Donny, and Ben all deny ever knowing about the "misallocation" scheme or any special computer printout for the purpose of tax evasion, and claim further that any improprieties that may have occurred ended with Rovinsky's dismissal.

They say Rovinsky devised and authorized the tax dodge schemes entirely on his own. He had demonstrated his brilliance as an accountant and they had complete faith in his honesty and ability. They claim that the only computer printouts they saw were ones which accurately reflected the profits and losses of their stores. They say they did not review the printout Rovinsky devised for tax purposes or compare that one with the printouts they used to operate the company, and add that by the time Rovinsky began to perpetrate his illegal schemes, Zale was too big and had too many subsidiaries for M.B. or anyone else to check everything. Taxes, according to the ruling family, were Shearn Rovinsky's responsibility. "Everybody's been asking us about the *emis*," Donny said in a recent interview. "I never heard that word used for one of our printouts until the trial."

This dispute will eventually have to be settled by the IRS and the courts, but as the corporate family well knows, there is almost no way Zale can emerge unscathed. If charged and found guilty of criminal fraud, the Zales and the Lipshys could face not only further disgrace and humiliation but also stiff fines and prison sentences. Even if they are not held responsible for the actual commission of crimes, the corporate family still stands to lose severely. Just as Rovinsky's theft trial led to a host of apparently unrelated disclosures about Zale's questionable activities with the Belgian fund, these allegations about the tax schemes could lead to still further embarrassing disclosures about other areas of company behavior. "Rovinsky's charges are just the tip of the iceberg," claims one former employee who had working access to the company's books.

Whatever the *emis* really is, both sides agree that this period in the company's history is filled with other examples of the tension between the family ways and the ways of the outside world, between tradition and modern corporate life. Perhaps the best sign of the times was the move from the old two-story building on Akard Street to the glittering bronzed-glass eighteen-story headquarters building on Stemmons Freeway. Set at a special angle to the freeway on a cul-de-sac appropriately named Diamond Park, the great toaster-shaped edifice is a prideful sight in the morning sun as it shimmers from gold to black and back to gold. But it is also the symbol of some significant changes in the corporate family and its leadership.

In 1971, as he was approaching the "mandatory" retirement age of seventy, M.B. moved from chairman of the board to chairman of the executive committee, leaving Ben Lipshy to take his place. Donny Zale, Marvin Zale, their cousin Leo Fields, and Marvin Rubin, the highest-ranking nonfamily member, were instructed to choose a president from among themselves. Though only the second-oldest of M.B.'s sons, Donny, then 37, won out.

Donny reacted to his new responsibility by becoming more tough-minded and somewhat more daring. One of the first assertions of his leadership was to change the very nature and identity of the Zale's store. The stores had been typical discount credit jewelers selling pots and pans and appliances alongside bracelets and rings. As Gordon's and other competitors determined that their clientele had become affluent enough for them to abandon the sale of these "traffic" items and become "jewelry boutiques," Donny decided Zale's, too, should become a pure specialty outfit for fine jewelry, "the diamond store," as the company's advertisements now say. "The decision was obvious but it took some balls to get it implemented," Donny said recently, looking back. "The decision to go into diamonds involved dropping about 20 per cent of our business. That's a hell of a risk."

These and other moves Donny made did pay off, but many company insiders who had been loyal to M.B. and to Ben Lipshy found Donny too concerned with proving himself, not only in charting new directions but also in handling people. Much of it they describe as Donny's overreaction to the company's increasing size. He always had to make it clear he was the boss, that he had 17,000 employees depending on him for their livelihood, that he could not be the same old Donny anymore. "M.B. and Ben were hard but compassionate," says one Zale veteran. "Donny was just hard."

The same was said about another family member who joined the top executive ranks in the early seventies, Ben Lipshy's son Bruce. Though born in Wichita Falls, Bruce was a child of Dallas and a graduate of SMU. He did not start out working in a jewelry store like his father, his Uncle Morris, and his cousin Donny, but went to law school and became one of the founding members of a prosperous Dallas law firm before deciding to join the Zale Corporation in 1972. When he came, at 29, he began as senior vice president.

Not surprisingly, Bruce quickly developed a reputation for being arrogant and impetuous, a kid who had gone too far too fast. Like his cousin Donny, Bruce seemed constantly concerned with proving himself. Symbolically, an assistant once gave him a poster, which hung in his office, titled "The Prince" after people around the building began calling him "Prince Bruce." Then he picked up the nickname "Mr. Impetuous" for his tendency to snap at decisions and people. Bruce faced other personal problems as well. Short, stocky, and frenetic, with handsome features and enormous green eyes, he gained a reputation as something of a ladies' man. His standing was not enhanced by a bitter divorce proceeding in 1975 in which he accused his wife of adultery and invoked all the powers of the corporate family, the local rabbinate, and even presumably confidential psychiatrist's files to aid in his custody fight.

But at the corporation, Bruce and Donny began to assert at least something of a modernizing second-generation influence on a company with one foot in the past and the other now firmly in the present. Though the executive committee of the corporation still held its official meetings over lunch at M.B.'s apartment, the coming of Bruce and Donny signaled a new and more impersonal style. M.B. began to stay away from Diamond Park and devoted his energies to foreign acquisitions, while the others began an increasing reliance on management systems and procedures.

As Bruce and Donny and their corporation grew in stature and sophistication, so did their chief financial officer, Shearn Rovinsky. On the surface, Rovinsky seemed a picture of success. He won considerable public praise from his peers and his employers for his apparent magic as a tax man, but he also distinguished himself in other areas. He saved the company $200,000 a year in overhead costs by integrating the accounting systems. He developed a highly accurate cash flow forecasting system and was instrumental in obtaining an A-1 rating from Standard and Poor and a Prime I rating from Moody's. Such ratings pave the way for a corporation to raise money by selling commercial paper to the public. In the tight-money days of 1974 and 1975, the company was thus able to draw on a cash reserve of some $75 million Rovinsky had built up through such sales.

Rovinsky himself was often the first to list these accomplishments, boasting that he was the best accountant west of the Mississippi and east of Jerusalem. But beneath his prideful facade, Rovinsky was a strange and troubled man, a tightening knot of opposites. His delicate build and propensity for almost childlike gestures, expressions, and postures conveyed an impression of weakness. He could sit cross-legged on the floor, simper like a schoolboy, or frown and flail his arms like a bad-tempered brat. He was a follower, not a leader. He craved acceptance in the Zale-Lipshy inner circle and worked hard to get it. He was gullible and trusting to a fault. But at the same time, he was sly and devious, capable of deceiving everyone from his employers and the IRS to his wife and family. Despite occasional diffidence, he was full of sharp prejudices, and he retained a bitter sense of personal superiority over those whose favor he sought. Perhaps more than anything, he was a character of the Walter Mitty style, a fellow who bounced from one fantasy world to the next. The only constant for him was numbers.

As Rovinsky's corporate success increased, he began to make his separate dream lives into separate realities. He began to wear shiny silk suits and flew first class on business trips instead of tourist class like M.B., Donny, and Ben. Privately he disdained them for what he called their "Jewishness."

Always drawn to the mathematics of games of chance, Rovinsky became ever more obsessed by the dream of quick, easy money and began to gamble heavily. He kept a television in his office to watch the sporting events he bet on and held what some have called the "biggest poker game in Dallas" at his house on Yamini every Tuesday night. He would later testify that he bet approximately $50,000 with a net loss of about $150,000 between 1971 and the end of 1975.

In addition, Rovinsky spent plenty of money on his family during these years. He sent his four children to private schools, helped put on a $20,000 bar mitzvah for his son Kirk, installed a pool in the backyard, and supplied his wife, Linda, with tens of thousands of dollars' worth of clothes and jewelry.

Unbeknownst to his family and most of his friends, Shearn lavished thousands more on his girl friend, Shari Oliver, who was simultaneously having an on-again-off-again relationship with Bruce Lipshy and several other boyfriends. Typically, Rovinsky lost his head over his new lover. He bought Shari new clothes, fine jewelry, and a Pontiac Grand Prix, paid the rent on the North Dallas townhouse apartment she shared with her seven-year-old daughter by a previous marriage, and took her on trips to Las Vegas.

Strangely enough, no one seemed to wonder where Shearn Rovinsky was getting the money to finance his swinging new lifestyle, perhaps because only Rovinsky himself knew about all the fragmented sides of it. His wife, an heiress to a blue-jeans manufacturing company, had some money, but she was not all that wealthy, and Rovinsky's take-home pay was only about $50,000 a year. Still, he was depositing hundreds of thousands of dollars in his accounts at Republic National Bank every year and spending the money fairly visibly and with speed. And despite his huge depositing, his personal bank account was almost constantly overdrawn, but with no apparent alarm to his bankers or to anyone else. "I always thought we were rather conserva-

tive," Rovinsky's wife, Linda, would remark after her husband's fall. "Most of the money we spent was my money, but I was never consulted on anything."

Finally, in late January 1976, the high times came crashing down. The beginning of the end came when Rovinsky's assistant Ronnie Hickerson stumbled across an irregular entry on the Zale Corporation books: one of the property tax accounts showed that $10,000 had been paid out. This was unusual because debits to the property tax account were typically odd-numbered figures like $5,768.95; property taxes were never nice round numbers like $10,000, and they were never quite that high. Further investigation revealed that the $10,000 had not been paid as a property tax expense: it had been withdrawn by Shearn Rovinsky. When Hickerson and his assistant Joe Underwood confronted Rovinsky with the entry, he kept giving them double-talk. First, Rovinsky said that the money was connected with a commercial paper transaction and that a check had been deposited to make up the balance. But Hickerson and Underwood discovered that story to be a lie when they learned that Rovinsky did not deposit a check to cover the $10,000 until after they had confronted him about the irregular entry.

Confronted a second time, Rovinsky did something his two assistants had never seen him do before: he broke into a cold sweat. He told Hickerson and Underwood that the money was "for political" and made it known by his stern facial expression that the matter should be dismissed. Hickerson and Underwood were not satisfied. The massive tax "misallocation" scheme they had been participating in for years had never prompted them to report to Donald Zale, but Rovinsky's inability to explain this curious $10,000 entry did. It appeared that Shearn might have had his hand in the till. A week-long investigation of company accounts by Hickerson and Touche Ross & Company, Zale's outside auditing firm, eventually determined that over $600,000 was missing. After a series of hotly contested private meetings with Donny and Ben, Rovinsky was given 24 hours to come up with a satisfactory explanation.

When Rovinsky went home on the fretful night of February 5, he got a telephone call from his brother-in-law Larry Burk, a Lipshy son-in-law not employed at Zale Corporation. "I understand you've committed some horrible misadventures," Burk jibed. Apparently, the word on him was already out. Shearn slammed down the phone without replying. "It sounds sort of silly," he would recall months later. "But that's when I decided I was going to have to kill myself."

No doubt both Rovinsky and the Zale people have at times wished the suicide attempt had been successful. For when Rovinsky came back from his flight with Shari Oliver to face the first set of theft charges against him, he and the Zale family began a legal battle which appears destined to continue until one or both are totally destroyed. The great shock so far is that round one—the first trial on theft charges—went to Rovinsky.

Having already convinced the Dallas County district attorney of the nobility of their enterprise, the Zales and the Lipshys apparently expected to march down to the courthouse and convince the jury, too. But Shearn Rovinsky turned out to be a marvelous witness on his own behalf, with his photographic memory spilling out detail after colorful detail. He claimed that part of the $600,000 he had taken was for political contributions made by his superiors. The rest, he said, was "secret compensation" for his work on the company's tax evasion schemes. When the trial judge ruled Rovinsky could not claim one illegal act as a defense against charges of committing another, Shearn modified his story to say the money was "loans" against a $2 million stock award Ben and Donny had promised him. Rovinsky's attorneys then pointed accusing fingers at Zale; in cross-examinations they concentrated on the family's own record and the questionable activities they admitted authorizing Rovinsky to pursue—the Belgian fund, the $25,000 in political contributions, and insider loans.

Ben and Donny, on the other hand, were terrible on the stand. Though their own well-known penury was perhaps the best counter to Rovinsky's claim of a $2 million stock award, they hemmed and hawed and claimed to know so little about their former chief financial officer and the way the company's accounts were handled that it seemed a wonder they could even sell a watch, much less run a great multi-national corporation. Though by no means convinced of Rovinsky's total innocence, the jury apparently felt that he was at worst just one rascal among many and should not be made to suffer while his masters got away. They voted to acquit.

The impact on the Zale corporate family was devastating. A clan that had built its business and its reputation on honor and integrity—*mazel und brucha*—had had that honor and integrity seriously impugned not only by a disgruntled former employee but also by the legal process. And more was yet to come: already stirred up by Rovinsky's pretrial allegations, the IRS, the SEC, and three groups of outside shareholders were sure to crank up their separate attacks with renewed vigor and credibility. In the meantime, to add insult, the bonding company that insures Zale against theft up to $5 million made it known that they had no intention of reimbursing the company for the $600,000 Rovinsky had been acquitted of stealing.

Characteristically, the family attempted stoicism and restraint: shortly after the verdict was announced, Donald Zale came out of his office, turned to a trusted employee, and simply quoted the cliché heading printed atop his Uncle Ben Lipshy's memo pads: "When the going gets tough the tough get going," then he addressed himself to the details of some routine jewelry transactions. But it was not easy to maintain the front for long, especially not for the older generation of family leadership. For weeks afterward, M.B. Zale wandered around the offices, thinking aloud, "Where did I go wrong? After fifty years, what was my mistake?" And for the first time in their living memories the women of the family feared what would happen the next time they showed their faces in public.

The reaction in the Jewish community was fascinating. A respected member of the rabbinate expressed the apparent consensus when he wondered aloud, "How could Morris not have known what Shearn was doing? This is what everyone cannot understand. Perhaps it is a symptom of size—that one man cannot control everything the way he used to." Among local Jewish businessmen, the reaction was harsher and more cynical. "Frankly, the last place you expect a Jewish businessman to get beat is on the books," said one, "especially when it's people who watch the books as closely as the Zales do. The worst part of it is that they let

themselves get caught by turning themselves in. That implies a serious error of judgment. No matter how bad things are, you just don't blow the whistle on your accountant, because he'll always have something on you, no matter how honestly you try to run your business."

Exactly when Zale's officers will do their explaining to stockholders remains to be seen. Because the SEC finds the company's proxy statement "inadequate," Zale has been unable to hold an annual shareholders' meeting for over a year and a half, and there is none scheduled for the near future.

Apart from the questions directed at Zale, Rovinsky's acquittal and the allegations he made before, during, and after the trial also raised serious questions about the behavior of Touche Ross & Company, the IRS, and Republic National Bank. How had Rovinsky been able to mislead them for so long? Why had they not been able to discover the irregularities, his tax evasion schemes, his profligate spending? Rovinsky's answer was that Touche Ross had "winked at" his tax evasion schemes and that he—the former IRS special agent—had simply used his wiles and experience to convince the IRS that the company's books were in order; he still does not know why the bank did not inquire into his incessant overdrafts. Meanwhile, Touche Ross, the IRS, and Republic National Bank all refuse to comment on the case.

Then came round two. Shortly after Rovinsky's acquittal, he and Ben Lipshy met in a series of face-to-face sessions at the Fairmont Hotel in downtown Dallas. At issue were three points of contention between Rovinsky and Zale: a $55.5 million civil suit the former chief accountant threatened to file against the corporation and the family; the extent to which Rovinsky would cooperate with the shareholders suing Zale or with media people researching stories on the company; and, of course, Rovinsky's testimony to the IRS. Although stressing he wanted to structure their agreement "legally," Rovinsky said his cooperation on this third area would have to be unwritten because "it might be obstruction of justice." Rovinsky said that he could shade his testimony either to exonerate the family or to implicate them in tax fraud.

Lipshy told Rovinsky he was not very interested in the first two areas since he did not consider them much of a problem. But he said that he and the other family members were concerned about Rovinsky's testimony before the IRS. So while maintaining his own innocence, Lipshy agreed to what he considered Rovinsky's "blackmail"; on their third meeting he brought a suitcase with $200,000 in cash. He told Rovinsky that the money was a token of good faith, the first installment in an agreed upon price of $4 million. Somewhat surprised, both at the speed and method of the payment, Rovinsky nevertheless accepted the money and began discussing the details of future payments and the role of their attorneys. He said he could guarantee delivery on his part of the bargain on each of the three points but added that he might have some trouble saving Donald Zale from the IRS. "Donny and I are handcuffed together," Rovinsky said several times. "If I go down, he goes down." But he assured Ben that he would do his utmost to save them both.

Moments later, as Rovinsky left the hotel room and started down the hall, he was arrested by two Texas Rangers and charged with theft by coercion, the new legalese for extortion. It turned out that the Dallas district attorney and the Zale people had been secretly tape recording the meetings and had over eight hours of reel-to-reel evidence to use in making their case. The DA had even been feeding Ben Lipshy the questions to ask in order to separate Rovinsky's proposals concerning the IRS from his proposals concerning the first two areas involving civil matters, because only Rovinsky's "threats" to implicate the Zales and Lipshys in a tax crime constituted an indictable offense.

The affair, then, has come full circle. Rovinsky has been indicted again and the Zale corporate family must again face the prospect of their corporate secrets being dragged into public view as they try to convict and discredit a former family member they now consider a common criminal. The trial is set to begin in Dallas on June 13.

In the meantime, the various government investigative agencies appear to be pursuing the Zale case with great vigor. IRS agents, who will not comment even to confirm who is the subject of their investigation, have taken up a special section of desks in Zale's accounting department and have reportedly read Rovinsky, Hickerson, and Underwood their Miranda rights, an indication that their investigation is for possible criminal fraud, not just possible civil violations. The SEC, which also operates under stringent disclosure prohibitions, gave some indication of the status of its investigation in early April when a Dallas judge granted SEC attorney Mary Lou Felsman's motion to compel Ben, Donny, and Bruce to testify before the commission: Felsman stated that at "every turn" in her investigation employees other than Rovinsky said that questions about Rovinsky's various allegations should be addressed to the three top men.

Should they find violations of federal securities and federal tax laws, both the IRS and the SEC investigations contain the possibility of indirectly forcing the resignation of top management. Short of that, the SEC could also compel changes in management practices and in the composition of the board of directors and force the family to relinquish the power to vote their stock.

As these investigations progress, Rovinsky has been living quite literally from day to day. Linda has divorced him and returned to work at her parents' blue-jeans manufacturing plant, but Shearn has won custody of their four children—unless or until he is convicted of a crime. For several weeks, Rovinsky and the kids stayed at Shari Oliver's townhouse-apartment—where he still paid the rent—but he recently won the right to reoccupy the family house on Yamini, and they have all moved back in. Rovinsky has no job, no visible means of support, and a great deal of litigation to face. "I'm finished in my profession and I'm finished in the Jewish community in Dallas," he says flatly. "No one wants the name Shearn Rovinsky at the bottom of their tax return; the IRS would be on it in a minute." Rovinsky's financial future now rests on continued support from his gambling friends, the civil suit he still intends to file against the Zale people, and the possibility of writing a book about his experiences. He knows full well that he could end up writing his book from behind bars.

But in spite of all that has happened, he still catches himself referring to the Zale family as "we," and he says that his nights are often disturbed by a recurring dream: that he is back at Zale working with Donny and Ben just as in the old days.

Shari Oliver has returned to Dallas after a sojourn in Oklahoma. With Shearn's help, she has found a job at a local jewelry company—not Zale's. She still bursts into tears when she recounts some of the more intimate details of the Rovinsky affair. "You may think she's a tramp because of all the men she's been with," Rovinsky concedes, "but Shari has been more loyal to me than anyone through the whole thing. After this is all over, maybe we'll get back together again. I don't know."

Life is not nearly so difficult for the members of the Zale corporate family, but there have been rumblings. In January of this year, M.B. Zale and his brother Bill officially moved off the company's executive committee to become "chairman emeritus" and "vice-chairman emeritus." M.B.'s oldest son, Marvin, who is head of the company's New York office, and Marvin Rubin, a non-family member who has been with the company since he was sixteen, took their places on the committee. Bruce Lipshy became executive vice president, and Wayne Majors, the highest-ranking gentile, took Bruce's place as senior vice president for administration.

Ostensibly, this titular changing of the guard has the effect of confirming the accession to power of the second generation and the second tier of the company's leadership ranks. M.B. Zale has been staying away from Diamond Park more than ever, but no one believes he has or ever will truly retire. But while continuing to display his frenetic work energy, Morris seems to some to be perplexed and preoccupied these days. "Morris does not want to let go," said a longtime friend. "I think he is still worried about what will happen to his work and how to provide for his succession."

M.B. and the rest of the corporate family fully expect to survive the remaining Rovinsky repercussions, but they have not eliminated the possibility of outside management—the divorce of the family from the family business—even if it is not forced upon them by the courts. However, they would clearly prefer to keep things in the hands of the emerging new generation headed by Donny and Bruce.

The problem, of course, is that neither of them, individually or together with Ben Lipshy, can match the standard set by M.B. At 66, Ben Lipshy is an introverted man who shows the scars of having been too long a protégé. "Decisions don't come easy for Ben," concedes a close friend. As if to remind himself, Lipshy keeps a plaque on his office wall which reads, "Nothing will happen unless *you* make it happen." He is only three years away from the mandatory retirement age, but will likely continue in some high capacity as long as he can.

The new master strategist of the group, to the extent that there is one, is Donny Zale. A disciplinarian in the past, he shows signs of becoming still tougher in the future. He and his cousin Leo Fields recently sold the family-connected Levine's chain, a longtime money loser, and are working on ways to refine what Donny calls a "concept of management which will take us from here to five years from now." That latter project so far appears to be about as vague as it sounds.

Company insiders fully expect that the next president of Zale Corporation will be Bruce Lipshy—probably in three years when his father hands the chairmanship over to

Donny. In the interim, Bruce has been helping with the development of a new management approach as well as supervising real estate acquisitions and working to improve the legal department of the company. He also took a rather active behind-the-scenes role in taping the meetings which led to Rovinsky's second arrest. Some participants and observers blame Bruce for letting the Rovinsky affair get "out of hand" in the first place, charging that in his jealousy and rage over Shari Oliver and in the mistaken belief that Rovinsky had committed suicide, he naively and impulsively convinced his elders to let him handle things, not knowing the sort of "secrets" Rovinsky could and would come back to tell. This Bruce angrily denies. "What were we supposed to do?" he asks. "Not turn him in?" But perhaps more than any other family member he was hurt by the experience of the Rovinsky affair. Nonetheless, knowledgeable family friends insist that Bruce is the only one who may be able to take M.B.'s place as the corporate family *mensh*.

If, and it's a big "if," they are able to survive the repercussions of the Rovinsky affair, Donny and Bruce could maintain the family dynasty well into the next century. There are also about half a dozen younger family members Donny says have a "damn good opportunity for a future with the company," a fact of which the youngsters were apprised not long ago in a special children's meeting.

The continuation of family management, however, has become more vital to the family than to the corporation it created. Insiders say the company is so well conceived, well functioning, and well organized, that it could run itself for years on present momentum even if some disaster wiped out every male Zale and Lipshy before the next sunrise. Before the Rovinsky problems arose, the company was bound for being a billion-dollar corporation by 1980. Now it will likely take two or three years longer. But it also seems likely that Zale will be able to weather whatever tax liability it is destined to pay, even if the figure is as high as Rovinsky estimates. The company's long-term debt is only $21 million, or approximately 6 per cent of Zale's $317 million net worth, which makes the company greatly "underleveraged" by big corporation standards and leaves plenty of room for additional bank borrowing should the need arise. Zale is so far ahead in its basic jewelry industry that no other company can hope to touch it for years to come. As an overall retailer, Zale ranks second in all of American capitalism—behind only McDonald's—in return on sales. It had another record season last Christmas, with one-day volume surpassing $10 million at the height of the rush, and will probably do even better this year.

Not surprisingly, both the corporate family and the employees are doing their best to get Rovinsky behind them and get back to running the company. In the wake of the Rovinsky affair, interested outsiders of all varieties have clamored for more controls, but there has been little response. In what some financial analysts consider an unusual and disturbing move, Zale and Touche Ross terminated their long-standing relationship by "mutual agreement" in March of this year. Then in what one outside observer characterized as "an apparent attempt to clean up their image," Zale managed to get Arthur Anderson & Co., reputedly the most upright of the Big Eight accounting firms, to be the company's new outside auditor. Zale found a replacement for Rovinsky in Richard Mitchell, a former department store accountant from Atlanta. The company also abandoned its multiple-corporation structure with the phaseout of the surtax exemption and has filed the first consolidated tax return in many years. But for the most part, Zale faces the future in exactly the same fashion it has faced the past. As usual, M.B. summed it up best.

"Listen, I want you to know something," he told his kin on the eighteenth floor when he heard the cry for more controls, "Morris Zale, you, or no one else built this business except all the people who are working for this company. Ninety-nine and ninety-nine one-hundredths of our people have never taken a penny. They've given an honest day's work for an honest day's pay. And I don't want anybody walking around here being suspicious of anybody. I can't live being suspicious of people. I'm in the diamond business. I spend a million dollars over the telephone without seeing a piece of merchandise. It's all on faith. And the day this business can't be run on faith, it ought to be closed down."

And that is one *emis* no one will argue about.

*—June 1977*

# EMPIRES OF PAPER

## by Griffin Smith, jr.

*Three of the nation's largest law firms are in Houston. They have kept their awesome power, their pervasive influence, and their closed societies out of the public eye. Until now.*

Three of the ten biggest law firms in the United States are located in Houston. Two of them rank as #3 and #4. In the past few months they have overtaken several Manhattan giants that were doyens of American law for decades before the men who lead the Texas firms were even born; their phenomenal growth shows no signs of slowing down. They are the talk of the legal profession.

These are the Big Three of Houston law:

• Vinson, Elkins, Searls, Connally & Smith (186 lawyers).

• Fulbright, Crooker & Jaworski (185 lawyers).

• Baker & Botts (160 lawyers).

Roughly two-fifths of the lawyers in each firm are partners, meaning they are senior men who own the institution and share its profits. The rest are "associates," younger men who work as salaried employees pending promotion to partnership status. There are currently 68 partners at Vinson Elkins, 69 at Fulbright Crooker, and 66 at Baker & Botts. The only firms in the country that remain larger than the two biggest Houston mammoths are the Wall Street firms of Shearman & Sterling with 226 lawyers; and Dewey, Ballantine, Bushby, Palmer & Wood with 197. No one outside New York is any longer even close: there is nothing in Chicago, Los Angeles, Philadelphia, Boston, or Washington to match them.

Nor is there anything in Texas either. Dallas has five firms over 30, but none over 45. San Antonio, Fort Worth, and Austin trail far behind. Houston lawyers speak of an "amoeba complex" that regularly causes Dallas firms to split into separate factions just as they approach the 50 mark. It doesn't happen in Houston.

Their elaborate structure of specialized departments and

*Griffin Smith, jr., is a former senior editor of* Texas Monthly *and an attorney. He is presently living in Washington, D.C., where he is working as a speechwriter for President Jimmy Carter.*

sections is a far cry from the days of the country lawyer who hung out his shingle on the courthouse square. Though the labels differ from firm to firm, each of the Big Three offers specialists in corporate finance, banking, patent law, utilities, real estate, labor, admiralty, bankruptcy, tax, wills, trusts, and public law. They also have a separate breed of trial lawyers, men who would not think of trading the rough-and-tumble of the courtroom for any sort of office practice.

Houston's Big Three have a national reputation for top-quality legal work. Local lawyers may sometimes joke about the big firms' peculiarities, but no one underestimates their skill at handling the law. A successful small-firm trial lawyer in Houston who opposes big firms in courtrooms all across the country says flatly, "The lawyers I face from the big firms here in Houston are the best anywhere. They're better than Wall Street, far in excess of O'Melveny & Myers [the top Los Angeles firm]. By and large, they've got the finest talent in the country." Even discounted for a little Texas brag, the statement is not far wrong, judging from the opinions of their colleagues in bar associations nationwide.

## THE BIG SIX: A FLOOR PLAN OF HOUSTON LAW

There are those who will argue that Houston law is dominated not by the Big Three but by the Big Five—or, as some would have it, the Big Six. The massive bulk of the giants does tend to obscure the fact that several other firms do a similar sort of legal practice with enough lawyers to make them giants in their own right if they were located in San Antonio, Dallas, or almost any other American city.

The oldest and most aristocratic of these middle-sized firms is Andrews, Kurth, Campbell & Jones, an exclusive group of 65 lawyers with many of the attributes of a social club. Very ingrown, they seldom fraternize with other members of the Houston bar. "It's like a closed fraternal order," says a successful solo practitioner who spent several years in another of the big firms. "They go to retreats together, that sort of thing. They judge your looks and your wife before they hire you—they take only handsome lawyers. They come to work late, and they quit early."

They are also more paternal than others: once accepted into the fold, a young lawyer is virtually assured of lifetime security without the desperate competition that characterizes the ladder of success elsewhere. Andrews Kurth once shared the cream of the Houston practice with Baker & Botts, but after the death of its driving force, Col. Frank Andrews, in 1936, it threatened to wither on the vine.

In the past 15 years, however, it has come back strongly and is now generally regarded as having one of the finest collections of legal ability in the city. It is also considered suffocatingly conservative, even by conservatives. Political involvement is strenuously discouraged, with a conspicuous exception for Hall Timanus, the one-time chairman of the Wallace-for-President forces in Texas. For years the firm's biggest client has been Howard Hughes' Hughes Tool Company. Among their other major clients is the Missouri Pacific Railroad. The dominant figures in the firm today are Mickey West and Harry Jones.

Although the firm of Butler, Binion, Rice, Cook & Knapp comprises 85 lawyers, it has been described as "a small firm that happens to have a lot of people in it." Formed in the 1940s, it has never gone in for representation of large corporate clients whose work requires concentrated teamwork, and therefore has developed into a collection of feudal fiefdoms instead of a monolithic empire. Each lawyer reputedly has his own set of articles of incorporation, for example.

One consequence of this informality, individualism, and lack of tradition has been a certain unevenness in the quality of the legal talent there. The firm has some very able lawyers at the top, and others who are not so able. "They've got 50 per cent good lawyers and 50 per cent bad lawyers, and they don't know which are which," is the harsh judgment of a lawyer in the Big Three. Their attrition rate is admittedly high; good lawyers like Bob Singleton, Bill Wright, and Percy Williams have departed for greener pastures. On the other hand, no major Houston firm has a more distinguished record of elevating its partners to the bench. James Noel, a federal district judge in Houston; Malcolm Wilkey, circuit judge on the U.S. Court of Appeals which heard the White House tapes appeal; and state district judge Bill Blanton, are the most notable. As might be expected from such an individualistic firm, Butler Binion is far more tolerant and flexible about the political involvement of its members. Partners and associates are readily granted leaves of absence for political work. Steve Oaks, a partner, currently serves as Executive Assistant to Lt. Governor Bill Hobby, and Jonathan Day acted as campaign manager for Houston mayoral candidate Fred Hofheinz. Since the November, 1972, death of the firm's remarkable managing partner, trial lawyer Jack Binion, its dominant figures have been B. Hunter Loftin and the "name" partners, Frank J. Knapp, Cecil N. Cook, and George W. Rice. It continues to do vast quantities of probate work, and counts among its clients the Bank of Texas.

With the Big Three, Andrews Kurth and Butler Binion make up Houston's traditional "Big Five." But the explosive growth of another business-oriented firm, Bracewell & Patterson, has stirred talk of a new "Big Six." It has more than doubled in size in the last four years and now stands at 42 lawyers. Plans are being made to hire 15 more next year. "It's a supergrowth firm, just going like crazy," says a wide-eyed solo practitioner. B&P's aggressiveness has clearly (and probably understandably) not met with the favor of the older, larger firms—in particular not with Baker & Botts, from whom B&P alienated the affections of an exceptionally able lawyer, Ed Marston, to strengthen their corporate department. The older firm steadfastly refuses to acknowledge B&P's aspirations to major firm status. They dealt the upstarts a gloved karate chop this spring, when Bracewell & Patterson audaciously offered one of their partners, Hal DeMoss, as a candidate for President of the Houston Bar Association. The Bar Association, it seems, has a cozy tradition that a partner in one of the "big firms" will serve as president in odd-numbered years and someone from the small firms can have the job in even-numbered years. Except for Fulbright Crooker, the large firms never do much with the office, but they guard the honor jealously. Baker & Botts scowled that it was their turn this time, and besides, that Bracewell bunch wasn't a big firm anyway. The contest became a colossal grudge match with both firms fighting for their self-esteem. "The activity at Baker & Botts was unbelievable," recalls one young associate who lived through the experience there. "Nobody seemed to be doing any work for a while—the associates certainly weren't. We were all on the phones, calling people to get out the vote. It was like saving Western Civilization." Baker & Botts' resources eventually succeeded in electing their candidate, Ralph Carrigan, but not without some hard feelings all around. In 1975, B&P may try again, and may win.

Bracewell & Patterson, like Butler Binion, is a firm of uneven quality—a situation due in part to its rapid growth. Unlike the other big firms, it is willing to hire experienced lawyers, men who have practiced elsewhere, to shore up departments that have grown faster than the firm could manage. Politically it maintains a moderate conservative tone that occasionally slides into super-conservatism. With Butler Binion, it shares the distinction of being the only major firm still directed by the men who created it—in this instance, Harry Patterson and the two Bracewell brothers, Fentress and Searcy. The latter is well-known as a former Harris County state senator, present-day lobbyist for the utilities during legislative sessions, and one of the handful of authentically powerful figures in the downtown Houston conservative political establishment. (During the furious last days of the 1971 Legislature's congressional redistricting fight, things came to a brief but firm halt while the members awaited a precinct-by-precinct map of the Harris County congressional districts prepared by Bracewell. It arrived with instructions that the legislators were not to change it by one iota. They didn't.) Among the firm's more prominent clients are the Houston Independent School District and Parker Brothers (the shell dredgers, not the manufacturers of games).

There are some areas of the law the big firms will not touch, principally divorce work, criminal defense work, and plaintiffs' personal injury cases. Mention to a partner in one of the Big Six that you would like him to handle your divorce, and he will react as though he has just discerned an unpleasant odor in the room. In rare instances involving a valued client, a personal friend, or an extraordinarily enticing fee, this rule may be suspended, but for the general public the big firms will politely suggest taking your divorce elsewhere. Percy Foreman is the acknowledged grand sachem in the divorce field.

Criminal defense work is regarded as far, far worse, a sullying pastime if ever there was one, and . . . well, not very lucrative either. There is no point in a criminal defendant's ever stepping aboard the elevator to one of the Big Six unless he happens to enjoy heights, or he has, by the luck of the draw, been assigned one of their lawyers by the court because he is indigent. (This sometimes happens, and occasionally a big firm lawyer whose practice is exclusively civil will acquit himself—and his client—brilliantly. Leon Jaworski at Fulbright Crooker argues forcefully that lawyers should welcome the professional duty of representing accused indigents, and has done so himself in state court cases.) The day-to-day criminal law practice, however, is handled by a largely penurious cross-section of specialists. Percy Foreman and his motorcycle-riding, pipe-smoking rival, Racehorse Haynes, are the most prominent criminal defense lawyers in the neighborhood.

Representation of plaintiffs in personal injury lawsuits is potentially the most lucrative branch of the law, but the big firms are effectively precluded from entering it because they already represent the defendants—manufacturers, railroads, insurance companies—who are being sued. It is a feast-or-famine business, but the feasts are regal indeed. One Houston lawyer who specializes in products liability cases (injuries caused by defective products) has two verdicts of more than $1.5 million to his credit, one over $1.6 million, and fifty over $100,000. The usual fee for successful representation in a personal injury case is about 30 per cent of the recovery, plus expenses. Handsome. The firm of Kronzer, Abraham & Watkins is generally regarded as the top personal injury firm in town, but Joe Jamail, the driving force behind the tiny firm of Jamail & Gano, is unquestionably the leading individual personal injury lawyer.

Any member of a bar association grievance committee will confirm that the vast majority of unethical practices are committed by lawyers on the fringes of divorce work, criminal law, and personal injury work. An observer of the Houston scene laments the reluctance of the big firms to become involved in these branches of the law (or at least in divorce and criminal cases, where no problems of conflict of interest arise). "If the large firms came down and got involved, the overall quality of the work would improve dramatically, I'm sure," he says. "They have the ability and they know what an ethical lawyer is supposed to do. But they're not interested because they're afraid they'll get themselves dirty. It's a vicious circle. And the reputation of all us lawyers, good and bad, gets hurt by it."

A variety of excellent smaller firms specialize in more or less esoteric branches of the law. Dixie, Wolf & Hall is the leader in the field of labor law on the unions' side and Neel & Hooper is highly regarded on the employers' side. Royston, Rayzor, Cook & Vickery is the top admiralty firm; like Butler Binion it is notably proficient at producing federal judges, including Carl Bue, a district judge, and John Brown, colorful chief judge of the Fifth Circuit. Arnold, White & Durkee take their hats off to no one in the patent

law field. Sheinfeld, Maley & Kay is excellent in bankruptcy cases. And there are several outstanding firms approaching 20 lawyers with a more general civil practice, including Hutcheson & Grundy; Childs, Fortenbach, Beck & Guyton; Liddell, Sapp, Zivley & Brown; Sewell, Junell & Riggs; and Foreman, Dyess, Prewett, Rosenburg & Henderson. Each is competitive with the giants, and each feels the pinch on legal business that the big firms' domination causes. There are, in addition, a number of solo practitioners and three- or four-man firms who vigorously defend their way of doing things. Many of them—too many to mention—are quite able. But the Big Three remain the singular, dominant feature of the Houston legal landscape.

# BAKER & BOTTS: DOING THE DEITY'S WORK

For many years Baker & Botts was the largest and most prestigious of the Houston law firms; until the late 1920s it held a virtual monopoly on the city's desirable law business, except for the share claimed by Andrews Kurth. From this commanding position it has now slipped in size to a somewhat distant third. But it has lost none of its classy reputation.

There is something remote . . . foreign . . . even *Yankee* . . . about Baker & Botts, despite its undeniable pedigree in the early Houston establishment. From its earliest days it has been the East Coast's team in southeast Texas, representing Northern brokerage houses, utilities, lumber companies and other absentee landlords, and railroads. From the 1870s to the 1930s, when the Southwest was just another province in an economic system that was centralized in the East, these interests required trustworthy lawyers to cultivate their Texas gardens, and they found them. Baker & Botts grew with its clients. One of their most prized documents is an original hand-written $10,000 retainer from a corporate predecessor of the Southern Pacific Railroad, dated 1872, six years after the law firm was founded in the wreckage of the war-torn South. The partner who handles Southern Pacific's business today preserves it in his files.

None of the other Houston firms has anything like this sort of tradition. It sustains the B&B lawyer in his serene detachment, a detachment that in turn goads other lawyers to mutter sourly of "the Baker-Botts halo" and dream of puncturing the self-righteous aura that surrounds the firm. Ask a member of Baker & Botts about his competitors and you will hear a scornful series of Olympian thunderbolts, two-thirds serious, concerning everyone but Andrews Kurth, the one firm to whom B&B graciously extends full diplomatic recognition because (some say) it is the only group of lawyers not suspected of scheming to lure away a valued client or two. He views his firm as "national" rather than regional, the equal (which in many ways it is) of practitioners in New York or Philadelphia.

Lawyers at Vinson Elkins and Fulbright Crooker are equally convinced of the superiority of their own firms, but they do not express their feelings with the same self-assured air of patrician certainty as the B&B man does. He seems satisfied to believe that his soul remains in Wall Street, Greenwich, Westchester, or Cape Cod, while his body has been temporarily assigned to these steamy Gulf Coast marshes in furtherance of the Deity's inscrutable barristerial design.

A strict sense of legal professionalism is the dominant concept—critics would call it an obsession—at Baker & Botts. More than any other of the Big Three, the firm scorns partisan political activity. Young associates are rigorously chosen for their grades and rank in class (''mental gear,'' says one). It is the firm least likely to be caught in a conflict of interest. It is also the firm least likely to have welcomed retiring Governor John Connally into its fold—in fact, they instinctively wouldn't have done it. ''We have a very formalized set of procedures around here,'' remarked one B&B member. ''To bring someone in from The Outside—anyone—just upsets our traditional way of doing things.'' Secrecy about the firm is almost a fetish; the managing partner never bothered to return calls or acknowledge letters from *Texas Monthly* requesting an interview. Said a young associate: ''It's just imprudent, unwise, and very unBottsian to talk to the press.'' Baker & Botts prides itself on the fact that it has never sued a client over an unpaid bill. From this tight little island the severest censure that can be hurled at another lawyer is the epithet, ''unprofessional.''

Baker & Botts' offices occupy all of the 29th, 30th, and 31st floors (and parts of two others) in Houston's tallest skyscraper, One Shell Plaza. A swift ascent in the building's famous leather-lined elevators deposits the visitor in a tastefully modernistic world of Vasarely wall hangings, glass tables, and stylish furniture. The rich blond wood called *prima vera* that panels the walls grows in just a single Central American country and represents (so the story goes) more than half the total world's supply. It is worth whatever they paid for it. The decor, so different from the traditional dark intimidating law office atmosphere, provides a cheerful feeling of airiness and openness.

Presiding over this legal department store is the most able group of senior partners in the city. Baker & Botts has its share of deadwood at the top—patriarchs who make $250,000 a year and do virtually no productive work—but one of the signal advantages of a giant firm is that it can afford to put its superannuated partners out to pasture as civic front men. (Similarly, lawyers who turn out to be duds can be hidden away as workhorses who never tarnish the reputation of the firm by coming into contact with clients or the courts.) The majority of B&B's senior partners are exceptionally fine, and among them power is more diffused than it is at Fulbright Crooker or Vinson Elkins.

Three men, however, stand out within the ruling executive committee: William Harvin, George Jewell, and John Mackin. Harvin is the mandarin of mandarins—a formidable trial lawyer who acts as managing partner. Associates view him as a frustrated corporate lawyer, a man who would be more at home in the gilded world of conference rooms and Boards of Directors. He keeps his cards close to his vest. Brilliant, poised, and cold-blooded, he first came to B&B as an associate whose mother was the firm's office manager. The anti-nepotism rules that prevented founder James A. Baker's great-grandson from joining the firm that bears his name (he went instead to Andrews Kurth, of course) did not apply to the sons of employees; and Harvin, bred in the firm as few others have been, has become perhaps its most tenaciously loyal leader.

Jewell runs the tax department. Affable and tough, he has leapfrogged over a score of older partners to reach his present position. Ability got him there.

Mackin is regarded as something of an enigma by everyone. A widely read man, he is powerful because his department (the corporate section) is itself so powerful.

Baker & Botts is now in the midst of a more-or-less orderly transfer of power from the men who arrived in the flush years of the late 1920s to those who belong to the postwar generation. (Only a handful of partners came in the 1930s.) Discreetly, they are fighting over the only things they consider worth fighting over: money, control, and the type of clients they will cultivate. Whatever the outcome, one thing is certain: the large clients like Pennzoil, who provide over a million dollars a year in fees, will continue to be taken care of.

# VINSON ELKINS:
# JET-SET SUPERLAWYERS

Vinson Elkins is not only the largest law firm in Texas: it is the third largest in the world and in reach of the top. If Baker & Botts is patterned after Wall Street practice, VE is the closest thing Houston has to the legendary Washington superlawyers. The analogy is not perfect because VE spends the overwhelming part of its time on very traditional types of legal business; but the rest of the time it is political to a degree that no other Texas firm can match.

The offices that sprawl across the 20th, 21st, 22nd, and 25th floors of Houston's First City National Bank building (and parts of two other floors as well) are a surprisingly prosaic setting for the power that emanates from within. The reception area is an elevator lobby unsuccessfully disguised as a living room. Paintings of scenes from ancient Rome and antique cabinets containing finely-bound but unread classic law books line the walls, and the view in either direction is down long corridors oppressively reminiscent of federal office buildings, suffused with a pink light. There is an air of intense activity; young lawyers in white shirtsleeves and respectable ties dart briskly from one door to another, bearing sheafs of papers and intent expressions. In a random five-minute period one afternoon, 37 people passed in front of the reception desk.

Both the building and the law firm are a striking monument to the tenacity of one man, although others have improved upon his original plan. He was James Elkins, a county judge in Walker County, who came to Houston in 1917, allied himself with the young law firm of Vinson & Townes, and founded the City National Bank. The firm's fortunes were the bank's fortunes; they grew together. Judge Elkins had a winning combination, and he played it for all it was worth. He lived to be 93, but the legend of his strong will may outlast him by a century. Said a lawyer who knew him in his heyday: ''There wasn't a man alive who could dominate anything Judge Elkins was in, except Judge Elkins.''

He made all the decisions at both institutions for practically half a century, never bothering to get anyone else's approval. Lawyers work on Saturdays, he said, and a hundred VE attorneys attired in coat and tie duly trooped to their desks each Saturday morning until 1969, almost a decade after the other firms had made such appearances optional.

Lawyers wear hats, he said, and hats were worn. It is conceivable that by the mid-sixties, half the hats sold in Houston were purchased by Vinson Elkins lawyers. A young Kennedyesque associate, new to the firm, vowed he would be damned if he would wear a hat. One day as he was leaving, he chanced to encounter Judge Elkins in the elevator. Granitic stares. Uncomfortable silence. Finally: "Young man, I *see* that you do not have a *hat*." Came the abashed and craven answer: "Sir, I *did* have a hat, but somebody stole it, and I'm on my way out right now to buy another one."

Vinson Elkins, unlike Baker & Botts, built its strength on local business. In the 1930s it was a "four-client firm": the Great Southern Life Insurance Company, Moody-Seagraves, the production end of United Gas Corporation, and Pure Oil Corporation. All but the last were headquartered in Houston. Judge Elkins saw another resource, however, and exploited it brilliantly. The local independent oil men had never catered to Baker & Botts; they always thought it was too close to the big oil companies and Eastern finance. The Judge, wearing his banker's hat as president of First National, gave them loans; VE in turn did their legal work. The firm prospered by carrying them on the cuff while they drilled dry holes and collecting when they finally hit. This neat little arrangement catapulted VE into the big time.

For VE's future, however, the worm in the apple was Judge Elkins' embarrassing penchant for hiring the sons of clients and judges, young men whose legal abilities were not always readily apparent. His purpose was to gain what lawyers call "client access," and it worked for a while: business boomed. But the firm became less and less able to handle that business properly. Enter, then, the second of VE's guiding lights, David Searls, whose influence grew as Elkins aged. Searls served only briefly as the official managing partner, but he was the dominant figure in the firm for over a decade, from 1960 until his death in October, 1972.

Searls, a nationally-known trial lawyer, recognized that the firm needed a transfusion of brainpower. He wrenched the hiring practices around to place a premium on merit. His efforts were rewarded in 1963 when VE swooped down on the University of Texas Law School and carried away practically all the top graduates of a class that is still remembered by professors as the finest in the school's history. It was an event that transformed VE and revolutionized the Houston legal scene. The new recruits set to work devising methods for winning others, and during the remainder of the decade their lavish recruiting program enjoyed success after success.

Searls gave an astonishing amount of authority to these younger men, particularly Harry Reasoner and Richard Keeton. Together they initiated most of the basic reforms that swept through the Big Three in the Sixties, reforms that included sharply increased salaries for new associates, a shortening of the time required to become a partner from ten or 12 years to six, and a wider system of participation to replace ironfisted one-man rule. VE developed a reputation as the most aware and enlightened firm in town.

Searls was genuinely beloved and widely mourned. Today his picture sits on the desk of many partners, a white-haired fatherly figure alongside snapshots of their wives and children. One can talk to Houston lawyers for weeks about their peers, past and present, without hearing an unflattering word about the man.

Since his death, there is a growing feeling that the firm has begun to slip a little. Control has shifted to A. Frank Smith, Marvin Collie, and of course John Connally. Although Connally has generally been regarded as a progressive force, his busy role as Presidential advisor and Republican politician has left him little time for day-to-day decision-making about VE's policies. As the official managing partner, Smith has increasingly set the tone. Those close to the firm perceive a definite reaction against "the liberals, long-hairs, and fancy dressers." Recruitment has changed, and less say is given to younger partners and associates.

The "45-year-old bracket"—men who for years felt voiceless as Searls passed them over to share his power with the younger men—dominate Smith's executive committee. (Smith himself is 58.) Rivalry between the two groups is subdued but obvious even to the outsider. Where it will lead is anybody's guess. Worried associates observe that the 45-year-old group built up a substantial body of resentment and discontent watching the younger generation enjoy fatter salaries and swifter promotions than they themselves had been privileged to receive at such an unseasoned age; deprived of their turn at power for so long, they are unlikely to relinquish it willingly. And they are still relatively young themselves.

Whatever problems Vinson Elkins may be having with its generation gap, however, nothing has interrupted the phenomenal growth of its already-high-quality clientele. The firm represents such corporate giants as Texas Eastern, Pan Am, Halliburton, and Occidental Petroleum (the last three, Connally is said to have brought in), as well as the extensive Cullen family interests. More are coming in every day, attracted from far beyond the borders of Texas by the former Treasury Secretary's reputation for thaumaturgy. "Everyone wants to hire him," smiles a VE partner, "because everyone wants to get acquainted with John Connally."

# FULBRIGHT CROOKER: TEXAN TO THE CORE

Fulbright, Crooker & Jaworski is the johnny-come-lately of the Big Three, a big gangling giant that seems as surprised as anyone else by its position as one of the nation's four largest firms. The Eastern pretensions of the other two are missing here: FC is Texan to the core. Aware that it lacks B&B's lofty tradition and VE's jet-set polish, it has stewed itself into a massive inferiority complex over the years. A lawyer at the other two who brags about his firm will simply take for granted that the listener considers it Number One; by contrast, a lawyer at FC is likely to say plaintively (as one did), "I hope you're going to be as fair to us as you are to the other two."

There is no question that Fulbright Crooker is a somewhat different genre: less sophisticated, less affected, more friendly, open, and down-home. It is much less secretive than the others. No one ever calls it stodgy. Says a former member: "Through the years, Fulbright Crooker has always wanted to hire the best, but only if they were Good Ole Boys." Asked for a capsule description of the Big Three, another Houston lawyer thought a moment and said, "Baker Botts plays golf; Vinson Elkins plays tennis; Fulbright Crooker hunts."

These differences provide fuel for one of the most popular (and catty) parlor games among Houston lawyers: making fun of Fulbright Crooker. "Their suits are shinier; mostly they wear Hong Kong silks," sniffs a VE wife. "They look a little bit corny, like they could wear a string tie to work." FC lawyers absorb this sort of thing with stoic indifference; but it hurts. They respond by redoubling their efforts to make a mark in various highly-visible civic and professional endeavors. It is no accident, for example, that FC always controls the Houston Junior Bar Association, now that its senior partner, Leon Jaworski, won election as President of the American Bar Association. The firm has an unquenchable thirst to gain acceptance by its peers.

The most persistent criticisms of Fulbright Crooker involve its alleged ruthlessness and disregard for the customary rules governing conflict of interest. "They don't see a conflict of interest . . . ever," charges one of their competitors. More than any other of the Big Six, Fulbright Crooker has been touched by scandal. The Haden will contest, the Andrau airport, and the *first* Sharpstown scandal (in 1957) are oft-cited examples. Similar accusations float like wraiths around the Houston bar. "There is a constant feeling of impropriety about the firm," remarks a middle-aged solo practitioner. "Conflict of interest is not a term often heard around there."

In fairness to Fulbright Crooker, one must readily admit that it is difficult to measure how much of this criticism is truly righteous indignation and how much is just meanspirited professional jealousy. As the solo practitioner acknowledged, "These older firms know how to use power and they are pretty proud of it. When somebody else comes along who is able to do the same thing, they get knocked."

Even the harshest critics of the firm are quick to praise the caliber of its work in many areas. FC is nationally recognized for its insurance defense trial section, headed by Newton Gresham. "They're probably the best firm in the country in that field," says a University of Texas law professor. Their labor law section, headed by Larry Clinton, is "far and away the best in town." Their admiralty work is likewise fine. And virtually every department is laced with men whose legal abilities match or exceed those of their rivals in other firms. Although Baker & Botts is considered preeminent in corporate financing and Vinson Elkins in oil & gas, the overall professional quality of the Big Three is remarkably close to being even.

Fulbright Crooker has also been something of a pioneer in chipping away racial barriers and other forms of discrimination. It hired its first Jewish lawyer about 15 years ago, well ahead of the other Big Six (one Jew did practice briefly at Baker & Botts in 1917). It is not the only firm to hire black law clerks in recent summers, but it topped all the rest by hiring a black woman and offering her an associateship at summer's end.

The firm is governed by a seven-member management committee, three of whom are among its most senior partners. But the dominant figure is Leon Jaworski, known to all as "the Colonel," who has been the committee's chairman for years. His rule is not the monolithic kind Judge Elkins practiced; other partners, particularly Kraft

Eidman and Gresham, possess real influence. Gibson Gayle is an up-and-coming figure. But Jaworski is the man that matters.

His corner office on the 8th floor of the Bank of the Southwest Building is cheerful, comfortable, and decorated as discreetly as possible with the avalanche of photographs, awards, and other memorabilia he has received during several decades of civic activity. (Students of the Houston skyline who associate elevation with status have noted that Baker & Botts looks down from its lofty perch on both of the other two, while Vinson Elkins has at least the satisfaction of looking down on Fulbright Crooker.) Sobriety is the keynote of the firm's reception area, where leather chairs and oriental vases are balanced by bookcases containing rare editions of Smollett's *History of England* and bound volumes of *The Spectator*. The mood of traditionalism and affluence is enhanced by portraits of Jefferson and Marshall along with an original landscape painting or two (of English pastoral scenes—not Hill Country bluebonnets).

It is impossible to dislike Jaworski. A winning blend of Legal Lion and small-town Chamber-of-Commerce booster, he never gives you a chance. His enthusiasm for Fulbright Crooker is infectious. Although he has never been fully accepted by the old Houston legal and social establishment, he is exempted from the reproofs that they sometimes levy against his firm. "The Colonel," says one, "is still a man who has *judgment*."

"Our really phenomenal growth has been in the last decade," Jaworski says. From 56 members in 1955, the firm grew to 108 in 1965 and has reached 185 "as of today." He recalls that a meeting of the entire firm two years ago had to be held in the auditorium of the Humble Building, five blocks away, because there was no room large enough to hold everyone at the Bank. (If they had all marched down there together, one supposes they would have needed a parade permit.)

He is convinced that the big firms will keep on growing. "There's not a psychological barrier at 200," he says. "Years ago I said that when we reach 100 lawyers we ought to put on the brakes because we'll be getting too unwieldy. I could not have had a more complete misconception. Either you keep growing or you run the risk of stagnation."

Fulbright Crooker got its start in 1919 through the liaison of John H. Crooker and R. C. Fulbright, an expert in tax and transportation who spent much of his time in Washington, D.C. (The firm has had an office there from the beginning.) Their principal client was Anderson Clayton & Co., a cotton compress company which had the perspicacity to corner the world market in cotton after World War I. As far as the firm's vigor was concerned, having Anderson Clayton for a client was like having a lifetime supply of Gatorade. The company is an even bigger giant today, although it has switched to food processing, insurance, and vegetable oils. After a merger in the years following World War II that brought in a large amount of high-quality insurance defense work, FC began to grow in earnest. Clients included legendary oilman Glenn McCarthy, the M.D. Anderson Foundation, and the Second National Bank, now the Bank of the Southwest.

Jaworski surveys his firm as a benign father might contemplate his happy family. "I have never seen a team work together like these boys do," he beams. "Why, the way these boys pitch in and help when someone else's ox is in the mire is amazing. They'll even stay down here at night.'' It is like being captain of the world's finest steamship.

Most vivid of all, perhaps, is his obvious, pardonably Texanish pride in the sheer *bigness* of it all—how it is booming, going great guns. "We've got men going all over the world," says the man who began his career when Houston was just another provincial city never dreaming that it might one day sit in the seats of the mighty. "We even have an office in London now." Did you send someone over there to run it? he is asked. "No, we didn't have to. About a year ago we got a man from Mobil Oil to head up the operation. He was already familiar with that part of the country."

## HOW THE BIG FIRMS GOT THAT WAY: THEY'RE BIG BECAUSE THEY'RE BIG BECAUSE . . .

**W**hy has Houston produced these immense law factories? The question is really two-fold: *Why did they become so big? And why do they stay so big?*

The conventional answer to the first question is that they grew because of their intimate associations with the big banks. This holds true for Vinson Elkins and Fulbright Crooker; for Baker & Botts, less so. But is not far wrong with B&B, either. The banks generated a lot of business for their allied firms, and more importantly, they *sent* a lot of business upstairs. Houston's banks have traditionally done business with a single firm, in contrast to those in Dallas which have parceled their business out and played one set of lawyers off against another. These different modes of operation were partly foreordained by the unusual way some Houston banks happened to develop: Judge Elkins' dual role as banker and lawyer is only the most obvious example.

An even more important reason, though, was the sheer forcefulness of the personalities who ruled the Big Three in their formative years. Men like Judge Elkins, John Crooker, and Captain Baker at Baker & Botts held the firms together by the strength of their own wills in the crucial 1920s and 1930s. The centrifugal forces that have held sway in Dallas—where the Turner firm reached 45 or 50 and split, the Carrington firm 30 or so and split—were held in check by these extraordinary men at precisely the time when their firms were still small enough to break apart. By avoiding the break then, they ensured it would probably never come.

As a partner at Vinson Elkins observed, "There comes a point of 'critical mass.' Beyond a certain point—perhaps 50 or so—large firms are so much more profitable because of the size of the clients they can attract and the specialization they can bring to bear." A group of partners could conceivably have walked off with half the clients of one of the Big Three in the Twenties; now they never could. One does not walk off with Texas Eastern, Pennzoil, or Anderson Clayton. They are too big to put in one's briefcase—and their loyalties now are to the firm itself and not to the lawyer who handles their business (or part of it) at a given moment. The real reason for the Big Three's size is to be found in history, rather than in anything that is happening today. It is

no riddle to say, "They are big . . . because they are big."

This is not to deny that there are other forces helping to *keep* them big. Some of these are common to law practice in other major cities: the sustained boom in legal business for the past decade, dumping more work than they can handle on the major firms; Houston's own growth; and, fascinatingly, the introduction of the jet airplane. By making Washington and New York as accessible as Austin, it has opened up new vistas in branches of the law heretofore monopolized by firms along the Eastern seaboard—representation of clients before federal agencies like the Federal Power Commission and the Securities and Exchange Commission, for example. As VE partner Evans Attwell observes, "As late as the Fifties, the only way you could get up there was by taking a three-day train trip or flying an uncomfortable DC-6. Now you can leave in the morning, be in DC by noon, have your conference, and be home that night. It's opened up a whole new world of federal practice to us."

There are also forces peculiar to Houston that help keep the big firms big. Foremost among them is the special status, the patina of prestige, that they have acquired in social and legal circles. A lawyer loses it if he leaves. In Dallas no one would care; in Houston they do. A lawyer who severs his ties with one of the Big Three must face the fact that he is choosing to be an outsider from then on; it is not an easy thing for some men to do. Leaving that elite peer group relationship takes a bite out of his ego.

If he is a partner, it may also take a sizeable bite out of his bank account. The lawyer on the move is always under economic pressure: the house always costs $10,000 more than he can afford. For a partner to abandon the built-in security of the big firm is usually judged to be a pretty poor gamble. Some of the firms have penalty clauses in their partnership agreements, requiring the departing ingrate to forfeit the value of his partnership interest, which can be substantial, and refrain from competing with Alma Mater's business for as long as five years. All in all, it is easier to stay put.

Besides, most of the people in the big firms *like* what they are doing. It is a simple thing, but it escapes most of their critics, who reason that lawyers in large firms must somehow be miserable. "The cement that's kept the big firms together," says a lawyer at Vinson Elkins, "is the fact that they mediate the economic life of Texas. They resolve the most intriguing problems a lawyer can imagine, and they do it every day." Another young associate puts it even more simply: "I like large firms," he says, "because I can work on interesting problems with qualified people . . . for money."

## IS BIG BEST? THE LARGE AND THE SMALL OF THINGS

**I**f you're looking for a lawyer to handle your business affairs, should you head for a big firm or seek out one of the smaller ones? It depends, naturally, on whom you ask.

Hank Webeldor (a pseudonym) is a promising young associate at Baker & Botts, wise beyond his years. He argues persuasively for the big firms. "Let's face it," he says, "they've got brand-name confidence. The client knows he's not going to get fly-by-night legal service. But even more importantly, he knows the big firm has as much to lose as *he* does if things aren't done right.

"You can find outstanding, brilliant lawyers who practice alone or in small groups. Look at their work and you can see they're worth their fee. But when you find an organization which is able *as an institution* to bring off work comparable in excellence to that of a brilliant, charismatic lawyer, then you've got a remarkable situation."

Webeldor concedes that big clients stand to gain the most from hiring a big firm. "A very big client can count on the firm to have all the available manpower he needs. Say you want to merge two companies and do it right. You'll have to merge their pension plans. That's intensely complicated. But there'll be a man in the big firm who does nothing but pension plans—and he'll be ready and available to talk to the client. The same things goes for anti-trust questions, securities, and so forth. If it's a big deal, you'll probably have two anti-trust guys, four corporate guys, two tax guys, a patent-trademark guy, and some real estate guys. The whole thing can be done in one place without winding up in the soup."

But what about the little man, the small businessman who just wants to set up a corporation and doesn't need all that expertise? What's the point of his going to one of the giants? Webeldor's answer sums up the big firms' self-perpetuating success story: "*A blue chip law firm gives instant credibility to a new business.*"

Ray Needham, an energetic and articulate young labor lawyer who has put his chips in with the four-man firm of Schlumberger, Hinsley & Westmoreland, sees, on the other hand, a new breed of businessman developing—one who doesn't want the same kind of relationship to his lawyer that his father had.

"Houston business was created by gunslinger-types," he says. "They were happy with the big firms because they'd grown up with them. But now their sons are taking over, and *they* want someone they can call 'their lawyer.' They want a guy whose advice they can trust, somebody who's not just a narrow specialist. They want a real person they can see, not a vast anonymous structure.

"They've been going to the big firms by default, because they know they can get good work done there; but they know the big firms are always going to give first attention to their big clients, and they'd much prefer to work instead with someone they *know*—if he's good. You're going to see things loosening up around here as they take over."

There are hazards for the small practice, though, attitudes which alarm solo practitioner Brooks Pollard (a pseudonym). Pollard was associated with one of the Big Six for several years; now on his own, he agrees that many good clients are intimidated by the larger firms. But he worries about some of them.

"You have a lot of businesses who don't particularly *want* the kind of professionalism the big firms represent," he says. "There are lots of lawyers in Houston making bundles of money with an eighth-rate practice. A client calls and says, 'I want a contract and I want it now and I want it on one page'—so the lawyer does it. It's gross, horrible, sloppy—but he does it. And the client is happy because he controls the lawyer.

"A large firm has the ability to maintain its professionalism and resist client wiles and manipulations much

better than someone who depends on that client for perhaps one-fourth of his total income."

You pays your money and you takes your choice.

# LIFE IN THE FIRM: THE BONDS OF AFFLUENCE

An article in *Forbes* magazine two years ago neatly capsuled the economic realities of a large law firm: Economically speaking, a law firm is a very simple structure. It buys brainpower wholesale—by the year, that is—and sells it retail—by the hour.

Less than half the members of the large firms are partners. The rest are associates, working long hours for a fixed wage and waiting for the day when they may be allowed to "make partner." The typical starting salary for someone fresh out of law school who goes to work for one of the Big Three is now $15,400 a year. This figure has risen dramatically in a short time. In 1967, $7500 was considered good; in 1969, the going rate was $13,200. Compensation for this wholesale brainpower increases by about $2400 each year the associate remains with the firm; about the time he is getting nervous about being made a partner, six or seven years after he arrived, he can expect to be earning in the neighborhood of $25,000 to $30,000.

This may seem like a lot of money, but it is actually only a small fraction of the revenue he *produces* for the firm. Therein lies the rub, as far as many an associate is concerned. Billing clients by the hour for his work, he may bring in $80,000 to $100,000 in annual receipts. His overhead is perhaps $10,000, and the remaining $40,000 or so (after his salary is taken out) is siphoned into the coffers of the firm, to reappear at the end of the year in the pockets of the partners. This difference between the money an associate produces and the cost of hiring him—billing cost versus talent cost—is what makes the big firms roll.

Obviously it is in the partners' interest to squeeze as much profitable labor as possible out of their associates. The associates don't get paid extra for doing more; the partners keep the revenue. "The only way they make so much money is for the associates to overproduce," says a bright young lawyer who left one of the Big Three.

To the outsider there is something chilling about the cynical ways associates are induced to "overproduce." Long hours are expected and demanded; it is not uncommon for a young associate to be at work before 8:30 a.m. and come home after 9 at night. Work regularly spills over onto Saturdays and Sundays. Wives, families, and outside interests are neglected; the firm is an all-consuming thing. Some lawyers often work sixty and seventy hour weeks. "There is a moral imperative to spend long hours at the office," says an associate at one of the Big Six.

Fear is what keep things going—fear of not being made a partner, fear of being resented as a laggard by one's peers. As an ex-Marine figuratively put it, "It's like basic training: if one guy falls behind on laps, the whole group has to do them over." An associate who tries to live a normal life is plagued by gnawing fears that one of his friends is back at the firm doing something he himself ought to be doing, and cussing him for it; or that displeased partners are preparing a package of switches and ashes for him at promotion time.

"The older men want to take too much out of the firm,"

says a young associate who left one of the Big Three considerably disillusioned. "By the time they draw a hundred-and-fifty, two-hundred, two-hundred-and-fifty thousand a year, they are rich men. But they derive satisfaction out of pushing it higher and higher, even though it's ordinary income and taxes take a huge bite. It hurts the firm and it discourages the associates. But it's a way of explaining to themselves that the treacherous climb to the top was worth it."

The firms are ruthless about exposing idlers who do not carry their share of the excessive load; conversely, they make certain that those who work themselves dizzy are properly rewarded—with praise, of course, not money. Baker & Botts annually circulates a sheet ranking the associates according to the number of hours each has billed during the year: woe betide the young man whose total slips much below 1750 hours, and 2000 is a safer figure. If an associate did nothing but "billable" work eight solid hours every workday for 50 weeks a year, he would barely reach the mark. Since, in the nature of things, it's impossible (ethically) to bill a client for every minute he spends at his desk—six billable hours out of eight is doing well—most associates work nights and weekends to make up the difference. Others skip their vacations. Vinson Elkins is even more domineering: the billing totals for each lawyer are circulated each *month*. The sheets are reviewed by older partners who worked even harder in *their* day and don't take kindly to young whippersnappers who fail to appreciate how lucky they are. They know if you've been bad or good, so be good for goodness' sake!

The physical working conditions are, of course, superb. Messengers, day and night secretarial shifts, comprehensive libraries, even (at Baker & Botts) desk switches that open and close office doors by remote control. "You don't have to bother with the details of running a law office," says a happy associate. "You can concentrate on the law."

But the price for these advantages is steep, and it must be paid in the coin of personal independence and freedom. The firms regiment their members' dress, their access to clients, even the decor of their offices. A story now making the rounds in Houston tells of a young associate at Vinson Elkins who decided that his north-facing office did not need curtains; "heresy," said the office managers, and they hung the curtains anyway. For a decorative plant he chose a hanging basket instead of one that sat on the floor like everybody else's; soon he was summoned by the managing partner and ordered to take it down. Except at Fulbright Crooker, which has a reputation for leniency, political activity by associates is notoriously restricted. They can vote for whomever they please, but to take an active role in a campaign is courting disaster unless the management approves. In the opinion of a VE partner, a lawyer is taking an "active" role if he receives calls about the campaign through the firm's switchboard during the day.

Even more burdensome to the self-respect of some proud associates is the knowledge that they are virtually forbidden to discuss their work—the major portion of their lives—with their best friends outside the firm. It is not a matter of disclosing professional secrets or confidential client relationships; no reputable lawyer will do that. They know that the censorship imposed on them is broader; if they are observed talking about even the most innocuous matters, like the leadership of the firm or its history, their trustworthiness

is made suspect and their advancement threatened.

This writer has interviewed political dissenters in Czechoslovakia and "banned" African revolutionaries in South Africa, meeting them in obscure cafes and parked cars to avoid detection. By all odds, associates in Houston's Big Three are more reticent and fearful than either. One old friend who did talk (but not about his firm) was obviously distressed by his sudden loss of freedom to discuss his work; he kept returning to the subject, trying to explain his predicament as the inexorable consequence of choosing to go to work there—like volunteering for the Army (a recurring image). "You obey orders in the Army," he said, "even if you're told to paint the tanks pink. You can question them logically, but if you're told to go ahead, you do it. The whole training of a lawyer in the big firms is to *know your place in the organization*—to avoid being presumptuous. One shines in one's work—not in extracurricular things. You don't talk about the firm unless you've been authorized to do it, any more than you allow a default judgment to be entered against your client. At all costs you have to avoid whatever can be seen as indiscreet."

Other young lawyers who come in contact with their friends at the big firms wonder out loud why they don't mutiny. "Why do they put up with it?" asks one. "Why don't they go on strike, why don't they get the hell out? I've never understood it."

The answer, not surprisingly, is the alluring promised land of a partnership. "Make partner" and your income almost doubles right away—suddenly you're a sixty-thousand-dollar-a-year man, and right at Christmastime, too. It *is* delicious. Who would risk taking a chance at losing that, especially when the firm is ominously dotted with graying 50-year-old relics who were judged a little too rambunctious in their day and were therefore kept as permanent associates, *pour encourager les autres*? When the alternative is finding yourself on the street, deprived of the monthly check and forced to develop a private practice or drown, most associates shudder, hurriedly clamp the lid on the abyss, and return to the warm glow of their respective firms. They are hooked. Predictable rationalizations ensue: their overworked existence is no longer thought of as exploitation, but rather as a prudent system of "forced savings," a way of depositing in the bosom of the firm a comfortable income for their future years, a kind of upper-middle-class Social Security.

Left unspoken to themselves and their families is the recognition that, like Social Security, the system depends upon steady, even increasing, contributions by the associates who succeed them; that it is premised on an ever-expanding economy and law business which may or may not materialize. Thus their fears become the same as those of their elders who hold them down: what if, when *I* become a partner, the associates demand their share at once? At that point, cynics say, they are ready for a partnership.

With so much riding on a partnership, there is agony as the time approaches. There is no appointed hour, just a minimum number of years (it varies from firm to firm) below which no one will be considered. But once that time passes, an associate begins to get the message. A year or two later, it is obvious to all that he is in trouble.

He can pack and go, or stick around and take his chances. The firm has very little incentive to kick him out: after all, he has eight or nine years' experience, he is bringing them perhaps a hundred thousand dollars in billings, and his replacement would be an inexperienced fellow fresh from law school. "Maybe he will improve." For those who remain, the suspense often becomes almost unbearable. One lawyer from a small firm vividly remembers the tension he has witnessed. "A fine young attorney at Baker & Botts got passed over when he should have made partner two years ago. His friends took him to lunch to console him, but he got sick. Next year the same thing happened, only this time he passed out in the street. Soon afterwards he moved to Dallas."

Merit is the main criterion for promotion, and the continuing quality of the big firms' work over the years indicates that their executive committees (whose list is almost never overruled by the full partnership) know what they are doing. Still, there is a measure of truth to the saying that "the only way you get to be a general is by not offending the generals." Every firm has those senior associates who have paid for their independence.

An element of caprice also enters in. In some firms, an associate is assigned to work with a particular lawyer; his advancement is sometimes unjustly affected by how highly the other partners regard his supervisor. In other cases the partner decides how many billing hours he will credit to himself and how many to his associates, when they have worked on the project together. "How many billing hours I get to show depends on how good a guy he is," says an associate. "And yet his decision rules my career."

The high degree of specialization in the Big Three gives some associates a running head start on others. "At Fulbright Crooker, the patent section is the way to dusty death," says a former associate there. Baker & Botts is dominated by the trial and corporate departments, whose strength is demonstrated at promotion and profit-sharing time. Says a disgruntled associate: "If they make a trial man a partner, they almost have to make a corporate man a partner. If you're in, say, oil & gas, your partners may be fighting for you, but they just don't have the same clout."

Ironically, a partner's life often turns out to be more of the same. The trappings change—they sell their homes in West University and Southgate to associates and move to Tanglewood or River Oaks—but they find themselves working harder than ever. Ingrained habits are hard to change. Some new partners tend to relax and coast, but most don't; they identify themselves completely with their firms. Partnership brings its own set of competitions for rank and power.

Alcoholism and the divorce rate are both high among the middle-aged partners, evidence of discontent and frustration that will not go away. In the Big Three, a partner finds that unless he sits on the firm's executive committee, he is still not likely to have much voice in its policies. "It would be very unusual for the partnership not to go along with the management," says Leon Jaworski, "but it can happen." For those so inclined, a struggle for influence within the firm replaces the struggle for promotion.

Why then do people do it? What do the big firms have to offer that make worthwhile the struggle to win a niche in a giant organization and the loss of personal independence it entails? Part of the reason is the excitement and exhilaration of the big firms' type of law practice; there are those who are happier—*professionally happier*—in a big firm than they could ever be outside. For most, however, it is money,

security, and social prestige. Money, because there are few Houston lawyers who make more than the top partners of the big firms, and those that do won their stripes in a very risky world where the losers outnumber the winners. Security, because a partnership carries with it a lifetime relief from fears of financial reversal. Social prestige, because those who have not previously moved in establishment society find the big firms an irresistibly easy path to acceptance and status.

These insights are not lost on the recruiters who leave the big firms each year and fan out to law school campuses in search of the ablest legal talent they can find. They know their winning cards.

# STUDENTS ON PEDESTALS: THE DAZZLE OF BIGTIME LAW RECRUITING

As recently as ten years ago, a law student who aspired to work for one of the Big Three went to their office, credentials in hand. All that has changed. Active recruiting now occupies a considerable portion of several partners' time, year-in, year-out. With more law business than they have lawyers to handle it, the big firms find themselves engaged in a bruising, escalating competition for top law graduates. And like college football stars at the height of the old AFL-NFL rivalry, the graduates love it.

The University of Texas Law School in Austin is the principal battleground for capturing this legal talent. While the old Texas prejudice against Ivy Leaguers has largely faded (each of the Big Three sends a recruiting team to Harvard), the old Ivy League prejudice against Texas hasn't, with the result that these sallies to New England are not notably successful. The big firms persist in showing icy indifference to most graduates of other Texas law schools, including Baylor, the University of Houston, and to a lesser extent, SMU. But almost any second- or third-year law student in the top ten per cent of his class at U.T. can, if he wants, savor the opulent delights of big-time law recruiting.

There is a round of parties in the fall, timed to coincide with a football weekend, and another in the spring, to coincide with the Law Review Banquet. These are nothing if not lavish, and Vinson Elkins (which started it all) is universally regarded as the most lavish of all.

A third-year law student who was invited to one of VE's early parties this fall was numbed by the experience. "There was this giant buffet at Green Pastures [a mansion-style restaurant in Austin]," he said. "It was huge—spread out through two or three rooms. And an *incredible* amount of liquor: I've never seen anything like it. An open bar beforehand, they kept filling your drinks while you ate, then Irish coffee. Amazing! Then they invited you up to their suite for *after-dinner drinks*! I never knew lawyers could drink that much." A moment later he added pensively, "You know, I don't think people today are as impressed by that sort of thing as they were a couple of years ago."

Like the Russian army mobilizing for war, Vinson Elkins sometimes sends as many as 30 young associates, partners, and their wives to Austin for a recruiting weekend. Each is fully briefed in advance on the salient details of the four or five law students for whom they have assumed particular responsibility. At a "structured" party, each couple may be assigned a specific prospect to entertain and shepherd around, usually without the prospect's prior knowledge. The atmosphere is reminiscent of fraternity rush—in some ways it is simply a continuation of fraternity rush—and in unguarded moments members of the big firms frequently slip back into the Greek terminology (rushee, rush party) until, grinning sheepishly at the outsider, they catch themselves.

The big impetus toward lavish recruitment came after the famous VE class of '63 had settled into the firm; the other firms were virtually forced to follow. The emphasis at VE has always been upon bountiful, conspicuous extravagance: the finest foods, the finest wines, a life of stylish prosperity. One young lawyer who went to VE describes the process as "an attempt to sway impressionable law students, an appeal to their ego. 'Here we are in Maxim's wine cellar; this is the life of the young VE lawyer.'" A Vinson Elkins dinner for a half dozen students held at Austin's prestigious Headliners Club in 1971 was, according to Club officials, the single most expensive meal ever served there.

Fulbright Crooker and Baker & Botts pursue the same pattern with varying degrees of success. The unreal atmosphere of a cocktail party does not afford a congenial home court advantage to the aloof lawyers at B&B, and despite their punctilious observance of all the proper rules, they sometimes trip over their feet when stepping down from their pedestal. A 1973 Law Review graduate of U.T. argues that "VE gives the best parties because they hire the best cocktail party people. [The recruiting technique at] Baker Botts is just awful, clearly the worst—they send people up to Austin who don't have any idea what to do at cocktail parties and that turns some guys off." He adds, "Of course, that may mean they are better lawyers. I've never thought good cocktail party people and good lawyers were particularly compatible."

Fulbright Crooker, as always, is honored more for their folksiness than their finesse. A typical FC recruiting weekend might feature a rock band at the Party Barn in Austin. A central Texas lawyer who was rushed by the big firms recalls that on his trip to Houston he and his wife went to see *Lucia di Lammermoor* with Beverly Sills at the Houston opera, courtesy of Vinson Elkins. "Fulbright Crooker," he says half-seriously, "would have taken us to the Astrodome." He neglected to mention that VE, keeping all its options open, has reserved a block of seats behind home plate.

Until quite recently, the most ferocious recruiting always took place within the Texas Law Review, a prestigious group of second- and third-year students who earned their positions strictly on the basis of their grade point average. But in late 1972 the Review began to admit members on an internship system that emphasized such things as a candidate's legal writing ability; only 15 (instead of 40) positions are now determined solely on grades. At about the same time, the Law School administration forbade firms to restrict their campus interviews to an exclusive group like the "top 10 per cent" or "Law Review only." They must now interview any student who asks to be interviewed.

The result of these reforms has been to make the grade-conscious Big Three increasingly suspicious of the students they interview on campus, with a correspondingly greater reliance on off-campus, informal party impressions. There are no more blanket Law Review invitations to parties, either; admission is now by individual invitation only. "It's a lot more like rush than it used to be," says one recent graduate. "If you are shy, introverted, don't talk easily, you are likely to suffer. You just don't have the chance to make the same impression. Good people have been hurt this way, especially with Vinson Elkins, who've been getting more and more toward the 'good ole boy' syndrome in the last year or so."

One of the most reliable methods the firms have developed to measure the abilities of a prospective associate is the system of "summer clerkships." Students whom the firm is interesting in hiring are given a chance between their second and third years in law school to do legal research at the firm, to pick up a little cash at $250 a week, and to show their stuff. Ostensibly it's just another summer job, but the firm and the clerks both regard it as a sort of trial run. In some ways it is deceptive (the clerks leave at 5 p.m. and don't see the young associates still working at 10:30), but each learns enough about the other that solid "offers" are frequently made, and accepted, for employment to commence after graduation. Some students thus return to law school for their final year already employed, in effect, by one of the Big Three. At least two of the big firms, and possibly the third as well, quietly provide expense accounts for them to entertain and recruit selected fellow students who are still uncommitted.

A third-year student who is being pursued by one or more of the Big Three can expect to receive a first-class trip to Houston at the firm's expense. One who recently returned from such a visit recalled that he and his wife were flown down and given a choice of staying in any hotel they desired. While he toured the office and met a succession of partners, his wife was taken on a tour of the city by several firm wives. During lunch at Neiman-Marcus the wives discussed the merits of housing and the Houston schools. Meanwhile he was having lunch at the Hyatt-Regency Windowbox with a few young associates. "There was no hard sell about it," he said. "Their attitude was, 'This is what we've got; be sure it's what you want.'" In the afternoon he continued to make the rounds of partners, impressed that the top lawyers in the firm would stop what they were doing to visit with him. His wife was also taken to meet several of the principal partners. "When it was over I was told that if I wanted an offer, I could have one," he said. "That was all there was to it, except we had dinner with some associates that evening. The rest of the weekend we were free to do as we wished; they made it clear we could stay as long as we wanted at their expense, but I had to get on back to school." A "moderately generous" check for taxis, meals, and miscellaneous expenses arrived at his Austin home a few days later.

The recruiting battle is fueled by the traditional feeling at U.T. that anyone who doesn't go to work for one of the big Houston firms probably isn't much good. The firms scrupulously strive to preserve their status by impressive recruiting tactics and generous gifts to the Law School Foundation. (Each of the three has endowed a $100,000 professorship.) By and large the strategy works: an offer from one of the Big Three is regarded as proof of professional ability even by their most cynical Naderesque classmates; like the winner of a Rhodes Scholarship, the recipient can never again be regarded as just another face in the crowd.

The firms' recruiting luck varies from year to year. Baker & Botts adroitly manages to spirit away a few of the highest-ranked students almost every time. Vinson Elkins dazzled the legal profession by snapping up great gobs of top graduates in the late 1960s, but their last vintage year was 1971. Fulbright Crooker outstripped the others in 1972, when they got four officers of the Law Review. A large proportion of the Class of 1973 opted for judicial clerkships, perhaps expressing a measure of distaste for the sort of work done by the Big Three. The current class talks even more radically than their predecessors, but at graduation they very likely will head for business-oriented firms.

If that doesn't happen—if the Big Three are spurned by yet another crop of activist, reform-minded U.T. law graduates—the firms may well be forced to reappraise some of their policies. One which is long overdue for some reexamination is their attitude toward legal work *pro bono publico*, lawyers' Latin for professional services provided free of charge to causes the lawyer deems worthy. Lawyers are traditionally even more tight-fisted than doctors when it comes to giving away their services for free, but this resistance has increasingly come under attack by young lawyers chagrined at the lack of legal representation available to poorly-financed consumer, environmental, and civil rights causes. In many of the larger New York and Washington firms, a substantial fraction of a lawyer's time may be devoted to *pro bono* work for which the firm receives no income. The failure of Texas firms to follow suit has made them something of a joke among Ivy League law students at recruiting time.

None of the Houston firms has a *pro bono* program worthy of the name. There is a story, possibly apocryphal, of a much-sought-after Harvard law senior who was being recruited by Vinson Elkins. His hosts happened to take him to the office of one of the firm's grand old men, a prominent insurance lawyer. Looking at the youngster, the senior partner said, "So you want to work for Vinson Elkins."

The young man acknowledged that he thought that might be nice, and the two chatted amiably for a while about the many splendors of the firm. Finally the student asked, "By the way, do you do any *pro bono* work?"

"Any *what?*"

An explanation ensued in which the student, somewhat taken aback, explained to the old gentleman the nature of that particular form of legal generosity. With an indulgent smile came the partner's response: "Well, son, I'm sure it's all right for you to do that, just as long as you do it on Saturdays."

A recent U.T. graduate who is well acquainted with the *pro bono* policies of Washington law firms was discussing them with several of the top partners at VE during a recruiting interview. "I was talking about one D.C. firm—one of the two or three best—that has a written firm policy that 20 per cent of the firm's time shall be spent on *pro bono* work. No ifs or buts—it's a written policy, and it's not just something nominal, it's 20 per cent. The bigwigs at VE just flatly refused to *believe* it. What can you say?"

Vinson Elkins is by no means the worst offender in the matter of *pro bono* work, although their progressive reputation in the Sixties makes their lack of initiative more conspicuous. Baker & Botts seems to discipline associates who stray too far from the moneymaking path by denying them

promotion to partner year after year, regardless of the merit of their outside work. At Fulbright Crooker, managing partner Jaworski was obviously discomforted by questions involving *pro bono* work. There, as at the other big firms, the crunch comes when an attorney is asked, say, by environmental groups like the Sierra Club or the League of Conservation Voters to contribute his time in a class action suit on behalf of citizens seeking to stop industrial pollution or freeway construction.

"How," Jaworski asks, "would a client who pays us a retainer react if he found that one of our boys was sitting on the other side helping to agitate a lawsuit against him? We can't trample on our clients' interests by turning one of our boys loose to foment litigation."

Most lawyers would acknowledge that he has a point. In one form or another, this is the persistent dilemma of the big firms: conflict of interest. A junior partner at Vinson Elkins candidly admits: "Most of our clients have environmental problems. We can't represent both sides in an environmental lawsuit anymore than we can in any other kind of suit, even if we represent one side for free. If someone wants to handle environmental litigation, he shouldn't come to a big firm." He means, of course, handling environmental work for the *plaintiff's* side, since the big firms defend such cases for their clients every day; they are happy to latch onto a young lawyer who knows environmental law, provided he wants to use his expertise in behalf of corporate defendants.

But lurking in the background is the realization that conflict of interest is not as final an answer as it seems. There are many environmental cases that even a lawyer in the Big Three could handle without placing himself in direct opposition to one of the firm's clients. What the big firms know, however, is that if one of their lawyers succeeds in winning a tough environmental ruling today in a case that does *not* involve one of their clients, the law thus made may be used tomorrow as a precedent in a case that *does*. In this sense, "conflict of interest" is a convenient excuse for refraining from doing anything that would impair the interests of corporate defendants *as a class*, regardless of whether there is an ethical conflict in a particular case. Critics of the big firms would regard this as a telling example of the way they confuse their own responsibilities as lawyers with the very different interests of the clients they serve.

Still, the Houston firms sense that something new is in the wind, and one suspects that they are preparing for the necessity of allowing *pro bono* work when and if they have to. Their desire to keep getting the top graduates is ultimately stronger than their distaste for *pro bono* work; if their favored graduates consistently start going somewhere else in pursuit of the greater personal opportunities that such a program offers, the Big Three will doubtless devise one of their own to win them back—but not until. Meanwhile, Houston managing partners do have fewer illusions than lawyers in other Texas cities about the nature of *pro bono* work. The graduate who had such difficulty convincing the VE brass that Washington firms actually did require *pro bono* work recalls: "At least the people in Houston know what the words mean—even if they are damned sure they aren't going to *do* any of it. At one of the biggest Dallas firms they said, 'You betcha we do *pro bono* work: one of our senior partners helps run the United Fund campaign every year.'"

# LAWYER'S WIVES: THE LONELINESS OF A CLOSED SOCIETY

**M**ost wives find that the firm dominates their lives as well as their husbands'. Emily Lowry (a pseudonym) is attractive, dark-haired, thirtyish. Her husband recently became a partner in one of the Big Three. Seated in the den of their comfortable two-story home in a fashionable neighborhood of Houston, she analyzes their climb.

"The first thing you have to understand about being a lawyer's wife is that it's very similar to being a doctor's wife. The first few years are hard and lonely. He's working long, long, hard hours—twelve to 15 hours is not unusual, for days at a time. You'll raise your family almost single-handedly for a while."

Whatever dreams a law student's wife may have, they probably do not include an image of herself sitting around an empty house day after day as the sun sets, the dinner hour passing unmarked and preschool children wanting to be cared for and entertained, while her husband works on downtown. The young lawyer's wife knows the firm's night number by heart. To combat the inevitable loneliness, the wives seek out others in the same situation. "They'll group together," says Emily. "For instance, they'll go over for a cocktail at 5:30 and pass the time with each other's children until eight or so. But it gets a lot better after a while."

Social life tends to revolve around the firm—about 50 per cent of the time, Emily estimates. "These are the men your husband is working with, so it's just easier that way." For the first three or four years, young lawyers are expected to shoulder the recruiting burden. When they do this sort of entertaining, whether at home or somewhere else, the firm picks up the check. Emily recalls "one of the more exuberant" parties during her husband's second year with the firm. "We went to the Petroleum Club; there were 30 of us, plus the rushee and his wife. So you see there's an advantage to entertaining—it's a very nice fringe benefit. The disadvantage for the wife, if she's only on her own budget, is that you have to have very nice clothes in order to go places with your rushees."

After the husband becomes a partner, he and his wife begin to entertain the firm's clients instead of prospective associates. For the wife this is often an emotional trial, since she is the one who is expected to see that things go smoothly. The degree of entertaining depends on the type of work her husband does. If he is in real estate, securities, or some other kind of predominantly office practice, the burden may be light. But if he is in trial work, especially insurance trial work, entertaining is a permanent part of their lives. If the wife does not like it—or if she doesn't like the people she is expected to entertain—"that can be a real problem," says Emily. "You will be constantly socializing with insurance people, going to meetings with insurance people, traveling here and there. You just have to say, 'I don't like 'em, but this is my job,' and go out and *do* it. And that isn't very pleasant, especially if you've had a hard day with six screaming children."

If the husband's line of work requires him to know a wide circle of other lawyers, his wife becomes a useful agent to help him establish and develop contacts. She may be expected to join and participate in a variety of women's clubs, civic projects, or charitable activities. If she balks, his advancement in the firm may be impaired.

When wives are so important to their husband's and the firm's success, it is not surprising that the firm scrutinizes them coldly but inconspicuously during the recruiting process. The associates' wives are often asked for their opinion of a rushee's spouse, although their judgment seems to carry weight in inverse proportion to the prospective young lawyer's grade point average. "If you're talking about a guy with super grades," says Emily, "then he'd have to have a pretty bad wife to lose out." But it does happen. "I remember a Harvard boy had married an actress from New York, a former prostitute. If she'd been able to cover all this up—not the actress part, but the former prostitute part—then I guess it would have been all right. But she didn't. She came to the firm and was quite loud, fairly obnoxious; and he was not offered a job because of her. They later got divorced."

"A good wife is rather unobtrusive," muses Emily. "She should be someone who can help entertain, to a degree. And yet there are some excellent lawyers whose wives you never see socially"—their husbands, presumably, had super grades. For the rest, feminine subordination to the husband's career is a basic premise of their life together. In the firm's eyes, the wife's activities are his activities, and the same ground rules apply to both. A wife conspicuously active in radical politics, for example, would be an unmitigated disaster for her husband. Life in the big firms is still very much a family affair, and the firm's threshold of embarrassment is low indeed.

An incident that occurred near the end of the interview forcefully (and unexpectedly) drove this point home. The telephone rang, and Emily's precocious seven-year-old daughter answered it. "Mommy's talking to the tape recorder," she told the caller, who turned out to be Daddy. His curiosity metamorphosed into great ire when Mommy told him she had been discussing the life of lawyers' wives. This writer took the phone to reassure him that the interview had begun with an understanding that neither Emily's identity nor the firm's would be disclosed. Unmollified, he insisted that the firm be supplied with a copy of the transcript and allowed to delete anything it did not want printed. He was told that this would be impossible, but that the writer would be happy to clear up any misconceptions about the terms of the interview on his visit to their offices the next day.

A somewhat-shaken Emily returned to the sofa and continued the discussion, but her animated manner was gone. About five minutes later the phone rang again. Daddy's message was unambiguous, *ex cathedra*: I have told the managing partner what you are doing, and he has ordered you to stop the interview. "I guess you'll have to destroy the tape," said Emily as she sat back down, stunned.

A few minutes of pleasantries were exchanged to save embarrassment all around, but the interview was over. Emily grew visibly unnerved by the occurrence, changing the subject every couple of minutes to say, "I suppose I should have checked with them first, but I never *thought* . . ." And her voice trailed off. Explanations were offered— "It's just a misunderstanding, we'll straighten it out tomorrow''—but one had the distinct impression of being present at a moment when another person realized for the first time the true extent of her confinement. A man for whom she did not even work, sitting in an office building five miles away, could casually *order* her to stop talking to someone else about her life. He not only could, he *had*, without even bothering to ask first what she had been saying. It was a sobering experience, and it spoke volumes about the way the Big Three firms sweep lawyers, wives, and families into their all-encompassing embrace.

# HIDDEN MANDARINS: THE LAW FIRMS AND POWER

The extraordinary edifice of power erected by the Big Three is built on two secure cornerstones: politics and economics. Their political power is enormous, but it is not displayed in the manner that the general public has come to expect. Seldom does a partner manage a campaign, even locally. Almost never does one seek public office. Judges, too, come from someplace else. There is no tradition of public service in the big Houston firms, no *noblesse oblige*. Their sense of dignity clashes with the realities of politics as they perceive it: politics is not a gentleman's game in this state; therefore gentleman lawyers do not sully themselves by becoming politicians. This distaste extends to other forms of public service as well. Dillon Anderson of Baker & Botts, who served as Special Assistant to Dwight Eisenhower, and John Crooker, Jr., of Fulbright Crooker, who took a leave of absence to assume the chairmanship of the Civil Aeronautics Board, are exceptions to a very rigid rule. Much more typical is John Heard at Vinson Elkins, who declined John Kennedy's request to serve as Commissioner of Internal Revenue because his firm objected.

The big firms, of course, cannot please their critics either way. The very people who deplore their unwillingness to share the responsibilities of public service would be furious if they decided to do so, considering the possibilities for conflict-of-interest charges that could be levied against a legislator whose law firm represented the multitudinous clients of the Big Three. In any event the question of direct political participation is academic. As one lawyer remarks, ''The big firms are conceived and bred like thoroughbred horses for one purpose: the practice of law. That is the end of their collective existence.''

The political power is instead *derivative*. It flows through the big firms—and from them—but is not generated by them. It belongs to the people who have the money: those who rule empires of insurance, lumber, shipping, petrochemicals, utilities, and banking, to name a few. It belongs, in other words, to their clients (except in the case of the banks, which are often run by the lawyers themselves).

The big Houston firms act as mediators between these men with money and the men who hold (or want to hold) public office. ''If you thought something needed to be done in Houston,'' muses a partner at Vinson Elkins, ''the managing partners of the big firms would be the logical place to start.'' The firms' endorsement is a sort of imprimatur that gives credibility to a candidate, a proposal, or an idea; their power comes primarily from the fact that their judgment is trusted.

''Nothing big is going to happen in Houston unless Houston Lighting and Power, Humble Oil, *et al*. want it to happen,'' a liberal-minded trial lawyer insists. ''And they're all represented by one of the Big Three. They go to their lawyer and have their lawyer tell the mayor.'' Not all the firms, however, have equal political clout. Baker & Botts seems at times to take a perverse pride in losing politically-tinged battles like the recent contest for Cable TV franchise rights, as though a certain degree of ineptness in dealing with politicians was the hallmark of a truly professional lawyer. Fulbright Crooker (which clobbered Baker & Botts in that fight) has a record of backing winners in political races without much regard to whether they were Republicans or Democrats. A study of the ''Houston Establishment'' last year placed FC at the apex of its pyramid. Vinson Elkins has for many years been the most politically astute of all, if one measures astuteness by success in seeing one's allies elected to public office; but their greatest impact has been on state, not local, politics.

To the outside observer, the role of the big Houston firms in state politics is a masterwork of subtlety. In essence it is a screening system that approves candidates and enables them to tap the great resources of establishment wealth.

''All the state officials go down and see them, hat in hand,'' says a wealthy, aristocratic former state legislator. But why bother with the lawyers, he is asked: it's the clients who have the big money. ''Of course,'' he says. ''But that's not the way it works. You have to go through the firm before you get to the client. You have to run the gauntlet first. In the old days you went to see Judge Elkins, or old man Crooker. . . . Now it's one of the other partners, but the routine is just the same. If the firm approves, you've got access to the client. Unless you could get their blessing, you couldn't get the money from the client. And the firms would charge their clients fees commensurate with the heat they'd taken off them.''

The last Texas governor who was not the candidate of the big firms (or substantially acceptable to them) was James Allred. He left office in 1939. The firms also take an abiding interest in the races for State Treasurer (held by Jesse James since 1941), Attorney General, the Railroad Commission, and of course, the Texas Supreme Court. Occasionally a candidate slips up on them, as did John Hill, a trial lawyer who made his reputation on the opposite side of the docket from the big firms and squeaked through to election as Attorney General in 1972. Hill's strategy was simple: he announced his candidacy at the last minute, preventing the big firms from fielding a third candidate who would split the anti-Crawford Martin vote. Hill has continued to be independent of them.

By reputation the Big Three have a hefty say in the selection of judges, particularly local judges. Partners in the firms seldom deign to accept judgeships themselves, but there is no doubt they keep close watch on those who do. Younger lawyers outside the big firms claim to see the malevolent hand of self-interest at work: ''Get a judge who doesn't know the law,'' says one aggressive young newcomer, ''and he has to depend on the reputation of the attorneys in the case . . . or of their firms.'' The quality of trial judges in Harris County is considered uneven, to say the least, but the appellate bench is exceptionally able for a state court. In the opinion of some experienced attorneys outside the big firms, it is at least the equal of the state Supreme

Court in character, integrity, and legal scholarship. There is no real evidence that the Big Three actively attempt to maneuver mediocre minds onto the bench, although they do frequently get the benefit of the doubt in mediocre judges' decisions.

Members of the Big Three candidly admit that the firms hold a virtual veto over Harris County judicial appointments. (Although judicial positions are elective in Texas, most vacancies occur by death or resignation and are filled by gubernatorial appointment. The new judge then runs at the next election with whatever advantage an incumbent might have.) One prominent trial lawyer views judicial appointments as merely another example of the comfortable, symbiotic power relationships between big law firms and their prosperous clients. "Say you have a governor who got oil money the last time he ran. The law firm has a guy they want to see appointed judge. All they have to do is pick up the phone and call the Chairman of the Board of one of those companies, who just happens to be their client, whom they've just happened to keep out of trouble in the courts, and ask him to mention to the governor that so-and-so would make a fine judge down here. I'm not saying it's dishonest. I'm saying they use the political tools available to them."

Once on the bench, moreover, a Texas judge faces a lifetime of re-election campaigns if he wishes to remain there. While it is true that incumbent judges are hard to beat, very few are reckless enough to risk their positions by ignoring the political niceties. And the indispensable ingredients for a political campaign—publicity and finances—are conveniently available through the big firms and their corporate clients.

No one familiar with the practice of law in Houston seriously contends that the judges who win appointment or re-election in this fashion put on their robes and step into the courtroom determined to disregard the law in order to reward the lawyers and litigants whose influence helped them get there. But the idea that some lawyers and some clients exercise a disproportionate influence over the accession of judges has an insidious effect on the confidence other lawyers feel for their courts. Like so much else, it perpetuates an "us and them" attitude in the Houston bar.

# POWER IS WHERE THE MONEY IS

The economic power of the firms is even more impressive than their political power. It can be traced to their special relationships with major Houston banks. National Democratic party chairman Robert Strauss, a Dallas lawyer, observes that while in most cities the big financial interests dominate the big law firms, in Houston the situation is reversed. And there is nothing at all derivative about that power.

On paper, the interpenetration is impressive: Jaworski is chairman of the executive committee of the Bank of the Southwest, and FC senior partner Hugh Buck also serves on the board. The firm also represents Houston-Citizens Bank, where two other partners, Newton Gresham and John Crooker, are on the board. Vinson Elkins is practically synonymous with First City National Bank, where senior partners John Connally and Marvin Collie serve on a board

chaired by Judge Elkins' non-lawyer son. Baker & Botts has its share of partners on various local boards, but it has no major "captive" bank of its own. Paradoxically, however, this situation has given them special influence over many medium-sized banks. As a giant firm with the largest corporate clientele of all, they automatically fall heir to much banking business, and the other banks tend to prefer doing business with them because they are *not* identified with Bank of the Southwest or First City National.

Economic power flows both ways, of course; the answer to the question of who controls whom is often murky. But the influence of lawyers from the Big Three is obviously substantial. The banks have channelled a disproportionate amount of their legal business to their allied law firms, in sharp contrast to the Dallas banking tradition of spreading the work around. Houston law practice is rife with tales of heavy-handed banking tactics. In effect the firms can use the banks to promote their own business. Lawyers from the small firms insist they often do.

Nor is the alliance of lawyers and banks limited to the downtown giants. Because the Texas constitution prohibits branch banking, there is nothing comparable to California's vast Bank of America with statewide offices. Instead there is a plethora of small suburban "community" banks, each ostensibly an independent business enterprise. But the names of directors at the big banks appear with uncanny regularity as proposed directors for community banks seeking operating charters from the State Banking Board in Austin. An observer who has watched the Banking Board for years says, "When an application comes up, you can always tell which big bank is interested in it, just by looking at the names." Through this system of interlocking directorates, the big banks have dominated the Texas banking scene far more than the casual observer might suspect.

This informal procedure came roaring out into the open after the Bank Holding Company Act was amended in 1970 to permit, in effect, the development of bank holding companies. More and more "downtown" Texas banks are acquiring direct control of community banks through this device, which enables them to dominate numerous smaller institutions without running afoul of the letter of the constitution. There are now twenty multibank holding companies in the state with 122 subsidiaries. They control almost 40 per cent of the total deposits. Two of the top four are First City Bancorporation of Texas and Southwest Bancshares. The lead bank in the former is Houston's First City National; in the latter, Bank of the Southwest. Even as this new technique flourishes, however, the quest for bank charters continues.

A bank charter is a very valuable piece of paper. "It's the next best thing to a Coors beer franchise," one lawyer quips. Charters are adjudged to be so valuable, in fact, that they are granted not by a single individual, but by the three-man State Banking Board, one member of which is called the Banking Commissioner and is appointed by the State Finance Commission. The second member is appointed by the governor for a two-year term, and the third is the State Treasurer himself. A majority vote is sufficient to award a charter. And a majority of the Board is, of course, composed of one elected official and one direct appointee of an elected official, both of whom have been required to mount expensive statewide campaigns every two years.

The cooperation of the big law firms has traditionally

been central to the success of gubernatorial candidates and Treasurer Jesse James. A disillusioned former member of the Banking Board sums up the situation thusly: "Millions of dollars in state funds are lying around in banks at very low interest rates. James has the authority to put the state's money pretty much where he pleases, and a lot of it winds up in Houston, at banks associated with law firms that have helped him stay in office. I'm not suggesting there's been any wrongdoing, but I am suggesting that they [the big Houston firms] understand his problem, and he understands theirs." A big transfusion of state money that can be invested at a profit is, of course, a very useful thing for a bank to have.

Lately the economic importance of the Big Three, especially Vinson Elkins, has been showing definite signs of going international, in a way that has very little to do with banks. The American oil industry, centered in Houston, is not without its influence in the Middle East. Most of the big companies already rely on their lawyers for advice that often transcends the merely technical. If the energy shortage worsens, American policy in that ticklish, oil-rich corner of the world may be affected even more by the judgments of oil men and their lawyers. Firms in New York have for decades influenced the development of American foreign policy, sending partners to counsel presidents and even to serve as Secretaries and Undersecretaries of State. Now it seems to be Houston's turn.

There is another little-noticed basis for the big firms' power. They are *enduring* institutions. A partner at Vinson Elkins reflected this when he remarked, "If you are going into Texas politics, you can assume that VE will be there throughout your career"—adding as an afterthought, "for good or ill, of course."

In a young city like Houston, their age and apparent permanence stand out sharply from the surrounding landscape. In one very real sense they are more powerful than their clients. A lawyer in government service muses on the relationship between Baker & Botts and their pollution-troubled client, Champion Paper. "They've been around longer than Champion Paper and they'll be here when Champion Paper is gone," he says. "The judges on the bench are there because of Baker & Botts, not because of Champion Paper. Whatever happens B&B will still be here: it's just like the government itself. They're going to suffer when their clients suffer, but they're going to bounce back."

The examples could be multiplied endlessly, but the message is the same. The big firms abide while other things change.

## WHAT THE FUTURE HOLDS

Where are the big firms headed? Despite their apparent immutability, they are actually at the threshold of a potentially dangerous transition. Control is passing inexorably from an older generation of generalists who had diverse knowledge of the law, to younger specialists who have spent their professional lives in one narrow "section" of their huge firms. "There is a generation of lawyers coming up who cannot try a lawsuit or set up a small corporation," says a worried freshman associate at a Big Three firm. The fear is that such men may make mistakes their seniors would never have committed because no one will be around to see the overall picture. Whatever may happen, it is clear that the trend toward specialization makes big firm lawyers even more dependent on their institutions, more than ever unable to leave if they are dissatisfied. A lawyer who does nothing but write pension plans is eventually trapped by his own expertise.

The big firms long ago reached a size where the day-to-day demands of managing their affairs became a full-time job for one or more partners. The relentless inroads of bureaucracy continue. Many lawyers who have left to set up practice on their own did so because they felt the management techniques placed an unacceptable barrier between them and their clients. "Time sheets, billing, all the mechanical details began to dominate," said one emigrant who gave up a successful partnership at a Big Six firm. "I kept sending the stuff back, or 'forgetting' to do it, and they put up with my idiosyncrasies because I brought in a hell of a lot of money every year. But that's the only reason I got away with it. Maybe they have to be that formalistic, but there's nothing in a time sheet that reflects the *quality* of the work you do. After a while you fall into the trap of working for your firm instead of your client."

A great lawyer has to have a certain individualistic spirit; the giants of the profession are not technicians. But the big firms put no premium on that quality. Those of their senior partners who have it, began their careers when the firms were still small. If the big firms expect to see it 20 years from now, they will have to pursue it by conscious choice.

As yet, however, they show every indication of moving in the opposite direction. Exhibiting the abundant caution of men who have already got what they want and are determined to keep it, their instinct is to play things safe. The really exotic corporate finance creativity lately, for example, came out of Wynne, Jaffe & Tinsley, a Dallas firm that represented James Ling in his conglomerate sorcery. Could it happen in Houston? Probably not; the tendency is not to be terribly bold. An inventive young lawyer who left one of the Big Three recalls an incident that helped him make up his mind: "We had a client who did business on the Ship Channel. He was worried to death about a proposed new Treasury Regulation that would have required him to report under-the-table payments to captains of foreign vessels—something that was pretty standard in his business. They were kickbacks, really. He didn't mind *reporting* them because they were deductible anyway. But the captains, who weren't reporting them as income, didn't want the government to have any record of them. Our client knew that his competitors would just ignore the Regulation, so that if it were adopted he would lose all his customers because the captains would just deal with his competitors and not with him.

"He was an honest man, and he was about to lose his shirt. So I went up to Washington and testified at a hearing in opposition to the Regulation. I must have been persuasive, because they didn't adopt it. After I got back I told the head of my section what I'd done. I thought he'd be delighted. Instead he was alarmed, and he told me in a stony tone, 'We *do not testify* on behalf of, or in opposition to, legislative matters, without the firm's approval.' What he meant was, 'If you go around changing the law to help one of our clients, you may hurt another, bigger client.' But if the firm had said, no, don't testify, where would that have left my client and me?''

That eternal incubus of the big firms, conflict of interest, subtly depresses their lawyers' creativity and sometimes stifles the free-swinging battling for the client's interest that all lawyers like to believe is their stock in trade.

For all their far-reaching involvement in the political and economic life of Texas, however, the big Houston firms are strangely insular places. Their power paradoxically isolates them from the society they oversee. They inhabit a curious high-rise world, peopled by men of undoubted power whose influence they share and sometimes even create, but disquietingly detached from the human consequences of the decisions they make. An individual who eventually will be affected by something they do may be strolling along Main Street 20 stories below, blithely unaware that his future is being determined in some small particular by a lawyer intent on ''the most intriguing legal problem imaginable,'' to whom he is a negligible abstraction. It happens all the time. The big firms take justifiable pride in their ability to resolve the most intractable legal problems and keep the engines of the Texas economy running smoothly for their clients. One looks in vain for a complementary sense of awe at the power they hold over other men's lives.

''They are law machines, my friend,'' said the trial lawyer who went on to praise them for being the finest concentration of legal talent in the country. He felt, quite rightly, that their ultimate justification lay in that fact. By their own professional lights, there is nothing wrong in siphoning off the best intellectual talent they can find and reshaping it into men whose first loyalty is to the wellbeing of the institution for which they work, rather than to the society of which they are citizens. If the firm's interest ever conflicted with the good of society, they tell themselves, we would of course defend the latter; but such is their perception of society's needs that that day never comes. And so the big Houston firms feel no sense of urgency to offer leadership in the reform of law, to improve the quality of the judiciary, or to elevate the tone of public life.

The source of the malaise is politics, and their inability to reach a reconciliation with it which they can regard as suitably professional. These thoughts were on the mind of a lawyer at one of the Big Three.

''What is a lawyer?'' he asked. ''Is he a professional man, an officer of the court? Or is he a tradesman who has mastered a lucrative craft? What the hell *is* a lawyer? Traditionally a professional man was respected because he was not just 'in it for the money'; he was a leader in the community and he took time away from his moneymaking to do it.

''Now, to a rather blatant degree, lawyers have become the tools of the propertied class. Instead of lawyers being the best read and wisest people in the community, they've become technocrats. Since you don't want to alienate your clients, you begin to think like them and act like them.

''Politics makes very cautious people out of us. When I think of the leadership that is lost to the community when lawyers are inhibited by these things, I become very discouraged indeed. We have a lot more to offer than we give, and we are the ones who are tying ourselves down.''

The clients of the big Houston firms gain excellence, of course; but the loss to the rest of us is considerable.

*—November 1973*

313

# POWER POLITICS

## by Paul Burka

*How one company's wheeling and dealing brought
the energy crisis into your life.*

When L. E. Norman opened his monthly utility bill from the San Antonio City Public Service Board last June he couldn't believe his eyes. Yes, the figures were in the correct column, all right, and they indeed read $101.97. But it had to be a mistake. His May bill had been only $32.93, and even that was a substantial increase over the March amount of $20.68. How could his bill have tripled in one month, *quintupled* in only three? Other San Antonians besieged City Hall with similar questions; to their dismay they learned there had been no mistake. Worse, they were told bluntly that their bills would continue to soar; another increase could be expected by August and still others would follow.

Austin was next, then Corpus Christi. Utility rates in both cities jumped markedly during the summer, stayed high all winter, and will certainly climb even higher during the hot months ahead. (An Austin-based engineer for the Lower Colorado River Authority, which provides electricity for rural Central Texas, predicts it will cost nearly $300 per month to keep his all-electric home functioning this summer.) Nor has the rest of the state escaped the malaise spreading like a plague from South Texas. Natural gas rates will rise in Fort Worth beginning May 1, while Dallas and Houston are fighting delaying actions against inevitable increases. Nothing, absolutely nothing, indicates that utility rates will decrease or even level off; on the contrary, all economic and political signs suggest that the situation will continue to worsen.

These cities, and the more than four million Texans who live in them, have one thing in common: all depend to some degree on a single company for the natural gas which heats their homes and generates their electricity. That company is the giant Coastal States Gas Corporation, an enterprise which—before it helped bring the energy crisis home to

*Paul Burka is an attorney and a senior editor of* Texas Monthly. *He received a grant from the Fund for Investigative Journalism to write "Power Politics."*

Texas—was one of the great success stories of American business. Today the company is fighting for its very existence; the value of its common stock has long ago collapsed, and its assets are threatened by lawsuits totaling more than a billion dollars. Behind it all is Oscar Wyatt, Coastal's founder and chairman of the board. Wyatt is tireless, innovative, daring, charismatic—a man compelling enough to have numbered among his friends Frank Erwin, Sissy Farenthold, Price Daniel, Ralph Yarborough, and Leon Jaworski. Once Wyatt was hailed as an entrepreneurial genius; now he is vilified by critics who seem to blame him for most of the world's evils since the Defenestration of Prague.

In order to understand what has happened to Coastal and its customers, it is first necessary to know something about the gas business. Natural gas is a form of petroleum, but for many years it remained the poor stepchild of crude oil. As late as the 1950s, oil producers wasted trillions of cubic feet of gas by flaring it—an oilfield euphemism for burning gas as a waste product. The usefulness of gas was limited to home heating or cooking; today gas used in this manner is described as *burner-tip gas* or *domestic gas*. Gradually, however, people began to recognize the potential of gas as a clean-burning, marvelously efficient form of energy. And cheap! Oh, was it ever cheap, sometimes as little as two cents per thousand cubic feet (2¢ per mcf). Natural gas could generate heat far more cheaply than its chief competitors, coal and fuel oil. This discovery led to the use of natural gas as *boiler fuel* in power plants: gas heated the water in the boiler, converting it into steam to drive the generators and produce electricity.

Everybody benefited; cheap boiler fuel meant cheap electricity. One of the major beneficiaries was Coastal States Gas Producing Company, the forerunner of Coastal States Gas Corporation. Between 1962 and 1968, Coastal secured contracts to supply virtually all of Central and South Texas with gas for power plants and domestic use; it also agreed to supply gas to companies that served the mammoth Houston and North Texas markets. On the strength of these contracts, Coastal borrowed money to expand its operations until its complex of 41 corporations and subsidiaries formed the eleventh largest corporation in Texas.

How did this corporate Goliath get us—and itself—into this mess? The answer is deceptively simple: Coastal ran out of gas. More precisely, it had more commitments to deliver gas than it had gas to deliver. That is another way of saying that Coastal sold what it turned out not to have—very much the same type of transaction that got Billie Sol Estes in trouble. There are a number of crucial differences, however, not the least of which is that Billie Sol dealt in fertilizer, a product which can be seen and, if necessary, touched and smelled. Natural gas, on the other hand, is buried far below the ground, and is invisible, intangible, even odorless; consequently, there is far greater chance of making a mistake about how much is actually there. The company blames its shortages on just such a mistake—its West Texas fields have produced far below expectations—but some of Coastal's customers believe otherwise. They say that Coastal sold reserves for high prices on the open market in defiance of its contractual obligation to supply local utilities at much lower prices. At the very least, they argue, Coastal failed to behave like a responsible public utility; some have even accused Coastal (and Wyatt personally) of fraud.

Setting aside for the moment the cause of the shortages, the effects have been chaotic. Unable to supply enough gas to satisfy the appetites of all of its customers, Lo-Vaca Gathering Company, the subsidiary that operates Coastal's intrastate pipeline network, had to cut back somewhere. Since domestic gas users have no substitute for burner-tip gas, Lo-Vaca chose to curtail deliveries to electric utilities, forcing local power companies to switch to fuel oil to heat their giant boilers. When the curtailments began in earnest during the severe winter of 1972–73, fuel oil was far more expensive than natural gas; each day a city generated electricity with oil instead of gas cost rate-payers dearly on their next electric bill. Consumers found a new phrase appearing on their monthly statements—"fuel adjustment cost"—which represented a 100 per cent pass-through of the added cost of fuel oil.

More bad news was on the way. In March 1973 Coastal asked the Texas Railroad Commission in effect to revoke the company's fixed-price contracts with the cities by granting Lo-Vaca a new rate reflecting the higher prices the company was paying producers for gas. Lo-Vaca was already paying more at the wellhead for new gas than it was receiving from local utilities under the long-term contracts Coastal signed in the early Sixties. Alarmed by what it learned in a public hearing, the Railroad Commission took formal control of Lo-Vaca away from Coastal and placed the subsidiary under court supervision. Meanwhile the federal Securities and Exchange Commission (SEC) suspended trading of Coastal's stock, which had plummeted from a 1972 high near 60 to 7½ by the time of the suspension in June 1973.

Nevertheless, Lo-Vaca got its rate increase, which of course hit the consumer in the pocketbook again; now he couldn't win even if Lo-Vaca actually delivered the gas it was obligated to supply. Lo-Vaca's customers are currently paying almost seven times the price called for in their contracts. Virtually every penny of the excess has been borne by the consumer, who through it all has steadfastly maintained an air of disbelief. Living in a state which has some

of the world's richest natural gas fields, often within an hour's drive of his beleaguered city, he asks, "How could it happen here?" The answer, as we shall see, is that it could happen *only* here.

# SUCCESS STORY

The pilot looked down from the cockpit at the gas flares burning at night in the Orange Grove Oil Field and knew he was almost home. Beneath him was the desolate South Texas landscape between Alice and Robstown; Corpus Christi, his destination, lay a little to the east. The field was a convenient landmark which the pilot knew well, for he was not a professional aviator but an oil and gas man, the president of Wymore Oil Company of Corpus Christi.

If he had mused about his own life that night, the pilot probably would have been rather satisfied with himself. In only five years he had parlayed a Texas A&M diploma (Class of '49) and a short stint as a roller bit salesman into the presidency of Wymore, a growing company which was developing the lucrative Saint Joseph's Field in Webb County. But if the pilot had been thinking such thoughts, his name would not have been Oscar Wyatt, Jr. Instead, Wyatt's active mind was working overtime. He looked at the flares and thought of all the gas that was going to waste because none of the big pipeline companies found it worthwhile to build a line into the Orange Grove Field. And he had an idea: why not build small lines into Orange Grove, collect the waste gas, and offer it as a package? If he could get enough gas together, perhaps one of the big companies might deal with him.

Wyatt's idea was the genesis of the Coastal States Gas story. By late 1955 Wyatt's enthusiasm for gas (and his enthusiasm in general) brought Wymore to the point of division; Wyatt took all of Wymore's gas properties and his partner got the oil interests. Now Wyatt needed capital. Somehow he coaxed a number of Wymore investors to buy stock in a new company he planned to call Coastal States Oil and Gas.

Coastal's founder may have been short of capital, but he did bring with him two invaluable assets. One was a penchant for hard work, a characteristic he retains even today. By the time Wyatt graduated from Texas A&M as a distinguished student, he had already held down jobs as a hayfield worker, a service station hand (afternoons and weekends for sixteen months), a shipfitter, and a roustabout (for Brown and Root). He had even tried his hand at rice farming while a student at Beaumont's Lamar Junior College, using the profits from a bumper crop to transfer to A&M. His other great asset was an intimate knowledge of the South Texas gas fields. As a salesman for the Reed Roller Bit Company, Wyatt had learned the history of every well.

George Farenthold operated several oil leases in the area when Wyatt was selling roller bits; he recalls that Wyatt was hungry for any information he could get his hands on. "As soon as we'd turn our backs, Oscar would sneak into the tool house and start checking the drilling logs to see what kind of luck we were having," Farenthold says with a grin. "Sometimes we'd have to tell him to keep his nose out of the books because we were running a tight [secret] hole, but that didn't seem to help much." (Farenthold and his wife—gubernatorial candidate Sissy—are the godparents of

Wyatt's eldest child.) Wyatt was doing his homework, learning where the gas was and who had it. With the formation of Coastal, he was ready to put that knowledge to use.

Coastal States was Wyatt's entry into a very tough league. It wasn't easy for a newcomer to break into the gas business in 1955. Unlike the oil business, which always seemed to have room for another independent, the gas industry was tightly controlled by a few large companies. There are at least three routes to wealth and power in the oil industry—production, refining, and marketing—but in the gas business in 1955 there was only one: transportation. An oil producer can ship his crude oil to a refinery by pipeline, truck, or rail; a gas producer has but a single option—gas can be transported only by pipeline. The big pipeline companies, therefore, had immense power over producers, for without a connecting pipeline, a gas well—no matter how productive—was useless.

The major pipeline companies—Tennessee Gas, Texas Eastern, United, perhaps one or two others—controlled the South Texas gas fields in the early Fifties. They would hook up with a gas field only if it had enough reserves; normally the company would build one mile of pipeline for each billion cubic feet of reserves. Because a federal court had ruled that the Texas Railroad Commission could not regulate gas production (as it did oil), the pipeline companies established their own rationing system. They handed out payments to all the owners in a field—regardless of whether they actually had wells on their property—in proportion to each owner's share of the underground reservoir. The companies even set their own daily allowable; they would take one million cubic feet of gas each day for each eight billion cubic feet of reserves, a formula designed to insure that the field would last for twenty years. Finally, the companies respected each other's territory, a sensible business decision which avoided duplication of expensive pipelines. It also avoided competition. Every gas field was a monopoly, a separate fiefdom subject to the absolute rule of the pipeline company.

Oscar Wyatt knew all this, of course, but he also realized that the very circumstances which gave the monopolies their power could be turned against them. Wyatt did the one thing the pipeline companies did not anticipate: he built his own pipeline network. Coastal States Oil and Gas (soon to become Coastal States Gas Producing Company) began in November 1955 with 68 miles of pipe into fields too small for the big companies to bother about. Before long Wyatt was ready to challenge their monopolies in the big fields. Wyatt signed contracts with small landowners (known in the industry as "town lot operators" because the tracts often were ten acres or less), who were effectively shut out by the big companies' practice of paying owners in proportion to their share of the field, whether they drilled or not. Wyatt would put in a pipeline and start hauling off gas. Coastal paid less for the gas than did the big companies, but the town lot owner was incomparably better off with his own well than he was under the proportional ownership formula imposed by the big companies. Wyatt sweetened his offer still further by promising to take one million cubic feet daily for each two billion cubic feet of reserves, a rate four times as fast as that used by the big companies.

Wyatt's tactics enraged both the larger producers and the established pipeline companies. The town lot operators were producing far more gas than lay underneath their own small tracts—much of the gas came from beneath the larger landowners in the field. True, it was all perfectly legal under the rule of capture (which declares that oil and gas are not owned until produced), but it was practically like stealing gas, or so the pipeline companies claimed.

Coastal's tactics did not win it many friends in the industry. Competitors whispered that Coastal pilfered gas in other ways that weren't so clearly within the law. Gas can be measured only with the aid of a complicated instrument known as an orifice meter, and even then the meter readings are subject to interpretation. Producers were always complaining about Coastal's calculations. In its early years the company was in and out of courthouses all over South Texas, getting sued by unhappy producers who felt shortchanged. One former Coastal employee says he has no doubt Coastal "took the benefit of the doubt on meter readings." There were other complaints about meters as well: some producers were convinced that Coastal tampered with meters by surreptitiously changing the diameter of the orifice. They installed their own meters as a check against Coastal's, an unusual but not unprecedented action. One San Antonio producer who is no admirer of Coastal States says he "never had double metering in his life with any pipeline company except Coastal." (Charges of meter-tampering were buttressed considerably by the fact that Coastal occasionally reported "negative line losses" to the Railroad Commission—in other words, more gas came out of Coastal's pipelines than went into them. On the other hand, this mysterious surplus could also be explained by reasonable ambiguities in meter-reading that Coastal resolved in favor of itself.)

Most of Coastal's tactics weren't new to the industry; other small operators used the town lot device, and every company interpreted meters to its own advantage. Coastal, however, refused to remain in the shadow of the major pipeline companies. Instead, it developed an entirely new concept in the gas business: the gathering company, which was neither a producer nor a major pipeline company, but rather a broker that bought and packaged gas for resale. Coastal revolutionized the gas industry in Texas; it broke the monopoly and went on to create an even larger one of its own. In the end it was not only Coastal's methods but also its successes that aroused such resentment in its competitors.

As Coastal's markets grew, so did its need for gas. Wyatt was already getting gas from town lot wells at low prices; now he began to outbid the big pipelines in other fields. To their consternation, the big companies now found that they actually *needed* Coastal. The big companies pegged all their payments to the highest prices they were paying in a field; if they started paying more for gas to any one producer, then they had to renegotiate all their contracts. So the large pipelines let Coastal outbid them, then purchased the gas from Coastal. The single purchase might be more expensive, but at least it wouldn't trigger the price escalation clauses in all their other contracts. Coastal, meanwhile, got a handsome profit for acting as a broker.

Oscar Wyatt had pulled it off. Not only had he successfully challenged the big boys, in the process he had made his company indispensable to them. He exuded optimism; in the early days the atmosphere at Coastal States was pervaded with a sense of destiny. "We knew we were going someplace—we didn't know how far, how fast, how big, but we did know there weren't any limits," says Ellis Brown, an attorney in Coastal's land department from 1958 to 1964. Wyatt developed a talented management team even though salaries started out well below the industry average. The staff was small, young, dedicated, and overworked. Wyatt himself was only 31 when he founded Coastal. As president he set the pace—driving, pushing, calling employees in middle of the night, working in his shirtsleeves, acting—in the words of one of his engineers—"like he was going to die if he didn't get the next dollar."

The tempo of life at Coastal was furious; time was precious, so important that sometimes it seemed as though time and not natural gas was Coastal's chief commodity. "Time is the most valuable thing in the world," Wyatt said in 1965. "When it is gone it can't be replaced." (His critics would add that much the same thing can be said about natural gas.) Almost 90 per cent of Coastal's top employees had pilot training (Wyatt had his license at age sixteen), and the company transacted much of its business by air. Wyatt's impatience with wasting time and his proclivity for taking over the controls occasionally caused complications for his passengers. Once when he was flying into Austin from Corpus Christi, Wyatt radioed the control tower for permission to land with the wind so that he wouldn't have to spend the time circling halfway around the field. On another flight into Austin he suddenly put the plane into a steep spiral dive when he saw a hole in the thick clouds enveloping the city. His uninformed passengers thought they were doomed. Usually, however, Wyatt did little actual flying even in Coastal's early years; he liked to take off and land, but the rest was too monotonous. It was a waste of time.

Wyatt has been described as a genius by both his critics and his admirers. His early associates remember that he could calculate in his head faster than engineers could operate a slide rule. Ellis Brown says that Wyatt could grasp a complex point of law better than any other layman and many lawyers; what's more, Brown says, Wyatt never forgot it.

Wyatt's creative energies matched his retentive powers. Almost everything about Coastal States during its early years was innovative: the concept of a gathering company, its method of attracting investors, and its approach to financing. Coastal paid no cash dividends—highly unusual for a company in the utility business—but was instead a growth stock. And what growth! The original stock was valued at $5 a share; by 1961 it was selling for $87.50 before splitting three-for-one. In 1963 it was first listed on the New York Stock Exchange, opening at 29. It crept upwards to 32¾ by mid-1965, and then began the phenomenal growth that made Coastal States Gas a darling of Wall Street: 49¾ in late 1967, a ten percent stock dividend in January 1968 and a high of 69⅝ in April of that year before splitting again, this time two-for-one. One hundred shares of stock purchased in 1955 for $500 would then have been worth $22,960.

Wyatt was equally successful in developing new forms of financing. Traditionally, pipeline companies offered their pipelines as security for bank loans. Coastal, on the other hand, made contracts to buy and sell gas, hoping to borrow money based on anticipated profits. There was some risk involved, to be sure, but Wyatt once explained his philosophy of business as "taking a reasonable risk and then working like hell to make sure it works."

Some of his former employees, looking back on their days with Coastal States, shake their heads and wonder how they survived. Most say they would never do it again, that the drain on their physical resources was too great; but all agree that working for Wyatt was an unforgettable experience. A former Coastal vice-president tried to explain how he felt: "In most big corporations, the only time you see the chairman of the board is on the cover of the annual report. If you work for Coastal States Gas, the chairman of the board will be in to see *you*. He wants to know if you're his kind of person—quick, ambitious, self-starting, willing to take a risk. The air is really electric around there, knowing that he might come through that door any minute." He paused for a minute, then added, "That's a lot of pressure."

Wyatt departed from traditional patterns in the political sphere, just as he did in the business world. He was somewhat unpopular for a time in financial circles for espousing liberal economic theories, but as usual he was ahead of his time, one of the few businessmen in the Fifties who understood how inflation worked to his advantage. Coastal was a growth company, short of capital and surviving on borrowed funds; he recognized that inflation enabled him to pay off loans with cheaper money. His first political ventures were on the liberal side in Corpus Christi; at one point in the early Sixties he was so popular he was urged to run for mayor. By 1964 he was known as a big liberal contributor on a statewide level, and during the U.S. Senate campaign that year he was cochairman of a Ralph Yarborough appreciation dinner. But his liberalism stopped at the plant gate. When Coastal bought the old Sinclair refinery in Corpus Christi in 1962, Wyatt spent heavily (and successfully) to beat an effort to unionize the plant.

An unusual aspect of Wyatt's political involvement is his interest in the judiciary, a branch of government often ignored by businessmen. He has contributed heavily to opponents of judges who have ruled against him, and is generally credited with the defeat of a Mission district judge named William Rogers Blalock in 1960. (Blalock, who now lives in Houston, says he was warned by a friendly lawyer after the trial that "ruling against Oscar Wyatt is serious business." Blalock's decision was later upheld by the Texas Supreme Court.) Wyatt is known to have entertained a number of state district judges lavishly at his South Texas ranches. Information collected by the Securities and Exchange Commission, which has been investigating Coastal States off and on for two years, confirms Wyatt's involvement in judicial politics.

## TOO GOOD TO BE TRUE

By 1960 Coastal had reached a plateau, just as Wymore had in 1954 when Oscar Wyatt flew over the Orange Grove Field. In less than five years, Coastal had increased its assets from $3.3 million to more than $48 million, and had carved out a strong foothold for itself in the gas industry. It had a somewhat unsavory reputation in the industry, and was decidedly unpopular among its competitors, but it was here to stay nevertheless. Coastal had carried Wyatt's original gas-gathering idea about as far as it would go; now Wyatt had to decide whether to continue to grow, or to slow down and consolidate his successes. The decision was inevitable from the beginning; growth it would be.

If the old idea had spent its force, then it was time for a new idea. Wyatt's first choice was a cross-state pipeline to supply El Paso Natural Gas, but that faded quickly under the threat of Federal Power Commission intervention. Then, just as Wyatt and Coastal were casting about for new markets, a series of fateful decisions in three Texas cities opened the way for Coastal to supply four million Texans with natural gas. The gas broker was about to become, at least in name, a public utility.

Most of the great success stories of American business involve a piece of luck, and the rise of Coastal States is no exception. Oscar Wyatt's good fortune was that long-term gas contracts in three large Texas cities—Corpus Christi, Austin, San Antonio—were up for bids between 1960 and 1962, which was perfect timing for Coastal States. The company was old enough to have a firm financial base, but young enough to remain innovative, daring, and, above all, hungry. If the contracts had lapsed even three years earlier, Coastal would have been in no position to make a move; a few years later the supply of gas was becoming so scarce that competition for new markets would have been virtually impossible.

Circumstances in all three cities were different—San Antonio owned both its gas and electric utilities; Austin controlled only its electric system; Corpus Christi owned the three gas distribution systems which served its residents—but in one essential way all three cities were alike. They all wanted cheap gas. Each was lured by the promise of low prices; each believed that gas would be available forever. The few spokesmen for restraint went unheard; the low bids were too attractive to pass up. In the end the cities bought twenty-year gas supplies with little more caution than if they were buying two years' worth of ball-point pens. The cities in the early Sixties did exactly what they later accused Coastal of doing in the early Seventies: they went after the quick dollar, the short-term gain, and ignored the long-range consequences. This is their story:

Corpus Christi, 1960. Everybody involved in local politics knew that Oscar Wyatt was a brash upstart, but this time he had gone too far. The city's gas advisory committee had just negotiated a twenty-year contract with Houston Natural Gas, which had supplied the main city distribution system since 1952; all that remained to make the contract effective was perfunctory approval by the city council and the voters. Then, with the election only six weeks away, here came a letter from Wyatt, questioning whether the proposed contract was the best one obtainable, and asking for a hearing before the committee.

Wyatt had a point. The old contract required the city to pay only 8.5¢ per mcf; the new agreement averaged 26.5¢ per mcf for eight years, with the remaining twelve years at cost-plus. But the advisory committee ignored him, and Wyatt vowed to fight. His attorneys questioned the legality of a negotiated contract, arguing that the city was required to take bids. Wyatt accused Mayor Ellroy King of playing political footsie with Houston Natural and trailed King and other supporters of the negotiated contract as they made the civic club circuit; whenever and wherever King spoke, Wyatt was present, monopolizing a microphone on the floor, turning a question-and-answer session into a debate. After four weeks of relentless pressure, Wyatt forced King to agree to a televised confrontation. It was no contest. The best argument King could muster was that the city had already come up with the best obtainable contract. Wyatt exploded that by offering to bid fifteen per cent lower than the Houston Natural price. He wasn't asking for Coastal States to get the contract, Wyatt kept saying, just for the chance to bid.

When he wasn't debating King, Wyatt was appearing at black churches, courting Mexican-Americans, and visiting union halls—putting together a potent political coalition of minority groups, labor, and white liberals. They were his natural allies, not because he was carrying the liberal banner—the gas contract fight had nothing to do with liberal-conservative issues—but because he was taking on the entrenched establishment, represented by King and the majority of the city council. Despite his business success and his contributions to the city (two downtown buildings and a third one planned, a payroll of $1.5 million, $10 million spent annually by Coastal in Corpus Christi), Wyatt was considered a pariah by the local establishment. They found him brash, cocky, and pushy, a young man in too much of a hurry; they hadn't accepted him by 1960 and they never did. But they were no match for him in open combat. Despite the relative obscurity of the gas contract issue, Wyatt's coalition turned out a record vote for a special election, and the Houston Natural contract was rejected by a 2–1 margin.

The city then drew up specifications for both a twenty-year contract and a short-term contract which the council could award without approval from the voters. Wyatt angrily charged that the specifications favored Houston Natural (one of the conditions could only be met by a company which was already supplying gas to the city), and promised another fight. Coastal was low bidder for the twenty-year period, but Houston Natural reduced its previous offer substantially to become low bidder for the five-year, short-term contract. To no one's surprise, a Houston engineering firm hired as the city's consultant recommended a short-term agreement with Houston Natural. The city council awarded the contract over Wyatt's protests that his twenty-year offer was a better deal. Wyatt promptly retaliated by filing suit as a taxpayer in state district court. When the trial judge found "fatal defects" in the contract and declared it void, it looked like Coastal might win after all; but an appellate court, without ruling on the validity of the contract, declared that Wyatt could not contest the procedure as a taxpayer, since no tax funds were involved. For a few days Wyatt blustered about appealing to the Texas Supreme Court, but eventually he accepted the adverse ruling. He had, after all, accomplished a great deal: through sheer force of personality, he had sliced fifteen years—and 3¢ per mcf—off Houston Natural's contract. What's more, the political coalition he forged had meanwhile grown into the Progress Party, which ousted the establishment-backed Action Party in the 1961 city elections. Coastal's president had proved himself a force to be reckoned with in local politics.

The point was not lost on Houston Natural. When the new city council asked for bids in 1962 on a twenty-year contract to become effective when the short-term Houston Natural contract expired in 1966, HNG didn't even enter a bid. In 1953, at the high water mark of its influence in Corpus Christi, Houston Natural had almost purchased the main city-owned gas system; it already owned a distribution system serving the fast-growing southeast area of the city near the Naval Air Station. Now, less than a decade later, it reluctantly prepared to withdraw from the lucrative Corpus Christi market. Houston Natural even sold its own distribution facilities to the city, retaining only an option to continue supplying the southeast area through 1977. The Corpus Christi gas market was wide open.

The immediate beneficiary, however, was not Coastal States, but a little-known Houston outfit called Lumar Gas Company. Coastal bid substantially lower than it had in 1960, but Lumar's offer, city officials said, was "a much lower figure than expected." Indeed, it was 6¢ per mcf lower than the existing HNG contract, an astounding bid of only 18.5 cents. Newspaper reports indicate that the city could hardly believe its good fortune; why, *it was almost too good to be true!* Not even Coastal States could match that price, and Lumar got the contract even though it was only two years old, had no major supply contracts, and had no guaranteed reserves.

Almost immediately there was trouble. Five months before Lumar was to start deliveries to Corpus Christi, it asked the city to put up $600,000 to help build a connecting pipeline. That ominous sign was followed by a letter to the city council from Coastal questioning Lumar's ability to live up to its contract. In fact, Lumar was in deep financial trouble, and so were two of its directors who had personally cosigned a loan to the company from the First City National Bank of Houston; one of those directors was a lawyer who was closely connected to the bank both personally and through the giant Vinson Elkins law firm. The company had paid no interest on the note, but time was running out. So was Lumar's gas; the hoped-for reserves hadn't panned out. Coastal bailed Lumar out by purchasing its Corpus Christi operations through an intermediary company called Hydrocarbon Development.

So Coastal now had the contract to supply the main Corpus Christi gas system that it had failed to get twice before—but for a substantially lower price than it had been willing to accept on either occasion. If this worried people in authority in Corpus Christi, then they kept it to themselves. Meanwhile, Coastal States was busily consolidating the remainder of the Corpus Christi market. Central Power and Light, the giant South Texas electric utility, made Coastal its chief supplier of natural gas for boiler fuel in 1964. One year later Coastal acquired the supply contract for the tiny city-owned Southern Community distribution system on the western edge of town. The Southern Community contract passed to Coastal when it purchased the previous supplier, Southern Coast Corporation, a small local company that had been operating more or less under Coastal's wing for several years.

The last holdout was the old Houston Natural Gas distribution system. HNG was still supplying the southeast area under a contract which required it to accept the same price paid to the supplier of the main city system. That worked fine from 1962 until 1966, so long as Houston Natural also supplied the main system. But when Lumar took over in 1966, Houston Natural's payoff dropped from 24.5¢ mcf to 18.5 cents. One year later HNG cancelled its option to renew and yielded its last foothold in Corpus Christi.

Now there was no one left but Coastal States. Suddenly the company—which had been so eager to supply gas at low prices—took a hard line: it informed the city the new price for the HNG system would be well above 18.5 cents. The city refused to negotiate and called for bids. But there was no one left to challenge Coastal. The new contract called for Coastal to receive 23.5 cents, with regular price escalations. Seven years after the Corpus Christi city council had given Houston Natural Gas a twenty-year contract over Oscar Wyatt's objections, Coastal States had a complete monopoly in Corpus Christi.

Austin, 1962. Frank Erwin's name was not yet a household word, but the Austin City Council knew very well who he was: a close associate of Vice President Lyndon Johnson and gubernatorial nominee John Connally, a power in state Democratic Party circles, and a highly skilled lobbyist with a shrewd mind and an acerbic tongue. He had made his political reputation in Washington by guiding a depletion allowance for brick manufacturers through Congress after numerous other lobbyists had tried and failed. He was a good advocate to have on your side in a tough fight; there was little chance his clients would not get a full and fair hearing. And his client, Coastal States Gas Producing Company, was in a *very* tough fight: it was bidding to supply Austin's power plants with natural gas, a contract which had been held for 37 years by United Gas of Shreveport.

A strange combination of circumstances brought Erwin before the council on behalf of Coastal. In the late Fifties, Councilwoman Emma Long got the idea that Austin shouldn't rely on United, but should find a permanent gas supply. She wanted the city to build its own pipeline to a field near Mineral Wells, but her male colleagues on the council had a well-developed habit of ignoring the somewhat iconoclastic Mrs. Long and this was no exception. So she approached former Governor Allan Shivers, who was more receptive. Shivers joined with oil and gas lawyer Clint Small and others to form a group known as Intra-Tex, which would seek the contract to supply Austin's proposed Holly Street power plant. They even obtained a conditional contract signed by the city manager, but, Small recalls, Mayor Tom Miller torpedoed the deal and forced the council to ask for bids. This touched off a wild fight among four companies, including Coastal States. Eventually the city hired a consultant to evaluate the bids; he turned out to be a former attorney for United, and when he recommended that United get a five-year contract, the Intra-Tex group headed for the courthouse. United agreed to resubmit the contract for bids, along with a new long-term contract to supply the city's other electrical generating stations. The two contracts were lumped together, and the Intra-Tex group prepared another bid. They retained Erwin to plead their case and made a contract with Coastal States for the gas.

Apparently Coastal had a change of heart and decided to bid on the contract in its own name, but first it had to get Intra-Tex out of the way. Coastal paid Small (Shivers had dropped out by this time) to release Coastal from its obligation to supply gas—and to keep Intra-Tex out of the bidding. This transaction has been characterized, somewhat unfairly, by San Antonio Congressman Henry B. Gonzalez as a "finder's fee," but the evidence does not support the charge. Intra-Tex obviously was not conceived as a front for Coastal; indeed, had the conditional contract become binding in 1960, Intra-Tex planned to purchase its gas from Houston Natural and not Coastal.

United, meanwhile, was not at all happy about how the situation was developing. The company had a huge capital investment in the Austin area—hundreds of miles of pipelines—which would be useless unless it won the bid. United argued strenuously, just as it was doing in San Antonio, that competitive bidding for the gas supply contract was an unwise course for the city. Any company could throw together a low bid just to win the contract, United contended. Further, they said, such bids meant nothing because a pipeline company is a public utility which by law is entitled to make a profit. If the contract price proved insufficient, the winning company could always go to the Railroad Commission and ask for a rate increase; the Commission would have to keep the company afloat in order to keep the gas coming into the city.

We'll put a stop to that, said the city. It included a clause in the contract extracting a promise from the winning company never to go to the Railroad Commission for rate relief. Coastal says the clause was the city's idea, but Erwin recalls that the concept originated with Coastal. "United was giving us a hard time, saying our bids didn't mean anything," Erwin says. "Oscar's number two man was up here for the negotiations, and he authorized me to say that we'd never go to the Railroad Commission."

Whoever idea it was, there is little doubt that the provision is meaningless. You can't contract away the jurisdiction of a regulatory body to act in the public interest; that is basic second-week-law-school stuff. Tracy DuBose, a Houston attorney who is handling most of Coastal's litigation, calls the paragraph "Mickey Mouse language." DuBose, who was with a Corpus Christi law firm in 1962 but did some work for Coastal, says he wasn't in on the contract negotiations, "but if I had been, I'd have advised, 'Sure, go ahead and sign it, it doesn't mean anything.'"

Three companies bid for the Austin contract: Coastal, United, and Humble. Coastal had filed an open offer with the city clerk *before* the bidding deadline, primarily to discourage competition. Humble beat Coastal's original price, but Coastal's sealed bid undercut its first proposal by $18 million. That ended Humble's chances. United's offer was more difficult to evaluate because it failed to meet contract specifications. For one thing, United refused to bid fixed prices for twenty years; for another, United would not agree to the provision never to seek rate relief. Erwin repeatedly stressed that Coastal was giving the city everything it wanted. On October 5, the Lower Colorado River Authority (LCRA) which had sought bids jointly with the City of Austin, awarded its contract to Coastal over Humble and United. One week later, Austin went with Coastal too.

Before another year had passed, Coastal won the residential gas contract for Austin over United, driving the Louisiana company out of the Central Texas market for good. Once again Coastal bid firm prices for twenty years, while United would bid for only ten years. Emma Long, back on the council after a four-year absence, was skeptical of Coastal's offer, and tried to get Coastal to dedicate specific reserves to the Austin contract. Again she received no support from her council colleagues. "Wyatt snowed them," she says, recalling his charm, optimism, and forcefulness. Coastal's founder spent most of his time in Austin during the contract fight; his ebullience and drive overwhelmed the council.

By this time, United had had just about all it could take; it asked the Federal Power Commission to put a stop to Coastal States' maneuvers. The FPC, whose function is to regulate interstate gas, said it had no jurisdiction over intrastate matters. United undoubtedly knew this all along; it probably went to the FPC out of utter frustration. United was an old company, somewhat stodgy and unquestionably arrogant toward its customers—but it was a basically sound and conservative organization, not given to making promises it might not be able to keep. Coastal, on the other hand, was a growing company, hungry for new markets and willing to gamble with its promises to get them. Furthermore—and this aspect cannot be underrated—it had Erwin to make its offer credible. Erwin himself says that "if the city council had known that Coastal was eventually going to go to the Railroad Commission, they'd never have let them have the contract." Erwin today feels little loyalty toward Coastal, his former client: "I think the bastards ought to be put in the penitentiary."

San Antonio, 1960. The City Public Service Board (CPSB), which operates the city-owned electric and gas utilities, wasn't getting anywhere in its discussions with United Gas. The Louisiana-based pipeline company had supplied the city with natural gas for 38 years, but the current contract was running out and negotiations for a new one were not going well for the city. United wanted to raise the price of its gas from 17¢ per mcf to 30 cents, an increase the CPSB equated with piracy. Nor was price the only point of contention: United refused to bid firm prices for a long-term contract, and it also declined to dedicate specific reserves to San Antonio's use. What really upset the CPSB, however, was United's attitude. The company owned the only pipeline capable of bringing gas to San Antonio, and it rarely missed an opportunity to remind the city negotiators of this monopoly position. Irritated by United arrogance, the City Public Service Board decided to teach its long-time gas supplier a lesson in power politics.

In most cities a government-owned utility like City Public Service would have been no match for a giant company like United Gas. But CPS was no ordinary municipal utility. It answered not to the city council but to a self-perpetuating board of trustees who constituted the essence of power in San Antonio. In 1960 the five-member board included (in addition to J. E. Kuykendall, the city's mayor) the president of Joske's, the president of Alamo Iron Works, an attorney for the King Ranch, and the chairman of the board of the National Bank of Commerce. The mayor was the only board member chosen by the public; the remainder had been selected by their predecessors and would in turn choose their successors.

Together they ran the utility system as if it were a private corporation, rarely consulting the city council or the city administration. This strange arrangement was designed to inspire confidence in potential bondholders by placing businessmen rather than politicians at the top of the utility's organizational chart, but it had another purpose as well. It supplied the rich and the powerful with a means of retaining control of the machinery of government in a city where they were fast becoming part of an ethnic minority. Regardless of the makeup of the city council, the old leadership could be sure of controlling the utility system and its rate structure. (Other special boards oversee other important functions of government—water, hospitals, and transportation.) Many of the board members through the years have been real heavyweights—financially, politically, and socially— and the CPS board in 1960 was no exception. These were not the people to have mad at you when you were after a $500-million gas contract.

United had been blithely ignoring these political realities for years. In fact, the CPSB had considered dumping United as far back as 1952, when the city's contract with the company still had ten years to run. Alarmed by the prospect of bargaining with a haughty monopoly, the board hired a consultant to assess three options the CPSB might choose when the contract expired: renew with United, put the contract up for competitive bids, or go into the natural gas business and become its own supplier. To the board's dismay, the consultant recommended renewing with United for as long a term as possible.

What the board really wanted was to go into business for itself—or to threaten United that it would do so. It needed *something* to use as leverage in the contract negotiations. But geologist William Spice (of whom more will be heard later) advised the board that there wasn't enough gas available within 150 miles of San Antonio to make public ownership a feasible business operation. That left competitive bids as the CPSB's only alternative to United.

Overconfident, United brushed off the danger. United contended that CPS could not legally put the contract up for bids and that competitive bidding for a utility contract was not in the public interest. San Antonio couldn't abandon United and its heavy investment in a pipeline network, the company argued, any more than United could refuse to sell gas to San Antonio when it had the only pipeline. If the city didn't like United's offer, then it should ask the Railroad Commission to set a fair price—not ask for competitive bids. After a few years of this, the CPSB and the city had heard enough. On July 8, 1960, they advertised for competitive bids on a twenty-year contract to supply two trillion feet of gas.

Three major companies bid for the contract: United, Houston Pipeline (a subsidiary of Houston Natural Gas), and Coastal States. Coastal's bid was far higher than the other two. But the low bidder was not one of those major companies; in fact, it was not a company at all. It was two San Antonio businessmen, Glen Martin and Fred Schoolfield, who decided they could supply gas more cheaply than anybody else.

Martin and Schoolfield had little more than an idea. They had no corporation, no pipeline, and no gas. They did, however, have one major asset: by this time the CPSB's relationship with United had so deteriorated that the board was looking for any excuse to avoid doing business with United. Martin and Schoolfield's proposed Alamo Gas Supply Company provided the necessary alternative. What's more, their backers included some of the most respected names in San Antonio oil and gas circles—all of them well known to the businessmen who sat on the City Public Service Board.

From this point on, strange things began to happen. Between October 1960 and January 1961, the CPSB staff prepared four different comparisons between the Alamo and United bids; their conclusion on each occasion was that the

gap between Alamo's bid and United's was even wider than it first appeared. (These were staff estimates, remember, not new bids.) Some of the staff's actions seem highly questionable; for example, they summarily reduced the estimated cost of Alamo's pipeline from $6.5 million to $1 million for no apparent reason. Best indications are that the final cost was indeed around $6 million. By the time the fourth and final comparison was made, the original spread of $14 million between the two bids had grown to—in theory at least—$33 million.

Other bids were not seriously considered. The best prices Coastal States could offer were anywhere from 2¢ to 6¢ per mcf higher than Alamo's. Houston Pipeline essentially matched United's bid, but offered firm prices only for the first 1.2 trillion cubic feet, reserving the right to charge cost-plus for the last 800 billion. Houston Pipeline's president prophetically warned the CPSB that a long-term, fixed-price contract was a gamble no responsible company would take, but the CPSB had heard that kind of talk from United and had ceased to listen.*

On January 12, 1961, the City Public Service Board tentatively decided in favor of Martin and Schoolfield. But the local oilmen still had work to do before the contract became final. Within a few months they would have to show that Alamo had 1.2 trillion cubic feet of gas under contract and dedicated to San Antonio. They would also have to arrange financing of Alamo's pipeline by responsible investment bankers. Five months earlier Martin and Schoolfield had begun with nothing; now they had a conditional contract and a corporation, but they still didn't have a single cubic foot of gas. The conditional contract was really little more than a "hunting license" to search for gas—or at least that's the way Alamo's New York underwriters described it. United Gas thought so too. It attacked the conditional contract before the Railroad Commission and in court, calling it "not a contract but a device to help Martin and Schoolfield obtain the gas reserves, pipeline system, and financing that they needed before they could enter into a gas supply contract."

Months of work and millions of dollars now depended upon whether Alamo could come up with the gas. Understandably worried about dealing with a wholly new entry in the pipeline business, the CPSB asked several San Antonio oilmen whether they thought Alamo could pull it off. The oilmen were dubious. (One later changed his mind and ended up on Alamo's board of directors.) Martin and Schoolfield eased CPSB fears by offering to use the best consultants in the business, DeGolyer and MacNaughton of Dallas, to verify the reserves. For financing, Alamo would use White, Weld & Co. of New York, another blue-ribbon firm. But things didn't quite work out that way. In early May, White, Weld broke off financing negotiations. As for

*The text of the letter from Houston Pipeline's president to the CPSB is worth noting:

"[A]nyone offering to supply your entire requirements at fixed prices must be gambling on his ability to buy or discover gas in the future as your requirements increase. In view of the great uncertainties as to what the future cost of gas will be and the large volumes involved, no responsible supplier can afford to assume the risk that the cost of gas in the field may approach or rise above the prices quoted for delivery to the City. This risk must be considered most substantial when it is recognized that the average wellhead price of gas has increased at the rate of approximately 1¢ per mcf for the past ten years."

the reserve study, DeGolyer-MacNaughton was never formally approached. Alamo's reserves were indeed verified, but by a roundabout method that at best can be described as highly irregular. At worst, well, a San Antonio grand jury spent several months in late 1974 studying the events leading to the award of the final Alamo contract for evidence of fraud and conspiracy. The grand jury didn't find an indictable offense, but District Attorney Ted Butler's staff is still looking. Because, you see, the ink was hardly dry on the final contract before Alamo's reserves proved to be short, hopelessly short, 99 per cent short in some cases.

Here's what happened: the CPSB hired its own independent geologist to survey Alamo's claimed reserves. Its choice was William Spice, the same consultant who several years before had found that there was not enough gas near San Antonio for the CPSB to go into the gas business. Now he found there was more than enough for Alamo, 1.340 trillion cubic feet, to be exact. The firm Alamo hired instead of DeGolyer and MacNaughton also came up with a figure topping the critical 1.2 trillion mark. But Spice's conclusions were far more important to the CPSB. He was working for the board, not for Alamo; furthermore, Alamo's consultants had relied heavily on Spice's data in their report. The Spice study clinched Alamo's bid. One week after Spice handed his report to the CPSB, the board gave Alamo the final contract.

The Spice report is filled with irregularities. A consulting engineer who analyzed Spice's work for the San Antonio grand jury concluded that "reserves were added with little, if any, supporting data." In one gas field, the giant Word field in Lavaca County, the grand jury's consultant determined that reserves "were simply added to the reserve tabulation in order to achieve the minimum total reserve" of 1.2 trillion feet called for in the bid specifications. Spice's report also contained "probable misrepresentation," and used reserve determinations that were "entirely opinion, unsupported with fact." By the time the grand jury began its probe of the Alamo Gas contract, it was apparent that no more than 40 per cent of the reserves verified by Spice were recoverable.

Did Spice fake the study? San Antonio Congressman Henry B. Gonzalez thinks so. In a series of speeches on the House floor he has accused Spice of falsifying his report to save the contract for Alamo Gas. Gonzalez points out that more than one-third of Spice's $34,200 fee was eventually paid by Alamo, which in 1962 reimbursed CPS $12,475 for Spice's work. The current CPS board chairman has described this transaction as "at best, a gigantic conflict of interest." There are also indications (which Martin denies) that Martin—who, more than his partner Schoolfield, was the force behind Alamo—was deep in debt in 1961. If this is true, the Alamo contract could have insured his financial recovery. Any hope of exploring Martin's financial dealings during this period was erased in 1974, however, when San Antonio District Judge Preston Dial quashed a grand jury subpoena for Martin and his records.

Spice himself says he doesn't know what happened to the gas. He points out that many of the fields had little production history, making it impossible to use the most accurate method of measuring reserves—comparing the volume of gas produced with the drop in pressure of the well. Any other reserve measurement, Spice says, is educated guesswork and could be off 15 to 25 per cent either way. He

also speculates that after Coastal States took over Alamo in 1963, it may have produced and sold the gas without telling anyone, including the Railroad Commission.

There is another explanation which lies somewhere between intentional fraud and honest mistake. People in the oil and gas industry joke that the first question a consultant asks when he is hired to verify reserves is, "Are you buying or selling?" Reserve estimates are exactly that; petroleum geology is an inexact science. One of the leading oil and gas consultants in Texas says that Spice is a good man to have when you're selling; he tends toward optimism. Ostensibly his client, the City Public Service Board, was buying—but were they? Spice must have known how badly the CPSB wanted to do business with Alamo and avoid going back to United. The CPSB wanted those reserves to be there just as much as Martin and Schoolfield did.

While Spice was completing his study of Alamo's reserves, White, Weld & Co. was having second thoughts about financing the venture. Martin said in a deposition taken in early 1975 that White, Weld withdrew its offer because United Gas had applied pressure in New York financial circles. (Alamo sued United in 1963, claiming that United had interfered with its financing arrangements, but never pursued the lawsuit.) White, Weld, on the other hand, recently told investigators from the Bexar County district attorney's office that it withdrew because Alamo's reserves were deficient. Both stories could be true, because United was proclaiming loudly to anyone who would listen that Alamo did not have enough gas.

Meanwhile, in Corpus Christi Oscar Wyatt and Coastal States Gas Producing Company had troubles of their own. Coastal had just swung its first big deal, an agreement with El Paso Natural Gas which required Coastal to build a pipeline to West Texas. Wyatt had already purchased tons of pipe when the Federal Power Commission ruled that Coastal's pipeline network would thereafter be subject to FPC regulation. Wyatt wanted no part of that, so he was left with a lot of pipe rusting away on the Corpus Christi docks. If ever two businessmen needed each other, it was Wyatt and Martin. Wyatt had pipe and money, but no market; Martin had the San Antonio market but no money for a pipeline. One of Alamo's directors knew of Wyatt's plight, mentioned it to Martin, and Alamo's promoter wasted no time. The same day White, Weld backed away from financing Alamo, Martin turned to Coastal States. That was May 2. By May 11, Coastal had arranged to finance the pipeline through an Illinois bank. Coastal would guarantee half the debt and in return would share ownership of the pipeline with Alamo.

At last Alamo was ready to satisfy the terms of the conditional contract. Its reserves were verified (though not by DeGolyer-MacNaughton) and its financing was assured (though not by White, Weld). But the City Public Service Board had gone too far with Alamo to back out now, even if Alamo by this time meant Alamo-Coastal States. On June 14, the CPSB awarded the final contract amid much ceremony and self-praise about saving rate-payers $33 million.

Coastal States was already a partner in supplying gas to San Antonio, and before long it became the dominant partner. The Illinois bank hedged on its financing offer when United sued to set aside the Alamo contract; the bank feared that a United victory would leave Alamo without funds to repay the loan. The bank asked for personal guarantees from

Alamo's directors, but only Martin agreed. That ended all hope of borrowing money; the pipeline would have to be financed through other means. Once again Alamo turned to Coastal States. This time Coastal purchased 25 per cent of the outstanding Alamo stock from Alamo's directors, who used the money for a pipeline. Martin, however, sold no stock, but placed his shares in a voting trust whose trustees were Martin, Schoolfield, and Coastal States attorney Norman Davis. Theoretically Alamo remained independent, but as a practical matter Martin sided with Davis and Coastal against Schoolfield, giving Coastal effective control of 51.18 per cent of Alamo. Schoolfield, judging by notes Davis took at the time, didn't like it but there wasn't much he could do about it. By the time Alamo delivered its first cubic foot of gas in April 1962, it was already little more than a subsidiary of Coastal, and Davis was referring to Alamo as "we" in his notes. In October 1963, Coastal States made it official: it acquired all the remaining Alamo stock and two years later dissolved Alamo entirely.

Looking back on the transactions that culminated in Coastal's takeovers, the company's critics have suggested that Coastal planned the entire scenario from the start—that Lumar, Alamo, and Intra-Tex were only fronts for Coastal States all along. As is usually the case with such theories, this one has some superficial supporting evidence, particularly in San Antonio, where Glen Martin can be tied in with Coastal States even before he submitted his bid. Two Coastal engineers, moonlighting to San Antonio on weekends, helped prepare Alamo's offer. Furthermore, Coastal was going to supply a portion of Alamo's reserves. Finally, Coastal was *very* generous about helping Martin financially after it acquired Alamo stock. The company authorized Martin to make gas deals for his personal benefit; it gave him a $3-million half-interest in an extracting plant in exchange for a $500,000 note—a transaction questioned by Coastal's auditors; and it agreed to buy gas from Martin for ten years or until he accumulated $425,000. But the history of Alamo indicates that Martin wanted the company to stand on its own—that is, until White, Weld's last-minute pull-out left him no alternative; if he didn't turn to Coastal he would have to give up his chance at a half-billion-dollar contract. After investigating the Alamo contract for almost a year, Bexar County assistant district attorneys have also reached this conclusion.

Coastal did not conceive and execute a master plan; rather, it took advantage of circumstances that never should have been allowed to exist. San Antonio and Austin could have dealt with United Gas, which at the time claimed 34 trillion cubic feet of reserves, including 4.5 trillion in the San Antonio area alone. Corpus Christi and San Antonio could have chosen Houston Natural, which many Texas oil and gas operators consider the best pipeline company in the business. Yet all three cities chose to risk their futures with new, unproven companies.

"If there's anything Oscar Wyatt understands better than the gas business," a former Coastal employee says, "it's politics and politicians." What Coastal's critics have described as a grand scheme was in reality nothing more than political acumen at work. Austin is a city of influence; Coastal reacted by first disposing of Intra-Tex (and its influential local backers) and then working through Frank Erwin. In Corpus Christi, Wyatt worked against the local establishment to drive out Houston Natural, while in San Antonio he worked *with* the local establishment, rescuing Alamo and saving the City Public Service Board from having to turn to much-loathed United Gas. The tactics were different, but the result was the same: Coastal States—and Oscar Wyatt—ended up firmly, completely, totally in control.

# THE WINTER OF DISCONTENT

With more than a billion dollars worth of long-term contracts safely tucked away, the company's net income doubled between 1962 (when Coastal began supplying gas to San Antonio through Alamo) and 1964. It doubled again by 1969. Earnings showed huge annual gains: up sixteen per cent in 1965, eighteen per cent in 1966, seventeen per cent in 1967, eighteen per cent again in 1968. Money was no problem. Coastal obtained a $75 million line of credit through Houston's Bank of the Southwest in 1965 without having to pledge any physical property as security; the contracts alone were enough to satisfy the bank.

"Every year a record year" became the Coastal slogan. The hometown newspapers, Corpus Christi's *Caller* and *Times*, seemed to run the same stories over and over in the late Sixties: "Local Gas Firm Shows New Highs," "Coastal's 1st [2nd, 3rd] Quarter Profits Up," "Coastal Sets New Record." The figures changed but not the theme.

The company that broke the monopoly of the big pipeline companies now started to put together a monopoly of its own. In December 1964 Coastal acquired Texas Gas Utilities and its 400 miles of pipelines serving Del Rio, Eagle Pass, Uvalde, and Carrizo Springs. A few months later Coastal purchased the facilities of Nueces Industrial Gas Company. In 1968 Coastal tied up the loose ends by purchasing United's useless 965 miles of pipelines near San Antonio, and by acquiring all the assets of Rio Grande Valley Gas—including 543 miles of pipelines and 834 miles of gas distribution lines.

The Rio takeover was a classic Oscar Wyatt maneuver, a combination power play and finesse. By 1967 Rio's management knew that Wyatt had his eye on their company. They wanted no part of Coastal, however, and started looking for anyone else who might be interested in acquiring their company. They found someone—Houston Natural Gas. On October 20, 1967, Rio and Houston Natural announced their agreement. Three weeks later Coastal's directors voted to go after Rio anyway. Wyatt set up a command post in the Coastal board room. He installed a battery of telephones and began contacting Rio's stockholders personally, promising each one that Coastal would beat Houston Natural's offer for Rio stock. Houston Natural had to throw in the towel—after all, the deal hadn't been its idea in the first place—and in January 1968 Rio's directors voted to accept Coastal's offer.

As Coastal continued to grow, Wyatt's personal star was also in ascendancy. In 1962, shortly after his third divorce had terminated a short and stormy marriage, Wyatt met a beautiful Houston divorcee at a Houston society party. Her name was Lynn Sakowitz Lippman, daughter of Houston merchant Bernard Sakowitz. They married in July 1963, and before long the man whom the Corpus Christi establishment had never accepted was a prominent jet-set socialite, flying off to New York for affairs like the April in Paris Ball at the Waldorf. In November 1963 the Wyatts bought the River Oaks Boulevard home of the late Hugh Roy Cullen, a Houston oilman who somehow had managed to spend $1.8 million on the six-bedroom, six-bath mansion. (The house listed in 1963 for $650,000.)

Coastal's momentum was irrepressible: gas was cheap, supplies were plentiful, business was good. Still . . . there were a few trouble signs here and there for anyone who wanted to look for them. The most serious of these was the Alamo Gas reserves—or rather the lack of them. In-house memos indicate that Coastal knew as early as January 1962 (after it had acquired one-fourth of Alamo but before Alamo started deliveries to San Antonio), that something was wrong with Alamo's gas supply. At the very least, some of Alamo's purchase contracts weren't properly drawn. Coastal admits it knew the contracts were defective, but denies knowing that the gas wasn't there to start with. The memos are too ambiguous to resolve that dispute, but Coastal must have known when it purchased the remaining Alamo stock in October 1963 that wells had already been abandoned in seventeen of Alamo's gas fields. However, Coastal did not admit publicly that Alamo's reserves were short until 1966, when it warned—accurately—that the deficiencies were more than 50 per cent. The City Public Service Board at first was not particularly concerned; it apparently expected Coastal to make up the shortages by purchasing new reserves. The price of gas was still low enough in 1966 that Coastal could have bought new gas and still made a profit on the contract price. Besides, Coastal had promised to perform all of Alamo's obligations—and Alamo had vouched that it would supply 1.2 trillion cubic feet of reserves.

The CPSB was in for a shock. Coastal said flatly that it had no legal obligation to replace Alamo's missing reserves at contract prices. Those prices, according to Coastal, applied only to the gas Alamo *actually* had in 1962, not to the 1.2 trillion cubic feet it *claimed* to have. If you want new gas, Coastal said in effect, you'll have to pay extra for it. This was the beginning of a bitter disagreement that led, inevitably, to the courthouse. (The suit was filed in 1972, but still has not come to trial.) It was also the beginning of a pattern that was to be repeated time after time in the coming years: whenever Coastal saw a chance to increase its profit margin, it grabbed the opportunity.

In addition to the Alamo reserve issue, a second, much more subtle problem became apparent to some members of the Coastal family in the middle Sixties. They sensed a change in the atmosphere around the company, a feeling that the company had outgrown and outstripped many of its employees. Coastal was growing so fast that more and more of the new jobs opening at upper management levels were being filled by outsiders. The new people were different; they were experts, technicians, specialists, aloof individuals sharing only a common entrepreneurial urge. The people who had built the company from nothing, who had won the war against the monopolies, no longer felt wanted. It was a different company now; *Coastal* was the monopoly. One by one, the original staff began to leave, a few of them more than a little disillusioned. Ellis Brown is one of those who left; today, eleven years after his departure, he believes that Coastal's downfall began when the company snuffed out the unique esprit de corps that marked its early years and substi-

tuted in its place a fixation on growth and profits.

The first hint of real trouble came in January 1968. For the first time Coastal curtailed gas deliveries to the San Antonio power plants. Fourteen months later the company imposed a second curtailment. (A curtailment is just a fancy name for rationing gas.) If customer demand exceeds the supply of gas, the pressure in the pipeline will drop so low that gas will no longer be able to flow through the system. Even domestic gas—gas for home heating and cooking—would be cut off, causing chaos in affected communities. (Every pilot light in town would go out. Imagine, say, Houston Natural Gas having to send a serviceman to every building in Houston with a gas connection in order to rekindle a half-million pilot lights. Imagine the danger if the gas flow resumed with so many pilot lights out.)

Coastal claimed that the 1968–69 curtailments were caused by factors beyond the company's control—compressors and regulators in the pipeline system failed, causing gas to "freeze" in the pipes. The City Public Service Board thought otherwise; it was convinced that Coastal had oversold its gas supply. During the next three years the CPSB repeatedly asked Coastal for information about the company's gas reserves and contract commitments. The company responded by handing the CPSB copies of Coastal's annual reports, which indicated that the company had plenty of gas under contract: 9.5 trillion cubic feet of reserves in 1968 had grown to 11.3 trillion cubic feet by 1971. The company also produced a finding by a Houston engineering firm which certified that Coastal's available gas supply would meet customer needs through 1989. (The CPSB was given no data, only the conclusion.) The board's concern over the curtailments may have accomplished something, however, for during 1970–72 Coastal did not cut back deliveries to San Antonio, although it did occasionally curtail Austin, Central Power and Light, and the Lower Colorado River Authority.

If the curtailments were a bad omen, far worse was to follow. The bad news came, as it so often does in this state, from the Texas Legislature—Senate Bill No. 540 and House Bill No. 1018 in the 1971 session. (The original House version was introduced by Carl Parker, cousin to one Oscar Wyatt, after it was prepared by Coastal States' registered lobbyist.) The bill gave the Texas Railroad Commission regulatory authority over natural gas pipelines—and authorized the commission to set rates *without regard to contract prices* so as to insure gas companies a fair rate of return. The bill became known in Capitol circles as the "S.O.S. bill," legislative shorthand for "Save Oscar's Shirt." Coastal backed the legislation with some high-sounding rhetoric. "Save Texas gas for Texans" was the theme of Coastal's argument; at this same time, however, Coastal was making highly profitable spot sales of gas to interstate pipeline companies.

Wyatt went to San Antonio to plead personally for support from the city, but for once he was outgunned. Everybody—majors, independents, customers—was against him, except for one small Panhandle gas company, and that was hardly enough backing. The bill never escaped committee in either house, but the message was clear enough: Coastal wanted out of its fixed-price contracts.

With its pet legislation doomed, Coastal tried to get its customers to renegotiate their contracts voluntarily. The company still claimed to have enough gas to fulfill current contracts. Wyatt wrote San Antonio in April 1971 that Coastal had bought substantial quantities of gas in West Texas at 16¢ to 20¢ per mcf, "and this puts Coastal States in an adequate position to supply the City of San Antonio for the remainder of its contract." The contracts had to be renegotiated, Coastal argued, because conditions in the gas industry were changing: gas was getting scarce, and the well-head price was climbing rapidly. Like it or not, the cities were stuck with Coastal and Lo-Vaca even after their contracts expired; no one else would have enough gas to challenge Coastal's monopoly. The purpose of renegotiation, the company said, was to keep Coastal and its gas-gathering subsidiary Lo-Vaca in a healthy competitive position for new gas, so that Coastal would continue to have an adequate supply through the Eighties and Nineties.

Negotiations got down to specifics on May 25, 1972, when Coastal gave its proposals to the City Public Service Board. A year earlier Wyatt had written the CPSB that "you are Coastal States' partner in the energy business." Now the board was learning that one partner was more equal than the other. Coastal's first offer was hard-line all the way: the old contracts and their fixed prices would be thrown out; instead, Coastal would supply gas on a cost-plus basis. And that was only the beginning. There were other onerous features, like an additional charge for cost-of-living increases. Somewhat stunned, San Antonio and the other customers at the bargaining session reverted to the position they had taken for three years: before we make any deals, we intend to find out just what is going on. They reiterated their requests for information about Coastal's reserves, its commitments, and the cost of its gas.

After a month of deliberation, Coastal agreed to the study—and then promptly sabotaged it. The city's consultant (Ryder Scott of Houston) tried to verify Coastal's reserves, but the company would permit only limited access to its information. Ryder Scott couldn't copy any data, nor could it examine all of Coastal's contracts with producers. Based on its over-the-shoulder examination, Ryder Scott guessed that Coastal had eight trillion cubic feet of reserves—some three trillion less than the company was claiming, but still ample.

The cost study never got even that close to Coastal's data. A Washington firm the city retained turned out to be on permanent retainer from Colorado Interstate Corporation, which Coastal was then acquiring through a merger—a potential conflict of interest which ended the study before it really had begun.

While these studies were going on, contract negotiations took a new turn. Coastal now proposed a "total fuels" contract, which would allow the company to substitute high-cost fuel oil (marketed by a Coastal subsidiary) for cheap natural gas whenever necessary. This arrangement was even more advantageous to Coastal than the company's first offer; not only would the old contracts be cancelled, but Coastal would also be relieved of any obligation to provide gas—and the decision of *what* fuel to supply *when* and *to whom* would rest wholly with them. An attorney involved in the bargaining took one look at Coastal's proposal and described it as a "total fools" contract. Nevertheless, Coastal did find one important taker, the giant South Texas electric utility, Central Power and Light. (In August 1974, CPL sued Coastal and Wyatt personally for $625 million, claiming willful fraud in the contract negotiations.)

Coastal's intransigence at the negotiating table was reminiscent of the high-handed attitude displayed by an earlier monopoly—United Gas—a dozen or more years earlier. When Coastal was fighting for long-term supply contracts in the early Sixties, the company had gone out of its way to appear cooperative; it even submitted its bid for the Austin contract in the form of a signed contract complying with all specifications. Once Coastal had driven off the competition, however, everything changed. Coastal appeared interested only in making the best possible deal for itself. The cities found themselves in the same position San Antonio had tried to avoid in the late Fifties: they had no leverage.

They soon had even more to worry about. On the morning of November 7, 1972, Lo-Vaca notified its power plant customers that pressure was declining in its pipeline system. The Coastal subsidiary blamed mechanical malfunctions and advised its customers to use fuel oil in their boilers until the problem was solved. That was the beginning. During the next six months, the electric utilities suffered curtailments on thirteen separate occasions, for periods ranging up to twelve days. Altogether Coastal cut back deliveries on 65 different days in the winter of 1972–73, a winter which brought the most severe weather in memory to Central Texas.

In January, ice covered the streets of Austin for three consecutive days; the thermometer remained below freezing for nearly a week; the University of Texas at Austin had to shut down for a week in January because gas supplies for the school's power plant were critically low. (There was an element of grim irony in the fact that one-time Coastal advocate Frank Erwin angrily watched all this happen from his seat on the UT Board of Regents.) Residents of Austin and San Antonio lowered thermostats despite the cold (this was almost a year before the Arab embargo made such practices commonplace throughout the country), and cities doused their lights at midnight.

The bitter winter accelerated demand for natural gas, both at the burner tip and for generating electricity, but Coastal and Lo-Vaca continued to fall short in their deliveries. Lo-Vaca and Coastal concealed the seriousness of the situation from their customers during November and December, continuing to blame mechanical problems for the curtailments. By January, Lo-Vaca's customers began to suspect that they were in a full-fledged crisis, one they were totally unprepared for. They had been told repeatedly by Coastal States that the company had plenty of gas to perform its current contracts—the problem was to begin planning for the future.

R. L. Hancock, general manager of Austin's electric utility, and the other customer representatives thought that the future meant the next decade, not the next few months. When the curtailments began in earnest, Austin had a fuel oil storage capacity of 3.5 million gallons. Since the city had burned only 1.25 million gallons in all of 1971 plus the first two months of 1972, that seemed more than ample. But in the last two months of 1972, Austin's boilers consumed 6.25 million gallons; in the first two months of 1973, the city burned an astonishing 7.25 million gallons. The situation was near-catastrophic. Austin and Coastal's other customers were burning fuel oil as fast as it could be hauled in by truck. Worse, they were competing against each other for limited supplies. San Antonio managed to survive the crisis only because a crusty, outspoken oilman named

Johnny Newman had been appointed to the City Public Service Board in the late Sixties, and had managed to push through a fuel oil storage program just before the curtailments hit in late 1972.

The drastic winter of 1972–73 doomed whatever hope was left for successful negotiations between Coastal and its customers—not that the chances were very good anyway so long as Coastal refused to reveal information about its reserves and commitments. Coastal was running out of time and alternatives. Both its customers and the legislature had declined to bail Coastal out of its fixed-price contracts. That left only one option: the Texas Railroad Commission, whose assigned role in state government has traditionally been to protect and nurture the oil and gas industry. In March 1973, Coastal and Lo-Vaca asked the commission to ignore the contract prices and establish a new rate for gas that would guarantee the company a fair rate of return— exactly what Frank Erwin had once promised the Austin City Council that Coastal States would never do.

# SHELL GAME

Coastal was doing a lot more between 1968 and 1972 than urging its customers to renegotiate their contracts. By the end of the Sixties, the company had reached another plateau, just as it had at the beginning of the decade. In the early Sixties, Coastal could have remained in its innovative role as a gas gatherer and broker; instead, it abandoned its comfortable niche in order to challenge industry giants like United Gas and Houston Natural Gas. Now the company faced a similar decision. It had virtually complete control over the intrastate pipeline market in an immense, irregular swath of Texas stretching east to west from Corpus Christi to Del Rio, and north to south from Brownsville to Austin. Was that enough, or was Coastal's destiny still unfulfilled? To ask the question was to answer it. Coastal again opted for new markets and continued growth.

The company decided to venture into the rapidly developing gas fields in West Texas, where gas was plentiful but inaccessible to the great population centers in the eastern half of the state. Coastal announced in March 1968 that it would build a $33-million line across 305 miles of West Texas semidesert to bring gas into the San Antonio area. By 1969 the first intrastate line into West Texas was operational.

One year later the company announced plans for a second West Texas line. But there was something peculiar about this one: instead of terminating in San Antonio, Austin, or some other city served by Coastal and Lo-Vaca, the new West Texas line headed northeast for, of all places, Dallas-Fort Worth, an area already served by one of the healthiest utilities in Texas, Lone Star Gas. If the location of the line was unusual, the financing arrangements were even more so. Coastal, through Lo-Vaca, put up only 40 per cent of the $60.7-million price tag for the 395-mile line in return for half-ownership. Texas Utilities Fuel Company (TUFCO), a subsidiary of a North Texas utility consortium, supplied 60 per cent of the funds for its half interest. Coastal also got the right to use TUFCO's Old Ocean pipeline from Dallas to the Gulf Coast. Not a bad deal for Coastal—except for one thing. Coastal turned over to TUFCO numerous Coastal contracts with producers totaling a whopping 500 billion

cubic feet in reserves. It also gave TUFCO an option to purchase another 500 billion cubic feet. In a single transaction, therefore, Coastal parted with a trillion cubic feet of natural gas. The entire twenty-year San Antonio contract calls for only two trillion cubic feet.

Why would Coastal States enter into a deal like this? Wyatt told a legislative committee last summer that his company had little choice. Coastal had substantial reserves available in West Texas, but had secured them by contracting either to start hauling gas at once or to pay for it anyway. This requirement is commonly found in gas purchase contracts today and is known as a "take-or-pay" clause. (Ironically, Coastal helped pioneer this device during the company's early years, using it to entice producers to deal with Coastal instead of an established pipeline company.) Wyatt and Coastal defend selling off the reserves to TUFCO as the only way the company could get even some of the gas to its regular South Texas customers. Their argument runs something like this: Coastal's original West Texas pipeline, completed a year earlier, was already filled to capacity, so a new line was the only way to get the gas out of West Texas. But Coastal couldn't build the second pipeline without financial help—and no one except TUFCO offered any assistance. Sure, TUFCO got half the gas, but Coastal's customers got the other half (via Dallas and the Old Ocean pipeline); without the TUFCO contract, Coastal would have had to dump the gas to a nearby interstate pipeline company and then the customers wouldn't have gotten any of it.

This is a nice little argument which sounds perfectly logical until it is measured against the facts. Yes, the original West Texas pipeline was filled to capacity—but not with gas for Coastal's customers. Much of the gas in the southern line belonged to a subsidiary of Houston Natural; Lo-Vaca was merely hauling it for a fee. If Coastal truly wanted to save its West Texas gas for customers like San Antonio and Austin, then why did it fill up its only pipeline with transportation gas? The answer, of course, is that Coastal did not intend the TUFCO pipeline into North Texas primarily for its long-term customers.

Wyatt himself explained the true purpose of the TUFCO deal in his 1970 message to Coastal's stockholders: "[T]he North Texas gathering system brings Coastal States into new areas for expansion. It will give the Company access to gas supplies previously unreached and to other opportunities in a territory that will be opened up to Coastal States for the first time." The specific "expansion" that Wyatt had in mind was Lone Star Gas. Coastal had been rumored to be interested in acquiring Lone Star for several years. One knowledgeable Texas gas consultant states flatly that Coastal wanted the North Texas line for leverage in its attempt to take over Lone Star: if Coastal had the only lines into West Texas, Lone Star might eventually become dependent upon Coastal for gas.

Unfortunately for Coastal—and for Coastal's customers—this was one gamble that didn't work. Lone Star responded by building its own 36-inch line. It was absurdly wasteful—two parallel lines from Dallas to West Texas, neither one close to being full—but it preserved Lone Star's independence. Eventually Coastal had to drop its merger efforts when the Justice Department refused to give antitrust clearance to the proposed union. Coastal had squandered billions of cubic feet of reserves in a losing gamble.

The TUFCO deal was only the first in a series of unusual

transactions that Lo-Vaca attempted between 1970 and 1972—unusual, that is, for a public utility pipeline company with a duty to act in the public interest. Most pipeline companies hoard their reserves; Coastal and Lo-Vaca, on the other hand, couldn't seem to get rid of theirs fast enough. These transactions fell into four categories:

*Spot sales to interstate pipeline companies.* Starting in 1969 Lo-Vaca agreed to furnish gas on a short-term basis to large interstate lines like Natural Gas Pipeline of America, Northern Natural Gas, Transcontinental Gas Pipeline, and Texas Eastern Transmission. These deals usually involved gas Lo-Vaca had purchased for 18¢ per mcf; its selling price ranged between 30.5 and 35 cents. (The San Antonio contract price for 1971 was 23.754 cents.) By 1972, Lo-Vaca was selling 200 million cubic feet of Texas gas to interstate pipeline companies every day.

*Sales of specific reserves.* The TUFCO deal was Lo-Vaca's most ambitious maneuver, but the company also sold off reserves to Dow Chemical, Clajon, and El Paso Natural Gas. In each case Lo-Vaca received a transportation fee for hauling the gas it once had under contract.

*Brokerage deals.* Occasionally Lo-Vaca would learn that a package of gas was available, but instead of increasing its own reserve supply, the company would locate a buyer for the gas. This tactic enabled Lo-Vaca to collect a brokerage fee (sometimes more than $1 million) for arranging the transaction, plus a transportation fee for carrying the gas.

*Gas banking deals.* Lo-Vaca acted as a depository for producers and purchasers who had temporary excess supplies of gas. The company accepted the gas, then promptly sold it through its system, assuming it could replace it later. Now it must redeliver the gas (to companies like AMOCO), but today it must buy gas for $1.50 per mcf and more, in order to replace gas it sold for less than 25 cents.

This wheeling and dealing is what really arouses the ire of Coastal's customers. All of these maneuvers occurred while Coastal was occasionally curtailing Austin, the LCRA, and Central Power and Light between 1969 and 1972. Lo-Vaca was already short of gas; yet it continued spot sales well into the crisis that propelled Coastal toward the Railroad Commission and its customers toward the courthouse. Nor did the arrival of the crisis end the sale of reserves: in December 1972 Lo-Vaca transferred reserves to El Paso Natural Gas for a $5.1 million fee. Knowing that they were facing an emergency, Coastal and Lo-Vaca nevertheless continued to do exactly as they pleased, making deals, as a lawyer for the San Antonio City Public Service Board put it, "designed to enhance the short-term interests of Oscar S. Wyatt Jr. and other stockholders of Coastal at the expense of the long-term interest of San Antonio and other customers."

The "extraordinary transactions," as the wheeling and dealing became known, served the useful purpose of staving off the evil day when the Coastal balloon might burst. The deals all had one feature in common: they produced quick, immediate income, allowing the company to achieve for a few more years Wyatt's projections for a fifteen per cent compounded annual growth rate. By 1973, however, not even spot sales and other short-term transactions could compensate for the rising cost of gas. Coastal was being squeezed by escalating gas prices on the one hand, and its long-term, fixed-price contracts on the other.

When the squeeze became unbearable, Coastal, through Lo-Vaca, requested relief on its long-term contracts from the Railroad Commission. In so doing it surrendered control over its own destiny. The future of this cornerstone of Oscar Wyatt's empire would be determined not in its own board room but in a drab hearing room in Austin and in a dozen or more courtrooms across Texas. Never again would Coastal States have the privilege of doing exactly as it pleased.

# JUDGMENT DAY

"You've got to give security to the carriers," Texas Governor Jim Hogg (1891–95) liked to say, arguing for his pet idea—creation of a new state agency to regulate the railroad industry. Concerned by the ruinous competition threatening to bankrupt the state's railroads, Hogg proposed the creation of a special commission which would establish a system of uniform rates. His idea won acceptance as the Texas Railroad Commission, an agency which from its inception was designed to protect the industry it regulated. When the commission was assigned the task of overseeing oil and gas activity in 1917, its approach to the problem was very much the same: the agency viewed itself as responsible for the care and feeding of the infant industry.

The commission's role as nursemaid to the oil and gas industry has remained largely unchanged for years, although from time to time the industry has violently disagreed with the commission's view of what was best for it. When the commission first attempted to regulate production in the East Texas oil fields back in the Thirties, producers threatened to lynch any agency employee foolish enough to set foot in the area. But the commission won that fight, just as it won the right to prohibit flaring of gas in the Fifties. Eventually the industry recognized that the commission had been right all along in both cases. The rest of the time the commission and the industry worked together closely and comfortably; they were, to borrow Oscar Wyatt's phrase, partners in the energy business.

This was the agency to which Coastal and Lo-Vaca turned in 1973 for relief from their long-term, fixed-price contracts. Coastal States had been contemplating this step for a long time. A confidential company memorandum written in March 1969, only five days after Coastal's long-term contract with Austin was amended, boasted that the negotiations had strengthened "our position to appeal to the Railroad Commission in the event this sale becomes monetarily burdensome to Lo-Vaca prior to the expiration of the original contract." Three months later, a second memo called attention to Frank Erwin's promise to the Austin City Council in 1962 that Coastal would never ask for rate relief, and suggested that it might "tend to shed a new light on our proposed filing with the Railroad Commission for a rate increase with the City of Austin." And so, four years before the actual request, Coastal was preparing to circumvent its promise not to appeal to the Railroad Commission, the promise that had helped win it the Austin contract in the first place.

One reason Coastal waited until 1973 before going to the Railroad Commission was Lo-Vaca's ability to keep afloat financially by making spot sales and other short-term deals—deals that would later leave the company unable to meet its contract commitments. But in January 1973 the

Railroad Commission ended Lo-Vaca's wheeling and dealing by prohibiting any pipeline company facing a curtailment situation from making spot sales. Within two weeks of that ruling Coastal and Lo-Vaca informed customers of their decision to ask the commission for new rates.

Lo-Vaca was in trouble in 1973, bad trouble. In order to replace the reserves it had sold for short-term profit, Lo-Vaca was buying new gas at more than three times its average sales price. Altogether the company's average cost for gas was 22.75¢ per mcf, much too close to its average selling price of 24.21 cents. (Those now seem like the Good Old Days; new gas is now over $2 and Lo-Vaca's average cost for gas is $1.27.) Part of the problem was beyond Lo-Vaca's control: demand for gas was up; discoveries of new reserves were down; most of the cheap, shallow gas had already been produced; and once-productive fields were running out. It was a sellers' market, and producers knew it. If a producer found a new package of gas, he made pipeline companies renegotiate old purchase contracts in order to get new supplies. New contracts with producers called for prices to be revised annually. The gas market was changing monthly, even weekly, and here in the middle of these fluid conditions was Lo-Vaca, stuck with its fixed-price contracts. Small wonder that Lo-Vaca argued to the commission that "because of drastic and unforeseen changes in the availability and prices of natural gas in Texas, especially in the past few months, the prices and rates being charged by Lo-Vaca in its gas sales agreements are unfair, unreasonable, confiscatory, and contrary to the public interest."

Greatly simplified, Lo-Vaca's argument was this: we are a gas utility; gas utilities are vital to the public interest and welfare; a utility can serve the public interest only when it is healthy; we are sick; a new rate will make us well again. Therefore, the commission should—indeed, it *must*—act in the public interest and give us a new rate, so that we will have the financial ability and incentive to compete for new gas supplies.

Lo-Vaca's customers, who turned out in force to oppose the rate request, were stunned by the company's presentation. For years they had been pressing Coastal for the true facts about its reserves, commitments, and costs. Now they were getting them, and the truth was far worse than they had suspected. The customers had long ago discounted Wyatt's glowing statements in Coastal's annual reports, but none of them realized how misled they had been: of Coastal's 9.4 trillion cubic feet in reserves, only 3.7 trillion—about a five-year supply—were available for Texas customers. Lo-Vaca had daily obligations of 1.9 billion cubic feet (2.4 billion on peak winter days), but had only enough gas available to deliver 1.4 billion cubic feet. And there was more bad news ahead. Beginning in November, TUFCO and North Texas would get 300 million cubic feet, 21 per cent of Lo-Vaca's already inadequate daily deliverability.

The customers entered the hearings with the attitude that their contract prices should not and could not be changed. As the gravity of Lo-Vaca's condition became clear, however, the focus of the argument shifted to how much, rather than whether, the rates should be changed. One lawyer explained his client's response to Lo-Vaca's argument this way: Assuming you get a new rate, our contract still shouldn't be ignored. All you should get is the minimum rate necessary to satisfy the public interest—just enough to pay operating and maintenance expenses, but not enough to give you a return on your investment. Rate-making bodies don't exist to get utilities out of bad bargains. Besides, you're not entitled to a full rate of return in any event; a full rate should be a reward for full service, and you have not provided it.

Lo-Vaca asked the Railroad Commission for a new rate based on its average cost of gas plus 15.10 cents. After three months of hearings and thousands of pages of testimony, the commission issued a temporary order on September 27 authorizing Lo-Vaca to charge cost plus a nickel. It wasn't what Lo-Vaca wanted, but it was enough: the fixed-price contracts were no longer an albatross around Lo-Vaca's neck.

The subsidiary was on its way back to health, but the parent's problems were just beginning. The Coastal family of corporations was reorganized at the end of 1972 to prepare for the acquisition of Colorado Interstate. A new parent company, Coastal States Gas Corporation, replaced Coastal States Gas Producing Company, which was reduced to the status of a wholly owned subsidiary. (Coastal Producing continued to own Lo-Vaca, which became a second-tier subsidiary.) Investment analysts did not consider the merger a good one, and the new corporation was soon in trouble on Wall Street. Its stock, which had climbed near 60 while the Producing Company was still the parent, opened 1973 in the mid-30s and soon nosedived below $10 per share. Institutional investors began unloading their shares in May. Spurred on by San Antonio Congressman Henry B. Gonzalez, Coastal's most persistent critic, the Securities and Exchange Commission suspended trading in Coastal stock on June 5, pending an investigation of rumors that Coastal had misrepresented its gas reserves.

The Railroad Commission struck the next blow at Coastal. After learning how desperate Lo-Vaca's situation really was, lawyers for Austin and the LCRA urged the commission to strip Coastal of all control over its subsidiary and place Lo-Vaca in receivership. The commission was unwilling to take such a drastic step; instead, it reached an agreement with Coastal which called for a partial separation of the two companies. Coastal Producing gave an Austin court an irrevocable proxy to vote its Lo-Vaca stock. Lo-Vaca's board of directors resigned and was replaced by a court-appointed board and a supervisor-manager, whose job was to oversee the operations of the company and report back to the court. Furthermore, Coastal agreed to supply Lo-Vaca $2.5 million per month for capital expenses (not operating costs) such as pipeline construction and advance payments for new gas. But Coastal and Lo-Vaca did not have to separate physically; they were allowed to remain in the same building, use the same telephone switchboard, and in some instances, share the same law firm (Houston's Fulbright and Jaworski).

There is considerable debate over the effect of this separation. Some critics believe that the Railroad Commission didn't go far enough; as San Antonio's Johnny Newman puts it, "Anybody who believes they are really separate is a damn fool." The separation agreement is designed to last for a maximum of five years, but can be terminated earlier if Lo-Vaca manages to accumulate enough gas to meet 90 per cent of its commitments—so Lo-Vaca's employees know that before too long they will be working for Coastal States again.

Lo-Vaca's new board may be independent, but as its

supervisor-manager James Hargrove points out, it also must be "conscious of its obligation to operate the corporation on behalf of its stockholders." Besides, as Hargrove says, on major issues like rate increases and liability to customers, Coastal's and Lo-Vaca's interests are essentially the same. Any real damage to Coastal's financial situation would equally damage Lo-Vaca, and vice-versa; the companies are tied together in complex financing arrangements because Lo-Vaca has never had independent borrowing power. If either goes bankrupt, the other will almost certainly follow. The partial separation of the two companies has not altered the fact that, in Hargrove's words, "It would be a form of suicide for us to jump in against the long-term interests of Coastal States. We're on the same umbilical cord."

The beneficial effects of the separation have been largely psychological. Customers have found Lo-Vaca far more communicative since the Railroad Commission's action. Now they have some idea how long curtailments will last and how serious they will be. Prior to the split, customers would receive only a terse message that pressure was dropping in Lo-Vaca's line and curtailments would be imposed in a matter of hours. R. L. Hancock, director of Austin's electric utility, says that Lo-Vaca's performance in the field and in the office has improved considerably. So has the company's ability to buy gas.

Coastal, too, has benefited from the present arrangement, despite having to supply up to $30 million annually in capital contributions. Prior to the winter of 1972–73, Lo-Vaca was buried in obscurity. True, Coastal had turned its long-term contracts over to Lo-Vaca as far back as 1963, but all of the customers continued to view Coastal as their gas supplier. Coastal treated the distinction between itself and its subsidiary fairly casually; the company's annual reports during the boom years of the late Sixties don't even refer to Lo-Vaca by name. Frank Erwin, who received continuing payments for his role in landing the Austin gas supply contract for Coastal, recalls that as late as 1971 his checks would come one month from Lo-Vaca, the next month from Coastal, in a random pattern.

But once the crisis hit, Coastal was eager to isolate its ills in one subsidiary. (In its 1970 annual report, Coastal reported that "the Company is the supplier of consumer gas for several major cities in Texas," but in 1973 these cities were described as Lo-Vaca's customers.) The separation agreement has also aided Coastal's efforts to avoid having its healthy non-utility functions subsidize its sick subsidiary. One SEC investigator believes that the Railroad Commission action was designed not to save Lo-Vaca but to bail Coastal out of its legal difficulties. Why else, he asks, would the commission have gone after the subsidiary instead of the parent? One possible answer is that the commission was uncertain of its jurisdiction over the parent; another is that the commission wanted to avoid a protracted legal battle and simply settled for what Wyatt would agree to.

By the end of the summer, the SEC was ready to proceed against Coastal itself. The federal agency filed suit against Coastal on September 11, but that was only for show; one day later Coastal signed a consent decree settling the controversy. Coastal agreed to refrain from making false or misleading statements about reserves, deliverability, and earnings. It also consented to a reorganization of its board of directors and its executive committee—two moves which

the agency hoped would end what one SEC source called "the dictatorial authority of the chief executive," that being, of course, Oscar Wyatt. The SEC plan called for four Coastal directors to step down. The remaining six directors were then joined by seven new appointees mutually acceptable to the SEC and the company. Two of the seven new members would join Wyatt on the three-member executive committee.

Whether the SEC achieved its goal is doubtful. Former Railroad Commission hearing examiner Walter Wendlandt, who handled the Lo-Vaca rate case for the commission, says Wyatt remains in control through "incredible ability and personal magnetism." Wyatt also had some help from Washington attorney Manuel Cohen, who handled the SEC investigation for Coastal. Cohen knows something about such matters; he was chairman of the commission from 1964 to 1969. (SEC sources have confirmed that Cohen became involved in the case at the request of one of Coastal's directors who later resigned to take a legal job of his own in Washington—the soon-to-be Special Prosecutor of the United States, Leon Jaworski.) SEC investigators are quick to point out that Cohen was totally cooperative in producing needed documents and in not impeding their work— "We've never had an investigation go so smoothly," one lawyer said—but *somebody* managed to convince the SEC chiefs in Washington to accept "independent" directors whose independence was open to question. One of the seven "independent" directors had already been nominated by the Coastal board; he was embraced by the SEC as one of its own. Another "independent" director, former Tenneco president Harold Burrow, has had close ties with Wyatt for many years.

If the public regulatory bodies had limited success in their legal battles with Coastal, they at least scored some points here and there. The customers, who were also lining up at the courthouse at the same time, so far have been shut out. Most of these lawsuits involve two types of claims. The customers have fixed-price, long-term contracts, but are required to pay an interim rate far higher than their contract price. They want Lo-Vaca and Coastal to make up the difference. Sometimes, however, Lo-Vaca hasn't been able to supply gas at any price. During these curtailment periods, customers have had to purchase fuel oil to keep their electrical generators running. They want to be reimbursed for that cost, too. San Antonio, the LCRA, Corpus Christi, and Central Power and Light are all suing Coastal, Lo-Vaca, and in some cases, Wyatt himself, for damages suffered in one or both of these ways. Austin will almost certainly join in after its spring city council runoffs. Each lawsuit is slightly different from the others (the LCRA, for example, contends that its contract is with Coastal, not Lo-Vaca), but the differences are such that only a lawyer could care.

One lawyer who definitely cares is Tracy DuBose, a former Coastal director and house counsel who now operates out of an office on the sixth floor of Houston's Lincoln Liberty Life Building. Lawyers for the customers have been tangling—usually unsuccessfully—with DuBose for years now, and yet they feel toward him none of the rancor they hold for Wyatt. Perhaps this is because lawyers reserve a special place in their fraternity for men like DuBose— tough, tenacious advocates who epitomize the adversary process, who display a command of rhetoric, logic, and the law itself but seldom let disputes touch on personalities.

DuBose professes little concern about the legal issues in the various cases. He does not see how Coastal or Lo-Vaca can be held liable for charging an interim rate approved by the Railroad Commission, nor does he believe that the companies can be faulted for following curtailment schedules which also had Railroad Commission approval. As for the possibility that Coastal's profits should be used to lower Lo-Vaca's gas rates, DuBose rejects that out of hand: "It is axiomatic that non-utility operations by a utility company do not subsidize utility operations." That doesn't mean DuBose is without problems, however. "The most frustrating thing I face is that I sincerely believe any lawyer taking an objective view would agree that we have the better side of the case," DuBose says. "But where do we get a fair trial? San Antonio, where customers who pay utility bills sit on the jury? Where do we go to find a forum where the case isn't tried in a lynch-mob, prejudicial atmosphere?" He pauses, pours himself a drink, looks up at the ceiling. "Oh, well, I always wanted to be a big-time lawyer. And when you're getting sued for a billion dollars, at least you know you're big time."

On the other side of the case, lawyers for the customers exude none of DuBose's confidence. They do not agree that the law is against them, but they do concede that their side has the more difficult task. Before they can recover damages from Coastal and Lo-Vaca for breach of contract, they must prove that the current shortages were caused not by factors beyond Lo-Vaca's control—the "energy crisis"—but by the wheeling and dealing maneuvers that took place between 1969 and 1972. They must also demonstrate that these "extraordinary transactions" were bad business judgments which Coastal and Lo-Vaca knew at the time to be detrimental to their long-term customers. That is not an easy burden to carry in a lawsuit.

The customers have already lost one round. Enraged because TUFCO received full deliveries of gas while other customers were being curtailed, San Antonio, the LCRA, and a new plaintiff, UT-Austin, asked the Railroad Commission to rescind the TUFCO contract and restore the gas to Lo-Vaca's long-term customers. At the very least, they argued, TUFCO should be put in the same category with Lo-Vaca's other customers and be forced to suffer curtailments. TUFCO was getting full deliveries of gas while Lo-Vaca's other customers were being curtailed. Coastal answered that the TUFCO contract had transferred specific reserves to TUFCO; the gas actually *belonged* to TUFCO, and Lo-Vaca was merely *transporting* it. The three elected commissioners took one look at this dispute and wanted no part of it, not when they were being asked to take gas away from Dallas-Fort Worth and redirect it to Austin-San Antonio. As one Fort Worth legislator said, "They can count the votes." The commission dismissed the request, saying it had no authority to set aside contracts. Wrong, said an Austin district court, overruling the Railroad Commission. Right, said the Texas Supreme Court, reversing the district court and upholding the commission. If you want to set aside a contract, the justices told the customers, then go to court.

One customer—Houston-based United Texas Transmission Company, formerly Pennzoil Pipeline—went to court in 1973 to contest the TUFCO contract and Lo-Vaca's other sales of reserves to Clajon, Dow, and El Paso Natural Gas. United Texas purchases gas from Lo-Vaca, then sells it to Houston Lighting and Power for boiler fuel. Other customers have joined in the action, but the case has yet to come to trial.

Trial lawyers have a saying about cases where the facts are hard to understand and even harder to prove: "Bad facts make bad law." If that is true, we may be headed for some very bad law. Nothing like this has ever happened before—a natural gas shortage, a runaway sellers' market, and a public utility apparently heedless to the public interest—and it will take all the ingenuity of courts and lawyers alike to fit traditional utility law, developed under far different circumstances, to the present problems. An even more serious danger, however, is that the rush of events has already passed the courts by. Suppose, for a moment, that the customers win their cases. What then? Where will Coastal find the money to settle $1 billion in damage claims? If Coastal has to pay huge judgments, or if Lo-Vaca has to live up to its contracts, the companies will be driven into bankruptcy, and how will that help get more gas to Austin, San Antonio, Corpus Christi, the Rio Grande Valley, Houston (Lo-Vaca supplies Pennzoil, remember), and even Dallas-Fort Worth (Lo-Vaca is a heavy supplier for Lone Star)? The answer, of course, is that it won't. This is the insolvable problem that confronts and frustrates lawyers for the customers: even if they win, they lose. No other pipeline company has enough gas to supply the millions of Texans who depend on Lo-Vaca; like it or not, the customers are stuck with their present supplier. They can deal with a bankrupt Lo-Vaca or a healthy one, but those are the only choices.

The worst consequence of bankruptcy is that Coastal could be turned over to a federal judge in New York or Delaware, who would appoint a trustee to operate the company (as bankruptcy law requires) for the benefit of its creditors rather than its customers. Coastal's assets, including its gas purchase contracts, could be sold to the highest bidder, possibly an interstate pipeline company. This is the version put forward by Coastal and the Railroad Commission, who speak grimly of Texas gas "going up Yankee smokestacks."

Most of the lawyers involved do not believe that bankruptcy would be so catastrophic. They say that utilities are different from ordinary corporations (an argument Coastal has been known to use), and that the system would undoubtedly be run for the benefit of the customers. On this issue the customers seem to have the better of the law. But bankruptcy would still not be pleasant; gas producers would hardly want to deal with a bankrupt company if they could avoid it. Gas supplies would be hard to come by, and rates surely would not improve. Nevertheless, more and more of the lawyers in the case are ready to put Coastal out of business if they can, and worry about the consequences later. But no one pretends that getting Coastal out of the picture will make it any easier for their cities to get gas. That dilemma will remain.

Is there a solution? Perhaps. Hearing examiner Walter Wendlandt thought he had one after listening to the evidence in Lo-Vaca's rate hearing before the Railroad Commission. In his recommendations to the commission, Wendlandt recognized that Lo-Vaca was a "sick corporation." He also found that "[Coastal's] management has vigorously pursued a rapidly increasing profit picture with little regard for the Public Interest." His aim was to give

Lo-Vaca a rate which would allow it "to become a strong, viable company able to purchase the gas necessary, but which does not unjustly enrich the Stockholders of Coastal States Gas Corporation. The Stockholders are the ones through their management who gambled on continued low field prices, lost, and must pay."

Wendlandt recommended that Lo-Vaca receive its cost of gas plus 6.16¢ per mcf. He also recommended that the Railroad Commission establish a contract reimbursement fund—and that all profits made by Lo-Vaca, Coastal States Gas Producing Company, and Coastal States Gas Corporation in future years go into this fund until customers receive the difference between their contract prices and the new rates they would have to pay. It was a clever, careful recommendation—recognizing the principle that utility operations are entitled to show a profit on their own, yet rejecting it. Customers describe it as "innovative," which it is; DuBose calls it "totally unrealistic" and "in conflict with established principles of law," which it also may be. One thing is certain: the Railroad Commission isn't saying anything. Wendlandt issued his recommendations last April; one year later, the commission has done nothing.

From the viewpoint of the rate-payer, the future looks bleak. Lo-Vaca has already applied to the Railroad Commission for a five-cent increase in its interim rate, and if the company is successful, the rate-payer will suffer still more. One bright spot is that the upcoming hearing will again raise the issue of whether Coastal's highly profitable nonutility operations should help subsidize Lo-Vaca—but so far the Railroad Commission has shown no inclination to decide this question. Even if Coastal has to reimburse its customers, there is little likelihood that the consumer would benefit immediately. All electric utilities are facing huge capital outlays in the next few years to convert from gas and oil to coal, lignite (low-grade coal), and nuclear power, and any extra money the cities receive would surely be used for new facilities. There is ample energy available, but it won't be cheap energy. Those days are gone forever. The energy crisis, it turns out, is just another facet of the economic crisis.

# POWER TO THE PEOPLE

Who is to blame for the gas crisis? Already overburdened by rising utility bills, the consumer wants easy answers. But there are none.

Coastal States and Oscar Wyatt are the obvious targets, and doubtless both do bear a heavy share of the responsibility. The company has continually ignored its obligations as a public utility; it was conceived as a gas broker in 1955, and a gas broker it has remained—wheeling and dealing, taking a short-term profit whenever it could, and seldom worrying about long-term consequences. Nothing illustrates this more vividly than the transactions which occurred between 1969 and 1972, when Coastal dealt away its reserves, knowing full well that a gas shortage was imminent. A high officer of Lo-Vaca admitted during the 1973 Railroad Commission rate hearings that he was aware of the "acuteness of the problem of the gas supply" in early 1972. Undaunted by such foreknowledge, Lo-Vaca went ahead and sold its precious reserves to Clajon and El Paso Natural Gas

later that year. In its numerous brokerage deals during 1972, it passed up the chance to buy gas in order to snatch a sales commission that could be reported as income.

There is some evidence that Coastal knew about an impending shortage even before the disastrous (for its customers) TUFCO contract in 1970. SEC investigators uncovered a five-year forecast written in 1969, estimating that Coastal's reserves were 4.1 trillion cubic feet short of its contract commitments through 1980. There is nothing particularly shocking about this; most pipeline companies don't have enough reserves to meet all their long-term commitments. But then most companies don't compute their reserves like Coastal did before the SEC cracked down in 1973. Coastal counted as reserves every cubic foot of gas that went into its pipeline, including gas it was hauling for others—gas that Coastal did not own, would never own, and could not make available to long-term customers. Coastal was claiming nine and ten trillion cubic feet of reserves when it had only about one-third of that amount available for its intrastate customers. So if Coastal was estimating a shortage of 4.1 trillion cubic feet, the actual shortage was more like nine trillion. (Coastal's reserve calculations have never been declared illegal, but the company did agree to change its reporting methods as part of its settlement with the SEC.)

If Coastal was not concerned about preventing a gas crisis, neither was it hesitant to take advantage of its customers once the crisis was upon them. In May 1973, just eleven days before San Antonio was hit with a drastic two-thirds curtailment, a Coastal memorandum discussed how the company could twist such a crisis to its own benefit by rushing to the rescue with fuel oil:

> Marketing policy with regard to solicitation of any "contemplated Texas utility deal" is to wait until the crisis develops. This position is taken for two primary reasons: First, these people [San Antonio, Austin, the LCRA] do not want to talk oil at this time as they view it a poor substitute for natural gas. Second, once they are in trouble, Coastal's availing of relief through liquid fuels should enhance Coastal's image. . . .

The memo concluded, "[W]hatever is done should be done in the best interests of Coastal States Gas Corporation."

The fuel oil memo underscores one seldom-discussed effect of the gas crisis: while Lo-Vaca has been suffering, other Coastal subsidiaries have profited from Lo-Vaca's sickness. Coastal States Marketing, where the memo originated, supplied fuel oil on an emergency basis to the same customers who were curtailed by Lo-Vaca. Austin even gave Coastal Marketing a $5-million contract for twenty million gallons of fuel oil. Coastal States Gas Producing Company has done all right for itself at Lo-Vaca's expense, too. Coastal supplies Lo-Vaca with about seven per cent of the pipeline company's gas; in the last year deliveries have remained constant at 80 million cubic feet per day, but the average price Lo-Vaca pays its parent has skyrocketed from 44¢ per mcf in December 1973 to 81 cents in November 1974. Why the sudden jump? No, Coastal isn't selling Lo-Vaca huge quantities of expensive newly discovered gas; rather, it persuaded Lo-Vaca's former supervisor-manager Mills Cox to renegotiate contract prices upward. The increase should bring in around $10 million annually for Coastal Producing—and $10 million less for Lo-Vaca. The overall effect is doubly beneficial to Coastal States Gas Corporation: one subsidiary gains when the other loses—and the one that loses is the utility, which can plead poverty before the Railroad Commission and recoup its losses at the expense of the rate-payer.

One further intracorporate transaction should be mentioned, primarily because it is so bizarre. Lo-Vaca delivers gas to the old Rio Grande Valley Gas distribution system, which for very complicated reasons is now operated by Coastal States Gas Corporation rather than by a subsidiary. Coastal, therefore, is buying gas from its own subsidiary—at the same high price everyone else in the state has to pay for Lo-Vaca's gas. Now Coastal wants to pass this cost on to its domestic customers in the Valley, whose reaction verges on apoplexy. They say Coastal will be making a killing at both ends of the pipeline (Lo-Vaca is actually paying very little for the gas) simply because it was clever enough to maneuver itself into this position.

These intra-family manipulations prove one thing: Coastal has never stopped wheeling and dealing. It continues to find ingenious ways to profit from the mess it created. This emphasis on profit and growth at the expense of utility obligations has been a Coastal characteristic for years. Other gas utilities like Houston Natural and Lone Star have a totally different philosophy from Coastal's. Both companies have avoided fixed-price, long-term contracts. Neither company has ever sold any reserves. Both companies store surplus gas in huge natural reservoirs. Houston Natural purchased an entire reservoir in 1965, the played-out Bammel field near Katy, to use for storage. (Natural gas can't be stored in tanks, like oil, but must be injected into a natural reservoir by expensive compressors.) Lone Star owns ten reservoir areas and is looking for more. The Bammel field will hold 85 billion cubic feet of gas, while Lone Star can store 57.7 billion.

Coastal States, on the other hand, has virtually no storage capacity. On days when demand for gas is slack, Houston Natural and Lone Star can pump gas underground for use on peak days; Coastal cannot. It must take gas from producers or pay for it anyway, and even if Coastal decides to take, it may have to unload the gas somewhere. Many of Coastal's most devastating deals during the 1969–72 period might not have been necessary if Coastal had owned storage facilities—but, as a Coastal spokesman said earlier this year, "Sure, we'd like to have storage, but the expense is prohibitive." What that means, a Houston Natural vice-president said, somewhat disgustedly, is that storage doesn't generate income. And income has always been Coastal's foremost concern—income and growth. Those were the concepts pushed at Wyatt by his New York financial advisor, German refugee Joachim Silberman. It was Silberman who worked the Wall Street investment crowd for Wyatt, and who pushed for a fifteen per cent annual growth rate. Many members of the original Coastal family hated "Joey," as they called him; they found him cold, aloof, and arrogant, but one early Coastal employee recalls that Silberman "was the only man I ever saw Oscar Wyatt treat as an equal."

The commitment to growth was responsible for the rise of Coastal, but it eventually led to the company's downfall. Once gas prices started rising, only spot sales, reserve transfers, and brokerage commissions could keep income at high levels. The importance of these transactions can be seen from the fact that in the last half of 1972, Coastal's gas

systems accounted for 66 percent of the company's profit; only 17 per cent of the profit came from refining. One year later, when the Railroad Commission had clamped down on the wheeling and dealing, the situation was radically different: refined products accounted for 92 per cent of the profit, while gas systems actually lost money.

Yet, Coastal is far from deserving *all* of the blame. The company may not have taken all the precautions of a responsible utility, but as long as gas was plentiful, that didn't matter. In the early years of its long-term contracts, Coastal brought millions of Texans cheaper gas than anyone else could, and still made a profit on it. When Lo-Vaca went to the Railroad Commission to ask for rate relief in 1973, most of its municipal customers were paying less than 25¢ per mcf; Houston Natural's rate was 38.3 cents and Lone Star was getting 43.7 cents. Any calculation of how much Coastal is costing rate-payers now should be balanced by how much the company saved them before 1973.

Furthermore, even the "extraordinary transactions" look worse in hindsight than they must have appeared at the time. Coastal may have anticipated that prices were going to rise—but did anyone in the industry guess how much and how fast? The company probably knew that gas would be expensive to replace—more expensive than it could afford under its contracts—but it sold its reserves anyway, hoping to bludgeon the Railroad Commission into giving Lo-Vaca a higher rate. What Coastal did not anticipate is that there would not be enough gas available at *any* price. Looking back, we know now that Coastal sold when it should have bought. It did nothing illegal, but it did gamble on the continued availability of gas, and it lost.

Oscar Wyatt lost too. Before the gas crisis engulfed Coastal, Wyatt and his relatives owned the largest single block of its stock—2,298,819 shares, or 11.9 per cent of all outstanding stock, worth close to $130 million. When the stock fell from its high of near 60 to 7½, Wyatt suffered a paper loss of more than $100 million.

In the face of adversity, Wyatt remains firm. He challenges everything, conceding nothing, battling much like he did fifteen years ago when he faced a hostile Corpus Christi City Council alone and vowed to fight the Houston Natural contract to the finish. Wyatt denies that Coastal oversold its reserves; instead, he attributes the company's shortages to failures in deliverability. We have the gas, Wyatt says—we just can't get it out of the ground as fast as we would like. He argues that the incriminating memos were just individual opinions, not company policy; in short, he admits no wrong except the failure to have perfect foresight. He lashes out at his critics at every opportunity, blaming the news media for intensifying Lo-Vaca's gas-buying problems, then blaming the cities for not listening to him back in the Sixties.

Wyatt is right. The cities did bring the crisis upon themselves—though not for the reasons he suggests. Like Coastal, like Wyatt, the cities also gambled, but theirs was a double gamble: not only that the gas market would remain stable, but also that they could risk abandoning their reliable, long-time suppliers. They were so sure of themselves, so certain that they were dealing in a buyers' market, that they forgot that twenty years is a long, long time.

The public regulatory bodies did not exactly cover themselves in glory, either. The Federal Power Commission, which regulates all aspects of the interstate gas market, helped create the gas crisis by keeping the wellhead price below what was needed to stimulate an active drilling program. Once again, the short-range view—providing cheap gas for the out-of-state consumer—prevailed. Nor was the Texas Railroad Commission any help. The commission had enough close ties with the Texas gas industry to know what Lo-Vaca was doing to its gas supply between 1968 and 1972. People in the gas industry certainly knew; a high official with Tenneco warned San Antonio's Johnny Newman in 1971 that "San Antonio's gas supply situation is going to be sick, sick, sick in a few more years." Where was the Railroad Commission while all of this was going on? Surely it had enough information to begin an investigation. But the commission preferred to wait for the crisis to come to it.

Even the Legislature cannot escape blame. For years it has debated—and rejected—proposals to establish a state utilities commission. Certainly a commission would be no panacea—the dismal record of the existing regulatory bodies in preventing the current crisis is evidence enough of that. But a utilities commission could have made some very real differences: for example, Coastal could never have built its North Texas pipeline—or entered into the TUFCO contract—without official scrutiny. It might never even have been able to get the city contracts in the first place.

In the end, nothing worked the way it was supposed to—not the economic system, not the political system, not the regulatory system. The saga of Coastal States Gas is the story of the American Dream—how one man, starting with nothing but an idea, can build an empire. But it is also the story of the American Nightmare—how the successful can become too big, too greedy, too arrogant, too obsessed with becoming still bigger. Coastal chose privilege over duty, reward over responsibility, and there was no one to say no. In the beginning, Oscar Wyatt and Coastal States epitomized the best in American business traditions; in the end, the worst.

*—May 1975*

Southwest Airlines' Lamar Muse

# THE GREAT AIRLINE WAR

by James Fallows

*Will TI's ''whiz kids'' fizzle?! Will sexy Southwest conquer all?! Will Braniff lose its routes?!*

Russell Thayer held the world between his outstretched hands. ''This, over here, is Hawaii,'' he said, jiggling his right hand, ''and this,'' jiggling his left, ''is Dallas. We fly a 747 between them, the only 747 we've got. To make a 747 pay off, you have to have a long haul with a lot of people on board. Now, it turns out that the distance between Dallas and Honolulu is exactly right. If it were any shorter, you couldn't fly it as efficiently. And if it were any longer, you couldn't turn it around for the daily round trip.''

Thayer lowered his hands and leaned across the desk. ''I decided that the islands were in the right place, and I didn't move 'em an inch.''

Russell Thayer laughed, a hearty, warm-natured laugh that rumbled up out of his football player's body. He was sitting in his office on the ninth floor of the Braniff Tower on the west side of Dallas. Around the airlines industry, Thayer is known as a genius, as the man who has helped turn Braniff into one of the most efficient money makers the business has ever seen. Five days a week he works in Dallas as Braniff's executive vice-president for Corporate and Market Planning. The other two days—this is the beauty of working for an airline—he spends at home in Princeton, New Jersey. Word is that he hates Texas.

One floor above Thayer, Harding Lawrence—with studied informality—came from behind his desk and gestured his visitor to the coffee table at the opposite end of the room. Perched on the table was a model of the supersonic Concorde jet, painted in bright Braniff colors. At Lawrence's elbow was a matching model of the Boeing 747.

When he became chairman and chief executive officer of Braniff ten years ago, Lawrence was often described as ''dashing'' and ''romantic.'' Now, his silver hair and deeply creased face make him look ten years older than 55;

*James Fallows is a former associate editor of* Texas Monthly *and has written for* The Washington Monthly, Harper's, Esquire, The Atlantic Monthly, *and other magazines. He is the chief speechwriter to President Carter.*

his appearance hovers on the line between ''distinguished'' and ''tired.'' A smile on his face, Lawrence offered his visitor an expensive cigar, then began chewing on an unlighted one himself as he talked about his airline.

''We have our creeds, our objectives. We know what we stand for. Our job is to promote the foreign and domestic commerce of the United States, the national defense, the postal service—and to do that in the public interest. You might say, in the *consumer's* interest. The airline industry is the most consumer-oriented business I know.''

As Lawrence spoke, a red and orange jet from Southwest Airlines, perfectly framed in the picture window behind him, settled in for a landing at Love Field. In addition to pursuing its high-flown goals, Braniff has spent almost five years trying to prevent this very occurrence. For its efforts, the company has been indicted by a federal grand jury for antitrust violations in trying to kill Southwest.

Serious as such a charge is, it is not the most serious challenge facing Lawrence and his airline. In Washington, an accusation of unprecedented gravity is now pending before the Civil Aeronautics Board (CAB). Based on revelations of a sizeable Braniff slush fund (generated through ''off the books'' sale of tickets and used to bribe ticket agents in South America), the complaint threatens Braniff's right to operate any route, foreign or domestic, as long as ''present management retains operational control.'' ''Present management,'' as everyone understands, means Harding L. Lawrence.

In Houston, Francisco Lorenzo was turning on the charm. Four years ago, when he had just turned 30, Lorenzo came down from the Northeast, trailing his Harvard Business School pedigree, to take control of Texas International Airlines. TI was in deep, deep trouble at the time; the year before Lorenzo became president, the airline lost more than $6 million. Now TI is in deep trouble again. During the first half of 1975, after TI's disastrous, five-month-long strike, the company was losing money even faster than it had in

1971. Like Braniff, TI is under federal indictment for anti-trust activities against Southwest. Nonetheless, Lorenzo was the picture of urbane good will as he listened to a question based on the latest appalling hypothesis about Texas International: that it had outlasted its reason for existence.

"Of course we don't agree with that," he said, attempting to suggest with his smile that no reasonable man possibly could agree. "We came to a company that was flat on its back, twenty million in the hole. It was in trouble not because it had bad routes, not because its employees weren't dedicated, but because management had made some bad mistakes. We've turned that around now. Until the strike, we were making money. We've paid off more than half of that twenty million. We are making long strides forward."

Lorenzo was ready for another question; whether, as many people suspect, he had taken over TI as a business pirate's booty, to be sold quickly at a profit.

"Texas International is not for sale. It has not been for sale. It will not be for sale," Lorenzo continues to smile, with apparently genuine graciousness.

"Are there any circumstances under which it might be for sale?"

"When we get to the bankruptcy courts."

Lamar Muse was a symphony in pink. On his bald spot and on the cheeks which framed his white mustache, his skin was as pink as a newborn baby's. His aviator's glasses were tinted pink. He wore a pink-striped tie, and a shirt of pink checks. His jacket was a plaid—gray and pink. He radiated, like a pastel sun, as he sat munching on a cheeseburger in Austin's Polonaise restaurant.

"There's a story I love to tell, about a man who ran a hamburger stand, whose children wanted to open up a fancy restaurant. He took them aside and told them, 'Boys, remember this: feed the rich, and grow poor; feed the poor, and grow rich.' That's really what we've done. We've made airline travel available to the average person."

Muse is president of Southwest Airlines, whose flights between Houston, Dallas, San Antonio, and the Rio Grande Valley cost 25 per cent, 40 per cent, 50 per cent less than do comparable ones on Braniff and TI. Muse, however, has spent at least as much time fighting the two other Texas airlines as in running his own. ("Mr. Muse hasn't been here in weeks," the Southwest office said at one point this fall. "He's been too busy with the suits.") Southwest has been tied up in virtually continuous litigation by its rivals, ever since it filed for its first routes in 1968.

"You know," Muse said between bites, "Harding Lawrence is probably the best chief executive officer of a trunk line in the United States. But he just got a hard-on about Southwest Airlines. It didn't make any difference to him whether it made economic sense to fight Southwest. He was just going to do us in. He had told hundreds of people in Dallas that we weren't going to make it, and he wasn't going to be proven wrong. He let his emotions get control of him."

Muse paused, and called the waitress over for a dish of butter-pecan ice cream. "The funny thing is," he continued, "every one of his tricks backfired on him. If he had just let us alone from the very beginning, we'd probably have gone under by now."

The dilemmas of Lawrence and Lorenzo have their own special drama, but it took the entry of Muse and Southwest to create the Great Texas Airline War. Like other grand episodes of commercial conflict, this one has all the requisite elements—jealousy, intrigue, back stabbing, high stakes, and occasional honor. The personal futures of several of the participants hang shakily in the balance, and a corporate future or two as well. This war is also a preview of the future for the American airlines. During the coming year, the airlines, along with their benign regulators in Washington, are in for a major assault. Waving banners of "competition" and "deregulation," their opponents will be storming the barricades of Braniff, American, United, and a dozen other carriers, as well as the CAB which nestles protectively over them; the assailants will ask that the industry be broken up the way the oil trust was at the end of the nineteenth century (for all the good that has done). And, as the national struggle wears on, every one of the potential outcomes will already be on display in Texas. Price competition, the decline of the "feeder" lines, shake-ups in long-entrenched management—you'll see it all first, right here.

As much as anything else, the struggle between the three Texas airlines is a contrast of styles—different styles of making money, different views of life. Lamar Muse may grumble about the $2 million Southwest has shelled out in its legal crusades since 1968 (during 1975, this came to $35 per flight), but he clearly relishes having the bullies of the block so relentlessly picking on him. The scrapbooks in Southwest's office in Dallas bulge with clippings describing the latest horror visited upon them by Braniff or TI. While recounting their troubles, the people of Southwest often resemble the conspiracy nuts who hang around so many newspaper offices, fitting every random occurrence into a seamless pattern of malign intent. The difference in this case is that Southwest's paranoia seems justified: there really are people out to get them. No vindication could have been sweeter than the day last February when the federal grand jury indicted Braniff and TI for their dirty tactics against the fledgling airline. Southwest is only too eager to take off its bandages, display its bruises, and point the finger at the man with the blackjack.

Meanwhile, everyone at Braniff feigns magisterial disdain for any other airline that might happen to be operating in the same corner of the country. The Braniff PR man, a corporate incarnation of Ron Ziegler named Jere Cox, at first affected not to understand references to an "airline war," and then, when the mystery was finally explained, said, "*Oh*, you must mean the controversies between Southwest and TI." The impression, up and down the Braniff organization, is of a classily dressed society lady who makes polite conversation while kneeing her neighbor in the groin.

On the other hand, Texas International's people are too preoccupied with survival to worry about appearances. Lorenzo and his friends grumble freely about the injuries they suffer at the hands of Southwest, and about the Texas Aeronautics Commission, a demon in their dark hierarchy second only to Southwest. They prepare position papers to plead their side of the story, they slug it out in the courts, they leave absolutely no doubt about who their enemy is.

The differences in the airlines are highlighted by the personal contrast between Muse, Lawrence, and Lorenzo.

Lamar Muse is as uninhibited as his airline's advertisements—the ones that refer to Southwest as "The Someone Else Up There Who Loves You," that manage to work a busty stewardess into every bit of publicity, that strove, at one point, to give the company an "Ali McGraw image." When the company's stock was introduced for trading on the American Stock Exchange in October, its chosen symbol was "LUV." Muse drives a flashy Mark IV, whose license plate reads FLY SWA. It is as difficult to imagine Harding Lawrence riding in that sort of car as it would be to see him with the white patent-leather shoes that would be the perfect complement to Muse's outfit.

If Muse is a specimen from the raw entrepreneurial end of the business spectrum, Harding Lawrence comes from the other extreme: he is the cold shark of the boardroom, charm and calculation mixed in his icy stares and fixed smiles. When Lawrence responds to a question, large sections of the answer are likely to be missing, as if he were producing a verbal Swiss cheese. When several of these answers are put together, something like deception is the result. (When asked about Braniff's two-fold reputation—as the most efficient, and the meanest, of the Texas airlines—Lawrence set off on a long spiel about Braniff's employment totals in Texas and its commitment to public service. Thirty minutes later he smiled and said, "I haven't really answered your question, have I?") Through his factotum, Jere Cox, Lawrence demurs on questions about the Latin American kickbacks, saying that it would be "inappropriate" to talk while the CAB investigation is going on. That may well be true, but it did not keep him from plastering a one-sided explanation, distorted by omission, before the Braniff stockholders in the latest annual report. Lawrence is a man who won on a fast track; not surprisingly, he is both suspicious and suspect. He is smart enough to have brought men like Russell Thayer to work for him, and smart enough to know now the kind of trouble he is in. Lamar Muse might look on the "airline war" as a kind of exhilarating sport; Harding Lawrence must sense that he is now involved in a struggle for his life.

In a different world, Francisco Lorenzo might have learned to play the part of Harding Lawrence. Since he is at Texas International, however, a more straightforward role has fallen to him. There are few ellipses in his answers, few obviously canned responses. He is trying to save the airline, and disguise or chicanery will not help him in that task. He is affable without being overtly manipulative. "Many people think that because Frank is so charming, he must be a real politician," says a man who has worked with him in Houston. "But he's not. You remember Lyndon Johnson's definition of a politician—a man who could walk into a room full of strangers and know, before anyone spoke a word, who was for him and who was against him. Frank can't do that. Most of the time he thinks everyone is for him, except on bad days, when he thinks everyone is against him." Harding Lawrence would pass the politician's test easily.

The arena in which these disparate spirits contend is one of the remaining romantic pockets of the business world. The shades of Lindbergh and Earhart may have departed the airlines business, but the romance they embody lives on. An accountant who works at General Foods might think of himself as an ac-

countant; an accountant who works at Pan Am would tell his friends that he is "in the airlines business." This pull of glamour and derring-do is felt all the way to the top of the corporate structure; most of the presidents and managers of airlines have had a life-long affair with the sky. Muse and Lawrence both got their start at the same time, as very young men, shortly after World War II. Lorenzo, twenty years their junior, was trained in finance but soon heard the seductive song of the airlines. If he had simply been interested in maximizing the return on his time and his capital, he would have sold TI long ago and sunk the money in real estate. He has not done that, because he too has been captured by the romance.

From casual glances at the business page, the industry's fortunes might also seem to be romantically unpredictable. During the Sixties the airlines were making money faster than they could carry it to the bank, but during most of the Seventies they have had to try desperately to avoid big losses. What this apparent riskiness conceals, however, is the basic secret of the airlines business. In some industries you make money by driving your competition out of business, or monopolizing the talent, or landing the big contract, or getting the best patents. In the airlines industry, you make money by being in business. Like broadcasting, though to a less grotesque extent, the airlines are government franchisees, whose product is almost guaranteed to sell. Management and intelligence can make a difference: bad managers have gotten many lines into trouble, and smart management, at a line like Braniff, can help it clean up on its competition. But the rules of the game are fixed far more than for most businesses. The most vicious competition—the efforts which will make the big difference in profit and loss—take place not before the customer but before the government: before the Civil Aeronautics Board, to be precise, which distributes routes to the various supplicant airlines. If you get a route from Dallas to Seattle, or Chicago to London, or Houston to Mexico City, then you should make money. It is like being given the right to operate a new TV station: the opportunity is there, yours for the taking. There is, of course, a whole subsidiary level of competition over scheduling and equipment, but the real battle is to get the route. This is why the airlines were so distraught with the CAB's "route freeze" of the last few years. While the CAB was awarding no new routes (they said they might start again last summer), airlines did what they could to squeeze extra profits out of their existing routes, but they knew they would not see any big changes. Those big changes were not under the customers' control or the managers', but under the CAB's.

Because of the CAB, the airlines business has been more stable than most others. Of the sixteen trunk lines (the cross-country carriers) chartered by the CAB in 1938 eleven are still in existence. Not one of them has gone bankrupt or out of business (five disappeared through mergers). Not one new competitor has been allowed to enter the market.

It is, of course, possible to lose money in the airlines business, even in good times. One of the quickest ways is to buy too many airplanes, or airplanes too big for your market. When the first commercial jets came rolling off the assembly line in the late Fifties, they were a godsend to the industry. The cost of carrying a passenger from point A to point B was cut dramatically, and the speed was dramatically increased. The airlines bought planes as fast as Boeing and Convair could turn them out; to get on the delivery list ahead of your competitor was to have a significant edge.

At the end of the Sixties, another generation of miracle planes was on the way. These were the "wide body" jets, the 747s and the DC-10s. Airlines stood in line to buy these, too; soon Delta had 20, Eastern 27, Continental 15—and these were only the smaller trunks; United had 45. But these planes were different from the jets of the early Sixties. They might bring the cost per passenger down, if you were flying full planes over long hauls (such as Braniff's flight to Honolulu), but they could run the cost per passenger right through the ceiling if they were only one-fifth full, or if they flew on unrealistically short routes. There were far fewer profitable markets for the 747 than the airlines had hoped, and two or three years after they made their first appearance the jumbo jets were looked on as one of the major threats to the airlines' financial stability. Continental had to park three 747s on the sand near Roswell, New Mexico; whatever rot and deterioration they suffered there would be less expensive than keeping them in the air. (Finally, last summer, Continental managed to unload them on the Iranians, who are able to afford such things.) Braniff was virtually the only line to avoid the 747 frenzy; the company bought only one big jet, and makes a profit flying it to Hawaii.

One class of airlines, however, was created to lose money, to fly routes where the passengers aren't. These were the "feeder" lines, the "local service" carriers, which included companies like Trans-Texas, the forebear of TI. Theirs has been a riskier life than that of the trunks; of the nineteen feeder lines that have sprung into brief existence since 1945 only nine remain. The rest have fallen to the bankruptcy courts, the license-renewal office at the CAB, or to mergers and name changes. The cost of serving the little towns, the Brownwoods and the Big Springs that generate a handful of passengers each day, continues to rise, while the money that the government will cheerfully devote to this cause keeps going down. The question running through many minds, both in Washington and in offices like the TI headquarters, is how long the feeders can last, and what contortions they might have to go through in order to survive. If the Texas Airline War is any indication, the outlook is not good.

This story will eventually roll through the muck, so it might as well start out on the high road, with the good things that Harding Lawrence has done for Braniff. Although the modern era of Braniff dates from Lawrence's arrival in 1965, the airline has been in business since 1930, three years after Thomas Braniff was bitten by the airline bug. Braniff, a businessman in his forties who was getting tired of running an insurance company, bought his own private plane during the excitement following Lindbergh's voyage over the Atlantic. Braniff soon put his plane to work flying commuter runs (with his brother at the controls) between Oklahoma City and Tulsa. Even after it expanded its operations over a broader network, Braniff was not dealt in on the first big federal subsidy to airlines—the payment for making space available for airmail. Braniff did not begin partaking of this nourishing sustenance until 1934, when—after a series of complaints from Braniff and other have-not carriers and a brief, disastrous fling at having the military fly the mail—the government re-awarded the contracts, cutting a few lines like Braniff in on the action.

Four years later, the carriers that had been getting airmail payments were enshrined in the Civil Aeronautics Act as the existing trunk lines; their position has been unassailable ever since.

Braniff remained under the control of its founder until 1954, when Thomas Braniff, irony of ironies, was killed in an airplane crash. Through the next decade, both ownership and management passed from hand to hand, until the big change in 1965. That year, the three major stockholders sold out to Dallas' Troy Post, head of the Greatamerica Corporation, for some $60 million. After a search through the ranks of the airlines business, Post recruited Harding Lawrence, then the number-two man at Continental, to come back home to Texas to be the new manager of his airline. Two years later both Braniff and Greatamerica were acquired by Ling-Temco-Vought, then in the headiest years of its conglomerating. In 1970 the Justice Department forced LTV to dump either Braniff or Jones and Laughlin Steel in an antitrust action; since the steel company was then worth twice as much as Braniff, LTV elected to get out of the airline business. Braniff was sold to a widely dispersed group of smaller investors. Through all the shuffling Harding Lawrence remained in control.

Lawrence had gotten into the industry during World War II by helping run a pilot-training school in Terrell, Texas. After the war he started at Pioneer Air Lines and zoomed up the corporate ranks at Continental when it acquired Pioneer. By the time he came to Braniff, the 44-year-old Lawrence was (in the words of the New York Times) "a dark-haired Texan who looks as though an agency had sent him over to play the part of a dynamic airline president." "Hardly a man alive looks more like the ideal head of an airline than Lawrence," Stanley Brown wrote in his book Ling. "His wavy hair, silvery at the sides, his careful attention to his modified modish dress (especially notable and colorful at the ranch), and the image his airline projects in its advertising and decor . . . all conspire to present Braniff's top manager as a jet-age personality."

That's just the part he played, too, on several fronts. The pre-Lawrence Braniff was something of a joke in the industry, its routes small, its performance poor. The most immediately visible of Lawrence's innovations was the change in the style of the airline—"The End of the Plain Plane," as the admen put it. Shortly after his arrival, Lawrence turned to a New York advertising agency, Jack Tinker and Partners, to give the airline a little pizzazz. The head of the team assigned to work with Lawrence was one Mary Wells, who helped develop the ideas that made Braniff gaudily famous—the brightly colored planes, the Pucci outfits for stewardesses, the retreat from stodginess on all fronts. The following year, Mary Wells and her associates struck out on their own to form a new advertising agency, the now famous Wells, Rich, Greene. The rest, as they say, is history: Harding Lawrence divorced the wife he had married in 1952, he and Mary Wells were married in Paris to the oohs and ahs of a planeload of American friends, and they have lived happily ever after, she working out of New York, he out of Dallas, pieds à terre in each city. "They're the sweethearts of American business," wrote Marilyn Bender of the New York Times, "the Mary Pickford and Douglas Fairbanks of the corporate realm." Bender quoted Wells: "I am stark staring in love with my husband, and he with me." To avoid all appearances of conflict, Wells, Rich dropped the Braniff account soon after the marriage; for consolation, they picked up TWA, with billings three times as large.

Even after the departure of Wells, Rich, the stylish imprint remains. In many of his annual reports Harding Lawrence talks in astonishing detail about chic innovations—the new hors d'oeuvres called "conchitas," the "air strip" costumes which his stewardesses peeled off as the planes headed south, the introduction of drinks like the "Capuccino" (unrecognizable to any Italian), containing coffee, hot chocolate, and brandy.

Beneath the bright colors, Harding Lawrence was doing something even more important: he was making big profits; 1974, the tenth year of Lawrence's regime, was the richest year in Braniff's history. Profits were $26.2 million, up thirteen per cent from the year before—which had been a record itself. In 1974, Braniff earned an 18.2 per cent return on equity, a staggering figure for the American business world as a whole and more than twice the average for the rest of the airlines. During Lawrence's ten years, profits had increased by an average of sixteen per cent, compounded, every single year. As one of the smaller trunk lines, Braniff takes in only *four* per cent of the industry's total revenues; but on that money, it makes *eleven* per cent of the industry's total profits.

It was the kind of picture that few executives in any industry besides oil could paint in these troubled times—least of all executives in the airlines business. Pan Am lost $82 million last year, and Eastern, whose revenues are three times as large as Braniff's, made less than half as much profit. (Only Delta, with one of the most favorable route structures in the industry, made proportionately more profit than Braniff in 1974.) The "secret" of Braniff's success lies with two principles that strike outsiders as obvious, but which have not been widely followed elsewhere. One is to build a network of routes and schedules sensitive to the passenger's demand—"You go when the passenger wants to go," says Russell Thayer. The other is to purchase the right kind of airplanes for those routes.

"The most important thing on a passenger's mind when he chooses an airline is the schedule," says Thayer, whose own high reputation depends on his having put these principles into effect. "There may be a little bit of loyalty to a certain line or hostility to another, but in general, if you go at five o'clock, and I want to go at five, I'm going to go with you. This means that you have to work back from the schedule, make your whole system start there."

Braniff has a "radial" route structure, with its center at Dallas, which is harder to coordinate than long cross-country routes like those of TWA, United, or American. "On a system like this," Thayer says, "the purpose of each connection is to feed the overall network. You try to start flights as far back as possible, so you can build up the traffic for the longer hauls. You start by analyzing traffic out of the smaller stations. Take Austin—a state capital, a lot of good traffic coming out of there. We found that the main long-haul destination from Austin was Washington. The next most important destination was Chicago. You keep that in mind, while you do the same thing with the other cities all over the system. You try to weave them together to make the connections. We're a high-frequency, short-haul airline, and we pay more attention than other lines do to the most convenient timing of the flights." Despite Braniff's reputation as the World's Largest Unscheduled Airline, it also

pays attention to getting the planes to their destination on time; in 1974, it had a better on-time record than most other trunks.

"Once you have the schedule, you look at the equipment and see what's going to be most effective for the specific market you're serving." The Braniff fleet is composed almost entirely of two tested if unromantic workhorses. One is the 727, used for flights inside the United States; the other, the DC-8, for the long hauls to South America. (If and when the Concorde goes on the market, Braniff may buy some for its South American routes, which have all the right qualities for a supersonic flight: long hauls, over water, and full of business travelers who don't mind paying the higher prices.) Because it has only two basic planes, Braniff doesn't have to juggle its equipment around; repairs and scheduling also become easier.

There is one other plane in the Braniff fleet—the famous 747. When Harding Lawrence comes close to letting down his guard and speaking from the heart, it is about this plane.

"All the other guys were going a different route than we did," he says, referring to the 747 orgy a few years back. "They were all buying the widebody planes, and we were out of step. You heard comments—'Lawrence has lost his touch.' A lot of bankers wondered what the hell we were doing." He lights his cigar and takes a puff. "We figured that it might be a mistake to buy the plane, or it might be a mistake not to buy it. If we were making a mistake by holding back, that would be fairly easy to rectify. But if purchasing it was the mistake, that would be very hard to rectify." In the twinkle in Lawrence's eye, one can see visions of poor Continental's jets, baking in the New Mexico sun.

Lawrence pulls out his scratch pad, and begins drawing a series of parallel lines. "You have your jumbo jet, costing X million dollars, and carrying so many passengers. You find that for the same money you can operate two smaller planes, carry the same load, and have them take off thirty minutes apart. Those thirty minutes may be very important to your customers. One of them wants to go at four-thirty, and another wants to go at five. You can serve both of them if you stay with the smaller planes." When Braniff finally did order its one 747, it did so for a tailor-made market. Braniff's 747 was the one hundredth plane off the Boeing assembly line, but it has already surpassed every other 747 in the world in number of hours flown, profitability, efficiency, and everything else. It is in the air nearly fifteen hours every day of the year.

"Once you've got the equipment and the scheduling," Thayer continues, "then you market the system, you tell people what you're offering. We have schedules at all our ticket counters; a lot of other lines think they're too expensive to print up. You don't use your advertising to talk about legroom or frills. [Braniff has reason to be modest about its legroom. Its coach seats are only 34 inches apart, compared to 36 inches for TWA.] You tell people where you go and when. It's all part of coordination—really, coordination is the key to our success. You have to coordinate four elements. First, the kind of equipment you purchase. Second, how much of it. Third, the scheduling, and fourth, the marketing. At some lines, the equipment is chosen by the engineers, and the amount is determined by how many planes they're getting rid of. The scheduling is set up for the convenience of the maintenance men, and marketing has to push what's left. That's no way to run a railroad."

While Harding Lawrence was painting his planes and helping his airline prosper, another side of his spirit was making its influence felt. The consequences have not yet fully run their course, but they came to a climax of sorts last summer, when a tenth-floor office at Braniff Towers was hurriedly vacated. In August 1975, ten years after he arrived, Braniff's president Edward Acker was leaving the airline business. An announcement in the *Wall Street Journal* brought the surprising news that Acker was going to New York—a city low in his esteem—to be second in command of the Transway Company, whose main business was ocean freight. In Braniff Tower, the official reaction was predictable: a mixture of heartbreak at the loss of a great and promising executive, and best wishes for Eddie's future. As Lawrence put it, with the faintest glint of a tear in his eye, "Ed is forty-six years old. That's a vulnerable age, a time when many people make changes in their careers. I made mine when I was forty-four. The man he's understudying at Transway is sixty-five years old. I am fifty-five. Now, Eddie's never said anything like that to me, but if I had to put forward a supposition about why he left, that would be it."

Lawrence continued, "Ed was my choice for president, my successor, but"—and here he flashes a steely grin—"I'm going to be around for a long time."

There is another view about Acker's departure, a view Lawrence flatly labels "nonsense" but which has somewhat wider credence outside his office. It involves Braniff's troubles with the CAB, and it begins—small world—with Watergate.

In the fall of 1973, Harding Lawrence was one of the many corporate officials who pled guilty to making illegal contributions to the Nixon Campaign. Braniff had given $40,000 to the Finance Committee for the Re-election of the President, in violation of federal law. The company was fined $5000; Lawrence himself was fined $1000. If its involvement in the Nixon scandal did not make Braniff unique among American businesses, the subsequent course of investigation did; for the government was soon much more interested in how Braniff had generated the money than in the uses to which it had been put.

According to the complaint now pending before the CAB, Braniff's political contribution to CREEP was only a droplet from a slush fund it had been illegally collecting for the previous three years. Beginning in the fall of 1969, Braniff distributed some 3626 tickets for "off the books" sales. The tickets looked like ordinary tickets, and the customers who bought them got to take their airplane rides. But the tickets were never recorded on the company's normal books, and their proceeds went into a special fund. In this manner, Braniff built up a sum of money which, the CAB has estimated, contained between $641,285 and $926,955.

Apart from the relatively small contribution to Nixon, the money (so Braniff says) went for kickbacks and bribes for ticket agents in South America. Because the CAB complaint inconveniently hit the headlines just as Lawrence was preparing his glorious ten-year report, he felt obliged to begin with a special explanation to his stockholders, designed to knock down the "erroneous and misleading publicity" the company had been receiving. The case he made, essentially, was that all the other fellas were doing it, and that Braniff had to play the game in order to survive. "The fact is," Lawrence wrote in the report, "the market in

South America in 1968 and 1969 was being diverted from Braniff to foreign carriers who were paying travel agents extra commissions." As responsible managers, the executives of Braniff had little choice: "Your company executives charged with responsibility for the Latin American division decided in late 1969 to defend the company by meeting the competitive practices used by other carriers, and thus to protect the company's revenues from continuing erosion." The same Harding Lawrence who felt it would be "inappropriate" to answer questions about the CAB complaint tossed a final plum to the shareholders in his report: he assured them for that modest investment of less than $1 million in kickbacks, the company had "protected" more than $13 million in revenues.

Inside the government, a somewhat colder eye is being cast on the Braniff affair. The CAB's Petition for Enforcement has an unmistakable voice-of-doom quality about it. (The petition is, in a way, Ralph Nader's doing. The Aviation Consumer Action Project, one of his organizations, is listed as the complainant, and it was largely at ACAP's insistence that the CAB began looking hard at Braniff.) It names six individual respondents (Lawrence and Acker; John Casey, the vice-president for sales and operations; Charles South, vice-president for the Latin American division; Robert Burck, executive vice-president for public affairs; and Camilo Fabrega, regional vice-president for Panama) and accuses them of scheming to "generate an 'off the books' source of funds for use by Braniff management, including Lawrence and Acker, as management saw fit, and at least in part for unlawful purposes." The six are accused of lying to the CAB investigators about the scope and nature of the program. Finally, at the end of the complaint, the boom comes crashing down. As part of its "Prayer for Relief" the Bureau of Enforcement not only makes the rather obvious point that Braniff should cease and desist from its illegal operations, but also asks the full CAB to answer the following question:

"Whether the public convenience and necessity require that Braniff's authority to operate in air transportation generally or to operate air transportation within Latin America should be altered, amended, modified, or suspended for such period of time as present management retains operations control over its activities, or be revoked for intentional failure to comply with the Act . . ."

Translated from the legalese, the question is whether the CAB will pull Lawrence from the helm. That the CAB does have the power to "alter, amend, modify, or suspend" Braniff's route authorities is beyond question, even though the agency has never exercised it in such circumstances before.

Whether Lawrence will actually bite the dust is quite another issue. One school of thought, as expressed by a Texas airline man, is that "If they're going after Harding, they're going after a mighty big hoss." In this view, the CAB's purpose was to strike a tough pose, and to give Braniff a scare in the process. Now that Acker, Lawrence's number-two man, has disappeared, the government will settle back, content with the "shakeup" in the management. But many familiar with the CAB's intentions think that the board actually does mean to depose Lawrence. When a man has so molded an airline in his own personal image, this argument runs, he can hardly escape liability when it comes to grief. Although officials at the CAB, in proper legal fashion, will say absolutely nothing about the case, outsiders point out that the new director of the Bureau of Enforcement is Thomas McBride, who has had his dealings with Braniff before. As part of the Watergate Special Prosecutor's office, he investigated Braniff's illegal campaign contributions. He is, in the words of *Business Week*, "an advocate of strong deterrent penalties."

Whatever their final legal consequences, the Latin American kickbacks suggest a certain frame of mind at Braniff, an inner voice saying, "When the going gets tough, the tough pay kickbacks too, rather than running like sissies to complain to the authorities." Perhaps the most interesting aspect of the Latin adventure, and about Braniff's run-ins with Southwest, is the light they shed on Harding Lawrence's character. More than most businesses, the airlines have traditionally borne the stamp of their romantic leaders; and it is Harding Lawrence, with his vanity and derring-do writ large, whom many people see embodied in the warfare with Southwest.

The Southwest concept, anathema as this may seem to local patriots, originated not here but in California. Ever since the Civil Aeronautics Act went into effect, people in the business knew that there were only two ways to escape the CAB's heavy-handed regulation. One was to operate small air-taxi services, of the variety that Metro, Rio, and Davis airlines now run in Texas. Their aircraft were so small that they could never hope to compete in the big leagues. The other solution was to operate wholly within the boundaries of one state, so that the power of the CAB, even when extended to its limits under the "interstate commerce" clause of the Constitution, could not apply. This second approach had some geographical limitations, however: to make an intrastate airline pay off, it took a special kind of state—one with several large cities separated by several hundred miles. If the cities were too small, there would not be enough traffic, and if they were too close together, airplanes could not compete with cars. California—with San Francisco and Los Angeles separated by more than 400 air miles—was the intrastate man's dream, and the local lines got their start there. More than a dozen of the lines rose and fell—this is the law of the marketplace—before one of them, Pacific Southwest Airlines (PSA), established itself as the model of a profitable, low-cost intrastate line.

Texas was the next most likely state on the list, and in 1967 a Harvard Business School contemporary of Francisco Lorenzo's named Rollin King decided to give the idea a try. That year he incorporated Air Southwest, and in January 1968 he filed with the Texas Aeronautics Commission for a license to fly commuter flights between Houston, Dallas, and San Antonio. The TAC, by every indication, was delighted to have this case fall into its lap. Established in 1945 to modernize and promote the air system within the state, it had up to this point divided its attention between the two-bit local air taxis and the rural air strips necessary to keep small, lonely towns in touch with the rest of the state. An intrastate commuter line, which could provide fast, cheap travel between the state's major cities, was part of its vision of a better Texas. Then as now, Southwest was supplied with ample political credentials. On its list of investors appear such names as Dolph Briscoe, Robert Strauss, Jake Jacobsen, George Brown, John D. Murchison, and several

others from the big time of Texas politics and finance. After the hearing in January 1968—at which Braniff and TI had made their own stab at political weight, being represented by Fulbright, Crooker of Houston and Clark, West, Keller, Clark, and Ginsberg of Dallas—the TAC voted unanimously to give Southwest its license. Then the troubles began.

Demonstrating the ancient truth that, with enough money to pay for enough good lawyers, a dedicated opponent can keep almost anything from happening for years and years, Braniff and TI ran Southwest through half the courts of the country. The first prolonged legal battle was over the TAC decision; that finally made its way to the Texas Supreme Court in 1970, where Southwest won a unanimous decision. Braniff and TI promptly appealed to the U.S. Supreme Court, but the Court refused to hear their case.

Not to be daunted, Southwest's opponents took another tack. This time they appealed to the CAB, saying that Southwest's operations would inevitably violate their "intrastate" limitations. Who could tell, their lawyers asked, whether someone journeying from another state into Dallas might step onto a Southwest flight into Houston, thereby making the airline part of the interstate system. The CAB, even though it is traditionally the trunk lines' friend, threw this case out promptly, at which point Braniff and TI appealed that decision to the courts. By the time this case was finally disposed of, in December 1972, the Senior Judge of the U.S. Court of Appeals for the District of Columbia let Braniff and TI know that he was on to their game:

"I have read carefully the pleading and briefs filed by all parties in the Texas Courts—a mass of material more than four inches thick—and have become familiar with the arguments advanced by the diligent and resourceful counsel for Braniff and Texas International. They have omitted no point which their ingenuity could devise in their attack upon Air Southwest . . . . It is now five years since Air Southwest applied to the Texas Aeronautics Commission for a certificate of public convenience and necessity. This litigation should have been terminated long ago; its undue prolongation approaches harassment."

While this case was bobbling through the courts, an equally bitter and even more complicated one was also keeping the lawyers occupied. This time the zeal of Braniff and TI was exceeded by that of the cities of Dallas and Fort Worth, who envisioned their mammoth, expensive, world's-largest airport turning into a municipal disaster at the hands of Southwest. The cities—which had been forced by the CAB to give up their downtown airports (Love Field in Dallas; Greater Southwest near Fort Worth) and join in a shotgun wedding to build the gala new facility—had made all the CAB-certificated carriers sign a blood oath that they would move out to DFW when it was built, so they could start paying enormous landing fees to help retire the bonds. The airlines were hardly delighted at the prospect; it was made palatable only by the fact that everyone was being forced to do it together.

There was one airline left out, however—Southwest, which had only been a gleam in Rollin King's eye when the DFW contracts were being signed. As opening day approached at the big field, Southwest was understandably reluctant to move its commuter flights twenty miles outside of the city—passengers would spend more time in their cars than they would in the plane. As Herbert Kelleher, the attorney from San Antonio who has fought Southwest's battles up and down the appellate system, likes to say, "The passenger has a right to travel from Dallas to Houston, and not from Grapevine to Conroe." Although this litigation probably has a few more appeals left before it finally dies, some of the panic seems to have left the city fathers of Dallas and Fort Worth. Everyone except Southwest is now at DFW, chipping away at the construction bonds, while Southwest continues to use Love Field and Hobby Airport in Houston.

This was the courtroom side of the story; and while it may illustrate the many evils to which the law is prey, it was aboveboard and legitimate. At the same time, efforts of a darker sort were underway—this, at least, is the contention of the U.S. government in its indictment of Braniff and TI for violations of the Sherman Anti-Trust Act. Everyone, even a corporation, is innocent until proven guilty, but the allegations, spelled out in a sixteen-page Bill of Particulars, tell a fascinating story of commercial intrigue.

According to the government, the collaboration between Braniff and TI began long before Southwest took to the skies. "On or about May 14, 1970," the Bill says, "the management of Braniff and TI held a meeting in Dallas. The purpose of the meeting was to promote more cooperation between the two airlines." Among the alleged fruits of that cooperation were not only the legal and administrative appeals, but other tactics of much less subtlety. Some of these were immediately obvious to the public: on June 18, 1971, the day that Southwest's first plane went aloft, Braniff and TI decided to cut their fares to competitive levels. Later, in 1973, Braniff embarked on a brief, and even more obvious, fare war with Southwest. The "Thirteen Dollar War," as it was called, saw Braniff dramatically slash its fares—but only on flights directly competitive with Southwest. This meant, for example, that passengers flying to Dallas from Hobby Field (where Southwest was a competitor) paid $13 on Braniff, while a flight from Houston's Intercontinental Airport, where Southwest was out of the picture, still cost $27. For a short time, Braniff charged less on flights from Dallas to San Antonio (where it competed with Southwest) than from Dallas to Austin (where it did not). With its brassy full-page newspaper ads, reading "No One's Going to Shoot Us Out of the Sky for a Lousy Thirteen Bucks," Southwest generated a handsome return in both business and public relations during the "war." "The Thirteen Dollar War was what really backfired on them," says Lamar Muse, who came to the company when it looked as if the planes would finally get off the ground (Rollin King became Southwest's number-one pilot). "It was so incredibly obvious what they were trying to do. They lost more sympathy on that than on anything else they did."

According to the government's allegations, Braniff and TI also took other steps which, if less evident to the outsider, were even more heavy-handed. One was to keep Southwest from using the fuel hydrant at Houston's Intercontinental Airport; another, to blackball Southwest's application from membership in the interline credit card system, an application all the other airlines were willing to support. When a flight on Braniff or TI was cancelled, passengers were allegedly funneled to the collaborating carrier; they would be picked up in a bus and taken to a waiting plane, rather than allowed to roam free in the terminal, where they might happen upon Southwest. There was a touch of the vindictive as

well; according to the Bill of Particulars, Braniff cancelled an agreement with a package pickup service, called Security Couriers, because Security had had the poor judgment to sign a contract with Southwest.

The Bill mentions one other incident, rendered thus in its dry prose: "On or about July, 1972, Edward Acker, president of Braniff, pressured First of Texas Co., a stock brokerage firm in Houston, to withdraw an investment research analysis which represented Southwest as a favorable speculative stock for high risk capital seeking growth." Lamar Muse tells the story with somewhat richer detail:

"We'd been in business about a year, when the vice-president for research at the First of Texas got real interested in us. He wrote up a beautiful investor's report on us, and when it came out he sent us a few copies. About a week later, I got a call from the guy. He said they'd found a mistake in the report that they needed to correct. He asked us to send all our copies back. So we sent them back. The weeks went by—two, three. There was no report. About six months or a year later, I was told in casual conversation—assuming that I already knew—that Braniff had called the top man at the First of Texas. The First owns Docutel, which had a contract to construct baggage-handling facilities at DFW. Braniff said that if you don't call that report off the streets, we'll cancel the contract with Docutel. That contract was about ninety per cent of Docutel's business."

If even one of these stories is true, the most interesting question is *why*—why Harding Lawrence's Braniff, which had only a small fraction of its business threatened by Southwest, would try with such vengeance to extinguish its tiny spark. Lamar Muse's theory that "Harding got a hard-on" may, in its own way, hit the mark. Lawrence has long been a creature of formidable pride. In *Ling*, Stanley Brown tells the story of Lawrence's twisting James Ling's arm for an enormous increase in pay, so that he could keep pace with his wife's bountiful earnings from Wells, Rich. As one of the industry's swashbucklers, Lawrence has a reputation as a man who can get away with things; indeed, among his colleagues the events of the last year seem actually to have improved Lawrence's reputation, since he has survived scandals that would have toppled less agile men. If the CAB does finally do Lawrence in, the psycho-historians may look back and decide that this was Lawrence's tragic flaw, the hubris that led him astray. The man at the top might have thought that anything was possible, that if you were smart enough you did not have to play by the rules, that there was no reason not to indulge a whim. (And it was not just the rules of fair play which fell by the wayside; simple business sense suffered too. Although Braniff disputes these estimates, Lamar Muse claims that Braniff lost $4 million during the course of the $13 war out of Hobby Airport—or about half of the entire profit from Braniff's domestic operations in that year, 1973.) It was this apparent absence of proportion, the loss of any sense of limitation, which has now endangered Lawrence in holding on to his very job, and will force his company to stand in the defendant's dock in San Antonio as well as before the CAB in Washington.

A very different question arises about relations between Southwest and Texas International. In *Braniff* the provocative element is the pointlessness of it all; Southwest was not going to put

Braniff out of business. For Texas International, the dangers are not illusory. Braniff has treated Southwest with exceeding politeness, ever since word of an antitrust indictment was bruited about in legal circles. Although most of TI's involvement in the antitrust mess took place before Lorenzo's ascent, the new regime has gone after Southwest with renewed vigor in the last year, fighting prolonged and bitter legal battles. Through August, September, and much of October, lawyers for Southwest and TI slugged it out in an Austin courtroom, fighting over Southwest's right to fly into the Rio Grande Valley, a fight emblematic of TI's entire dilemma.

Southwest had first gone into Harlingen during the TI strike last winter. It might seem graceless of TI to protest this incursion while its own planes were grounded, but even before its strike was settled it took two quick steps. One was to file a suit asking that Southwest be removed from the Valley—or more formally, that the TAC's decision granting it the route be reversed. The other was a filing with the CAB, asking that if Southwest stayed in Harlingen TI be allowed to move out. The hard fact is that TI can't compete with Southwest; Southwest can offer lower fares out of the Valley, or anywhere else it flies.

There are several reasons for Southwest's advantage. One is labor costs; Southwest, which is not only non-union but aggressively anti-union, still gives its employees the feeling of working in a family business, and thereby manages to shell out less hard cash. Its pilots, unlike TI's, have not fallen into the clutches of the Air Line Pilots Association. Francisco Lorenzo says that the average pilot at TI makes close to $30,000; at Southwest, the figure is closer to $25,000. (Lamar Muse does claim, however, that his pilots will make as much as TI's when they have accumulated the same amount of seniority. Twenty of Southwest's 39 pilots have been hired since the beginning of 1974.) Another reason goes to the heart of the controversy between "regulated" and "non-regulated" carriers. Because Southwest doesn't have to arrange elaborate reservations through other carriers, sell interline tickets, check baggage from one line to another, or do anything but get passengers from one city to another, it shrugs off much of the overhead which burdens down TI and the other CAB carriers. ("Say that these expenses came to five per cent of our costs, which is just a guess," Lorenzo says. "When you consider that in the best years we're just making a two or three per cent profit, the cost is significant.") Finally, and what has the TI management most steamed up, is that Southwest is free to pay travel agents extra commissions without having the CAB breath down its neck. For all these reasons, TI must either push Southwest out of the market, or find a new reason to justify its own survival.

Francisco Lorenzo inherited this burden when he came to TI. The airline had already mastered one of the secrets of losing money—it served a network of tiny towns that never generated enough income to pay off, even with the government subsidies. Until 1966, when the line was bought by a group of investors from Minnesota, the situation had not been so bleak, and Trans-Texas (as it was known until 1969) had earned steady, if modest, profits. But with the arrival of the Minnesotans, and the musical-chairs sequences of presidents who came in their wake, the airline did not see another profitable month. The figures were those usually associated with impending backruptcy: TI lost more

than $6 million in 1969, and even more than that the following year. By the end of 1971, it was $20 million in debt. The TI stock, which had sold for as much as 29¼ early in 1969, was selling for as little as 3½ by the end of 1971.

This may not be everyone's idea of a dream business, but to Lorenzo it had its charms. While still in their midtwenties, he and Robert Carney had put together Lorenzo-Carney Enterprises; a few years later they converted it to Jet Capital Inc., a financing company whose purpose was to serve, as they put it, as "a meaningful platform for successful participation in the exciting but beleaguered field of air transportation." In other words, to buy their way onto a sinking ship, and hope to keep it afloat. They had made the try before, at Mohawk before it disappeared (by merger) into the maw of Allegheny, but with TI they had a much clearer shot. In April 1971, they became consultants to TI's panicked management, earning $15,000 per month to help pull the airline out of its nose dive. One year later they were sitting at the controls, on the strength of a refinancing deal that temporarily pacified the creditors.

Even though TI was in trouble, others in the airline business had hoped to take it over and make it pay. There was, consequently, widespread incredulity about how Lorenzo and Carney finally won control. By lining up the refinancing for the $20-million debt—admittedly no small feat—Lorenzo and Carney took over TI on extremely attractive terms. For their part, the two men, through Jet Capital, put up $1,150,000 in cash. Actually, since they had been paid some $180,000 in consulting fees over the previous months, and got a $60,000 "finders fee" for arranging the refinancing as well, the cash was easier to raise than it might otherwise have been. In return for their money, they got 59 per cent of the voting stock of the company. (The flier which went out to stockholders explaining the deal, 64 pages of small type and obscure accountants' terms, drily told the present stockholders that what used to be 100 per cent of the voting stock would now count for only 35 per cent.) They also received 2,040,000 shares of "series C" stock, convertible after a few years to 1,020,000 shares of TI common stock. Even at the greatly depressed market prices of TI right now, the stock alone is worth as much as Lorenzo and Carney paid for the airline. Lorenzo was also made president of the company and Carney executive vice-president. One of the rival suitors for TI's hand, Hughes Air West (run by Howard Hughes) in California, filed a statement with the CAB, saying that the deal was unfair. Lorenzo and Carney were getting too much, the Hughes men said, they were paying too little, and they had twisted the stockholders' arms in a moment of duress. The protest was to no avail.

In Lorenzo and Carney's defense it must be said that TI's stockholders are better off as diluted owners of a going business than as full owners of a business in the bankruptcy courts, and that, once installed, the new managers did everything sensible and possible to get the airline back in business. They angled for the rich routes, most notably one between Houston and Mexico City, which has turned into a steady money maker; they have also improved service routes to Albuquerque, Denver, and other cities not in the Brownwood/Big Spring category. At the same time, they begged the CAB to let them out of service to some "marginal" cities, like Pine Bluff and Lufkin. (The normal process for terminating service owes a great deal to the railroad industry. To win a route-suspension case before the CAB, an airline usually has to demonstrate that there is no real demand for its services from the torpid small town. There is no better way to dampen such demand than to schedule the required two-daily round trips, for, say, five in the morning and ten at night, so that they become just as inconvenient for the passengers as the railroads became when they were trying to discourage all but the hardiest riders.) In 1973, Lorenzo and Carney saw TI make a modest profit of $319,000. The next year, the profit was $401,000. These sorts of figures would be laughed out of the boardroom if they were announced at Braniff, but they were a welcome relief for an airline that had, in its bleakest periods, been losing a million dollars a month.

But all of these well-intentioned efforts went to hell over Thanksgiving weekend of 1974, when the long siege of the TI strike began. The airline lost $3.2 million in the first half of 1975, and traffic depressed through most of the year. The strike also revealed the basic oil-and-water nature of TI's management. Lorenzo and the earnest young people he has brought with him seem uniformly decent and capable, but there was something about their background that sat ill with the rest of the company. "You often get the feeling," says a lawyer who has been close to the events, "that Frank and his people came down from Harvard, saw the TI employees driving pickup trucks with gun racks in the back, and thought to themselves, 'We can handle these guys.' There was never any kind of natural relationship between the handful of people at the top and everyone beneath them. You saw the results of the bitterness when it took four months to settle the strike."

For their part, Lorenzo and his associates deny that there is anything like a class division at TI; they also deny that the strike has done any permanent damage to company morale. Lorenzo claims that the management had to weather the strike to keep the company afloat. "It's the easiest thing in the world to avoid a strike," he says. "All you have to do is give in. It's harder to make the necessary judgment of what the company can sustain in the long run." In this case, the "necessary judgment" was that the company needed to squeeze two concessions out of the union—the right to hire part-time employees (without laying off any of the permanent staff), and the right to let employees voluntarily work split shifts, at a premium in pay. "This is a business of peaks and valleys," says James O'Donnell, the company's young PR man who is now becoming one of its six regional managers. "At Lufkin, for example, you'll have one flurry of business at eight in the morning, and another at five in the afternoon. If you can't hire anybody to work part-time or on a split shift, you have to hire two full shifts and you're going to go broke." (On both these points, the union finally gave in.)

Time, the great arbiter, will give the final answer about TI's wisdom in taking on the strike, and about class divisions within the airline as well. But one other problem spawned by the strike already has TI screaming. The strike let Southwest into the Valley.

The litigation between Southwest and TI is likely to drag on until the pages of this magazine have turned to dust, and many of the disputes are quite recondite and confusing. If the case were to be distilled to familiar clichés, however, each side would be saying roughly the following: TI tells Southwest that this town ain't big enough for both of them—that TI can't compete with Southwest's fares, and so one or the other of them must get out of town. ("Town," in this case, is the airports at Harlingen and McAllen; TI now serves both cities, while Southwest flies only into Harlingen.) Southwest, on the other side, contends that a growing pie means bigger slices for all. In its court case and in its appearances before the TAC, Southwest has produced dozens of the Little People of the Valley, citizens of modest wealth who testify gladly that Southwest—with its $25 fare, compared to $40 for TI—has given them wings out of the Valley: they fly to Houston to be treated by Dr. Cooley (how they pay for *that* is another question), they fly to San Antonio to visit their long-lost children. For those who like numbers, Southwest also has one particularly impressive piece of evidence; in 1973, before Southwest got into the picture, TI was carrying an average of 305 passengers each day out of its two airports in the Valley; in 1974, the average was 331. During August of 1975, Southwest alone carried 785 passengers a day out of its one airport at Harlingen. Southwest, which can afford such sentiments, has a live-and-let-live attitude about the Valley. "TI's own estimates show that sixty per cent of the traffic out of the Valley is connecting on for out-of-state flights," says Lamar Muse. We're not allowed to carry those people. Anyway, they want to fly to DFW and not Love Field. If TI would just get on the ball and put on two daily nonstops between Harlingen and DFW, they could make $985,000 each year on that route." To this, Lorenzo replies, "Mister Muse is full of S-H-I-T. He knows very well that there's no single flight that will cater to the needs of that market. He also knows that we were operating that very flight during August and couldn't make a fifty per cent load factor on it. So he is just spewing smoke." Nonetheless, TI's diffidence about this kind of competition is only one of several illustrations that airlines aficionados cite to show that Lorenzo and company, while decent and honest, just haven't figured out how to give their airline a winning image.

Far from digging into the competition with Southwest, TI feels so spurned by Southwest, the TAC, and the ungrateful cities of the Valley that it has decided to turn its back on the "Texas Philosophy." The "Texas Philosophy" was TI's dream, at least as expressed to local chambers of commerce. Lorenzo told them that the airline would give first allegiance to the state, that the Lufkins and Brownwoods would prosper under its aegis. Now, Lorenzo says, "We've had to make a wholesale change in the business strategy of the company during the last six months. We have to change in order to allow the company to operate as a viable concern in the business environment of the state [for "business environment," read "competition from Southwest"]. It's made us de-emphasize Texas. We had announced service between Hobby Field and Austin. If you look out at Hobby, you'll see a nice facility that's never been used. We decided not to offer the service. The current environment prohibits us from making business investments in the state of Texas, if they can be snapped up by someone with different costs and incentives than we have." And so TI is broadening its horizons, looking toward Las Vegas, La Paz, and Mazatlán, rather than to Longview, McAllen, and Austin. October was the first month that TI's "revenue passenger miles" pulled ahead of the previous year's level; and that, says Lorenzo, is because "we've succeeded in redeploying the aircraft outside of the state of Texas." Southwest, meanwhile, is preparing to expand, filing for service to Austin, Corpus Christi, El Paso, Lubbock and Midland-Odessa.

From a profit-and-loss point of view, it is hard to fault Lorenzo's decision. For more than a decade, the old local service carriers have been trying their best to become baby trunk lines. When the government got tired of paying exorbitant subsidies to lines like TI, it decided to give the feeder lines a few plums to offset the lemons they'd been assigned to handle: that is why TI got its routes to Los Angeles, Denver, and Mexico City. Seeing that these big cities make money while Waco continues to be a loser, TI, like many other feeder lines, is drawing the obvious conclusion: why bother with the Wacos at all?

It is difficult to have an evil thought about TI. It wears its heart on its sleeve, it puts the state's name right there on its airplanes. It is trying very hard. Its managers are so appealing, and much more savory than the hard-boiled toughies at the top of Braniff. Its predicament is so touchingly similar to that of the corner candy store being muscled out of existence by the new, shiny, soulless emporium of a national chain supermarket. Still, the question remains: why is TI still in business? What purpose remains for it to serve?

This is connected to the large question now making the rounds in Washington, which is: what lies ahead for regulation of the airline business? Hearings have been held, reports prepared, and, in the inimitable government fashion, detail amassed in quantities sure to stun all inquiring outsiders. The only trend clearly visible through the chaos is that the CAB is going to get it in the neck. A good number of politicians have decided that the airlines can now be portrayed as a conspiracy against the public, and so the CAB and its clients are the more and more frequent targets of rhetorical abuse. Last spring, for example, Senator Edward Kennedy held a long series of hearings, during which he lost no opportunities to point out the difference between the low fares of Southwest and the high fares of the CAB's carriers.

On their side, the airline men do make several plausible points. The first is that the American airline system is, as Russell Thayer of Braniff puts it, "the most remarkable system of transportation in the history of mankind," and that the "high" fares it charges are only half as high as those charged everywhere else in the world. Anyone who has ever invested a year's savings in a short flight from, say, London to Rome, knows the truth of this statement. The second point the industry makes is that reduced fares—which are the main goal of "deregulation"—really make very little difference to most travelers. On Braniff, for example, some 70 per cent of the customers are businessmen, traveling on expense accounts; for them, convenient scheduling and speedy flights are far more important than price. One of Thayer's prize examples of this point is the record of the "Bi-Centennial" excursion fares which United Airlines introduced last summer, and which the other lines reluctantly tagged along with. This special deal offered a twenty per cent reduction on certain journeys; during the first few weeks it applied, Thayer gleefully points out, its most common use was by people who had already traveled and turned their tickets back in for refunds. Even now, he says, it has not enticed many more passengers to fly; it has only allowed the ones who would have flown anyway to fly cheaper.

Even Lamar Muse would agree with this proposition—that modest fare cuts make no substantial difference in the market. "Twenty per cent's not enough," he says, "you have to cut the fare by half." And, short of dismantling the scheduled airline system or bringing on the transportation anarchy that the industry spokesmen constantly warn against, there *should* be some ways to bring the fares down. Charter flights, group travel free of the awkward administrative burdens that now restrict it—these are the ways to benefit the customers not traveling on expense account who pay some attention to price. All CAB fares are now set on the assumption that the average "load factor" on the trunk lines will be 55 per cent—that is, that 45 per cent of the available seats will be empty, carried for free. (In practice annual average load factors fall below that level.) This means, in effect, that the passengers who do travel must pay almost twice as much as they would if the airplane were completely full. Russell Thayer, among others, contends that lines like Braniff, with all their intricate interconnections, could not tolerate a load factor any higher than 55 per cent; if they did, bottlenecks would start developing all over the system. That may be true. But there seem to be clear opportunities for additional service where passengers would trade the inconvenience of worse scheduling for the benefit of half-price fares. The popularity of the old student standby fares and constant demand for charter flights on long hauls from coast-to-coast or to Europe seem to support this principle. (The restrictions against charters often leave the CAB in the grotesque position of spending most of its energy keeping non-bona-fide group members from stealing aboard a cutrate flight, rather than encouraging the trunk lines to find more efficient ways to carry the passengers.)

The inertia of vested interests means that few of these changes, if they come at all, will come very soon. The CAB, tired of being the most maligned agency in Washington, announced last fall the beginning of an "experimental" program of freer competition that would allow the existing trunks to cut fares by modest levels—ten to twenty per cent—and to add or drop routes, also within modest limitations. This is what radicals used to call incremental change; it is hardly enough to satisfy the doughty theorists of Southwest, who would like to see the entire business thrown open to competition. The strong would survive, the weak would die, and for several years there would be chaos in transportation. But, when the dust had settled, passengers would be riding in inexpensive splendor—so this theory goes. Sadly, it seems at least as probable that three or four large trunks would squeeze everybody else out of business, and then impose an oligopolistic control over pricing like that of the guardians of the public's automotive interest in Detroit. Even Braniff might be too small a fry to survive in this sort of free market. "What you'll see under President Ford's proposals," says Francisco Lorenzo, "is two types of airlines. You'll see United Airlines, and you'll see some lines like Southwest." Braniff, TI, and all other inhabitants of the middle tier would be squeezed out of the market.

In the short run, it may not be necessary to make such dire predictions. The deliberate, not to say glacial, pace of governmental reform virtually guarantees that such changes as come at the CAB will come very slowly. But in the longer run someone will win in the national airline war, and the outcome will be presaged in Texas.

—*December 1975*

# DOWN TO EARTH

**"I**n the beginning, before any people, was the land. . . ." So begins T. R. Fehrenbach's epic history of Texas, *Lone Star*. If Texans are united by anything, it is by their continued ties to an abundance of land, 267,339 square miles of it. If in the history of our nation New York is the melting pot and California the promised land, then Texas is surely the frontier. The land, since it sustained, nourished, and protected, even as it challenged, was the foundation of this culture, and the land remains something special in Texas today.

Griffin Smith, jr.'s "Forgotten Places" are the first four in a series of sketches Smith wrote on those hidden corners of Texas that remain more or less as the pioneers found them. Smith's story links us with what Texas once was, and never will be again. John Graves' "Coping," the first in a series of Country Notes columns Graves has been writing for *Texas Monthly*, is one man's musings on going back to the land. In a state rushing to an urban future, Graves is a strong but ironic voice from our country past.

Richard West's "The Last Frontier" explores the life of Presidio County out in the Big Bend, a sprawling, rugged land—still living the frontier past. The setting for the movie *Giant*, Presidio County stands foursquare in the Texas myth, a ranching empire resistant so far to fast-food franchises, psychiatrists, and suburbs.

Appropriately T. R. Fehrenbach ends this volume, just as he began this brief introduction. "The Americanization of Texas" is his elegiac exploration of modern Texas for remnants of a distinctive "Texas" culture. Fehrenbach is too much the realist to underestimate the homogenizing strength of the larger American culture. But he also knows Texas, and he knows Texans. We still have our land; with it, something essentially Texas will endure.

# FORGOTTEN PLACES

by Griffin Smith, jr.

## *Where something of the original Texas still survives.*

"In the beginning," writes Texan historian T. R. Fehrenbach, "in the beginning, before any people, was the land: an immense region 265,000 square miles in area rising out of the warm muck of the green Gulf of Mexico, running for countless leagues of rich coastal prairies, forests, and savannahs; reaching out hugely 770 miles from boundary to boundary south to north and east to west, to enclose a series of magnificent, rising limestone plateaus, ending in the thin, hot air of blue-shadowed mountains."

Newcomers we are, intruders on a wilderness with purposes of our own: varied purposes that have until quite lately not included the determination to preserve some islands of wildness among the workshops we have constructed to hammer out our dreams. Unique among the states, Texas chose and was permitted to keep its public lands upon admission to the union; 170 million acres were thus withheld from federal supervision and distributed indiscriminately for the balance of the century. Much of the modern history of Texas is the story of the fortunes that were built and broken through speculation in those lands. Less has been said about the consequences of their loss.

One consequence is that Texas is dismayingly poor in public recreational land and wilderness preserves. Federal lands in other states, especially in the West, have done much to fill the need for open space demanded by crowded city dwellers as outlets for their growing leisure. Except for two important but remote national parks in far West Texas, Padre Island National Seashore, and a few national forests in the East, the state is devoid of federal land that can now be used for this purpose. Most Texans must choose between private lands and scrawny state parks, and for all but a handful who have access to some property of their own, there is actually no choice at all. The need for wilderness

*Griffin Smith, jr., served as project editor for the Lyndon Baines Johnson School of Public Affairs' Natural Areas Survey in 1973. Formerly a senior editor of* Texas Monthly, *he is now a speechwriter for President Jimmy Carter.*

and recreational land has become acute, even if it could not have been foreseen by the nineteenth-century politicians to whom the Texas earth surface seemed an inexhaustible resource.

Many significant natural sites still in private hands have never been adequately studied and classified; scientifically speaking, they remain unexplored territory. At the instigation of former State Senator Don Kennard—a canoeist, *raconteur,* and lover of the wilderness—the Lyndon B. Johnson School of Public Affairs at The University of Texas at Austin set about last year to rectify this situation. Establishing the Natural Areas Survey Project with Kennard himself as director, the School assembled a team of botanists, zoologists, geologists, and anthropologists to examine four sites that ranged, quite literally, from the warm muck of the Gulf to several of the tallest blue-shadowed mountains in the state: Matagorda Island on the coast northeast of Corpus Christi, the Davis Mountains of West Texas, Victorio Canyon near Van Horn, and Capote Falls—a place so isolated that the nearest city (the remote settlement of Presidio) is nearly two hours' drive away. Another team will consider five more sites this summer.

The four sites included in the first project are among the most memorable works of nature in the state. Each has long ago been disturbed to the point where it can no longer be called wilderness, but none has yet been blighted beyond recovery. They are wild places still.

In wildness, we are told, is the preservation of the world. To visit them is to know that is so.

One cold dawn in January 1881, Texas Rangers attacked a small Apache camp in the Sierra Diablo twenty miles northwest of Van Horn. The Rangers saw the camp as merely the most recent base for Indian raids by followers of the Mescalero military genius, Victorio, whose depredations in the region had reached their greatest intensity in late summer and fall of the previous year. History records it instead as the site of the last Indian battle in Texas—a trivial episode in itself, but marking the fateful moment when the white man took unchallenged dominion over the Lone Star State's contested western lands.

The Indian survivors fled southward with their wounded, pursued by a party of Rangers. Today the quiet arroyo conjures images of Rangers, washed and rested, waiting impatiently for their fellow officers to return, wandering away from the corpse-strewn field across the desolate Diablo Plain to a slight, rocky rise, there to stand in numbed astonishment at the spectacular scene suddenly spread out below: a canyon 2000 feet deep and five miles long. The majestic power of Victorio Canyon is heightened by the improbability that such a natural drama could be played out silently, without warning, in the midst of featureless desert that gives no hint of what lies beyond. The impact of seeing Victorio for the first time comes from realizing that one has failed to take a true measure of the land. There is an unsettling awareness that eyes can grow lazy with flatlands' predictable dimensions and monotonous probabilities, leaving one unprepared for canyons sliced through multicolored rock and successions of windworked statuary looming on steep walls like faceless apostles around some weathered Royal Portal. If the Rangers did not see it, it is their loss: the land is worthy of the moment.

Though in area relatively small, Victorio Canyon and Peak are stunning examples of Basin and Range physiography. The rugged Sierra Diablo typifies the limestone bank reefs that ring the Delaware Basin. Its prominent kin is the towering El Capitan Reef in Guadalupe Mountains National Park to the north. The mysterious narrow side canyons resulted from uplift, intense fracturing, and desert erosion. Eastward beyond the canyon mouth a bleached Salt Basin shimmers through turbulent air. An ever-present wind intensifies the immense solitude and grandeur.

Botanically the area contains climax grama and tobosagrasses with isolated stands of pinyon pine, juniper, and small-leaf oak. Eleven rare and endangered species of plants have been identified in the vicinity, and a shaded fork of Little Victorio Canyon narrows above 5000 feet to a moist, fertile oasis where ferns, oaks, fragrant ash, barberry, and bigtooth maples survive. Found throughout the Sierra Diablo are the native spines of giant yucca, agave, ocotillo, and cactus.

The lower canyon's fauna is typical of the Chihuahuan Desert. Wildlife, after all, is unimpressed by scenery, and neither the vegetation nor the terrain differs sufficiently from surrounding areas for a unique habitat to have developed. Areas above the rim, however, constitute a transitional zone with some of the characteristics of the Guadalupe Mountains. The Sierra Diablo and Victorio Canyon have been insufficiently studied by biologists, but apparently the region has been an important route for the exchange of wildlife north and south between the Navahonian Biotic Province and the Chihuahuan Biotic Province.

The most unusual features of the canyon's wildlife are the bighorn sheep, recently restored to a corner of the state that witnessed their "last stand" two decades ago. As late as 1939 zoologists estimated that 300 bighorns survived in the Sierra Diablo and nearby mountains. By 1956 the estimate had fallen to five. The Texas Parks and Wildlife Department, which last year released bighorns into the Sierra Diablo Wildlife Management Area of southern Victorio Canyon, hopes eventually to reestablish them throughout the mountains.

Inhospitable climate and physical inaccessibility have rendered the Sierra Diablo an area of few archeological sites. Spanish rule left no mark on Victorio. Traces of prehistoric man persist as burned rock middens and lithic debris scattered along small stream terraces above the canyon floor, but the absence of dependable water supplies evidently thwarted human habitation in the area for many centuries. A short distance from the rim, perhaps a half-mile from the precise spot where local legend says the Rangers surprised the last embattled Apaches, the homestead of J. V. McAdoo stands. Built in 1917 by the first white man ever to own the surrounding land, the two-room dwelling served until 1945 as the home for a family of six. Often they cooked and slept outside. The widowed matriarch now lives in a modern ranch house several miles away. Her vivid recollections are a sobering reminder that the white man's presence in the Sierra Diablo has been so brief that its beginnings were witnessed by those still living.

The self-centered arrogance so characteristic of settled, civilized man is impossible at Victorio. He who lives in London or Cairo, Shanghai or Boston—even the man who lives in Houston, Fort Worth, or Alpine—can scarcely imagine the land without himself or his kind upon it, even though he knows intuitively that it once was empty of his people and will surely be empty again. Victorio permits no such illusions. Man's presence—any man's—is revealed for the superficial thing it is. Those who live in the Sierra Diablo reminisce with stories of men who vanished without a trace, sensing uneasily that those stories are symbolic of their own tenuous existence here.

Nothing lasts in this ruthless country. The well-tended McAdoo cemetery stands beside the crumbling homestead, but the hollyhocks are clipped and carried from the ranch house beyond the hills, and the sound of human voices is not heard. Braced against treacherous winds at the lip of the empty canyon, one knows that everything men have fashioned for this land will sooner or later be an archaeological site, a spot marked "ruins" on the map—and probably sooner. Men do not "develop" the Sierra Diablo: they cling to it.

A student of the past has observed that Texas history is a story of racial and cultural conflict. The blood shed at Victorio is a poignant reminder of his insight. But the empty horizon, the weathered homestead, and the dry canyon filled with silences give ironic witness that the land outlasts the men who occupy it.

Capote Falls, the highest waterfall in Texas, drops 150 feet from the volcanic rim of the Sierra Vieja 70 miles northwest of Presidio near the Rio Grande. Although its waters disappear into the desert sands before they reach the banks of that famous river, they form a brief dramatic oasis in the barren countryside.

The falls derive their name from a sloping capelike travertine deposit that backs the lower cascade. For countless years mineral-saturated spring water has plunged over the falls to evaporate in the intense summer heat and form this unusual geologic feature.

Sheer box canyon walls rise on three sides, appended with the brown, pot-bellied nests of hundreds of cliff swallows. Rich banks of maidenhair fern and columbine line the lower reaches, moistened by seeping springs and blowing

The Davis Mountains. *Photography by Reagan Bradshaw*

mist. Sunlight rarely penetrates to these sheltered walls where deep shadows and the awesome vertical scale evoke the mystery of cathedrals.

Less than a hundred miles away, the ancient Spanish settlement of La Junta de los Rios (now Presidio-Ojinaga) was a remote way-station for travelers during centuries of colonial rule. Many expeditions passed within a few miles of the falls themselves, yet with the single exception of the wayward explorer Antonio de Espejo, there is not the slightest evidence that European eyes ever observed them. History swirled around Capote and left it untouched, its natural isolation reinforced by the unwitting neglect of men preoccupied with dreams of empire, until 1885 when Luke Brite and his cattle brought a new dispensation to the land.

The stream which convenes the life of this oasis is born and dies in the vast solitudes of the *despoblado*, a stark and angular region that summons to the mind's eye an image of Texas as the world imagines it. Afternoon light cleaves across the broad, mostly dry Rio Grande Valley, drawing the eye beyond narrow stands of willow and salt cedar, shining like some furious beacon with promise of a greener land wet with winter snows where the thirsty river has its source.

Red weathered Old Mountains of faulted Tertiary stone address the massive Mexican escarpment rising west across the river like the breastworks of two gigantic baronial castles menacing each other across some fancied North American Rhine. In all directions angles lie upon angles, forming a steepness that shuts out civilization and divides mankind into the billions above and the dozens below the savage, sunlit rim.

Through this harsh landscape Capote Creek conveys life-giving water, tempering the desert with foxtails, ferns, and cotton woods, abrading the rocks to smoothness, comforting the eye wearied by too much masculine country with the gentler ornaments of rills and arabesques. The creek and its feed-springs in the *cienega* above the falls form a unique biological island in an isolated corner of the state that fewer than one Texan in a thousand has ever seen. What would otherwise be a desert shrub canyon is instead the home of water-loving ash and hackberry growing over a carpet of green grass and goldenrod. Nine rare, endangered, or endemic species of plants still exist in the vicinity. Below the mouth of the last warm spring, willows and chloris appear; they accompany the gradually-diminishing stream through inhospitable country where afternoon summer temperatures average 110 degrees, to the point a short distance from the Rio Grande where it finally sinks below parched stones.

In a region of staggering distances where miles are meaningless, life or death is paradoxically determined by inches. A few steps away from the water's edge, typical dry canyon vegetation appears: prickly pear, lotebush, catclaw, stickyleaf acacia, grama grass, cockroach plant, and pale-face rosemallow. Farther back, mesquite and creosote bush visibly confirm the inexorable transition from oasis to Chihuahuan Desert.

The canyon below the falls is a narrow passage through old volcanic tuff. This secluded shelter forms a protective environment for a variety of wildlife like the canyon-wren, whose clear descending stairstep song echoes distinctively within the walls. Seventy-five other bird species have been recorded in the canyon, among them the black vulture, which is rarely seen in other parts of Texas. Twenty-nine species of mammals are known to exist along the creek, of which the colony of rare mastiff bats is perhaps the most remarkable. Mountain lions range the area, and bobcats, mule deer, badgers, and porcupines inhabit the banks of this perennial stream. Unusual reptiles like the all-female whiptail lizards, who reproduce through the immaculate conception of parthenogenesis, and the ornate whipsnake, which may be a distinct subspecies unique to Capote Canyon, help make it a wild preserve of significant value.

Aquatic insects skate across the creek surface, while knotleaf rush and smooth flatsedge thrive in the streambed. Beneath the shallow, fast-flowing water an occasional brilliant glint betrays a fragment of opalescent moonstone, dislodged from the ignimbrite along the highest reaches of Capote Rim. Washed into the creek, the crystal faces of gems catch the sun and reflect iridescent blue light to the astonished eye.

Despite the expectation that Capote Canyon must have been an irresistible magnet to Indian tribesmen, European explorers, and nineteenth-century westward travelers, its recent archaeology affords no indication that it was cherished as the oasis we now perceive. Capote Canyon's interest to archaeologists comes from the fact that it lay on a border between desert-adapted Jumano huntsmen ranging beyond the Chisos Mountains, and river-adapted Jumano and Patarabuey Pueblo farmers in the Rio Grande and Rio Conchos valleys.

Military rifle shells dated 1915 and 1918 are silent reminders of Pancho Villa's fellow bandits who raided across the Sierra Vieja rimrock to the Brite Ranch above the *cienega* little more than a half-century ago.

Today, accelerated erosion attributable to reckless overgrazing in the basin above the falls threatens destruction of the delicate cape. A massive section of the capote has broken away since 1964 and the plunge pool—fifteen feet deep in 1966—is now no more than a shallow, gravel-filled basin. Extensively exposed mesquite roots along the canyon are striking examples of the damage taking place. The combined impact of man and nature on this fragile oasis is alarming. To expect that it will be the same ten years from now is perhaps to make the same mistake made by vistors who admired the plunge pool and perfect cape in 1963. Although the past of Capote Falls is measured in centuries, its future may be measured in years.

To the casual traveler the mountains of West Texas are a pleasant scenic interlude in the long monotonous journey across hundreds of miles of arid plains; to the naturalist, however, they are rare remnants of an ancient environment that once sustained vast areas of plants and wildlife similar to those in the Rocky Mountains. Receding under the implacable pressure of a drying climate, that verdant past now survives only on the higher elevations of the Chisos, Guadalupe, and Davis Mountains. These true biological islands preserve living fragments of an existence that has otherwise completely disappeared from Texas.

The only significant history of the Davis Mountains, especially of the unique central Sawtooth-Livermore area, is *natural* history. Their importance as a slowly vanishing remnant of Rocky Mountain environment far exceeds their importance as a stage for human endeavor. Their recorded history is so meager as to be disconcerting: despite Spanish title dating from the sixteenth century, not a single expedition penetrated these mountains until the 1850s. They served only as a haven for Comanches and Mescalero Apaches ranging across the plains. The savagery of both tribes made ranching impossible, regardless of how tempting the water and thick grass of this region might have seemed. Not until 1849, when Captain William Whiting opened the first trail through Limpia Canyon and Wild Rose Pass, skirting the mountains and linking San Antonio with El Paso, did the white man begin to make his presence felt. The founding of Fort Davis in 1854 helped secure the area against infuriated Indians, but this outpost was temporarily lost when the fort was abandoned during the Civil War. Only after the rampaging Victorio's death in 1880 was the region safe for white men. "Ancient history" in Jeff Davis County carries dates like 1889, when the Bloy's Camp Meeting ground was founded six miles south of Mount Livermore, and 1903, when the Reynolds ranch (which now owns Sawtooth Mountain) began its operations. The devotee of history must seek other diversions here.

The archaeological record appears even less rewarding. Only three sites are recorded within the Davis Mountains, compared to more than 1100 in adjacent Brewster County. Apart from a few cliff paintings, pictographs, and scattered projectile points, the only substantial archaeological discovery in the Sawtooth-Livermore area was made in 1895 when the Janes party unearthed a cache of 1200 highly distinctive arrowpoints in a pit at the very summit of Mount Livermore. No finds of even remotely similar extent have been made in the intervening years, reinforcing a popular supposition that the site had ceremonial significance to unknown prehistoric peoples.

For the naturalist and the seeker of wild beauty, these mountains hold infinitely greater rewards. Their ecological importance is undisputed, even if they are not protected by national park status as are the only two comparable areas, the Chisos and the Guadalupes. The fauna of the Sawtooth-Livermore area in particular is remarkable. Animals living above 5000 feet, isolated from other species on similar mountain ranges by the Plains Life Belt at lower elevations, include some of the most interesting wildlife to be found in Texas. Among the unusual species occurring here are Pinyon Jays, Steller's Jays, Clark's Nutcrackers, Cassin's Finches, Golden Eagles, Black-headed Grosbeaks, Grace's Warblers, Trans-Pecos Rat Snakes, Baird's Rat Snakes, Short-horned Lizards, and Pocket Gophers. The Harlequinn, or Mearn's Quail, which once was widely distributed in Texas, is now confined to the Davis Mountains and hovers on the verge of extinction. The only known specimen of a unique species of grizzly bear, *Ursus texensis*, was killed at the head of Limpia Creek in 1890. Black bears are occasionally seen, although the last verified sighting occurred in 1965. Gray wolves once prowled these mountains but are now considered extinct, despite periodic reports of wolflike tracks. Roaming mountain lions have reappeared with increasing frequency in recent years.

The cool, moist northern slopes are covered by montane forests containing plant forms widely distributed in the Rocky Mountains. Madera Canyon shelters a thick stand of quaking aspen. The southern slopes are dominated by pinyon pine, gray oak, alligator juniper, Texas madrone, and mountain mahogany. Cholla, yucca, grass, and dry land

herbs dominate the lower elevations of the foothills. Eleven rare and endangered species of plants have been identified along with six other species familiar to the western states but rare in Texas.

Scenically the Davis Mountains have no peer in Texas. Both the Chisos and the Guadalupes have situations of exhilarating splendor, but neither can match the spacious, sustained beauty of the Davis. The visitor who savors the magnificent panorama from McDonald Observatory on the summit of Mount Locke after a rain may be pardoned for disbelieving that such mellow and seductive country actually exists in Texas. The land appears richer than it is, as fertile as Denmark. From a distance the abundant grasses obscure its roughness, leaving only the jagged rim of Sawtooth and a few eroded volcanic cliffs to interrupt the deceptive velvet surface.

The special appeal of the Davis Mountains lies in such vistas as this. The wooded canyon and grassy hillsides have the feel of wilderness, but the unique quality of the region consists in the opportunity for a visitor to perceive himself *in the midst of mountains*, rather than simply *upon* a mountain. Unregulated development can destroy these perfect vistas. Even a smattering of development on a mere fraction of the total land surface can produce a checkerboard abomination that permanently disfigures an entire panorama. For one who wishes to comprehend the Davis Mountains, every resident becomes a neighbor.

At night lights are visible 40 miles away. Fortunately they still are few, a fact which helps to maintain the continued preeminence of astronomical research at McDonald Observatory. But even now, mercury vapor lamps from the Davis Mountain Resort, owned by the Global Land Development Corporation and situated in a sheltered area opposite Mount Livermore, adversely affect viewing from Mount Locke. Continued subdivision of ranch land into resort developments will not only mutilate the irreplaceable perspectives of the mountains; it will also eliminate, in a way unlikely ever to be undone, their exceptional advantages as a site for scientific inquiry.

If ever a case could be made for preservation of an entire region of Texas as a wild or primitive area, it is here. The form such preservation takes is less crucial than the fact that preservation be assured; a stewardship program which left the care of this land in private hands while guaranteeing responsible public access might well be compatible with Texas customs. Continued governmental indifference to development of the Davis Mountains may, however, ensure that this beautiful land without a history will be consumed and destroyed by strangers seeking to make its future their own.

Texas is blessed not only with dramatic desert landscapes, prairie vistas, and dense forests, but also with the third longest coastline of any state. Unique in this 624-mile seashore is Matagorda Island—isolated, only brushed by history, curiously detached from the steady throb of mainland activity. With the single exception of adjacent St. Joseph Island, no other part of the coast has remained so nearly undisturbed by the destructive encroachments of man. Only the grazing of cows and the exploding of Air Force practice bombs threaten the island as a wilderness preserve and wildlife sanctuary.

Spanish explorers sailed around Matagorda and Spanish

cartographers made note of its dimensions. In 1685 the long, grand rivalry of France and Spain first touched Matagorda when LaSalle's well-stocked provision ship, the *Aimable*, ran aground on shoals along its northern tip, dooming French colonial hopes west of Louisiana. But not until 1793, seventeen years after American independence, did the Spaniards explore the island itself, and even then persistent mosquitoes and flies forced them into prompt retreat, hurling the epithet "purgatory" at the inhospitable place.

If any figure from the past haunts Matagorda, it is doubtless the swaggering shade of Jean Lafitte. Privateering and smuggling dominated the region in the late eighteenth century. While there is no concrete evidence that Lafitte actually used Matagorda as a base, he regularly plied the nearby waters, and his legends captured the imagination of settlers in the decades that followed. One privateer who did attempt to establish himself at Matagorda, only to meet with mysterious disaster, was Louis-Michel d'Aury. Annihilation of his island forces comprising thirteen ships and over a hundred men occurred in 1817 and has never been explained, although recent historical speculation suggests that Aury's rival, Lafitte, may have cinched his domination of the area in one terrible and destructive blow.

A generation later, the clash of privateers had given way to the purposeful footsteps of European settlers like the Irishmen who arrived with their families aboard the *Albion* in 1829. The first immigrants merely landed at Matagorda on their way to mainland colonies of American impresarios, but by the 1850s settlements had been established on Matagorda and St. Joseph islands. Two-masted schooners provided regular transportation between villages, although the residents (mostly ranchers or shipping entrepreneurs) could, if they wished, travel on a thriving stage coach line operated by two sea captains.

Few traces remain today of these towns. One of them, Saluria, has fallen victim to a locally eroding coastline where almost nothing man-made has survived a century of hurricanes. Most of the site itself is now under water. The location of another, named Calhoun, can no longer be identified with precision. A Confederate installation called Fort Esperanza has vanished except for a line of zigzag trenches, overgrown with vegetation and detectable only from the air. There is something altogether transitory about the island, symbolized perhaps by the small United States Air Force Base whose personnel (except for a skeleton crew) return to the mainland shore at night. Matagorda seems destined to be exploited but not inhabited. It is a strong yet passive place, and those who have tried to force it to yield them a home and a living have for the most part left disappointed.

The land they have left is a migrating barrier island, cast up perhaps 5000 years ago and suitable for human habitation no sooner than 2000 years before Christ. In the few seconds of geologic time since it first formed, it has grown seaward nearly a mile, developing sandy beaches of exceptional width—as much as 2000 feet at some points. Thirty-eight miles long and two to four miles wide, Matagorda Island is one of the few areas along the Texas coast possessed of a long beach that is not actively eroding. So few are its visitors that shells and piles of rubbish brought in by tides lie largely undisturbed along the strand, jumbled relics of human civilization and the life of the sea.

Chains of old primary and younger secondary dunes separate the beach from the storm-built back island, where shell spits, ridges, and flood deltas probe into the shallow bays. The rich broth of marine life could not exist if deprived of these indispensable spawning grounds.

The island's two sides afford a striking contrast of mood. Compared to the rich bayside vegetation around pools teeming with half-seen aquatic creatures, the beach itself seems monotonous and barren. Along the bay the wind is gentle, almost still, and the white birds proclaim their indignation at the visitor's intrusion; there is a human scale to things. On the Gulf the unrelenting sea dwarfs everything, dominating each moment without the possibility of refuge or escape. The beach at Matagorda is for those who are not intimidated by the sea; but the quiet bay is closer to the pulse of life.

The isolation of the island makes it ideal for the study of zoological geography. Restricted travel and the lack of a causeway to the mainland differentiate Matagorda from every other major barrier island on the Texas coast. Since it is not a geological remnant of the continent, it has no stranded faunal forms. It is populated only by animals capable of making passage across the bay. As a result its wildlife is limited but remarkable. Raccoons have adapted to an unaccustomed habitat by living in burrows dug into sand banks and eating a diet of insects and crabs. The rare and endangered red wolf hunts jack rabbits and rodents on grass covered dunes. Alligators, fresh water pond turtles, terrapins, and diamondback rattlesnakes are established residents, and unique specimens of six-lined racerunners inhabit a shell island in Matagorda bay. Because conditions are ideal for all kinds of aquatic and semiaquatic waterfowl, most North American species can be found on Matagorda in one season or another. Hawks, turkey vultures, and other nonaquatic birds live on the island year round. Endangered whooping cranes that winter at the nearby Aransas National Refuge doubtless stray to Matagorda. Bobwhite quail, wild turkeys, and a herd of whitetail deer are cultivated by Air Force personnel for sport shooting.

Vegetation on Matagorda is typical of the Texas Coast. Plants on the low-lying island are greatly influenced by slight differences in elevation and tidal inundation. Sea-beach morning glory, beach primrose, and portulaca temporarily anchor the sand above high-tide. Sea oats and long grass ride the shifting dunes, while the back dune region is dominated by dense grasses, sedges, and forbs familiar to coastal prairies. The greatest diversity occurs on the barrier flats stretching across the width of the island between dune ridges and bayside marshes. Needlesharp leaves of gulf cord-grass often grow in the company of Indian blankets, pineleaf sundrops, silver leaf sunflowers, panic grass, frogfruit, bluets, daisies, yuccae, prickly pear cacti, and corpus christi fleabane. Despite the near absence of trees, there is a wholly unexpected lushness to the island that invites close contemplation.

Owing to the geologically recent formation of the Gulf barrier islands, and to their demanding living conditions, archaeologists have found on them relatively few traces of early man. Matagorda is part of the region historically occupied by hunters and gatherers of the Karankawa Indian tribes. The nomadic Karankawa moved seasonally from the offshore islands to the bays, lagoons, and inland areas, taking advantage of the different resources offered by each.

The ultimate beauty of Matagorda rests not in any biological or historical uniqueness—for it resembles other islands along the Texas coast in many more ways than it differs from them—but in its isolation. The sensation of remoteness, of being set apart from mainland Texas in time as well as distance, penetrates more deeply than other aesthetic pleasures the island has to offer. Should its inaccessibility be lost, Matagorda would be little more than another piece of coastal real estate. Causeways and settlements unmake an island, and it is the knowledge that one is truly upon an island that gives the visitor to Matagorda a special sort of emotional liberation.

It also fires his imagination. That detachment from the everyday world enables him to gaze across the Gulf at night, moonlight layering the breakers, and see the ghostly sails of long-sunk privateers or hear the low voices of Lafitte's lieutenants contriving Aury's doom. Bring the mainland over and the ghosts will leave.

If you go, you probably can't get in. All of the areas described here have limited accessibility to the public, either because they are under private ownership or because of government restrictions of some kind. Trespass has always been taken seriously in West Texas and with the adoption of the new Penal Code on January 1 of this year it has become a criminal offense.

—*July 1974*

Presidio County vista. *Photography by John Bintliff*

# THE LAST FRONTIER

by Richard West

## *What Texas once was, Marfa still is.*

**N**ot one member of the Big Bend Dance Club of Marfa doubted this would be a fine July Friday night. One of their favorite bands, Al Dean and his four All Stars, had driven in 470 miles from Freer. Friends from Fort Davis, Alpine, Pecos, Valentine, Van Horn, and Presidio would be here, couples that the vast expanse of country seemed to swallow up between ritual events like weddings, funerals, high school football games, or the Bloy's Camp Meeting.

Although it was midsummer, outside the air was a cool 57 degrees. At an elevation of 4800 feet, Marfa is virtually as high as Denver, and during this July its evening temperature would average a degree or so lower than in Anchorage, Alaska. Marfa's neighbors 25 miles to the east had been so enamored of the climate between the Davis Mountains and the Rio Grande that they named their town Alpine. The people of this most isolated part of Texas are proud of their weather, just as they are, in a quiet, secure sort of way, proud of the way of life they have sustained more or less unchanged since the high days of the cattle kingdom. But what made this particular night special was the light rain that began falling as the pickups and sedans circled and parked around the Beta Sigma Phi Community Center, like buzzards coming to roost at dusk. Rain was a tonic that changed facial expressions, erased wrinkles, lightened voice tones. Rain had the same effect on the Big Bend Dance Clubbers as getting money in the mail, and in this semiarid region of Texas, where a wet year would see barely fifteen inches of rainfall, it amounted to the same thing.

Inside, Al and the boys with the glamorous Maxine on drums blended ballads, waltzes, jitterbugs, put-your-little-foots, cotton-eyed Joes, and schottisches, 25 songs a set thrown out with the regularity of a Wurlitzer jukebox full of

*Senior editor Richard West has been with* Texas Monthly *since its early days. He was the first editor of ''The Texas Monthly Reporter'' section of the magazine.*

dimes. Everybody danced. No one refused an offer. Within the first hour, coats were abandoned, and hairdos unraveled as the temperature on the dance floor climbed with the pace of the dancers' enthusiasm. The dancing styles varied from ice-skating champions to dippers and heel lifters, energetic old boys unconsciously imitating oil-field pumps, and dancing fanatics whose years of practice had transformed them into mechanical windup dolls.

While the men wore variations of their daily work clothes, the women on the dance floor stood out. In this ranching county, women play not subordinate but supporting roles. As teachers, shop clerks, waitresses, government clerks, wives, and mothers, they blend into the fabric of daily life without a hint of contrast. But, every other month at the Big Bend Dance Club, they had sanction to spread their wings and show their plumage. They wore formal evening gowns, pajama pants suits, slacks, slit evening gowns, long granny dresses, cowgirl pants so tight you could read the date on a quarter in the hip pocket; they sported bouffants, fluff-outs, ponytails, pageboys, a chignon or two, and they wore an astounding number of shoe styles. Each outfit was a statement that, since it would have to suffice until the next dance two months away, carried few subtleties.

The land around Marfa also cradles no subtlety. It is hard country, so four-square in the Texas myth that it was the location for that most mythic of Texas movies, *Giant*. The lack of rain, the wind and sun, the sharp drainage and hungry animals keep the fat and drapery from this near bare-bones territory. A touch of soft gentleness appears only in time of rain when the thick skin of grama grass springs to life on the Marfa Highland Plain. Here, among the 3892 square miles of Presidio County's mountains and barrancas, washes, cliffs, valleys, tors, and screes, man is an insignificant figure. There is one of his species per square mile, just as there was in 1850.

If space and aridity define this country, so does silence.

There is not the rich polyphony of forest noises—frogs, birds, cicadas—nor the marsh sounds of the coastal plains —Southern bullfrog belches or spring peeper chirps. It is as if the land was so full of silence that there was no room for sound. Presidio County would remain virtually as quiet in 1977 as in 1885 except for the whirring of the windmill, the swishhhh-bang of a ranch-house screen door, the hum of Border Patrol aircraft, the comings and goings of a few thousand people, and the most important sound heard in the frontier, the low three-toned wail of the railroad whistle announcing a link with the outside world.

When the newly arrived founder of the county's most historic ranch, Lucas Brite, climbed atop Capote Peak on Columbus Day, 1885, he wrote in his journal that he saw no sign of man. No windmills, no roads, no watering places or domestic livestock. By Christmas the next year there were 60,000 cattle in the county and the new ranchers had leased all available water. The way of life they transplanted here became associated the world over with Texas. Although larger forces are gathering that may soon end it forever, it is a way of life that continues in Presidio County to this day.

What Brite and other pioneers discovered was really two countries. On the north are the rolling plains and grasslands of the Marfa Highland, a plateau 75 miles long and 35 miles wide that benefits from moderate rainfall. To the south is the hot, merciless Chihuahuan Desert—sotol, ocotillo, maguey, creosote, and mesquite—country as angular as the Spanish dagger plant. Here only the meager Rio Grande provides a thin ribbon oasis. Separating grassland from the desert floor is a continuous east-west range topped with 6000-foot peaks—the Sierra Viejas, Chinatis, Bofecillos, Chisos. Brite stood on the edge of the highland grasses on the Rimrock, an eight-million-year-old, 6000-foot igneous uplift, and gazed hundreds of feet below to the desert, marveling at this definitive break in nature.

The Rimrock divides cultures as well as landscape. South is Presidio and the home of the *brujo* and *curandero*, a 400-year-old Hispanic way of life, an agrarian civilization huddled near the Rio Grande. North of the mountains would rise the Anglo culture of Lucas Brite—railroads, ranching empires, Rotary Clubs. The Hispanic and Anglo cultures mingled on the ranches, in Marfa and Presidio stores, in the high schools; but not at parties, clubs, churches, or in the cemetery, where Presidio County's deceased Mexicans lie buried on either side of the Anglos in the middle.

As the residents of this isolated, rough county are insignificant, so are the few towns. Scattered south along the Rio Grande are the villages of Presidio, Redford, Candelaria, and Ruidosa. On the Highland Plain to the north, Marfa, the county seat, exists as a ranching-supply center and Border Patrol headquarters, in some ways almost an ideal American village of Thoreau, of Whitman, of early Mark Twain, Hamlin Garland, and Owen Wister, of the village store cracker barrel, but set instead on the open road and far horizon, a small town on the clear uncluttered sweep of a high grassy plateau. Named by the wife of a railroad president for the princess in the Russian novella *Marfa Posadnitsa*, the town grew from a whistle-stop on a frontier railroad. Once it was the center of a vast county stretching from Van Horn to Sanderson, an area the size of Connecticut and Rhode Island. In 1887, to appease the residents of Fort Davis and Alpine, portions of Presidio County were taken to form Jeff Davis and Brewster counties.

In 1955 George Stevens came to Presidio County to film Edna Ferber's novel, *Giant*, the epic of how oil changed Texans and their relation to the land. The movie presented a tale of Texans true to their individuality until the land unexpectedly, almost effortlessly, yielded unimagined riches. The wealth made new creatures of the people; their tragedy was in their yielding to the wealth and forsaking the old values. Not one acre of Presidio County, however, has ever yielded a drop of oil or gas. The filmmakers had to build their own oil field in miniature out on the Evans Ranch. Yet the ghost of the movie still lingers in the county, even as the last few timbers of Riata, the *Giant* ranch house, stand black and weathered next to a brand-new ranch-style mansion Clay Evans has built west of town.

No matter how evocative these Texas myths may be, the land remains, as always, cattle and desert country where making a profit depends on rainfall; where the quotidian beat of the county rarely changes; where for some the metronome regularity of life is paralyzing, warping and narrowing the spirit; where for others the exclusive devotion to the land and cattle, the well-worn paths of conduct, and the total immersion in nature mean serenity and salvation. As Texans become more and more urban, Presidio County becomes more and more a special place, beyond even the myth-making power of Hollywood.

In Presidio County a nineteenth-century way of life clings to a last foothold. This story is about the county and the people who have made it. While women and Mexican Americans have played crucial roles in the county's history, the main shaping influences of the county's dominant way of life have been Anglo males. Whether rancher, farmer, or miner, they followed their dreams to a landscape almost determinedly impervious to their ambitions. This is the story of what they have made, of the small town that anchors their far-flung pursuits, and of an old homesteader, still living as a frontiersman, who ties them all to the past that dwells so clearly in their present.

As in many small towns, the high school is a major unifying institution. The Marfa Independent School District covers 3048 square miles, which means that students scattered in an area the size of Dallas, Harris, and Galveston counties attend the same high school. The head of the district is therefore an important man. In the midst of the dancers, Marfa School Superintendent Carl Robinson looked worried as he moved counterclockwise to "Red Necks, White Socks, and Blue-Ribbon Beer." Always formal, Robinson was easy to spot in his dark suit and horn-rims, with a high forehead marching back to meet reddish, riffling hair. He more than slightly resembled the radio commentator Paul Harvey. He was not the sort of man to take off his coat.

Robinson was worried about finding a band director. Phil Rogers had been a good one, but after four years was moving to Midland to work for Merrill Lynch. Robinson couldn't blame him. Being band director was an incredibly demanding job. You had to instruct all ages in instruments, sight reading, and marching, as well as pacify the Marfa Shorthorn Booster Club and keep peace with the faculty. Where to find such a paradigm? There were other worries, too. West Texas Utilities was proposing additional stadium lights, and the trustees had to fill two vacancies on the board. There was always dope to worry about and pregnancies (four last year), not to mention how to provide transportation for the 25 Mexican American students from Redford, 76 miles away. At least the Redford kids, as they were known, were all fine children, and that reminded Robinson of other blessings. The new coach, Jim Bartlett, had a winning season last year, the first in a while, thanks largely to Espy Howard, a great linebacker and fullback who received a scholarship to West Texas State. Despite being almost deaf, Espy had done well in class. He didn't have to hear anything on the field. He could smell that ball. A fine, even-tempered Christian young man, he made his dad and granddad, who ran Exxon and Mobil stations across from each other at one of Marfa's two blinking lights, puff up with pride like old toads.

There was more to be thankful for. Thirty-four kids had made the National Honor Society; Lee Bennett's Junior Historians had done well in Austin at the state competition; and the tennis team had placed second both in boys' and girls' doubles. Once again a majority of last spring's forty-member graduating class (fourteen boys, eight girls, more Mexican Americans than Anglos) had college plans. For those high school seniors not going to college, however, particularly if their parents did not own a ranch or business, the future in Marfa and Presidio County looked bleak.

A few young men were coming back after graduation, but almost without exception their last names had been on the property rolls for fifty years. Jim Miller, Tom Wood, Bodie Means, Chili Bean Ridley, Robert White. Jimmy White III, Jim White's son working out on the Brite Ranch, was a lucky one. His dad had married Jane Brite, one of the heirs to the Brite Ranch, 88,573 acres. In this masculine country, many penniless young men gained their fiefdoms by marrying high school sweethearts who happened to be heirs apparent to big ranches. No one thought that gaining a ranch by marriage was unusual or belittling. It was simply that parents owned ranches and worked land in Presidio County rather than owning town houses and working for corporations. But ownership of such vast fiefdoms created a local aristocracy far more obvious and important than a townhouse empire could ever be. And marriage into such an aristocracy was not without its historic responsibilities.

The Texas cattle industry grew from its origins in the mesquite brush country in South Texas, along the Nueces and San Antonio rivers, where Anglo herders traded techniques, tools, and stock with Hispanic vaqueros. One great thrust traveled north through the Cross Timbers region—near Jacksboro, Fort Belknap, and the Brazos River—on up the Chisholm, Great Western, and Shawnee cattle trails to Dodge City, Wichita, and Abilene, Kansas, and Sedalia, Missouri. Another headed west over the Edwards Plateau, crossing the Devils and Pecos rivers to the Trans-Pecos, bringing to Presidio County the vaquero and a hardy crossbreed called the Texas longhorn.

When Lucas Brite left Frio County in the spring of 1885 with half a dozen friends and 730 cattle (140 were his), the range country east of the Pecos River was practically full. Cowmen back in San Antonio and Austin knew the buffalo were gone and that Colonel Ranald Mackenzie and the Army were ridding the vast West Texas lands of the last Comanches, Kiowas, Mescaleros, and other Apaches. So they came west with their longhorns and Durhams, by trail

drive or railroad, into Pecos and Van Horn on the Texas & Pacific and into Alpine on the Southern Pacific. In 1884, a rancher named Jim Hiler forever changed the face of the Presidio County cattle business when he brought in the first Hereford. With its meaty carcass, the Hereford, first imported into the United States in 1817 to replace scrub-range stock in Kentucky, quickly replaced the tougher longhorn and became famous to cattlemen around the country as the Marfa Highland Hereford.

Since the beginning, whether you raised fat, prize-winning Highland Herefords, or sheep and goats, or alfalfa, livelihood in Presidio County has relied on one thing: water. No matter how rich the man, how large the ranch, whether he depended on pipe, windmill, Jake Tanks, divining rod, or witching stick, there has never been enough water. The word "rain" dominates every conversation. Did you get any, how much, where, hope you do. Its absence is the common denominator of the American West.

The ranchers' favorite Bible verse is Psalm 121:1-2: "I will lift up mine eyes unto the hills, from whence cometh my help. My help cometh from the Lord which made Heaven and Earth," although they don't always agree with verse 6 ("The Sun shall not smite thee by day").

Many ranchers in Presidio County remember when help cameth not for seven years. The great drought began in 1950 amidst the celebrations and rodeos marking the county's centennial year, a trial by blistering sun, hot winds and dust, and dying cattle. In the end came bankruptcy and the death throes of a way of life. Cattle bought at $250 a head in 1950 sold for $65 in 1956. The familiar penurious sequence began with a rancher taking larger loans on his land, trying to hold his herd together, hoping for rain. When the rain still didn't come, the productivity of the land no longer carried the service on the debt. Then the rancher had to borrow more money from the production credit association and perhaps touch his friend at the Marfa National Bank for one more loan. He pleaded with the Federal Land Bank for help to pay inheritance taxes, mortgages, operating expenses. Finally, when the rain never came, there was nothing left to do but sell the land, pay the bills, and leave.

Roy H. "Happy" Godbold watched this destructive spiral in the 1950s as a board member of the Marfa National Bank and from his office as owner and operator of Godbold Feed and Supply, Marfa's largest employer next to the federal government. From his military nest egg after World War II, Happy spent $6000 for an elevator from an old mica mine and $5200 for an Army quartermaster warehouse, and began Godbold Feeds. He is a strong-looking man in his early fifties with a comfortable paunch, clear blue eyes, a benign grandfather smile. He always wears a soiled Stetson to match his khaki shirt and khaki pants. When the bank board meets, however, he dresses up in a clean Stetson, blue shirt, and khaki pants.

Inside the warehouse, Happy and his manager, Chili Bean Ridley, make supplemental dry cattle feed. A 75-ton press mixes molasses and steam with ground milo, alfalfa, phosphorous, vitamin A, and salt to produce Godbold's 37 per cent protein Grass Buster feed block. From mid-November to May, Chili Ridley oversees around-the-clock crews who load 50,000 pounds of blocks and pellets on each Godbold truck for delivery to hungry cattle around Texas. Ridley and Godbold deal only in pellets and blocks of dry feed, and not in the liquid feeds that are gaining

Moving cattle near Marfa. *Photography by John Bintliff*

popularity. A ton of blocks costs $146; the same amount of pellets is $20 cheaper.

Both liquid and dry feed have their committed advocates. The advantage of liquid feed is the same as relying on a butane gas company delivery man. For the price, you get the liquid feed, the delivery man, and his truck. He assumes control of your supplemental feed operation, periodically bringing the liquid feed for your scattered troughs. However convenient the liquid feed operation may be for humans, dry feed advocates say cattle get too accustomed to the liquid, consuming five, six, or seven pounds a day. They also believe dry feed is better for the cow's digestion, since it does not alter the bacterial action in its first stomach as liquid feed is supposed to do. Many ranchers simply limit the intake of liquid feed by scheduling less frequent deliveries. But, in whatever form, supplemental feeding is necessary, and adds to the cost of raising cattle.

"There is no way to make a living in the cattle business in this country," says Happy Godbold, riding to his six-section ranch (a section is one square mile or 640 acres) down the Casa Piedra road, southeast of Marfa in the creosote-mesquite country. "If your family has been here seventy years and has no land payment, you might make a little money, but not a living. No rancher I know has a savings account. Damn, that old steer is getting some flesh on him, ain't he, Chili?"

Where could the flesh have come from? Eating what? The four or five head of cattle, masticating under the aegis of Godbold and Ridley's Squat Cattle Company, seemed surrounded by thorns, inedible creosote, and pronged cactus a Cyclops wouldn't nibble on. If there was grass at all, it was knee-high to a cicada.

"Down here you run a much smaller number of head per section, not the twenty-five or thirty they run near Marfa. You better have half your grass on the ground come the first of May to last until the late summer rains. If it rains. In a dry year like this one, you cut your numbers to what the land will feed to keep the cows alive. You can't rely solely on buying feed from me or trucking in hay. You'll go broke even quicker. So you have to go to market."

While most cattle ranchers in Presidio County are not turning much profit because of poor cattle prices, little rainfall, and high costs, some do quite well. It helps to have no land debts, to be favored with shallow wells, and to be able to raise other stock—sheep and goats—for added income. This works particularly well in the mid-county mountain areas where one family with 23,000 acres netted $50,000 last year. But such a profit is rare. Expenses and cattle prices see to that. A ranch bought in 1945 with 700 head could be operated for $10,000 yearly. Today, insurance alone for a big ranch costs $15,000. Feed costs have risen from $30 per ton in 1945 to $150. Today, a rancher pays $140 a calf and typically incurs expenses—leasing, taxes, insurance, labor, medicine—of $190 per calf in the nine months it takes to raise it to market weight. If the calf then sells, as they have been selling, for $220, the rancher is looking at a $110 loss.

Ranchers survive with a constant hope that cattle prices will improve and by a constant effort to cut costs. They hate vegetarians as much as drought and rising expenses. The only way to meet expenses is to borrow against future cattle sales. However, there have been only three good years for cattlemen since 1945: 1950, 1963, and 1973. The Siren's song to sell and get out is sweet and compelling. Land appreciated 11 per cent last year and plenty of oil-rich Texans are seeking tax shelters and playgrounds in this beautiful, rugged country. But most Presidio County ranchers try to hold out. Like Ulysses' men, they fill their ears with wax, resisting the sweet music of instant cash that would end their perpetual indebtedness.

On his own ranch Happy was studying the progress of the two things he hoped would better his land. One was root plowing. A bulldozer had dragged a twelve-foot, four-ton blade shaped like a cowcatcher across 2500 acres, snapping off and uprooting unwanted shrubs at root level. Moving the cattle to another section, he had reseeded the ground with either Layman's Love or one of the grama grasses. After six months, the plowed land resembled a strip of AstroTurf carpet next to a desert field. But at a cost of $13 per acre, Happy was still not sure the effort was worth it.

Happy Godbold and Chili Ridley were also trying something else: four-wing saltbrush chamiza (FSC), a fodder shrub that cattle eat in the arid regions of the Mideast and Australia and which has spread into Texas from New Mexico. On his son Carlton's lease, Happy was pleasantly surprised to see the forty cows fleshy despite low grass and no supplements. One morning at dawn he saddled a horse and followed the steers out to pasture. They led him to a bush he had recognized before, FSC, an edible shrub with a 35-foot taproot and no lateral roots to compete with other grasses. The hope of Australia, Israel, and Saudi Arabia may also be the hope of the Godbold Ranch and the Squat Cattle Company. Now, much of Happy's land is sown with chamiza seed and the four-foot plants dot the landscape.

From Alpine to Marfa to Valentine, 63 miles east to west, everybody knows you don't call Chili Bean Ridley, "Chili Bean." Either "Chili" or "Bean" but never both. It is doubtful he would look up or turn his head if someone, in an instance as rare as high cattle prices, addressed him by his given Christian name, Edward Alton. It was "Chili" or "Bean" or something more vulgar to his seven fellow graduating seniors in Valentine High School nine years ago; or to his rowdy friends at Sul Ross, devising schemes to cut all the range animal science courses for the week for a Juárez run; or to the boys on Happy Godbold's loading dock. The Mexicans in Valentine couldn't exactly pronounce Chili's father's name, Chilton, so it got shortened to Chili. When Uncle Noel Everett came to see the newborn second son of Chili Ridley, the water-well driller, he decreed the babe "Chili Bean" and the name stuck.

Like his name, Chili's features reflect the desert Southwest: hair gold as sunshine, parted in the middle like his nineteenth-century ancestors'; sky blue eyes that stare minutes without the normal restful blink; a clear gaze; reddish-brown complexion; a son of Mother Nature. He has the same deliberate unexcited air as his boss, a quiet manner that embodies his whole philosophy. Chili Ridley has never been to a disco, would as soon be shot as endure the people, the smoke, the noise. He would rather think that the word refers to part of a plow.

He only leaves the county to see his friend B. C. Bennett, a cattle buyer for the Clifton Cattle Company, Clifton, Texas; or for weddings and funerals; or to water ski and fish and eat seafood with rancher friends near Corpus Christi; or in search of single women, the reason most single men leave Presidio County. Single women are also as rare as high cattle prices. Chili knows he may be missing something in life, staying around, running his ranch west of Valentine and helping Happy with the Squat Cattle Company. But another place is always hotter, always colder or drier, certainly more polluted, more crowded and noisier, and besides all that, he admits he can't escape the land any more than he could spend his paycheck on Nik-Nik shirts and command a table at Maxim's.

If there is a common feeling binding people together here, it is a distaste for cities. Chili Ridley and all the rest would no doubt apply Mark Twain's phrase about mankind—"a museum of disease, a home of impurities"—to Dallas, Houston, and so on. City folk, they say, don't understand the peace that comes from living with eighty-mile vistas. City claustrophobia leads to narrow thoughts and mean spirits. So many defenses for self-protection in cities: defenses against freeways, against hustlers, noises, criminals, architectural ugliness, against all kinds of obscenities that offend mind and eye, and, worst of all, defenses and masks that people wear for protection against each other.

Life was hard enough without masks. Chili Ridley loved his open country because, simply, it made him feel real. After returning from his occasional trips to Houston or Dallas he felt he was one of them, one of the living dead, all style, no substance, a victim of misapprehensions of what life was all about. No matter how good it was to see friends, he always felt guilty for having left the country.

Chili knew how to read the country. All his life he had worked it, ridden over it, helped his dad throw up windmills on it. He knew that fewer rattlesnakes seen in the summer meant drought. By July, he had killed only six, three times less than midsummer's usual harvest. Rabbits and deer coming to the paved county highway at night meant that pastures were burned up since animals were seeking the only green grass left—that watered by runoffs along the road. Chili knew that the best thing to scatter in the shallow water of a cattle tank or lake to attract minnows was Gravy Train. He knew that mule deer and jackrabbits were behavioral kin as were cottontails and white-tailed deer. A mule deer and a jackrabbit will run off and stop in mid-clearing curiously looking back at you, unconcerned about blending into cover. Cottontails and white-tailed deer will disappear into the bush, seeking camouflage at any cost. Chili knew all this as he knew his own habits.

He followed the unwritten codes of conduct that seemed more important to cattlemen than written laws. These governings were the historical adaptation, like the windmill, barbed wire, and six-shooter, to an unfamiliar country where laws and customs of the more civilized East did not apply. Out here other customs prevailed. Never go on a man's land without permission. Don't ask how many sections he has. Never step over a man sleeping on the floor. Don't mess with a man's hat, and, of course, never throw a hat on a bed. Never rope another man's cow that has wandered on your land. Corral it. Never take a man's last chaw. Chili especially followed that one. He was a fervent dipper of Skoal chewing tobacco—worm dirt, some of his disgusted friends called it.

If Chili Ridley was long in gaze he was short in speech. Ridley on after-dinner plans in Marfa:

"Chili, what do you want to do tonight?"

"Can't do it here."

On *chile serrano* potency:

"Bean, that pepper hot?"

"It's got chances."

He was married once, to a schoolteacher from California, but it didn't take. So Chili takes his thoughts and desires—building a house in the canyon on his ranch, or putting a lot of money together, or lucking into a good woman—he takes them to the country, out to Happy's place to check on Squat's cattle. Maybe it will be a lucky day. Maybe the ground will be hubcap deep in runoff rainwater and the cows will have gained hundreds of pounds eating creosote and mesquite. Who knows? But at least out there it will be open and roomy, and part of him.

Happy Godbold and Chili Ridley's Squat Cattle Company does in fact make money, but not because of rain or high prices or lush grassland. It is a small, carefully planned venture that they operate themselves, on horseback. In February 1976, Squat paid Clifton Cattle Company $34,770 for 225 head of cattle for a steer operation. Expenses amounted to $14,500 for the usual: medicine, freight, feed, ranch repair, and miscellaneous (scale fees, interest, horseshoeing, chute charges). After 257 days and an average of 325 pounds added per animal, they sold them in October for $55,000, leaving them a small profit of $13,000, including $6000 from hedging in the commodities market. They were not fooled. Luckily, it was a way of life, not a living.

With so many variables and expenses and being at the mercy of cattle prices and government policy set far away, perhaps Chili Ridley and Happy Godbold's smaller, controlled operation was the future of the cattle business. Perhaps the huge ranches and cattle herds of *Giant* and the Texas mythology are withering away into smaller, more economically sound entities. Perhaps the secluded imperial domains and cattle empires are destined to disappear forever from the West. But that future, like so much else, will be shaped far from Presidio County—in Congress, in big corporations, in the government bureaucracies. The same is true for farming.

Mike O'Connor watched the dancers whirl by, eyeing the heiress to the convenience store franchise in Alpine, the only Farrah Fawcett-Majors hairdo in the Beta Hall. Was she married or not? The answer was important because O'Connor had been down on his farm in Presidio for two months straight supervising the pitiful harvest of his partnership's alfalfa, cantaloupes, onions, and long green chile peppers. Mike O'Connor, like his across-the-yard neighbor, Chili Ridley, was in the cattle feed business—liquid, not dry—and had done well. But his first agricultural operation had left him deep in debt. Thanks to the United States government—as we shall see—he had reaped only a whirlwind.

But tonight he was going to enjoy himself. He was glad to be out of the hot Presidio sun, to have a drink, to dance and eye the ladies and to see old friends like Wilburn Elliott, the local beekeeper and producer of Elliott's Best Pure Honey, certainly the best Mike O'Connor had ever had. As always, Wilburn seemed to be preceded by his cinemascopic smile.

"Well, Wilburn, bet these girls look good to you being as you been down in the country with just your bees."

"I don't know, Mike. Looks to me like these ranchers took the girls to the market and the pigs to the dance." Wilburn's grin threatened to circle his ears and lap itself.

"Don't you be eyeing that Alpine gal, she's married." Wilburn, a lifelong bachelor in his fifties, would know, thought Mike. Besides she's danced with the same guy three straight dances and looked bored during "An Empty Bottle, a Broken Heart, and You're Still on My Mind." Must be married.

"Mike, you do any good down there in Lapland?" Wilburn knew he hadn't. For the second time, Mike took his eyes off the dancers and looked at Wilburn. "Lapland, where's that?"

"Lapland. Presidio. Where Mexico laps over into Texas," said the beekeeper, immensely pleased with his joke, his grin setting new girth records.

"You know we didn't. We lost everything but a few cantaloupes and onions, some of the alfalfa. About all we have left is Ratón, that Mexican-hating German shepherd. You remember him, don't you, Wilburn, the one whose mother was a Border Patrol dog? Ratón hasn't done too well in Presidio. He hears mariachi music and acts like I'm getting knifed. How was your spring honey crop? I guess those bees loaf now that the weeds aren't blooming?"

"No sir, Mike, no sir. They're on vacation. They made me twelve thousand pounds of catclaw-mesquite honey this spring. Those little bitty fellers are tired. Come on down and I'll show you how it works. I'll show you the business end of a bee," Elliott said, grinning as he left to shake hands with Sheriff Rick Thompson.

Farms are as rare in Presidio County as beekeepers. Without irrigation from the Rio Grande, and more important, the Rio Conchos flowing in through Ojinaga from Mexico, there would be none. Annual rainfall along the Rio Grande in Presidio County measures a bit over eight inches. Geographers save their dustiest term, "arid," for any area receiving less than ten inches of rain a year: the Mideast, the Patagonian Desert, North Africa, and the Presidio Valley.

Seventy-two years before the founding of Jamestown in 1607, Cabeza de Vaca marched through the area of Presidio, where 225 years later, in 1760, Rubín de Celis founded what the Spanish called a *presidio*, a general store, fort, and mission of adobe where the clergy lived and worked on Christianizing Indians and Mexicans. Two years after Texas joined the Union, John Spencer, founder of one of Presidio's most powerful families, laid out the plans for the present-day town. It is indeed "Lapland." The Latin pulse and philosophy of life lap into all aspects of Presidio economics and social structures. Unlike South Texas, where the numerically superior Mexicans live under Anglo political and economic dominance, Presidio more resembles Laredo or Eagle Pass, where the Anglos have been a small minority for a hundred years and the two peoples blend together.

Still, Presidio is more like a Mexican village than a Texas border town. It has a rigid class structure. The wealthier Mexican Americans, along with a few Anglos, control the town's purse. Its middle class—storekeepers, mechanics, cafe owners—provide rudimentary services for the population. Presidio is not incorporated, has no city hall, police department, paved streets (except the county-maintained highway), public library, waterworks, or sewer system; no barber, dentist, or baker; no newspaper, radio station, or public swimming pool. There is one doctor, a 79-year-old osteopath named Clyde Vaught, one lawyer, one motel, four cafes, a television cable company, six department stores, five grocery stores, a honey farm, four service stations, a justice of the peace, a bank, post office, and three bars. Presidio's gay bar closed last spring.

Incorporation would mean Presidio would be eligible for federal revenue-sharing funds and could pave streets, build sewers, erect a waterworks similar to the one across the border in Ojinaga, and qualify for low-cost housing loans for the poorer of its 1200 citizens. But it would also mean higher taxes for the merchants, taxes for a mayor's salary, police, city officers. The ruling families—the Nietos, Spencers, Armendarizes, Herreras—don't mind the present tax rates. Pete Herrera's new $50,000 home is listed on the rolls at $10,000, while no adobe hovel, no matter how squalid, is listed under $1000.

The effects of Presidio's property tax inequities are nowhere better seen than at the high school on the eastern edge of town. The forty-year-old building is falling apart. Teachers need buckets in the classrooms during infrequent rains. Termites have enjoyed most of the floor molding in the typing room. Recently, the old steam-heated boiler exploded, and the administration had to dig deep for $12,000 for a new butane system. The gym is partitioned into classrooms on the south end and a library on the north. The new gym has no lights or bleachers. The football field is a stark green patch, no seats, among the cactus and sand. People have suggested lining up cars and using the headlights for illumination.

Presidio's famous heat is overpowering. The heat and dust, dazing and relentless, turn Presidio into a brick kiln during the summer. The sun sucks everything dry. It is a hard, worn, rocky country, Hell's Half Acre, no quarter asked, none given. The chronicler of Presidio's heat is Oliver Harper, who came to Presidio in November 1929 and opened a hardware store, planning to stick it out awhile and then return to Marfa. He ended up staying, and Harper Hardware prospered. For 26 years Harper served as the town's official weatherman, faithfully recording those harrowing statistics that compose its most meaningful history. Night after night he reported to the nation that Presidio was the hottest spot in the country. No longer the official weatherman, Harper still keeps his records. On June 17 and 18 this year the temperature climbed to 112 degrees, well below the record 117 recorded in June of 1953, 1957, and 1960. In 1956, during the seven-year drought, total rainfall in Presidio was 1.52 inches. "Now that's dry," admits Oliver Harper, white-haired, twinkle-eyed, sitting at his hardware store desk beneath prints suggesting the Rockies and snow: grizzlies, moose, mountain goats, eagles soaring over white-capped peaks.

Presidio County has never seen the violent wars between cattlemen and farmers, because its farms were restricted to this corridor of the Rio Grande far south of the High Plains cattle country. The newest unsuccessful farmer, Mike O'Connor, came here to work as an accountant for Presidio County's largest ranch and biggest taxpayer, the Diamond A Cattle Company (191,391 acres), 25 miles east of Presidio, after graduating from New Mexico State University. He had grown up in Carlsbad as a friend of the sons of oilman Robert O. Anderson, who owned the Diamond A and five other ranches in New Mexico. Mike knew the ranching business and he loved the wild country of Presidio County more every time he passed through.

He and his brother formed the O'Connor Brothers Loomix liquid supplemental feed franchise to keep Happy Godbold and Chili Bean Ridley on their toes. Last fall came the opportunity to buy a farm in Presidio: 170 acres on the Rio Grande floodplain, facing the river, half a mile south of Presidio's main street. You could look over the fields of O'Connor Farms and see the neon signs of Ojinaga's dusty red-light district across the river. The O'Connors paid $270,000 for it, including $145,000 down, which they had to borrow.

By the following spring the O'Connors had 50 acres in cantaloupes, 50 acres in long green chiles, 37 acres in alfalfa, and 25 acres in transplanted onions. Vegetable farming is a risk; it requires hard labor and costs three to four times more than producing row crops such as cotton or wheat. Not only that, it is impossible to know each year which vegetable will bring the highest price. Last year, onions didn't pay production costs. The year before onions paid the bills. Farmers can never tell how much of what they are growing is being produced by other farmers. Too much of a good crop floods the market. And if costs become too high and consumers have to pay too much, they quit buying, and once again the market is flooded.

But the vagaries of the market were unimportant from the moment in late April when Border Patrol agents H. C. Murphy and J. W. Reed informed the group of stunned farmers gathered in the Oil Flyer Cafe that from May 9 to June 9 an additional detail of nineteen patrolmen would be in Presidio to pick up all illegal aliens. This harvest season the farmers would not have the traditional labor force from Ojinaga to help bring in the valley's 5000 acres. That meant, simply, that the O'Connor enterprise was doomed.

The farmers fought back. They applied to the U.S. Department of Labor for temporary visas for Ojinaga citizens. The Labor Department denied the request, saying that the farmers had not advertised enough around the county for workers; that they had no adequate housing for laborers; and that they had balked at paying $2.83 an hour, which, although higher than the minimum wage of $2.20, was a figure the government determined would have "no adverse effect" on U.S. wage rates. So far as the farmers were concerned, they had advertised and no one came. They were willing to pay the minimum wage and a bit more. Were they supposed to build housing for nonexistent workers? They had no money for housing and were not eligible for federal low-cost housing loans because they had no sewers. They had no sewers because they were not a city—no sewers, no federal loan, no housing. But there were no American workers anyway.

For the inevitable remake of *Mr. Smith Goes to Washington*, Hollywood could do worse than hire Mike O'Connor for James Stewart's role. Six feet two, green eyes, cowboy-lean, a fine honest face, O'Connor decided to do what any American would do: sue the bastards. Actually, the Presidio Valley Growers Association petitioned the El Paso district judge for a court review of the government's decision, but O'Connor found the lawyer and pressed the case. Sufficiently impressed with the magnitude of the crisis, President Carter on June 9 ordered Leonel Castillo, the new commissioner of immigration and naturalization, to issue an order allowing Mexican workers to proceed across the bridge and save the harvest. But the long delay had been too much. Forty per cent of the valley's onion crop was lost. The O'Connors suffered disastrous low yields with onions,

cantaloupe, and alfalfa. They harvested 3 of the 47 acres of chiles. In July, when Mike closed the books on O'Connor Farms' first season, the final figure was $46,264—in the red.

It was typical of O'Connor that the experience did not leave him bitter. He would try during the summer to borrow money from Marfa National Bank to start again. He felt the American system of redress had worked. No one, not presidents, immigration officials, or bureaucrats in Washington, stood above a judge. On his wall O'Connor hung Judge William Sessions' order to the Department of Labor to get cracking. O'Connor knew its contents as well as he knew his name.

For 400 years there have been farmers in Presidio County. There have been ranchers since 1850 and since 1883 there have been miners. The land has proved no easier for people seeking profits below the land than for farmers and ranchers coaxing along crops and livestock. In 1883, General W. R. Shafter from Fort Davis found evidence of silver twenty miles north of Presidio in the Chinati Mountains and organized the Presidio Mining Company. On Armistice Day 1918, the Texas Secretary of State issued a charter to the Capote Nitrate Company, capitalized at $100,000. Another $50,000 was spent in the fruitless pursuit of commercial nitrate before the company's death in 1950. Meanwhile, American Metals had bought Presidio Mining Company's silver operation, now in the town of Shafter, and mined $25 million worth of the metal from 700-foot-deep mine shafts in the nearby Chinati foothills before giving it up in the early 1940s when silver prices dropped to 25 cents per ounce. The mountains surrounding Shafter are still bare from the sacrifice of timber to the mine companys' wood-burning boilers before they switched to oil burners.

There may or may not be oil in the county. If there is, it would be a true wildcat, one hundred miles from any known production. There may or may not be copper, nitrate, molybdenum, or more silver. Azcon, a mining company from Colorado, has invested half a million dollars in a mining operation at Shafter, moving people into Mollie Biediger's mobile home camp, leasing Russ White's land, where you can spot silver slivers on the ground, and taking an office next to Mollie's Big Bend Travel Agency in the old school building. Since 1968, a handful of companies have sunk millions of dollars into empty holes in search of uranium.

Pat Kenney, a geologist for Meeker and Company, still insists that the grandmother of all uranium lodes sits under Presidio County's soil, bigger than the $30 million Utah-Colorado lode found in 1949. Kenney has spent a million of Meeker's dollars to prove the theory that eons ago the large uranium deposits near Karnes City and Three Rivers in South Texas flowed out of the igneous volcanic intrusions and uplifts of Presidio County and down the ancestral Pecos River and the Rio Grande. It would follow that the mother lode would still be in Presidio County. The geology is right. Uranium comes from volcanic rock, either igneous flow rocks (which are lava beds), volcanic ash flows (the white tuffs seen in the mesa sides), or igneous uplifts (mountains like Santiago Peak, Chinati Peak, Mount Livermore).

The first thing Kenney learned nine years ago was that it was cheaper to lease a whole ranch than to pay surveyors to subdivide it. He leased the 125,000-acre Pope Ranch south of Marathon, some 25,000-acre spreads in Presidio County, and ranches along Highway 90 toward Valentine. He flew over much of it with a scintillometer, a device to detect gamma radiation. Uranium, however, emits only low levels of gamma rays. A deposit the size of Rhode Island could be located under a one-foot layer of shale and the scintillometer would pass over it and the needle would not move.

After learning about the geology of the county, he eliminated all areas of worthless Cretaceous limestone and the gravel and sand alluvial areas south of the Rimrock. Equipment and money are the main problems. Local water-well drillers have the rigs to cut through anything, but they can't go deep enough. South Texas outfits, rigged to go deep in soft rock near the Gulf, can't go through lava. Kenney spent $20,000 trying to drill deeper than 720 feet in one lava bed. He drilled five 1500-foot holes in the C. T. Mitchell Ranch before dropping the lease. Nine years and a million dollars later he has still found nothing.

Some summer nights geologists, miners, and prospectors discuss rocks, current theories, and the temperament of local ranchers at Willis Williams' Shafter House restaurant. His wife, Virginia, cooks with plenty of sweet Presidio onions, and her Mexican-style food is spicier than the dishes served at the equally venerated Old Borunda cafe in Marfa. Sitting out on the Shafter House screened porch overlooking the ghost town on those evenings, the men can watch the circling buzzards drifting like black ash against the blue sky before coming to roost in the cottonwood trees along nearby Cibolo Creek. The buzzards are probably symbolic of the whole mining venture in Presidio County.

Still, after the years, the money, the frustrations, and the failures, Kenney keeps at it, an old prospector convinced that tomorrow will bring the big strike. He knows it's there—the biggest uranium deposit of all— buried safe from all his machines and knowledge, waiting to be unearthed. Perhaps next week. Perhaps never.

If the buzzards circled over uranium's carcass, so should they over petroleum's. Kenney knew as well as his signature the leases Atlantic-Richfield, Phillips, Gulf, Exxon, and El Paso Natural Gas had taken over the years and the location of attempted wells: the El Paso Natural Gas well southeast of Marfa near the radio observatory on the C. T. Mitchell land; the 18,000-foot Exxon try near Plata that cost $4 million over a year's time; the geothermal wells Atlantic-Richfield drilled near Presidio; and Gulf's well up on the Rimrock on the King Ranch's Chilicothe property. Now Atlantic-Richfield is trying again, this time a 9000-footer on the C. T. Mitchell place, not far from the last dry hole. Out on the Williamses' porch feeling the cool breeze, with two of the biggest and best burritos ever served to a man handily dispatched, anything seemed possible. Perhaps as much oil lay undiscovered as uranium. Perhaps none. If anything could change this country, it would be another Petrolia- or Ranger-size oil discovery or another Utah-Colorado uranium strike.

The lack of oil and gas sets Presidio County apart. The huge strikes in West Texas after World War II transformed Midland, Ector, and Scurry counties, creating cities such as Midland and Odessa and filling them with aggressive, rootless people, alien to their surroundings and intertwined with industry and speculative, shallow-rooted enterprises. While guaranteeing fortune, oil degraded the land and people's feelings toward it. The land, which had been heroic and mystical, a link to one's past as well as to one's sustenance, became merely speculative capital. For better or worse, Presidio County has escaped the amenities and deformities, the population spurts and cash flows, the drastic psychic changes that accompany the discovery of oil.

It is not that the place couldn't use the money a big oil find would create. Marfa's economy depends on the predictable bureaucratic cash flow of the Border Patrol and the unpredictable spending power of the ranchers. Presidio County, like two-thirds of the state's rural counties, lost population according to the 1970 Census. There were fewer businesses and fewer heads of households under fifty years of age, and the median family income was half that of the state's average of $8490.

The future was painted in rosy rather than dark hues in the early forties when Marfa's stores were filled with uniformed American boys. The 2700 acres of Fort D. A. Russell on the southern edge of town were packed with cadets and officers of the Second Battalion, 77th Field Artillery, and later, a contingent of German POWs. But the end of World War II brought the end of Marfa's brief boom. Then came the drought of the fifties and the town sank in gloom.

Only when Hollywood came to Marfa in 1955 to film *Giant* did people stop thinking of going broke, of starving cattle, of monstrous mortgages, if only for awhile. Rock Hudson, Chill Wills (everybody's favorite), and James Dean stayed up at Lee Bennett's mother's house in town. But what really made a man forget the drought was the impact of meeting Elizabeth Taylor at age 23 carrying a plate of barbecued ribs. At the barbecues Warner Brothers hosted for the townfolk working as extras or giving a hand with the livestock or, like Worth Evans, lending a ranch, her lithe young body, her eyes the color of Parma violets, her grin that promised everything literally stopped Marfa men in their tracks. She stayed up at the Charlie Hancock house with her hairdresser and came into town often, especially to eat enchiladas at the Old Borunda.

Hollywood had discovered Presidio County way back in 1929, when *Below the Border, Flashing Spurs, The Texas Battle,* and *West of the Rockies* were churned out, all in the year the country was going broke. But folks didn't pay much attention to these oaters. Ranchers were making money and the grass was high. The Depression and Dust Bowl were yet to come. In 1955, however, Marfans needed that additional $10 a day they could make as extras in the barbecue scene or in the funeral filmed over at the Valentine cemetery.

Noland Kelley, Marfa's funeral director, got to bury Sal Mineo, who played the poor Mexican boy whose family worked for Bick Benedict. For his beatitudes and lowering device he made more than the others, $1000 a day. Since director George Stevens liked the West Texas sunsets, the scene was shot at dusk. Kelley lowered and raised Mineo time and again through three sunsets until Stevens was satisfied. Besides earning $3000, Kelley learned cosmetic techniques—always helpful in his work—from the studio's makeup crew. When filming was finished, his makeup friends gave him their cosmetic case (which he still has), a black tray with "Warner Brothers" stenciled on the top. Before his retirement in 1976, Kelley had buried 2497 people in 33 years, a bit over the current living population of Marfa.

Movie star memories still linger, but the physical evidence of that brief exciting period is almost gone. The Benedict mansion has fallen victim to the weather and is now only a series of boards supported by telephone poles. The handful of tiny oil derricks that Hollywood magic turned into miles of James Dean's wells are rusting on their sides behind Evans' son's house. Sal Mineo lies in another cemetery. George Stevens is dead. James Dean wrapped his Porsche around a tree and was killed the same year *Giant* was filmed, Chill Wills is making commercials for television, and the old Paisano Hotel is closed.

Marfa is a town where no one is rich but no one starves, although avoiding the latter isn't easy. People rarely take vacations. Noland Kelley and his wife, Mary Lou, did not take one long trip during the 33 years he owned Kelley Funeral Home. Marfa stores reflect the no-nonsense character of the land. Their signs advertise necessities: "Feed," "U-Gas-Um," "Patent Medicines," "Groceries," "Furniture," "Credit." The only allusions to leisure are the beer joints, a pool hall, two liquor stores (one run by the county's only Jew, Walter Polsky), Mando's Arcade, and the Branding Iron (the last vestige of the Paisano Hotel and Presidio County's only private club). There are no fast food franchises in the county, no golden arches, Kentucky colonels, or huts selling pizza; no karate studios, health-food restaurants, radio stations; no massage parlors, pornographic theatres, or XXX-rated bookstores. These offerings exist in places with money and people, where the fat of the land permits citizens such luxuries as learning karate or being massaged.

There are few street signs in Marfa and fewer street numbers. Everyone knows where everyone else lives. Leave 50 cents in an empty egg carton inside your unlocked front door and the egg man will replace it with fresh farm eggs. A lazy fullback ordered to run the stadium steps wouldn't mind—there are only seven. Everyone knows that airport manager Fritz Kahl's house is the only one with a windsock on top, and they know about the town's occasional affairs. All the kids know Marfa's motorized zombies who cruise Highway 90 every night looking for something to happen and they know the two best places for parking, one down from the cemetery behind the drive-in, the other on the opposite side of town, down a road near Texas' highest golf course. The kids know that at dusk, in the westering light, the sign for the Stardust Motel, a vertical Stardust atop a horizontal Motel, casts a scandalous shadow resembling an upraised third finger on the embankment across the road.

Marfa's eccentrics—the dog man who wanders town with a cur trotting along behind on a leash, or the shell-shocked Mexican, Polito Alvarado, who travels everywhere in hightopped hiking boots, unlaced and without socks, and a cloth hat pulled tight over his head covering everything but one ear—are known and catalogued and accepted as are those who have fallen deep into sin—a handful of alcoholics, one or two high school girls seized with nymphomania, the young hellions getting busted for dope and drunkenness.

As in every small town, covert truths and scandals are never mentioned, only alluded to by knowing glances, winks, uplifted eyebrows. For the most part, the people of Presidio County are decent and hard working and show little narrowness of spirit or other qualities of small-town Babbittry: smugness, hypocrisy, gross materialism, moral cant.

Everybody knows who works where and everybody knows that balancing the budget takes two wage earners—not father and son, but in many families, father and mother. Everybody in town comes to the post office at least once a day, since home delivery is for bigger cities. Bill Shannon sells stamps and money orders, while his wife, Mildred, teaches at Marfa Elementary. Going north across the Southern Pacific tracks that bisect Highland, the main street, the first store on the right is Jerry's Uniforms, where Jerry Dickson clothes her husband, Gene, and the rest of his Border Patrol colleagues. Nasario Hernandez repairs boots at his shoe shop next door, while across Highland, his wife, Virginia, works in the bank. Past Nasario is the county's only newspaper, the *Big Bend Sentinel*, published by Pat Ryan. Dorothy Ryan is the high school librarian.

On north, past Gloria's beauty salon, is the Palace Theater, which is closed in the summer while Joan and Paul Buren transfer their films to the Marfa Drive Inn next to the cemetery on Highway 90. Joan also works as District Judge Bill Earney's secretary and Paul is manager of the Montgomery Ward order-store. Across Highland at the north end is the courthouse, which is still a desert-sand color after a June 1969 hailstorm battered away the previous pink stucco.

Coming back down Highland there's Marfa Car Parts, Worth Evans' town house in the old Texas Theatre, the Paisano (handsomest hotel in the West), and Baker Jewelers. At the University of Texas, Smitty Baker met and later married Nancy Rawls, daughter of an old ranching family. Smitty soon learned he hated ranching, something the Rawls had done in the county since 1888, so he opened what was to be the first of three jewelry stores in West Texas. Next to Baker's is the Marfa National Bank, whose president is a Marfa native. Then comes Gary and Carolyn Rogers' real estate office.

Out on the highway, Eddie Pierce is king. Since arriving in 1946 from Rockwall to cure his asthma, Pierce has done well. He owns Eddie Pierce Ford and the town's social nexus, the Thunderbird Restaurant. Pierce also owns the Holiday Capri Inn, the Eddie Pierce Apartments, and the Thunderbird Motel.

Aside from the landscape and the lack of people, life in Marfa differs from the city mostly in how its citizens live with time. In urban areas, hour-by-hour events, clock time, is the most important. There is no time to reflect on one's history and sense of place. In Marfa, and more so in Presidio and the county's other small settlements on the river, people live with history. Each moment of their lives is conditioned not only by that moment's experience but also by the sum of experiences up to that time. Around them are the immutable mountains, plains, and sky, keeping a kind of unchanging time against which mere human comings and goings assume their appropriate, subordinate place.

No Mexican Americans attended the Big Bend Dance Club's Friday night party, although they sometimes came as guests. There is one Mexican name listed on the 250-membership roster. Seventy-five per cent of the county's 4800 people are of Mexican descent. Mexican Americans serve as jailer, county clerk, chief deputy tax assessor-collector, parole officer, county treasurer, and county commissioner (three out of the four). They own many of Marfa's businesses. But no Mexican Americans are members of the Marfa Roping Club, the Beta Sigma Phi Club, the West of the Pecos Cowbelles, or the Marfa Rotary Club. Socially, the races stay apart. Most Mexican Americans don't like to dance to George Jones and few Anglos know what a *cumbia* is, much less how to dance to it.

Although the schools have long been integrated, there are few mixed parties and few intermarriages, except between out-of-state Border patrolmen and local women like Delfina Heredia, a 1975 Marfa High School graduate who recently married Ed McCabe of Buffalo, New York. Delfina's sisters, Pilar and Rosario, also married Border patrolmen.

Mexicans came to Marfa for the same reason Anglos did: economic opportunity. Despite their greater numbers, they hold no real political or economic power. Most are semi-skilled or unskilled laborers, although a number derive their incomes from managing or owning the smaller businesses in town. The loyalty to their mother tongue, plus the popularity of Mexican films, Spanish-language radio and Mexican TV programs, and Mexican bands and singers, all reflect a persistence to keep their distinctive culture. Like other Americans, most want to get ahead in their work; they want work that gives them satisfaction, job security, and a higher income. But in sparse, unyielding Presidio County, moving up the status ladder is hard.

Still, Presidio County, like other Texas border counties, is where Anglo ranch life confronts the numerically superior Third World society of Latin America. Prejudices exist, mostly regarding job opportunities and salaries. It is the lower pay of Mexican Americans that is reflected in the county's low median income. In Marfa's public-housing project 10 Anglo families live among 46 Mexican American ones. Of the 26 welfare cases in the county, only one father is Anglo, and he is the head of a mixed family.

Some Mexican American families have done very well. The Prietos own the building in which sits Jerry's Uniforms, a grocery, Exxon station, beauty salon, welding shop, two coin-operated laundries, and rental property. Genevive Prieto runs her beauty shop. Her husband, Mel, teaches at Marfa Elementary and works part-time for George Cross at the downtown pharmacy. Chon Prieto manages one of the laundries, works at Safeway, and oversees the ranch at Candelaria. The Zubiate family has a furniture store, cafe, Sixto's Liquor, apartments, New Star Grocery, and until recently the Western Auto Store. Jesse Vizcaino serves on the bank board, runs the family department stores, and manages an 8529-acre ranch. Conrado Vasquez has had a ranch down near Casa Piedra for many years. Conrado is a retired postal worker. His son, Mando, runs Mando's Auto Shop. Mexican Americans own all the bars, one of the lumberyards, one of the cleaners, all the beauty shops and laundries, the mobile home park, and at one time two businesses, now gone, with the wonderful names of the "Chopin Block Lounge" and the "Lye and Brag." But for most Mexican Americans, life here is just as it is all along the border: hard.

Only two people (his deputy, Gary Painter, six five, 250 pounds, and his jailer, Robert Guevara, six six, 260 pounds) would be bigger than Sheriff Rick Thompson at the Big Bend Dance Club, and they were elsewhere. At six four, 210 pounds, Thompson was the runt of the sheriff's office. Thompson had been appointed to the job in 1973, six days after a retired Air Force major named George Duckworth put five bullets into Sheriff Hank Hamilton as Hank opened Duckworth's car door to order him off the Rolston Ranch. Most people thought Duckworth was crazy, especially when they learned he had tape recorded the whole episode, including Hamilton's last cries. He gave no reason at his trial for the murder. The jury found him guilty of murder and sentenced him to life in prison.

Hamilton had always been embarrassed wearing a gun and didn't for the first few years as sheriff. He had one that day, but it made no difference. Not that there weren't enough guns in the county. On any midmorning coffee break at the Thunderbird Restaurant pistols outnumber straw hats. In this isolated, barely populated county where crime is rare, there are more than forty Border patrolmen, two game wardens, two Department of Public Safety officers, four sheriff's officers, ten U.S. Customs officials, three constables, and two city cops, or about 1.5 uniformed, armed lawmen for every 100 citizens.

Sheriff Thompson was glad to see the end of 1976, Bicentennial year or not. He had barely survived an old-fashioned, all-American, mud-slinging reelection campaign against Mañuel Rodriguez, a former city policeman. Rodriguez beat him in the May primary by nine votes. After the recount, Rodriguez still had a five-vote margin. Thompson contested the election, and visiting District Judge Sam Paxson ruled Thompson the winner by five. Rodriguez appealed and a month after the country's 200th birthday, the appellate court ruled Thompson the winner by three votes. Like most good politicians Thompson hadn't forgotten the source of Rodriguez' support: the Prietos, Vizcainos, Zubiates, Alex Leos, and other prominent Mexican American families. Thompson had gained enough Mexican American votes to win, but before next election he would have to do some fence mending.

To Thompson, dancing with his wife, Barbara Jean, on this cool Friday night a year later, the election seemed a lifetime away. Tempers envenomed by the campaign had cooled and the animosity had disappeared almost immediately, as if most Marfans were grateful it was over and could turn their concerns back to the basics, like rain. As sheriff, tax assessor-collector, and custodian of the jail and courthouse, Thompson received $860 a month. The hours were long, the distances far, but he was thankful for the low crime rate. June's rap sheet showed twenty arrests; two assaults; four auto thefts; a break-in; some traffic offenses. Most of the offenders were transients.

The real center for law enforcement in the county, however, is the Border Patrol. Drifting past Sheriff Thompson and his wife on the dance floor was Carey Clement "Doc" Whitman, the best tracker and best dancer in the Marfa sector Border Patrol. Dancing and tracking wets for 22 years had kept Doc slim as a flagpole. His green-eyed gaze was mild, and he could even look contemplative and dreamy, thinking of his upcoming January retirement and his homestead near Marble Falls. Doc was two years older than the Marfa sector Border Patrol headquarters, which was founded in Fort D. A. Russell in 1924 with a cadre of four. Liquor smuggling was the main challenge in those days. The old-timers still remember the group of Mexicans stopped on the Presidio Highway hauling a wagonload of fish. Inside each fish was a full bottle of whiskey on its way to the speakeasies. Now the problems are illegal aliens and dope. The Marfa sector covers the biggest geographical area in the country, 92,000 square miles with 22 counties in Texas, 18 in Oklahoma, and contains over a million people.

In Doc Whitman's 22 years, the "little fellers," as he called the illegals, had learned a lot. They could still walk 25 miles at night across the Marfa Plain from the Sierra Viejas north to Mount Livermore, avoiding rattlers and cactus. They still carried Clorox water bottles and plastic bags filled with sardines, flour tortillas, *chiles serranos*, and a few limes to quench their thirst. But huaraches had given way to Viet Nam jungle boots and tennis shoes, and the stronger, long-haired young men outnumbered their papas. They had learned to avoid making tracks on the smooth-raked dirt road paralleling the railroad track by wrapping their feet in burlap. Once a man had even attached horseshoes on his hands and feet and clomped across the path, up to a fence, and over into the pasture. Sometimes Doc wondered whether what he had done for so many years made any difference. It always seemed contradictory, tracking down people he knew wanted to work, while so many of his fellow citizens lived on welfare and food stamps. But he had done his job to the letter and considered himself lucky to have lived in Marfa his whole career.

When internal politics or politics between the green-uniformed Border Patrol and the blue uniformed U.S. Customs got bad, Doc thought maybe Evans Means had the right idea. In his whole life, Doc had never met anyone like Evans, a loner, a mountainman, a tough old man of 85 who had lived by himself in his adobe and rock house below Sierra Vieja Pass, 35 hard miles from the highway, since 1913. There had been a wife, Louise, along the way, and time overseas in France during World War I, but Evans had always been a vaquero, a cowboy who wore a six-shooter and could handle ten mules and a wagon.

In 1901, when Evans was nine years old, he had come 500 miles with his family in a wagon train from Lampasas and settled at the old Double Wells Ranch, eleven miles west of Valentine. His mother had homesteaded the first of his sections in 1911, and Evans had staked out the rest two years later, 3019½ acres all together at $1.50 an acre.

Evans had killed a man during his military service, not one from Germany but one from New Jersey. A big Italian doughboy who hated Mexicans thought he had found one and spent most of his off-time hours trying to pick a fight with the walnut-colored Means. Means recalled the scene as if it were yesterday while he stirred the two pots of apricots that had come off the trees his mother planted 66 years ago. They simmered in sugar and juice over the coals on his backyard grill. A cow and a few birds dug into the weeds and cans and bottles behind his house near the spring. After swishing the apricots about, he glanced toward his orchard where pomegranates, peaches, and figs were budding.

"I told him he was too damn big to hit with my fist and to cut it out. He said, 'I been trying to get a fight out of you for three months. I'm gonna kick your ass and make you fight.' I said, 'You kick my ass and you'll die.' He came at me with a stick and I said, 'What you going to do with that stick?'

"He come at me and I never seen a feller jump as fast when my gun came out and went WRRRRRUP. It was kinda dark and I couldn't see, but I hit him. That gun came out and went WRRRRRUP. That bullet hit him right in the navel and carried him from here to my pickup. He lived about ten hours. Sumbitch still dead."

Evans served two years in Leavenworth and was back by the end of 1920, working his place and getting free rides into town from rookie Border patrolmen who invariably thought Means was an illegal alien. He didn't bother to let them know different until they got to Marfa so he could do his shopping: 100 pounds of sugar, 100 pounds of flour, 300 pounds of frijoles, salt, coffee, Bull Durham, bullets, and a fifth of Jim Beam. Usually Doc Whitman brought him back.

His kin had always thought him a scapegrace, half crazy for staying down in the country, sleeping in that dirty room, and never going to the doctor, but they were all dead and he was 85 and planting pecan trees and thinking how he'd laugh when he hid behind his door and threw hot stuff, High Life or Clearlight they called it, on the next wetback who broke his lock. "The Lord says that man shall live by the sweat of his brow. If you get too damn smart to work and sit on your ass, you'll die in six months."

Evans worked in his orchard, watched a few cattle and horses, and kept on making horsehair ropes. From time to time he did missionary work, armed with his .44 pistol. He needed to take another load of New Testaments to the Mexicans on the river and down below Ojinaga. The Rio Grande River Ministry people were all right but they couldn't reach those hombres like he could. And he'd better get doing the Lord's work because He had been good to him. Evans often thought, if the Lord gave him another life, only two things would he do different: raise cattle instead of horses and do more missionary work. To hell with the rest.

From El Paso to Presidio, Evans Means is a legend, a man who, for whatever reason, has gone it alone. He is a bridge from young Lucas Brite, whose ambition was curtailed only by how hard he worked, to the present-day cowman, bound securely by paperwork, the Department of Agriculture, and inheritance taxes. Doc Whitman wasn't the only man who daydreamed about the tough old man. Many men did, especially when thinking of all the ways in which they had trapped themselves into mild versions of slavery: jobs, class convention, families, materialism, affectations, pomposity, laziness.

Evans Means has tested society and will have nothing of it. Like Huck Finn, he was just a young man with little education and great confidence in omens and his own clairvoyance. He embodies the inescapable dilemma of all frontiers and emerging new towns. To what degree must one person live alone and free and to what extent must he submit to society? Is man a social being, responsible to others, or an independent individual, accountable only to his conscience? This democratic paradox was the central quesion of America's last century, recorded in her literature from Natty Bumppo, to Huck Finn, to Emerson's "Divine Individual," to Whitman's *Leaves of Grass*, to the anguish of Billy Budd. Evans Means, at least, has made his choice.

The country is changing hands. More than half of Presidio County's acreage is now held by out-of-county residents: 750,000 acres, 30 per cent, bought by West Texas oilmen like Bobby French and Bill

Blakemore or politicians like Wayne Connally, Forrest Harding, or Cletus (Cowboy) Davis. Even the governor's brother, Andy Briscoe, has a place down near Jack Kingston's hot springs.

Whether they are politicians, like John Connally, Lyndon Johnson, Dolph Briscoe (the state's largest landowner), or John Hill, or accountants, lawyers, or bankers, rich Texans still don't feel they have done anything unless they own a ranch. Making money doesn't matter as much, really. A ranch is the most powerful status object, more meaningful than a Highland Park mansion or a membership in the Houston Country Club.

There are ranches for sale, since many of the families of Presidio County are caught between the romantic view of their own past and the realistic facts of their present situation. Cattle ranching is feasible only if they have outside income. Some are financially strapped. Some are just tired. And they are selling. A fellow from League City and a rich gas man named James Dyer bought Bryant and Alice Harris' Kelly Ranch, 30,000 acres, for $115 an acre. Bobby French, Odessa oilman, bought Lorraine Johnson's old Dipper Ranch, 34,000 acres, in 1974 for $132.50 an acre. Bill Shurley bought Joe Tom Bishop's Alamito Springs Ranch for his son-in-law Gene Nixon. Joe Tom moved west and bought a place in the salt flats near Van Horn. Some of the old families are holding on: the Brites, of course; the Mitchells, Crossens, Humphreys, Howards, Pools, the Espys, all of whose ranches were founded between 1881 and 1890. But a few more ranches seem to change hands each year.

Gary and Carolyn Rogers from Houston are the agents of change. Gary Rogers Ranch Brokerage handled the French, Bishop, Harris sales. The Rogers arrived in Marfa seven years ago to take on an ultimately unsuccessful effort to resurrect the Paisano Hotel. Gary then handled ranch properties for his Houston friend Julio La Guarta, and became more familiar with ranch property in his next venture, taking hunters out in old Houston Light and Power half-tracks to herds of pronghorn antelope and letting them blast away at the curious animals. One year Rogers ran 102 antelope hunters through Presidio County in the eight-day season. Since 1973, Rogers and his wife have sold ranches exclusively, $23 million worth. Rogers says the ranches are basically uneconomical and sell for only one reason: the buyers are "double-barreled rich and they just want that land."

As it was in the beginning, so shall it always be in Presidio County: "A great place for men and dogs but hell on women and horses." "If it doesn't bite it'll stick you with a thorn." "It's got to rain enough to bog down a house cat before I'm satisfied." No amount of grousing or cussing will ever end the quest for land in this country. For there is little else. Presidio County is not like East Texas where the small cotton and corn farms engender problems, not prestige. Or the Gulf Coast where land is something to force pipelines through. Or West Texas where the petroleum culture cheapens its ultimate worth. Only in South Texas with its rich bicultural ranching tradition does owning land mean the same as in the Trans-Pecos.

However furious the changing of ranch titles, the country will remain the same. It is too far, too isolated from mainstream Texas, too wild and rough to become urbanized. The land has a way of repelling the get-rich schemes of "Davis Mountains Resorts," or the "Lost Frontier," or the plans by the Gulf Coast Real Estate people to develop the 96 Ranch near Evans Means' place. Of all three, only weather-cracked billboards remain.

In Presidio County, neither the auto nor pickup nor hordes of new residents will ever blur the distinction between farm and ranch and town as it has in other Texas regions such as the Rio Grande Valley. Here the town is less important than the farm or ranch. The county, not the city, remains the more important political unit. Marfa's population will continue to drop. Unless new Border patrolmen are assigned to the Marfa sector, the 23 houses on the market will sell slowly, if ever.

Marfa High graduates will continue to leave for brighter lights and bigger cities. The franchise restaurants will stay away, venturing only as close as Alpine, 25 miles east. So will freeways and smog, new factories, people, high burglary rates, and rape crisis centers. For some, Presidio County will always be interminably dull and mediocre, almost lifeless. For others, topping the hill and seeing the lights of Marfa will be like coming into harbor after a storm. For Marfa and Presidio County and the people living there, the land is their blessing and their curse.

At the Big Bend Dance Club hoedown, Friday was now Saturday and Carl Robinson still had his coat on as he danced with his wife, Ellen, to Al Dean's finale, "Cotton-eyed Joe." As if he was clairvoyant like Evans Means, his worried look had disappeared. In a month he would have a new band director and two new trustees, and he would be working on schedule changes. He was thankful the Legislature had again defeated Land Commissioner Bob Armstrong's project of buying the Diamond A Cattle Company's Big Bend Ranch, the largest taxpayer in the county. Despite the politicians' promises and assurances, where would he have come up with the $10,000 the Diamond A paid last year in revenue for the school? Not from new cities or new factories or a migration of residents from Buffalo, New York, seeking warmth. Like everything else, it would have to come from the land.

*—November 1977*

# COPING

## by John Graves

---

*Life in the country may have its rewards,*
*but easy living isn't one of them.*

---

"The hell with it," said the seventeenth-century specialist."I spent nine years working on a PhD and fifteen years making full professor and here I am shoveling rocks out of a ditch. I'm moving back to town."

"You don't mean it," I said, visitant free labor, leaning on the pick that had loosened the rocks of which he spoke.

He shook his head and grinned. "I guess maybe not. But one of these times I will."

No figures exist nor is there much demand for them, but I suspect that electrical malfunctions, leaky roofs, busted pipes, jammed sewers, rampaging storm waters, and the like have more bearing on the number of back-to-the-landers who eventually return to the cities than do other strong factors like wifely lonesomeness and the generally dismal economics, these days, of a functional existence on the land. Not that city dwellers and suburbanites don't have to face similar troubles in their brick-veneer "machines for living." But they don't have to face them quite so squarely and so miserably alone unless they choose to, nor is the possible range of problems half as extensive in town as out among the hoot owls and coyotes.

Consider if you will the question of human waste, to designate it by one of the numerous euphemisms which have been tailored for it and which attest to its grubby importance. Except for anal-stage babies and certain happy coprophiles and a billion or so Third World vegetable gardeners, not many people have much affection for the stuff, but it is one of the more central facts of life.

A scant century ago if that much (let's not stray into tales of mythical Thomas Crapper and his invention and all that), Western man devised a means of whisking this substance out of sight and mind so fast that for most of us these days it is possible to pretend that it doesn't exist, except as an epithet. Whether this evasion is good for us philosophically

*John Graves is the author of several books and is a contributing editor of* Texas Monthly.

is an unresolved question. Whether it's good for our world is all too clearly resolved on the nay side, as a boat trip down any stream that has to absorb even standardly "treated" mass wastes will show. But that's a social problem, not a personal one, unless you happen to live too close to the bank of such a stream. The average urban or suburban householder can keep his mind on higher things like bass lures and Archie Bunker, except on rare occasions when T. Crapper's invention backfires or tree roots clog the short house sewer that connects him to the public main. And on those occasions he can call a nearby plumber, whose charges are theoretically kept within reason by competition from hordes of other nearby plumbers, and with spouse, offspring, and intact dignity can quit the house till the trouble has been fixed and the air has cleared.

Not so in the boondocks. Here flows no public sewer main, but instead an intricate disposal system, consisting usually of a septic tank or two whose population of a friendly bacteria digests solids (a second euphemism, though it includes other matter that gets flushed too), and a "field" of tile or perforated plastic pipe to disperse into the soil the clear effluent that results. Indigestible sludge results also, building up slowly in the bottom of the tank. This system isn't a social problem but normally belongs to the sturdy homesteader alone. It costs large heaps of money to install, and if he neglects it, letting sludge accumulate to the point that it spills over and clogs his disposal field, it costs heaps more to replace. Hence a returner to the land, after one or two sour experiences, is likely to spend a portion of his time digging down to inspection boxes to lift their lids and make certain his effluent is unclouded, or searching for damp fragrant spots in grass that hasn't been rained on in weeks.

And after a couple of other sour experiences with the payment demanded and received by one of the scarce and uncompetitive plumbers willing to drive out from a town and view his trouble and maybe cope with it, he is likely to spend a good bit more time manipulating a pick and shovel and certain more specialized tools such as snakes and sewer rods. Spouse and offspring may leave the premises with dignity at such times, but not he. Few of us neo-rustics (or paleo-rustics either) have the fortitude to tackle a sludge-packed septic tank on our own; we call in a specialist with a tank truck and· a suction pump, who gets revenge for the general unpleasantness and lack of social cachet attaching to his job by charging hell out of us. But most of the rest of it we learn how to do, because we have to.

So too do we learn about water systems that begin at the bottom of a 200-foot well and progress through pumps and pressure tanks to an underground network of leak-prone pipes running to far-flung cattle troughs and kitchen sinks and what all, with swarms of differently sized and functioning valves and outlets along the way. And about high lines, ground rods, breaker boxes, and shorted motors. And diversion ditches, and chimney flashings, and one-lung gasoline engines, and termites, and even such mechanisms as water heaters and automatic washers, though with some of these latter you do have the sweaty alternative of detaching the offending object from its moorings, wrestling it aboard your pickup, and hauling it to some shop in town that will not charge you more for repairs than it charges suburbanites. In the course of this education you acquire boxes and shelves and walls full of tools, a good many of which you never heard of before you headed countryward and some few of which you will use exactly one time in your life—because for instance on one sole occasion you had urgent need for a 1¼-inch crow's-foot wrench and nowhere to borrow one. All for the dubious reward of leading a technological life in a place where it possibly doesn't belong. And all aside from other technological maintenance with which your pursuit of agriculture, if any, may embroil you.

The only true alternative would seem to be a return to the simple forthright ways of old, which for that matter are still pretty much the ways of most of mankind. Privies and water buckets, mules and muscles, handcarts and firewood and candles. Most of us who go to the country from a city background have some nostalgia for all that, even if it only manifests itself in a wagon wheel hung over the gate and an expensive fieldstone fireplace and a deluxe edition of Thoreau on the coffee table. And a certain number of us believe in principle that the old ways were more honorable in basic terms, since they fed on local renewable resources and individual effort and didn't gnaw at the earth's guts and disrupt the complex rich flow of its processes. (Not that some old ways of farming and grazing and hunting meat haven't been hugely disrupting the scheme of things since way back in prehistory...)

Yet, except for very pure and young and vigorous home-steaders of the Mother Earth persuasion, may God bless them one and all, the old-way alternative is a tough one. Rewiring a barn and unstopping a sewer and sweating joints in copper pipe are very small potatoes, in terms of effort and, above all, of expended time, when compared to the endless hauling and pounding and scrubbing and lifting and digging and chopping that characterized the day-to-day life of our rural ancestors unless they were landlords with serfs and peasants to command or else the hard-handed fathers of large families. Or Henry David Thoreau, who was only responsible for his own basic needs and could dine in Concord when he felt like it.

We have tasted the fruit of the tree, and technology seems to be with us, even if there's room for a little hope that in time it may grow less destructive. Few women, having grown used to a Maytag, are willingly going to boil dirty clothes in a washpot or carry them to a creek and flog them clean on stones. And while there must be folks who consider a January outhouse preferable to a heated bathroom, I haven't spoken with any of them lately.

Hence, stuck, one copes or one goes back to town. Most of us end up coping most of the time, and paying through the nose for help when we can't. And most of us too end up taking a perverse pride in the acquisition of such blue-collar skills, since it represents survival in a way of life we have picked. In the company of others afflicted with the same disease, be they academics or Baptist preachers or businessmen or hairy dropouts, we can always find a bridge for conversation in such topics as PVC drainage systems, tick invasions, and the merits of jet versus submersible pumps, and can brag to a discerning audience, impatient to start bragging themselves, about occasions on which we have tracked down and rectified esoteric troubles. The high point of my own career in this respect came one winter day after an ice storm when turning on the electric range mysteriously caused various lights in the house to come on and flicker dimly. By deduction and much snapping of switches and breakers and an uneasy rejection of my wife's theory of poltergeists, I traced this phenomenon to a meter pole split-bolt connector, loosened by the ice's weight and jiggling in the wind, that was intermittently letting the juice from one of the range's hot wires flow out through the—well, never mind. It was not much of a triumph, but it was mine alone.

You can go for months without much trouble and then have ten different sorts of it in a week, all urgent. I won't pretend that under such assaults pride doesn't often succumb to weariness and anger, especially as the years pile up. You're supposed to be whatever it is that you are, in my case a writer, and you find that you've ended up a part-time, unpaid, and often unthanked jack-of-all-trades. It is possible at such moments of realization, like my professor friend, to consider quitting or to yearn back illiberally and vainly toward a class society that would furnish you with a smart peasant or two or three to do such work and allow you, in the traditional manner of patricians and intellectuals, to take pride not in grubby blue-collar skills but in soft hands and happy ignorance of how things function.

Not that such wishfulness does much good when eleven heifers are bawling their thirsty heads off at an empty water trough and finding and patching the cause of its emptiness is up to you and nobody else. And not that it usually lasts long. You go ahead and cope because you chose to be where you are and still like being there, and the coping is part of the bargain. And in it, too, you attain sometimes the pleasant illusion, rare these days, of dominating the world around you, technology and all.

*—February 1977*

# THE AMERICANIZATION OF TEXAS

by T. R. Fehrenbach

*Has the independent Texan disappeared into the melting pot?*

Once there was an independent Texan. But no more—finding a truly independent Texan today is about as rare as hearing a real Texas accent in the Galleria or Northpark. The myth lives on, as myths do; the reality survives only among a few old coots, flaming radicals, or rugged individualists. There is an H. L. Hunt, a Ramsey Clark, a Howard Hughes, a Don Meredith, and a Sissy Farenthold, independent Texans all, and whether we damn them or praise them or would like to bury them, they evoke that haunting uneasiness and sense of loss that we have come to associate with endangered species.

There never were as many independent Texans as our folklore insists. But there were enough to make that folklore and to color our whole Texas consciousness: tall men who could die valiantly at the Alamo or San Jacinto but who took orders with poor grace; Rangers who rode alone like paladins; cattlemen who held their ranges against wire and writs as stubbornly as any baron facing the king's cannon; farmers who took their families to scratched-out corn fields in the Post Oak belt when it was Comanche country and lived by choice miles from every neighbor; statesmen like Sam Houston who damned and dared the popular fury—heroes in heroic times, who made and stood for an attitude, a frame of mind rich in Texan symbolism and mythology. The independent Texan was both a real person and a folk hero, part historical figure and part social invention, satisfying deep-seated longings in the Anglo-Texan soul. The man is almost gone; the memory and the few scattered survivors remain.

Like so many things Texan, this folk hero was and is reactionary and futuristic at the same time. The oldtime cattleman or the early wildcatter clings to this image. But the independent Texan had and has another image, or series of

*T. R. Fehrenbach of San Antonio is the author of* Lone Star, Fire and Blood, *and* Comanches: The Destruction of a People.

images, too: that uninhibited or unencumbered spirit who jeers at the hypocrisies and pretensions of over-organized society, Yankee or Texan, who speaks his or her mind in pungent, sometimes barnyard-flavored phrases, who ignores, outwits, or overcomes the absurdities and humiliations foisted on most of us by this modern mess of pottage, twentieth-century civilization. This hero can be a cowboy or cow king, a multimillionaire or a jackleg without the proverbial pot. He can be right-wing or radical, a tycoon or football player, politico or country doctor. It doesn't matter the view or style, just that the independent Texan has both and can thumb his nose at some part of the world and make it stick.

All of these manifestations are admired, though each more in some circles than in others. In Texas, even the words "independent s.o.b." are usually spoken in a tone of rueful admiration.

It is obviously harder to define what the independent Texan is than what he is not. The type would appear to some to be anti-social, but the independent Texan has always really been more asocial; that is, he is not against society in general and does not oppose it so long as society goes along with him, or leaves him alone. The independent Texan is distinctly not a revolutionary in the common modern meaning of the word; when he rebels it is not to reform or change society so much as to secure his own freedoms from or within it. The independent Texan has few desires to push his own prejudices or leanings on others except in self-defense. Yet the independent Texan has never been a peaceful type, although with the possible exception of big-city bars the six-shooter era in Texas is over. An aura of tension, even violence, surrounds this folk hero, which comes from the effort of getting and keeping his vital independence. He seems always to be "agin" something or somebody—because independence is not a natural human condition. It is achieved with strain, and held only by isolation or effort. The independent Texas is *not* a dropout

—he works at it. And the independent Texan is the antithesis of the "organization man" although he may and sometimes does own his own organization.

The type, of course, is not found only in Texas. Some have been exported to other states, and some have evolved elsewhere naturally. However, it is peculiarly prevalent historically in Texas, and is much rarer east of the Sabine and north of the Red River. Say "independent Ohioan" and nothing whatever comes to mind; say "independent Easterners" and there are visions of droves of angry voters all splitting ballots in exactly the same way. Independent Texans do not form droves, and they are basically incapable of leading one. This is why independent Texans, though they often get the urge, are usually fiascos in politics, whether they run in Texas or New York. Independence and the American political system, as the late Sam Rayburn said in slightly different words, are two different things. Nevertheless, the virtue—or curse, as some would put it—of independence is not exclusively Texan but American, frontier American, to the core. It still permeates Texan thinking so strongly because Texas is far closer in time and spirit and society to the frontier than is most of America.

Across most of these United States independence is something celebrated each July 4th but which remains wishful thinking the rest of the year. For most Americans independence is still an unrealized ideal. Although the reality has vanished, the word itself still has a fine sound to the American ear; it can hardly be given a bad connotation. It is, for millions, about the last living heritage of the old frontier.

Most Americans do not act or think independently, whether voting, buying, dressing, investing, or holding forth in intellectual circles. However, to be called or thought independent at the polls, on Wall Street, in educational or intellectual circles, or in the entertainment world is a supreme compliment. Whether the truly independent thinker is tolerated in any circle, he or she is often praised. Financial independence, rather than riches, is probably the most desired American goal, which Merrill Lynch, land developers, and the Social Security administrators have all learned to exploit expertly. Millions of Americans claim to be political Independents, which makes thousands of office-seekers run as Independent Republicans or Democrats. The word still has magic for millions now submerged in a vast socio-economic-political system that in fact has made most forms of independence—other than financial—obsolete.

It is this still unsurrendered ideal that keeps some men slaving eighteen hours a day in gas stations or selling insurance on their own when they could make more at wages. It drives women lawyers to compete and sustains would-be entrepreneurs. It hounds some families from the rat race to cabins in Alaska, or more likely, from the polluted sidewalks of New York to the smogs of Houston or Denver. Most people would prefer to be their own man or woman, live their own lives, do work they enjoy, and be beholden to no one. Modern American social and economic organization has not allowed this for a long time; this is for most the impossible dream. A handful achieve it; others rush about, unhappy, afraid, suffering heart attacks and ending up in nursing homes on Social Security and Medicare.

What has happened in modern-day America, including Texas, is the development of irreconcilable imperatives. As Raymond Aron, perhaps the most astute foreign observer of the American scene since de Tocqueville, has said, Western civilization since the democratic revolutions of the eighteenth century has fostered strong and splendid ideals of personal freedom, but at the same time has created industrial, economic, and social forms in which genuine liberty for the individual is severely limited. Here "capitalism" is not the villain, but the social organization required in a society increasingly geared to provide mass employment, production, and consumption. Under either a "capitalist" or "socialist" system, the modern roles—and education, status, and psychological problems—of file clerks, sanitary workers, production-line personnel, and rocket engineers remain the same. This is not a dichotomy peculiar to the modern industrial world. Human history is scarred by the clash of opposing social imperatives. The Indian wars in Texas are a splendid case in point.

The conflict between whites and Indians was not a struggle between "right" and "wrong" although great wrongs were done and suffered by each side, but a fight for cultural life and death between two conflicting rights or cultural imperatives. It was not possible to leave the land to the Comanches as a hunting preserve and still spread the Anglo-American brand of agrarian civilization across the continent. In this battle the stronger forces won; the Indians were killed, pushed out, or reduced to beggary on reservations.

But this was not the last struggle for cultural life or death on the plains. A battle has continued from the day the Indians were removed within the conquering civilization itself. All Americans know the story, which forms both American history and legend: the Indians' hunting grounds were appropriated by free-range cattlemen, whose "rights" gave way, not without violence, to agrarian stock-raisers with barbed wire and windmills, who themselves fell to railroads and held on only with the greatest difficulty against hordes of incoming homesteaders. The cattle culture —that semi-feudal way of life that exploded Texas longhorns and the cowboy across half the continent—was vanquished like the Indian, replaced by a less colorful but more profitable cattle "business." And the hoemen who destroyed the vast freedoms of the cattle kings and their riders were themselves oppressed and finally driven from the land by great impersonal forces beyond their individual or collective control, as despite all the Granges and Peoples' Party protests the Texas farmer was reduced to debt and tenantry and finally forced from his way of life. Each successive fight for cultural life and death on the prairies left its mark upon the land and upon the American soul. These form the stuff of Western literature, that most peculiarly American of all art forms, in which for some single, independent hero arrayed against vast odds it is always High Noon.

This culmination in the West was and is inherent in the whole Anglo-American experience in America. The origin of the independent Texan in both reality and myth lies in that experience, and the type was formed long before the first Anglo-Texan colonists crossed the Sabine.

The frontier people who spilled over the Appalachians into the dark and bloody battleground of Kentucky were men and women determined to make their own destiny. This colonial advance violated British treaties with the Indians, and each further advance was to break or abrogate

*Illustrated by Tom Ballenger*

treaties of the American government with Indians for a hundred years. Government could not and did not control this restless tide of individual humanity. The frontier had its own imperatives, which were the hopes and dreams for opportunity and independence of millions of pioneer families. The advancing frontier did not take society and government and organized religion with it into the wilderness; it sucked them after it, something not always seen. And the frontier soon found a voice in this rough and ready male democracy. It learned to exploit the powers of government, while usually avoiding its direction or control.

The frontiersmen set their own goals and carried them out in their own way, but they demanded services from government: protection, roads, bridges and other communications, and the removal of the Indians. Here grew up a pattern that foreign historians have noted: a government that did not plan or direct society and in fact had almost no control over it, but which was forced to be responsive to its wants and demands.

The frontier was atomistic. Families were often separated by many miles as they carved out homesteads and farms, banding together only in times of extreme danger such as Indians uprisings. Each family was enormously self-sufficient, growing or making almost everything it needed and used except for nails, firearms, and ammunition. It was a brutally hard existence for most on this hardscrabble frontier, but it was free and enterprising, and perhaps the very hardness and freeness of life made a society of enormous strength and vigor. Many who went West failed: they died, remained indigent, or sometimes had to retreat back in defeat. A majority, probably, lacked the skills, endurance, or sheer luck to make it there. These failures became the poor "white trash," the slovenly farmers, the hired hands or tenants of more successful men. But enough succeeded not only to keep the dream alive generation after generation from the Alleghenies to the Pacific but to shape the American consciousness in powerful ways. Restless, rootless until they found what they came for, ruthless to whatever opposed them, these pioneers lived by a code sometimes called "rugged individualism." Their mottos were asocial and showed a certain appalling ruthlessness: *Root, hog, or die; God helps them who help themselves; the Devil take the hindmost.*

This people poured over the continent, the despair of Indians, Mexicans, and European powers who distrusted the rise of an American colossus. It was this sort of people who formed the Anglo-American vanguard into Texas, seeking an opportunity that was then and later defined in terms of land.

The advertisements of Stephen F. Austin and other impresarios created a vision of empire in Texas which lasted. Texas soil was for all practical purposes free, thousands of acres for each family head for the asking if he could develop it. Anglo-American history in Texas began with a land rush, which was to continue through revolution and war throughout the century. The Mexican government, desperate to colonize Texas as a buffer against both the Comanches and the United States, made generous land grants to all qualified applicants, but also other vast concessions, such as freedom from tithes and taxes and customs duties as well as virtual freedom, for many years, from government itself. Mexican-Texas became the frontier paradise of

America. Thousands of substantial Americans changed citizenship to become Texans, showing, perhaps, how little the early American frontier was conscious of government. In Austin's colony, and in many others, every immigrant acquired land he was permitted to develop according to his abilities and inclinations. Families could expect little assistance from anyone; there was no credit, virtually no money, and what little commerce there was was carried out by barter. Early Texas had neither banks nor jails, nor any real need for either. All that was asked of a colonist was that he mind his business and interfere in no one else's. A few people who could not live by these rules, troublemakers or idlers, were ejected from Austin's colony, sometimes with a whipping for emphasis.

Texas was the antithesis of an organic or corporately organized society. Each family head was a peer among equals; there was no hierarchy or web of social obligations beyond the family. Inevitably, some men, more capable or energetic, gained more prosperity, and like Jared Groce or the McNeels, acquired prestige or leadership. But the notion of a basic social, not economic, equality was very strong on the American frontier and went hand in hand with the insistence upon individual independence.

This was a frontier paradise that could not last. The Anglo-American presence by its very energy and activity inevitably sucked in Mexican government, which came in forms strange and distasteful to this free population. And, as a British minister to Mexico had warned, in 1836 the American frontiersmen in Texas repeated against the Mexicans what their forefathers had wrought against the British Crown 60 years before.

The pattern, and the society, of Texas was very similar to the American experience of 1775-1789. All Texas colonists resisted incorporation and control by Mexican authority, though they did not oppose Mexican sovereignty. The majority of substantial settlers, such as Austin's Old Three Hundred, were reluctant rebels, remaining loyal to Mexico until events finally forced their hand. The prime agitators of Texan independence were largely lawyers, latecomers, and adventurers from the United States who had small stake in the old scheme of things. The Texas Revolution, like the American, left society basically unchanged, but with families now entirely free to pursue their individual goals without fear of distant authority.

The founders of the Republic of Texas consciously attempted to create a society of freeholding citizens. This concept underlay the Republic's and the later State's constitutions. The Texas government granted large acreages freely to its citizens and to all new immigrants who applied for land. The dominant theory in Texas, so far as theory meant anything, was of Jeffersonian democracy. It was believed that only a society in which most citizens owned real property—income-producing property, not a house and car with mortgage—could practice the true democracy of an independent citizenry.

The major pressure for annexation by the United States came from the substantial property owners in East Texas, who saw little future in a raw nation of 23-odd counties too poor to build a road or issue sound currency and who, like the founding fathers of the United States, wanted a government strong enough to protect the social order and private property. The small-farmer frontier, then moving through the post-oak belts of central Texas and being rapidly swelled by constant immigration from the southern and border states, was less interested in annexation or even what was happening "back East" in Houston. The westerners' main concerns were the Indian and Mexican dangers, and the Republic, primarily because of financial difficulties, was never able to solve the frontier problems. Economic and strategic necessity, more than any call of "blood to blood," was the big factor in the Texans' decision to join the American Union in 1845. The cotton-exporting East understood the advantages of entering the American common market and customs union; the western and southern border regions expected federal troops to handle the ever-threatening Mexicans and constantly rampaging Comanche Indians. It is certain that Texans believed that entry into the Union was an act somewhat like the entry of European nations into the European Common Market and NATO. They expected enormous benefits but without any real loss of independence or sovereignty over their local affairs.

Significantly, quarrels arose almost at once, although the annexation settlement, granting the State title to its public lands, paying its existing debts, and even allowing for the formation of four more states from Texan territory, was extremely favorable to the Texans. But the Texans wanted the federal apparatus to solve the Indian problem and pay all the bills to boot, and further, to carry out the job according to Texan wishes. As Walter Prescott Webb wrote, when Washington tried to apply humanitarian doctrines to the tribes blocking the advance of the frontier or grant them territories, Texan impatience with the national government became "colossal." This souring played no small part in the coming Secession. The overwhelming majority of white Texas settlers held no slaves, but they were extremely touchy about any kind of interference in their lives or with their desires by distant government. This was to be a pattern of continuing confrontation, with impatience on both sides, that has lasted, over changing issues, to the present.

The society and ethos of Anglo-Texas were largely formed in the period prior to the War Between the States. The state remained a rough and ready frontier male democracy, with the citizenry usually able to apply direct and irresistible pressure on local office holders. There was no insulating bureaucracy. There were strong traditions of local or county government. The wholesale granting of land to citizens and immigrants by the state government realized something very close to the original dream of creating a freeholder society. Only a few Texans became really rich; these were mostly the great cotton planters along the Brazos and other eastern rivers who could export crops for cash. The majority of Texans raised corn and cows and hogs and beans on hardscrabble farms, trading for necessities. But most Texans, whether in plantation houses or frontier dog-run cabins or even in the few towns, owned land—which held promise if few immediate benefits. This fact caused the emergence of a genuine landowner ethos throughout the population.

Owners and property interests dominated society and politics. Property meant not only independence but status. Every Texan who had a piece of property saw himself as a petty emperor on his mini-empire; he was jealous of both the independence of his "country"—as some West Texans still call their ranches—and his property lines. Land acquired symbolic as well as economic value, powerfully affecting attitudes and law.

The larger owners always understood the essentially colonial nature of the Texan economy, exporting raw materials and agricultural products against money or manufactured goods, and consequently they were never very strong for "territorial" sovereignty. In 1860 few great planters, slaveholders all, really wanted Secession; if they hated Abolitionists and Black Republicans, they feared disorder more. Again, lawyers and politicians and the vociferous small-holder frontier forced the issue. This time the larger land owners lost everything, and the State of Texas lost whatever pretensions to sovereignty within the Union it had retained upon annexation, at least through our time.

But the "War," as it is still called along the Brazos, was not really the downfall of the old independent Texan. The Union victory, once the traumatic Reconstruction was done with, restored very much the old state of affairs. The Texas government continued to sell off lands to incoming settlers, and Texas farmers and ranchers dominated the writing of the state constitution of 1876. Nothing could have been more apparent in this document than that the old, thorny self-determination of the frontier folk remained intact. Texans rejected all efforts to give the state a government along the lines of the Northern states, with strong governors, longterm office holders, and laws that facilitated railroads, banks, and other corporate interests. Texans were resentful of government, including their own. Landholders saw banks and business corporations as class enemies. The 1876 constitution thus went a long way toward preventing Texas from becoming a major industrial state like Michigan or Illinois; it hamstrung central authority, harassed corporations of all kinds, and halted the formation of most large financial institutions. These stubborn farm and ranch types have been much criticized, above all by those who came to see the Texas future in further industrialization. But perhaps they saw something that Toynbee had expressed in 1929: that the democratic revolution and the industrial revolution were not complementary, but really hostile.

Texan society had begun to proceed now along quite divergent lines from that of most Eastern or Northern states. Something approaching a genuine "Texas character" was being formed. In most states the frontier was ephemeral, lasting a decade at most. The Texan frontier—a bloody, embattled frontier both in the West and along the Rio Grande—lasted some three generations. While the great majority of Americans who peopled the rising urban complexes of the North from New York to Milwaukee to Omaha were nineteenth-century immigrants who completely bypassed the old trans-Appalachian frontier experience, Texas was populated overwhelmingly by Old Americans, who had buried their grandparents on native soil. Texans had created a sense of peoplehood, or blood and soil, common in the Old World, rare in the restless United States. Texans had fought for their land, and since there was very little immigration from Europe or anywhere else into the state after 1875 until the middle of the twentieth century, the feeling for the land and people was preserved.

The early Texas towns were formed largely by certain types of immigrants, usually mercantilists and professional people, both European and American. The Texas cities—San Antonio remained the largest until the 1930s—were trading and distribution centers, nothing more. They remained relatively small well into the twentieth century. In

1880, Washington County was the richest and most populous in the state, and Washington County had no towns or cities then worthy of the name. And finally, when the vast trend of urbanization began, the first waves of migrants to the Texas cities were Texans from the surrounding countryside—former farmers and other rural residents who rarely migrated more than 200 miles. Thus well into this century the outlooks and mores of a nineteenth-century frontier ethos (which had vanished in the Northern urban melting pots) survived in Texas.

But the Texan independence, if not quite the Texan sense of time and blood and place, was in this same period inexorably destroyed. While railroads and wire and windmills made settlements of the entire state possible, concurrent economic and social developments within the nation—high rail rates, falling commodity prices, hard money, and tight credit—rapidly made it impossible for the great majority of independent landowners to survive on the land. Two statistics tell a story of heartbreak that all the Populist tides and tirades could not stem: in 1860 80 per cent of all white Texans were freeholders and self-employed; by 1915 more than 50 per cent of all Texans—white, black, and brown—had become share croppers or tenant farmers on the soil. The next step was the vast flight to the cities, two-thirds of all Texas counties losing population decade after decade while the refugees found employment in a developing industrial society with firms like Republic Insurance or Texaco.

It was the second cycle of the industrial revolution in America, beginning about 1875, that made the independent Texan an endangered species.

Industrialism created huge abundance, supported large populations, and fueled the rise of an enormously powerful American nation state. But it also required the formation of vast, impersonal pools of capital and called forth new disciplines, social organizations, and social hierarchies. The gods give bad things with the good.

The tendency of American business enterprise (which invariably began from a powerful entrepreneurial thrust and ethos) to reorganize itself into large private bureaucracies had profound influence. The eventual social product—for enterprise affected every aspect of society and government—was the so-called industrial society, organized for mass production and consumption, affluent but marked by its tendency to reduce men and women to role-playing functions rather than primary productive work, or to professional service within interconnected and mutually supporting private and public bureaucracies. These bureaucracies, whether General Motors or Exxon, government or education, are increasingly the same in their internal organization and direction and control. Society has become "managerial," with a loss of individual independence that no high salaries and permissin to wear exotic dress or hair styles or pursue esoteric sex lives can quite replace.

The chief executive officers of major corporations in Texas like to think of themselves as entrepreneurs and demand entrepreneurial rewards—but the word no longer has meaning in most of America. Few presidents have ever met a payroll from their own resources; they have advanced as role-playing bureaucrats, only risking their careers, by maneuvers resembling those in the Army or Department of State. Below the high executive ranks what was once an American middle class—bankers, merchants, professional people, manufacturers, farmers—has become a New Class of hired hands, salaried, but hired hands all the same. They find the same fragmentation of emotion and intellect in their their work, which is rarely productive and at which they are judged less by results than the approval of superiors and peers. No part of life, from the university to the highway department, has escaped this profound reorganization, as the old drive to frontier independence based on self-reliance became, and had to become, a newer discipline of conformity. Even professionals, with the precious privilege of defining their own jobs, have succumbed to a new-guilding in which their true independence has been surrendered to peer group strictures, poor reward for relief from pressures from the outside.

The basic struggle of the independent Texan—man or woman, rancher, wildcatter, small businessman, writer, or jackleg insurance peddler—has been against incorporation within this social tide. It is a struggle more deeply felt than articulated. And because the industrial society has come late to Texas, and in fact has only made large beachheads in certain areas—Houston-Baytown, Dallas-Arlington come to mind—the image of the independent Texan still has force. The resistance is fierce, and probably hopeless. Already many Texans, with others, have retreated into refuge, like the street people of Austin, who are not so much people who have preserved their independence against a world they hate, but people who survive almost by beggary on the fringes of society.

However, the independent Texan may survive. The old society of Texas still lingers in many ways. Texas is still basically a colonial economy, exporting beef and cotton and wool, sulphur and petroleum—a giant agrarian and mining complex, with a social outlook to match. The "owner" is still the most important and respected figure in Texan society, never the "manager" or the professional, who unless he is a prince in his own right is still regarded in most Texas circles as a hired hand. Here arises a continual confusion in the mind of the recent immigrant from the true industrial society of the North, where managers at various levels direct things, and have become accustomed to respect. They are not yet awarded such status in Texas, where a symphony conductor in Dallas, while recognized as a skilled professional, remains something of a hired hand who must answer to the owner's beck and call.

There is still an instinctive clinging to a sense of uniqueness, however battered by a national insistence upon total pluralism. There is still a deep attachment to the soil—almost every Texan would like to have a place, call it ranch or lake cabin, of his own. There is a sense of time and place—of history, lost in other cities and states. This is what Texans mean when they say they are proud to be Texans, thereby baffling newcomers who have shown their own pride and attachment to the places of their birth by their alacrity to leave it forever.

There is also a national turning inward now, following a lead Texans have long shown. There is a rising concern with personal goals and local interests, clashing with the purely technical demands for more and more outside coercion, direction, and cooperation. Emotional needs for true independence, not just territorial but personal, may grow stronger in this watershed world of 1975. Within our now interdependent civilization, this may be either a splendid or a destructive force. It should be remembered that social systems and civilizations rarely collapse from outside pressures, but because their denizens, either out of disgust or weariness, no longer sustain them.

If the independent Texan lives—crusty old coot, or flaming radical calling into question all the conventional wisdom of mass man—his survival may be the harbinger of the rise of a genuine Texan-American civilization. In the final analysis a few people, not masses, create high civilizations. Frontier Texas culture was aborted by modern American civilization, just as white culture destroyed the Indians—but historians, searching for the origin of the aristocracy and bourgeoisie who rose in the debacle of the European Dark Ages, making a new scheme of things and creating our

Western culture on the bones of the Roman civilization, have found the nobles and proud burgers among small minorities who refused to be overwhelmed. The family that kept its vital independence on the land while all around it sank into comfortable serfdom emerged as chivalry. A few refugees from territorial or spiritual lords forged vital town communities—not drop-out places, but spots where things got done in new and splendid ways, by independent souls who had new visions.

There are still a few independent Texans, in dubious battle against a suspicious, even hostile world. If enough of them remain great-hearted and optimistic, retaining above all else that quality that makes them special in our state and culture, they may prevail, not only for themselves but for all of us.

*—January 1975*

William Brazler Paul Burka Gregory ... Jo...
Alexander Cockburn Bill Martin... Al Rein...
Prudence Mackintosh ... ... ... L. Kin...
John Graves Billy Lee Brammer Richard West Willi...
James Fallows A.C. Greene Jan Reid...
william c. martin John Davidson Stephen Harrigan Pru...
W. Fehrenbach Shelby Hearon Nancy Neut III
Paul Burka Gregory ... John Deaton
Alexander Cockburn Bill Martin... Al Rein...
Prudence Mackintosh ... ... ... L. Kin...
John Graves Billy Lee Brammer Richard West Willi...
James Fallows A.C. Greene Jan Reid...
william c. martin John Davidson Stephen Harrigan Pru...
W. Fehrenbach Shelby Hearon Nancy Neut III
Paul Burka Gregory ... John Deaton
Alexander Cockburn Bill Martin... Al Rein...
Prudence Mackintosh ... ... ... L. Kin...
John Graves Billy Lee Brammer Richard West Willi...